T0189270

IFIP Advances in Information and Communication Technology

676

Editor-in-Chief

Kai Rannenberg, Goethe University Frankfurt, Germany

Editorial Board Members

TC 1 – Foundations of Computer Science
  Luís Soares Barbosa, University of Minho, Braga, Portugal

TC 2 – Software: Theory and Practice
  Michael Goedicke, University of Duisburg-Essen, Germany

TC 3 – Education
  Arthur Tatnall, Victoria University, Melbourne, Australia

TC 5 – Information Technology Applications
  Erich J. Neuhold, University of Vienna, Austria

TC 6 – Communication Systems
  Burkhard Stiller, University of Zurich, Zürich, Switzerland

TC 7 – System Modeling and Optimization
  Lukasz Stettner, Institute of Mathematics, Polish Academy of Sciences, Warsaw, Poland

TC 8 – Information Systems
  Jan Pries-Heje, Roskilde University, Denmark

TC 9 – ICT and Society
  David Kreps, National University of Ireland, Galway, Ireland

TC 10 – Computer Systems Technology
  Achim Rettberg, Hamm-Lippstadt University of Applied Sciences, Hamm, Germany

TC 11 – Security and Privacy Protection in Information Processing Systems
  Steven Furnell, Plymouth University, UK

TC 12 – Artificial Intelligence
  Eunika Mercier-Laurent, University of Reims Champagne-Ardenne, Reims, France

TC 13 – Human-Computer Interaction
  Marco Winckler, University of Nice Sophia Antipolis, France

TC 14 – Entertainment Computing
  Rainer Malaka, University of Bremen, Germany

IFIP Advances in Information and Communication Technology

The IFIP AICT series publishes state-of-the-art results in the sciences and technologies of information and communication. The scope of the series includes: foundations of computer science; software theory and practice; education; computer applications in technology; communication systems; systems modeling and optimization; information systems; ICT and society; computer systems technology; security and protection in information processing systems; artificial intelligence; and human-computer interaction.

Edited volumes and proceedings of refereed international conferences in computer science and interdisciplinary fields are featured. These results often precede journal publication and represent the most current research.

The principal aim of the IFIP AICT series is to encourage education and the dissemination and exchange of information about all aspects of computing.

More information about this series at https://link.springer.com/bookseries/6102

Ilias Maglogiannis · Lazaros Iliadis ·
John MacIntyre · Manuel Dominguez
Editors

Artificial Intelligence Applications and Innovations

19th IFIP WG 12.5 International Conference, AIAI 2023
León, Spain, June 14–17, 2023
Proceedings, Part II

 Springer

Editors
Ilias Maglogiannis (iD)
University of Piraeus
Piraeus, Greece

Lazaros Iliadis (iD)
Democritus University of Thrace
Xanthi, Greece

John MacIntyre (iD)
University of Sunderland
Sunderland, UK

Manuel Dominguez (iD)
University of Leon
León, Spain

ISSN 1868-4238   ISSN 1868-422X (electronic)
IFIP Advances in Information and Communication Technology
ISBN 978-3-031-34109-0   ISBN 978-3-031-34107-6   (eBook)
https://doi.org/10.1007/978-3-031-34107-6

© IFIP International Federation for Information Processing 2023

This work is subject to copyright. All rights are reserved by the Publisher, whether the whole or part of the material is concerned, specifically the rights of translation, reprinting, reuse of illustrations, recitation, broadcasting, reproduction on microfilms or in any other physical way, and transmission or information storage and retrieval, electronic adaptation, computer software, or by similar or dissimilar methodology now known or hereafter developed.

The use of general descriptive names, registered names, trademarks, service marks, etc. in this publication does not imply, even in the absence of a specific statement, that such names are exempt from the relevant protective laws and regulations and therefore free for general use.

The publisher, the authors, and the editors are safe to assume that the advice and information in this book are believed to be true and accurate at the date of publication. Neither the publisher nor the authors or the editors give a warranty, expressed or implied, with respect to the material contained herein or for any errors or omissions that may have been made. The publisher remains neutral with regard to jurisdictional claims in published maps and institutional affiliations.

This Springer imprint is published by the registered company Springer Nature Switzerland AG
The registered company address is: Gewerbestrasse 11, 6330 Cham, Switzerland

Preface

The 19th *Artificial Intelligence Applications and Innovations* (AIAI) conference offered a deep insight into all recent scientific advances and timely challenges of AI. From a technical point of view, novel algorithms and potential prototypes suitable to offer solutions in a multidisciplinary spectrum of applications (e.g., industry, finance, healthcare, cybersecurity, education) were introduced.

Moreover, it discussed ethical aspects and moral questions arising from the ability of AI to act autonomously, something that calls for the development of new legislative frameworks.

AIAI is a long-standing, well-established, mature international scientific conference, that has been held all over the world continuously for 19 years in the row. Its history is long and very successful, following and spreading the evolution of intelligent systems.

The first event was organized in Toulouse, France in 2004. Since then, it has had a continuous and dynamic presence as a major global, but mainly European scientific event. More specifically, it has been organized in China, Greece, Cyprus, Australia, and France. It has always been technically supported by the International Federation for Information Processing (IFIP) and more specifically by the Working Group 12.5, which is interested in AI applications.

Following a long-standing tradition, this Springer volume belongs to the IFIP AICT Springer Series, and it contains the papers that were accepted to be presented orally at the AIAI 2023 conference. An additional volume comprises the papers that were accepted and presented at the workshops that were held as parallel events. The event was held during June 14–17, 2023, at the University of León, Spain. The diverse nature of papers presented demonstrates the vitality of AI algorithms and approaches. It certainly proves the very wide range of AI applications as well.

The response of the international scientific community to the AIAI 2023 main event call for papers was more than satisfactory, with 185 papers initially submitted. All papers were peer reviewed (single blind) by at least two independent academic referees. Where needed, a third referee was consulted to resolve any potential conflicts. A total of 75 papers (40.5% of the submitted manuscripts) were accepted to be published in the proceedings as full papers (12+ pages long) while at the same time 17 short papers (9 to 11 pages) were accepted due to their significant academic strength.

Workshops

In total, the following five (5) scientific workshops on timely AI subjects were organized under the framework of AIAI 2023.

- The **12th** *Mining Humanistic Data Workshop* **(MHDW 2023)**

Coordinators: Spyros Sioutas, University of Patras, Greece, Ioannis Karydis and Katia Lida Kermanidis, Ionian University, Greece. It aimed to bring together interdisciplinary approaches that focus on the application of innovative as well as existing artificial intelligence, data matching, fusion and mining, and knowledge discovery and management techniques to data derived from all areas of Humanistic Sciences. The abundance of available data, which is retrieved from or is related to the areas of Humanities and the human condition, challenges the research community in processing and analyzing it. The aim was two-fold: on the one hand, to understand human behavior, creativity, way of thinking, reasoning, learning, decision making, socializing and respective biological processes; on the other hand, to exploit the extracted knowledge by incorporating it into intelligent systems that will support humans in their everyday activities.

- The **8th Workshop on** *5G-Putting Intelligence to the Network Edge (5G-PINE 2023)*

Coordinator: Ioannis Chochliouros, Hellenic Organization of Telecommunications, Greece (OTE). The 8th 5G-PINE workshop was organized by the research team of the *Hellenic Telecommunications Organization* (OTE) in cooperation with many major partner companies. The 8th 5G-PINE Workshop was established to disseminate knowledge obtained from ongoing EU projects as well as from other actions of EU-funded research in the wider thematic area of "*5G Innovative Activities – Putting Intelligence to the Network Edge*", and had the aim of focusing on Artificial Intelligence in modern 5G telecommunications infrastructures. It emphasized associated results, methodologies, trials, concepts and/or findings originating from technical reports/deliverables, from related pilot actions and/or any other relevant 5G-based applications intending to enhance intelligence to the network edges.

- The **3rd Workshop on** *AI and Ethics* **(AIETH 2023)**

Coordinator: John Macintyre, University of Sunderland, UK.

The 3rd AIETH workshop included short presentations from the panel members and an open Q&A session where the audience members were able to ask, and answer, important questions about the current and future development of *Generative AI* models. It aimed to emphasize the need for responsible global AI. The respective scientific community must be preparing to act preemptively and ensure that our societies will avoid negative effects of AI and of the 4th Industrial Revolution in general.

- **The 1st Workshop on** *Visual Analytics Approaches for Complex Problems in Engineering and Biomedicine* **(VAA-CP-EB)**

Coordinators: Ignacio Díaz Blanco, Jose María Enguita Gonzalez, University of Oviedo, Spain.

Many problems in the fields of Biomedicine and Engineering involve huge volumes of data, and an extended spectrum of variables under highly complex underlying processes. Numerous factors influence their behavior, resulting in common challenges in diagnosis, prognosis, estimation, anomaly detection, explainability, image analysis or knowledge discovery.

Machine learning (ML) algorithms allow modeling of complex processes from massive data, as they are able to surpass humans in well-defined tasks. However, they are prone to error under changes in the context or in the problem's definition. Also, they are often "black box" models, which makes their integration with an expert's domain knowledge difficult. Humans, in turn, although less precise, can work with poorly posed problems, perform well on a wide range of tasks, and are able to find connections and improve responses through an iterative, exploratory process. Aiming to embrace both approaches, Visual Analytics (VA) has emerged in recent years as a powerful paradigm based on the integration of ML and human reasoning by means of data visualization and interaction for complex problem solving.

- **The 2nd Workshop on *AI in Energy, Buildings and Micro-Grids* (AIBMG 2023)**

Coordinators: Iakovos Michailidis (CERTH Greece), Stelios Krinidis (IHU, CERTH, Greece), Elias Kosmatopoulos (DUTh, CERTH, Greece) and Dimosthenis Ioannidis (CERTH, Greece). Sustainable energy is hands down one of the biggest challenges of our times. As the EU sets its focus to reach its 2030 and 2050 goals, the role of artificial intelligence in the energy domain at building, district and micro-grid level becomes prevalent. The EU and member states are increasingly highlighting the need to complement IoT capacity (e.g., appliances and meters) with artificial intelligence capabilities (e.g., building management systems, proactive optimization, prescriptive maintenance). Moreover, moving away from the centralized production schema of the grid, novel approaches are needed for the optimal management/balancing of local (or remote aggregated net metering) generation and consumption rather than only reducing energy consumption for communities.

The aim of the AIBMG Workshop was to bring together interdisciplinary approaches that focus on the application of AI-driven solutions for increasing and improving energy efficiency of residential and tertiary buildings without compromising the occupants' well-being. Applied directly on either the device, building or district management system, the proposed solutions should enable more energy efficient and sustainable operation of devices, buildings, districts and micro-grids. The workshop also welcomed cross-domain approaches that investigate how to support energy efficiency by exploiting decentralized, proactive, plug-n-play solutions.

The accepted papers of the AIAI 2023 conference are related to the following AI algorithms, thematic topics and application areas:

Algorithms and Areas of Research:

Active Learning	Augmented Reality
Adversarial attacks	Autoencoders
Adversarial Neural Networks	Biomedical
Agents	Boosting
Anomaly Detection	Case-Based Reasoning
Artificial Neural Networks	Classification

Constraint Programming
Convolutional Neural Networks
  (YOLO)
Cyber Security
Deep Learning
Deep Neural Networks
Explainable AI
Federated Learning
Fuzzy Modeling
Generative Adversarial Neural
  Networks
Genetic – Evolution
Gradient Boosting
Graph Neural Networks

Image Analysis
IoT
Long-Short Term Memory
Machine Learning
Natural Language
Optimization
Recurrent Neural Networks
Reinforcement Learning
Robotics
Sentiment Analysis
Social Impact of AI
Spiking Neural Networks
Text Mining
Transfer Learning

The authors of the AIAI 2023 accepted papers came from the following **32** different countries from **5** continents.

Algeria
Austria
Brazil
People's Republic of China
Croatia
Cyprus
Czech Republic
France
Germany
Greece
Hungary
India
Israel
Italy
Lebanon
Malaysia

Malta
Montenegro
The Netherlands
New Zealand
Norway
Oman
Poland
Portugal
Romania
Saudi Arabia
Spain
Sweden
Turkey
UK
United Arab Emirates
USA

June 2023

Ilias Maglogiannis
Lazaros Iliadis
John MacIntyre
Paulo Cortez

Organization

Executive Committee

General Co-chairs

Ilias Maglogiannis	University of Piraeus, Greece
John Macintyre	University of Sunderland, UK
Manuel Domínguez	University of León, Spain

Program Co-chairs

Lazaros Iliadis	Democritus University of Thrace, Greece
Serafin Alonso	University of León, Spain

Steering Committee

Ilias Maglogiannis	University of Piraeus, Greece
Lazaros Iliadis	Democritus University of Thrace, Greece
Eunika Mercier-Laurent	University of Reims Champagne-Ardenne, France

Honorary Co-chairs

Nikola Kasabov	Auckland University of Technology, New Zealand
Vera Kurkova	Czech Academy of Sciences, Czech Republic

Organizing Co-chairs

Antonios Papaleonidas	Democritus University of Thrace, Greece
Antonio Moran	University of León, Spain

Advisory Co-chairs

George Magoulas	Birkbeck, University of London, UK
Paulo Cortez	University of Minho, Portugal
Plamen Angelov	Lancaster University, UK

Doctoral Consortium Co-chairs

Valerio Bellandi	Università degli Studi di Milano, Italy
Ioannis Anagnostopoulos	University of Thessaly, Greece

Publication and Publicity Co-chairs

Antonios Papaleonidas	Democritus University of Thrace, Greece
Anastasios Panagiotis Psathas	Democritus University of Thrace, Greece
Athanasios Kallipolitis	Hellenic Air Force (HAF)/University of Piraeus, Greece
Dionysios Koulouris	University of Piraeus, Greece

Liaison Chair

Ioannis Chochliouros	Hellenic Telecommunication Organization (OTE), Greece

Workshops Co-chairs

Spyros Sioutas	University of Patras, Greece
Peter Hajek	University of Pardubice, Czech Republic

Special Sessions and Tutorials Chair

Luca Magri	Politecnico di Milano, Italy

Program Committee

Alexander Ryjov	Lomonosov Moscow State University, Russia
Alexander Zender	Hochschule Darmstadt, Germany
Aliki Stefanopoulou	CERTH, Greece
Anastasios Panagiotis Psathas	Democritus University of Thrace, Greece
Andreas Kanavos	University of Patras, Greece
Andreas Menychtas	University of Piraeus, Greece
Ángel Lareo	Universidad Autónoma de Madrid, Spain
Antonino Staiano	University of Naples Parthenope, Italy
Antonio José Serrano-López	University of Valencia, Spain
Antonio Morán	University of León, Spain
Antonios Kalampakas	AUM, Kuwait
Antonios Papaleonidas	DUTh, Greece
Aristidis Likas	University of Ioannina, Greece
Asimina Dimara	CERTH, Greece
Athanasios Alexiou	NGCEF, Australia
Athanasios Kallipolitis	University of Piraeus, Greece
Athanasios Koutras	University of the Peloponnese, Greece
Athanasios Tsadiras	Aristotle University of Thessaloniki, Greece
Bernhard Humm	Darmstadt University of Applied Sciences, Germany
Boudjelal Meftah	University of Mustapha Stambouli, Mascara, Algeria
Catalin Stoean	University of Craiova, Romania
Cen Wan	Birkbeck, University of London, UK

Christos Diou	Harokopio University of Athens, Greece
Christos Makris	University of Patras, Greece
Christos Timplalexis	CERTH/ITI, Greece
Daniel Pérez	University of León, Spain
Daniel Stamate	Goldsmiths, University of London, UK
Davide Zambrano	CWI, The Netherlands
Denise Gorse	University College London, UK
Doina Logofatu	Frankfurt University of Applied Sciences, Germany
Duc-Hong Pham	Vietnam National University, Hanoi, Vietnam
Efstratios Georgopoulos	University of the Peloponnese, Greece
Elias Pimenidis	University of the West of England, UK
Emilio Soria Olivas	University of Valencia, Spain
Fabio Pereira	Universidade Nove de Julho, Brazil
Florin Leon	Technical University of Iasi, Romania
Francesco Marcelloni	University of Pisa, Italy
Francisco Carvalho	Universidade Federal de Pernambuco, Brazil
Francisco Zamora-Martinez	VERIDAS SL, Spain
George Anastassopoulos	Democritus University of Thrace, Greece
George Caridakis	National Technical University of Athens, Greece
George Magoulas	Birkbeck, University of London, UK
Georgios Alexandridis	University of the Aegean, Greece
Georgios Drakopoulos	Ionian University, Greece
Gerasimos Vonitsanos	University of Patras, Greece
Gul Muhammad Khan	UET Peshawar, Pakistan
Hakan Haberdar	University of Houston, USA
Harris Papadopoulos	Frederick University, Cyprus
Ignacio Díaz	University of Oviedo, Spain
Ilias Maglogiannis	University of Piraeus, Greece
Ioannis Chamodrakas	National and Kapodistrian University of Athens, Greece
Ioannis Chochliouros	Hellenic Telecommunications Organization S.A. (OTE), Greece
Ioannis Hatzilygeroudis	University of Patras, Greece
Ioannis Karydis	Ionian University, Greece
Ioannis Livieris	University of Patras, Greece
Isidoros Perikos	University of Patras, Greece
Ivo Bukovsky	University of South Bohemia, Czech Republic
Jielin Qiu	Shanghai Jiao Tong University, China
Joan Vila-Francés	University of Valencia, Spain
Jose Maria Enguita	University of Oviedo, Spain
Juan Jose Fuertes	University of León, Spain
Katia Lida Kermanidis	Ionian University, Greece
Kazuhiko Takahashi	Doshisha University, Japan
Kazuyuki Hara	Nihon University, Japan
Kleanthis Malialis	University of Cyprus, Cyprus
Konstantinos Delibasis	University of Thessaly, Greece

Konstantinos Demertzis	Democritus University of Thrace, Greece
Konstantinos Moutselos	University of Piraeus, Greece
Kostas Karatzas	Aristotle University of Thessaloniki, Greece
Kostas Karpouzis	ICCS-NTUA, Greece
Lazaros Iliadis	Democritus University of Thrace, Greece
Lei Shi	Durham University, UK
Leon Bobrowski	Bialystok University of Technology, Poland
Luca Oneto	University of Genoa, Italy
Manuel Domínguez Gonzalez	Universidad de León, Spain
Mario Malcangi	Università degli Studi di Milano, Italy
Michel Aldanondo	IMT Mines Albi, France
Miguel Ángel Prada	Universidad de León, Spain
Mihaela Oprea	Petroleum-Gas University of Ploiesti, Romania
Mikko Kolehmainen	University of Eastern Finland, Finland
Mirjana Ivanovic	University of Novi Sad, Serbia
Napoleon Bezas	Centre for Research & Technology Hellas (CERTH), Greece
Neslihan Serap Sengor	Istanbul Technical University, Turkey
Nikolaos Mitianoudis	Democritus University of Thrace, Greece
Nikolaos Passalis	Aristotle University of Thessaloniki, Greece
Nikolaos Polatidis	University of Brighton, UK
Nikolaos Stylianou	Aristotle University of Thessaloniki, Greece
Nikos Kanakaris	University of Patras, Greece
Nikos Karacapilidis	University of Patras, Greece
Panagiotis Pintelas	University of Patras, Greece
Paraskevas Koukaras	Centre for Research and Technology Hellas, Greece
Paulo Cortez	University of Minho, Portugal
Paulo Vitor Campos Souza	CEFET-MG, Brazil
Petia Koprinkova-Hristova	Bulgarian Academy of Sciences, Bulgaria
Petr Hajek	University of Pardubice, Czech Republic
Petra Vidnerová	Czech Academy of Sciences, Czech Republic
Petros Kefalas	University of Sheffield International Faculty, Greece
Phivos Mylonas	National Technical University of Athens, Greece
Hassan Kazemian	London Metropolitan University, UK
Raffaele Giancarlo	University of Palermo, Italy
Riccardo Rizzo	National Research Council of Italy, Italy
Salvatore Aiello	Politecnico di Torino, Italy
Samira Maghool	University of Milan, Italy
Sebastian Otte	University of Tübingen, Germany
Serafin Alonso	University of León, Spain
Sergey Dolenko	D.V. Skobeltsyn Institute of Nuclear Physics, M.V. Lomonosov Moscow State University, Russia
Shareeful Islam	Anglia Ruskin University, UK
Simone Bonechi	University of Siena, Italy
Sotiris Kotsiantis	University of Patras, Greece

Sotiris Koussouris	Suite5 Data Intelligence Solutions ltd, Cyprus
Spiros Likothanassis	University of Patras, Greece
Stefan Reitmann	TU Bergakademie Freiberg, Germany
Stefanos Kollias	University of Lincoln, UK
Stefanos Nikiforos	Ionian University, Greece
Stelios Krinidis	International Hellenic University (IHU), Greece
Vaios Papaioannou	University of Patras, Greece
Vasileios Mezaris	CERTH, Greece
Vilson Luiz Dalle Mole	UTFPR, Brazil
Vincenzo Piuri	University of Milan, Italy
Will Serrano	University College London, UK
Yiannis Kontos	Aristotle University of Thessaloniki, Greece
Ziad Doughan	Beirut Arab University, Lebanon

Local Organizing/Hybrid Facilitation Committee

Anastasios Panagiotis Psathas	Democritus University of Thrace, Greece
Athanasios Kallipolitis	University of Piraeus, Greece
Dionysios Koulouris	University of Piraeus, Greece
Guzmán González Mateos	Universidad de León, Spain
Héctor Alaiz Moretón	Universidad de León, Spain
Ioanna-Maria Erentzi	Democritus University of Thrace, Greece
Ioannis Skopelitis	Democritus University of Thrace, Greece
José Ramón Rodriguez Ossorio	Universidad de León, Spain
Lambros Kazelis	Democritus University of Thrace, Greece
Leandros Tsatsaronis	Democritus University of Thrace, Greece
María del Carmen Benavides Cuéllar	Universidad de León, Spain
Maria Teresa García Ordás	Universidad de León, Spain
Natalia Prieto Fernández	Universidad de León, Spain
Nikiforos Mpotzoris	Democritus University of Thrace, Greece
Nikos Zervis	Democritus University of Thrace, Greece
Panagiotis Restos	Democritus University of Thrace, Greece
Raúl González Herbón	Universidad de León, Spain
Tassos Giannakopoulos	Democritus University of Thrace, Greece

AIAI 2023 Doctoral Track

For the first time, the 19th International Conference on Artificial Intelligence Applications and Innovations (AIAI 2023) set up a Doctoral Track which was a special meeting place for all PhD Students on all conference subjects and topics.

The AIAI 2023 Doctoral Track was not configured just as a mentoring track. It was an open forum in which all PhD students could present their ideas and their "up to now" work, and exchange ideas and thoughts about their research and their ideas.

All PhD student authors of accepted AIAI 2023 papers together with PhD students who separately submitted for the doctoral track participated in this session.

In total there were 5 extra submissions for the doctoral track (apart from the student submissions at the main event). All those submissions were reviewed by the Program Co-Chairs of AIAI 2023 and based on their score the following one was selected for full oral presentation in the main event.

Keynote Lectures

Five keynote speakers gave state-of-the-art lectures (after invitation) on timely aspects and applications of Artificial Intelligence.

Evolutionary Neural Architecture Search: Computational Efficiency, Privacy Preservation and Robustness Enhancement

Yaochu Jin

Bielefeld University, Germany and University of Surrey, UK

Abstract. Evolutionary neural architecture search has received considerable attention in deep learning. This talk begins with a presentation of computationally efficient evolutionary neural architecture search algorithms by means of sampled training and partial weight sharing. Then, we introduce communication-efficient deep neural architecture search in a federated learning environment. Finally, a surrogate-assisted evolutionary search algorithm for neural architectures that are robust to adversarial attacks is described. The talk is concluded with a brief discussion of open questions for future research.

Interpretable-By-Design Prototype-Based Deep Learning

Plamen Angelov

Lancaster University, UK

Abstract. Deep Learning has justifiably attracted the attention and interest of the scientific community and industry as well as of the wider society and even policy makers. However, the predominant architectures (from Convolutional Neural Networks to Transformers) are hyper-parametric models with weights/parameters that are detached from the physical meaning of the object of modelling. They are, essentially, embedded functions of functions which do provide the power of deep learning; however, they are also the main reason for diminished transparency and difficulties in explaining and interpreting the decisions made by deep neural network classifiers. Some dub this the "black box" approach. This makes problematic the use of such algorithms in high-stakes complex problems such as aviation, health, bailing from jail, etc. where the clear rationale for a particular decision is very important and errors are very costly. This motivated researchers and regulators to focus efforts on the quest for "explainable" yet highly efficient models. Most of the solutions proposed in this direction so far are, however, post hoc and only partially address the problem. At the same time, it is remarkable that humans learn in a principally different manner (by examples, using similarities) and not by fitting (hyper-) parametric models, and can easily perform so-called "zero-shot learning". Current deep learning is focused primarily on accuracy and overlooks explainability, the semantic meaning of the internal model representation, reasoning and decision making, and its link with the specific problem domain. Once trained, such models are inflexible to new knowledge. They cannot dynamically evolve their internal structure to start recognising new classes. They are good only for what they were originally trained for. The empirical results achieved by these types of methods according to Terry Sejnowski "should not be possible according to sample complexity in statistics and nonconvex optimization theory". The challenge is to bring together the high levels of accuracy with the semantically meaningful and theoretically sound and provable solutions.

All these challenges and identified gaps require a dramatic paradigm shift and a radical new approach. In this talk, we present such a new approach towards the next generation of explainable-by-design deep learning. It is based on prototypes and uses kernel-like functions, making it interpretable-by-design. It is dramatically easier to train and adapt without the need for complete re-training, can start learning from few training data samples, explore the data space, detect and learn from unseen data patterns. Indeed, the ability to detect the unseen and unexpected and start learning this new class/es in real time with no or very little supervision is critically important and is something that no currently existing classifier can offer. This method was applied to a range of applications including but not limited to remote sensing, autonomous driving, health and others.

Intelligent Mobile Sensing For Understanding Human Behaviour

Oresti Baños Legrán

University of Granada, Spain

Abstract. Understanding people's behaviour is essential to characterise patient progress, make treatment decisions and elicit effective and relevant coaching actions. Hence, a great deal of research has been devoted in recent years to the automatic sensing and intelligent analysis of human behaviour. Among all sensing options, smartphones stand out as they enable the unobtrusive observation and detection of a wide variety of behaviours as we go about our physical and virtual interactions with the world. This talk aims to give the audience a taste of the unparalleled potential that mobile sensing in combination with artificial intelligence offers for the study of human individual and collective behaviour.

Secure, Efficient and High Performance Computing: A Computer Architecture Perspective

Tamara Silbergleit Lehman

University of Colorado Boulder, USA

Abstract. Distributed systems and new architectures introduce new sets of security risks. Microarchitectural attacks have presented many challenges in the computer architecture community and this talk will present a few of the methods that the Boulder Computer Architecture Lab (BCAL) has been studying in order to address these vulnerabilities. The talk will first introduce physical and microarchitectural attacks and why they are hard to mitigate. Then, the talk will introduce an efficient implementation of speculative integrity verification, Poisonivy, to construct an efficient and high-performance secure memory system. Finally, the talk will show how we can leverage emerging memory technologies such as near memory processing to defend and identify microarchitectural side-channel attacks. The talk will end by briefly introducing a new research direction that is investigating the Rowhammer attack impact on neural network accuracy running on GPUs and how we can leverage secure memory to protect the accuracy of the models.

How AI/Machine Learning Has the Power of Revolutionizing (for Good?) Cybersecurity?

Javier Alonso Lopez

Amazon, USA

Abstract. As we already know, Machine Learning is already used in various cybersecurity tasks such as malware identification/classification, intrusion detection, botnet identification, phishing detection, predicting cyberattacks like denial of service, fraud detection, etc. However, during recent years there has been a revolution in machine learning, specifically deep learning, that creates not only an unbelievable opportunity to develop more effective solutions but also represents a new threat and a new tool to be used to attack and gain control over systems, organizations and even countries.

In this talk, we will overview the major applications of Machine Learning in the field of cybersecurity both to prevent attacks but also to pose a threat. We will review the main advances of Deep Learning in the last 5 years and their applications in Cybersecurity. Finally, we will discuss the possible future trends we can expect (I do not expect high accuracy, but high recall :D) at the intersection of Deep Learning and Cybersecurity.

Contents – Part II

Graph Neural Networks/Constraint Programming

IoT/Fuzzy Modeling/Augmented Reality

Learning (Active-AutoEncoders-Federated)

Natural Language

Optimization-Genetic Programming

Robotics

Spiking NN

Text Mining/Transfer Learning

Contents – Part I

Agents/Case Based Reasoning/Sentiment Analysis

CNN - Convolutional Neural Networks YOLO CNN

Doctoral Track

Cyber Security/Anomaly Detection

Implicit Directed Acyclic Graphs (DAGs) for Parallel Outlier/Anomaly Detection Ensembles

David Muhr[1,2(✉)] , Michael Affenzeller[2,4] , and Josef Küng[3]

[1] BMW Group, Steyr, Austria
david.muhr@bmw.com
[2] Institute for Formal Models and Verification, JKU Linz, Linz, Austria
[3] Institute for Application-oriented Knowledge Processing, JKU Linz, Linz, Austria
[4] Heuristic and Evolutionary Algorithms Laboratory, UAS Hagenberg,
Hagenberg, Austria

Abstract. We present a methodology to automatically parallelize outlier detection ensemble models using directed acyclic graphs embedding the MapReduce paradigm. The DAGs are built implicitly such that naive sequential computations can be transformed into efficient parallel computations without changing the underlying implementation. We show that the proposed parallelization approach is an effective strategy to combat the computational complexity inherent to ensemble learning models, leading to a near-optimal speedup in a theoretical setting, and a substantial speedup in a practical setting.

Keywords: outlier detection · anomaly detection · ensemble learning

1 Introduction

The key motivation behind ensemble learning is that a combination of individual judgments improve upon a single judgment in terms of bias and/or variance. The effectiveness of ensemble models for outlier detection has repeatedly been shown in the literature [3,4,32,40], yet little research addresses the parallelization problem of outlier ensembles. The computational complexity inherent to ensemble models limits the acceptance and usage of this kind of models and, as a result, the progress in this promising area of research. To tackle this challenge, we propose an abstraction of outlier ensembles in the form of implicitly generated DAGs, drastically simplifying the definition of highly parallel ensembles without additional implementation effort.

Ensemble models for classification and regression have been extensively studied for decades. Breiman [10] famously described a parallel ensemble known as bagging, which consists of multiple models trained on subsamples of the data using a plurality vote to classify the data. It has been shown that bagging reduces the variance of a predictor by equalizing the influence of individual training examples [13,23]. Other ensemble methods, collectively known as boosting [21], aim to reduce the bias of weak predictors by iteratively combining them to a

© IFIP International Federation for Information Processing 2023
Published by Springer Nature Switzerland AG 2023
I. Maglogiannis et al. (Eds.): AIAI 2023, IFIP AICT 676, pp. 3–15, 2023.
https://doi.org/10.1007/978-3-031-34107-6_1

weighted ensemble. In contrast to classification and regression, ensemble learning for outlier detection has been neglected for a long time [39]. Outlier detection is the process of identifying observations that deviate from the remaining data, which is sometimes also referred to as anomaly detection or novelty detection. An outlier is (vaguely) described as "an observation (or subset of observations) which appears to be inconsistent with the remainder of that set of data" [7]. Outliers are infrequent by definition; thus, labels are often infeasible to obtain, and the ground truth is typically missing in outlier detection tasks. Outlier detection is mainly used in fields that process large amounts of unlabeled data, such as network intrusion detection, fraud detection, medical diagnostics, or industrial quality control, which further exacerbates the challenges regarding computational complexity in outlier ensembles. Aggarwal [2] differentiates between sequential and independent ensembles. Sequential ensembles are sequentially applied algorithms such that the previous applications impact the future application of the algorithms, as in boosting. Independent ensembles use different instantiations of algorithms or data, which are independent of the results obtained from mutual instantiations as, for example, in bagging. Sequential ensemble techniques are difficult to employ for outlier detection tasks because of the missing ground truth; therefore, outlier ensembles predominantly consist of independent, unsupervised approaches [4]. Consequently, we focus our work on independent ensembles and structure our work as follows. In Sect. 2, we categorize and differentiate ensemble learning approaches for outlier detection and review the current state of the art. In Sect. 3, we show how complex ensemble models can be modeled as implicitly generated DAGs. In Sect. 4, we show how the implicitly generated DAGs can efficiently be parallelized by embedding MapReduce. In Sect. 5, we show how our proposed method improves outlier detection ensembles in theoretical and practical settings. Finally, in Sect. 6, we summarize our contributions and propose research areas for future works.

2   Types of Outlier Ensembles

In a similar vein to the ensemble learning categorization efforts of Aggarwal [2] or Sagi and Rokach [34], we differentiate between the following strategies to induce diversity in the ensemble learning process.

Transformation and embedding. Each model in the ensemble is learned using a transformed version of the input data such that a variety of inputs are used for the different models. A transformation of the input data can be achieved by using different data augmentations such as CutPaste [28] or using different feature embeddings as in PatchCore ensembles [5].

Subspacing and subsampling. In this category of methods, different samples of the data are utilized to build an ensemble. This general idea has been explored from various angles, such as learning models from subsamples of the data, as in bagging [10], learning models from different subspaces, as in feature bagging [27], or learning models from a partitioning of the data, as in divide and conquer detection [32].

Model adaptation. Ensembles using model adaptation combine entirely different outlier detection models, randomized versions of the same model, or the same model over different choices of parameters. Isolation methods, for example, build an ensemble of tree-based [29] or hypersphere-based [6] detectors to determine the outlierness of an instance.

The unifying aspect of the categories above is that all of them yield multiple outlier detection models as a result of the training process. An outlier detection model is typically formalized as a scoring function $q : \mathcal{M} \rightarrow \mathbb{R}$ on a metric space $\mathcal{M}$, which assigns a real-valued *outlier score* or simply *score* to each sample. A question arising in the context of outlier detection ensemble learning is: How can the scores from the models in the ensemble be combined? To answer that question, there are two major issues that need to be solved, namely, score *normalization* and score *combination* [2]. Normalization addresses the problem that different models may output scores that are not directly comparable. For example, a distance-based method might output some form of distance as an outlier score while a probabilistic method might use a negative log-likelihood estimate as a measure of outlierness. The simplest way of bringing outlier scores to a common scale is to apply a linear transformation such that the minimum score is mapped to 0 and the maximum score is mapped to 1. [22] propose an expectation maximization approach to learn the parameters of a sigmoid calibration function or mixture model to convert the outlier scores to probability estimates. [26] point out that the expectation maximization models often converge to a "no outliers" or "all outlier" model and propose instead to use a Gaussian or Gamma distribution instead to transform the scores. [35] note that "a key for building good ensembles is to use ensemble members that make uncorrelated errors", proposing that the *selection* of ensemble members can be an important additional step. Ensemble model selection, however, is often missing in ensemble research and would greatly benefit from reduced processing time and parallelization.

The normalized scores of the models in the ensemble finally have to be combined to a single outlier score for the ensemble. The commonly used strategies to combine normalized scores is to average the scores or take the maximum of scores for a specific sample [3]. Aggarwal and Sathe [3] further propose to combine the average and maximum to counter their individual drawbacks, which appears to be useful for very large ensembles. Other authors [27] propose to discard the scores entirely and use the maximum ranks instead.

In summary, an (independent) outlier ensemble can be formulated as a process of diversification, normalization and combination as shown in Fig. 1.

3   Ensembles as DAGs

We formalize outlier detection ensemble models as directed acyclic graphs and show that this specification brings several advantages for such models. The composition of machine learning models as graphs has already been described machine learning toolboxes [8], outlier detection frameworks [31], automated machine learning [24] or federated machine learning [30]. Following [8], we define a node in the

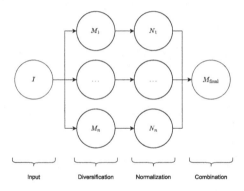

Fig. 1. Generic outlier detection ensemble model, where the abstract input is diversified into a set of individual outlier detection models $M_1, \ldots, M_n$, that are processed using normalization functions $N_1, \ldots, N_n$ to a final model M_{final}.

graph as a lazily evaluated expression f with optional input arguments. Each node in the graph is assigned a unique name. We denote a hypothetical node a in the graph as $f_a()$ or short f_a, where () indicates that the node a does not have any input arguments. An edge in a graph describes a directed dependency, such that the evaluation of an unnamed node $f(f_1, \ldots, f_n)$ with arguments $f_1, \ldots, f_n$ defines the directed dependencies from f to $f_1, \ldots, f_n$ and requires an evaluation of the dependencies before f can be evaluated. Using this formalization, we can infer the underlying computational graph G with no explicit definition of the graph structure. The described specification, by definition, leads to a directed graph, but, because a node depends on the evaluation of its dependencies, there must not be any circular dependencies. For example, if a node a depends on b, then the node b cannot depend on a because those dependencies could not be resolved. We define a dependency chain as a walk on the graph such that the walk $(a \rightarrow b \rightarrow c)$ describes a dependency chain, whereby c depends on b, and b depends on a. To ensure that no circular dependencies exist in the specified graph, we require that there exists no walk that begins and ends with the same node. For instance, the graph implicitly determined by a set of nodes $G(\{f_a(f_c), f_b(f_a), f_c(f_b)\})$ would not be valid, because the inferred walk $(a \rightarrow b \rightarrow c \rightarrow a)$ begins with a and ends with a and, therefore, is not acyclic. Using the introduced formalization, we can provide a concrete example of a feature bagging ensemble. For a detailed definition of the individual steps of the feature bagging approach, we refer to [27]. Also note that the decision as to what defines a node in the graph is given by a specified set of interrelated functions, which implicitly determine the granularity at which to exploit the concurrency. The granularity refers to the amount of work associated with a node in the graph and leads to a trade-off between many nodes with high overhead or fewer nodes with decreased load balance [16].

$$G(\{f_{\text{data}}, f_{\text{subspace}}(f_{\text{data}}), f_{\text{model}}(f_{\text{subspace}}), f_{\text{combine}}(f_{\text{model}})\}) \qquad (1)$$

In this case, the implicit graph is a simple walk of (data → subspace → model → combine) and the graph contains no branches, which is sometimes referred to as a pipeline [33]. Note that it is only possible to determine a *static* graph implicitly. In the feature bagging example of definition 1, we do not necessarily know how many subspaces are generated from the data, because the determination of the number of subspaces could depend on the dimensionality of the data, which is only known after f_{data} is evaluated and, hence, leads to a *dynamic* graph. Alternatively, we can define a fully static feature bagging ensemble with a fixed number of three rounds as follows.

$$
\begin{aligned}
G(\{ & f_{\mathrm{data}}, f_{\mathrm{subspace}_1}(f_{\mathrm{data}}), f_{\mathrm{subspace}_2}(f_{\mathrm{data}}), f_{\mathrm{subspace}_3}(f_{\mathrm{data}}), \\
& f_{\mathrm{model}_1}(f_{\mathrm{subspace}_1}), f_{\mathrm{model}_2}(f_{\mathrm{subspace}_2}), f_{\mathrm{model}_3}(f_{\mathrm{subspace}_3}), \qquad (2) \\
& f_{\mathrm{combine}}(f_{\mathrm{model}_1}, f_{\mathrm{model}_2}, f_{\mathrm{model}_3})\})
\end{aligned}
$$

Because the graph is directed and acyclic, it is possible to generate a topological ordering of the graph, which, in this example, is unique, but this does not have to be the case. The underlying ordered graph is depicted in Fig. 2.

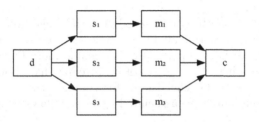

Fig. 2. Topologically ordered feature bagging graph where the data is denoted by d, the subspaces by s_1, s_2, s_3, the models by m_1, m_2, m_3 combined by c.

Formally, for a DAG with nodes $v_1, v_2, \ldots, v_n$, a topological ordering describes linear ordering of its nodes such that, for every edge (v_i, v_j), it holds that $i < j$. It can be proven that, if a graph has a topological ordering, then the graph is a DAG and vice versa [25]. In the following section, we will discuss how such a topological ordering can be used to parallelize DAGs.

4   Parallelization of DAGs

As apparent from the feature bagging example with a fixed number of rounds, a topological ordering can result in a number of nodes that do not depend on each other and may be parallelized, such as the nodes s_1, s_2, s_3 and m_1, m_2, m_3 in Fig. 2. We say that a topological ordering results in a number of topological generations, sometimes called levels, such that each descendant of a node is guaranteed to be in a following generation. Each node in a generation can be executed in parallel, because it is guaranteed that all dependencies have already been resolved in the previous generation. Schedulers may not parallelize entire generations, but schedule individual nodes that are *ready*, meaning that all dependencies are resolved for the specific node, for example, based on a first-in first-out queue. Scheduling computational DAGs has been extensively explored in multiprocessor scheduling [17,19] and cloud workflow scheduling [1,15,38]. The scheduler can follow different goals depending on the application, see [1] for an extensive overview of scheduling objectives. In our theoretical and practical analysis in Sect. 5, we focus on the *makespan* objective, which reflects the total execution time of the DAG. Parallelization of DAGs leads to multiple challenges: (1) a scheduler may not have knowledge of the entire DAG beforehand, thus, it has to learn about the structure of the DAG online and use dynamic scheduling [9], (2) the individual nodes in the DAG vary in their computational and resource requirements leading to resource scheduling challenges [38], and (3) the graph structure can result in deeply nested parallel workloads, leading to bad timing behavior [37]. Due to stated scheduling challenges and the highly complex and heterogeneous workloads in ensemble learning, we propose to embed a MapReduce [18] workflow in the DAG to enable more fine-grained resource and workflow scheduling. The success of MapReduce has shown that a simple processing model can be beneficial even for complex tasks. Conceptually, the map and reduce functions have associated types as follows

$$\textbf{map } (k, v) \rightarrow \text{list}(k', v')$$
$$\textbf{reduce } (k', \text{list}(v')) \rightarrow \text{list}(v'), \tag{3}$$

where the input keys k and values v are drawn from a different domain than the output keys k' and values v' [18]. Embedding MapReduce in a DAG allows the DAG to be statically defined and the dynamic portions of the DAG can be efficiently handled by MapReduce. The high-level query languages for MapReduce extend the original processing model [36], however, Fegaras [20] shows that a simple algebra underlies those so-called data-intensive computing environments [12]. Using the previously declared feature bagging ensemble, Fig. 3 shows the static DAG with embedded MapReduce edges. To embed MapReduce in a statically determined DAG, we annotate dynamic edges of the graph as map or reduce edges. We can then define the total amount of work of a DAG T as the sum of work of the static nodes $w^{(\text{static})}$ plus the sum of work of the dynamic nodes $w^{(\text{dynamic})}$ times the extent of their dynamic edges s.

$$T = \sum_{i=1}^{n} w_i^{(\text{static})} + \sum_{k=1}^{m} s_k \cdot w_k^{(\text{dynamic})}, \tag{4}$$

where n is the number of static nodes and m is the number of dynamic nodes. The work required to compute a node is also referred to as a node's

Fig. 3. The feature bagging graph where the data is denoted by d, the variable number of subspaces by s, the corresponding number of models by m which are combined by c. The map edge denotes a mapping step, such that each subspace s yields a model m. The reduce edge, in this case, consists of a single reducer.

weight. In terms of parallelization, we further differentiate between static and dynamic parallelization as visible in Fig. 4. The optimal level of parallelism can be defined as T/L, where L is the total work of the nodes in the critical path. For the example in Fig. 4, if we assume that each node's weight is equal to one, the critical path's total work is $L = 5$, the total work is $T = 11$, and the optimal level of parallelism for this DAG is $T/L = 2.2$, which is also referred to as the optimal *speedup* or average parallelism under infinite resources [16].

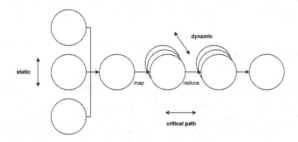

Fig. 4. Static and dynamic parallelization of MapReduce DAGs.

We do not prescribe a specific computational backend for the generated MapReduce DAGs; instead, we allow any computational backend representable by the algebra defined in [20]. The algebra is based on the concept of a *monoid* in abstract algebra, and the authors show that a small number of operations based on collection monoids are a good basis for various computational backends. For a collection monoid $\oplus$ and a collection monoid $\otimes$, the partial order $\otimes \preceq \oplus$ indicates that $\oplus$ obeys all the laws of $\otimes$. For example, using the Boom Hierarchy [14], it can be seen that list-concat $\preceq$ set-concat since set-concat is commutative, while list-concat is not. The MapReduce paradigm in definition 3 can be implemented using two of the operations of the collection monoid algebra described in [20], namely *concat-map* and *group-by*. The concat-map function embodies the concept of data parallelism, in which multiple processing nodes execute identical code on distinct sets of data. Given two collection monoids $\oplus$ and $\otimes$ with $\otimes \preceq \oplus$, concat-map maps a collection $\mathfrak{X}$ with parametric data type $\mathbb{T}_\oplus(\alpha)$ to a collection of type $\mathbb{T}_\otimes(\beta)$, by applying a mapping function of type $\alpha \to \mathbb{T}_\otimes(\beta)$. In contrast, the group-by function redistributes data among nodes based on the grouping key, such that data sharing the same key are directed to a single node. Given a type κ that supports value equality, a type α and a collection $\mathfrak{X}$ of type $\mathbb{T}_\oplus(\kappa \times \alpha)$, the group-by operation groups elements by their key, returning a collection of type $\kappa \times \mathbb{T}_\oplus(\alpha)$. Using concat-map and group-by, we can define MapReduce in the monoid algebra as

$$\mathbf{mapReduce}(m, r, X) = \text{concatMap}(r, \text{groupBy}(\text{concatMap}(m, X))), \quad (5)$$

where m is a mapping function and r is a reduce function. Note that, if a node specifies a dependency as a map or reduce edge, it has to be defined in terms of a mapping function m or reduce function r, and it is possible to transform the node into concat-map and group-by, which allows for a translation to computational backends that can be represented in the collection monoid algebra.

5   Implementation and Results

To test the potential of our approach, we first examine a theoretical example, using a resource-independent computational workload and a low-overhead computational backend. Second, we test our approach using a realistic outlier detection ensemble with different computational backends. For the theoretical example, we want to test the static and dynamic parallelization and a combination thereof. We generate a graph with a variable number of static and dynamic nodes and assume that each node in the graph waits for 100 ms before its execution finishes. We define the sequential lower bound as $T \cdot 100$ ms, which would only be achievable without any computational overhead. The parallel lower bound is defined as $L \cdot 100$ ms corresponding to the minimal time required for the critical path with no overhead. We conduct three experiments as shown in Fig. 5 where we increase the static and dynamic depth using n workers. Using a lightweight threading backend, we observe that an almost optimal level of parallelism can be achieved when the number of threads n equals the static or dynamic depth as visible when compared to the parallel lower bound.

For the realistic case study, we hypothetically devise a novel outlier detection ensemble model combining bagging with feature bagging, therefore training multiple models on simultaneous subspaces and subsamples of the data. We are interested in the overall speedup of the makespan objective compared to the sequential execution of the nodes in the graph, representing a naive, unoptimized implementation. Note that the exact same function definitions are used to implement the sequential and parallel approach. We use decorators to annotate each function and implicitly generate the underlying DAG and MapReduce edges from the annotations, which allows us to parallelize the DAG without

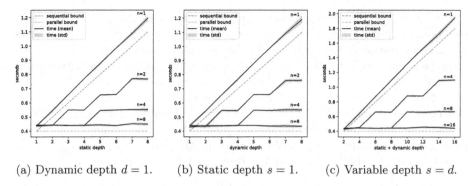

(a) Dynamic depth $d = 1$.   (b) Static depth $s = 1$.   (c) Variable depth $s = d$.

Fig. 5. Parallelization behavior with different depths, where (a) shows the parallelization using n threads under a fixed dynamic depth, but variable static depth, (b) shows a fixed static and variable dynamic depth and (c) shows the parallelization behavior with increasing static and dynamic depth.

changing any underlying function definitions.[1] As a computational backend for parallelization, we use a mixture of thread-based parallelism and process-based parallelism. Because the same function definitions are used for the sequential and parallel implementation, both sequential and parallel execution lead to the same results; therefore, we are not interested in a comparison of the resulting scores and use randomized synthetic data for all experiments. We generate standard-normal data with a fixed dataset size of 1024 samples and 128 features. We draw 50% of the samples for each bootstrap and 50% of the features. To determine the outlier scores for each bootstrap, we use the Local Outlier Factor [11] model implemented in scikit-learn [33].

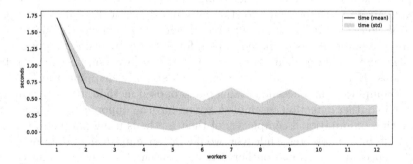

Fig. 6. Makespan objective of an implicitly parallelized outlier detection ensemble with varying number of workers consisting of threads and processes.

---

[1] It should be noted that the DAG could equivalently be inferred by other means.

As visible in Fig. 6, a sequential implementation of the proposed ensemble model requires 1.71 ± 0.01 s to compute the entire graph, which consists of the computation of the outlier scores for ten subspaces and subsamples. With increasing numbers of workers, the performance saturates the underlying computational resources at about ten workers with 0.23 ± 0.16 s to complete the DAG. Note that 25 executions are performed to determine the mean execution time and corresponding standard deviation. The high standard deviation is mainly an implementation detail due to process pool initialization. Using ten workers, we achieve a speedup of ~ 7.4 without changing the underlying naive implementation and implicitly generating a MapReduce DAG from annotations.[2]

6   Conclusion

We show an effective approach to automatically parallelize outlier detection ensembles by implicitly generating and parallelizing the underlying DAG. The effectiveness is achieved by embedding MapReduce in the DAG, such that MapReduce handles the dynamic parts of the DAG which drastically simplifies scheduling of the entire graph. Previous works in outlier detection ensemble learning often resulted in models with high computational complexity, limiting their usefulness and adoption. We show that these outlier detection ensembles, implemented in a naive, sequential manner can be automatically parallelized without additional implementation effort. A limitation of our work is that it focuses only on independent outlier detection ensembles, which include a majority of the existing methods, but non-independent models would also benefit from parallelization. A future extension to our approach could include support for sequential ensemble methods that are not independent of their previous executions. More generally, the described implicit parallelization approach could also be applied to a wide range of other computational tasks in the future. We use a simple algebra to represent the statically and dynamically parallelized parts based on collection monoids. Future researchers could extend the algebra and MapReduce paradigm as proposed in [20], for example by fusing mapping operations for improved parallelization or including improved support for join-type operations. Extending the algebra could also simplify mapping the DAGs to various computational backends. Using our proposed method, future researchers working in outlier detection ensemble learning have an opportunity to drastically reduce the computational complexity of their methods using parallelization. An important future research endeavor would be an empirical evaluation of the possible speedup of common outlier detection ensembles using different computational backends. In general, parallelization aspects should be discussed more thoroughly in future outlier detection ensemble learning research.

---

[2] We publish the code to reproduce our experiments including all dependencies at: https://github.com/davnn/implicit-dag.

References

1. Adhikari, M., Amgoth, T., Srirama, S.N.: A survey on scheduling strategies for workflows in cloud environment and emerging trends. ACM Comput. Surv. **52**(4), 1–36 (2020). https://doi.org/10.1145/3325097. ISSN 0360-0300, 1557-7341
2. Aggarwal, C.C.: Outlier ensembles: position paper. ACM SIGKDD Explor. Newslett. **14**(2), 49–58 (2013). https://doi.org/10.1145/2481244.2481252. ISSN 1931-0145, 1931-0153
3. Aggarwal, C.C., Sathe, S.: Theoretical foundations and algorithms for outlier ensembles. ACM SIGKDD Explor. Newslett. **17**(1), 24–47 (2015). https://doi.org/10.1145/2830544.2830549. ISSN 1931-145
4. Aggarwal, C.C., Sathe, S.: Outlier Ensembles. Springer, Cham (2017). https://doi.org/10.1007/978-3-319-54765-7. ISBN 978-3-319-54764-0 978-3-319-54765-7
5. Bae, J., Lee, J.H., Kim, S.: Image Anomaly Detection and Localization with Position and Neighborhood Information (2022)
6. Bandaragoda, T.R., Ting, K.M., Albrecht, D., Liu, F.T., Zhu, Y., Wells, J.R.: Isolation-based anomaly detection using nearest-neighbor ensembles. Comput. Intell. **34**(4), 968–998 (2018). https://doi.org/10.1111/coin.12156. ISSN 1467-8640
7. Barnett, V., Lewis, T.: Outliers in Statistical Data. Wiley, Hoboken (1978). ISBN 978-0-471-99599-9
8. Blaom, A.D., Vollmer, S.J.: Flexible model composition in machine learning and its implementation in MLJ. arXiv:2012.15505 (2020)
9. Blelloch, G.E., Gibbons, P.B., Matias, Y.: Provably efficient scheduling for languages with fine-grained parallelism. J. ACM **46**(2), 281–321 (1999). https://doi.org/10.1145/301970.301974. ISSN 0004-5411
10. Breiman, L.: Bagging predictors. Mach. Learn. **24**(2), 123–140 (1996). https://doi.org/10.1007/BF00058655. ISSN 1573-0565
11. Breunig, M.M., Kriegel, H.P., Ng, R.T., Sander, J.: LOF: identifying density-based local outliers. In: Dunham, M., Naughton, J.F., Chen, W., Koudas, N. (eds.) Proceedings of the 2000 ACM SIGMOD International Conference on Management of Data: 2000, Dallas, Texas, United States, 15–18 May 2000, pp. 93–104. Association for Computing Machinery, New York (2000). https://doi.org/10.1145/342009.335388. ISBN 1-58113-217-4
12. Bryant, R.E.: Data-intensive scalable computing for scientific applications. Comput. Sci. Eng. **13**(6), 25–33 (2011). https://doi.org/10.1109/MCSE.2011.73. ISSN 1558-366X
13. Bühlmann, P., Yu, B.: Analyzing bagging. Ann. Stat. **30**(4) (2002). https://doi.org/10.1214/aos/1031689014. ISSN 0090-5364
14. Bunkenburg, A.: The boom hierarchy. In: O'Donnell, J.T., Hammond, K. (eds.) Functional Programming, pp. 1–8. Springer, London (1994). https://doi.org/10.1007/978-1-4471-3236-3_1 ISBN 978-1-4471-3236-3
15. Convolbo, M.W., Chou, J.: Cost-aware DAG scheduling algorithms for minimizing execution cost on cloud resources. J. Supercomput. **72**(3), 985–1012 (2016). https://doi.org/10.1007/s11227-016-1637-7
16. Culler, D., Singh, J.P., Ph.D, A.G.: Parallel Computer Architecture: A Hardware/Software Approach, 1st edn. Morgan Kaufmann, San Francisco (1998). ISBN 978-1-55860-343-1
17. da Silva, E.C., Gabriel, P.H.R.: A comprehensive review of evolutionary algorithms for multiprocessor DAG scheduling. Computation **8**(2), 26 (2020). https://doi.org/10.3390/computation8020026. ISSN 2079-3197

18. Dean, J., Ghemawat, S.: MapReduce: simplified data processing on large clusters. Commun. ACM **51**(1), 107–113 (2008). https://doi.org/10.1145/1327452.1327492. ISSN 0001-0782

19. Drozdowski, M.: Scheduling multiprocessor tasks — an overview. Eur. J. Oper. Res. **94**(2), 215–230 (1996). https://doi.org/10.1016/0377-2217(96)00123-3. ISSN 0377-2217

20. Fegaras, L.: An algebra for distributed big data analytics. J. Funct. Program. **27**, e27 (2017). https://doi.org/10.1017/S0956796817000193. ISSN 0956-7968, 1469-7653

21. Freund, Y., Schapire, R.E.: A decision-theoretic generalization of on-line learning and an application to boosting. J. Comput. Syst. Sci. **55**(1), 119–139 (1997). https://doi.org/10.1006/jcss.1997.1504. ISSN 0022-0000

22. Gao, J., Tan, P.N.: Converting output scores from outlier detection algorithms into probability estimates. In: Sixth International Conference on Data Mining (ICDM 2006), pp. 212–221 (2006). https://doi.org/10.1109/ICDM.2006.43. ISSN 2374-8486

23. Grandvalet, Y.: Bagging equalizes influence. Mach. Learn. **55**(3), 251–270 (2004). https://doi.org/10.1023/B:MACH.0000027783.34431.42. ISSN 0885-6125

24. He, X., Zhao, K., Chu, X.: AutoML: a survey of the state-of-the-art. Knowl.-Based Syst. **212**, 106622 (2021). https://doi.org/10.1016/j.knosys.2020.106622. ISSN 0950-7051

25. Kleinberg, J., Tardos, E.: Algorithm Design, 1st edn. Addison-Wesley Educational Publishers Inc, Boston (2005). ISBN 978-0-321-29535-4

26. Kriegel, H.P., Kroger, P., Schubert, E., Zimek, A.: Interpreting and unifying outlier scores. In: Liu, B., Liu, H., Clifton, C., Washio, T., Kamath, C. (eds.) Proceedings of the 2011 SIAM International Conference on Data Mining, pp. 13–24. Society for Industrial and Applied Mathematics, Philadelphia (2011). https://doi.org/10.1137/1.9781611972818.2. ISBN 978-0-89871-992-5

27. Lazarevic, A., Kumar, V.: Feature bagging for outlier detection. In: Proceedings of the Eleventh ACM SIGKDD International Conference on Knowledge Discovery in Data Mining, KDD 2005, pp. 157–166. Association for Computing Machinery, New York (2005). https://doi.org/10.1145/1081870.1081891. ISBN 978-1-59593-135-1

28. Li, C.L., Sohn, K., Yoon, J., Pfister, T.: CutPaste: self-supervised learning for anomaly detection and localization. In: 2021 IEEE/CVF Conference on Computer Vision and Pattern Recognition (CVPR), Nashville, TN, USA, pp. 9659–9669. IEEE (2021). https://doi.org/10.1109/CVPR46437.2021.00954. ISBN 978-1-66544-509-2

29. Liu, F.T., Ting, K.M., Zhou, Z.H.: Isolation forest. In: 2008 Eighth IEEE International Conference on Data Mining, Pisa, Italy, pp. 413–422. IEEE (2008). https://doi.org/10.1109/ICDM.2008.17. ISBN 978-0-7695-3502-9

30. Liu, J., Huang, J., Zhou, Y., Li, X., Ji, S., Xiong, H., Dou, D.: From distributed machine learning to federated learning: a survey. Knowl. Inf. Syst. **64**(4), 885–917 (2022). https://doi.org/10.1007/s10115-022-01664-x

31. Muhr, D., Affenzeller, M., Blaom, A.D.: OutlierDetection.jl: a modular outlier detection ecosystem for the Julia programming language (2022)

32. Muhr, D., Tripathi, S., Jodlbauer, H.: Divide and conquer anomaly detection: a case study predicting defective engines. Procedia Manuf. **42**, 57–61 (2020). https://doi.org/10.1016/j.promfg.2020.02.090. ISSN 23519789

33. Pedregosa, F., et al.: Scikit-learn: machine learning in python. J. Mach. Learn. Res. **12**, 2825–2830 (2011)

34. Sagi, O., Rokach, L.: Ensemble learning: a survey. WIREs Data Mining Knowl. Discov. **8**(4), e1249 (2018). https://doi.org/10.1002/widm.1249. ISSN 1942-4795

35. Schubert, E., Wojdanowski, R., Zimek, A., Kriegel, H.P.: On evaluation of outlier rankings and outlier scores. In: Ghosh, J., Liu, H., Davidson, I., Domeniconi, C., Kamath, C. (eds.) Proceedings of the 2012 SIAM International Conference on Data Mining, pp. 1047–1058. Society for Industrial and Applied Mathematics, Philadelphia (2012). https://doi.org/10.1137/1.9781611972825.90. ISBN 978-1-61197-232-0

36. Stewart, R.J., Trinder, P.W., Loidl, H.-W.: Comparing high level mapreduce query languages. In: Temam, O., Yew, P.-C., Zang, B. (eds.) APPT 2011. LNCS, vol. 6965, pp. 58–72. Springer, Heidelberg (2011). https://doi.org/10.1007/978-3-642-24151-2_5

37. Sun, J., Guan, N., Li, F., Gao, H., Shi, C., Yi, W.: Real-time scheduling and analysis of OpenMP DAG tasks supporting nested parallelism. IEEE Trans. Comput. **69**(9), 1335–1348 (2020). https://doi.org/10.1109/TC.2020.2972385. ISSN 1557-9956

38. Zhan, Z.H., Liu, X.F., Gong, Y.J., Zhang, J., Chung, H.S.H., Li, Y.: Cloud computing resource scheduling and a survey of its evolutionary approaches. ACM Comput. Surv. **47**(4), 1–33 (2015). https://doi.org/10.1145/2788397. ISSN 0360-0300, 1557-7341

39. Zimek, A., Campello, R.J., Sander, J.: Ensembles for unsupervised outlier detection: challenges and research questions. ACM SIGKDD Explor. Newslett. **15**(1), 11–22 (2014). https://doi.org/10.1145/2594473.2594476. ISSN 1931-0145

40. Zimek, A., Gaudet, M., Campello, R.J., Sander, J.: Subsampling for efficient and effective unsupervised outlier detection ensembles. In: Proceedings of the 19th ACM SIGKDD International Conference on Knowledge Discovery and Data Mining, KDD 2013, pp. 428–436. Association for Computing Machinery, New York (2013). https://doi.org/10.1145/2487575.2487676. ISBN 978-1-4503-2174-7

Next Generation Automated Reservoir Computing for Cyber Defense

Konstantinos Demertzis[1]([✉]) and Lazaros Iliadis[2]

[1] School of Science and Technology, Informatics Studies, Hellenic Open University, Patra,
Greece
demertzis.konstantinos@ac.eap.gr
[2] School of Engineering, Department of Civil Engineering, Faculty of Mathematics
Programming and General Courses, Democritus University of Thrace, Kimmeria, Xanthi, Greece
liliadis@civil.duth.gr

Abstract. It is a fact, that important information related to systems' behavior and dynamics, can be revealed as time passes. Observing changes over time, can often lead to the detection of patterns and trends that might not be immediately apparent from a single system's snapshot. Additionally, the concept of time can be essential in understanding cause-and-effect relationships. Observing how changes in one variable over time affect changes in another, can gain insights into the causal relationships between different system components. Time series analysis of data that change over time, can be a powerful tool for understanding complex systems in the field of cyber security. Reservoir Computing (RC) is a Machine Learning technique, using a fixed and randomly generated high-dimensional dynamic system, called a Reservoir, to transform and classify input data. The reservoir acts as a nonlinear and temporal filter of the input data, which is then readout by a linear output layer. Continuous-Time Reservoir Computing (CTRC) is a type of recurrent neural network, aiming to model the continuous-time dynamics of the network's neurons. It is particularly useful for applications where time is critical and it can provide insights into the underlying system's dynamics. This paper proposes a next-generation CTRC for cyber defense, where the reservoir neurons are modeled as continuous-time dynamical systems. This means that their behavior is described by a system of differential equations that change over time. In order to model the drift phenomenon, identify the abnormal changes in the data, and adaptively stabilize the learning system. The CTRC parameters are optimized using the Reinforcement Learning (RL) method. The proposed system, as proved experimentally, has several advantages over discrete systems, including the ability to handle signals with high sampling rates and to effectively capture real cyber security signals' continuous nature.

Keywords: Reservoir Computing · Continuous-Time Reservoir Computing · Cyber Defense · Time Series Analysis

© IFIP International Federation for Information Processing 2023
Published by Springer Nature Switzerland AG 2023
I. Maglogiannis et al. (Eds.): AIAI 2023, IFIP AICT 676, pp. 16–27, 2023.
https://doi.org/10.1007/978-3-031-34107-6_2

1 Introduction

RC is a computational framework that utilizes the dynamics of a high-dimensional, randomly connected network to process and learn from input signals [1]. It is an efficient and powerful technique for solving complex machine-learning tasks, particularly those involving time-series data. At the heart of a reservoir computing system is a reservoir, which is a randomly connected network of nodes. The nodes in the reservoir are typically arranged recurrently, meaning they have connections to each other that allow information to be processed over time. The input signal is fed into the reservoir, interacting with the network's dynamics to produce a high-dimensional state vector. The state vector represents the current state of the reservoir, and it captures the temporal patterns and features of the input signal. The state vector is then fed into a readout layer, a simple, linear layer that maps the reservoir states to the desired output [2]. The readout layer is typically trained using linear regression or another simple learning algorithm. It learns to produce the correct output based on the input signal and the current state of the reservoir [3].

Reservoir computing is a machine learning algorithm employing linear optimization. It is suitable for processing information generated by dynamical systems, using observed time-series data. It is important that it requires very small training data sets, and thus it has small requirements of computing resources. One of the key advantages of reservoir computing is that the reservoir itself is not trained. Instead, the reservoir's random connections and internal dynamics are fixed, and the readout layer is the only trained part of the system. This greatly simplifies the training process and makes it more efficient. Another advantage of RC is that it can have many nodes, enabling it to capture the input signal's complex temporal patterns and features. This makes it particularly well-suited to sophisticated tasks where the input signal is a complex, time-varying waveform [4].

Next-generation automated RC [5] is an emerging technology that has the potential to enhance cyber defense greatly. It involves applying the basic principles of RC to analyze network traffic [6] and identify anomalies indicative of cyberattacks or other security threats. The basic concept of the next-generation automated RC is that a high-dimensional, randomly connected network can be used to model complex data patterns and relationships on cyber security prospects. This can be particularly useful when traditional rule-based detection methods are ineffective, such as zero-day attacks or other advanced persistent threats.

One extremely novel application of next-generation automated RC for cyber defence is the CTRC [7]. It is an extension of the RC paradigm that operates in continuous rather than discrete time. In a traditional discrete-time reservoir computing system, input signals are fed into the reservoir at discrete intervals. In contrast, the input signal is processed in real-time without discretization in a CTRC system. Specifically, in CTRC, the reservoir dynamics are described by continuous-time differential equations. The input signal drives the reservoir dynamics, producing an output signal. The output signal is then passed through a readout layer to produce the desired output. The continuous-time nature of the system enables the reservoir to process input signals in real time without discretization. This is particularly useful in applications where the input signal is a continuous data stream, such as large-scale network traffic analyses, which can be used to make predictions and detect anomalies in continuous data streams [8].

One of the challenges of CTRC is that it can be more difficult to train and optimize than discrete-time RC. This is because the reservoir dynamics are described by continuous-time differential equations, which can be more complex to model and optimize than discrete-time ones. Specifically, the biggest challenge with continuous-time differential equations is that they require numerical integration, which can be computationally expensive and lead to instability or accuracy issues if not implemented correctly. Furthermore, optimizing continuous-time differential equations can be more difficult than that discrete-time equations, as the optimization problem becomes a Partial Differential Equation (PDE) instead of a simple algebraic equation. In order to overcome these challenges, the proposed CTRC's system parameters are optimized using RL method.

2 Methodology

The proposed CTRC system is modelled using continuous-time differential equations, and the system parameters are optimized using the RL method and, specifically, the Q-Learning approach. The following paragraphs are presenting the specific steps required to combine these approaches:

2.1 Defining the CTRC System

The architecture of a CTRC system, includes the input, reservoir, and output layers. The respective connection and input weights are random in RC. The reservoir weights are scaled in such a way as to ensure the *Echo State Property* (ESP), which is defined as the state in which the reservoir is an "echo" of the entire input history. Of course, this is partly determined by its architecture [9]. The discrete layers of the CTRC are only those of input $u(n)$ and output $y(n)$ as they are defined by the problem. The hidden layers are clustered in an RC region, and their number is indistinguishable. The neurons in the RC, $x(n)$, are connected by some percentage, which determines how sparsity the RC will be. A depiction of the RC architecture [10] is presented in the following Fig. 1.

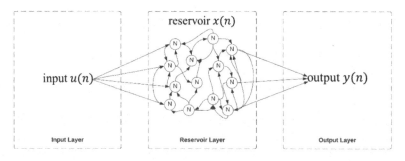

Fig. 1. RC architecture

The synaptic associations that link the levels together and the RC are characterized by a value that identifies the weights [11]. In CTRC, each input neuron is connected via

W^{in}_{ij} weights (i-input neuron, j-neuron in the RC) to each neuron from the RC. Although normalized, these weights are determined randomly before training, and their values are the final ones as they do not change during training. Also, each RC neuron is connected to each other neuron, via weights W_{jk} (j-neuron in RC, k-neuron RC, and $j \neq k$). The respective weights, although normalized, are randomly determined before training and their values do not change. We use $x^{(l)}(t) \in R^{N_R}$ to declare the status of level l at time t. By omitting the bias conditions, the first level state transition function is defined by the following Eq. 1, [12, 13]:

$$x^{(1)}(t) = \left(1 - a^{(1)}\right)x^{(1)}(t-1) + a^{(1)} \tanh\left(W_{in}u(t) + \hat{W}^{(1)}x^{(1)}(t-1)\right) \quad (1)$$

For each level higher than $l > 1$ Eq. 1, has the following form (2) [7, 14]:

$$x^{(l)}(t) = \left(1 - a^{(l)}\right)x^{(l)}(t-1) + a^{(l)} \tanh\left(W^l x^{l-1}(t) + \hat{W}^{(l)}x^{(l)}(t-1)\right) \quad (2)$$

where $W_{in} \in R^{N_R \times N_U}$ is the input weight matrix, $\hat{W}^{(l)} \in R^{N_R \times N_R}$ is the recurrent weight matrix for layer l, $W^{(l)} \in R^{N_R \times N_R}$ is the matrix containing the connection weights between layer l-1 and l, $a^{(l)}$ is the leaky parameter of layer l and $tanh$ is the Tangent Hyperbolic function. Finally, each RC neuron is connected via W^{out}_{jm} weights (j-neuron in the RC, m-neuron input) to the neurons in the output layer. The weights, located in the readout layer, are the only ones trained to get their final values [1, 15].

2.2 Defining the Differential Equations

The differential Eqs. 3 and 4, govern the behaviour of the state vectors $x1(t)$ and $x2(t)$ in the continuous-time reservoir computing system, enable the system to capture both temporal and spatial patterns of the network's traffic data. They are given by [16, 17]:

$$dx1/dt = -x1(t) + f1(W1x1(t) + Win1u(t)) \quad (3)$$

$$dx2/dt = -x2(t) + f2(W2x2(t) + Win2u(t) + Vx1(t)) \quad (4)$$

In the above Eqs. 3, 4, $x1(t)$ represents the state vector that captures the temporal patterns of the network traffic data, while x2(t) represents the state vector that captures the spatial patterns of the data. In Eq. 3, the term $-x1(t)$ represents the leaky integrator, which causes the state vector to decay over time. The term $f1(W1 \times 1(t) + Win1u(t))$ represents the nonlinear activation function, which maps the input signal and the current state of the reservoir to a new state vector [18]. In Eq. 4, the term $-x2(t)$ represents the leaky integrator, and the term f2(W2 × 2(t) + Win2u(t) + V × 1(t)) represents the nonlinear activation function. Moreover, V is a weight matrix that captures the interaction between the temporal and spatial patterns of the network traffic data. The above differential equations describe how the state vectors $x1(t)$ and $x2(t)$ change over time in response to the input signal u(t) and the current state of the reservoir. The weight matrices W1, W2, Win1, Win2, and V are optimized using Q-Learning algorithm to minimize the difference between the predicted output of the system and the true labels in a training dataset in order to model the drift phenomenon, identify the abnormal changes in the data, and adaptively stabilize the learning system.

2.3 Defining the RL Algorithm

The RL algorithm optimizes the CTRC system parameters. This involves using the Q-learning algorithm. Q-learning is a RL algorithm, and the following are the exact methodology steps to use Q-learning to optimize the CTRC system parameters [19, 20]:

1. Defining the state space: The state space for the Q-learning algorithm is based on the output of the CTRC system. The state space captures relevant information about the current network traffic analysis of the cyber defense scenario. The state space, denoted by S, represents the possible states of the cyber defense system at any given time. The state space can be defined in terms of the output of the CTRC system, which might include features such as network traffic patterns, system logs, or other relevant data. The state space can be discretized into a set of discrete states, $S = \{s_1, s_2,..., s_n\}$, where n is the number of discrete states.
2. Defining the action space: The action space for the Q-learning algorithm is based on the possible actions that the agent can take to mitigate cyber-attacks. For example, the action space might include blocking traffic from a specific IP address, shutting down a compromised system, or initiating a backup of critical data. The action space, denoted by A, represents the set of actions that the agent can take to mitigate cyber-attacks. The action space can be defined based on the available defensive actions, such as blocking traffic from a specific IP address, shutting down a compromised system, or initiating a backup of critical data. The action space can be discretized into a set of discrete actions, $A = \{a_1, a_2,..., a_m\}$, where m is the number of discrete actions.
3. Defining the reward function: The reward function for the Q-learning algorithm is based on the agent's performance in the cyber defence task. The reward function encourages the agent to mitigate cyber-attacks effectively and discourage ineffective or harmful actions. The reward function, denoted by R, is a function that maps a state-action pair to a scalar reward value. The reward function should encourage the agent to mitigate cyber-attacks effectively and discourage ineffective or harmful actions. The reward function 5, can be defined as follows [21]:

$$R(s, a) = r(s, a) \tag{5}$$

where $r(s, a)$ is the immediate reward associated with taking action a in state s.
4. Initializing the Q-table: The Q-table is a lookup table that maps states and actions to expected rewards. The Q-table is initially set to arbitrary values. The Q-table, denoted by Q, is a lookup table that maps states and actions to expected rewards. The Q-table is initially set to arbitrary values. The Q-value for a state-action pair (s, a) is denoted by $Q(s, a)$.
5. Running the Q-learning algorithm: The use of the Q-learning algorithm to update the Q-table by iteratively selecting actions based on the current state and the values in the Q-table. The Q-table is updated using the Bellman equation, which estimates the expected future reward from the current state and action. The algorithm works as follows [19, 22]:
    a. At each time step t, the agent observes the current state st and selects an action at based on an exploration-exploitation tradeoff.
    b. The agent receives an immediate reward $rt = r(st, at)$ and transitions to a new state $st + 1$.

c. The Q-value for the current state-action pair (st, at) is updated using the Bellman Eq. 6:

$$Q(st, at) \leftarrow Q(st, at) + \alpha[rt + \gamma \max aa'Q(st + 1, a') - Q(st, at)] \quad (6)$$

where α is the learning rate, γ is the discount factor, and $max a'Q(st + 1, a')$ is the maximum expected reward over all actions in the next state $st + 1$.

d. The Q-table is updated at each time step, and the process continues until convergence is achieved.

6. Training the CTRC system: The Q-table adjusts the CTRC system parameters, such as the weight matrices and bias terms. The CTRC system is trained to optimize the expected future reward as the Q-table estimates.

7. Evaluating the performance: The performance evaluation process of the trained CTRC system is implemented based on a test dataset. This involves measuring accuracy, precision, recall, and F1-score metrics.

8. Refining the system: The CTRC algorithm parameters are refined based on the evaluation results. This involves automatically adjusting the set of parameters optimized in the Q-learning process.

3   Experiments

To provide a perfect simulation environment, the *Factry.io* data collecting platform and the *InfluxDB* were used [23]. Factry.io is a data collection and visualization platform that enables users to easily collect, monitor, and analyze data from various sources, such as machines, sensors, and devices [24]. It provides a user-friendly interface to connect to different data sources, set up data collection parameters, and visualize data in real-time. InfluxDB, on the other hand, is a time-series database designed to handle high volumes of data that are time-stamped. It is optimized for storing and retrieving time-stamped data and enables fast queries and data analysis. InfluxDB supports a variety of data types and formats, including numerical, string, and Boolean data, and provides a SQL-like query language to access and manipulate data. Factry.io can integrate with InfluxDB to store and query time-series data collected from various sources. Users can configure Factry.io to send data to InfluxDB, which can then be used for further analysis or visualization. InfluxDB's efficient data storage and retrieval capabilities make it an ideal choice for managing large volumes of time-series data collected by Factry.io.

The goal was to gather data about the industrial environment using the open-source OPC-UA collector protocol [25]. It is a time series of sensor data that has been compiled. In order to store sensor data in InfluxDB, programmable PLC controllers, SCADA systems, and construction equipment are used to collect the data. Time series or timestamps are best served by the storage database. Measurements or events that are tracked throughout time and gathered as time series data are used to create them. Such occurrences may include transactions, application performance monitoring, and server analytics [26]. Sensors or different kinds of analytics are examples of potential sources. In this instance, data for one year was gathered from three sensors' hourly quantifiable values within the context of a machine condition that runs continuously. The attack modifies the sensor settings to alter how some mechanisms operate, but the meters and displays of the entire system are not aware of this.

There is a tank specifically for raw water storage. A water level sensor is part of this, along with a valve that opens when the sensor detects a level of less than or equal to 0.5 m and closes when the level is higher than 0.8 m. Also, it has a pump whose operation is based on a procedure that separates the pressure levels through a semipermeable membrane. This is seen as a safety device because the pump shuts off immediately if the water level in the tank falls below 0.25 m. The attacker wants to increase the water without being noticed by a typical detection system that looks for irregularities. This is accomplished by altering the sensor and actuator information and creating the proper packets, which are altered so that the devices' functionality can be changed by the fieldbus communication.

The model was trained to recognize anomalies during the operation of the SCADA automations that manage the water tank in the situation under examination using the above-described technique. The success or failure of the anomaly recognition approach is largely dependent on the class separation threshold. This research suggests a trustworthy heuristic approach of selection, based only on assessment criteria, to identify an ideal threshold. The suggested technique specifically implies that a distance function, which calculates the distance d between the objects and the appropriate target category, is constructed during the training phase. For the binary class separation (normal or abnormal), a threshold is utilized.

The proposed algorithm calculating the density around each data point in order to identify the dynamic threshold. This is achieved by counting the number of points in a user-defined neighborhood (*Eps*-Neighbourhood) with the definition of thresholds. The purpose is to locate points in the center of the areas (core), on their borders (border), and points that involve noise (noise). The extra data points are added to the center of the regions if they are densely accessible, i.e., there is a chain of core points where each one belongs to the neighborhood (*Eps*-Neighborhood) of the next point and therefore to distinguish the extreme values for each time frame. Specifically, the neighborhood area of a point p is defined as the set of points for which the Euclidean distance between the points p, q is smaller than the parameter *Eps* [27, 28]:

$$N_{Eps}(p) = \{q \in D|\ dist(p, q) \leq Eps\} \tag{7}$$

provided that $p = (p1, p2)$ and $q = (q1, q2)$, the Euclidean distance is defined as:

$$\sqrt{(q_1 - p_1)^2 + (q_2 - p_2)^2} \tag{8}$$

So, a point p is considered to be reachable from a point q based on a density determined by the parameters *Eps*, *MinPts* if:

$$p \in N_{Eps}(q) \text{ and } N_{Eps}(q) \geq MinPts \tag{9}$$

Two plots to visualize the dynamic threshold calculation depicted in the following Fig. 2.

Samples (outliers) are considered abnormal when the anomaly score departs from the expected behavior by the application of the dynamic threshold.

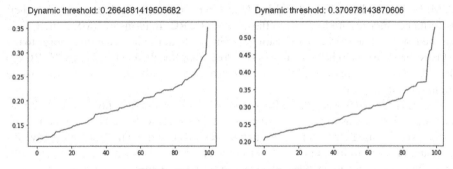

Fig. 2. Dynamic threshold calculation

Evaluating the performance of anomaly detection algorithms is important to understand how well they are able to detect anomalies in a given dataset. Here are the used performance metrics for anomaly detection [29–31]:

1. Accuracy: The percentage of correctly classified data points as normal or anomalous.
2. RMSE: It measures the average distance between the predicted and actual values in a dataset taking into account the scale of the values.
3. Precision: The proportion of true positive predictions out of all positive predictions.
4. Recall (Sensitivity): The proportion of true positive predictions out of all actual positives
5. F-Score: The harmonic mean of precision and recall.
6. AUC: A metric that measures the performance of the model across different thresholds for labeling data as normal or anomalous. It is calculated as the area under the ROC curve, which plots the true positive rate (sensitivity) against the false positive rate (1-specificity) at different threshold values. A higher AUC indicates better performance.

Table 1 shows the classification accuracy and performance metrics of five different classifiers: CTRC, One Class SVM, Long Short-Term Memory (LSTM), Isolation Forest and k-NN.

Table 1. Classification Accuracy and Performance Metrics

Classifier	Accuracy	RMSE	Precision	Recall	F-Score	AUC
CTRC	97.89%	0.0821	0.980	0.980	0.978	0.9887
One Class SVM	93.66%	0.0912	0.937	0.936	0.937	0.9752
LSTM	93.17%	0.0932	0.932	0.933	0.933	0.9703
Isolation Forest	91.38%	0.1007	0.914	0.914	0.913	0.9588
k-NN	87.99%	0.1185	0.880	0.880	0.880	0.9502

In the above Table 1, it is shown that the CTRC has the highest accuracy (97.89%) and AUC (0.9887), as well as the highest precision, recall, and F-score. One Class

SVM, LSTM, Isolation Forest and k-NN also have relatively high accuracy, but their performance metrics are lower than those of the CTRC. In terms of RMSE, the CTRC has the lowest value (0.0821), indicating that its predictions are on average closer to the actual values than the other classifiers. The Precision, Recall, and F-score for CTRC are also relatively high, indicating that it is able to correctly identify positive cases while minimizing false positives.

The CTRC model as a type of Recurrent Neural Network has shown to be effective for time series forecasting and classification tasks. Specifically, CTRC can be trained easily, using a single forward pass through the reservoir, making it computationally efficient and faster to train than other recurrent neural networks such as LSTM networks. This efficiency is beneficial for real-time applications where the model needs to make predictions quickly. In addition is robust to noise in the input data and to perform well even when the input data is corrupted or contains missing values. This robustness is useful in real-world cybersecurity applications where the data may not be perfectly clean. Moreover, CTRC is relatively easy to implement and does not require complex optimization algorithms or hyperparameter tuning. This make it more accessible to researchers and practitioners who may not have extensive experience with machine learning. Finally, it adapts to changing input data over time due to the differential equation, allowing it to continuously learn and improve its predictions based on Q-learning algorithm. This adaptability is extremely useful in the cyber defense applications where the input data changes frequently or where there are multiple sources of variability.

Overall, the CTRC model's efficiency, robustness, ease of implementation, and adaptability make it a promising approach for time series classification and forecasting tasks, and it may outperform other classifiers in certain scenarios. In conclusion, based on the obtained values of the performance indices and considering the objective difficulties raised in this research, the proposed model has been proven very efficient, able to cope with complex situations and to recognize anomalies.

4   Discussion and Conclusions

This research presents a next-generation anomaly detection model for cyber defence where the reservoir neurons are modelled as continuous-time dynamical systems. The CTRC system uses the dynamics of a high-dimensional, randomly connected network to process and learn from complicated input signals. In particular, CTRC expands the constantly operating reservoir computing paradigm. It provides discretization-free real-time processing of input signals, and the Q-Learning method is used to optimize the system parameters. The fundamental goal of CTRC is to convert the time-series data input into a high-dimensional representation that can be applied to tasks involving classification or prediction. The input is transformed through the reservoir, a fixed network of nonlinear dynamical systems with random initialization. Differential equations with a continuous time are used to describe reservoir dynamics. The output layer is trained to distinguish between normal (i.e., non-anomalous) and abnormal data to apply CTRC for anomaly detection.

The proposed approach is extremely helpful when conventional rule-based detection techniques fall short, such as zero-day assaults or other sophisticated, persistent threats.

It also has several advantages over other machine learning methods, such as a quick and easy training procedure and the ability to interpret time-series data effectively.

While Continuous-Time Reservoir Computing (CTRC) has shown promising results, there are two specific limitations to consider in future research using this model:

1. Model Complexity: CTRC can have a high model complexity due to many reservoir nodes and recurrent connections. This can make it difficult to interpret and analyze the model and make it prone to overfitting.
2. Limited Memory: The reservoir in CTRC has a limited memory capacity, which means that it may struggle to process long-term dependencies in data. This makes it less suitable for applications with important long-term patterns or trends.

References

1. Bala, A., Ismail, I., Ibrahim, R., Sait, S.M.: Applications of metaheuristics in reservoir computing techniques: a review. IEEE Access **6**, 58012–58029 (2018). https://doi.org/10.1109/ACCESS.2018.2873770
2. Demertzis, K., Iliadis, L., Pimenidis, E.: Geo-AI to aid disaster response by memory-augmented deep reservoir computing. Integr. Comput.-Aided Eng. **28**(4), 383–398 (2021). https://doi.org/10.3233/ICA-210657
3. Freiberger, M., Katumba, A., Bienstman, P., Dambre, J.: Training passive photonic reservoirs with integrated optical readout. IEEE Trans. Neural Netw. Learn. Syst. **30**(7), 1943–1953 (2019). https://doi.org/10.1109/TNNLS.2018.2874571
4. Li, S., Pachnicke, S.: Photonic reservoir computing in optical transmission systems. In: 2020 IEEE Photonics Society Summer Topicals Meeting Series (SUM), pp. 1–2 (2020). https://doi.org/10.1109/SUM48678.2020.9161045
5. Gauthier, D.J., Bollt, E., Griffith, A., Barbosa, W.A.S.: Next generation reservoir computing. Nat. Commun. **12**(1), Art. no. 1 (2021). https://doi.org/10.1038/s41467-021-25801-2
6. Demertzis, K., Kikiras, P., Tziritas, N., Sanchez, S.L., Iliadis, L.: The next generation cognitive security operations center: network flow forensics using cybersecurity intelligence. Big Data Cogn. Comput. **2**(4), Art. no. 4 (2018). https://doi.org/10.3390/bdcc2040035
7. Hart, A.: Generalised Synchronisation for Continuous Time Reservoir Computers. Rochester, NY (2021). https://doi.org/10.2139/ssrn.3987856
8. Smith, L.M., Kim, J.Z., Lu, Z., Bassett, D.S.: Learning continuous chaotic attractors with a reservoir computer. Chaos Interdiscip. J. Nonlinear Sci. **32**(1), 011101 (2022). https://doi.org/10.1063/5.0075572
9. Abu, U.A., Folly, K.A., Jayawardene, I., Venayagamoorthy, G.K.: Echo state network (ESN) based generator speed prediction of wide area signals in a multimachine power system. In: 2020 International SAUPEC/RobMech/PRASA Conference, pp. 1–5 (2020). https://doi.org/10.1109/SAUPEC/RobMech/PRASA48453.2020.9041236
10. Duport, F., Smerieri, A., Akrout, A., Haelterman, M., Massar, S.: Fully analogue photonic reservoir computer. Sci. Rep. **6**(1), Art. no. 1 (2016). https://doi.org/10.1038/srep22381
11. Manjunath, G.: An echo state network imparts a curve fitting. IEEE Trans. Neural Netw. Learn. Syst. **33**(6), 2596–2604 (2022). https://doi.org/10.1109/TNNLS.2021.3099091
12. Wang, Z., Yao, X., Huang, Z., Liu, L.: Deep echo state network with multiple adaptive reservoirs for time series prediction. IEEE Trans. Cogn. Dev. Syst. **13**(3), 693–704 (2021). https://doi.org/10.1109/TCDS.2021.3062177

13. Whiteaker, B., Gerstoft, P.: Memory in echo state networks and the controllability matrix rank. In: ICASSP 2022 - 2022 IEEE International Conference on Acoustics, Speech and Signal Processing (ICASSP), pp. 3948–3952 (2022). https://doi.org/10.1109/ICASSP43922.2022. 9746766

14. Shao, Y., Yao, X., Wang, G., Cao, S.: A new improved echo state network with multiple output layers for time series prediction. In: 2021 6th International Conference on Robotics and Automation Engineering (ICRAE), pp. 7–11 (2021). https://doi.org/10.1109/ICRAE5 3653.2021.9657812

15. Li, X., Bi, F., Yang, X., Bi, X.: An echo state network with improved topology for time series prediction. IEEE Sens. J. **22**(6), 5869–5878 (2022). https://doi.org/10.1109/JSEN.2022.314 8742

16. Kidger, P.: On Neural Differential Equations. arXiv (2022). https://doi.org/10.48550/arXiv. 2202.02435

17. Physics-informed neural networks: A deep learning framework for solving forward and inverse problems involving nonlinear partial differential equations. J. Comput. Phys. **378**, 686–707 (2019). https://doi.org/10.1016/j.jcp.2018.10.045

18. Demertzis, K., Iliadis, L.: Adaptive elitist differential evolution extreme learning machines on big data: intelligent recognition of invasive species. In: Angelov, P., Manolopoulos, Y., Iliadis, L., Roy, A., Vellasco, M. (eds.) INNS 2016. AISC, vol. 529, pp. 333–345. Springer, Cham (2017). https://doi.org/10.1007/978-3-319-47898-2_34

19. Bai, Z., Pang, H., Liu, M., Wang, M.: An improved Q-Learning algorithm and its application to the optimized path planning for unmanned ground robot with obstacle avoidance. In: 2022 6th CAA International Conference on Vehicular Control and Intelligence (CVCI), pp. 1–6 (2022). https://doi.org/10.1109/CVCI56766.2022.9964859

20. Huang, D., Zhu, H., Lin, X., Wang, L.: Application of massive parallel computation based Q-learning in system control. In: 2022 5th International Conference on Pattern Recognition and Artificial Intelligence (PRAI), pp. 1–5 (2022). https://doi.org/10.1109/PRAI55851.2022. 9904213

21. Yin, Z., Cao, W., Song, T., Yang, X., Zhang, T.: Reinforcement learning path planning based on step batch Q-learning algorithm. In: 2022 IEEE International Conference on Artificial Intelligence and Computer Applications (ICAICA), pp. 630–633 (2022). https://doi.org/10. 1109/ICAICA54878.2022.9844553

22. Chouiekh, C., Yahyaouy, A., Aarab, A., Sabri, A.: Road traffic: deep q-learning agent control traffic lights in the intersection. In: 2022 International Conference on Intelligent Systems and Computer Vision (ISCV), pp. 1–5 (2022). https://doi.org/10.1109/ISCV54655.2022.9806135

23. InfluxDB Times Series Data Platform. InfluxData (2022). https://www.influxdata.com/home/. Accessed 28 Feb 2023

24. Industrial IoT (IIoT) solutions for smart industries – Factry. Factry - Open Manufacturing Intelligence. https://www.factry.io/. Accessed 28 Feb 2023

25. Nguyen, Q.-D., Dhouib, S., Chanet, J.-P., Bellot, P.: Towards a web-of-things approach for OPC UA field device discovery in the industrial IoT. In: 2022 IEEE 18th International Conference on Factory Communication Systems (WFCS), pp. 1–4 (2022). https://doi.org/10.1109/ WFCS53837.2022.9779181

26. Demertzis, K., Iliadis, L.S., Anezakis, V.-D.: An innovative soft computing system for smart energy grids cybersecurity. Adv. Build. Energy Res. **12**(1), 3–24 (2018). https://doi.org/10. 1080/17512549.2017.1325401

27. Wang, H., Wang, Y., Wan, S.: A density-based clustering algorithm for uncertain data. In: 2012 International Conference on Computer Science and Electronics Engineering, vol. 3, pp. 102–105 (2012). https://doi.org/10.1109/ICCSEE.2012.91

28. Khan, M.M.R., Siddique, M.A.B., Arif, R.B., Oishe, M.R.: ADBSCAN: adaptive density-based spatial clustering of applications with noise for identifying clusters with varying densities. In: 2018 4th International Conference on Electrical Engineering and Information & Communication Technology (iCEEiCT), pp. 107–111 (2018). https://doi.org/10.1109/CEE ICT.2018.8628138

29. Botchkarev, A.: Performance metrics (error measures) in machine learning regression, forecasting and prognostics: properties and typology. Interdiscip. J. Inf. Knowl. Manag. **14**, 045–076 (2019). https://doi.org/10.28945/4184

30. Koyejo, O.O., Natarajan, N., Ravikumar, P.K., Dhillon, I.S.: Consistent binary classification with generalized performance metrics. In: Advances in Neural Information Processing Systems, vol. 27 (2014). https://papers.nips.cc/paper/2014/hash/30c8e1ca872524fbf7ea5c519ca 397ee-Abstract.html. Accessed 24 Oct 2021

31. Liu, Y., Zhou, Y., Wen, S., Tang, C.: A strategy on selecting performance metrics for classifier evaluation. Int. J. Mob. Comput. Multimed. Commun. IJMCMC **6**(4), 20–35 (2014). https://doi.org/10.4018/IJMCMC.2014100102

One-Class Models for Intrusion Detection at ISP Customer Networks

Nuno Schumacher[1], Pedro M. Santos[2,3](✉), Pedro F. Souto[1,3],
Nuno Martins[4], Joana Sousa[4], João M. Ferreira[4], and Luís Almeida[1,3]

[1] Universidade do Porto - Faculdade de Engenharia, Porto, Portugal
{nuno.schumacher,pfs,lda}@fe.up.pt
[2] Instituto Superior de Engenharia do Porto - Instituto Politécnico do Porto,
Porto, Portugal
pss@isep.ipp.pt
[3] CISTER Research Unit, Porto, Portugal
[4] NOS Inovação, Lisboa, Portugal
{nuno.mmartins,joana.sousa,joao.MFerreira}@nos.pt

Abstract. Despite the explosion of IoT deployments at Internet Service Provider (ISP) customer networks, such devices remain vulnerable to cyber-attacks. We present a ML-based anomaly detection system, to be deployed at the Customer Premises Equipment (CPE), that leverages several One-Class Classification algorithms and majority voting to detect anomalous network traffic. We train these models using not only conventional per-flow features but also features extracted from sliding windows of flows. An extensive evaluation, using publicly available datasets shows that our algorithm has a higher detection rate than commonly supervised-learning algorithms, which require the use of labelled datasets. Our evaluation suggests that the detection capabilities of our algorithm are only marginally affected by Packet Acceleration, a technique used by CPEs to improve throughput but that reduces the number of packets (per flow) available to extract features from.

Keywords: IoT · Intrusion Detection System · One-Class Classification

1 Introduction

By the end of 2020, cybercrime-derived losses approached $1 trillion [3]. A particular type of cyberattacks is Denial-of-Service (DoS), in which a malicious agent floods a target server with a number of requests that exceeds the server's capacity, thus denying access to legitimate users. A Distributed DoS (DDoS) attack generates traffic from a very large number of sources that have been infected previously with malware (*botnet*) that is under remote control from a Command and Control (C&C) server. The distributed nature of this attack makes it hard to counteract, because the traffic pattern generated by the devices may be difficult to distinguish from regular traffic. A well-known malware used in DDoS

© IFIP International Federation for Information Processing 2023
Published by Springer Nature Switzerland AG 2023
I. Maglogiannis et al. (Eds.): AIAI 2023, IFIP AICT 676, pp. 28–41, 2023.
https://doi.org/10.1007/978-3-031-34107-6_3

attacks is Mirai, which targeted domestic IoT devices such as surveillance cameras, DVRs and routers, and was responsible, among others, for a DDoS attack to French webhost and cloud service provider OVH that peaked at 1.1 Tbps [6].

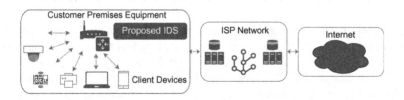

Fig. 1. Context of operation and placement of proposed IDS

IoT devices are often not equipped with levels of protection similar to personal devices (e.g., laptops, smart phones), and attackers explore such ill-protected devices for infection and attack. With the growing number of IoT devices deployed at their customer premises, Internet Service Providers (ISPs) are interested in protecting their customers networks as well as their own. In this paper we describe Machine Learning (ML) models for an Intrusion Detection System (IDS) to be deployed at the Customer Premises Equipment (CPE), an ISP-provided equipment that enables Internet connectivity and local networking, as shown in Fig. 1. The goal is to monitor the network traffic at the CPE and use ML techniques to detect anomalies. More specifically, we present an anomaly detector that uses several one-class classification (OCC) models and majority voting to classify network traffic as either legitimate or (potentially) malicious. Model training can happen either at the CPE or be offloaded to the cloud. As CPEs have limited computing power, we foresee training to be cloud-based and trained models to be deployed at the CPE for inference; however, we do not address this aspect of the system in this paper.

The deployment of the IDS at the CPE runs into another specific challenge: CPEs typically resort to packet accelerators (PA) to speed up packet processing. As a result, the IDS only has access to the first few packets of each traffic flow, i.e. it must make predictions based only on those packets.

Our contributions can be summarized as follows.

– **Use of features of a sliding window of traffic flows** in combination with traditional traffic flow features.
– **Use of a refined hyperparameter tuning strategy** for training each of the OCC models and of **majority voting** for prediction. This combination leads to a model that has a higher detection rate than models using supervised learning.
– An extensive evaluation of the prediction accuracy with and without **packet acceleration** (PA), indicating that PA does not affect performance significantly.

The remainder of this paper is as follows. Section 2 reviews the relevant state-of-the-art. Section 3 details the datasets identified and used in this work, followed by the developed ML pipeline. A performance evaluation of the system is presented in Sect. 4. Section 5 draws final remarks.

2   Related Work on ML-Based IDS for IoT Networks

In this section, we focus our review on detection of (D)DoS and Botnet infections in IoT networks, due to the growing relevance of such attacks. A broader review of the research on the application of ML to IDS for IoT networks can be found in survey papers like [2] and [4]. Nõmm and Bahşi [17] developed an anomaly-based detection system with emphasis on reducing model dimension. They compared a common model with device-specific models using iForest and SVM and concluded that, for some devices, a common model had significantly lower detection performance, due to the complexity and uniqueness of some devices. Lima Filho et al. [14] developed *Smart Detection*, an ML system for DoS/DDoS detection. The authors used a dataset of their own and three public datasets to validate their Random Forest based model; results showed that the system was capable of accurately detecting different types of DoS attacks such as TCP/UDP/HTTP floods. Yuan et al. [21] developed *DeepDefense*, a Deep Learning detection system with emphasis on DDoS. By using various types of Recurrent Neural Networks (RNN), such as LSTM, authors achieved a reduction of the error rate from 7.517% to 2.103%, with respect to Random Forest. Other line of research is the detection as early as possible of infection by botnets such as Mirai. Kumar and Lim [13] developed *Early Detection of IoT Malware Network Activity* (EDIMA), a botnet detection system aimed at identifying malware activity during the scanning and infection phases. They used their own dataset to simulate the characteristics of the original Mirai code during the initial phases and this data was fed to models based on Random Forest, k-NN and Naive Bayes, obtaining good results on the scoring metrics. Meidan et al. [16] developed an anomaly-based IDS for botnet detection using deep learning techniques. They trained an autoencoder for each IoT device to capture their normal traffic behavior, and evaluated their method by deploying the Mirai and BASHLITE botnets. Every attack was successfully detected with a low false positive rate. McDermott et al. [15] deployed a Deep Learning approach to detect botnet activity, based on Bidirectional Long Short Term Memory based Recurrent Neural Networks (BLSTM-RNN). The authors produced their own dataset with Mirai attack samples; BLSTM-RNN was compared to LSTM-RNN and the results showed high accuracy in the detection of botnets and other related attacks.

Our work focus on one-class classification (OCC) algorithms, as [17], but it considers a larger number of algorithms and uses majority voting to improve the detection rate and reduce the false positive rate. Furthermore, it uses inter-flow (sliding window) features to improve those metrics, and evaluates the effect of packet acceleration, a feature typically used by CPEs to increase their bandwidth. To develop our system, we carried out a careful review of publicly-available datasets and judiciously combined them to obtain a composite dataset that features both personal and IoT traffic with adequate representativeness.

3   Machine Learning Models for Anomaly Detection

We describe the training of the Machine Learning models used in this Intrusion Detection System. The goal of this system is to detect anomalous traffic at or to/from the customer network, i.e., traffic that differs considerably from the typical observed behaviour and that can be presumed to be malicious traffic.

Two particular decisions have influenced our approach. The first one was to train ML models solely with legitimate data, under the assumption that malicious traffic datasets are hard to obtain or of little use, as unknown attacks may operate differently than existing ones. As mentioned in Sect. 1, this option lead to the use of OCC models. The second one was to use two types of legitimate traffic: *IoT* and *normal* traffic. By IoT traffic, we mean traffic generated by devices that collect data or perform simple home tasks. IoT devices connected to a home network include IP security cameras, smart bulbs and door sensors. The traffic volume generated by these devices is typically low (with exceptions such as camera video streams), the connections are periodic and relatively repetitive [1]. Normal traffic is usually generated directly by humans on their personal devices, such as laptops and smartphones; examples are web browsing, gaming and video conferencing.

The two above decisions informed our selection of publicly available datasets; these are described in Sect. 3.1. Used features and extraction procedure are described in Sect. 3.2. Lastly, in Sect. 3.3, we describe the selected OCC ML models, the majority voting procedure developed to aggregate the output of the various models into a single classification, and the hyperparameter tuning procedure carried out at training to improve accuracy.

3.1   Public Datasets Description

The datasets relevant to this work, and that would be captured by the Customer Premises Equipment (CPE), are composed of packet capture traces. Sequences of packets that have similar characteristics (e.g., same source and destination nodes) and occur in temporal proximity can be aggregated in **flows**. In TCP-based transactions, flows are named *connections*, and the start and end of transactions are explicitly identified with dedicated packets. Our OCC models use as features mainly statistical characteristics of flows. After introducing the used datasets, we discuss the process of mapping raw packet captures into flow descriptions.

Used datasets were the **UNSW-IoT** [19], **Bot-IoT** [7–12], **IoT-23** [5], **CTU-Normal** [20], and the **NOS** dataset (produced by portuguese ISP NOS and not publicly disclosed at this moment). The combination of these provides sets of IoT and normal traffic samples from different scenarios, as well as samples from different types of attacks that commonly affect the devices in question. Table 1 outlines the types of samples present in each of these datasets.

The **UNSW-IoT** dataset was separated into two subsets with devices of similar types, as shown in Table 2. The first set (**UNSW-IoT #1**) was used

Table 1. Selected datasets and types of traces.

Datasets	IoT Traces	Normal Traces	Attack Traces
UNSW-IoT	√	X	√
Bot-IoT	√	X	√
IoT-23	√	X	√
CTU-Normal	X	√	X
NOS provided	√	√	X

Table 2. Traces Used For Training And Validating The Models

	Dataset	Training	Hyperparameter Tuning	Evaluation	Capture details
Benign	UNSW-IoT #1	2000	2000	1832	Amazon Echo, Netatmo camera, Lixf light, WEMO power switch
	UNSW-IoT #2	–	–	5331	iHome, Samsung camera, Hue bulb, TP Link plug
	IoT-23	–	–	486	Amazon Echo, Hue bulb, Somfy door lock
	NOS - IoT	–	–	10	Smart plug, temperature and humidity sensors
	CTU-Normal #1	2000	2000	27639	Automated capture, top 500 websites: 1-30, 61-120, 241-360
	CTU-Normal #2	–	–	31790	Automated capture, top 500 websites: 31-60, 150-240, 361-500 and manual capture of web traffic
	NOS -Normal	–	–	295	Manual capture of web traffic
Malign	Bot-IoT - TCP DDoS	–	2000	35585	TCP floods generated using hping3
	Bot-IoT - HTTP DDoS	–	–	19180	HTTP request floods using Golden-eye
	Bot-IoT - OS Scan	–	–	68	OS fingerprinting using Nmap and Xprobe2
	Bot-IoT - Service Scan	–	2000	34885	Different port scans using Nmap and Hping3
	Bot-IoT - Keylogging	–	–	1464	Record keystrokes with Logkeys or exploits
	Bot-IoT - Data Theft	–	–	197	Directory exfiltration through system exploits
	IoT-23 - DDoS	–	–	114	DDoS attack part of a botnet
	IoT-23 - Port Scan	–	–	68	Port scans part of a botnet
	IoT-23 - C&C	–	–	4094	C&C communication part of a botnet

for the hyperparameter tuning selection, as described in Sect. 3.3, and training with different samples from that subset afterwards. The remaining samples are used for evaluation. The second set (**UNSW-IoT #2**) is used solely for inference, to evaluate the model's ability to correctly recognise new traffic of a similar type. We took a similar approach for the normal traffic, with the first set (**CTU-Normal #1**) being used for training and hyperparameter tuning and the second (**CTU-Normal #2**) for evaluation. The rest of the benign samples from the remaining datasets (**IoT-23** and **NOS**) was used solely for evaluating the models.

Selected datasets typically either do not have absolute *Ground Truth* labels, i.e., a label indicating whether a given flow is legitimate or malicious, or use rule-based external tools to attribute labels, such as *Zeek* (https://zeek.org/) or *Argus* (https://openargus.org/), which is not appropriate for inference on unseen anomalous traffic patterns since their rules are too specific. In our work, we resort in great measure to the *tstat* (http://tstat.polito.it/) tool (discussed in the next section) to extract flows from raw packet captures. The issue arises to map one tool's flows (e.g., *tstat*) into another tool's flows (*Zeek* or *Argus*). For that, we developed a tool that allows us to map the labels of existing datasets into

Table 3. *Tstat* (top) and sliding window (bottom) features

Feature	Unit	Description
packets	-	total number of packets observed form the client/server
RST sent	0/1	0 = no RST segment has been sent by the client/server
ACK sent	-	number of segments with the ACK field set to 1
PURE ACK sent	-	number of segments with ACK field set to 1 and no data
unique bytes	bytes	number of bytes sent in the payload
data pkts	-	number of segments with payload
data bytes	bytes	number of bytes transmitted in the payload, including retransmissions
rexmit pkts	-	number of retransmitted segments
rexmit bytes	bytes	number of retransmitted bytes
out seq pkts	-	number of segments observed out of sequence
SYN count	-	number of SYN segments observed (including rtx)
FIN count	-	number of FIN segments observed (including rtx)
Completion time	ms	Flow duration since first packet to last packet
C first payload	ms	Client first segment with payload since the first flow segment
S first payload	ms	Server first segment with payload since the first flow segment
C last payload	ms	Client last segment with payload since the first flow segment
S last payload	ms	Server last segment with payload since the first flow segment
C first ack	ms	Client first ACK segment (without SYN) since the first flow segment
S first ack	ms	Server first ACK segment (without SYN) since the first flow segment
sw_fRate_IPSrc	flows/s	Rate of flows with same origin IP
sw_bRate_IPSrc	bytes/s	Rate of bytes with same origin IP
sw_pRate_IPSrc	pkts/s	Rate of packets with same origin IP
sw_fRate_IpPortDst	flows/s	Rate of flows with same destination IP and Port
sw_bRate_IpPortDst	bytes/s	Rate of bytes with same destination IP and Port
sw_pRate_IpPortDst	pkts/s	Rate of packets with same destination IP and Port
sw_isComplete_percentage	-	Percentage of flows that are complete

tstat generated logs, thus allowing us to use those datasets to train the models and still have the large feature set generated by *tstat*.

3.2 Feature Extraction and Description

The raw packet captures are processed to extract flow and inter-flow characteristics that serve as features in the model training and evaluation procedures.

Flow-Based Features: The publicly available packet traces were parsed with *tstat*, a tool that identifies flows from packet traces. Features that have no statistical relevance are removed, such as identifiers (e.g., IP addresses), timestamps and highly-contextual characteristics (e.g., whether address are anonimized/internal or not). Table 3 presents the flow descriptions produced by *tstat* that we use to train our models. The feature values were normalized before applied to the models via Min-Max normalization (rescaling the training data to $[0, 1]$). Figure 2 shows a boxplot of the numerical normalized features for the benign and malign sets for hyperparameter tuning (see Table 2). It shows that some features have different distributions for each class, and therefore should

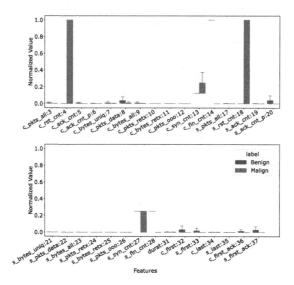

Fig. 2. Boxplot of *tstat*-generated features for both classes

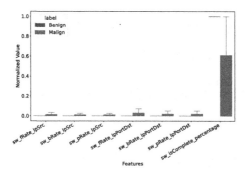

Fig. 3. Boxplot of the window-based features per traffic class.

be used to improve the classifiers' performance. Note that the hyperparameter tuning and evaluation data is rescaled using the same reference values as the training set.

Sliding Window Features: While informative, observing specific flows does not directly give network context (e.g., network throughput) or device context (e.g., device throughput), and it does not provide much information at a packet level either. We generated extra features (from *tstat*'s) using a sliding window of 100 flows (a value selected empirically), that are also shown in Table 3 (bottom section).

The rate of flows/bytes/packets are calculated by the number of flows/bytes/ packets that occurred in that window, divided by the elapsed time of that window, respectively. These rates are calculated per original IP address (refered to

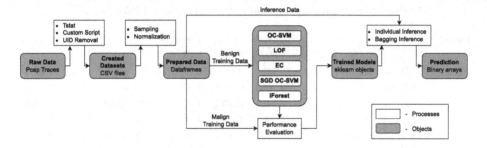

Fig. 4. Developed prediction pipeline for the proposed IDS

as client by *tstat*, thus specifying the origin device) and per destination (ref-ered to server by *tstat*) IP address and port (thus specifying the destination device/service). Lastly, the percentage of flow that are classified as complete is calculated. Complete flows are properly initiated (by a three-way handshake) and closed (by a FIN or RST flag, or after a certain timeout).

Figure 3 shows the normalized distribution of these derived features per traf-fic class. We observe larger values for the malign class, as expected for flood attacks, thus indicating potential usefulness to the classifiers. Additionally, the percentage of complete flows feature is nearly maximum for the benign class, indicating most benign flows are correctly terminated, but low for the malign class, which is expected as many attacks never get to properly initiate and ter-minate the connections.

3.3   Selected ML Methods, Decision and Tuning

As refered earlier, we focus on the use of one-class classification (OCC) algo-rithms. OCC models receive only benign/legitimate (or negative class) data and attempt to fit boundaries around these data points. The OCC models used in this work are:

- **One-Class Support Vector Machine** (OC-SVM)
- **Stochastic Gradient Descent One-Class Support Vector Machine** (SGD OC-SVM)
- **Local Outlier Factor** (LOF)
- **Elliptic Curve** (EC)
- **Isolation Forest** (iForest)

Model implementations were provided by the *scikit-learn* library [18]. At the end, a single classification output must be provided. Once the models are trained and a classification is requested, we implement a **majority vote strategy**, in which the class with the highest number of votes is output. Figure 4 describes the complete prediction ML pipeline, including the feature extraction stage described earlier.

Table 4. Performance of optimized, supervised and PA models

Dataset		Tuning		Supervised				PA
		Default	Tuned	SVM	RF	NB	KNN	
Benign	UNSW-IoT #1 (T,V)	0.9333	**0.9890**	1.0000	0.9996	0.9976	0.9999	0.9239
	UNSW-IoT #2	0.9650	**0.9923**	1.0000	0.9998	0.9999	0.9999	0.9939
	IoT-23	0.5483	**0.9055**	1.0000	1.0000	1.0000	1.0000	0.8704
	NOS - IoT	1.0000	**1.0000**	1.0000	1.0000	0.9836	0.9979	1.0000
	CTU-Normal #1 (T,V)	0.8392	**0.9801**	1.0000	0.9995	0.9964	0.9998	0.9893
	CTU-Normal #2	0.8378	**0.9822**	1.0000	0.9997	0.9957	0.9999	0.9929
	NOS - Normal	0.0946	**0.4358**	1.0000	1.0000	0.9223	1.0000	0.4257
Malign	Bot-IoT - TCP DDoS (T,V)	1.0000	**1.0000**	0.9931	1.0000	1.0000	1.0000	1.0000
	Bot-IoT - HTTP DDoS	1.0000	**0.8612**	0.3163	0.9767	0.4203	0.3905	0.9174
	Bot-IoT - OS Scan	0.9980	**0.9696**	0.6419	0.9956	0.9668	0.9594	0.9693
	Bot-IoT - Service Scan (T,V)	0.9986	**0.9926**	0.8118	0.9994	0.9890	0.9946	0.9914
	Bot-IoT - Keylogging	1.0000	**0.9590**	0.0000	0.9980	0.9495	0.8198	0.9235
	Bot-IoT - Data Theft	0.9898	**0.7959**	0.0102	0.9796	0.7602	0.6633	0.7449
	IoT-23 - Port Scan	1.0000	**1.0000**	0.0000	0.0142	1.0000	1.0000	N/A
	IoT-23 - DDoS	1.0000	**1.0000**	0.0000	0.9913	0.9826	0.9913	N/A
	IoT-23 - C&C	0.9995	**0.9900**	0.0000	0.0139	1.0000	1.0000	N/A

During the training stage, each model has a set of user-defined parameters (i.e., hyperparameters) that can be changed as part of a validation process. Optimizing these based on performance for only the benign class (i.e., true negative rate) might lead to large or underfit boundaries that maximize performance for the benign class, but then incorrectly classify malicious samples as also benign leading to high false negative rates. To compensate for this factor, we used samples of both classes (benign and malign) when calculating the accuracy of the model with the chosen parameters. The models are still trained with only benign data, but this validation informed by the two classes allows for the selection of a good set of hyperparameters that can be later on used for training new models without the need for validation and, consequently, any malign samples.

Considering the number of samples is limited in one of the chosen datasets, and that models size can increase drastically with number of training samples, each training and hyperparameter tuning set is sampled to **n = 2000 samples**, while the remaining samples are used for evaluation.

4   Results and Discussion

We evaluate the models for different scenarios. The main metric used is **accuracy**; since the datasets are separated by class, this directly translates to the True Negative Rate (**TNR**) and True Positive Rate (**TPR**) when predicting for benign or malign traffic, respectively. Note that the results that combine different datasets are a simple average of the performance for each dataset, i.e. it doesn't take into account the size of theses datasets.

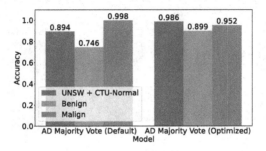

Fig. 5. Comparison between models with untuned (default) and tuned (optimized) parameters

4.1 Baseline and Tuned Classification Performance

We assess the ability of the ML models to correctly classify unseen traffic samples of the devices present in a network, as well as from other devices similar to those seen during training. The models were trained with traffic from **UNSW-IoT #1** and **CTU-Normal #1**. The most relevant test datasets of benign traffic are the **UNSW-IoT #2** and **CTU-Normal #2**, since these constitute (different) traffic generated in the same networks. This subset of data is hereby refered to as **UNSW+CTU** for simplicity. The other benign datasets serve the purpose of assessing correct benign classification of captures in different conditions.

Table 4 (*Default* column) shows the accuracy when evaluating the ML models for each benign test dataset without any parameter tuning. Figure 5 (left side) summarizes the accuracy of the majority voting of the models with the untuned hyperparameters. The aggregated decision has a 89.4% accuracy, i.e., TNR, when inferring on **UNSW+CTU**, but the average (non-weighted) of the model accuracy per benign dataset is 74.6%. For the malign datasets, the average of the per-dataset accuracy, i.e. TPR, is 99.8%.

We perform the hyperparameter tuning process (Sect. 3.3) to decrease the false positive rate of the models. This procedure uses samples from **UNSW-IoT #1** and **CTU-Normal #1**, and also samples from **Bot-IoT TCP DDoS** and **Bot-IoT Service Scan** for the positive class. Afterwards, we evaluate the tuned models using the datasets previously used for evaluating the models with default hyperparameters. As earlier, Table 4 (*Tuned* column) shows the classification performance per dataset aggregated across all tuned models, and Fig. 5 (right side) summarizes the accuracy of the majority voting of the models with tuned hyperparameters. The majority vote of the tuned models achieves a performance of 98.6% for the **UNSW+CTU** subset, and an overall TNR of 89.9% and TPR of 95.2%.

Comparing default and tuned, hyperparameter tuning increases the TNR for the **UNSW+CTU** subset from 89.4% to 98.6%. In general, tuned models outperform untuned ones for benign datasets, resulting in an increased TNR from 74.6% to 89.9%. This comes at the cost of the TPR, that decreases from 99.8% to 95.2%. Overall, this trade-off alone is advantageous, since the FNR is still under

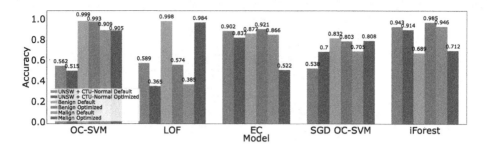

Fig. 6. Performance of individual models with default and tuned parameters.

a reasonable 5%, but the FPR is lower (particularly for the **UNSW+CTU** dataset), which is important to avoid raising too many false alerts to the ISP.

Finally, Fig. 6 presents the performance of individual models with default and tuned parameters aggregated per class. It is worth noting that some models clearly under-perform with the training data **UNSW+CTU** dataset (e.g., OC-SVM, LOF), but provide reasonable accuracy when classifying the other benign datasets. This may indicate statistical differences between the training data and the other benign datasets. Nevertheless, we observe that the aggregated classification accuracy, obtained through majority vote of the classifications of all models, improves over the accuracy of the individual models.

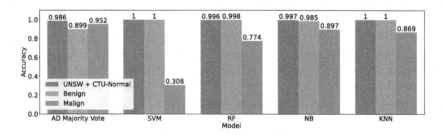

Fig. 7. Performance comparison between the anomaly detector and supervised models

4.2   Anomaly Detection vs. Supervised Learning Comparison

In order to assess how the proposed one-class models compare to traditional supervised methods, we trained four models of similar nature using traditional SVM, Random Forests (RF), Naive Bayes (NB) and k-Nearest Neighbors (KNN), more specifically their respective *scikit-learn* implementations. We trained these models using the datasets used for training and for hyperparameter tuning of the one-class models. For hyperparameter tunning, we used disjoint subsets of the datasets used for training.

Figure 7 summarizes the accuracy of these supervised models for the evaluation datasets previously used. Overall, the models present a higher TNR (most over 99%) but lower TPR (the highest being under 90%) than the OCC AD counterpart. The performance results for the supervised models are shown in Table 4 (*Supervised* columns).

The supervised models are better at inferring legitimate traffic correctly than the tuned version of the OCC models, including datasets for which OCC performed poorly (e.g., *NOS-Normal* dataset). Interestingly enough, **they generally perform worse for malign traffic**. Therefore, opting for a supervised solution would likely lead to less false alerts delivered to the ISP, but allow more malicious connections to go through unnoticed. This trade-off has to be assessed for each use-case, as the acceptable rates of each kind may vary, e.g., in accordance to Service Level Agreements.

4.3   Impact of Packet Acceleration (PA) on Model Accuracy

As described in Sect. 1, CPEs can be equipped with a packet accelerator to improve network throughput. This means that the classifiers deployed at the CPE may only have access to the first few packets of each flow for the inference process (the remaining packets of the flow are forwarded directly to the outgress port).

To simulate the effect of PA on the available datasets, we trimmed the flows according to what a PA would do. To do so, **NOS** (a portuguese ISP) provided datasets containing samples of flows with the PA deactivated (untrimmed flows) and activated (trimmed flows) captured on an actual CPE. We computed the probability mass functions (PMF) of these two sets of data, and configured *tstat* to trim flows in all datasets in a way that the resulting PMF mimics, to the extent possible, the PMF of the **NOS** trimmed dataset. This procedure was done by instructing *tstat* to trim flows to 5 packets – the value that we found, by visual inspection, to provide the best results. While the PMF of the new trimmed datasets did not replicate exactly the PMF of the **NOS** trimmed data, we consider a sufficiently similar result was obtained.

We trained and tuned the hyperparameters of the various one-class models using the same datasets as before, but now using the trimmed versions. Figure 8 summarizes the accuracy of these models for the evaluation datasets previously

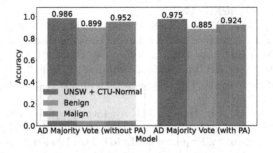

Fig. 8. Performance with or without PA.

used, but with the respective flows trimmed. Table 4 (*PA* column) shows the complete results. Overall, TNR is about 1.5% lower whereas TPR is about 3.3% lower. This suggests that PA does not to significantly affect the models classification capability, even when they are built with trimmed flows.

5 Conclusion

We report the development of ML-based anomaly detection (AD) techniques to be integrated in an Intrusion Detection System (IDS). The system is able to learn the typical traffic behaviour in the customer network and flag any anomalous traffic. We trained a range of AD methods with different underlying operating natures and combine their outputs into a single verdict using majority voting. To this end, we developed an ML pipeline that includes, at the training phase, an hyperparameter tuning stage that uses examples of malicious traffic for refinement. Lastly, we list the publicly-sourced datasets that were used for training and evaluating the models, and that encompass the different types of traffic expected in home networks. Performance evaluation showed correct classification rates of around 90% for legitimate traffic; this value increases to around 99% when considering traffic generated within same network conditions as the training data. It also detects different types of attacks with an average accuracy of around 95%.

Acknowledgements. This work was partially supported by National Funds through FCT/MCTES (Portuguese Foundation for Science and Technology), within the CIS-TER Research Unit (UIDB/04234/2020), and by the Portuguese National Innovation Agency (ANI) through the Operational Competitiveness Programme and Internationalization (COMPETE 2020) under the PT2020 Partnership Agreement, through the European Regional Development Fund (ERDF), within project(s) grant nr. 69522, POCI-01-0247-FEDER-069522 (MIRAI). The authors thank João Tagaio for creating the **NOS** dataset.

References

1. Apthorpe, N., Reisman, D., Feamster, N.: A Smart Home is No Castle: Privacy Vulnerabilities of Encrypted IoT Traffic. arXiv:1705.06805 (2017). http://arxiv.org/abs/1705.06805. arXiv: 1705.06805
2. Benkhelifa, E., Welsh, T., Hamouda, W.: A critical review of practices and challenges in intrusion detection systems for IoT: toward universal and resilient systems. IEEE Commun. Surv. Tutor. **20**(4), 3496–3509 (2018)
3. Center for Strategic and International Studies (CSIS): The Hidden Costs of Cybercrime. Technical report (2020). https://www.csis.org/analysis/hidden-costs-cybercrime
4. Elrawy, M.F., Awad, A.I., Hamed, H.F.A.: Intrusion detection systems for IoT-based smart environments: a survey. J. Cloud Comput. **7**(1), 21 (2018)
5. Garcia, S., Parmisano, A., Erquiaga, M.J.: IoT-23: a labeled dataset with malicious and benign IoT network traffic (version 1.0.0) [data set]. Stratosphere Lab., Praha, Czech Republic, Technical report (2020). https://doi.org/10.5281/zenodo.4743746

6. Kolias, C., Kambourakis, G., Stavrou, A., Voas, J.: DDoS in the IoT: Mirai and other botnets. Computer **50**(7), 80–84 (2017). https://doi.org/10.1109/MC.2017. 201

7. Koroniotis, N.: Designing an effective network forensic framework for the investigation of botnets in the Internet of Things. Ph.D. thesis, UNSW Sydney (2020)

8. Koroniotis, N., Moustafa, N.: Enhancing network forensics with particle swarm and deep learning: the particle deep framework. arXiv preprint arXiv:2005.00722 (2020)

9. Koroniotis, N., Moustafa, N., Schiliro, F., Gauravaram, P., Janicke, H.: A holistic review of cybersecurity and reliability perspectives in smart airports. IEEE Access **8**, 209802–209834 (2020). https://doi.org/10.1109/ACCESS.2020.3036728

10. Koroniotis, N., Moustafa, N., Sitnikova, E.: A new network forensic framework based on deep learning for internet of things networks: a particle deep framework. Futur. Gener. Comput. Syst. **110**, 91–106 (2020)

11. Koroniotis, N., Moustafa, N., Sitnikova, E., Slay, J.: Towards developing network forensic mechanism for botnet activities in the IoT based on machine learning techniques. In: Hu, J., Khalil, I., Tari, Z., Wen, S. (eds.) MONAMI 2017. LNICST, vol. 235, pp. 30–44. Springer, Cham (2018). https://doi.org/10.1007/978-3-319-90775-8_3

12. Koroniotis, N., Moustafa, N., Sitnikova, E., Turnbull, B.: Towards the development of realistic botnet dataset in the internet of things for network forensic analytics: bot-IoT dataset. Futur. Gener. Comput. Syst. **100**, 779–796 (2019)

13. Kumar, A., Lim, T.J.: EDIMA: early detection of IoT malware network activity using machine learning techniques. In: 2019 IEEE 5th World Forum on Internet of Things (WF-IoT), pp. 289–294 (2019). https://doi.org/10.1109/WF-IoT.2019. 8767194

14. Lima Filho, F.S.D., Silveira, F.A.F., de Medeiros Brito Junior, A., Vargas-Solar, G., Silveira, L.F.: Smart detection: an online approach for DoS/DDoS attack detection using machine learning. Secur. Commun. Netw. **2019**, 1–15 (2019)

15. McDermott, C.D., Majdani, F., Petrovski, A.V.: Botnet detection in the internet of things using deep learning approaches. In: 2018 International Joint Conference on Neural Networks (IJCNN), pp. 1–8 (2018). https://doi.org/10.1109/IJCNN.2018. 8489489

16. Meidan, Y., et al.: N-BaIoT-network-based detection of IoT botnet attacks using deep autoencoders. IEEE Pervasive Comput. **17**(3), 12–22 (2018)

17. Nõmm, S., Bahşi, H.: Unsupervised anomaly based botnet detection in IoT networks. In: 2018 17th IEEE International Conference on Machine Learning and Applications (ICMLA), pp. 1048–1053 (2018)

18. Pedregosa, F., et al.: Scikit-learn: machine learning in Python. J. Mach. Learn. Res. **12**, 2825–2830 (2011)

19. Sivanathan, A., et al.: Classifying IoT devices in smart environments using network traffic characteristics. IEEE Trans. Mob. Comput. **18**(8), 1745–1759 (2018)

20. Strasak, Garcia, S., Parmisano, A., Erquiaga, M.J.: Detecting malware even when it is encrypted - machine learning for network https analysis. Stratosphere Lab., Praha, Czech Republic, Technical report (2017)

21. Yuan, X., Li, C., Li, X.: DeepDefense: identifying DDoS attack via deep learning. In: 2017 IEEE International Conference on Smart Computing, pp. 1–8 (2017)

Explainable AI/Social Impact of AI

An Innovative Method to Study the Social Impact of AI on the Work Environment Based on a Multi-dimensional Human-Centred Analysis of the Worker-AI Team

Simona D'Attanasio[(⊠)] [iD], Sara De Martino, and Yann Ferguson [iD]

Icam, Toulouse, France
simona.dattanasio@icam.fr

Abstract. This paper presents an innovative method to analyse the impact of artificial intelligence (AI) technologies in the work environment. These technologies are becoming more and more widespread in workplaces, integrating the cognitive processes of workflows, provoking an important disruption in the worker environment. At present, the state of the art lacks tools and methods to understand what we call the worker-AI team. The method presented in the paper is based on a four-dimensional model considering the social, the strategic, the structural, the core framework dimensions that contribute to determine the dynamics of this team within an organisation. Each dimension is related to one or more involved stakeholders, providers, workers, managers, policy-makers and social partners. An experimental protocol has been derived from the model and deployed to retrieve data from use-cases in different fields of activity and for different specific tasks. The analysis of the initial set of data allowed the identification of a preliminary taxonomy that is presented in the conclusions. The eight worker profiles that have been identified can help to provide a human-centred integration of AI technologies in the workplace.

Keywords: Social impact of AI · taxonomy · worker-AI team

1 Introduction

It is widely recognised that artificial intelligence (AI) technologies can provide economic and societal benefits for organisations[1]. The condition for a successful integration of such technologies in the workplace is that all stakeholders in the AI environment - AI providers, AI users, managers integrating AI, policy-makers and social partners - provide a safe framework for all workers, from the technological, strategical, social and ethical points of view, based on a human-centred approach [1]. The "shape" of this framework is not well defined yet. Models and clear guidelines need to be established to lead the

---

[1] With the term "organisation" we refer here to public and private organisations, including companies and small and medium enterprises.

© IFIP International Federation for Information Processing 2023
Published by Springer Nature Switzerland AG 2023
I. Maglogiannis et al. (Eds.): AIAI 2023, IFIP AICT 676, pp. 45–56, 2023.
https://doi.org/10.1007/978-3-031-34107-6_4

development and the deployment of AI. Shneiderman [2] proposes a two-dimensional framework of HCAI Human-Centred Artificial Intelligence, with the aim of producing new and more complete guidelines for the design of computer applications which are Reliable, Safe and Trustworthy, RST [3]. To achieve this goal, Shneiderman brilliantly discusses the need of "technical practices that support reliability", "management strategies that create cultures of safety", and "independent oversight structures that support trust". This approach suggests a three-party contribution leading to RST AI applications: product providers that implement "good" technical practices, managers that implement strategies and structures that support trust. The AI final user, the worker at the workplace, is part of the technical practices through audit trails, but doesn't constitute a party itself. The European Union [4, 5] on the other hand clearly states that human agency and oversight are some of the main key requirements for a trustworthy AI: "the overall wellbeing of the user should be central to the system's functionality". The report points out the need for transparency, i.e. the "explainability of the algorithmic decision-making process, adapted to the persons involved, should be provided to the extent possible". In addition, "it is important to adequately communicate the AI system's capabilities and limitations to the different stakeholders involved in a manner appropriate to the use case at hand". In the most part of the literature the impact of AI on work has been analysed and measured just in terms of job loss and risk of automation. In this direction goes The impact of Artificial Intelligence on Work report from Frontier Economics [6] that focuses on the forecast of the labour market (job suppression and creation). McKinsey's analysis targets more than 400 use-cases to identify the applications that have the greatest potential to create economic value [7]. Hence the recent public debate has tried to outline the future of the work and the evolution of work and working relations in the light of the digitalization waves [8, 9]. Notwithstanding, the way in which the working relations and the work itself change under the influence of the introduction of AI solutions, is still not deeply explored. For these reasons, the paper aims at understanding the impact of AI technologies on working environment in the following way:

- By identifying the main features that have a role in the dynamics of the worker-AI team and worker-worker interactions.
- By taking into consideration the interactions with the whole constellation of stakeholders and social-territorial partners.

The paper is organised as follows. The next section defines the context of the research and the use-case selection presented in the paper. The multi-dimensional model section provides a description of the model that we implemented to describe the worker-AI team dynamics. The research methodology and use-cases selection section details the use-case list and the experimental protocol deployed. The analysis of the results presents the taxonomy derived from the verbatim of the interviews. The conclusion and future work section will conclude the paper illustrating the next steps of the research.

2 The Research Context

The starting hypothesis of this research is that the building of the worker-AI team is not only finalised to perform a working task more efficiently and better, as stated by the majority of AI designers, but also to enhance the workers' expertise. Since the human counterpart is significantly impacted by the introduction of AI solutions in the workplace, it is important to focus the analysis on the workers' experience evolution at several levels. More specifically we propose to analyse the diverse features emerging from different working contexts in order to identify common patterns that could allow the definition of a generalised framework of worker-AI team typologies at work. The ultimate related objective is to use the different observed working experiences and workers' perspectives to provide guidelines for future design of more human-centred AI systems. To define the context of our research, we refer to the definition given by the European Union [10]: "Artificial intelligent systems are software (and possibly also hardware) systems designed by humans that, given a complex goal, act in the physical or digital dimension by perceiving their environment through data acquisition, interpreting the collected structured or unstructured data [...] to achieve the given goal". This definition explicitly mentions the possible double nature of AI systems, hardware and software, thus including robots. The use-cases that we consider do not include fully automated systems, like robot manipulators acting in a production line, as we focus on worker-AI teams, showing interaction and/or synergy between them. More in particular, we consider AI systems that are integrated in a workplace and play a role in the workflow and/or in the task planning, execution or decision strategy of the worker. In other words, we consider AI-systems that change the "ordinary way of doing a job".

As the main objective is to focus on the human partner of the team, the research is conducted by an interdisciplinary team, including researchers in human sciences, such as sociology, psychology, ergonomics, design, semiotics, political science, and in technical sciences, such as robotics and computer science. The research mainly focuses on social impacts and does not consider other important aspects of AI, such as explicability and cybersecurity. Since the research is financed by the Occitanie region in France in the framework of the ICENTRA project[2], we only focused on use-cases in this area. The limit of the study lies within the mono-cultural representativity of our experimental data, as we believe that observed behaviours are typical of occidental democratic countries. Nevertheless, we believe that the study provides architecture and analysis that can be generally applied.

3 The Multi-dimensional Model

The goal of our research is to identify the main features of the worker-AI team that impact human work mainly under the worker perspective. Economic benefits are in most of the cases well defined and easily accessible. Intelligent automation can in fact provide metrics to evaluate their performance: for example, increase in quantity (faster,

---

[2] ICENTRA project. "Intelligence artificielle CENtrée sur le TRAvail. Work-centered artificial intelligence." Funded in the framework of the Research and Society call of the Occitanie region (France). Toulouse and Nîmes (France), 2022–2023.

more output in less time) and quality (better, identification of poor results). On the other hand, it is difficult to evaluate social impacts, positive or negative, of the introduction of the AI system in the work environment. Workers' well-being and thus engagement and motivation are considered essential to the health and productivity of an organisation and strongly contribute to a virtuous circle [11]. When talking about well-being, motivation, engagement, indicators become qualitative, hardly measurable, application dependent and strongly correlated among them. Ferguson et al. propose a tool to measure the impact of AI systems on well-being at work [12]. The tool is declined in 3 criteria: acknowledgement, social relationships, and monitoring and control. A questionnaire allows quantitative evaluation in the workplace of the risk of undermining acknowledgement, relational disengagement, and monitoring feeling. This research was highly inspiring for the social dimension of our model. We also took inspiration from the key high-level dimensions of the Organisation for Economic Co-operation and Development, OECD, Framework [13]. The dimensions and their interaction are depicted in Fig. 1.

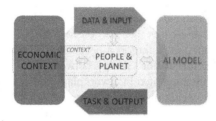

Fig. 1. The OECD dimensions for classification of AI systems.

The dimension People & Planet at the centre of the picture clearly (graphically) defines the human-centred approach of the framework. This dimension considers among other criteria the impacted stakeholders. The Economic Context refers to the economic environment and sector in which the AI system is implemented. Data & Input refers to the data/input used in the AI system. The AI model is the computational representation of the system. Task & Output refers to system tasks and evaluation methods. To build our model, we extracted several criteria adapting them to our purpose. Our final model is depicted in Fig. 2 and consists of four dimensions, each with well-defined features. The human-machine (worker/AI system) team is at the centre. The dimensions are described in the following paragraphs.

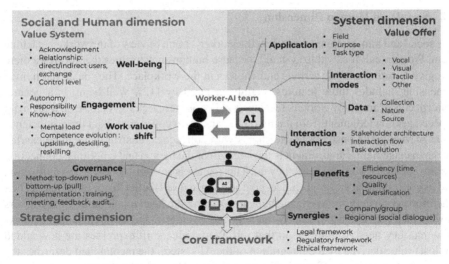

Fig. 2. The four-dimensional architecture of our research.

3.1 System Dimension

The system dimension contributes to describe the main characteristics and attributes of the technological solution, in other words what the AI system has been designed for and how it works. It offers the solution provider point of view. We also call it "value offer", because the provider of an AI system has some goals and problems to solve in mind for the designed solution. The system dimension includes five features. Application concerns the field of the AI system, e.g. financial, human resources, maintenance or medical among others[3]. It also concerns the specific purpose of the application and the particular task in which the AI system is involved. For example, an AI system in the transportation field, can be used in maintenance to organise maintenance operations (AI purpose), generating operator sequence of interventions (task). Interaction modes define the modality of the human-machine interface: visual, vocal, tactile or other. Data helps to understand some non-technical issues about the data used by the AI system [13]: the way of collecting them, manually or autonomously; their origin, who or what inputs them; their nature with respect to time, real-time or static. Interaction dynamics defines who does what, when and how, enhancing the interaction point of view. The stakeholder architecture describes the interaction among stakeholders in the workflow. The interaction flow allows the description of the flow of information in terms of sequence of interactions (worker-AI, worker-worker, AI-AI). Task evolution provides a comparison of flows before and after the introduction of the AI system.

---

[3] A full list of fields of application is given by the International Standard Industrial Classification of All Economic Activities Autonomy https://unstats.un.org/unsd/publication/seriesm/seriesm_4rev4e.pdf

3.2   Social and Human Dimension

The social and human dimension offers the worker's point of view of the worker-machine team. We also call it a "value system", because humans have values that motivate them and give meaning to their actions and choices in the workplace. The social and human dimension includes three features, mainly inspired by [12]. Well-being is a general concept concerning how workers feel at work. For our research we focalise on three main aspects: acknowledgment from the hierarchy and from colleagues from the competence point of view, relationship and exchanges with colleagues, control that can be exerted by the management. Engagement is the strength of the mental and emotional connection employees feel toward the work they do. This feature is strongly connected to motivation and its core components, goal choice, goal striving and self-belief in goal attainment [11]. Therefore, contributions to engagement at work are: the level of autonomy that workers have in their job, the responsibility that they are given from the hierarchy and the know-how that they need to mobilise in that job. Work value shift expresses the new added (or lost) value derived by the integration of the AI system: the mental load describes the change in the cognitive effort involved in managing the task; the competence evolution is an indicator on the impact on the skills in terms of upskilling, deskilling – increasing or decreasing skill level - or reskilling – learning new skills.

3.3   Strategic Dimension

The strategic dimension offers the opportunity to understand the framework in which the managers decided to introduce a specific AI system. More specifically the strategic dimension allows, on one hand, to describe the reasons and the modalities through which the integration process of the AI technology happened within the organisation, and on the other, to better understand the working relational system. The strategic dimension includes three features. Benefit aims to identify the reason for the integration. The AI system may allow improved efficiency, in terms of time – doing a task faster – and/or in terms of resources – doing a task with less resources. The AI system may also provide a better quality or allow the development of new products and/or services, thus improving diversification of the organisation. Governance describes the modality through which an organisation decides to implement the IA solution and explains the mechanisms needed to balance the knowledge and the competencies required among the different actors. More in depth the governance focuses on the integration process of the AI system explaining if it has been vertically imposed (top-down) or horizontally discussed with and proposed by the workers (bottom-up). This allows the understanding of the degree of the workers' involvement in the decisions concerning the introduction of a "new (AI-based) working tool" within the organisation and consequently the degree of appropriation of it. Synergies aim at measuring the involvement of territorial and social actors and other stakeholders within the decisional process that has led to the introduction in a specific organisation. This feature helps in describing the extension of the decisional process and it strengthens the diverse governance approach of the managers (decision-makers).

3.4 Core Framework

The core framework includes the overall normative, regulatory and ethical context in which are embedded the cases-studies. More specifically it offers the opportunity to evaluate the integration of an AI solution within an organisation, in the light of the evolution of national and supranational strategies [14, 15]. This dimension helps to understand to what extent the decisions taken by the different organisations and stakeholders are in line with the current regulatory framework and if these respect the officially defined main principles and values of AI. The core framework is still under development and for this reason it has been really complicated to analyse this dimension in our case-studies. There is still a lack of a proper awareness concerning all the risks and opportunities deriving from the integration of AI at the workplace.

4 The Research Methodology and Use-Cases Selection

Starting from the abovementioned model we have constructed a semi-directive questionnaire whose objective is to investigate the four dimensions. A second related step has been to categorise the stakeholders to be interviewed: the designer/provider of the solution, the managers and the users (workers).

Table 1. The table shows nine use-cases, grouped according to the field of application. For each field, we interviewed different stakeholders belonging to diverse hierarchical levels. The code is the following M = manager, SW = senior worker, W = worker, P = provider. The People column indicated the number of people interviewed.

Field	Stakeholders	Purpose	People	Type of organisation
Transportation	M, SW, W	Maintenance	3	Public
	W	Design	1	Private
Banking	SW, W, P	Advisor support	5	Private
Public Administration	M, W	Advisor support	2	Public
Spatial	SW, P	Recruitment	2	Public
Marketing	M	Design	1	Private
Manufacturing	W	Maintenance	1	Private
Justice	SW, P	Support	2	Private
	P		1	Public

This allows us to adapt the questionnaire in function of the different stakeholders involved in the research. In total we have done 18 qualitative in-depth interviews conducted at least by 3 experts, 2 in the field of social sciences (semiotics, political science, sociology, design), 1 in the technological field (robotics and AI). As a consequence of the deployment of the questionnaire, an adjustment of the model has been iteratively performed. The Table 1 summarises the use-cases interviewed.

A two-steps methodological approach is proposed. The first step is descriptive and consists in extracting and structuring data from the verbatim of the interviews. The goal of this step is to highlight the structure and dynamics of the interactions among stakeholders and within the worker-AI team, and the integration process within the organisation. In particular, a focus on the comparison between the period before and after the introduction of the solution has allowed a better understanding of its impact on the work. This descriptive analysis can be conducted using graphical architectures and comparative tables, whose introduction is out of the scope of this article. The second step, which is analytical and demands a use-case oriented interpretation of verbatim, is presented and discussed in detail in the following paragraphs.

5   The Analysis of the Results: The Preliminary Taxonomy

From the analysis of verbatims, three main axes seem to emerge, each one corresponding to a dimension of the model (excluding the Core framework dimension). These three axes allow the identification of a three-dimensional space that defines 8 areas characterising the worker attitude in teaming with an AI system, as shown in Fig. 3.

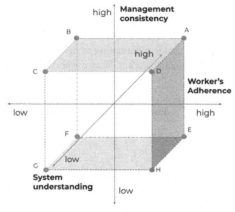

Fig. 3. The three-dimensional taxonomy. As an example, the point A is in the area having high management consistency, high worker's adherence and high system understanding. The point C is in the area having high management consistency, low work awareness and low system understanding.

The axes of the taxonomy are described in the following paragraphs, where some extracts of the interviews expressed in quotations will be introduced to support the research results. In order to respect the confidentiality of the interviewed actors the exact sources of quotations are omitted.

5.1   Management Consistency

The "Management Consistency" axis is related to the role of the management in the deployment of the AI system, imposing a use that can be more or less consistent with the recommendations of the solution provider. When an AI tool is deployed, in fact, recommendations and rules are often provided to be able to achieve the best benefits from the solution. Concerning this aspect, we have observed two main kinds of behaviours presented in different case-studies. The first behaviour is the answer to a management that imposes the tool but that still allows a certain degree of freedom to the worker in its deployment. Some of the interviewed workers state "I made my own method", "I don't have to report the results to my hierarchy", "The tool provides enormous flexibility but only because we allow it" "I trust the AI solution but I do not use this at the beginning of the process but only after in a second step". The second behaviour derives from a management that imposes not only the use of the AI solution but also the information flow and the exact sequencing of use. Hence "the control is there [...] we are tracked daily". A provider states that the worker can "project his/her intuition on the model [..] that can distort the results", "our main recommendation is to use our tool as early as possible in the [...] process, since the models are much more reliable and [...] much more relevant".

5.2 System Understanding

The "System Understanding" axis is the understanding of the system "intelligence", in terms of data sources, and the workers' contribution (if allowed) to it. Independently from the specific technology at the base of the intelligent solution (e.g. chatbot, deep neural networks for data classification, optimization algorithms, physical robots), we have observed that the understanding of the fundamental principles of the solution (e.g. parameters used and their meaning, associated database, basic principles) has an impact on the worker-AI team dynamics. "We spend a lot of time with users to explain what the robot can't do, because there is a real difference between what people expect a robot to do and what a robot actually can do". "I never use their models, I only use the model we create", "[the provider] has studied its algorithms very well", "the tool is very thoughtful. There are algorithms and people who think about it, that's why it can put my opinion in perspective". The deeper the understanding the more positive is the dynamics that is created and the adoption rate of the solution. "It is a system that we have shaped at our image", "it's a system imposed but we do not understand the working mechanisms behind, we stop at what it shows us, we do not try to go further!".

5.3 Worker's Adherence

The "Worker's Adherence" is the adherence of the worker to the values offered by the AI system. In other words, it represents the match between the value offer and the value system, as described in the model. All workers interviewed were committed to doing a good job. They are in the best position to know how. A good job is "when you have a real feeling of choice". Workers demonstrate mastery of the skills and of the workflow associated with their job. If the AI system meets their needs, it is adopted and supported. "You need this motivation, this involvement, because a tool (...) if it is not kept up to date if it is not managed it won't be used and it will be obsolete". Its use can also be diverted: "I don't read the result [..], because it introduces a bias for me", "it influences our judgement". Adherence can influence the trust of workers, even if it is not always based on a real understanding, as pointed out before. This trust can be instrumentalized to serve the worker's convenience and "develop sometimes complicated discussions by saying - it's not me, it's neutral, it's the tool. What do you think?". "I know the physics, the machine just validates my previous intuitions".

5.4 Worker's Profiling

The structure highlighted with the introduction of the three axes can lead to the identification of different worker's profiles as illustrated in Fig. 4.

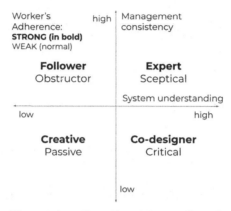

Fig. 4. The worker's profiling consists of 8 profiles. In the two-dimensional diagram, 4 profiles are shown according to the level (high or low) of manager consistency and of system understanding. The 4 profiles written in bold characters refer to a strong worker's adherence. The 4 profiles written in normal characters refer to a weak worker's adherence.

Since the research is still ongoing, the taxonomy is based on a limited set of interviews and cannot allow us to adequately define all the different worker profiles. Nevertheless, even if the collected data are related to field-dependent, individual, and specific work practices, we could highlight common characteristics of the worker-AI teaming dynamics and similar worker attitude. It is important to point out that within the same organisation, different attitudes can coexist depending on the worker teaming perception. This perception can evolve and can be influenced by human-centred management and AI design practices. Whenever the worker's adherence is met, for a high level of understanding of the AI system, the Expert is aware of its benefits and fully endorses its deployment. Whenever freedom is allowed, the Co-designer is capable of truly exploiting it by adapting the system to a specific task. If the level of understanding is low, the Creative has the freedom to modify the decisional flow, introducing alternative working modes. The Follower, unlike the Creative, hasn't this freedom and applies the workflow suggested by recommendations. In the absence of worker's adherence, the risk of a failure in the deployment of the AI system can be important. For a high level of conformity imposed by the management, the Sceptical can understand the AI system but the cooperation to the deployment can be minimal. This low level of involvement becomes obstructive if there is a lack of understanding of the system (Obstructor profile). The worker's attitude can be less adversarial, but still far from constructive, if more freedom is given. In this context, the Critical clearly "does" otherwise and uses shortcuts whenever possible. The Passive doesn't care at all and often doesn't use the system.

6 Conclusions and Future Work

A method to evaluate the impact of AI systems on workers has been proposed. The method is based on a four-dimensional model derived from what we believe to be the most relevant features that impact work from the human perspective, thus in a human-centred approach. We studied nine use-cases and interviewed 18 stakeholders, workers, managers and providers. The analysis of the verbatims allowed the introduction of a preliminary taxonomy and the identification of 8 worker profiles, that describe the worker's attitude in teaming with the AI system. The taxonomy reflects the impactful features of each dimension of the model, system, social and strategic. The taxonomy is an attempt to synthesise the data and it will certainly evolve and gain in pertinence and consistency as more use-cases will be analysed in the future. Nevertheless, the preliminary results highlight common trends and reveal some points of attention in the design and deployment of an AI system. Firstly, the understanding of the AI system by the worker and, if possible, the involvement in the system design is critical to promote the successful adoption of an AI solution by workers. Secondly, management strategy and decisions in the deployment of AI is mandatory to promote motivation and engagement. Providing clear and motivated guidelines is important but another factor should be considered. Allowing creativity and freedom to workers in the decisional process to modulate the AI implementation according to the context of the workplace, thus choosing the teaming mode with AI, can be a winning strategy for an even more successful implementation. This can contribute to finding self-motivation and personal fulfilment in the workplace. Finally, coherence between the value offer and value system can create trust, establishing a positive dynamic in the worker-AI team. Providers can have a huge impact on the worker-AI team: to obtain a constructive acceptance of the AI system, understanding and creativity must be stimulated and not inhibited. Together with managers, they are thus responsible to build a motivated trust on the technology deployed. Finally, this first part of the research revealed the fundamental importance of applying a human-centred approach when integrating AI systems in the work environment.

By considering the overall results of the research, we can conclude that the main weakness of the model consists in the difficulty to reach and to include in the analysis the effective beneficiaries of the study: the workers. Solution providers are often unable to give us customers' contact information. As in the case of managers, their point of view can be easily biased and does not always provide a clear insight of the impact of the AI solution on workers. Hence, particular attention must be payed when analysing data.

In contrast, the main strength of the model is the capability to provide a general framework to observe and analyse the impacts of AI tools on the work environment, regardless of the specificity of the technical solution deployed, the field of application and the particular context of a use-case. The insight offered by the interdisciplinary approach of the research, allowed to observe patterns in worker's behaviours with respect to the introduction of an AI tool in the workflow. The model has therefore the potential to be generally applied, and useful to shift towards a positive impact of AI tool in the workplace.

References

1. Auernhammer, J.: Human-centered AI: the role of human-centered design research in the development of AI. In: Boess, S., Cheung, M. and Cain, R. (eds.) Synergy - DRS International Conference 2020, 11–14 August, Held online (2020)
2. Shneiderman, B.: Human-centered artificial intelligence: realiable, safe & trustworthy. Int. J. Hum.-Comput. Interact. 495–504 (2020)
3. Shneiderman, B.: Human-Centered AI. Oxford University Press, Oxford (2022)
4. European Commission: Building Trust in Human-Centric Artificial Intelligence. Communication from the Commission to the European Parliament, the Council, the European Economic and Social Committee and the Committee of the Regions, Brussels (2019)
5. High-Level Expert Group on Artificial Intelligence: The Assessment List for Trustworthy Artificial Intelligence (ALTAI). Report, European Commission, Brussels (2020)
6. Frontier Economics: The Impact of Artificial Intelligence on Work. Report (2018)
7. McKinsey Global Institute - McKinsey & Company: Notes from the AI Frontier Insights from Hundreds of Use Cases. Report (2018)
8. Villani, C.: Donner un sense à l'intelligence artificielle: pour une stratégie nationale et européenne. Report of a parliamentary mission, September 2017–March 2018 (2018)
9. GPAI (Global Partnership on Artificial Intelligence): Future of work AI observatory at workplace. Report, Paris Summit (2021)
10. Independent High-Level Expert Group on Artificial Intelligence set up by the European Commission: A Definition of AI: Main Capabilities and Disciplines. Brussels (2019)
11. Hughes, C., Robert, L.P., Frady, K., Arroyos, A.: Artificial intelligence, employee engagement, fairness, and job outcomes. In: Managing Technology and Middle- and Low-Skilled Employees, pp. 61–68 (2019)
12. Ferguson, Y., Pecoste, C.: L'IA au travail: proposition pour outiller la confiance. In: CNIA National Conference on Artificial Intelligence. Saint-Etienne, France, pp. 71–78 (2022)
13. OECD: OECD Framework for the Classification of AI Systems. OECD Publishing (2022)
14. European Commission: White Paper on Artificial Intelligence - A European Approach to Excellence and Confidence (2020)
15. European Commission: Regulation of the European Parliament and of the Council laying down harmonised rules on artificial intelligence (Artificial Intelligence Act) and amending certain legislative acts (2021)

CaTabRa: Efficient Analysis and Predictive Modeling of Tabular Data

Alexander Maletzky$^{(\boxtimes)}$ [iD], Sophie Kaltenleithner[iD], Philipp Moser[iD], and Michael Giretzlehner[iD]

Research Department Medical Informatics, RISC Software GmbH, Softwarepark 32a, 4232 Hagenberg, Austria
{alexander.maletzky,sophie.kaltenleithner,philipp.moser, michael.giretzlehner}@risc-software.at

Abstract. We present CaTabRa, a novel open-source Python package for the efficient and largely automated analysis of tabular data. It combines a variety of established frameworks and libraries for data processing, automated machine learning, explainable AI and out-of-distribution detection into one coherent system. Thanks to its simple user interface, CaTabRa can be used by practitioners who want to quickly gain insights into their data and the potential of predictive modeling, but it also provides added value for data-science experts through its function library. We demonstrate CaTabRa's usefulness in two example applications.

Keywords: Machine learning · Tabular data · AutoML · OOD detection · Explainable AI

1 Introduction

Tabular data are ubiquitous in many domains, including the health sector, business intelligence, industrial applications, empirical research, and many more. Effectively and efficiently utilizing these data, e.g. for predictive and prescriptive modeling, for a long time required profound expertise in data science. While this remains true to a certain extent, in recent years there has been a trend towards automating ever more aspects of data science, both to generate more and better output in shorter time, but also to make it accessible to non-experts. Automation affects machine learning (AutoML [4,11]), feature engineering [7,17] and report generation, implemented in frameworks, systems and tools of different kinds (Sect. 1.1). Yet, we found none of them offer the right degree of automation for being able to efficiently solve problems of varying complexity.

Therefore, our goal was to develop a user-friendly data analysis system that supports simple and complex tasks alike, and as such provides added value for both non-experts (or *domain* experts) and experienced data science professionals. Simple tasks should be handled in an entirely automatic way, to quickly gain insights into data and the potential of predictive modeling; complex tasks should be solvable by combining powerful data wrangling functions to clean,

© IFIP International Federation for Information Processing 2023
Published by Springer Nature Switzerland AG 2023
I. Maglogiannis et al. (Eds.): AIAI 2023, IFIP AICT 676, pp. 57–68, 2023.
https://doi.org/10.1007/978-3-031-34107-6_5

efficient programs. The resulting *CaTabRa* system builds upon established tools and frameworks for data processing, automated machine learning (AutoML), explainable AI and out-of-distribution detection (OOD-detection). It integrates them into a coherent whole, adding glue code [30] where necessary and implementing useful functionality missing in the constituent frameworks as readily available Python functions.

CaTabRa's design is inspired by one key principle: *Automate what can reasonably be automated, don't try to automate everything.* Unlike many related systems, CaTabRa neither claims nor aims to automate all aspects of the typical data analysis workflow. With increasing data complexity, according to our own experience, some programming and data-science skills will always be necessary to obtain high-quality prediction models from raw data [19]. Above all this concerns the definition and extraction of meaningful target labels for supervised learning. Even if all feature engineering can be automated, as claimed in [17], label extraction generally cannot. Especially in the medical domain, label- and sample definitions can become fairly complicated (see [14] for an example) and do not fit into predefined 'templates' offered by related systems like [2].

CaTabRa is both a ready-to-use command-line tool and a function library. The command-line interface automates the parts of the data analysis workflow that can reasonably be automated, and the function library exposes the functionality of the command-line interface through a simple API and furthermore provides building blocks for the steps that cannot be automated easily.

Summarizing, our main contributions in this paper are:

– A novel, open-source tabular data analysis system and library (Sect. 2), available at https://github.com/risc-mi/catabra.
– A largely automated workflow (Sect. 2.1) encompassing not only model training (Sect. 2.2), but also model evaluation and explanation (Sect. 2.4), OOD-detection (Sect. 2.5), and the creation of publication-ready descriptive statistics and visualizations (Sect. 2.3).
– Functions for efficient data preparation and feature extraction, especially from longitudinal data (Sect. 2.6).
– Two specific, real-world use-cases for demonstrating the practical applicability and usefulness of the system (Sect. 3).

1.1   Related Work

Frameworks similar to CaTabRa have been proposed in the past for different goals and end users. A brief overview of these solutions including their main differences to CaTabRa is given below; a more thorough comparison of CaTabRa to related work is not in the scope of this paper.

PyCaret [1] is perhaps the system most similar to CaTabRa. The Python library is essentially a wrapper around well-known machine learning libraries and frameworks, such as scikit-learn, optuna and spaCy. It aims to reduce the technological knowledge necessary to perform moderately difficult data analysis tasks (supervised and unsupervised). In contrast to CaTabRa's default auto-sklearn AutoML backend, data preprocessing is not considered during optimization and more manual effort is required for executing a complete pipeline including data analysis, model training and evaluation. *MLJAR* [26] is another similar solution focusing on supervised machine learning tasks. It aims at reducing development time for data scientists by offering multiple training modes depending on whether the goal is explainability, a production-ready pipeline or a highly-tuned model. It includes preprocessing, ensemble-construction, hyperparameter tuning, evaluation and explanation. However, including custom building blocks (e.g., new model classes) is not straightforward. *AMLBID* [12] is a Python framework focusing on facilitating model-training and analysis for non-data-scientists. It consists of two main components: A recommender that proposes a training pipeline based on meta-learning and an explainer that starts a dashboard providing data level explanations (correlations, missing values), model level explanations (feature importance, decision paths) and performance evaluations. As algorithm selection is done by meta learning, where hyperparameters are guessed from experiments with other datasets, the user is limited to the eight algorithms built into the system. Further, preprocessing is not included in the optimization pipeline.

Besides these generic solutions, some more specialized ones have been proposed in the medical field: *Cardea* [2] is a general end-to-end framework specialized on electronic health records. It takes data from a relational database and applies automatic feature engineering. Prediction models are generated using *ML Bazaar* [32] and hyperopt [4] for a fixed set of problem definitions, which limits its general applicability. Performance reports are not as thorough as in CaTabRa and an explanation component is not included by default. *Clairvoyance* [15] is a generic pipeline for processing time-series medical data and training prediction models including model building and hyperparameter optimization. The system lacks flexibility due to implicit assumptions on the format of the input data and limited options for defining target labels. *AutoDC* [3] is a framework for disease classification based on gene expression data using AutoML. While it comprises many interesting functionalities (e.g., optimizations of preprocessing steps and model training, model explanations), its focus on a specific application makes it unusable for other tasks without extensive code refactoring.

Cloud-based solutions like Google's Vertex AI [13] and Azure Machine Learning [21] are platform-dependent, not free-to-use or open-source and require data to be uploaded to external servers, which could be problematic in terms of data protection. We consider these solutions to be aimed at a different target group.

In summary, while solutions exist that resemble CaTabRa's functionality in some ways, they differ in the degree of automation, flexibility, extensibility and accessibility. Also, none of them considers the applicability of prediction models to new data, as CaTabRa does through its OOD detection component (Sect. 2.5).

2   The CaTabRa System

2.1   General Workflow

CaTabRa covers all aspects of tabular data analysis, ranging from generating descriptive statistics over training prediction models, evaluating and explaining

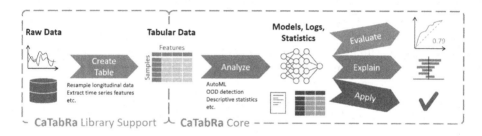

Fig. 1. CaTabRa workflow.

them on test data to applying them to new data for making predictions. Although data preparation (transforming raw, unstructured/semi-structured data into tabular form) is not part of CaTabRa's largely automated core functionality by design, the system also provides some ready-to-use data preparation tools through its function library (Sect. 2.6).

The general CaTabRa workflow is summarized in Fig. 1. It essentially consists of four main steps: *analyze, evaluate, explain* and *apply*. Each of these steps can be easily invoked both through CaTabRa's command-line interface and through corresponding library functions, and requires relatively little user input.

Analyze takes a single data table, with rows corresponding to samples and columns corresponding to attributes, as input and thoroughly analyzes it. This includes generating descriptive statistics for each attribute, training prediction models if one or more target attributes are specified (Sect. 2.2), setting up model explainers (Sect. 2.4) and creating OOD detection models (Sect. 2.5). All generated artifacts are stored in a local directory that serves as input for the other steps.

Evaluate applies prediction models trained in *analyze* to test data and creates thorough performance reports, both in tabular form and as static and/or interactive plots (Sect. 2.3). It automatically ensures that the given test data has the same format as the data originally analyzed, and in addition applies the OOD detector to identify potential issues in the data distribution.

Explain explains the trained prediction model. The required input and generated output largely depend on the used backend (Sect. 2.4).

Apply applies the trained model to (unlabeled) data, generating predictions and OOD-scores. It optionally explains how the model arrived at its predictions.

2.2   Model Training and Hyperparameter Tuning: AutoML

CaTabRa leverages state-of-the-art automated machine learning (AutoML) systems to quickly produce top-performing prediction models for four widespread prediction tasks (binary/multi-class/multilabel classification, regression) without cumbersome manual pipeline configuration and hyperparameter tuning. The default AutoML backend is auto-sklearn [10,11], which constructs and optimizes whole pipelines, including data- and feature preprocessing (imputation, encoding, feature selection, etc.) and the final ML algorithm. Other backends can be incorporated easily if auto-sklearn's built-in capabilities turn out insufficient for a given use-case.

It is of course also possible to extend auto-sklearn itself, for instance by adding preprocessing steps or machine learning algorithms. CaTabRa by default adds extreme gradient boosting (XGBoost) [6] to the arsenal of readily available machine learning algorithms, and provides convenience features that facilitate interacting with auto-sklearn. For example, it implements additional resampling strategies for internal validation during hyperparameter optimization, in particular, train-test splits where samples can be assigned to groups and all samples of a group are put into the same data partition ('grouped splitting'). Another convenience feature is the ability to abort hyperparameter optimization at any time through simple keyboard interrupts, and still combine the models trained so far to a final ensemble.

Classification models are often ill-calibrated even if they perform well in terms of area under the receiver operating characteristic curve and related metrics [23]. Therefore, classifiers created with CaTabRa can be calibrated easily, either immediately during model training by specifying the subset of the data to calibrate on, or through a stand-alone command/function.

2.3   Performance Reports

CaTabRa automatically generates extensive performance reports when evaluating trained prediction models on test data, consisting of both tables with numerical data and static and/or interactive plots. Numerical results include all suitable performance metrics available in scikit-learn [24], with micro-, macro- and weighted averaging for prediction tasks with multiple targets. Classification metrics that depend on a specific decision threshold rather than a continuous probability (like precision and recall) are by default evaluated for multiple thresholds to allow users select the optimal threshold based on their own preference. In addition, several widely used strategies for selecting decision thresholds based on objective criteria are implemented as well, for instance, minimizing the difference between sensitivity and specificity, the closest-to-$(0, 1)$ criterion [25], or maximizing any given metric. Bootstrapping [9] is an integral part of CaTabRa's performance evaluation tools as well, which can be activated on demand and returns both aggregate (mean, standard deviation, etc.) and detailed information about the corresponding random subsamples of the test data.

Model performance is visualized in publication-ready static plots and interactive plots generated with plotly [27], without any user interaction required. The kind of data visualized depends on the prediction task, but includes all common plot types like scatter plots of ground truth vs. predictions in regression settings, ROC- and precision-recall (PR) curves in binary classification, and confusion matrices in binary- and multiclass classification. Examples can be found in Sect. 3.1.

2.4   Model Explanations

CaTabRa uses SHAP [18] as its default model explanation framework. SHAP explains models by calculating sample-wise feature importance values and works particularly well on tabular data. It was thus the natural choice for our system, but other explanation backends can be added, too.

Since SHAP is able to explain any (black-box) machine learning model it can be readily applied to ensembles and pipelines of preprocessing steps and final estimators, two model-types frequently returned by AutoML systems. This approach has two downsides, though: it is relatively slow and only gives approximate SHAP values. Fast and exact methods exist for tree-based models, like random forests, but cannot be applied to pipelines that include preprocessing steps. The overcome this limitation CaTabRa implements rules for back-propagating feature importance through some of the most common preprocessing transformations, like rescaling, one-hot encoding, or feature selection. This means that dedicated explanation techniques can be applied despite the presence of (some types of) data preprocessing.

Similar to the performance reports described in Sect. 2.3, explaining a model automatically creates visually appealing plots of the obtained feature importance.

2.5   Out-of-Distribution Detection

Machine learning models generally assume that test data follows the same distribution as the data they were initially trained on. If this assumption is violated, for instance due to semantic- or covariate shifts, the models' predictions can become unreliable. CaTabRa therefore integrates a set of OOD detectors to identify samples that are likely OOD. They are trained during initial data analysis and automatically applied when dealing with new (unseen) data.

CaTabRa offers five methods for OOD detection: *Bins Detector*: A simple detector that divides each feature into equally sized bins. A new value that falls within a bin without any instances in the training data is considered OOD. *Autoencoder*: A neural network that consists of an encoder, which maps features to a lower dimensional space, and a decoder, which aims to reconstruct the original values. This assumes that OOD samples have a higher reconstruction error than in-distribution (ID) samples [34]. *Soft Brownian Offset Detector* [22]: A detector based on a method to generate synthetic OOD samples from the training data. Once they have been generated, a classifier is trained to distinguish the OOD and ID samples. *Kolmogorov-Smirnov-Test* (KS-Test) [31]: A statistical test assessing whether two samples are likely to stem from the same distribution. *PyOD Detector*: A wrapper for algorithms included in the PyOD [33] framework. This framework contains a collection of classes for outlier and anomaly detection which can double as OOD detectors.

2.6 Utilities for Working with Longitudinal Data

CaTabRa offers a couple of useful tools for transforming raw data into the tabular form required by its core workflow. One of these tools allows to efficiently work with large amounts of irregularly-sampled longitudinal data, as can be often found in electronic health records, for instance. Each entry in such data corresponds to an observation of a certain attribute for a certain entity (e.g., subject) at a given time. Converting longitudinal data into the 'samples × features' format usually amounts to aggregating over the temporal dimension, e.g., by computing the first, last, average, etc. observed value of each entity and attribute over time. Many standard machine learning libraries (like Pandas [20] and tsfresh [7]) implement related functions, but they all lack support for *efficiently* aggregating values over a given set of (non-uniform, overlapping) time windows individually: assuming the observations are stored in a table in long table format and the windows are contained in a table as well, with columns for entity-identifiers, start- and end times, aggregate observed values per time window and store the results in a table with one row per window and one column per attribute. The solution implemented in CaTabRa consists of a function with a simple interface, that takes the tables of observations and windows, and the requested aggregations, as input, and returns the output table as described above. It is implemented highly efficiently and even supports parallel and distributed execution through Dask DataFrames [8]. An example use-case is sketched in Sect. 3.2.

3 Use-Cases

3.1 Use-Case 1: COVID-19 Prediction

Roland et al. have recently evaluated machine learning models for the prediction of COVID-19 diagnosis based on routinely acquired blood tests [29]. By comparing evaluation metrics obtained with different train-test splits, they showed (a) that their data exhibited domain shifts over time (e.g., changes in disease prevalence, testing procedures and virus mutations) and (b) that these had diminishing effects on the predictive performance and reliability of COVID-19 diagnosis predictions. The dataset contained 127,115 samples (1.24% positives) and included 100 features ranging from age and sex to various blood test parameters (e.g., leucocyte count).

Since CaTabRa was not used in the original publication, we showcase in this use-case how CaTabRa allows to tackle this supervised classification problem, covering all steps from initial data inspection to final model evaluation. We opted to reproduce only the temporal split scenario from the original publication, but the minimal coding effort required by CaTabRa would allow to easily extend our analysis to a variety of splits and classifiers. Using CaTabRa's *analyze* functionality we first generated descriptive statistics about the dataset which also encompasses inferential tests for significant differences between the negative- and positive classes. For testing whether the expected domain shifts can be picked

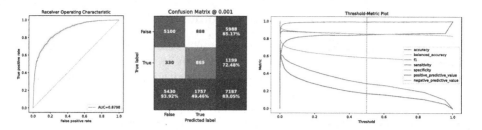

Fig. 2. Performance figures for the Use-Case 1 (COVID-19 prediction) using the XGBoost classifier on the test set. CaTabRa produces a variety of publication-ready figures including ROC-AUC curves (the 95% confidence interval is shown as shaded area around the curve), confusion matrices and threshold-dependency plots for various metrics.

up by the framework, the KS-test was used for OOD detection. This detector was chosen as it checks for an overall change of distribution in features in contrast to a per-sample approach. The model training including hyperparameter tuning described in Sect. 2.2 was performed with two classifier approaches: (a) an XGBoost trained for 15 min and (b) an ensemble of 25 classifiers trained for 120 min. The first was chosen as it outperformed other model classes in the original publication, while the ensemble should highlight CaTabRa's diversity in classifiers. After model training, CaTabRa's *evaluate* functionality was applied to the test set using 1000 repetitions of bootstrapping, thereby generating a comprehensive performance report (Sect. 2.3) comprised of various plots (Fig. 2) and performance metrics. Our results for the area under the ROC curve (ROC-AUC) were 0.8797 ± 0.0054 (XGBoost) and 0.8935 ± 0.0052 (ensemble). For the PR-AUC we obtained 0.6530 ± 0.0143 (XGBoost) and 0.6843 ± 0.0148 (ensemble). Our results compared favourably with the best results in [29], which were 0.8142 ± 0.0000 (ROC-AUC) and 0.7077 ± 0.0000 (PR-AUC). Further, the OOD detector created during the *analyze* phase was automatically applied during *evaluate*. 81 of 95 continuous features were flagged as stemming from a different distribution. In contrast, only 18 features were considered OOD when applying the same detector to a validation set sampled closer in time to the training set. This illustrates that CaTabRa successfully detected the domain shift reported in [29].

In summary, CaTabRa allowed us to easily implement machine learning models to predict COVID-19 diagnoses. Data loading, model training and evaluation were coded in about 10 lines of Python code in less than 30 min of work.

3.2   Use-Case 2: ICU Mortality Prediction

MIMIC-III is a large-scale public database with electronic health records of an intensive care unit (ICU) [16]. It has been used in a wide variety of data analysis projects, for instance ICU mortality prediction [5]. In order to objectively compare results produced by our framework to those presented in [5], we prepared

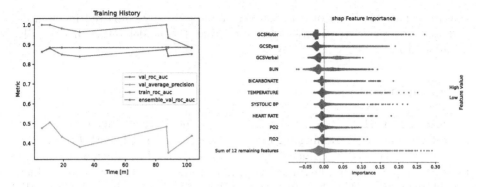

Fig. 3. Training and explanation plots for Use-Case 2 (ICU mortality prediction) Left: Train and validation metrics over time Right: Local feature explanations for one model on the test set.

the raw data following the exact same prepreprocessing steps. In summary, this comprises (1) selecting a proper data subset based on patient age and length of ICU stay, (2) extracting medical measurements (laboratory tests, vital signs) in a certain time frame, and (3) data harmonization, validation and imputation. The resulting data set consisted of six static features and 16 dynamic features with one value per hour in the first 48 h of each ICU stay.

For extracting the measurements in (2), the longitudinal data preparation utilities from Sect. 2.6 could be employed. We then again used CaTabRa's *analyze* functionality to train prediction models. In this scenario, an ensemble of 5 classifiers was trained. Different training times were configured with 10, 30, 60 and 120 min. During training, CaTabRa logs model performance and creates corresponding plots (Fig. 3) for inspecting the training process. This revealed that the number of trained ensembles increased from 0 to 7 with longer training, explaining the test-set ROC-AUC scores obtained when running *evaluate* with 1000 bootstrapping repetitions: 0.5 ± 0.0000, 0.8445 ± 0.0090, 0.8842 ± 0.0079 and 0.8866 ± 0.0084. A longer training time allowed more models to be trained, which lead to better results. However, a good performance could be achieved in less than an hour. The quality of our best model is comparable to the one of [5], with a ROC-AUC of 0.8735 ± 0.0025.

A central aspect of [5] is explaining the prediction models in terms of feature importance, something supported by CaTabRa out of the box (Sect. 2.4). At the end of the initial *analyze* phase, a SHAP explainer was automatically fitted on the final ensemble. In the *explain* phase this explainer is loaded and used for explaining the ensemble on a given data set. For each model in the ensemble feature importance scores are calculated and visualized in the form of a so-called 'beeswarm' plot. Figure 3 shows one for a random forest classifier part of the ensemble trained for 120 min. The ten most important features as well as the total importance of remaining features are depicted. Each dot corresponds to a sample with its color indicating the feature value. The three components of the Glasgow Coma Scale all rank highly compared to other features. This score assesses a patient's level of consciousness and is already employed in research and ICU scoring systems [28], suggesting that the model relies on clinically meaningful features.

4   Conclusion

We presented CaTabRa, a novel software tool and Python library for analyzing tabular data and training high-quality prediction models with little effort. Thanks to its key design principle it can be readily used by domain experts for tackling simple machine learning tasks and at the same time provides added value for experienced Python developers in large-scale data science projects. We successfully used it in our own projects already, for instance in predicting organ failure after blood transfusions, determining whether patients discharged from an intensive care unit will be readmitted within a short time, and predicting functional outcomes after surgical clipping of brain aneurysms.[1] Although these projects and the two use cases in Sect. 3 are concerned with medical data analysis, CaTabRa itself can be applied to tabular data from any domain. Examples can be found in the GitHub repository (https://github.com/risc-mi/catabra).

CaTabRa is ready to be used, but there are a couple of potential limitations that might have to be addressed in the future. For instance, integrating feature extraction (e.g., from longitudinal data) into the existing AutoML component is currently not easily possible, owing to the limited pipeline configuration capabilities of the default auto-sklearn backend. Second, *big data* and distributed computing are currently only fully supported by the data preparation tools described in Sect. 2.6, but corresponding functionality is yet to be integrated into the core workflow. And third, a graphical user interface could even further lower the entrance barrier for users unacquainted with Python and the command-line.

Acknowledgements. This project is financed by research subsidies granted by the government of Upper Austria. RISC Software GmbH is Member of UAR (Upper Austrian Research) Innovation Network.

We thank the anonymous reviewers for their valuable comments.

References

1. Ali, M., et al.: PyCaret. https://pycaret.org/. Accessed 30 Mar 2023
2. Alnegheimish, S., et al.: Cardea: an open automated machine learning framework for electronic health records. In: 2020 IEEE 7th International Conference on Data Science and Advanced Analytics (DSAA), pp. 536–545 (2020). https://doi.org/10.1109/DSAA49011.2020.00068
3. Bai, Y., Li, Y., Shen, Y., Yang, M., Zhang, W., Cui, B.: AutoDC: an automatic machine learning framework for disease classification. Bioinformatics **38**(13), 3415–3421 (2022). https://doi.org/10.1093/bioinformatics/btac334

[1] Scientific publications describing these projects are currently in preparation.

4. Bergstra, J., Yamins, D., Cox, D.: Making a science of model search: hyperparameter optimization in hundreds of dimensions for vision architectures. In: Dasgupta, S., McAllester, D. (eds.) Proceedings of the 30th International Conference on Machine Learning. Proceedings of Machine Learning Research, Atlanta, Georgia, USA, vol. 28, pp. 115–123. PMLR (2013). https://proceedings.mlr.press/v28/bergstra13.html
5. Caicedo-Torres, W., Gutierrez, J.: ISeeU: visually interpretable deep learning for mortality prediction inside the ICU. J. Biomed. Inform. **98**, 103269 (2019). https://doi.org/10.1016/j.jbi.2019.103269
6. Chen, T., Guestrin, C.: XGBoost: a scalable tree boosting system. In: Proceedings of the 22nd ACM SIGKDD International Conference on Knowledge Discovery and Data Mining, KDD 2016, pp. 785–794. ACM, New York (2016). https://doi.org/10.1145/2939672.2939785
7. Christ, M., Braun, N., Neuffer, J., Kempa-Liehr, A.W.: Time series feature extraction on basis of scalable hypothesis tests (tsfresh - a python package). Neurocomputing **307**, 72–77 (2018). https://doi.org/10.1016/j.neucom.2018.03.067
8. Dask Development Team: Dask: Library for dynamic task scheduling (2016). https://dask.org. Accessed 30 Mar 2023
9. Efron, B.: Bootstrap methods: another look at the jackknife. Ann. Stat. **7**, 1–26 (1979). https://doi.org/10.1214/aos/1176344552
10. Feurer, M., Eggensperger, K., Falkner, S., Lindauer, M., Hutter, F.: Auto-Sklearn 2.0: Hands-free AutoML via Meta-Learning. Technical report. arXiv:2007.04074 (2021)
11. Feurer, M., Klein, A., Eggensperger, K., Springenberg, J., Blum, M., Hutter, F.: Efficient and robust automated machine learning. In: Advances in Neural Information Processing Systems, vol. 28. Curran Associates Inc. (2015). https://papers.neurips.cc/paper/2015/hash/11d0e6287202fced83f79975ec59a3a6-Abstract.html
12. Garouani, M., Ahmad, A., Bouneffa, M., Hamlich, M.: AMLBID: an auto-explained automated machine learning tool for big industrial data. SoftwareX **17**, 100919 (2022). https://doi.org/10.1016/j.softx.2021.100919
13. Google: Vertex AI. https://cloud.google.com/vertex-ai?hl=en. Accessed 30 Mar 2023
14. Hatib, F., et al.: Machine-learning algorithm to predict hypotension based on high-fidelity arterial pressure waveform analysis. Anesthesiology **129**(4), 663–674 (2018). https://doi.org/10.1097/ALN.0000000000002300
15. Jarrett, D., Bica, I., Ercole, A., Yoon, J., Qian, Z., van der Schaar, M.: Clairvoyance: a pipeline toolkit for medical time series. In: Proceedings of ICLR 2021, p. 32 (2021)
16. Johnson, A.E.W., Stone, D.J., Celi, L.A., Pollard, T.J.: The MIMIC code repository: enabling reproducibility in critical care research. J. Am. Med. Inform. Assoc. **25**(1), 32–39 (2018). https://doi.org/10.1093/jamia/ocx084
17. Kanter, J.M., Veeramachaneni, K.: Deep feature synthesis: towards automating data science endeavors. In: 2015 IEEE International Conference on Data Science and Advanced Analytics (DSAA), pp. 1–10 (2015). https://doi.org/10.1109/DSAA.2015.7344858
18. Lundberg, S.M., Lee, S.I.: A unified approach to interpreting model predictions. In: Guyon, I., et al. (eds.) Advances in Neural Information Processing Systems, vol. 30, pp. 4765–4774. Curran Associates Inc. (2017). https://papers.nips.cc/paper/7062-a-unified-approach-to-interpreting-model-predictions.pdf

19. Maletzky, A., et al.: Lifting hospital electronic health record data treasures: challenges and opportunities. JMIR Med. Inform. **10**(10), e38557 (2022). https://doi.org/10.2196/38557

20. McKinney, W.: Data structures for statistical computing in python. In: van der Walt, S., Millman, J. (eds.) Proceedings of the 9th Python in Science Conference, pp. 56–61 (2010). https://doi.org/10.25080/Majora-92bf1922-00a

21. Microsoft: Azure Machine Learning - ML as a Service. https://azure.microsoft.com/en-us/products/machine-learning. Accessed 30 Mar 2023

22. Müller, F., Botache, D., Huseljic, D., Heidecker, F., Bieshaar, M., Sick, B.: Out-of-distribution Detection and Generation using Soft Brownian Offset Sampling and Autoencoders. arXiv:2105.02965 (2021)

23. Niculescu-Mizil, A., Caruana, R.: Predicting good probabilities with supervised learning. In: Proceedings of the 22nd International Conference on Machine Learning, ICML 2005, pp. 625–632. Association for Computing Machinery, New York (2005). https://doi.org/10.1145/1102351.1102430

24. Pedregosa, F., et al.: Scikit-learn: machine learning in Python. J. Mach. Learn. Res. **12**, 2825–2830 (2011)

25. Perkins, N.J., Schisterman, E.F.: The inconsistency of 'optimal' cutpoints obtained using two criteria based on the receiver operating characteristic curve. Am. J. Epidemiol. **163**, 670–675 (2006). https://doi.org/10.1093/aje/kwj063

26. Płońska, A., Płoński, P.: Mljar: state-of-the-art automated machine learning framework for tabular data. version 0.10.3 (2021). https://github.com/mljar/mljar-supervised. Accessed 30 Mar 2023

27. Plotly Technologies Inc.: Collaborative data science (2015). https://plotly.com. Accessed 30 Mar 2023

28. Reith, F.C.M., Van den Brande, R., Synnot, A., Gruen, R., Maas, A.I.R.: The reliability of the Glasgow Coma Scale: a systematic review. Intensive Care Med. **42**(1), 3–15 (2015). https://doi.org/10.1007/s00134-015-4124-3

29. Roland, T., et al.: Domain shifts in machine learning based Covid-19 diagnosis from blood tests. J. Med. Syst. **46**(5), 1–12 (2022). https://doi.org/10.1007/s10916-022-01807-1

30. Sculley, D., et al.: Hidden technical debt in machine learning systems. In: Proceedings of the 28th International Conference on Neural Information Processing Systems - Volume 2, NIPS 2015, pp. 2503–2511. MIT Press, Cambridge (2015)

31. Smirnov, N.V.: Estimate of deviation between empirical distribution functions in two independent samples. Bull. Moscow Univ. **2**(2), 3–16 (1939)

32. Smith, M.J., Sala, C., Kanter, J.M., Veeramachaneni, K.: The machine learning bazaar: harnessing the ML ecosystem for effective system development. In: Proceedings of the 2020 ACM SIGMOD International Conference on Management of Data, SIGMOD 2020, pp. 785–800. Association for Computing Machinery, New York (2020). https://doi.org/10.1145/3318464.3386146

33. Zhao, Y., Nasrullah, Z., Li, Z.: Pyod: a python toolbox for scalable outlier detection. J. Mach. Learn. Res. **20**(96), 1–7 (2019). https://jmlr.org/papers/v20/19-011.html

34. Zhou, Y.: Rethinking reconstruction autoencoder-based out-of-distribution detection. In: 2022 IEEE/CVF Conference on Computer Vision and Pattern Recognition (CVPR), New Orleans, LA, USA, pp. 7369–7377. IEEE (2022). https://doi.org/10.1109/CVPR52688.2022.00723

Explaining Machine Learning-Based Feature Selection of IDS for IoT and CPS Devices

Sesan Akintade[✉], Seongtae Kim, and Kaushik Roy

North Carolina Agricultural and Technical State University, 1601 E Market Street, Greensboro, NC 27411, USA
sfakintade@aggies.ncat.edu, {skim,kroy}@ncat.edu

Abstract. In training machine learning and artificial intelligence models for Intrusion Detection Systems (IDS), feature selection plays a critical role in evaluating the prediction performance and explainability of the trained model. The feature selection in designing the IDS is often hindered by the volume, variety, and veracity of the data generated from Internet-of-Things (IoT) and Cyber-Physical Systems (CPS) devices. In this paper, we explored selecting the best subset of features to reduce the feature space of high-dimensional datasets and thereby improve performance, explainability, and computing time. We incorporated the feature selection method of permutation importance in XGB models and prediction explainability methods, such as SHAP and LIME. Using two publicly available IDS datasets, NSL-KDD and CCID-V1, our feature selection-based XBG model for the NSL-KDD data reduced features from 42 to 20 with an AUC score of 0.8751 from the previous 0.8530 with 60% improvement in training time. A similar model for the CCID-V1 data reduced the features from 82 to 22 and achieved an AUC of 0.9999 with a 46% improvement in computing time. We also observed that SHAP and LIME explanations of the prediction showed consistent results in selecting important features. Our study demonstrated that the feature selection achieved an improvement in performance and explainability along with lower training time, which increases the usability of our model for the design of IDS.

Keywords: Internet-of-Things · Cyber Physical Systems · Intrusion Detection Systems · Explainability · Feature Selection

1 Introduction

Cloud computing entails the process of provisioning computing services like storage, software, and networking over the Internet. The ever-increasing availability of cloud platforms, inexpensive sensors, and continuous advances in Artificial Intelligence (AI) technologies have led to the proliferation of devices with the Internet of Things (IoT) and Cyber-Physical Systems (CPS). An IoT is a

© IFIP International Federation for Information Processing 2023
Published by Springer Nature Switzerland AG 2023
I. Maglogiannis et al. (Eds.): AIAI 2023, IFIP AICT 676, pp. 69–80, 2023.
https://doi.org/10.1007/978-3-031-34107-6_6

technology that connects and shares information between devices through the Internet. At the same time, a CPS is an interconnected intelligent system that uses digital control to manage the physical environment. The diverse applications of IoT and CPS, with the concurrent offering of different services, have exposed the connected devices to threats and attacks [4,12]. Some of the common attacks include phishing, SQL injections, denial-of-service (DoS) attacks, malware attacks, remote-to-local attacks (R2L), and zero-day exploitations [13]. Cybersecurity offers a solution to protecting interconnected networks, cloud computing devices, and the information transmitted from cyber-attacks [18]. One of the significant cybersecurity technologies is the Intrusion Detection System (IDS). IDS monitors networks, data transmission, policies, and activities of connected devices to identify attacks within the networks and reports such attacks to a network administrator [2].

The design and network architecture of IoT devices are always in a state of flux, with many constraints being added to meet emerging needs and challenges. IoT devices usually have low computing power, making them ideal for designing numerous and complex smart devices [13]. This limited computation exposes them to compromises and threats of DoS and other attacks. These pose unusual challenges for IDS in safeguarding IoT and CPS from attacks. Therefore, IDS must be practical and nimble enough to correctly identify cyber anomalies and appropriately classify different attacks on the network [13].

Despite the effectiveness and successes of Machine Learning (ML) and Artificial Intelligence (AI) models in designing IDS for traffic attack detection of IoT and CPS, such models are still vastly regarded as black-box models. Understanding the mathematical concept that undergirds such models notwithstanding, they lack clear declarative knowledge representation [10]. This lack of knowledge, coupled with the absence of human involvement in the decisions of AI/ML models, has made the need for the explainability of ML/AI models imperative.

Explainable AI (XAI) is a series of processes and methods establishing the rationale behind the ML algorithms' working mechanism and output. XAI has become a rapidly growing ML/AI research field [3]. XAI is essential in cybersecurity as it reconciles discrepancies and gaps in our knowledge of the cyber systems and the outputs of its predictions [12]. It is important that ML/AI algorithms make decisions that are interpretable, understandable, and explainable. The availability of enormous data for training AI models does not guarantee that a particular dataset is appropriate for tackling a cybersecurity challenge. If a dataset inherently contains bias, then the trained model using this dataset will also be biased [24]. It is therefore essential to safeguard against bias in AI. Feature selection can help make a model more explainable. Feature selection helps to uncover noisy features, and removing such features reduces overfitting, which in turn improves the model's performance. In addition, a model with fewer features is more manageable and interpretable [7].

The objectives of this work are two-fold: (1) To select a subset of features for high-dimensional datasets that give the best predictive performance, and (2)

To understand the explainability of features selected in the ML/AI prediction models.

Our contributions to this work include: (1) We compare the effectiveness of various traditional ML models in finding the model with the highest predictive performance. It is unnecessary to select features that are non-predictive for a model. Feature selection presupposes that there exist features that are significant toward prediction in the model; (2) We explore two feature selection approaches, feature importance, and permutation importance, to select the best-contributing features. We then compute performance metrics on the selected features to see the improvement in terms of accuracy and time, and (3) We explain the decisions of the ML/AI model both at the individual observation (local) level and the collective dataset (global) level. This explanation will help increase the model's reliability and will help discover when adjustments may be necessary for the training of the model.

Section 2 discusses the feature selection techniques and explainable AI tools. In Sect. 3, we introduce the two datasets and describe data preprocessing. Section 4 presents the results of the analysis along with a discussion. Last, we provide our study's conclusions and propose future research directions in Sect. 5.

2   Description of Methodology

2.1   Permutation Importance and Feature Selection

Permutation feature importance is the increase in the prediction error of a model after a feature's values have been randomly shuffled [17]. Randomly shuffling the values of a feature breaks the relationship between the feature and the true outcome. Based on the permutation feature importance for a Random Forest in [5], Fisher *et al.* [8] proposed a model-agnostic alternative to feature importance. Motivated by [5], the algorithm for the permutation feature importance used in this work is shown below.

Permutation Feature Algorithm

1. Input: Trained model $\hat{f}$, feature matrix X, performance score m
2. For each feature j (columns of X):
   (a) For each repetition k in 1, ..., K:
       i. Shuffle column j of matrix X randomly which produce an altered feature matrix $\hat{X}_{k,j}$
       ii. Calculate the metrics (*e.g., accuracy* score), $m_{k,j}$ of model $\hat{f}$ on the altered data $\hat{X}_{k,j}$
   (b) Calculate the permutation importance, $permImp_j$, for feature j as:

$$permImp_j = m - \frac{1}{K}\sum_{k=1}^{K} m_{k,j}$$

3. Output: Sort the *permImp* importance in a descending order.

We employ *Algorithm 1* to select a set of important features in the training data. Before we apply this algorithm, we first create two random features, one categorical and one numerical, called *random_cat* and *random_num*, and add them to the original feature matrix X to yield a new feature matrix X_{wrf} (with *random feature*). *Algorithm 1* is now applied to the X_{wrf} dataset. Since these two random features have no prediction power in an ML model, any other features ranked below them do not contribute to prediction, so we can remove those insignificant features.

2.2 Explainable AI Tools

There are two broadly used techniques for explaining ML models: *intrinsic* (or *ante-hoc*) and *post-hoc* explanations. Ante-hoc systems are interpretable by design toward glass-box approaches [11]. These systems are inherently explainable and are model-specific. Some examples include linear regression and decision trees. Post-hoc systems perform explainability on already constructed models, which are typically complex with high accuracy [1]. The post-hoc systems of explainability are model-agnostic such that they are not tied to a particular AI model. Two of the most popular post-hoc systems are *Local Interpretable Model-Agnostic Explanations (LIME)* [20] and *SHapley Additive exPlanations (SHAP)* [14].

LIME. LIME was first introduced by Ribeiro *et al.* (2016) [20]. LIME is designed to explain the prediction of any classifier in a way that is understandable and reliable by learning a simpler and more interpretable model around the local prediction. LIME does not provide a global explanation of an AI model; instead, it gives a local explanation that is locally faithful within the neighborhood of the prediction being explained. LIME achieves this by training a local surrogate model. LIME is also model-agnostic and can explain any existing model [1]. LIME trains an interpretable model such as linear models, decision trees, or falling rules lists [17,20]. LIME's execution speed is an advantage over SHAP, but it is also limited to local interpretation, whereas SHAP can explain the importance of features both locally and globally. Mathematically, LIME can be expressed as:

$$\text{explanation}(x) = \arg\min_{g \in G}\ L(f, g, \pi_x) + \Omega(g) \tag{1}$$

where x is the instance being explained, L is the model that minimizes the loss, f is the loss being minimized, Ω regularizes the model complexity which is kept low, G the family of possible explanations and π_x is the nearness or proximity measure.

SHAP. SHAP aims to explain a prediction by evaluating the effect of each of the features on the prediction. SHAP was first proposed by Lundberg *et al.* (2017) [14] to address the inconsistency of feature importance of some classifiers, *e.g.*, Random Forest. SHAP enhances Shapley values. The Shapley value refers to the average marginal contribution of a feature across all possible sets [16,21]. That is, the value of a feature contribution to a prediction should be considered vis-a-vis all possible subsets. The 'Shapley values' was originally developed for a cooperative game by Lloyd Shapley [16,21–23].

To extend the measurement of the features' contribution to any model (*i.e.*, making it agnostic), the cooperative game theory concept is employed. SHAP satisfies the properties of efficiency, symmetry, dummy, and additivity. It also fulfills the properties of local accuracy, missingness, and consistency [17]. One advantage of SHAP is that it can be used for local and global explanations. One disadvantage is the long computation time. In this paper, we applied SHAP and LIME to explain the entire dataset model's predictions and the individual sample prediction.

3   Datasets and Preprocessing

3.1   IDS Datasets

The NSL-KDD dataset is one of the most popular public data, which has been used as a benchmark dataset to facilitate the comparison of different IDS. NSL-KDD was first provided as an alternative to solve the problems in the KDD'99 dataset [25]. Those problems include numerous duplicates in the training and test sets. The NSL-KDD dataset contains 125,973 samples with 42 features and one label (target), which is the status of a cyber-attack. The number of normal traffic and malicious traffic (*i.e.* attacks) are approximately 67,343 and 58,630 samples, respectively. The dataset also provided a separate test dataset with 22,544 samples (9,711 normal and 12,833 attack samples) and 42 predictors. The types of attacks in this data are DoS, User to Root Attacks (U2R), R2L, and Probing Attacks.

The CCID-V1 dataset, publicly available, was generated by the researchers in [13]. The data were collected in both smart homes and intelligent lab environments. NetFlow, which dissects smart devices' network behavior, was used to monitor the network traffic while real cyberattacks were injected into the traffic. The attacks used in the creation of the dataset are Address Resolution Protocol (ARP) Poisoning, ARP Denial-of-Service (DoS), User Datagram Protocol (UDP) Flood, Hydra Bruteforce with Asterisk protocol, and SlowLoris.

The original raw data of CCID-V1 contained some instances with missing values. The ratio of the cases with missing values to the total number of observations was less than 0.5%. This made the author remove those instances, as their removal has a negligible effect on the model's performance. The resulting processed CCID-V1 datasets contain 91,665 traffic samples with 82 predictors with one label as the attack type. The distribution of the normal traffic to the malicious traffic is 47,231 to 44,434. The CCID-V1 dataset did not provide a separate test dataset, so the original dataset was split into a training set and test set to train the samples and validate, respectively. The training set was 75% of the total dataset, while the test set was 25% of the total dataset.

3.2   Data Preprocessing

The raw data in the NSL-KDD and CCID-V1 datasets are hardly usable as they are messy, inconsistent, and incomplete. In this raw state, the data cannot be used for modeling as they will lead to poor results. Using the Python Pandas package [15], the data were checked for feature type, missing values, and duplicates, with the duplicate values removed. We also checked the label's balance in both NSL-KDD and CCID-V1 datasets, which turned out to be fairly balanced. Scikit-Learn Pipelines [19] were used for data transformations. Data imputation of missing values and one-hot encoding were implemented on the categorical features of both datasets using pipelines. Imputation and scaling were performed on the numeric features of the two datasets with pipelines. We also checked multi-collinearities among the features and removed highly correlated features.

3.3   ML Models and Hyperparameter Selection

Eight models were used in this research, and they are eXtreme Gradient Boosting (XGB), Random Forest, Logistic Regression, K-Nearest Neighbour (KNN), Multi-layer Perceptron (MLP), Stochastic Gradient Descent, Naïve Bayes and Support Vector Classifier (SVC). These classifiers have parameters that need to be tuned to get optimal performance. These parameters are called hyperparameters. The classifiers perform well with the default values provided by the software packages. However, to be able to compare the performances of all the classifiers and to get the best of them, there is a need to tune the parameters for optimal values. In this research, GridSearchCV [19] was used to search for the optimal hyperparameters while using cross-validation to prevent overfitting. Some of the classifiers' hyperparameters considered include *learning_rate, max_depth, min_child_weight, n_estimators* for XGB [6] , *max_depth, min_samples_split* for Random Forest and *C, penalty* for Logistic Regression.

4   Result and Discussion

Performance Metrics. Table 1 and Table 2 show the various metrics for both NSL-KDD and CCID-V1 for all eight classifiers. The assessment metrics for the datasets with the two random features included are slightly higher than the original datasets without the two random features for both NSL-KDD and CCID-V1 datasets except for *MLP* classifiers. This result indicates that there is a presence of other non-informative features in the datasets that are not useful for the classification. The *XGB* classifier outperforms the other classifiers across all metrics for both datasets except *Recall* and *F*1, where it slightly lags *MLP*. Only *MLP* is comparable to *XGB* for all the metrics, but the amount of execution time is substantially higher for *MLP*. The training time of *MLP* on the moderately complex *NSL-KDD* dataset with 42 features is 65.44 s, which is more than five times the training time for *XGB* on the same dataset. With the more complex *CCID-V1* dataset with 82 features, the difference in training time is even more pronounced: 209.98 to 6.02 s. This disparity in training time makes *XGB* a preferred choice over *MLP* as the classification model for IDS and CPS, which require a quick response in predicting network attacks. *KNN* and *GaussianNB* have particularly short training time. This result is unsurprising, especially for *GaussianNB* which assumes independence among all the features. That assumption often fails in the real world. Despite their training time advantage, the performances of both *KNN* and *GaussianNB* lag those of *XGB*. Besides, the training time for *XGB* is reasonable enough to make it a better choice over *KNN* and *GaussianNB*.

Table 1. Prediction Metrics for NSL-KDD Dataset with and without Random Features

Model	Train_Acc	Test_Acc	AUC	Precision	Recall	F1	Time(s)
Without Random Features							
XGB	1.0000	0.8365	0.8530	0.9726	0.7333	0.8362	11.60
Random Forest	1.0000	0.7797	0.8032	0.9687	0.6334	0.7660	16.92
Logistic Regress	0.9898	0.8099	0.8231	0.9215	0.7281	0.8135	4.23
KNN	0.9993	0.8324	0.8488	0.9677	0.7299	0.8321	0.50
MLP	0.9993	0.8412	0.8514	0.9321	0.7776	0.8479	65.44
SGD	0.9893	0.8078	0.8213	0.9218	0.7238	0.8109	2.12
GaussianNB	0.8592	0.5661	0.6179	0.9760	0.2437	0.3901	0.80
SVC	0.9977	0.8357	0.8509	0.9611	0.7414	0.8371	67.98
with Random Features							
XGB	1.0000	0.8403	0.8564	0.9728	0.7401	0.8406	14.86
Random Forest	1.0000	0.7879	0.8104	0.9693	0.6479	0.7767	19.17
Logistic Regress	0.9898	0.8097	0.8229	0.9215	0.7276	0.8132	4.07
KNN	0.9986	0.8331	0.8495	0.9680	0.7310	0.8330	0.54
MLP	0.9996	0.8382	0.8488	0.9314	0.7727	0.8447	80.93
SGD	0.9891	0.8069	0.8206	0.9218	0.7220	0.8098	1.77
GaussianNB	0.8592	0.5661	0.6179	0.9760	0.2437	0.3901	0.97
SVC	0.9976	0.8380	0.8528	0.9607	0.7460	0.8398	90.26

Feature Selection. Permutation importance gives a realistic indication of usefulness in feature selection as it does not depend on the training dataset statistics [19]. In feature importance by impurity, tree-based models consider a feature important depending on the number of split points by the feature for the model to make a decision [5]. The feature importance in gradient booting also resembles that of the tree-based feature importance only that gradient boosting employs entropy, instead of impurity, in calculating the importance [9]. However, both impurity and entropy-based feature importance can inflate the importance of a

Table 2. Prediction Metrics for CCID-V1 Dataset with and without Random Features

Model	Train_Acc	Test_Acc	AUC	Precision	Recall	F1	Time(s)
Without Random Features							
XGB	1.0000	0.9999	0.9999	0.9999	0.9999	0.9999	6.02
Random Forest	1.0000	0.9992	0.9992	0.9995	0.9988	0.9991	8.11
Logistic Regress	0.8985	0.8980	0.8976	0.9016	0.8862	0.8939	1.99
KNN	0.9836	0.9764	0.9765	0.9701	0.9815	0.9758	0.39
MLP	0.9919	0.9907	0.9905	0.9964	0.9843	0.9904	209.98
SGD	0.9170	0.9159	0.9151	0.9324	0.8911	0.9113	1.63
GaussianNB	0.6938	0.6922	0.6827	0.9870	0.3700	0.5382	0.61
SVC	0.9735	0.9725	0.9722	0.9793	0.9636	0.9714	138.70
With Random Features							
XGB	1.0000	0.9999	0.9999	0.9998	0.9999	0.9999	6.52
Random Forest	1.0000	0.9992	0.9992	0.9995	0.9987	0.9991	8.05
Logistic Regress	0.8997	0.8997	0.8991	0.9097	0.8805	0.8948	2.04
KNN	0.9567	0.9327	0.9328	0.9262	0.9357	0.9310	0.46
MLP	0.9898	0.9871	0.9873	0.9805	0.9931	0.9868	136.46
SGD	0.9332	0.9340	0.9327	0.9725	0.8890	0.9289	1.96
GaussianNB	0.6938	0.6923	0.6827	0.9870	0.3701	0.5383	0.75
SVC	0.9734	0.9723	0.9720	0.9788	0.9637	0.9712	181.44

feature that may not have a prediction power in a test dataset, especially when a model is overfitted. The impurity-based feature importance is also biased towards a feature with high cardinality, *e.g.*, a numeric feature. Impurity-based feature importance is calculated using the training dataset statistics, and it does not always generalize to unseen dataset [19]. On the other hand, the permutation importance method uses the decrease in evaluation metric caused by the random jumbling of the non-informative features [5]. The process renders a feature unpredictive of the target. As a result, a decrease in the model metric due to the random jumbling indicates how important a particular feature is on the target. With some non-informative columns removed for brevity, the results of the permutation importance of the XGBoost model in NSL-KDD is shown in Fig. 1. The figure shows that the importances of both random features are higher than some of the features, which could be removed in the final model.

Explainability. SHAP and LIME were used to explain the prediction of the XGB model. Whereas LIME is best for local interpretation, SHAP can be utilized for local and global interpretation. In Figs. 2 and 3, LIME is used to explain which features are important in predicting one observation from each of the two datasets NSL-KDD and CCID-V1. LIME shows that the model predicts an attack for an instance of the NSL-KDD data in Fig. 2 because of the indicated range of values for src_bytes, $service\_tim_i$, $service\_IRC$, $service\_private$,

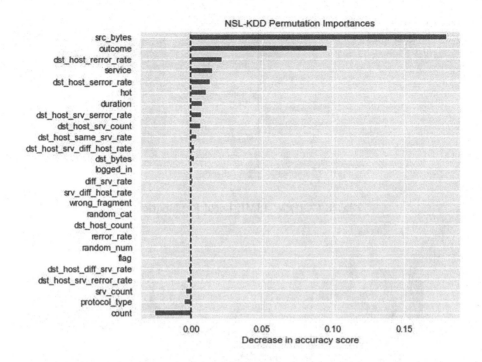

Fig. 1. NSL-KDD Permutation Importance

service_pop_3 and *service_shell*. In Fig. 3, LIME shows that the model predicts normal traffic for an instance of the CCID-V1 data because of the range of values for *src_ip*, *dst2src_first_seen_ms*, *src2dst_fin_packets*, *src2dst_mean_ps*, and *dst2src_fin_packets*. Figure 4 shows the global explanation of the predictions on CCID datasets. It shows that *scr_ip*, *dst_ip*, *scr_port*, *bidirectional_mean_ps* are all important in predicting whether a traffic signal is an attack. This is consistent with the output of the permutation importance processes.

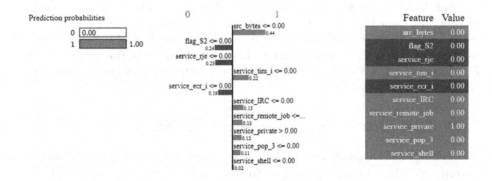

Fig. 2. NSL-KDD LIME Local Explanation

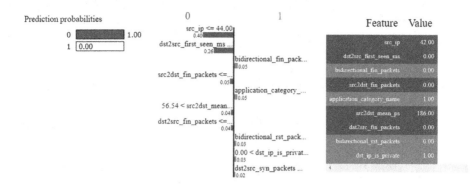

Fig. 3. CCID_VI LIME Local Explanation

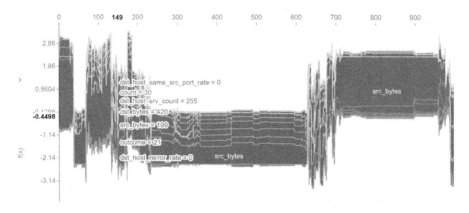

Fig. 4. CCID SHAP Global Explanation

The final metrics from the selected features are shown in Table 3. Only 20 features were finally selected for NSL-KDD from the 42 original features. Similarly, 22 features were selected from the 82 original features for the CCID-V1 dataset. From Table 3, we can see that with the NSL-KDD dataset, there is an improvement of 2.49% in the test accuracy and 2.21% in AUC. The time was reduced by over 50% from 11.60 to 4.49 s. The significant improvement for the CCID-V1 dataset is the time of execution which reduces to almost half of the initial time from 6.02 to 3.27 s. These improvements make the feature selection process ideal for the design of IDS and CPS, requiring traffic attacks to be quickly detected and promptly neutralized.

Table 3. The Final Metrics For NSL-KDD and CCID-V1 Datasets

Dataset	Model	Train_Acc	Test_Acc	AUC	Precision	Recall	F1	Time(s)
NSL-KDD	XGB	1.0000	0.8614	0.8751	0.9750	0.7764	0.8645	4.49
CCID-V1	XGB	1.0000	0.9999	0.9999	1.0000	0.9998	0.9999	3.27

5   Conclusion

In this paper, we compared the performances of eight different ML models on two IoT-network-based datasets. *XGBoost, Random Forest, Multi-Layer Perceptron (MLP) and Support Vector Classifier (SVC)* all did quite well in predicting attacks on the network traffic, but the long time *MLP* and *SVC* took to train the model subordinates them to *XGBoost*. With *XGBoost* performing the best among the models, we elicited the most important features by permuting each of the features and discovering the ones with the most impact on the accuracy score of the model. With this process, we achieved on a separate test dataset of NSL-KDD an AUC score of 0.8751 with a runtime of 4.49 s as against a previous run of 0.8530 AUC in 11.60 s. Although the process did not improve the metrics for the CCID-V1 dataset much, it reduced the time to almost half, from 6.2 s to 3.27 s. We also used SHAP and LIME to explain the outcome of our predictions. SHAP was used for global explanation, while LIME was able to explain the features that were locally important. The high metric scores and low training time make our process ideal for the design of an IDS. The fewer features selected also reduce the time it will take to collect more data for future training. This work can also be extended to other Machine Learning applications with high dimensional data like customer churn prediction, credit card fraud detection, mortgage loan defaults prediction, and intelligent home applications. In the future, we plan to extend the work to multi-class classification. We will also explore deep learning instead of the fully connected multi-layer perceptron, which was considered in this project.

Acknowledgements. This research was funded by the National Centers of Academic Excellence in Cybersecurity Grant (H98230-21-1-0326), which is part of the National Security Agency. The views and conclusions contained herein are those of the authors and should not be interpreted as necessarily representing the official policies or endorsements, either expressed or implied, of the U.S.

References

1. Adadi, A., Berrada, M.: Peeking inside the black-box: a survey on explainable artificial intelligence (XAI). IEEE Access **6**, 52138–52160 (2018)
2. Antunes, N., Balby, L., Figueiredo, F., Lourenco, N., Meira, W., Santos, W.: Fairness and transparency of machine learning for trustworthy cloud services. In: 2018 48th Annual IEEE/IFIP International Conference on Dependable Systems and Networks Workshops (DSN-W), pp. 188–193. IEEE (2018)
3. Arrieta, A.B., et al.: Explainable artificial intelligence (XAI): concepts, taxonomies, opportunities and challenges toward responsible ai. Inf. Fusion **58**, 82–115 (2020)
4. Atzori, L., Iera, A., Morabito, G.: The internet of things: a survey. Comput. Netw. **54**(15), 2787–2805 (2010)
5. Breiman, L.: Random forests. Mach. Learn. **45**, 5–32 (2001)
6. Chen, T., Guestrin, C.: Proceedings of the 22nd ACM SIGKDD International Conference on Knowledge Discovery and Data Mining (2016)

7. Figueroa Barraza, J., López Droguett, E., Martins, M.R.: Towards interpretable deep learning: a feature selection framework for prognostics and health management using deep neural networks. Sensors **21**(17), 5888 (2021)

8. Fisher, A., Rudin, C., Dominici, F.: All models are wrong, but many are useful: learning a variable's importance by studying an entire class of prediction models simultaneously. J. Mach. Learn. Res. **20**(177), 1–81 (2019)

9. Friedman, J.H.: Greedy function approximation: a gradient boosting machine. Ann. Stat. 1189–1232 (2001)

10. Holzinger, A., Biemann, C., Pattichis, C.S., Kell, D.B.: What do we need to build explainable ai systems for the medical domain? arXiv preprint arXiv:1712.09923 (2017)

11. Holzinger, A., Plass, M., Holzinger, K., Crisan, G.C., Pintea, C.M., Palade, V.: A glass-box interactive machine learning approach for solving np-hard problems with the human-in-the-loop. arXiv preprint arXiv:1708.01104 (2017)

12. Kumar, J.S., Patel, D.R.: A survey on internet of things: security and privacy issues. Int. J. Comput. Appl. **90**(11) (2014)

13. Liu, Z., et al.: Using embedded feature selection and CNN for classification on CCD-INID-V1-A new IoT dataset. Sensors **21**(14), 4834 (2021)

14. Lundberg, S.M., Lee, S.I.: A unified approach to interpreting model predictions. In: Advances in Neural Information Processing Systems, vol. 30 (2017)

15. McKinney, W., et al.: Data structures for statistical computing in python. In: Proceedings of the 9th Python in Science Conference, Austin, TX, vol. 445, pp. 51–56 (2010)

16. Mitchell, R., Cooper, J., Frank, E., Holmes, G.: Sampling permutations for shapley value estimation (2022)

17. Molnar, C.: Interpretable machine learning. Lulu.com (2020)

18. Morris, B.: Explainable anomaly and intrusion detection intelligence for platform information technology using dimensionality reduction and ensemble learning. In: 2019 IEEE AUTOTESTCON, pp. 1–5. IEEE (2019)

19. Pedregosa, F., et al.: Scikit-learn: machine learning in Python. J. Mach. Learn. Res. **12**, 2825–2830 (2011)

20. Ribeiro, M.T., Singh, S., Guestrin, C.: Model-agnostic interpretability of machine learning. arXiv preprint arXiv:1606.05386 (2016)

21. Serrano, R.: Cooperative games: core and shapley value. Technical report, Working Paper (2007)

22. Shapley, L.: A value for n-person games. In: Kuhn, H., Tucker, A. (eds.) Contributions to the Theory of Games II (1953)

23. Sundararajan, M., Najmi, A.: The many shapley values for model explanation. In: International Conference on Machine Learning, pp. 9269–9278. PMLR (2020)

24. Sweeney, L.: Discrimination in online ad delivery. Commun. ACM **56**(5), 44–54 (2013)

25. Tavallaee, M., Bagheri, E., Lu, W., Ghorbani, A.A.: A detailed analysis of the KDD cup 99 data set. In: 2009 IEEE Symposium on Computational Intelligence for Security and Defense Applications, pp. 1–6. IEEE (2009)

Explaining the Unexplainable: Role of XAI for Flight Take-Off Time Delay Prediction

Waleed Jmoona[1]($\boxtimes$) , Mobyen Uddin Ahmed[1] , Mir Riyanul Islam[1],
Shaibal Barua[1] , Shahina Begum[1] , Ana Ferreira[2], and Nicola Cavagnetto[2]

[1] School of Innovation, Design and Engineering, Mälardalen University, 72123
Västerås, Sweden
{waleed.jmoona,mobyen.uddin.ahmed,mir.riyanul.islam,
shaibal.barua,shahina.begum}@mdu.se
[2] Deep Blue, Rome, Italy
{ana.ferreira,nicola.cavagnetto}@dblue.it

Abstract. Flight Take-Off Time (TOT) delay prediction is essential to optimizing capacity-related tasks in Air Traffic Management (ATM) systems. Recently, the ATM domain has put afforded to predict TOT delays using machine learning (ML) algorithms, often seen as "black boxes", therefore it is difficult for air traffic controllers (ATCOs) to understand how the algorithms have made this decision. Hence, the ATCOs are reluctant to trust the decisions or predictions provided by the algorithms. This research paper explores the use of explainable artificial intelligence (XAI) in explaining flight TOT delay to ATCOs predicted by ML-based predictive models. Here, three post hoc explanation methods are employed to explain the models' predictions. Quantitative and user evaluations are conducted to assess the acceptability and usability of the XAI methods in explaining the predictions to ATCOs. The results show that the post hoc methods can successfully mimic the inference mechanism and explain the models' individual predictions. The user evaluation reveals that user-centric explanation is more usable and preferred by ATCOs. These findings demonstrate the potential of XAI to improve the transparency and interpretability of ML models in the ATM domain.

Keywords: Explainable Artificial Intelligence · LIME · SHAP · DALEX · Flight Take-off Time Delay Prediction · Air Traffic Management

1 Introduction

Artificial Intelligence (AI) has seen a surge in interest over the past decade due to the availability of massive volumes of data and the efficient calculation of learning algorithms using computer graphics card processors[1]. AI has been applied to

---

[1] https://www.coe.int/en/web/artificial-intelligence/history-of-ai.

© IFIP International Federation for Information Processing 2023
Published by Springer Nature Switzerland AG 2023
I. Maglogiannis et al. (Eds.): AIAI 2023, IFIP AICT 676, pp. 81–93, 2023.
https://doi.org/10.1007/978-3-031-34107-6_7

various domains, including ATM [8]. The availability of vast amounts of data in aviation compared to other transportation modes has contributed to this trend [15]. However, despite previous research in AI for the ATM domain, it has not been fully operational, nor has it brought significant benefits to end-users [8]. The slow progress in the application of AI in ATM is due to safety concerns, as the domain involves critical situations with human lives at stake. Nevertheless, the use of AI models such as Deep Convolutional Neural Networks (DCNN), Random Forest (RF), Extreme Gradient Boosting (XGBoost), and Gradient Boosting Machine (GBM) has gained significant attention for predicting delays in the ATM, as evidenced by recent studies [1,6,9,18]. Understanding the reasons behind congestion, trajectory routes, and delay is essential for enhancing traffic. However, one of the challenges in using these algorithms is their lack of explainability, which has prompted the XAI community to focus on developing techniques such as Local Interpretable Model-agnostic Explanation (LIME) [14], Shapley Additive Explanations (SHAP) [13], and Model-Agnostic Language for Exploration and Explanations (DALEX) [2] to enhance the transparency of these models. XAI has emerged as a field of research that aims to provide transparency to high-consequence decisions made by AI systems in various domains, including healthcare, criminal justice, and ATM [11]. Further, in the XAI domain, the aim is to empower users in data analysis and decision-making processes.

This research focuses on XAI techniques applied to flight TOT delay prediction, which deals with capacity optimization in the ATM domain. The main contribution of the study is to investigate the acceptability and usability of different XAI methods using both quantitative and user evaluation processes. Here, RF and XGBoost are used to develop two predictive models for delay predictions. The SHAP, LIME, and DALEX are employed to explain the predictions. The performance of ML models and the goodness of explanations are compared in the quantitative evaluation. Two rounds of experiments were conducted in user evaluation to compare the acceptability and usability of the three XAI methods in explaining the prediction to ATCOs. In general, the initial results demonstrate the feasibility and effectiveness of XAI techniques in enhancing the transparency, interpretability, and performance of AI models in ATM, particularly for TOT delay prediction.

2   Materials and Methods

2.1   Dataset

The dataset used in this study was acquired from EUROCONTROL[2], which contained the flight data messages from Enhanced Tactical Flow Management System (ETFMS) for all flights during the period of May - October 2019. In particular, the dataset contains approximately 9.5 million instances of EFD messages. The messages include basic information about the flights, their status, information on the previous flight legs, Air Traffic Flow Management (ATFM) regulations, calendar information, etc. A detailed description of the features can be found in the previous research work conducted with similar tasks of delay prediction [6].

---

[2] https://www.eurocontrol.int/.

2.2   Prediction Models

A vast range of ML and AI models has been developed regarding ATM tasks. However, RF and XGBoost have been mostly used in prediction tasks (regression) based on our previous literature study reported in [11]. Therefore, in this paper, two different prediction models were developed with RF and XGBoost. The RF algorithm, which consists of a collection of randomised decision trees, is one of the well-known ensemble algorithms of ML utilised in numerous ATM-linked tasks [3]. The motivation behind using RF is that it can generalise better with both tabular and categorical data without assuming the independence of the features [3]. Concurrently, XGBoost was chosen with a view to enhance the performance of flight TOT delay prediction models developed with predecessor algorithms in the previous work by Dalmau et al. [7]. In particular, XGBoost is a scalable ML algorithm for tree boosting used in regression and classification applications [5]. It uses an ensemble of weak prediction models to make the final prediction, and a weak prediction model refers to the randomised decision trees.

2.3   Explanation Models

To explain the flight TOT delay prediction, LIME and SHAP were chosen as the most widely used explanation generation tool for heterogeneous data [11]. These tools can produce an explanation of the prediction from the models perspective. In addition, DALEX was invoked to provide users with provisions of interactions by selecting their preferred features while generating explanations. LIME [14] is a tool that uses an interpretable model to approximate each individual prediction made by any black box ML model. LIME uses a three-step process to determine the specific contributions of the chosen features: perturbing the original data points, feeding them to the black-box model, and then observing the related predictions. For example, in our delay prediction case, each prediction of a flight TOT delay is shown together with a list of features that contributes to the delay and their weights in that prediction. SHAP is a mathematical technique [13] that was developed based on the "Shapley Values" proposed by Shapley in the cooperative game theory [16]. Shapley values are a mechanism to fairly assign impact to features that might not have an equal influence on the predictions. To generate additive explanations for predictions from black-box models, the Shapley value concept was incorporated. In delay prediction, to explain the decisions from the model (i.e., prediction), SHAP calculates the contribution of each feature in the prediction from the model. DALEX is a python library built upon the software for explainable machine learning proposed by Biecek [2]. The main goal of the DALEX tool is to create a level of abstraction around a model that makes it easier to explore and explain the model. Explanation deals with two uncertainty levels, model level and explanation level. The underlying idea is to capture the contribution of a feature to the model's prediction by computing the shift in the expected value of the prediction while fixing the values of other features. In this paper, for delay prediction, DALEX was used to generate an interactive Breakdown plot, which detects local interactions of user-selected features.

2.4   Validation Approaches

Evaluation Metrics. In this study, evaluation metrics are used as prediction accuracy metrics, namely Mean Absolute Error (MAE), for both the prediction and explanation models. MAE is computed as the average difference between the actual values (y_i) and the observed values $(\hat{y}_i)$ from the model using the following equation:

$$MAE = \frac{1}{n} \sum_{i=1}^{n} |y_i - \hat{y}_i| \tag{1}$$

For the prediction models, MAE was calculated using Eq. 1, considering the delays from the test dataset as actual values in comparison with the predicted delays by the developed regression models as the observed values.

To assess the similarity between the inference mechanisms of the prediction and explanation models, the evaluation prediction has been carried out. This involves calculating the MAE by comparing the observed values of the explanation model predictions with the actual values obtained from the regression models. This metric will be termed as the *local accuracy* in the discussions presented in Sect. 4.

To assess the quality of the feature attribution from the explanation models with respect to the prediction models, Normalised Discounted Cumulative Gain (nDCG) scores were examined. By definition, the nDCG score compares the order of retrieved documents in information retrieval tasks [4,17]. Here, nDCG scores were observed to compare the order of the features from the regression and explanation models in terms of their importance scores resulting in the corresponding predictions.

Table 1. Questionnaires to assess ATCOs' satisfaction and acceptance of the delay prediction XAI tool.

Objective	Questionnaire
Level of Understanding (Post Condition)	**Question 1:** ATCOs' understand why the delay value (time) is influenced by the selected features
	Question 2: ATCOs' understand the contribution of each feature to the overall delay value (time)
	Question 3: ATCOs' understand why the tool selected the features based on their operational relevance
	Question 4: Having access to an explanation would increase ATCOs' accuracy in making an impact assessment in operations.
Overall Delay Prediction Outcome (Final Questionnaire)	**Question 5:** ATCOs' find the information presented is clear and understandable
	Question 6: The unit in which information is presented is usable in operations
	Question 7: Knowing the features that influence the overall delay would help ATCOs' optimize runway use

User Evaluation on the Satisfaction of Explanation. The objective of the user evaluation was to assess the impact of different levels of explainability on controllers' acceptance. The hypothesis was: ATCOs self-reported acceptance would differ between the explanation methods and explanation levels. Hoffman et al. [10] suggested using a list of checklists through questionnaires to measure user satisfaction that addresses key attributes of explanation e.g., understandability, the sufficiency of detail, usefulness, etc. Therefore, to assess user satisfaction and acceptance of the explanation, the study utilized self-report questionnaires designed using a Likert scale [12]. The Likert scale used a five-level format ranging from "Strongly disagree" to "Strongly agree". Two categories of questionnaires were administered (see Table 1) - one after each condition i.e., explanations generated by SHAP, LIME, and DALEX, and one final questionnaire after all tasks were completed. The "post condition" questionnaire focused on understanding the AI outcome and the impact on work performance, while the final questionnaire evaluated the general usability and impact on work performance of a delay prediction tool.

3 Explaining Take-Off Delay Prediction

This section outlines the methodology we followed to answer the research question of this study. The methodology consists of three phases: Data Preparation, Model Development, and Validation. This section provides an overview of each phase and describes how they are related to each other. Figure 1 illustrates the phases of our research study.

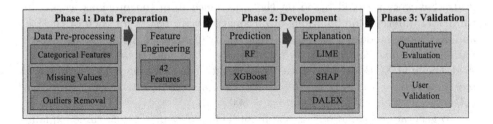

Fig. 1. Experimental methodology of explaining flight TOT delay prediction.

3.1 Phase 1: Data Preparation

The success of any machine learning model depends heavily on the quality and relevance of the dataset used for training. In this phase, we describe the steps taken data pre-processing and feature engineering to optimise the models' performances. During pre-processing, all the messages in the dataset with missing features and outliers were dropped to contain complete information of the flights. Considering the time of pre-tactical phase, i.e., 6 h [6], only those messages were considered which were received within the time interval from zero (inclusive) to three-hundred and sixty minutes (exclusive): (0,360] from the Estimated Off-Block Time (EOBT). In summary, the dataset was analyzed to extract 42 features based on air traffic control experts' determination, as described in [6]. The target variable was calculated from the difference between the Actual Take-off Time (ATOT) and the Estimated Take-off Time (ETOT). The features are classified as categorical or numerical, and whether it changes (dynamic) or not (static) during the progress of the flight, from the individual flight plan (IFP) to the ATOT. The final dataset contained 7,613,584 instances for 609,202 flights flown by 18,214 distinct aircraft with an average of 12 flights per day and approximately 15 min of average take-off delay. Finally, to improve the prediction performance of the trained models, a split of the time series data was performed where the training set consisted of instances from May to August, while the test set included instances from September to October. This split was preferred over the more standard 80/20 training/testing split as it preserved the chronological order of the data (i.e., each row of data in the time series has a time dependency) and accounted for any seasonal patterns or trends in the time series, leading to more accurate predictions.

3.2 Phase 2: Development

In the second phase, the focus is on developing predictive and explainable models for the study. Once the data has been prepared in Phase 1, it is then processed in Phase 2 to implement two AI models and three explainability tools.

Both the models, RF and XGBoost were trained with the parameter values selected through a grid search 5-fold cross-validation with arbitrary value grids that were selected based on the experience from the previous works. In total, 144 different combinations of parameters were tested for each of the RF and XGBoost models. Finally, the RF was trained with the following hyperparameters: $max\_depth = 7$, $max\_features = 16$ and $n\_estimators = 500$. And, the final XGBoost model was trained with the following hyperparameters: $learning\_rate = 0.1$, $max\_depth = 7$, $min\_child\_weight = 1$, $subsample = 0.5$, $colsample\_bytree = 0.5$, $n_e stimators = 500$.

To generate explanations on the flight TOT delay prediction, three explainability tools, namely, SHAP, LIME and DALEX were used. Each of the two trained prediction models and the test dataset were fed into the tools to compute the individual contributions of each features to the final prediction for each instance. To present the individual contributions of the features in a comprehensible manner to the users, breakdown plots were drawn. Figure 2c illustrates a breakdown plot that explains the prediction of 7.31 min. In the figure, the blue bar corresponds to the predicted delay. The red and green bars with corresponding values represent increase and decrease of delay time respectively.

3.3 Phase 3: Validation

The final phase of this methodology involves two validation scenarios: quantitative evaluation and user validation.

Quantitative Evaluation. The evaluation of the take-off delay prediction was performed from two perspectives: prediction models and explainability methods. To show the performance of our models (RF and XGBoost), two TOT delay prediction models reported in Dalmau's work [6], ETFMS and gradient-boosted decision tree (GBDT), were selected to comprehensively compare prediction models. The ETFMS was used as a benchmark for comparison as it is widely used in aviation for delay prediction. Besides, to investigate its potential in flight delay prediction, our aim was to explore the performance of the GBDT model, given its good results in other time series prediction tasks. Additionally, two explainability methods, LIME and SHAP, were used to explain the predictions of the XGBoost model based on the previous results of the model.

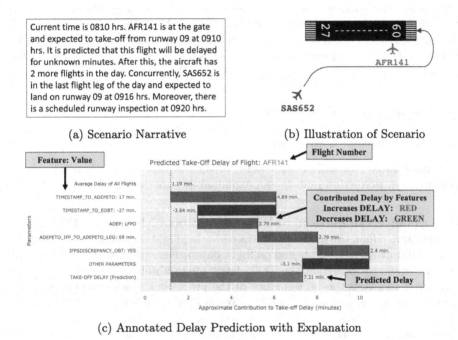

(a) Scenario Narrative   (b) Illustration of Scenario

(c) Annotated Delay Prediction with Explanation

Fig. 2. An example of scenario presentation and associated prediction of delay with explanation for user validation.

User Evaluation. In the user evaluation phase, a web platform was developed to conduct the evaluation of three XAI methods used to explain the prediction results to end users. The selected methods were LIME, SHAP, and DALEX. In the user validation exercise, a group of 9 Air Traffic Controllers (ATCOs) with varying levels of expertise participated. The participants, who were all male and aged between 30 and 60, had a minimum of 5 years of experience as ATCOs. For LIME and SHAP, each participant watched an introductory video and was presented with a scenario context with narrative (Fig. 2a) and illustration (Fig. 2b) of a delayed flight. In addition, a prediction of the delay with explanation was also presented (Fig. 2c) which varied based on the explainability tool used to generate the explanation. The system based on LIME and SHAP then presented a breakdown plot that contained the most important features contributing to the delay. At the end of each scenario, the participant was asked to fill in questions 1 to 4 in the questionnaire presented in Table 1 to evaluate factors linked to human performance. For DALEX, each participant watched an introductory video and was presented with a scenario context of a delayed flight. They are then asked to select five features from a list of features. Based on the chosen features, the system presented a breakdown plot containing the five selected features contributing to the delay. At the end of the scenario, participants were asked to report the questionnaire (questions 1 to 4). Once all scenarios were completed, the participants were asked to answer a final questionnaire (questions 5 to 7) to evaluate the effectiveness of the XAI methods in explaining the prediction results. Further, qualitative feedback was collected with open-ended questions from the representative of ANACNA (Italian Air Traffic Controllers Association).

4 Results and Discussion

4.1 Quantitative Evaluation

The quantitative evaluation of the delay prediction task was performed from two perspectives: prediction models and explainability methods.

Performance Comparison of RF and XGBoost Models for TOT Delay Prediction. Here, the models were trained using flight data from May to August 2019 (5.9M instances) and tested on flight data from September to October 2019 (1.7M instances) to predict the TOT delay. Mean absolute error (MAE) values were used to assess the performance of the predictors. Both models performed better than previous similar work [6] in terms of MAE when predicting the take-off delay on the whole test set. To assess performance in more detail, the dataset was sliced based on the time remaining in minutes until the EOBT. Table 2 lists the chunks with the prediction performance of existing ETFMS, GBDT [6], RF, and XGBoost. The table shows that RF and XGBoost performed better than previous models for all intervals, with XGBoost outperforming RF.

Interpretation and Explanation of XGBoost Model's Decision-making Process Using LIME and SHAP. Based on the outcome, XGBoost outperforms RF models, so we have only considered explanation models to explain the predictions of XGBoost only. As described in Sect. 2, LIME and SHAP were used to explain the predictions on the flight TOT delay made by the XGBoost model. These tools try to mimic the prediction of the trained models and determine the important features to explain the prediction. To evaluate the similarity between the predictions of the explanation tools and XGBoost, local accuracy

Table 2. Comparison of performances on take-off delay prediction from ETFMS, GBDT, RF and XGBoost using the MAE (in minutes), lower is better, and the lowest values are highlighted. The MAE values for the ETFMS and GBDT are considered as a reference from experimentation performed by Dalmau et al. [6].

Time to EOBT	ETFMS [6]	GBDT [6]	RF	XGBoost
(0, 15]	10.7	8.8	**7.22**	7.51
(15, 30]	12.4	10.2	8.75	**8.47**
(30, 60]	13.3	10.5	**9.05**	9.05
(60, 90]	14.3	10.8	9.46	**9.12**
(90, 120]	14.3	11.1	9.83	**9.50**
(120, 180]	19.1	13.5	11.09	**10.50**
(180, 240]	23.0	15.4	11.58	**11.46**
(240, 360]	21.2	15.1	**11.93**	12.02

was considered as MAE in minutes. The conditions of comparison for LIME and SHAP are consistent as both generate prediction model-centric explanations. Therefore, the results of their comparison are summarised in Table 3 for all instances, top 100k instances, and top 67k instances with the most accurate predictions, respectively. However, DALEX provides a user-centric explanation that is subjective and varies, which is different from LIME and SHAP. Due to this difference in the characteristics of the explanations, DALEX was excluded from the quantitative evaluation. Finally, based on the comparison, SHAP was used to generate visualisations to explain the predicted flight TOT delay prediction. Figure 2c illustrates an example of a visualisation explaining a single instance of flight TOT delay prediction.

Table 3. Comparison of *local accuracy* and nDCG values for SHAP and LIME. For local accuracy, lower is better, and for nDCG, higher is better. The best values are highlighted.

XAI Model	SHAP		LIME	
Metric	Local Accuracy	nDCG	Local Accuracy	nDCG
All	3.3×10^{-6}	0.806	8.62	**0.882**
100k	1.1×10^{-6}	0.722	4.75	**0.847**
67k	6.2×10^{-7}	0.717	3.13	**0.800**

4.2   User Evaluation

The user evaluation of the delay prediction task followed Phase 3 as shown in Fig. 1.

Post Condition Assessment. The aim was to evaluate the impact of LIME, SHAP and DALEX on the understanding of the influence of selected features and their contribution to the final output, as well as their impact on work performance. The results showed that LIME and DALEX received the highest positive feedback for understanding the influence of selected features. Moreover, SHAP received no negative feedback, resulting in a more balanced condition for the understanding of the influence of the features on the final delay. In contrast, DALEX was the most effective in understanding the contribution of each feature to the final output. Therefore, we could say that the user-centric selection of the features can positively influence the understanding of the contribution to the final delay value. However, none of the conditions received positive feedback about understanding the selected features' operational relevance. This could mean that, even if the influence and the contribution on the final delay of the selected features for SHAP and LIME, and the contribution of the features selected by the users for DALEX, is high, this would not impact the operational relevance of the information received. The rationalization is reflected in the qualitative interview discussed in the Qualitative Feedback section. Additionally, the impact on work performance was generally positive for all three tools, with DALEX being the most useful for operations, confirming the slight preference expressed by the users in the last understanding item (question 4). These findings suggest that the user-centric selection of features can improve understanding of the contribution to the final output value. However, further efforts are needed to improve the understanding of the operational relevance of the selected features. The three methods are compared per question (see Fig. 3).

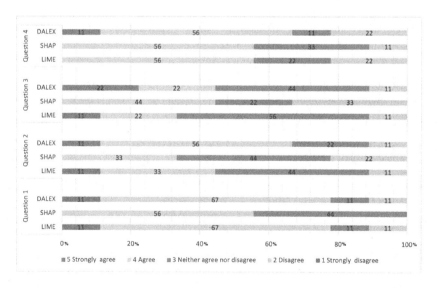

Fig. 3. ATCOs' response on the level of understanding of the explanation using LIME, SHAP, and DALEX.

Final Questionnaire. The final questionnaire revealed that the unit's usability in which information was presented was generally rated positively, with no negative feedback on this first usability item, as shown in Fig. 4. The second usability item regarding the clarity and understandability of the information presented also received positive feedback. The question about the impact on work performance showed that only 22% of participants reported negative feedback about the usefulness of a delay prediction tool in optimising the use of a runway, regardless of their condition.

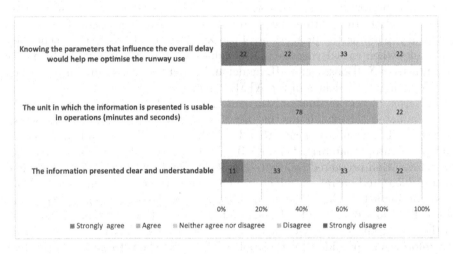

Fig. 4. Overall Delay Prediction outcomes.

Qualitative Feedback. An Open-ended question interview revealed that most ATCOs found the validation exercise clear and understandable, but some users found some details and features unclear. The tool has the potential for several operational tasks, such as generating the best sequence of departures and optimizing runway usage, optimizing Target Start-up Approval Time (TSAT), Air Traffic Flow and Capacity Management (ATFCM) delay, and airport strategic planning. However, The representative from the ANACNA pointed out that improvements to the DALEX condition should be needed to reduce the variables involved in selecting features. Also, an important finding was that basic training on AI is required for ATCOs to understand such AI tools for better communication with the end user.

Overall, these results highlight the potential and limitations of XAI tools in the aviation industry and can inform the development of future AI tools for air traffic management. Extensive details on user validation can be found in the project's deliverable 6.2[3].

---

[3] https://doi.org/10.5281/zenodo.7486982.

5   Conclusions

This study investigates ML and post hoc XAI methods to provide explanations of TOT delay prediction to the ATCOs, and presents a comparative analysis regarding usability and acceptance of the explanation offered by these XAI methods in the ATM domain. Here, we have compared the XGBoost and RF models as prediction models, along with their explanations provided by LIME, SHAP, and DALEX. The results indicate that XGBoost outperforms RF regarding MAE values for predicting TOT delays. Besides, XGBoost is more scalable, faster, and better at optimizing errors than RF and GBDT from an algorithmic perspective. In addition, the study finds that SHAP is more effective than LIME in explaining the predictions of the XGBoost model. SHAP presents better results when considering the nDCG values. Overall, the study highlights the advantages of XGBoost as an ML model and SHAP as an explainability method for predicting TOT delays in the ATM domain.

In terms of user evaluation, three XAI tools (SHAP, LIME, and DALEX) were evaluated for explaining the decisions of the XGBoost model to human operators. The results indicate that DALEX is more usable and preferred by human operators than SHAP and LIME. Feedback from the ATCOs showed that the information presented by the tool was clear and understandable, attributed to the videos and narration, which communicated the content intelligibly. However, the impact of the features on the estimated delay and take-off time was not self-explanatory for all ATCOs, and the level of clarity was an issue due to the synchronisation of video, text, and colour. Most ATCOs suggested that the information provided by the tool would allow them to generate the best sequence of departures, optimising runway usage, increasing the airside capacity of the airport, and reducing runway occupation time.

In conclusion, the study demonstrates the potential of XAI in improving the transparency and interpretability of machine learning models in the ATM domain, particularly in predicting flight TOT delays. The DALEX tool was found to be more effective and usable for explaining the decisions of the XGBoost model to human operators. Further research is needed to identify the most relevant features that should be shown event by event to the ATCOs.

Acknowledgements. This work was financed by the European Union's Horizon 2020 within the framework SESAR 2020 research and innovation program under grant agreement N. 894238, project Transparent Artificial Intelligence and Automation to Air Traffic Management Systems (ARTIMATION) and BrainSafeDrive, co-funded by the Vetenskapsrådet - The Swedish Research Council and the Ministero dell'Istruzione dell'Università e della Ricerca della Repubblica Italiana under Italy-Sweden Cooperation Program.

References

1. Bardach, M., Gringinger, E., Schrefl, M., Schuetz, C.G.: Predicting flight delay risk using a random forest classifier based on air traffic scenarios and environmental conditions. In: 2020 AIAA/IEEE 39th Digital Avionics Systems Conference (DASC), pp. 1–8. IEEE (2020)
2. Biecek, P.: Dalex: explainers for complex predictive models in R. J. Mach. Learn. Res. **19**(1), 3245–3249 (2018)
3. Breiman, L.: Bagging predictors. Mach. Learn. **24**, 123–140 (1996)
4. Busa-Fekete, R., Szarvas, G., Elteto, T., Kégl, B.: An apple-to-apple comparison of learning-to-rank algorithms in terms of normalized discounted cumulative gain. In: ECAI 2012-20th European Conference on Artificial Intelligence: Preference Learning: Problems and Applications in AI Workshop, vol. 242. IOS Press (2012)
5. Chen, T., Guestrin, C.: Xgboost: a scalable tree boosting system. In: Proceedings of the 22nd ACM SIGKDD International Conference on Knowledge Discovery and Data Mining, pp. 785–794 (2016)
6. Dalmau, R., Ballerini, F., Naessens, H., Belkoura, S., Wangnick, S.: An explainable machine learning approach to improve take-off time predictions. J. Air Transp. Manag. **95**, 102090 (2021)
7. Dalmau Codina, R., Belkoura, S., Naessens, H., Ballerini, F., Wagnick, S.: Improving the predictability of take-off times with machine learning: a case study for the maastricht upper area control centre area of responsibility. In: Proceedings of the 9th SESAR Innovation Days, pp. 1–8 (2019)
8. Degas, A., et al.: A survey on artificial intelligence (AI) and explainable AI in air traffic management: current trends and development with future research trajectory. Appl. Sci. **12**(3), 1295 (2022)
9. Guo, Z., et al.: SGDAN-a spatio-temporal graph dual-attention neural network for quantified flight delay prediction. Sensors **20**(22), 6433 (2020)
10. Hoffman, R.R., Mueller, S.T., Klein, G., Litman, J.: Metrics for explainable AI: challenges and prospects. arXiv abs/1812.04608 (2018)
11. Islam, M.R., Ahmed, M.U., Barua, S., Begum, S.: A systematic review of explainable artificial intelligence in terms of different application domains and tasks. Appl. Sci. **12**(3), 1353 (2022)
12. Joshi, A., Kale, S., Chandel, S., Pal, D.K.: Likert scale: explored and explained. Br. J. Appl. Sci. Technol. **7**(4), 396 (2015)
13. Lundberg, S.M., Lee, S.I.: A unified approach to interpreting model predictions. In: Advances in Neural Information Processing Systems, vol. 30 (2017)
14. Ribeiro, M.T., Singh, S., Guestrin, C.: "why should i trust you?" explaining the predictions of any classifier. In: Proceedings of the 22nd ACM SIGKDD International Conference on Knowledge Discovery and Data Mining, pp. 1135–1144 (2016)
15. Sanaei, R., Pinto, B.A., Gollnick, V.: Toward ATM resiliency: a deep CNN to predict number of delayed flights and ATFM delay. Aerospace **8**(2), 28 (2021)
16. Shapley, L.S.: A value for n-person games. In: Classics in Game Theory, vol. 69 (1997)
17. Wang, Y., Wang, L., Li, Y., He, D., Liu, T.Y.: A theoretical analysis of NDCG type ranking measures. In: Conference on Learning Theory, pp. 25–54. PMLR (2013)
18. Yu, B., Guo, Z., Asian, S., Wang, H., Chen, G.: Flight delay prediction for commercial air transport: a deep learning approach. Transp. Res. Part E Logist. Transp. Rev. **125**, 203–221 (2019)

Towards Autonomous Developmental Artificial Intelligence: Case Study for Explainable AI

Andrew Starkey[1]([✉]) [iD] and Chinedu Pascal Ezenkwu[2] [iD]

[1] Aberdeen University, Aberdeen, UK
a.starkey@abdn.ac.uk
[2] Robert Gordon University, Aberdeen, UK
p.ezenkwu@rgu.ac.uk

Abstract. State-of-the-art autonomous AI algorithms such as reinforcement learning and deep learning techniques suffer from high computational complexity, poor explainability ability, and a limited capacity for incremental adaptive learning. In response to these challenges, this paper highlights the TMGWR-based algorithm, developed by the present authors, as a case study towards self-adaptive unsupervised learning in autonomous developmental AI, and makes the following contributions: it presents and reviews essential requirements for today's autonomous AI and includes analysis for their potential for Green AI; it demonstrates that, unlike these state-of-the-art algorithms, TMGWR possesses explainability potentials that can be further developed and exploited for autonomous learning applications. In addition to shaping researchers' choice of metrics for selecting autonomous learning strategies, this paper will help to motivate further innovative research in autonomous AI.

Keywords: Autonomous AI · Green AI · Unsupervised learning

1 Introduction

A great deal of effort has been invested in autonomous artificial intelligence utilising high-performing machine learning algorithms, such as deep learning. However, these techniques continue to suffer from high computational costs, lack of explainability, and a limited capacity for incremental adaptive learning – which can lead to catastrophic forgetting and lack of self-recoverability in dynamic contexts. With the increasing adoption of AI in the global economy, a responsible application of Green AI techniques (with reduced carbon footprint) has become an important consideration alongside performance. In addition, there have been reports of catastrophic failures leading to casualties in the use of self-driving cars (Schmelzer, 2021). Therefore, to achieve a safe autonomous intelligent system, the system should be computationally efficient and meet Green AI criteria, be adaptable to changes in its environment, and should provide explainable outputs.

This study is amongst AI papers recommending a strategy based on the unsupervised learning paradigm as the way towards truly autonomous AI (LeCun, Bengio and Hinton,

© IFIP International Federation for Information Processing 2023
Published by Springer Nature Switzerland AG 2023
I. Maglogiannis et al. (Eds.): AIAI 2023, IFIP AICT 676, pp. 94–105, 2023.
https://doi.org/10.1007/978-3-031-34107-6_8

2015; Marcus, 2018). The Temporospatial Merge Grow When Required (TMGWR) network has recently been proposed to address the challenges of self-organising approaches and can compete favourably with traditional reinforcement learning in autonomous agent behaviours when incorporated with value iteration (Ezenkwu and Starkey, 2019, 2022). TMGWR and other self-adaptive unsupervised mechanisms are suitable for autonomous agents and neurorobotics due to their ability to support lifelong learning (Tenzer, Rasheed and Shafique, 2022).

While previous research into TMGWR has demonstrated that it is sample-efficient, self-adaptive, and can cope with unpredictable scenarios through dynamic planning, its explainability potential has not been explored further. With our belief in self-adaptive unsupervised learning as an effective approach to true autonomous agents, this paper makes the following contributions:

1. it reviews essential requirements for today's autonomous AI.
2. it demonstrates that, unlike reinforcement learning, TMGWR can be developed to give explainable outputs to a human observer that can be further developed and exploited for important autonomous learning applications.

Although this paper emphasises TMGWR, it is due to its superiority over other sensorimotor map learning strategies as presented in our previous paper (Ezenkwu and Starkey, 2019). Moreover, TMGWR is only a case study for reviewing the potential of self-adaptive unsupervised learning as well as discussing general desiderata for today's autonomous AI.

2 Requirements for Today's Autonomous Artificial Intelligence

Despite the significant successes recorded by sophisticated AI algorithms such as deep learning and reinforcement learning, they are neither safe nor suitable for autonomous learning due to the following reasons: (a) the environmental risks associated with high-performing but expensive AI techniques, (b) the inflexibility of these techniques due to their data-hungry nature, (c) their lack of explainability due to their black box architectures. These challenges can be presented under categories such as data intensiveness, task inflexibility, explainability, bias, and societal integration.

Based on the above challenges with the state-of-the-art AI techniques, the goal of all autonomous AI research should be to realise an AI technique with the potential to address these limitations as detailed in the following sections.

2.1 Computational Efficiency of Learning Algorithms

Some sophisticated AI techniques have revealed promising results in different areas of application. For example, in 2015 DeepMind Technologies developed AlphaGo, a deep reinforcement learning algorithm that became the first to defeat a master in the game of Go (Silver et al., 2016); deep learning has also proven to be a popular method in different classes of AI problems such as computer vision, natural language processing (NLP), self-driving cars and so on (LeCun et al., 2015). Another example is that despite being reported as the best performer in natural language processing (NLP) tasks in terms of accuracy (Edwards, 2021; Wang, Niu, Zhao, Wang, Hao and Che, 2021), the carbon dioxide emissions of training and applying a transformer are even more substantial than the lifetime emissions of an automobile (Strubell, Ganesh and McCallum, 2019).

The success of AlexNet in the 2010 ImageNet Large-Scale Visual Recognition Challenge (ILSVRC) has demonstrated that the depth of a deep learning model is significant for its high performance (Krizhevsky, Sutskever and Hinton, 2012), hence leading to competition in achieving the deepest neural networks in the field. The number of parameters a deep neural network has appears to correlate with the performance accuracy, with deeper neural network architectures emerging in recent times. For example, with 175 billion parameters and 96 total layers, GPT-3 has been ranked the best in NLP (Brown, Mann, Ryder, Subbiah, Kaplan, Dhariwal, Neelakantan, Shyam, Sastry, Askell et al., 2020). Similarly, EfficientNet-L2 has been ranked the best performing image classifier to date, with 480 million parameters trained on 130 million images (Xie, Luong, Hovy and Le, 2020).

These requirements raise clear concerns around the cost and the carbon footprint due to the use of energy-intensive hardware (Strubell et al., 2019; Anthony, Kanding and Selvan, 2020; Justus, Brennan, Bonner and McGough, 2018) and do not meet requirements for a Green AI.

Table 1. Summary of computational costs of learning algorithms. N = number of observations, D = vector size, M = number of hidden neurons, O = number of output values, C = number of clusters, S = size of state space, P = population size, G = size of chromosome

Learning algorithm	Time complexity	Order of complexity
SVM with Newton	N3	$O(n^3)$
Feed-forward neural networks	D.M.O.N	$O(n^4)$
Decision tree	N^2.D	$O(n^3)$
K-means	C.N.D	$O(n^3)$
SOM	N.D	$O(n^2)$
Growing SOM	N.D	$O(n^2)$
Q-learning	S3	$O(n^3)$
Value iteration	S2	$O(n^2)$
Genetic algorithms	P.log(P).G	$O(n.\log(n^2))$

Table 1 summarises the time complexities of the most common learning algorithms (Kearns, 1990; Koenig and Simmons, 1993; Nicolas, 2017; Kearns, Vazirani and Vazirani, 1994). The computational complexities of algorithms are crucial in deciding which best fits a given scenario.

SOM and growing SOM have computational advantage over most of the methods in Table 1. The number of nodes affects the speed of the algorithm, with the correct number of nodes crucial for improving the efficiency and representational ability of the algorithm. For the two planning algorithms in Table 1, model-based RL algorithms such as value iteration have a better time complexity than model-free RL algorithms such as Q-learning. Unlike Q-learning, which does not know the effect of an action before it is executed at least once, value iteration only needs to enter a state at least once to discover all of its successor-states (Koenig and Simmons, 1993). However, the model of an environment may not always be available or constant for that environment—in these cases, model-based RL will fail.

2.2 Self-adaptation

A desirable attribute of an autonomous system is the ability to cope with changing scenarios, especially when the environment is unpredictable. Because the real world is very complex and uncertain, it is probable that an agent designer will not capture all the possibilities of a given task during design time.

For example, a notorious consequence of lack of self-adaptation is the catastrophic failure of self-driving cars (Schmelzer, 2021). Self-driving cars make judgments based on their perceptions of their surroundings and pre-set traffic rules (Kang, Zhao, Qi and Banerjee, 2018). As a result, road construction, traffic signal failures, challenging weather conditions, confusing parking signs, and further unimagined circumstances could cause a self-driving car to fail (Kang et al., 2018). Gheibi et al. have studied the extent to which different machine learning paradigms have been applied to self-adaption tasks (Gheibi et al. 2021), and shown that reinforcement learning (RL), specifically model-free RL, is the most used learning method for self-adaption, followed by supervised learning, with little attention paid to unsupervised learning.

However, each of these popular methods has inherent problems that can restrict their self-adaptivity. For example, RL agents require a task-dependent reward function. A reward function is an indirect way in which the agent designers infuse their domain expertise into the design. The design of the reward function often requires understanding of the environment and can pose a challenge if the agent's world changes in a manner not anticipated during the design. Unlike RL agents, supervised learning agents require explicit provisions of ground truths by a teacher, meaning that they need humans in the loop to adapt to new changes. So, with a slight change in a task, a RL or supervised learning agent may need modification in its learning mechanism and retraining to overwrite the previous knowledge for the new task. This problem is known as catastrophic forgetting (Kirkpatrick et al., 2017).

2.3 Explainability of Learning Algorithms

One perspective adopted in the explainability of a learning algorithm is transparency (Belle and Papantonis, 2021). Transparency is the extent to which a human can understand the learning mechanisms of an algorithm (Lipton, 2018). It is possible to achieve the explainability of an already trained model through post-hoc processing (Tan et al., 2020; Belle and Papantonis, 2021). Since post-hoc processing adds computational overheads to the process of training and deploying a learning algorithm, this paper favours an inherently transparent learning model.

Belle and Papantonis present and compare three aspects of learning transparency—simulatability, decomposability, and algorithmic transparency (Belle and Papantonis,

2021). Simulatability is a model's ability to be replicable in human thought. Decomposability is the ability of a human to break down a model into inputs, parameters and computations and then explain these parts, while algorithmic transparency is the ability of a human to understand and explain the mechanism by which a model generates its output. While complex methods such as SVM, ensemble learning and multilayer neural networks are opaque and require post-hoc processing for explainability, simpler methods such as logistic regression, K-nearest neighbour algorithm, and rule-based learners are inherently transparent and do not require any post-hoc processing to understand the model.

In addition to the models considered in the paper by Belle and Papantonis, SOM and other neighbourhood-based algorithms such as K-means algorithm and Vector Quantisation have been considered transparent (Tan et al., 2020; Aliyu, 2018). While the transparency of evolutionary algorithms such as genetic algorithms is dependent on the cost function they are meant to optimise, they have been used for post-hoc processing (Pickering and Cohen, 2021). RL has the same explainability issue as evolutionary algorithms. Explainable RL, especially in complex environments, is an open research question (Kuhnle, May, Schafer and Lanza, 2021). Works by Belle and Papntonis (Belle and Papantonis, 2021) and Chazette et al. (Chazette, Brunotte and Speith, 2021) have provided in-depth reviews on explainability.

2.4 Summary of Desired Learning Attributes

The above sections describe the problems with current approaches; they are computationally intensive and do not satisfy Green AI, cannot adapt to changes, and cannot explain their decision making processes. These attributes then form the goals for a truly autonomous method: low compute satisfying Green AI; adapting automatically to changes; and explainable to the human operator.

3 Case Study of Self-adaptive Unsupervised Learning: TMGWR

A sensorimotor map is an agent's self-model of the world. Using the learned sensorimotor map of an environment or an agent's experiences, the agent can exhibit autonomous behaviours—either self-motivated or goal-directed. Previous work described the limitations of unsupervised learning approaches for sensorimotor map learning, such as Connectionist World Model (CWM) (Toussaint, 2004) using Growing Neural Gas (GNG) (Fritzke, 1995). This motivated the proposal of the TMGWR (Ezenkwu and Starkey, 2019), which is an adaptive neural architecture that learns the topological map and the sensorimotor links (Butz et al., 2008) between neurons using a time series self-organising strategy (Strickert and Hammer, 2005). The TMGWR network connects nodes based on their sensorimotor proximities, such that these edges can encode the transition possibilities as well as the motor signals that can cause transitions between nodes.

The experiment for this case study was designed on a simple maze environment, with a randomly changing goal within this maze and also new walls being added to the maze on a random basis. Although this is a simple problem, current solutions require human design and highlight the lack of adaptive learning properties described above.

The performance of the TMGWR-based agent with those of model-free and model-based RL agents was compared (Ezenkwu and Starkey, 2022). Although the TMGWR-based agent can be classified as a model-based RL agent, it differs from the traditional model-based agent in the sense that instead of requiring a human designer to encode the dynamics of the environment, it self-learns its world model using the TMGWR algorithm. The work by the authors evaluated the algorithms' sample complexities and their abilities to self-adapt to a sudden change in the environment or goal state. This work has shown that the TMGWR network gave more efficient representations of the environment in a computationally more efficient manner, and that it also showed the potential for online adaptation to changes in goal state or changes in the environment. However, the approach did not meet the requirements for Explainability as discussed in earlier sections.

The TMGWR framework consists of four main modules - the sensorimotor map learning module, the sensory preprocessor, the motivation estimator and the action selector (Ezenkwu and Starkey, 2022). An autonomous agent is equipped with suitable sensors and actuators which enable it to observe the environment and react to these observations using the actuators. The observations or sensory inputs can be preprocessed or transformed into a form that conveys meaningful or contextual information to the agent. The preprocessed sensory observations are passed on to the sensorimotor map learning module which enables the agent to develop or refine its mental model of the scenario. The sensorimotor map learning occurs continually in an open-ended manner to enable the agent to keep track of changes in the environment by continuously updating the sensorimotor map. The motivation estimator provides the motivation signal that enables the agent to plan towards a goal or behave in a given manner in the environment. The action selector considers the current observation and the agent's motivation in selecting the best action using the sensorimotor map. Execution of this action causes a change in the environment and the cycle continues.

3.1 Sensorimotor Map Learning

This section examines the TMGWR algorithm as a sensorimotor map learning method. The key features of TMGWR are that:

- the nodes are linked based on their sensorimotor proximities to one another;
- it uses the temporal context vector similar to Merge Grow Neural Gas (MNG) (Strickert and Hammer, 2005b) to keep track of the sensorimotor history;
- the GWR strategy of adding new nodes is employed to enable the system to keep track of changes in the environment;
- all the hyperparameters are kept constant throughout the lifetime of the agent to encourage continual learning.

The action map learns the codebook vector for each motor activity while the sensorimotor map learns the input weight vectors and the possible action vectors linking them to each other. At each time step, the activated action vector on the action map is associated with the sensorimotor-link from the previous winning node i to the current winning node j in the sensorimotor map. The algorithm uses a similarity function that compares the activated action vector at a given time with the action vector that has already been associated with the sensorimotor-link from node i to node j. This similarity function has been chosen to be a Gaussian function so that if the two activation vectors are similar then it tends towards 1 otherwise it will tend towards 0.

The advantage of introducing this similarity function in the update equation is that it increases the weight of the sensorimotor-link if the same action vector results in the same transition all the time and decreases it if the transition is possible with different action vectors. This modification is motivated by Hebbian associative learning, which reinforces the association between two neurons that fire together and discourages those which do not (Frolov and Murav'ev, 1993). This is a way of representing reliability in the agent's mental model and it is useful during planning as the agent is more likely to select reliable actions for each experience in the environment.

A full description of the TMGWR algorithm is presented in in Ezenkwu and Starkey, 2022 and the reader is directed there for further information on the algorithm.

3.2 Suitability for Autonomous Learning

Compared to both model-free and model-based RL agents, the TMGWR-based goal-directed agent has proven to be far more self-adaptive in situations of changing environment or changing goal state. In addition, the experiments demonstrated that the TMGWR-based algorithm shows a similar sample complexity to the model-based RL agent but is better than the model-free RL agent. The TMGWR-based agent requires less time to self-adapt to changing goal states than the model-free RL agent and a change in the environment, than the other algorithms, with the model-based agent being completely intolerant to a slight change in the environment.

Short demonstrations of the change of goal scenario for the Model-free RL[1], TMGWR-based[2] and the Model-based RL[3] agents, and for the responses of the Model-free RL[4], TMGWR-based[5] and model-based RL[6] agents to dynamic environments are available on YouTube for view.

---

[1] Demonstration: response of the model-free RL agent to change in goal state: https://www.you tube.com/watch?v=_j0z6B1RFjs.

[2] Demonstration: response of the TMGWR-based agent to change in goal state: https://www.you tube.com/watch?v=x9U0r-6Sct0.

[3] Demonstration: response of model-based RL agent to change in goal state: https://youtu.be/4GNbxYvJPhM.

[4] Demonstration: response of the model-free RL agent to change in the environment: https://youtu.be/aRr4Ja9TspQ.

[5] Demonstration: response of the TMGWR-based agent to change in the environment: https://youtu.be/-YpxGEjRoXA

[6] Demonstration: response of model-based RL agent to change in the environment: https://www.youtube.com/watch?v=peEYriVEK2k

3.3 Explainability in the TMGWR-Based Algorithm

This section discusses the development of the explanation mechanism of the TMGWR-based algorithm, exploiting the transparent nature of the algorithm and thereby how it can provide explanations to a human observer.

The TMGWR-based agent makes decisions using the sensorimotor map. An effective sensorimotor map should be able to represent the reality of the agent's environment. One benefit of this representation is that the agent can anticipate the outcome of its actions. For example, if the sensorimotor map represents that the agent takes action, a_{ik}, at node i, its next state will be a node, k, then the agent can anticipate this next state each time action, a_{ik}, is to be executed at node i. If the environment does not change as expected following this action, then this means that the sensorimotor map no longer represents the reality of the agent's world and can imply a change in the environment. This then represents the main contribution of this paper and the changes made to the algorithm that permits feedback to the human observer in terms of any change in the environment or goal state, since any expected change in the environment that is not met means that the TMGWR's internal representation of the environment is no longer current and will require to be changed. This change can be communicated to the human observer and more importantly can be described in terms of the actions and environment states that the algorithm expected to take place. As an example, if a new wall is introduced into the maze, then the previous learning will predict that the agent can move into the space now occupied by the wall. The algorithm will detect the lack of change in the sensor values (i.e. position in the maze) following the action having been taken (i.e. move to space now occupied by the wall). This can immediately be communicated to the human observer by the agent: I expected to be able to move forward; the world has changed since I cannot.

Therefore, the procedure for keeping track of a change in the environment is as follows:

- after selecting action a_{ik} at the current node i;
- use the sensorimotor map to anticipate the next state node k as follows: $k = argmax_n V(n)$, for all node n in the sensorimotor neighbourhood of node i, while $V(n)$ is the motivation potential at node n;
- execute action a_{ik} and identify the actual resulting node r;
- if k does not equal r (i.e. a different node has been activated) then the world has changed;
- otherwise, no observable change in the world.

Figure 1 demonstrates how a TMGWR-based agent responds to a change in the environment. After the agent's world changes, the agent will lose its ability to anticipate the outcomes of its actions. To the agent, these anticipation failures mean that the world has changed. However, the agent will self-adapt its mental model to correctly anticipate the outcomes of its actions to cope with the new state of the world. The rate of change for the TMGWR algorithm depends on a single parameter that can be modified so that it is more sensitive to changes in the environment, otherwise it will gradually change its model so that eventually it will choose a different action in order to reach its goal. The TMGWR approach thereby meets the requirements for explainability in terms of......

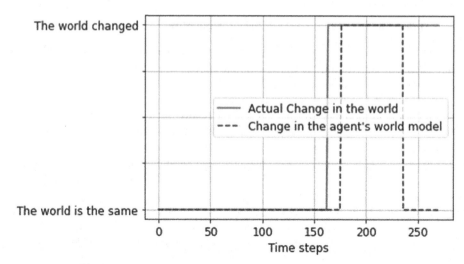

Fig. 1. TMGWR-based agent's response to a change in the world.

Learning paradigms such as RL and supervised learning lack this explainability potential because their world models are not interpretable. A video demonstration of this procedure has been provided here[7].

Explanation Mechanism in the TMGWR-Based Agent During a Change of Goal
The TMGWR-based algorithm uses a motivation estimator to compute motivation potentials of all the nodes in the sensorimotor map. The motivational potential of a node is a function of how similar the node is to the goal node and the availability of sensorimotor links from that node to the goal node. Therefore, after each run of the motivation estimator, the goal node will always have the highest motivation potential because it is the most similar to itself and the most easily reachable from itself. Based on this, the TMGWR-based agent can keep track of a change in goal by computing motivation potentials after each step and identifying any changes in the node with the largest motivation potential.

Figure 2 demonstrates how the sensorimotor map due to TMGWR can therefore immediately and correctly reflect a change in goal following the above procedure. There is no straightforward way of realising a similar interpretation of goal change in RL agents. The video demonstration can be found in this link[8].

---

[7] Demonstration: Change in environment: https://www.youtube.com/watch?v=CSooq2abq4g.

[8] Demonstration: Change in goal - https://www.youtube.com/watch?v=Mv0s79CFBtI.

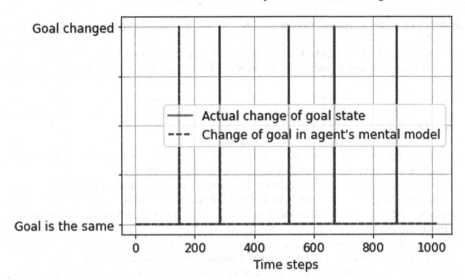

Fig. 2. Identification of change in goal state using TMGWR-based approach

4 Conclusions

This paper has highlighted the requirement for a learning framework that is self-adaptive, sample efficient, and requires less compute power thereby meeting requirements for Green AI. Currently popular AI techniques such as deep learning and deep reinforcement learning are sample inefficient, inflexible, and require significant designer input and huge compute power and so do not meet these requirements. The paper reviews different learning algorithms with respect to considerations such as computational efficiency, self-adaptivity and explainability. Based on this review, growing SOM has been identified as the most suitable learning paradigm for future autonomous learning agents. It is unsupervised, self-adaptive and inherently transparent and has an efficient computational cost when compared to popular methods such as deep learning, SVM and ensemble learning. The paper recommends an autonomous agent architecture based on the TMGWR network for continuous sensorimotor map learning and shows how improvements to this meet the requirements above by giving an effective demonstration of the explanation potential of the TMGWR-based framework for changes in goal and also changes in environment. Future work will focus on applying the TMGWR approach to more sophisticated environments and to different domain problems.

References

Aliyu, A.U.: Automated data classification using feature weighted self-organising map (FWSOM). University of Aberdeen, Ph.D. thesis (2018)

Anthony, L.F.W., Kanding, B., Selvan, R.: Carbontracker: Tracking and predicting the carbon footprint of training deep learning models. arXiv preprint arXiv:2007.03051 (2020)

Belle, V., Papantonis, I.: Principles and practice of explainable machine learning. Front. Big Data 39 (2021)

Brown, T.B., et al.: Language models are few-shot learners. arXiv preprint arXiv:2005.14165 (2020)

Butz, M.V., Reif, K., Herbort, O.: Bridging the gap: learning sensorimotor-linked population codes for planning and motor control. In: International Conference on Cognitive Systems, CogSys (2008)

Chazette, L., Brunotte, W., Speith, T.: Exploring explainability: a definition, a model, and a knowledge catalogue. In: 2021 IEEE 29th International Requirements Engineering Conference (RE), pp. 197–208. IEEE (2021)

Edwards, C.: The best of NLP. Commun. ACM **64**, 9–11 (2021)

Ezenkwu, C.P., Starkey, A.: Unsupervised temporospatial neural architecture for sensorimotor map learning. IEEE Trans. Cogn. Dev. Syst. **13**(1), 223–230 (2019)

Ezenkwu, C.P., Starkey, A.: An unsupervised autonomous learning framework for goal-directed behaviours in dynamic contexts. Adv. Comput. Intell. **2**, 1–14 (2022)

Fritzke, B.: A growing neural gas network learns topologies. In: Advances in Neural Information Processing Systems, pp. 625–632 (1995)

Frolov, A., Murav'ev, I.: Informational characteristics of neural networks capable of associative learning based on hebbian plasticity. Netw. Comput. Neural Syst. **4**, 495–536 (1993)

Gheibi, O., Weyns, D., Quin, F.: Applying machine learning in self-adaptive systems: a systematic literature review. arXiv preprint arXiv:2103.04112 (2021)

Justus, D., Brennan, J., Bonner, S., McGough, A.S.: Predicting the computational cost of deep learning models. In: 2018 IEEE International Conference on Big Data (Big Data), pp. 3873–3882. IEEE (2018)

Kang, L., Zhao, W., Qi, B., Banerjee, S.: Augmenting self-driving with remote control: challenges and directions. In: Proceedings of the 19th International Workshop on Mobile Computing Systems & Applications, pp. 19–24 (2018)

Kearns, M.J.: The Computational Complexity of Machine Learning. MIT Press, Cambridge (1990)

Kearns, M.J., Vazirani, U.V., Vazirani, U.: An Introduction to Computational Learning Theory. MIT Press, Cambridge (1994)

Kirkpatrick, J., et al.: Over-coming catastrophic forgetting in neural networks. Proc. Natl. Acad. Sci. **114**, 3521–3526 (2017)

Koenig, S., Simmons, R.G.: Complexity analysis of real-time reinforcement learning. In: AAAI, pp. 99–107 (1993)

Krizhevsky, A., Sutskever, I., Hinton, G.E.: Imagenet classification with deep convolutional neural networks. Adv. Neural. Inf. Process. Syst. **25**, 1097–1105 (2012)

Kuhnle, A., May, M.C., Schafer, L., Lanza, G.: Explainable reinforcement learning in production control of job shop manufacturing system. Int. J. Prod. Res. **60**(19), 5812–5834 (2021)

LeCun, Y., Bengio, Y., Hinton, G.: Deep learning. Nature **521**, 436–444 (2015)

Lipton, Z.C.: The mythos of model interpretability: In machine learning, the concept of interpretability is both important and slippery. Queue **16**, 31–57 (2018)

Marcus, G.: Deep learning: a critical appraisal. arXiv preprint arXiv:1801.00631 (2018)

Nicolas, P.R.: Scala for Machine Learning: Data processing, ML algorithms, smart analytics, and more. Packt Publishing Ltd. (2017)

Pickering, L., Cohen, K.: Toward explainable AI—genetic fuzzy systems—a use case. In: Rayz, J., Raskin, V., Dick, S., Kreinovich, V. (eds.) NAFIPS 2021. LNNS, vol. 258, pp. 343–354. Springer, Cham (2022). https://doi.org/10.1007/978-3-030-82099-2_31

Schmelzer, R.: What happens when self-driving cars kill people? (2021). https://www.forbes.com/sites/cognitiveworld/2019/09/26/what-happens-with-self-driving-cars-kill-people/

Silver, D., et al.: Mastering the game of go with deep neural networks and tree search. Nature **529**, 484–489 (2016)

Strickert, M., Hammer, B.: Merge som for temporal data. Neurocomputing **64**, 39–71 (2005)

Strubell, E., Ganesh, A., McCallum, A.: Energy and policy considerations for deep learning in NLP. arXiv preprint arXiv:1906.02243 (2019)

Tan, R., Khan, N.M., Guan, L.: Locality guided neural networks for explainable artificial intelligence. CoRR abs/2007.06131. https://arxiv.org/abs/2007.06131, arXiv:2007.06131 (2020)

Tenzer, M., Rasheed, Z., Shafique, K.: Learning citywide patterns of life from trajectory monitoring. arXiv preprint arXiv:2206.15352 (2022)

Toussaint, M.: Learning a world model and planning with a self-organizing, dynamic neural system. In: Advances in Neural Information Processing Systems, pp. 926–936 (2004)

Wang, L., Niu, D., Zhao, X., Wang, X., Hao, M., Che, H.: A comparative analysis of novel deep learning and ensemble learning models to predict the allergenicity of food proteins. Foods **10**, 809 (2021)

Xie, Q., Luong, M.T., Hovy, E., Le, Q.V.: Self-training with noisy student improves imagenet classification. In: Proceedings of the IEEE/CVF Conference on Computer Vision and Pattern Recognition, pp. 10687–10698 (2020)

Graph Neural Networks/Constraint Programming

Efficient Spatio-Temporal Graph Neural Networks for Traffic Forecasting

Yackov Lubarsky$^{(\boxtimes)}$, Alexei Gaissinski, and Pavel Kisilev

Toga Networks, Huawei Tel Aviv Research Center, Hod Hasharon, Israel
{yackov.lubarsky,alexei.gaissinski,pavel.kisilev}@huawei.com

Abstract. Urban Traffic Forecasting has recently seen a lot of research activity as it entails a compelling combination of multivariate temporal data with geo-spatial dependencies between multiple data collection sensors. Current top approaches to this task tend to use costly spatio-temporal pipelines, where the model complexities typically have linear dependency on the time-series length and quadratic on the number of nodes. In this paper, we propose a number of steps to dramatically improve the runtime efficiency of the traffic forecasting solutions. First, we use a temporal pooling stack prior to spatial processing to effectively eliminate the time dimension before applying the spatial components. This removes the linear dependency of the model on the length of the time series. Second, we construct learnable graph pooling blocks inside the spatial stack which progressively reduce the size of the graph and facilitate better data flow between far away nodes. Experimental results on the standard METR-LA and PEMSBAY benchmarks show that the proposed approach yields significant inference and training speedups of up to x5 in the 1-h prediction task and x27 in the 24-h prediction task, while keeping or surpassing the state-of-the-art results. Our findings call into question the need for time-consuming spatio-temporal processing blocks, used in many of latest solutions for the traffic forecasting task.

1 Introduction

Spatio-temporal signal modeling has recently seen a lot of activity with the rise in popularity of Graph Neural Networks (GNNs) and Attention-based neural architectures. These architectures, typically model the given real world data as a discrete set of entities, where each entity has both spatial attributes (e.g. geo-spatial location) and a temporal signal such as a series of sensor readings. Such a model can be applied to many real-world problems including weather forecasting [13], telecommunications network analysis [20] and many others [26]. In this work, we focus on the Urban Traffic Forecasting task, which is one of the most popular applications of this kind of data modeling.

In the canonical setting, data is collected using multiple sensors deployed at different locations in a particular area, each one measuring a time-varying signal such as the speed at a road segment. Given a series of history measurements of the sensors, the task is to forecast the future measurements up to some prediction horizon. The data can

---

Y. Lubarsky and A. Gaissinski—Equal contribution.

© IFIP International Federation for Information Processing 2023
Published by Springer Nature Switzerland AG 2023
I. Maglogiannis et al. (Eds.): AIAI 2023, IFIP AICT 676, pp. 109–120, 2023.
https://doi.org/10.1007/978-3-031-34107-6_9

be structured as a graph where nodes represent the sensors, each carrying a temporal signal, and edges reflect the distance measure between them.

The top scoring solutions for this kind of setup employ deep neural networks that process the data via a series of computational blocks. Some of these blocks process the data along the temporal dimension, e.g. temporal convolutions or LSTM blocks [7], while others work along the spatial (i.e. graph) dimension, such as GCN [12] or self-attention layers [21]. These components are typically interleaved to build dependencies between spatial and temporal processing steps.

However, such an approach often comes at a high computational cost. As an example, the complexity of a single block of the popular Graph WaveNet model [22] is $O(TN^2D)$ where T is the time series length, N is the number of nodes and D is the internal representation size. Such a model may be computationally too heavy to operate in a real-life production system where there is often a shortage in resources such as time, power, compute and memory. In addition, when the time-series are very long, training the models becomes increasingly demanding and in the extreme case, may be unfeasible due to out of memory condition.

In this work, we propose a method to dramatically improve the scalability and running times of existing traffic forecasting solutions without sacrificing the accuracy. It involves applying two architecture modifications to a given spatio-temporal model. First, a stack of gated convolutions is employed prior to spatial processing, reducing the size of the temporal dimension, while also functioning as a feature extractor for the subsequent layers. Second, sparse graph pooling blocks are added in the spatial processing layers to progressively reduce the size of the graph and facilitate better information propagation between far away nodes. To the best of our knowledge this is the first time a sparse and learnable pooling operation is used in the spatio-temporal modeling domain.

To validate our method, we use the Graph WaveNet architecture [22], a SOTA spatio-temporal architecture as shown in [11]. Using the proposed method, we develop efficient variants GWNET-TSQ and GWNET-SPOOL-TSQ. Our experiments show that these variants yield substantial x5-x27 speedups, while keeping or surpassing the state-of-the-art results. Furthermore, the speedup advantage is increased with the length of the input sequences.

The contributions of this paper can be summarized as follows:

– We propose a general method for significantly improving the runtime efficiency of spatio-temporal GNN models. It consists of preprocessing the input using a temporal pooling mechanism to reduce the temporal dimension into a fixed size representation and a novel application of learnable sparse graph pooling operators within the spatial blocks of the model, to reduce the runtime of the model and improve data flow between far away nodes.
– Using our method, we develop GWNET-TSQ and GWNET-SPOOL-TSQ architectures, a highly efficient solution for urban traffic forecasting. The proposed models are comparable or surpassing SOTA in the standard traffic forecasting benchmarks, while achieving a significant x5 speedup in training and inference.
– We evaluate the scalability of our proposed architectures using a long time-series forecasting task of 6-h and 24-h and observe dramatic speedups of up to x13 and x27 respectively, without any accuracy degradation compared to the top solutions.

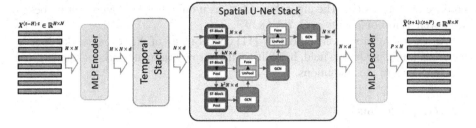

Fig. 1. The proposed GWNET-SPOOL-TSQ architecture. The temporal stack encodes the temporal signal for each node into a fixed size representation, removing the dependency of spatial processing on the length of time series. The subsequent spatial processing block employs sparse learnable U-Net pooling blocks to progressively reduce the graph size, improving the runtime and the data flow between far away nodes.

2 Related Work

2.1 Traffic Forecasting

The majority of recent Traffic Forecasting solutions, can be divided to two groups. 1) The spatio-temporal data is represented as a graph, where each node stores temporal data, and the nodes are connected by weighted edges, i.e. the distance between the sensors. 2) The a priori spatial correlation is neglected, and the data is treated as a multivariate prediction task.

Early GNN based works, such as [24], used a GRU [3] based architecture. In these works, the spatial graph features were extracted by a GNN and fed to a GRU unit to learn the temporal mechanics, which also produced the future predictions. These architectures are generally slow and fail on long-term forecasting horizons.

Modern Traffic Forecasting architectures use an interleaving processing of spatial GNNs and temporal convolutions, making the whole network fully convolutional and fast to train. In addition, all the predicted timesteps are produced at once by a single prediction block. A good representative of such architecture is [22]. This architecture uses a gated convolution for temporal feature extraction iterleaved with a slightly modified GCN [12] for message passing along the spatial dimension.

Some recent works neglect the underlying graph data and substitute it with an attention block, claiming that the correlation between nodes is dynamic and should be learned in an end-to-end manner. One of such works is GMAN [25]. In this work, the convolutional and GCN layers are substituted with attention blocks. There is a spatial attention block that operates over the different nodes, and temporal attention block working separately over the temporal dimension of each node. The blocks are then fused using weighted sum, to produce a single spatio-temporal representation of the data.

FC-GAGA [18] neglect the spatial information, and approached it as a multivariate prediction challenge. A learnable node embedding is used to measure the correlation between all node pairs, then each node is concatenated with a weighted representation of all other nodes, and this representation goes through fully connected (FC) layers to produce the forecasting. The algorithm is fast, as it only uses FC layers, but it doesn't scale well as its complexity is $O(TN^2)$.

An extensive survey carried out by [11] covers many of the recent works done in the urban traffic prediction field. In addition, they provide a framework for standardized benchmarking of these solutions.

2.2 Graph Pooling

Graph pooling is an essential component of many GNN architectures. Similarly to pooling operator in convolutional neural networks (CNNs) [1, 19], its role is to reduce the number of nodes in the graph, while preserving the graph representation. Graph data is missing the grid-like structure of images, making the pooling operation an open problem with a lot of research groups proposing novel pooling algorithms.

Early GNN works used simple pooling techniques as a post-processing step for obtaining a graph representation [4, 8, 15]. The GNN would extract a feature representation of each node in the graph, and the final representation layer would globally pool these features into a single representation vector using mean or max pooling. Then this vector would be used by the classification layer for the final prediction.

One of the first works to utilize a learnable graph pooling module for hierarchical coarsening of the GNN architectures was DiffPool [26]. In this work, the pooling decision was learned using an additional GNN, that would generate a dense assignment matrix S, effectively making a soft clustering of the nodes.

A later work, Graph U-Nets [6], adopted the U-Net style architecture [19] to the GNN domain, introducing a learnable sparse pooling and unpooling architecture. In this work, all nodes are ranked with an importance score, the top-K important nodes are pooled to the next layer and the rest are dropped. In the unpooling stage, features from higher hierarchy nodes are combined with their previous layer representations and then a GNN propagates the data to the rest.

Since then, many pooling approaches have been introduced as shown in [9, 16, 17]. In particular, [9] introduced a taxonomy of different pooling operators.

3   The Proposed Efficient Spatio-Temporal Net

3.1 Preliminaries

The data is represented in the form of a graph $G = (V, E, X)$ where V is the set of nodes and E is the set of edges. We denote $N = |V|$, the number of nodes. An adjacency matrix derived from the graph is denoted by $A \in \mathbb{R}^{N \times N}$, such that $A_{i,j} = 1$ if the edge $(v_i, v_j) \in E$. At each time step t the graph node features are represented by $X^{(t)} \in \mathbb{R}^{N \times D}$. Given a graph G, time t, history length H and prediction horizon P, the forecasting task is to learn a function which maps $X^{(t-H:t)}$ to $X^{(t+1:t+P)}$.

3.2 Temporal Pooling

Recently proposed spatio-temporal architectures process the temporal dependency with interleaved CNN-GNN operations, or using recurrent networks, such as GRU or LSTM,

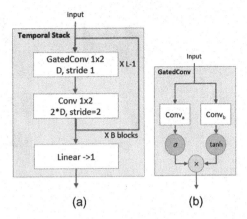

(a)   (b)

Fig. 2. a) Temporal pooling module. It consists of B consecutive blocks. Each block has a total of L convolutions, out of which $L - 1$ are gated convolutions followed by a single pooling convolution with stride 2 and a temporary channel expansion. The temporal dimension is halved after each block. The final linear layer is used to reduce the size to exactly one timestep. b) Gated Convolution block. The block has two identical layers, with different activation functions. One serving as a multiplicative gate to control the output of the other. The gate can be modeled as $h = tanh(\Theta_a * X + \beta_a) \odot \sigma(\Theta_b * X + \beta_b)$ where X is the input, $\Theta_a, \Theta_b, \beta_a, \beta_b$ are learnable weights and biases of the convolutions and σ the sigmoid activation.

over the graph representation of the data. Contrary to this paradigm, we use a Temporal Pooling module to extract the temporal data before applying the spatial processing. The Temporal Pooling module compresses the information stored in the temporal dimension of a given signal into a fixed vector representation. This design choice makes the spatial processing much more efficient as it needs to process only a single feature vector per node, decreasing the time complexity and allowing an efficient modeling of very long input sequences.

We implement the Temporal Pooling module using the following guiding principles: 1) all time steps should be accounted for, 2) low computational overhead and 3) powerful feature extraction. A detailed diagram of our temporal pooling stack is shown in Fig. 2. We employ a stack of gated convolutions as our Temporal Pooling module, since it fits well the above principals. It offers faster run-times compared to the recurrent architectures, while the gating mechanism is useful for overcoming the vanishing gradients problem in long sequences [5,10,22]. We use solely convolutional layers to keep the computational overhead linear in the input size. To reduce the size of the temporal dimension, a periodic stride of two is used to halve the input. One final linear layer is placed at the end of the stack to make the temporal dimension size exactly one.

3.3   Graph Pooling

The graph pooling block in our architecture serves two purposes: 1) as each consequent GNN layer receives less nodes, it also has less calculations, making the network more

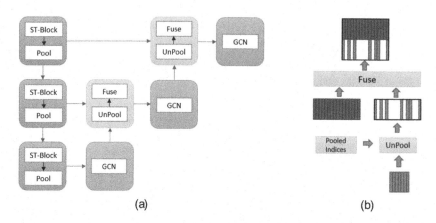

(a)   (b)

Fig. 3. (a) Graph U-Net architecture. The blue block represents the original Spatio-Temporal layer, enhanced with the node pooling mechanism. Each yellow block fuses the unpooled data, which is sparse, with the dense data coming from the skip connection. Lastly, each green block does a message passing step between all received nodes and un-pools the data before fusing it again with the higher block. (b) Un-Pooling architecture. In the UnPool block, the green features from the sparse layer are padded with zero features to accommodate for the pooled nodes. Then the unpooled features are fused with the nodes representation from the dense layer. In our architecture, the fusion step is performed by concatenation. (Color figure online)

efficient, 2) the pooling and unpooling operators improve the data propagation between distant nodes.

In this work, we propose to use the top-K pooling [6] operator. It allows end-to-end training, and alleviates the unpooling operator to produce dense predictions for all the nodes. The graph pooling architecture is shown in Fig. 3(a).

During the feature extraction phase, each consequent spatial processing block receives only the top-K chosen nodes from the previous layer. The importance score is derived by projecting node features on a learnable vector. In the proposed architecture, each consequent block has progressively less nodes which need to be accounted for by the un-pooling operation.

The unpooling stage is shown in Fig. 3(b). In the unpooling stage the low resolution features are upsampled with zeros, similarly to [1], and concatenated to the features extracted from the higher resolution block. After concatenation, the data between nodes is propagated using another GNN layer.

3.4   Architecture

Graph WaveNet. To demonstrate the effectiveness of the proposed approach, we use the Graph WaveNet model [22]. Based on the survey [11], Graph WaveNet consistently shows top results on the traffic forecasting task. The base architecture consists of a series of spatio-temporal blocks applied sequentially. The temporal component used is gated convolutions with dilation. The spatial component is a graph diffusion convolution layer applied on normalized forward an backward adjacency matrix as well as on a self-adaptive adjacency matrix. The model also has residual and skip connections for better gradient propagation. Due to use of non-sparse adjacency matrix in the GCN component, the operating cost of each layer is $O(TN|E|D)$ or $O(TN^2D)$ if using the non-sparse self-adaptive matrix.

Using the components proposed in previous sections, we develop three variants to the base architecture.

- GWNET-TSQ: Temporal pooling stack is used after the first convolution layer to reduce the temporal dimension size to one. The gated convolutions are removed from the spatio-temporal blocks as they are no longer needed. This improves the runtime to $O(N^2D)$.
- GWNET-SPOOL: A sparse graph pooling mechanism is added in each layer, reducing the size of the graph by a constant factor. This results in geometric decrease in the number of nodes processed in each following GCN layer.
- GWNET-SPOOL-TSQ: Combines the two mentioned modifications - both temporal stack and pooling modules are added, and the temporal gated convolutions are removed from the spatio-temporal layers. This variant is shown in Fig. 1.

GMAN. GMAN [25] is another popular model for the spatio-temporal traffic data. Here, the model relies on the powerful multi-head attention mechanism [21] for feature extraction. The model consists of an encoder processing the history signal and a decoder producing the predictions, connected by transform attention. Both encoder and decoder are stacks of fused spatio-temporal blocks where one self-attention layer is applied among the nodes and another among the time steps of each node. This is a canonical example of applying self-attention in an interleaved manner to a signal that has more than one dimension of interest.

We modify the GMAN architecture with the proposed Temporal pooling stack and develop the GMAN-TSQ variant. The temporal stack is applied before the encoder, eliminating the self-attention processing done along the temporal dimension. We avoid modifying the decoder since it relies on temporal attention along the predicted signal. Although, it is possible to separate temporal and spatial processing there as well, it may seem as too excessive a change from the original architecture. At any rate, replacing even just the encoder with a temporal pooling stack results in dramatic reduction in operating cost as shown in the next section.

4 Experiments

4.1 Datasets

We verify our approach on METR-LA and PEMS-BAY, two of the most widely used public traffic network datasets released by [14]. METR-LA contains four months of traffic speed recordings collected from 2012/3/1 to 2012/6/30 by 207 sensors on the highways of Los Angeles County. PEMS-BAY contains six months of traffic speed recordings, collected from 2017/1/1 to 2017/5/31 by 325 sensors in the Bay area. As mentioned in [11] these two datasets have been used in quite a lot of studies and can

Table 1. Performance comparison of our and baseline models on METR-LA and PEMS-BAY datasets with one hour history and prediction horizon and a five minute resolution.

Model	15 min./3 steps			30 min./6 steps			60 min./12 steps			MACs [G]	MAC compr
	MAE	RMSE	MAPE	MAE	RMSE	MAPE	MAE	RMSE	MAPE		
METR-LA											
Graph WaveNet	**2.73**	5.25	**7.04**	**3.12**	6.30	**8.48**	3.60	7.45	**10.15**	0.67	–
GWNET-TSQ	2.74	**5.22**	7.12	3.13	**6.21**	8.61	3.60	**7.30**	10.32	**0.14**	0.21
GWNET-SPOOL	2.77	5.30	7.16	3.16	6.32	8.65	3.63	7.43	10.40	0.45	0.68
GWNET-SPOOL-TSQ	2.75	**5.22**	7.13	3.13	6.25	8.49	3.60	7.38	10.19	0.23	0.34
GMAN	3.52	7.17	10.48	3.59	7.34	10.70	4.12	8.39	12.24	0.61	–
GMAN-TSQ	3.17	6.13	8.63	3.30	6.49	9.12	3.98	8.04	11.31	0.35	0.57
GMAN-TSQ-4H	3.12	6.06	8.70	3.24	6.40	9.18	3.91	7.91	11.32	**0.14**	0.23
FC-GAGA	2.81	5.48	7.43	3.19	6.49	8.81	3.65	7.59	10.53	0.88	–
MTGNN	2.82	5.57	7.56	3.18	6.53	8.94	**3.58**	7.45	10.32	–	–
AGCRN	2.88	5.59	7.63	3.25	6.56	9.00	3.65	7.51	10.31	–	–
PEMS-BAY											
Graph WaveNet	**1.31**	2.76	**2.76**	1.64	3.74	**3.71**	1.95	4.53	4.59	1.43	–
GWNET-TSQ	**1.31**	**2.74**	2.77	**1.63**	**3.67**	**3.71**	**1.94**	**4.44**	**4.57**	0.29	0.20
GWNET-SPOOL	1.34	2.78	2.84	1.68	3.77	3.84	1.99	4.54	4.74	1.09	0.76
GWNET-SPOOL-TSQ	1.34	2.78	2.88	1.67	3.75	3.87	1.99	4.54	4.81	0.44	0.31
GMAN	1.76	4.04	4.17	1.79	4.11	4.22	2.24	5.22	5.29	1.09	–
GMAN-TSQ	1.59	3.54	3.71	1.66	3.71	3.86	2.16	4.97	5.08	0.61	0.56
GMAN-TSQ-4H	1.54	3.38	3.47	1.66	3.70	3.76	2.20	5.11	5.10	**0.26**	0.23
FC-GAGA	1.37	2.89	2.90	1.70	3.84	3.86	1.99	4.56	4.71	2.09	–
MTGNN	1.33	2.85	2.84	1.66	3.80	3.77	1.95	4.49	4.59	–	–
AGCRN	1.35	2.86	2.94	1.67	3.82	3.84	1.96	4.57	4.69	–	–

be considered a standard benchmark for the traffic forecasting task. The sensor readings in both datasets are aggregated into 5-minute windows and the data is split in chronological order with 70% for training, 10% for validation and 20% for testing. As in other studies using these datasets, we use one hour (12 time steps) history length and one hour prediction in our forecasting task. To analyze model performances at longer time sequences, we introduce METR-LA-6H and METR-LA-24H configurations of the METR-LA data, having six hour (72 time steps) and 24 h (288 time steps) history and prediction horizons respectively.

4.2   Experimental Settings

In our experiments, we use Graph WaveNet [22], GMAN [25], FC-GAGA [18], MTGNN [23] and AGCRN [2] models as well as the variants presented in Sect. 3. For the one-hour (12 step) prediction task, we use the configuration found in the corresponding original publications. The temporal pooling stacks in GWNET-TSQ and GWNET-SPOOL-TSQ use $B = 2$ blocks in METR-LA and $B = 4$ in PEMS-BAY, with $L = 2$ layers and 32 channels. The spatial pooling in GWNET-SPOOL and GWNET-SPOOL-TSQ uses a pooling factor of 0.7.

For the longer time sequence experiments, in METR-LA-6H (72 step) we modify Graph WaveNet structure in order to cover the increased time dimension of 72 steps. The number of spatio-temporal blocks is increased to 5 and the dilation in gated convolutions is set to 4. In the temporal pooling stacks we use $B = 5$ blocks of $L = 2$ layers with 32 channels. We keep GMAN architecture unchanged. In METR-LA-24 (288 step) experiments, the Graph WaveNet structure uses 5 blocks of 3 spatio-temporal layers with dilation 4. The temporal pooling stack uses $B = 6$ blocks with $L = 2$ layers. All of the reported results are averaged over 3 runs with different seeds.

To compare the runtime efficiency of different models we compute and report the number of forward pass Multiply-Accumulate Operations (MACs) [27]. This serves as a common comparison metric, agnostic to the specific type of CPU or GPU used to run the model. For our proposed models, we also report the ratio between MACs of our model and MACs of the original.

Implementation. Our changes are implemented using the framework published by [11] for a standardized comparison of traffic forecasting methods. We introduce two main changes to the standardized setup of the framework. First, we use masked MAE loss instead of plain MAE (as is the framework default), in order to prevent the model learning from timesteps with missing data labels. Second, for the Graph WaveNet model, we reintroduce dropout of 0.3 as was done in the original publication [22]. Both of these changes are consistent with the original publications of the models we use for comparison. MAC estimates are computed using the THOP library [27], which we extend to support the benchmarked models.

4.3 Experimental Results

METR-LA. Table 1 summarizes the results. Notably, all the proposed Graph WaveNet variants perform on par with the baseline model, in particular for the far horizon of 12 time steps, often considered an indication for good modeling of long time-series dependencies. Furthermore, all the proposed variants use substantially less MACs to operate. GWNET-SPOOL and GWNET-SPOOL-TSQ reduce MACs used to 68% and 34% respectively compared to the original model. GWNET-TSQ uses only 21% of the original - a x4.76 speedup. GMAN performance is consistently worse than that of Graph WaveNet. Notably, GMAN-TSQ variants actually improve the prediction accuracy, while also using less computations. GMAN-TSQ variant reduces MACs to 57% of the original. We also consider reducing the number of attention heads in the GMAN-TSQ model to 4. Such a model GMAN-TSQ-4H further reduces the MACs to 23% of the original. In our experiments, FC-GAGA model did not reach better results than the baseline Graph WaveNet model while the MACs used indicate a slightly higher operational cost. It is worth noting that we were able to reproduce the results published in [18] when using their particular data setup. However, we couldn't reproduce the claimed results with a standard data pipeline.

PEMS-BAY. Table 1 summarizes the results. Here, the proposed variants show similar behavior to the METR-LA prediction task. GWNET-TSQ achieves the lowest errors while running 5 times faster than Graph WaveNet. GWNET-SPOOL and GWNET-SPOOL-TSQ reduce MACs used to 76% and 31% respectively and get slightly higher errors. GMAN-TSQ and GMAN-TSQ-4H variants result in lower errors than the original GMAN architecture using only 56% and 23% of the original MACs.

Table 2. Performance comparison on METR-LA with a 6-h history and 6-h prediction horizons at a five minute resolution.

Model	2 h/24 steps			4 h/48 steps			6 h/72 steps			MACs	MAC
	MAE	RMSE	MAPE	MAE	RMSE	MAPE	MAE	RMSE	MAPE	[G]	compr
Graph WaveNet	4.17	8.73	12.75	4.31	9.00	13.64	4.49	9.29	14.49	4.90	–
FC-GAGA	4.33	8.56	13.35	4.49	8.89	14.52	4.72	9.17	15.34	4.88	–
GWNET-TSQ	4.11	8.40	12.51	4.29	8.80	13.56	4.50	9.17	14.74	**0.38**	0.08
GWNET-SPOOL	4.10	**8.30**	12.48	4.30	**8.67**	**13.35**	4.49	**9.00**	14.45	1.70	0.35
GWNET-SPOOL-TSQ	**4.09**	8.45	**12.38**	**4.26**	8.86	13.60	**4.40**	9.10	**14.09**	0.44	0.09
GMAN	5.24	10.71	18.55	5.19	10.60	18.29	6.47	12.55	22.17	4.05	–
GMAN-TSQ	5.17	10.52	18.34	5.16	10.42	18.17	6.45	12.37	22.15	2.21	0.55
GMAN-TSQ-4H	5.15	10.49	18.29	5.19	10.47	18.18	6.57	12.55	22.39	0.91	0.22

Table 3. Performance comparison on METR-LA with a 24-h history and 24-h prediction horizons at a five minute resolution.

Model	6 h/72 steps			12 h/144 steps			24 h/288 steps			MACs	MAC
	MAE	RMSE	MAPE	MAE	RMSE	MAPE	MAE	RMSE	MAPE	[G]	compr
Graph WaveNet	4.32	8.86	13.60	4.44	9.04	13.82	4.59	9.32	15.35	32.18	–
GWNET-TSQ	4.31	8.66	14.05	4.39	8.77	14.01	4.57	9.20	15.49	**1.18**	0.04
GWNET-SPOOL-TSQ	**4.21**	**8.36**	**13.26**	**4.30**	**8.55**	**13.31**	**4.44**	**8.78**	**14.18**	1.81	0.06

METR-LA-6H. Table 2 summarizes the results. Here the time dimension is 6 times larger than in 1-h prediction task. The baseline models Graph WaveNet, FC-GAGA and GMAN run at a roughly similar computational cost of 4-5 GMACs. In comparison, the proposed variants run at a dramatically lower operational cost. GWNET-SPOOL reduces MACs used to 35% of the original, while GWNET-SPOOL-TSQ and GWNET-TSQ reduce to 9% and 8% with speedups of x11.1 and x12.9. Error-wise, we note that the proposed variants either improve on the baseline or perform on par. In particular, for the longest horizon of 72 steps our variants give the lowest errors compared to the baseline. Notably, while both GWNET-TSQ and GWNET-SPOOL reduce the error compared to the original models, the best variant is GWNET-SPOOL-TSQ which combines the temporal pooling stack and the spatial pooling components. GMAN-TSQ gives lower errors than the GMAN baseline while using only 55% of the original MACs. The GMAN-TSQ-4H variant performs on par or better than the GMAN baseline and 2-h and 4-h horizons and has a slightly higher errors in the 6-h horizon, while using only 22% MACs compared to the original.

METR-LA-24H. Table 3 summarizes the results. Here, we again note the dramatic difference in MACs used in our proposed variants compared to the baseline, paired with similar or better accuracies. GWNET-TSQ runs at only 4% MACs compared to original - a x27.3 speedup - with slightly lower MAE scores and slightly higher MAPE (less than 0.5%). GWNET-SPOOL-TSQ runs at 6% MACs compared to baseline - a x17.8 speedup - and yields lower errors in all prediction horizons - a reduction of 0.15 in MAE and 1.17 MAPE in the longest 288-step score. This again suggests that the combination of Temporal Pooling stack with the spatial pooling produces the most accurate model for the longer time horizons.

5   Conclusion

In this paper, we proposed a new framework to dramatically improve the runtime efficiency of the traffic forecasting solutions. We deploy a new temporal pooling block prior to spatial processing, which effectively compresses the time dimension prior to applying the message passing modules. We also embed graph pooling blocks to progressively reduce the size of the graph and to facilitate better information propagation between distant nodes. Our approach effectively reduces the linear dependency of the spatio-temporal network on the time dimension. Therefore, the achieved speedup scales with the size of the input time-series, and allows effective modeling of long-range dependencies. Our experiments demonstrate that the proposed method yields substantial speedups in both training and inference times, ranging from x5 speedup in the standard 1-h forecasting task and up to x27 for longer time series forecast of 24-h, while keeping or surpassing the accuracy of state-of-the-art methods.

References

1. Badrinarayanan, V., Kendall, A., Cipolla, R.: Segnet: a deep convolutional encoder-decoder architecture for image segmentation. IEEE Trans. Pattern Anal. Mach. Intell. **39**(12), 2481–2495 (2017)
2. Bai, L., Yao, L., Li, C., Wang, X., Wang, C.: Adaptive graph convolutional recurrent network for traffic forecasting. Adv. Neural. Inf. Process. Syst. **33**, 17804–17815 (2020)
3. Cho, K., Van Merriënboer, B., Bahdanau, D., Bengio, Y.: On the properties of neural machine translation: encoder-decoder approaches. arXiv preprint arXiv:1409.1259 (2014)
4. Dai, H., Dai, B., Song, L.: Discriminative embeddings of latent variable models for structured data. In: International Conference on Machine Learning, pp. 2702–2711. PMLR (2016)
5. Dauphin, Y.N., Fan, A., Auli, M., Grangier, D.: Language modeling with gated convolutional networks. In: International Conference on Machine Learning, pp. 933–941. PMLR (2017)
6. Gao, H., Ji, S.: Graph u-nets. In: International Conference on Machine Learning, pp. 2083–2092. PMLR (2019)
7. Gers, F.A., Schmidhuber, J., Cummins, F.: Learning to forget: continual prediction with LSTM. Neural Comput. **12**(10), 2451–2471 (2000)
8. Gilmer, J., Schoenholz, S.S., Riley, P.F., Vinyals, O., Dahl, G.E.: Neural message passing for quantum chemistry. In: International Conference on Machine Learning, pp. 1263–1272. PMLR (2017)
9. Grattarola, D., Zambon, D., Bianchi, F.M., Alippi, C.: Understanding pooling in graph neural networks. IEEE Trans. Neural Netw. Learn. Syst. (2022)

10. Heinrich, K., Zschech, P., Janiesch, C., Bonin, M.: Process data properties matter: introducing gated convolutional neural networks (GCNN) and key-value-predict attention networks (KVP) for next event prediction with deep learning. Decis. Support Syst. **143**, 113494 (2021)

11. Jiang, R., et al.: DL-Traff: survey and benchmark of deep learning models for urban traffic prediction. In: Proceedings of the 30th ACM International Conference on Information & Knowledge Management, pp. 4515–4525 (2021)

12. Kipf, T.N., Welling, M.: Semi-supervised classification with graph convolutional networks. arXiv preprint arXiv:1609.02907 (2016)

13. Lam, R., et al.: Graphcast: learning skillful medium-range global weather forecasting. arXiv preprint arXiv:2212.12794 (2022)

14. Li, Y., Yu, R., Shahabi, C., Liu, Y.: Diffusion convolutional recurrent neural network: data-driven traffic forecasting. In: International Conference on Learning Representations (ICLR 2018) (2018)

15. Li, Y., Tarlow, D., Brockschmidt, M., Zemel, R.: Gated graph sequence neural networks. arXiv preprint arXiv:1511.05493 (2015)

16. Liu, C., et al.: Graph pooling for graph neural networks: progress, challenges, and opportunities. arXiv preprint arXiv:2204.07321 (2022)

17. Mesquita, D., Souza, A., Kaski, S.: Rethinking pooling in graph neural networks. Adv. Neural. Inf. Process. Syst. **33**, 2220–2231 (2020)

18. Oreshkin, B.N., Amini, A., Coyle, L., Coates, M.: FC-GAGA: fully connected gated graph architecture for spatio-temporal traffic forecasting. In: Proceedings of the AAAI Conference on Artificial Intelligence, vol. 35, pp. 9233–9241 (2021)

19. Ronneberger, O., Fischer, P., Brox, T.: U-Net: convolutional networks for biomedical image segmentation. In: Navab, N., Hornegger, J., Wells, W.M., Frangi, A.F. (eds.) MICCAI 2015. LNCS, vol. 9351, pp. 234–241. Springer, Cham (2015). https://doi.org/10.1007/978-3-319-24574-4_28

20. Rusek, K., Suárez-Varela, J., Almasan, P., Barlet-Ros, P., Cabellos-Aparicio, A.: Routenet: leveraging graph neural networks for network modeling and optimization in SDN. IEEE J. Sel. Areas Commun. **38**(10), 2260–2270 (2020)

21. Vaswani, A., et al.: Attention is all you need. In: Advances in Neural Information Processing Systems, vol. 30 (2017)

22. Wu, Z., Pan, S., Long, G., Jiang, J., Zhang, C.: Graph wavenet for deep spatial-temporal graph modeling. In: The 28th International Joint Conference on Artificial Intelligence (IJCAI). International Joint Conferences on Artificial Intelligence Organization (2019)

23. Wu, Z., Pan, S., Long, G., Jiang, J., Chang, X., Zhang, C.: Connecting the dots: multivariate time series forecasting with graph neural networks. In: Proceedings of the 26th ACM SIGKDD International Conference on Knowledge Discovery & Data Mining, pp. 753–763 (2020)

24. Zhao, L., et al.: T-GCN: a temporal graph convolutional network for traffic prediction. IEEE Trans. Intell. Transp. Syst. **21**(9), 3848–3858 (2019)

25. Zheng, C., Fan, X., Wang, C., Qi, J.: GMAN: a graph multi-attention network for traffic prediction. In: Proceedings of the AAAI Conference on Artificial Intelligence, vol. 34, pp. 1234–1241 (2020)

26. Zhou, J., et al.: Graph neural networks: a review of methods and applications. AI Open **1**, 57–81 (2020)

27. Zhu, L.: THOP: PyTorch-OpCounter (2019). https://github.com/Lyken17/pytorch-OpCounter

GCN-based Reinforcement Learning Approach for Scheduling DAG Applications

Julius Roeder[1](✉) , Andy D. Pimentel[1] , and Clemens Grelck[1,2]

[1] University of Amsterdam, Amsterdam, The Netherlands
{j.roeder,a.d.pimentel,c.grelck}@uva.nl
[2] Friedrich Schiller University Jena, Jena, Germany
clemens.grelck@uni-jena.de

Abstract. Applications in various fields such as embedded systems or High-Performance-Computing are often represented as Directed Acyclic Graphs (DAG), also known as taskgraphs. DAGs represent the data flow between tasks in an application and can be used for scheduling. When scheduling taskgraphs, a scheduler needs to decide when and on which core each task is executed, while minimising the runtime of the schedule.

This paper explores offline scheduling of dependent tasks using a Reinforcement Learning (RL) approach. We propose two RL schedulers, one using a Fully Connected Network (FCN) and another one using a Graph Convolutional Network (GCN). First, we detail the different components of our two RL schedulers and illustrate how they schedule a task. Then, we compare our RL schedulers to a Forward List Scheduling (FLS) approach based on two different datasets. We demonstrate that our GCN-based scheduler produces schedules that are as good or better than the schedules produced by the FLS approach in over 85% of the cases for a dataset with small taskgraphs. The same scheduler performs very similar to the FLS scheduler (at most 5% degradation) in almost 76% of the cases for a more challenging dataset.

Keywords: DAGs · static scheduling · reinforcement learning · graph convolutional networks

1 Introduction

Directed Acyclic Graphs (DAGs) can be used in various fields (e.g. embedded systems, High-Performance-Computing) to represent applications. In a DAG, the nodes represent tasks and the edges between nodes represent the data dependency between tasks. Applications that can be represented as DAGs include, among others, augmented reality (AR) and AI applications in robotics and automotive [2], computer vision applications for precision agriculture [17], big data analytics applications that are implemented with Hive, Spark or Tez.

© IFIP International Federation for Information Processing 2023
Published by Springer Nature Switzerland AG 2023
I. Maglogiannis et al. (Eds.): AIAI 2023, IFIP AICT 676, pp. 121–134, 2023.
https://doi.org/10.1007/978-3-031-34107-6_10

These applications are executed on multi-core and many-core platforms. In the area of embedded systems the Nvidia Jetson lineup [1] and the Odroid-XU4 [10] are good examples. To fully utilise the hardware we need to ensure that our applications can take advantage of the multiple CPU cores, the GPU and other available accelerators. Targeting the different available Compute Units (CU) (e.g. CPU, GPU) can be done during the scheduling of an application.

It is advantageous for scheduling to represent applications as DAGs because the DAG naturally provides options for concurrency and thus simplifies targeting multiple CUs. However, this concurrency also provides a challenge, as the scheduler also has to adhere to the data dependency inferred from the DAG (i.e. partial ordering). This process of deciding when and where a task of an application is executed is called scheduling. Scheduling can be done online (i.e. dynamically at runtime) or offline (i.e. statically). In this paper, we focus on static scheduling as dynamic scheduling can introduce significant overhead which may be problematic, especially for embedded systems.

Previous research on scheduling DAG applications mainly focused on using heuristics such as Forward List Scheduling (FLS) or Integer Linear Programming (ILP) (for surveys see [3,8,22,23]). The later provides an optimal solution (e.g. minimising makespan, also known as execution time or run-time)), but does not scale well with increasing state space. The state space of a scheduling problem can depend on many different criteria such as the number of tasks in an application and the number of CUs available. Optimising for energy consumption adds another dimension to the state space. Heuristics scale better with the problem size. However, most scheduling heuristics require a total order [13,18,19,24]. Thus, the first step in scheduling heuristics is to rank all tasks in a DAG (while preserving the partial order) and then scheduling them one-by-one in a greedy fashion. It has been shown that no ranking strategy always outperforms all other ranking strategies (see [18,19]). Finding near-optimal static schedules for larger DAGs within a reasonable solving time is still an open problem.

Artificial intelligence (AI) may provide a feasible solution. However, supervised learning is not a suitable approach because it requires (large) datasets of examples with solutions (labels). This is especially problematic for large state-spaces, as for example in [18] where finding an optimal solution for DAGs containing more than 15 tasks takes more than 24 h. Extrapolating the execution times from [18] shows that finding an optimal solution for a DAGs of 100 tasks would take approximately 35 years. Thus, we could never make a large enough dataset for more complex problems. Additionally, the authors [18] show that, other AI approaches, such as evolutionary algorithms, are also not well suited for the task at hand. Reinforcement Learning (RL), however, may still provide a promising approach. Recent advances in Reinforcement Learning have enabled computers to find good solutions for a variety of challenges, e.g., RL methods can build near-optimal solutions (up to 100 nodes) for combinatorial problems such as the Travelling Salesmen Problem [15]. RL approaches combined with supervised learning can schedule DAG task graphs and outperform heuristics such as Heterogeneous Earliest Finish Time (HEFT), Critical-Path-on-a-Processor

(CPOP) and Graphene [13,26]. The combination of RL and supervised methods was required to stabilise the training. However, by pre-training neural networks in a supervised manner, they learn to imitate heuristics, whereas it has been shown that learning from scratch can outperform both heuristics and humans [21].

We propose a Deep Q-learning (DQN) approach that learns to build offline schedules from scratch (i.e., not relying on supervised learning to learn to imitate a heuristic). We propose two different RL-agents: one with a Fully Connected Neural Network (FCNN) backbone, and one with a Graph Convolutional Neural Network (GCN) backbone that can leverage graph information. To train and evaluate the models, we build two large datasets of 11,000 DAG taskgraphs each: one with small and simple graphs, and one with larger and complex graphs. Our experiments show that a Q-learning approach quickly learns static DAG scheduling without pre-training. Our experiments further show a comparison between a Forward List Scheduling (FLS) algorithm and the schedules generated by the two RL schedulers. Lastly, we show that incorporating graph information via GCN layers significantly improves the scheduling of DAG applications. Both the code[1] and the two datasets[2] are open source.

The remainder of this paper is structured as follows. In Sect. 2, we give a high level explanation of our RL-based scheduling approach, explain our DAG task model, layout the target architecture and discuss the most important components of our novel RL-scheduler. In Sect. 3, we discuss our experimental setup, followed by the results in Sect. 4. Section 5 discusses the related work. Lastly, Sect. 6 presents our conclusions and future work.

2   RL Scheduling

Let us start with a high-level overview of our RL scheduling approach. Figure 1 shows the interactions between the RL agent and the scheduling environment.

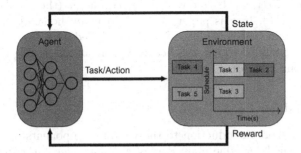

Fig. 1. Reinforcement Learning Framework

---

[1] https://bitbucket.org/jroeder/simple_rl_scheduling.
[2] https://bitbucket.org/jroeder/gnn_tgff_data.

The environment updates the ready-queue at the beginning of each scheduling step, i.e., it collects all tasks that can be scheduled. Only tasks whose predecessors have already been scheduled can be scheduled. Hence, at any given point in time, we might have multiple tasks that can be scheduled.

Then the features of all tasks (states) in the ready-queue are collected and passed to the agent. The agent evaluates all eligible tasks and selects the task/action pair with the highest expected reward.

The task/action pair is returned to the environment, and the environment adds the task to the schedule in a *as-soon-as-possible* fashion, respecting both predecessor run-times and preventing tasks from being scheduled to execute at the same time on the same CU. The environment then returns the reward for the task/action pair and the states for the next tasks in the ready-queue. This is repeated until all tasks in all applications have been added to the schedule.

2.1   System Model

Task Model. We consider applications represented as Directed Acyclic Graphs (DAG). In a graph, $G = (\tau, E)$ the set of nodes/vertices τ represents the tasks, and the set of edges E represents data dependencies between tasks, i.e., a source task needs to be completed before the corresponding sink task may start executing. Our task model supports multiple sources and sinks. Additionally, we support a multi-graph setup (i.e., multiple applications).

A task is a sub-part of an application that needs a certain input, then executes without additional input until it finalises and passes its output to the following tasks in the application. Each task has a runtime, also called worst-case execution time (WCET). Our model does not limit the number of incoming or outgoing edges of a task. We assume that multiple tasks cannot run concurrently on one processing unit.

Architecture Model. Our approach is fully platform-independent and can be applied to a wide range of homogeneous system architectures. The number of Compute Units (CU) can be altered via a parameter (the number of actions the agent can make). In this paper, we only focus on homogeneous quad-core systems to determine the feasibility of RL based schedulers. However, the model could easily be extended to heterogeneous systems by increasing the number of CU and including additional features.

2.2   RL Scheduler Components

Next, we give a short introduction to the various components of our reinforcement learning scheduler. One main part of the scheduler is the neural network agent that makes all the decisions. We investigate two different agents: one based on a Fully Connected Neural Network (FCNN), and an extention of the first one by incorporating Graph Convolutional (GCN) layers to leverage additional information inherent to the graph structure of the DAG.

Environment. The environment contains the task graph, the schedule and a representation of the target architecture. It can evaluate the impact of different scheduling decisions and update its internal states.

Fully Connected Agent. The main backbone of our agent consists of a fully connected neural network (FCNN). The network consists of *4* layers having *2048, 2048, 4096, 4096* neurons, respectively. We use ELU activation functions after each layer [5]. This network architecture performed the best across a range of different configurations while searching the hyperparameter space. The hyperparameter space search was performed using the Bayesian sweep function provided by *Weights and Biases* [4].

The input to a neural network depends on the type of neural network used. For our FCNN based approach, the state is a list of features for a task (i.e. node-specific and global features that are common to all tasks). The node-specific features are: (1) runtime of a task, (2) best start time at which a task can start (i.e. the end time across all predecessors), (3) actual start time of a task if it has been scheduled, and (4) target core if a task has been scheduled. The global features are: (1) normalised values of the min, max and mean of all tasks in the ready queue, (2) normalised values of the min, max and mean runtime of all tasks in the done queue, (3) number of tasks in the DAG, (4) number of tasks available for scheduling, and (5) number of tasks that still need to be scheduled. All normalised features are normalised with the maximum runtime of any task in the graph. This results in a total of 13 features for each task.

Graph Convolutional Network Agent. As our problem is in the form of a graph it was natural to turn to GCNs [14] in order to attempt to leverage the additional information inherent to the graph structure. The input to our GCNs consist of the same node features as for the FCNN, plus the edge information (i.e. which nodes are connected). We propose 3 different types of edge information: a node's predecessors, all previously scheduled nodes (i.e. they may hold information about gaps in the schedule) or all successors of a node. We create three different GCNs, that each take as input the node features and one of the three edge information. Each GCN consists of 4 SAGEConv [9] layers with *8, 16, 32, 64* neurons per layer respectively. Each layer is followed by an ELU activation function. The input to each GCN are the node information (runtime, best start time, actual start time and target core). However, the edge information for each GCN differ slightly depending on whether it is supposed to learn about predecessors, previously scheduled nodes or successor nodes. The output of the three GCNs is then concatenated to the original node information and to the same global features as for the FCNN agent. All this information is fed into the same FCNN agent as above (4 layers with *2048, 2048, 4096, 4096* neurons, respectively) and ELU activation functions to return what is the most valuable action.

Actions. The action is the CU on which a given task is scheduled. For example, in the case of a quad-core system, the action space is between 0 and 3. The number of possible actions depends on the target system.

Rewards. The reward function (Equation (1)) returns the value of a given state s_t. In our case, the reward is the negative release time $(-rt_0)$ of the action (i.e. start time of a task) plus the expected reward of future actions, where γ is the discount rate ($[0, 1)$) of future actions. We used a γ of 0.65. There are no positive rewards; the best possible reward is 0. If a task (t_0) starts at the 5 s mark, the reward is -5 minus the expected reward of future actions. That means if we expect the next task (t_1) to start at the 8 s mark, then the reward for t_0 is -13.

$$V(s_0) = -rt_0 + E_{t=1}^{\infty}\left[\gamma^t \times (-rt_t)\right] \tag{1}$$

RL Approach Description. We use a double DQN approach [11] with fixed Q-targets, where two networks (*NN1* and *NN2*) are initialised with the same weights. *NN1* and *NN2* are used to update each other. A simplified representation of a single training step is shown in Fig. 2. During training, the environment passes a state (S_t) to *NN1*, which predicts the *expected reward* of all actions at step t. The action with the highest *expected reward* is selected and passed to the environment, which evaluates it and computes a *reward*. At the same time, the environment passes the updated state S_{t+1} to *NN2*, which predicts the *expected reward* for the new state. The *reward* at t is combined with the *expected reward* at $t+1$ to form the *actual reward* at t. The *actual reward* is then used to update the weights of *NN1*. The weights of *NN2* are updated every τ steps with the weights of *NN1*. *NN2* is the network used for inference.

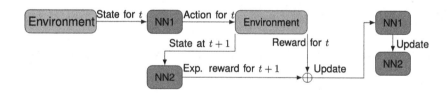

Fig. 2. RL agent training pipeline.

Furthermore, our approach uses prioritised experience replay [20], where training samples of higher impact are more likely to be in the training batch. The impact of a sample is the absolute percentage difference between the predicted and the actual reward.

3   Experiments

Data. We use Task Graphs For Free (*TGFF*) [7] to generate random DAG task graphs. TGFF generates 10,000 tasks, where each task has a different runtime. Using a random selection of the tasks, different DAGs are generated. We generate two datasets to run our experiments. One dataset with smaller, less diverse and simple graphs, and a second dataset with large, diverse and complex graphs.

The main difference between the two datasets is the number of tasks per graph. The small DAGs (Dataset 1) are set to 10 tasks with a multiplier of 1. This does not mean that all graphs have 10 tasks, as the number of tasks also depends on other characteristics. The larger taskgrahs (Dataset 2) are set to an average of 20 tasks with a multiplier of 5. This means that the larger DAGs are more challenging as they, for example, contain more potential parallelism, which is especially important as the target system only has 4 cores. All datasets are roughly uniformly distributed with respect to the number of tasks in a DAG.

Both datasets consist of a training dataset with 10,000 task graphs and a test dataset containing 1,000 task graphs. The graphs in the test and training datasets were generated separately with different seeds. Table 1 contains a summary of the graph statistics for the small and large DAG datasets. The training and test dataset do not differ much with respect to the number of tasks in the DAGs.

Table 1. The table shows the statistics with respect to the number of tasks in the train and test sets that contain the small and large DAGs.

	Mean	Min	Max	Std
Small Train	12.7	6	24	6.3
Small Test	13.0	6	24	6.4
Large Train	25.5	9	55	13.1
Large Test	25.5	9	54	13.4

The difference between the type of graphs generated for the two datasets can be well seen when comparing Figs. 3a and 3b.

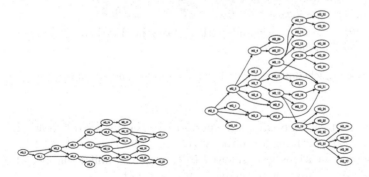

(a) Example DAG from the small DAG test dataset.

(b) Example DAG from the large DAG test dataset.

Fig. 3. Comparing example DAGs from the two generated datasets.

Comparison with Existing Method. We compare the RL generated schedules to schedules generated by a Forward List Scheduler (FLS) [6]. FLS first orders the tasks and then adds them one by one to the schedule without backtracking. FLS iteratively computes the impact on the makespan (i.e. run-time) of scheduling a task on a specific compute unit (CU) (e.g. CPU, GPU) and greedily selects the best CU with respect to the makespan. The performance of FLS heavily depends on the initial ranking of the tasks. Thus, it is common practice to try multiple ranking algorithms as none consistently outperforms the others [19]. In this case, we use 3 different rankings: BFS, DFS and BFS with Laxity.

4   Results

In general, the RL scheduler learns to schedule DAGs quickly. Figure 4a shows the schedule produced by an untrained, randomly initialised RL agent. We can see that all 27 tasks from the original graph are simply put after each other on a single core. However, after some training the scheduler improves. Figure 4b shows a schedule produced for the same graph by the same RL agent after some training (before convergence). The decisions are not necessarily optimal but we can clearly observe that the scheduler learns that distributing tasks over different cores is better (i.e. increases its rewards).

by one of our

(b) Schedule of a taskgraph with 27 tasks produced by one of our trained RL schedulers.

Fig. 4. Comparing schedules generated by an untrained and a trained RL-based scheduler.

In Sects. 4.1 to 4.4, we discuss the performance of the two different schedulers (FCNN and GCN) with regard to the two different datasets (Dataset 1 & Dataset 2). All four combinations were allowed to train for a similar number of epochs and the best performing neural network was selected.

4.1   Dataset 1 - FCNN Agent

The FCNN agent performs fairly well on the dataset consisting of smaller DAGs. The degradation distribution between the FCNN agent and the FLS scheduler can be seen in Fig. 5. In 69.6% of the cases the FCNN agent produces schedules that are the same or better. In 90.0% of the DAGs the FCNN agent results in schedules that perform similarly (at most 5% degradation) or better. The average degradation is 1.2% and at best the resulting schedule is 6.9% shorter than the schedule generated by the FLS approach. At worst, the FCNN scheduler results in a 19.7% higher makespan. Despite this good performance the FCNN scheduler had a L1Loss of 35.9 which is higher than the L1Loss of the GCNN scheduler.

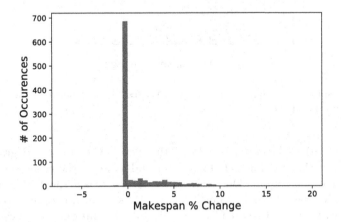

Fig. 5. Makespan degradation of the small DAG test dataset between the FCNN generated schedules and the FLS schedules.

4.2   Dataset 2 - FCNN Agent

The FCNN agent performs significantly worse for the dataset containing larger DAGs than for the dataset of small DAGs. The degradation spread is shown in Fig. 6. Overall, the FCNN agent only manages to produce schedules that are the same or better in 18.9% of the DAGs. Additionally, it finds schedules that perform similarly (at most 5% degradation) or better in only 42.3% of the cases. Overall, the degradation is 7.1%. And at best, the generated schedule results in 6.5% lower makespan but at worst we see a degradation of 35.3%. The L1Loss (45.5) is higher than the L1Loss in Sect. 4.1. Showing that the additional complexity of the large DAGs and possibly the larger variance of DAGs may require a more advanced approach.

4.3   Dataset 1 - GCN Based Network

On Dataset 1, the GCN agent performs better than the FCNN agent. The degradation is shown in Fig. 7. The distribution looks similar to the one shown in Fig. 5. Overall, the GCN approach generates schedules that are the same or better in 85.2% of the cases. And it finds schedules that perform similarly (at most

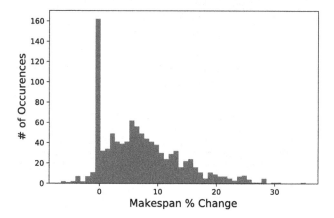

Fig. 6. Makespan degradation of the large DAG test dataset between the FCNN generated schedules and the FLS schedules.

5% degradation) or better in 98.1% of the cases. The average degradation is 0.29%. At best the schedule is 6.9% shorter and at worst the found schedule has a 20.4% longer makespan. One more difference between the FCNN scheduler and the GCN scheduler is the much lower L1Loss, which dropped to 5.9. This clearly shows that the three GCNs provide valuable information, even though, the information do not appear to add much value in the case of the smaller DAG dataset.

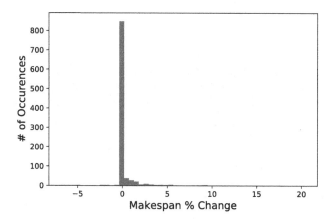

Fig. 7. Makespan degradation of the small DAG test dataset between the GCN based RL scheduler and the FLS scheduler.

4.4   Dataset 2 - GCN Based Network

We can see a clear improvement in the schedules generated by the GCN scheduler in comparison to the FCNN scheduler for the dataset of large DAGs. This
improvement can also be seen when comparing the degradation distributions in
Fig. 8 (GCN scheduler) and Fig. 6 (FCNN scheduler). In total, we find that the
GCN agent generates schedules that are the same or better in 38.7% of the cases.
Furthermore, the GCN scheduler finds schedules that perform similarly (at most
5% degradation) or better in 75.6% of the cases. The average degradation drops
from 7.1% for the FCNN agent to 2.8% for the GCNN agent. At best we see
schedules that are 11.2% shorter and at worst the schedules are 34.4% longer
than the FLS generated schedules. The final L1Loss is 11.0. In comparison, to
the GCN approach on smaller DAGs this L1Loss is slightly higher. However,
the L1Loss is also significantly lower than the L1Loss of the FCNN agent. This
clearly shows that the additional information provided by the GCN layers is
valuable.

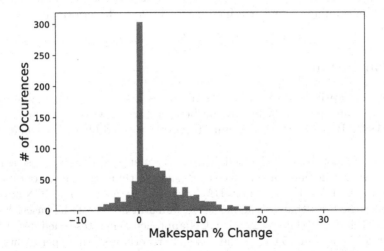

Fig. 8. Makespan degradation of the large DAG test dataset between the GCN based
RL scheduler and the FLS scheduler.

Across all four experiments, we cannot draw conclusions on whether the
number of tasks in a taskgraph impacts the performance of a RL-scheduler,
i.e., a larger taskgraph does not necessarily lead to a higher degradation.

5   Comparative Analysis with Existing Algorithms

Wu et al. [26] use the REINFORCE agent [25] from 1992 to schedule DAG
taskgraphs. The paper shows that this approach outperforms Heterogeneous
Earliest Finish Time (HEFT) and Critical-Path-on-a-Processor (CPOP) by up

to 25%. However, REINFORCE agents tend to be unstable in the training process. More modern approaches like our approach address this stability issue. Furthermore, the approach by Wu et al. depends on the original ranking of the tasks in the task graph.

Hu, Tu and Li [13] have proposed a new approach (called *Spear*) that uses Monte Carlo Tree Search (MCTS) combined with RL. *Spear* outperforms the Graphene heuristic by 20%. *Spear* determines the ranking of the tasks, i.e., it determines in what order the tasks are scheduled, whereas we use RL to schedule the task end-to-end. Additionally, *spear* initialises the network with supervised learning, i.e., it learns to imitate the behaviour of a heuristic. This means that the agent might learn undesirable behaviour from the heuristic. And is exactly the opposite of what we want, as it has been shown that RL agents are capable of learning strategies on their own and, in some cases outperforming both humans and heuristics [21].

Mao et al. [16] use Reinforcement Learning to schedule independent tasks, whereas we focus on dependent tasks. Hu et al. [12] introduce an RL agent for online scheduling of dependent tasks. Our approach focuses on offline scheduling as online scheduling can incur a high overhead on high-performance embedded systems.

6   Conclusion

Finding near-optimal static schedules for large DAGs in a reasonable solving time is still an open problem. To the best of our knowledge, we are the first to use DQN Reinforcement Learning to tackle this problem in an end-to-end fashion.

We show that RL-based schedulers can outperform FLS-based schedulers. The resulting schedules are up to 11.2% shorter than the corresponding FLS generated schedules. For the small DAG dataset (Dataset 1) our GCN approach generates schedules that are at most 5% worse in 98.1% of the cases. For the large DAG dataset (Dataset 2) our GCN approach generates schedules that are at most 5% worse in 75.6% of the cases. Furthermore, our experiments show that the additional information obtained by the GCN layers add value to our RL-based scheduler. However, this additional information only seems to result in significantly better schedules (on average) if the target dataset is more diverse or contains larger taskgraphs. Furthermore, we show that the selected reward function works (i.e. lower loss = better performance).

In the future, we plan to investigate deeper networks, the performance of the RL scheduler for heterogeneous systems and the use of sparse rewards. Additionally, we plan to investigate which one of the three GCNs adds most value. Lastly, we plan to experiment with policy learning instead of action-value learning.

Acknowledgement. We would like to thank the reviewers for their time and feedback.

This work has received funding from the European Union's Horizon 2020 research and innovation program under grant agreement No. 871259 (ADMORPH project).

This article is based upon work from COST Action CERCIRAS, supported by COST (European Cooperation in Science and Technology)

References

1. Jetson,   N.:   https://www.nvidia.com/en-us/autonomous-machines/embedded-systems/. Accessed 21 Jan 2023
2. Andreozzi, M., Gabrielli, G., Venu, B., Travaglini, G.: Industrial challenge 2022: a high-performance real-time case study on arm. In: ECRTS 2022. Schloss Dagstuhl-Leibniz-Zentrum für Informatik (2022)
3. Bambagini, M., Marinoni, M., Aydin, H., Buttazzo, G.: Energy-aware scheduling for real-time systems. TECS $15(1)$, 1–34 (2016)
4. Biewald, L.: Experiment tracking with weights and biases (2020). https://www.wandb.com/
5. Clevert, D., Unterthiner, T., Hochreiter, S.: Fast and accurate deep network learning by exponential linear units (ELUS). arXiv preprint arXiv:1511.07289 (2015)
6. Cooper, K.D., Schielke, P.J., Subramanian, D.: An Experimental Evaluation of List Scheduling. TR98 326 (1998)
7. Dick, R., Rhodes, D., Wolf, W.: TGFF: task graphs for free. In: 6th CODES/CASHE. IEEE (1998)
8. Gerards, M.E.T., Hurink, J.L., Hölzenspies, P.K.F.: A survey of offline algorithms for energy minimization under deadline constraints. J. Sched. $19(1)$, 3–19 (2016). https://doi.org/10.1007/s10951-015-0463-8
9. Hamilton, W., Ying, Z., Leskovec, J.: Inductive representation learning on large graphs. In: Advances in Neural Information Processing Systems, vol. 30 (2017)
10. Hardkernel Co., Ltd: Odroid-XU4. https://wiki.odroid.com/odroid-xu4/odroid-xu4. Accessed 06 Sep 2019
11. Hasselt, H.: Double Q-learning. In: 24th NIPS, vol. 23, pp. 2613–2621 (2010)
12. Hu, Y., de Laat, C., Zhao, Z.: Learning workflow scheduling on multi-resource clusters. In: 2019 NAS, pp. 1–8. IEEE (2019)
13. Hu, Z., Tu, J., Li, B.: Spear: optimized dependency-aware task scheduling with deep reinforcement learning. In: 39th ICDCS, pp. 2037–2046. IEEE (2019)
14. Kipf, T.N., Welling, M.: Semi-supervised classification with graph convolutional networks. arXiv preprint arXiv:1609.02907 (2016)
15. Kool, W., van Hoof, H., Welling, M.: Attention, learn to solve routing problems! In: 7th ICLR (2019)
16. Mao, H., Alizadeh, M., Menache, I., Kandula, S.: Resource management with deep reinforcement learning. In: Proceedings of the 15th ACM hot topics in Workshop on Networks, pp. 50–56 (2016)
17. Patrício, D.I., Rieder, R.: Computer vision and artificial intelligence in precision agriculture for grain crops: a systematic review. Comput. Electron. Agric. 153, 69–81 (2018)
18. Roeder, J., Rouxel, B., Altmeyer, S., Grelck, C.: Energy-aware scheduling of multi-version tasks on heterogeneous real-time systems. In: 2021 36th SAC, pp. 501–510 (2021)
19. Rouxel, B., Skalistis, S., Derrien, S., Puaut, I.: Hiding communication delays in contention-free execution for SPM-based multi-core architectures. In: 31st ECRTS19 (2019)
20. Schaul, T., Quan, J., Antonoglou, I., Silver, D.: Prioritized Experience Replay. arXiv:1511.05952 (2015)

21. Silver, D., et al.: Mastering the game of Go without human knowledge. Nature **550**, 354–379 (2017)
22. Singh, A.K., Dziurzanski, P., Mendis, H.R., Indrusiak, L.S.: A survey and comparative study of hard and soft real-time dynamic resource allocation strategies for multi-/many-core systems. ACM Comput. Surv. (CSUR) **50**(2), 1–40 (2017)
23. Singh, A.K., Shafique, M., Kumar, A., Henkel, J.: Mapping on multi/many-core systems: survey of current and emerging trends. In: 2013 50th DAC, pp. 1–10. IEEE (2013)
24. Ullah Tariq, U., Ali, H., Liu, L., Panneerselvam, J., Zhai, X.: Energy-efficient static task scheduling on VFI based NoC-HMPSoCs for intelligent edge devices in cyber-physical systems. TIST 1(1) (2019)
25. Williams, R.J.: Simple statistical gradient-following algorithms for connectionist reinforcement learning. Mach. Learn. **8**(3–4), 229–256 (1992)
26. Wu, Q., Wu, Z., Zhuang, Y., Cheng, Y.: Adaptive DAG tasks scheduling with deep reinforcement learning. In: Vaidya, J., Li, J. (eds.) ICA3PP 2018. LNCS, vol. 11335, pp. 477–490. Springer, Cham (2018). https://doi.org/10.1007/978-3-030-05054-2_37

Prediction of Drug Interactions Using Graph-Topological Features and GNN

Navyasree Balamuralidhar, Pranav Surendran, Gaurav Singh$^{(\boxtimes)}$,
Shrutilipi Bhattacharjee, and Ramya D. Shetty

Department of Information Technology, National Institute of Technology Karnataka,
Surathkal Mangaluru, India
{navya.191it135,pranavsurendran.191it239,gauravsingh.191it218,
shrutilipi,ramyadshetty.207it004}@nitk.edu.in

Abstract. The risk of side effects is sometimes inevitable every time two or more drugs are prescribed together, and these side effects of varying adversity levels can be referred to as drug-drug interactions (DDI). Massive amounts of data and the constraints of experimental circumstances result in clinical trials for medication compatibility being time-consuming, risky, expensive, and impractical. Recent research has demonstrated that DDI can be modelled as graphs and experimentally shown that deep learning on graphs can be a practical choice for determining the correlation and side effects of taking multiple medications simultaneously. We propose a novel approach to use inductive graph learning with GraphSAGE, along with topological features, to leverage the structural information of a graph along with the node attributes. An experimental study of the approach is done on a publicly available subset of the DrugBank dataset. We achieve our best results that are comparable with state-of-the-art works using degree, closeness and PageRank centrality measures as additional features with less computational complexity. This study can provide a reliable and cost-effective alternative to clinical trials to predict dangerous side effects, ensuring the safety of patients.

Keywords: Graph Neural Network · centrality measures · drug-drug interaction · topological feature generation · GraphSAGE

1 Introduction

Experimentation on drug compatibility is time-consuming, expensive, infeasible for large-scale data, and sometimes dangerous [1]. While there exist significant amounts of biomedical data regarding the phenotypic structures of the drugs themselves, only a tiny percentage of the total combinations have known and recorded side effects [2]. To avoid risks of damage to humans and, at the same time, to maintain a high confidence level of interaction prediction, artificial intelligence and deep neural networks have made significant progress. Due to the critical need for accurate predictions of drug interaction events, the research area

© IFIP International Federation for Information Processing 2023
Published by Springer Nature Switzerland AG 2023
I. Maglogiannis et al. (Eds.): AIAI 2023, IFIP AICT 676, pp. 135–144, 2023.
https://doi.org/10.1007/978-3-031-34107-6_11

has been increasingly gaining focus. On the other hand, graph neural networks have been gaining popularity in various research domains. The edge classification tasks aim to predict the exact type of interaction or link that occurs between two entities. More crucial domains, such as the pharmacological field [4], also require a similar type of behavioural analysis on substances and compounds that are currently being prescribed to patients all over the world. The drug-drug interactions (DDI) can be modelled as a graph with each drug as a node and the edges connecting them representing side effects. Information about the drugs in node embedding can be given as input to the graph neural network. Node embeddings are the vectors that describe the node properties, here, drug features, in a network. An edge classification approach can be used to predict the edge type or interaction event between two drugs.

Recent studies [2,3] have experimentally shown that deep learning on graphs can be a viable option when it comes to an understanding the correlation and side effects of taking different drugs concurrently and hence provide a degree of safety with fewer resources. Graph neural networks (GNNs) have been gaining popularity because graphs can easily represent different types of real world objects, such as images, text, object entities, and their inter-relationships with each other. Nguyen *et al.* [6] assumes the existence of latent features with latent interactions in a hypergraph created by linking two drugs and their associated side effect with one edge. The drug features and the hypergraph are encoded to preserve the sparsity of the data. Rohani *et al.* [2] selects the most informative and less redundant subset of similarity types by a heuristic process and is integrated by a non-linear similarity fusion method. Liu *et al.* [3] employs the attention neural network to learn attention vectors of each of the specific drug-drug pairs to predict interactions. Acharya *et al.* [5] extends the feature selection algorithm to GNNs with a ranking algorithm for extracted features. Lin. *et al.* [1] predicts DDI events based on multi-source drug fusion, multi-source feature fusion and a transformer self-attention mechanism with auto-encoders to learn latent representations of the drugs. Cui *et al.* [7] does an empirical study to shed light on the importance of artificial positional and structural node features in a GNN.

Most of the works [11,12] that have adopted graphical approaches for the DDI problem only deal with link prediction between two drugs using similarity measures. Our work provides a way to classify the interaction event into one of the hundred different interaction types recorded by DrugBank. Hypergraph link prediction [3] can also predict the side-effect between two drugs, however, the creation, manipulation and the learning of hypergraphs is more complex than that of regular graphs as is used in our study. We use the GraphSAGE model to learn the topological features (centrality measures) of the graph to predict interaction events [10]. Therefore, the main contributions of this study are as follows:

– This work effectively adds the topological features information of the graph into node embedding, which is learnt with a model that is compatible with dynamic data for when the need arises

- We propose a computationally efficient methodology using GraphSAGE to tackle the task of DDI prediction
- Our experiments conclusively prove that the use of topologically derived features improves the performance of the GraphSAGE model.

The rest of the paper is organized as follows. Section 2 describes the working of the GraphSAGE model. It also outlines the topological feature generation techniques experimented with in this work. In Sect. 3, we present the proposed model's experimental results with each feature generation type and summarize our findings. Finally, we present our conclusions and future scope in Sect. 4.

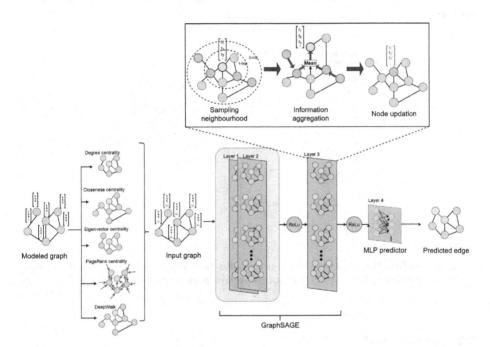

Fig. 1. Architecture of the proposed model. Graph centrality measures are computed for each node in the graphical network to generate new features, provided as input to the GraphSAGE network to obtain the predicted edge class, which is the type of side-effect between the two drugs.

2   Methodology

The diagrammatic representation of the methodology followed in this study is shown in Fig. 1. The following section deals with the details of each stage of the proposed model architecture.

2.1   Graph Neural Network for DDI Modeling

The primary motivation for using GNNs for the DDI analysis is their ability to represent real-world objects and behaviours in a way that their inherent structural properties can be leveraged. The interactions between drugs are represented as a graph with the drugs represented as nodes and the side-effect as the edges between the two drug nodes, as shown in Fig. 2. The ability to represent information about each drug as a low-dimensional node embedding is another merit of GNNs. Let $G = (V, E)$, where V is the set of vertices representing the drug, and E is the edges representing their mutual side effects. The features of a given node v are represented as the vector f_v, and the complete set of node feature vectors as $\{f_v, \forall v \in V\}$.

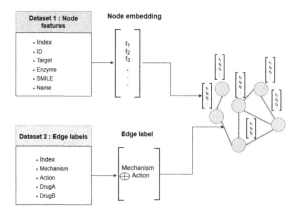

Fig. 2. Modeling the datasets into a graph with the drugs as the nodes and the side effects as the edges. Every node has its respective node embeddings.

2.2   GraphSAGE

GraphSAGE [10] is a representation learning algorithm useful for static and dynamic graphs as it can predict the embedding of a new node without retraining the model. It works on the assumption that the nodes that are in the neighbourhood will have similar embeddings. The main advantage of using GraphSAGE is that this model can be easily modified to work with dynamic graphs as and when the need to test new drugs arises. This paper focuses on the learning of static graphs, assuming that the nodes are the drugs and the interactions are the edges of the graphs. There are two major components of GraphSAGE, as follows:

– Context Construction: GraphSAGE works under the assumption that the nodes present in the same neighbourhood are likely to have similar node embeddings. The definition of a neighbourhood in relation to GraphSAGE is a sample of a uniformly picked fixed number of nodes.

– Information Aggregation: Aggregation functions take the neighbourhood as input and combine the neighbours' embeddings with weights to create an embedding of the neighbourhood. The mean aggregator provides a nearly similar propagation rule as is currently prevalent in graph convolutional neural networks. The only difference being that it does not concatenate the previous node embeddings with the current embeddings generated after information aggregation from the neighbouring nodes. At the beginning of each iteration, the node's vicinity is sampled, and the data from the sampled nodes are combined into a single vector. Hence, at the kth layer, the node v will have information aggregated as an embedding $h_N^t(v)$ given by:

$$h_N^t(v) = AGG_k(h_u^{(k-1)}) \tag{1}$$

$h_u^{(k-1)}$ represents the embeddings of node $u, \forall u \in U$, where U is the set of all the sampled neighbouring nodes of the node v and AGG_k represents the aggregator function at the kth layer. This aggregated embedding is then combined with the embedding of the node from the previous layer $h_v^{(k-1)}$ which is then followed by applying the weights of the model and the result is passed through an activation function. The embedding is calculated for the layer k, node v as:

$$h_v^k = \sigma(W^k CONCAT(h_v^{(k-1)}, h_N(v)^k)) \tag{2}$$

where W^k is the weight matrix and σ is the ReLU activation function. This work uses the mean aggregator due to its high performance with least expensive computational power and time complexity.

The RAdam Optimiser with focal loss is used due to its improved performance in cases of class imbalance. RAdam Optimiser is a variant of the Adam Optimiser as it rectifies the issue with variance and generalisation apparent with the Adam optimiser and other adaptive learning optimisers.

2.3   Feature Generation

Feature generation [7] techniques involve processing existing features and information to create more effective features that can help neural networks in their respective tasks. In graph analytics, centrality measures are used to find the degree of importance of a node in a network [15,16]. These measures give meaningful insight into the structural and positional information of a node and hence can be used as node embeddings [7,9]. Another node embedding technique, namely, DeepWalk, [13] has also been implemented and discussed below.

Degree Centrality. The degree centrality [14] of a node is the number of connections or edges it has. The degree of each node can also be assigned the fraction of edges it has compared to the node with the maximum number of connections. This centrality measure uses the intuitive principle that the more connections a node has, the more important it is.

Closeness Centrality. As the name suggests, closeness centrality [9] indicates how close a node is to the remaining nodes in the graph. It is inversely proportional to the sum of the shortest path lengths of the given node from the rest of the nodes in a connected graph. The formula for calculating the closeness centrality is given by,

$$Cx = \frac{1}{\sum_y d(x,y)} \tag{3}$$

Eigenvector Centrality. Eigenvector centrality [7] allows us to measure the transitive influence of the nodes. A higher eigenvector score means that a node is in turn connected to several nodes who are themselves connected to many nodes, or have high scores. It is calculated as follows:

$$x_v = \frac{1}{\lambda} \sum_{t \in M(v)} x_t \tag{4}$$

Here $M(v)$, is a set of the neighbours of node v, λ is a constant and x_v, x_t represent the relative centrality score for the vertex v and t respectively.

PageRank. PageRank [3] is a technique of using the incoming links in a directed graph to generate a ranking structure for the nodes in a graph. Furthermore, it takes into account the centrality or the importance of the nodes from which it receives incoming links. Let $A = (a_{i,j})$ be the adjacency matrix of a directed graph. The PageRank centrality x_i of node i is given by :

$$x_i = \alpha \sum_k \frac{a_{k,i}}{d_k} x_k + \beta \tag{5}$$

where α and β are constants and d_k is the out-degree of node k if such degree is positive, or $d_k = 1$ if the out-degree of k is null.

DeepWalk. DeepWalk [13] is a simple neural network that captures the co-interactions within graphs and encode them into node embeddings which can be used by GNNs to improve their performance. DeepWalk utilizes this for learning latent representations of the nodes in the graph.

These centrality measures are calculated for each node and appended to the list of node features before it is provided as input to GraphSAGE. Once the value for the particular centrality measure is obtained, it is added to the existing list of features. A different approach to incorporating the centrality measures is also implemented in which we consider one subgraph at a time. This subgraph consists of all the edges of a single type, and the centrality measures are calculated for each of these subgraphs. Hence, each node gets K generated features where K is the number of edge types. Here, $K = 100$. These values form a vector of size K which is appended to the list of existing features. This method is hereby referred to as the 100-vector approach.

3   Experiments and Results

This section presents a detailed experimental analysis of the dataset used and the different feature generation techniques implemented and evaluated.

3.1   Dataset

A combination of two datasets [8] is used for evaluating the approach. The first dataset consists of drug information, such as drug ID, drug name, target, enzyme and the structure of chemical species of the drug, known as SMILE (Simplified Molecular Input Line Entry). The second dataset has the mechanism and action between different pairs of drugs. The combination of the mechanism and action indicates the side-effect between the pair of drugs and hence acts as the class label. The data consists of 1258 drugs and 100 interaction event types with a total of 323539 DDI information.

3.2   Experimental Setup

The train-val-test split of the data is 80%, 10% and 10%, respectively. The input features after centrality computation are passed to the GraphSAGE model which consists of one GraphSAGE block with two layers and an additional layer. The mean aggregator function used in all layers. RAdam optimizer is used with a learning rate of 0.01, and the focal loss function is used with a γ value equal to 2. The training was carried on for 700 epochs; however the optimum results were reached at around 400-500 epochs. The evaluation metrics used are Area under ROC curve (AUC), F1 score, precision and recall. The evaluation of the experiments carried out is recorded in Table 1 and the variation of AUC scores with each epoch during training is shown in Fig. 3.

The initial stage of the experiment is carried out with default features available in the dataset (recorded as without feature generation experiment in Table 1). In further stages of the experiment, we incorporated the significant centrality measures such as degree, closeness, eigenvector and PageRank and another embedding technique, DeepWalk, along with its combinations. All these different experiment combinations have been conducted using the standard GraphSAGE model.

The 100-vector approach of incorporating centrality measures has also been implemented. Table 2 shows the results after running K-Fold cross validation on the dataset with $K = 5$.

The results in Table 2 show that degree centrality outperforms all other experiments. A rationale of why degree centrality is so high performing likely comes from how it relays information to the model about the nodes with high degree

Table 1. Evaluation metrics of experiments with and without feature generation techniques

Experiment	AUC	F1 Score	Precision	Recall
Without feature generation	0.9981	0.8772	0.8778	0.8785
Closeness centrality	0.9988	0.9003	0.9006	0.9011
Degree centrality	0.9995	0.9318	0.9320	0.9318
Degree + Closeness	0.9990	0.9090	0.9093	0.9098
Eigenvector Centrality	0.9965	0.8518	0.8531	0.8538
PageRank	0.9990	0.9104	0.9104	0.9109
Combined measures	0.9896	0.5869	0.6905	0.5959
DeepWalk	0.9982	0.8836	0.8839	0.8841
DeepWalk + PageRank	0.9968	0.8522	0.8545	0.8534

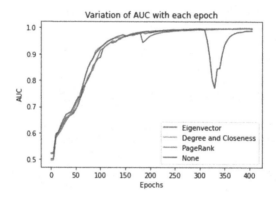

Fig. 3. AUC score variation during training of GraphSAGE model

Table 2. Averaged evaluation metrics of experiments with and without feature generation techniques for 5-fold crossvalidation training

Experiment	AUC	F1 Score	Precision	Recall
Without feature generation	0.9966	0.9077	0.9084	0.9085
Degree	0.9985	0.9162	0.9165	0.9165
Closeness	0.9980	0.8958	0.8962	0.8962
Degree + Closeness	0.9981	0.8817	0.8849	0.8823
PageRank	0.9982	0.8916	0.8942	0.8945
DeepWalk	0.9978	0.9294	0.9294	0.9297
Eigenvector	0.9982	0.8928	0.8935	0.8940

centrality. A high degree centrality of a node (drug) implies that there is a side effect for a wide range of drugs paired with the one in question which implies that a new unseen node in the network also has a strong probability of having a side effect with the high centrality node of that given interaction type (class label). The 100-vector approach provides similar results to that of the regular approach because while it provides more categorical context with respect to the edge type for the classification task, the limitation remains that the final vector is very sparse.

4 Conclusions

Prediction of side effects between medically prescribed drugs is highly critical for safe, effective treatment of patients globally. This study can offer a trustworthy and affordable substitute for clinical trials to forecast harmful side effects while maintaining patient safety. Predictive models with graph convolutional neural networks is an emerging field of interest that has not been intensively studied for drug-drug interactions. Graph centrality measures as new features in the DDI prediction task is one of the novel approach that has been studied here. Our work takes the interaction mechanism of various drugs and information about the enzyme, target and structural information of the drug compound to perform feature generation on this conceptualised graph. It is observed that the centrality measures play a crucial role in network analysis by which important nodes in a network are identified from a structural context. This work looks at closeness, degree, eigenvector and PageRank centrality along with DeepWalk to analyse a drug network where drugs as the nodes are connected based on their side effects. The empirical results show that centrality measures do play a critical role in determining drug-drug interactions. The performance of the proposed model with GraphSAGE has been validated on a subset of the standard Drug-Bank dataset and has achieved improved results for degree centrality measure. This work can provide significant contributions to the field and has a high scope for further research studies. Several improvements can be made on this approach, such as the use of data augmentation techniques and the classification of interaction events based on severity levels. We are currently working on implementing the Graph Attention Network (GAT) and Graph Convolutional Network (GCN) models and creating a comparative analysis to further our study.

References

1. Lin, S., et al.: MDF-SA-DDI: predicting drug-drug interaction events based on multi-source drug fusion, multi-source feature fusion and transformer self-attention mechanism. In: Briefings in Bioinformatics, vol. 23, January 2022. https://doi.org/10.1093/bib/bbab421
2. Rohani, N., Eslahchi, C.: Drug-drug interaction predicting by neural network using integrated similarity. Sci. Rep. **9**, 13645 (2019). https://doi.org/10.1038/s41598-019-50121-3

3. Liu, S., et al.: Enhancing drug-drug interaction prediction using deep attention neural networks. IEEE/ACM Trans. Comput. Biol. Bioinform. **20**, 976–985 (2022). https://doi.org/10.1109/TCBB.2022.3172421

4. Yan, C., Duan, G., Zhang, Y., Wu, F.-X., Pan, Y., Wang, J.: Predicting drug-drug interactions based on integrated similarity and semi-supervised learning. IEEE/ACM Trans. Comput. Biol. Bioinform. **19**(1), 168–179 (2022). https://doi.org/10.1109/TCBB.2020.2988018

5. Acharya, D.B., Zhang, H.: Feature Selection and Extraction for Graph Neural Networks. In: Proceedings of the 2020 ACM Southeast Conference (ACM SE 2020), pp. 252–255 (2019)

6. Nguyen, D.A., Nguyen, C.H., Petschner, P., Mamitsuka, H.: SPARSE: a sparse hypergraph neural network for learning multiple types of latent combinations to accurately predict drug-drug interactions. Bioinformatics. **38**, i333–i341 (2022). https://doi.org/10.1093/bioinformatics/btac250

7. Cui, H., Lu, Z., Li, P., Yang, C.: On positional and structural node features for graph neural networks on non-attributed graphs. In: Proceedings of the 31st ACM International Conference on Information & Knowledge Management, pp. 3898–3902 (2022). https://doi.org/10.1145/3511808.3557661

8. Zhou, J., et al.: Graph neural networks: a review of methods and applications. AI Open. 1, 57–81 (2020). https://doi.org/10.1016/j.aiopen.2021.01.001

9. Kenga, Y.Y., Kwa, K.H., Ratnavelu, K.: Centrality analysis in a drug network and its application to drug repositioning. In: Applied Mathematics and Computation, vol. 395 (2021)

10. Hamilton, W.L., Ying, R., Leskovec, J.: Inductive representation learning on large graphs. In: Proceedings of the 31st International Conference on Neural Information Processing Systems, pp. 1025–1035 (2017)

11. Abbas, K., et al.: Application of network link prediction in drug discovery. BMC Bioinform. **22**, 187 (2021). https://doi.org/10.1186/s12859-021-04082-y

12. Lu, Y., Guo, Y., Korhonen, A.: Link prediction in drug-target interactions network using similarity indices. BMC Bioinform. **18**, 1–9 (2017). https://doi.org/10.1186/s12859-017-1460-z

13. Perozzi, B., Al-Rfou, R., Skiena, S.: DeepWalk: online learning of social representations. In: Proceedings of the 20th ACM SIGKDD International Conference on Knowledge Discovery and Data Mining, pp. 701–710 (2014). https://doi.org/10.1145/2623330.2623732

14. Powell, J., Hopkins, M.: Graph analytics techniques. in A Librarian's Guide to Graphs. Chandos Publishing, Data and the Semantic Web (2015). ch. 19

15. Shetty, R.D., Bhattacharjee, S., Dutta, A., Namtirtha, A.: GSI: an influential node detection approach in heterogeneous net- work using COVID-19 as use case. In: IEEE Transactions on Computational Social Systems, pp. 1–15 (2022). https://doi.org/10.1109/TCSS.2022.3180177

16. Shetty, R.D., Bhattacharjee, S.: Weighted GNN-based betweenness centrality considering stability and connection structure. In: 15th International Conference on Communication Systems & NETworkS (COMSNETS), Bangalore, India, 2023, pp. 304–308 (2023). https://doi.org/10.1109/COMSNETS56262.2023.10041296

Scheduling the Service of Cargo Vessels in a Single Port with Spatial and Temporal Constraints

Loukas Chatzivasili[1]([✉]), Emmanouil S. Rigas[2], and Nick Bassiliades[3]

[1] Department of Computer Science, University of Cyprus, Nicosia, Cyprus
lchatz01@ucy.ac.cy
[2] School of Medicine, Aristotle University of Thessaloniki, Thessaloniki, Greece
erigas@auth.gr
[3] School of Informatics, Aristotle University of Thessaloniki, Thessaloniki, Greece
nbassili@csd.auth.gr

Abstract. Nowadays, a large number of cargo vessels arrive at ports and need to be serviced on a daily basis. This creates a hard to solve problem related to finding the most efficient order to service these vessels. In this context, we study the problem of scheduling the service of cargo vessels arriving at a single port and considering certain spatial and temporal constraints. We propose an optimal scheduling algorithm and two equivalent greedy ones. The optimal algorithm is based on Integer Linear Programming (ILP). The first greedy approach is a First Come First Served (FCFS) heuristic algorithm, meaning that whichever vessel arrives first at the port will be served first. The second greedy algorithm, which we refer to as "Smart" applies a heuristic mechanism, that considers vessels' latest preferred departure time from the port after being serviced and the maximum unloading/loading speed of each dock. Through a detailed evaluation that uses realistic data, we observe that the optimal algorithm outperformed the two greedy ones in terms of the average waiting time, delay, and unloading times of vessels to be serviced, but with a significantly higher execution time.

Keywords: scheduling · heuristic · search · vessel · port management

1 Introduction

From antiquity, the transport of goods and people from one part of the Earth to another was conducted mainly through sea, with various types of vessels. A *vessel* is a broader notion than a *ship* and refers to anything that can float and be moved or guided, either manually or with the help of another person or object.[1] As a normal result of the huge industrial development of the last years, vessels

---

[1] https://www.shippingandfreightresource.com/difference-between-a-ship-and-a-vessel/.

© IFIP International Federation for Information Processing 2023
Published by Springer Nature Switzerland AG 2023
I. Maglogiannis et al. (Eds.): AIAI 2023, IFIP AICT 676, pp. 145–156, 2023.
https://doi.org/10.1007/978-3-031-34107-6_12

in general and more specifically merchant ships are classified into various categories and types based on the construction material, the means of propulsion, the equipment they have, the type of cargo they carry, etc. The most common merchant ship regarding cargo transportation, not people transportation, is cargo ship. A cargo ship can carry all kinds of cargo such as raw materials, operating and maintenance materials of industrial plants, or other marketable products that may be consumed by humans.[2]

Despite the fact that vessels/ships are the number one means of transportation of materials, in contrast to land vehicle scheduling, relatively little work has been done in vessel routing and scheduling. In general, vessel 'scheduling' is mainly related to time windows attached to the calls of the vessels in the ports [11]. Service scheduling of vessels refers to the proper coordination of vessels to or within a port, or multiple ports, in order to achieve the most efficient service concerning time, space, energy and other affected factors. To satisfy and optimize such scheduling problems, it is extremely important to take into account a number of factors and constraints such as the speed of the vessels, the type and size of the vessels' cargo, the size of the port of reference, docks and quay cranes at the port [6], amongst others. Vessel scheduling is important not only to ensure the safe and efficient handling of traffic on busy waterways [12] but also to minimize fuel consumption and the related emissions [10] and bunker consumption from maritime transport [1] in liner shipping with either certain or uncertain port times.

The existing related literature [5] can be divided into three main categories: 1) General ship routing and scheduling problems, 2) Vessel scheduling problems at a port of reference, and 3) "Green" vessel scheduling problems. In the first category, Gatica and Miranda [7] propose a network-based model that includes discrete time windows for picking and delivering cargo. This allows for a broad variety of features and practical constraints to be implicitly included in the model. Whereas, in [2] a heuristic algorithm is used that is based on a variable neighborhood search, considering a number of neighborhood structures to find a solution to the problem. In [9], assuming fixed ship speeds, the problem of maximising profit is addressed. Then, a variable neighborhood search metaheuristic is proposed. In the second category, Golias et al. [8] describe an approach aiming at: (a) increasing berth productivity by cutting down on the total service time and delayed departures for all ships, and (b) cutting down on the total emissions and fuel used by all ships as they travel to their next port of reference. Another common problem is crane scheduling to service vessels arriving in the port of reference while minimizing their aggregate cost of delay [3]. In the third category, Dulebenets [4] presents a non-linear mathematical model which directly accounts for the carbon dioxide (CO_2) emission costs in the sea and at ports of call. In a similar study [10], an optimal vessel schedule in the liner shipping route is designed to minimize fuel consumption and emissions considering uncertain port times and frequency requirements.

---

[2] https://www.marineinsight.com/types-of-ships/what-are-cargo-ships/.

This work aims to present a simplified version of the problem of service scheduling of cargo vessels in a port taking into account the following factors: (a) number of vessels arriving to a port of reference, (b) number of docks of the port, (c) attributes of vessels (e.g., average sailing speed, cargo volume etc.) (d) port's elements (e.g. number of docks and average unload speed of their cranes). More specifically, the problem aims to figure out the proper order of service of various cargo vessels in a specific port to which they arrive in order to be serviced as quickly as possible and to reduce possible delays. The problem is solved using an optimal approach and two greedy heuristic algorithms, influenced by the algorithms of the related literature.

2   Problem Definition

This paper considers the problem of several cargo vessels arriving at a single port that need to be serviced. The port can serve at the same time as many vessels as the docks it has, assuming that each vessel can be assigned to a maximum of one dock. Also, two or more vessels can arrive at the port at exactly the same time and expect to be serviced as soon as possible. The goal is to service all vessels arriving at a port in a certain period of time as quickly as possible and reduce possible delays observed in relation to the service of ships in a port (i.e.,their waiting time outside the port if there is no dock available in the port to enter it). Towards this, some spatial and temporal constraints (e.g., length, cargo, sailing speed) concerning the vessels and the port are taken into account.

More specifically, we denote the set of cargo vessels $\alpha \in A \subseteq \mathbb{N}$ and the port of reference p, which has a number of docks $d \in D \subseteq \mathbb{N}$ each one equipped with a crane, for unloading cargo from ships/vessels. Moreover, we assume a set of discrete time points $t \in T \subseteq \mathbb{N}$ to exist. Every vessel α has its length $l_\alpha \subseteq \mathbb{R}$, its volume of carried cargo $U_a \subseteq \mathbb{R}$ and two types of velocity. One is the average velocity of the vessel α, $V_a^{aver} \subseteq \mathbb{R}$ and the other is the velocity of the vessel α at a specific time point, $V_{\alpha,t} \subseteq \mathbb{R}$. As already mentioned, the port of reference has a number of docks $d \in D \subseteq \mathbb{N}$ and each one of them has a length $\mu_d \subseteq \mathbb{R}$ and an unloading speed $s_d \subseteq \mathbb{R}$ concerning its crane.

On the same date and time t all vessels start from a different initial position to reach the port of reference. Depending on its velocity (i.e., we assume each ship to travel with a fixed average velocity) and its initial position, a vessel α arrives at the port at a specific time point $t_\alpha^{arr} \subseteq \mathbb{T}$, departs from the port at another specific time point $t_\alpha^{dep} > t_\alpha^{arr} \subseteq \mathbb{T}$ and has a latest departure time $t_\alpha^{latest} \geq t_\alpha^{dep} > t_\alpha^{arr} \subseteq \mathbb{T}$ after its cargo has been unloaded at a dock d_i of the port. Given the vessels' and the port of reference constraints, the port applies a scheduling algorithm to decide the sequence that the vessels should be serviced. In cases where it is not possible for all vessels to be served in time, the algorithm finds a solution that satisfies as many vessels as possible. For better specification of the problem, a set of restrictions has been determined:

1. A vessel α enters a dock d of the port of reference p only if the dock is *available* and its length l_α is less than or equal to the length of the dock μ_d that is trying to enter ($l_\alpha \leq \mu_d$).

2. In case of a vessel α arrives at a port p and cannot enter one of its docks d, as assumption 1 is not satisfied, then waits outside the port until both of the aforementioned constraints apply.
3. A vessel α enters a port p, is serviced and departs from this port until a deadline called latest departure time t_α^{latest}.

3   Proposed Scheduling Algorithms

To solve the proposed problem of scheduling cargo vessels in a single port, an optimal and two greedy heuristic approaches are developed, all of the three being offline algorithms meaning the requests of the vessels are known in advance. All three approaches take into account spatial and temporal constraints and are aiming to serve all vessels arriving at a port of reference while minimizing delays. In the case that a vessel arrives at a port but there is no free dock to enter, it is forced to wait outside the port for some time (wait time). Also, if a vessel's real departure time from the port (after its cargo has been unloaded) exceeds its latest allowed departure time (deadline), a delay occurs.

3.1   Optimal Algorithm

In this section, we present a centralized, static, optimal Mixed Integer Programming (MIP) formulation of the problem, which is used for benchmarking purposes, using CPLEX component libraries[3]. More specifically, in this work, we used the Python programming language and corresponding CPLEX's libraries for Python to implement the optimal algorithm for our problem. The aim of this formulation is to find the optimal order of service for the vessels so as to maximize the number of vessels serviced and minimize delays regarding vessels' departures from the port of reference after being serviced. The formulation contains two binary decision variables: 1) decision variable $\epsilon_{\alpha,d} \in \{0,1\}$ denoting whether a vessel α is serviced at the dock d and 2) $\delta_{\alpha,d,t} \in \{0,1\}$ denoting whether a vessel α is at dock d at time point t. Thus, the following objective function is used under a number of constraints:

Objective Function:

$$\text{Maximize} \left(\sum_{\alpha \in A} \sum_{d \in D} \epsilon_{\alpha,d} - 0.000001 \times \sum_{\alpha \in A} \sum_{d \in D} \sum_{t \in T} (\delta_{\alpha,d,t} \times t) \right) \quad (1)$$

The first part of the function is a double-sum that represents the number of vessels that are serviced at a dock of the port of reference (ideally all vessels arriving to the port). The second part of the function is a triple-sum that stands for the service time of a vessel at the port aiming at minimizing this time. The set of discrete time points T is equal to the difference of the latest t_{latest} of all vessels and the common starting date and time of all vessels' towards the port

---

[3] https://www.ibm.com/docs/en/icos/20.1.0?topic=mc-what-is-cplex.

of reference. Notice that, we multiply the second part of the function by a very small number so that it never becomes greater than the first part and results in a negative number.

Constraints:

$$\forall \alpha \sum_{d \in D} \epsilon_{\alpha,d} \leq 1 \tag{2}$$

$$\forall \alpha \forall d \sum_{t_{\alpha}^{arr} \leq t_{\alpha} \leq t_{\alpha}^{latest}} \delta_{\alpha,d,t} = [\ (\ u_{\alpha}/s_d)] \times \epsilon_{\alpha,d} \tag{3}$$

$$\forall \alpha \forall d \sum_{t=1}^{T} |\delta_{\alpha,d,t+1} - \delta_{\alpha,d,t}| = 2 \times \epsilon_{\alpha,d} \tag{4}$$

$$\forall \alpha \forall d \epsilon_{\alpha,d} \leq [\ \mu_{\delta}/l_{\alpha}] \tag{5}$$

$$\forall d \forall t \sum_{a=1}^{A} \delta_{\alpha,d,t} \leq 1 \tag{6}$$

In more detail, every vessel can be assigned to a maximum of one dock of a port of reference (constraint 2) and stays at this dock as long time as it takes the dock's crane to unload its cargo (constraint 3). Also, a vessel remains at a dock for consecutive discrete time points (constraint 4) and a vessel is able to enter a dock and be serviced only when its length l_{α} is less than or equal to the length of the dock μ_d that is trying to enter (constraint 5). Lastly, if a dock is already occupied by a vessel, then no more vessels can enter it (constraint 6). In simple words, a dock can only service one vessel at a time. These constraints also hold in the heuristic algorithms that are presented below.

3.2 FCFS Heuristic Algorithm

In this case, vessels are serviced by the order they arrive at the port of reference, which means that whichever vessel arrives first at the port will be also served first (First Come First Served). Initially, the distance between each vessel and the port of reference is calculated according to the Euclidean distance between two points in the Euclidean space. According to the average velocity of each vessel, the travel time for each one to arrive from an initial starting location to the port of reference is estimated. Given that all vessels start their voyage towards the port at a specific time point (date-time) and having calculated the travel time for each vessel, it is now easy to find the arrival times of vessels. Up to this point the same procedure is followed in the "Smart" heuristic algorithm that is described next. Based on the order in which vessels arrive at the port along with random selection of dock, each vessel enters a specific dock where its cargo is unloaded by a dock crane. As soon as this procedure is completed, the vessel departs from the port of reference.

3.3 "Smart" Heuristic Algorithm

To solve the problem more effectively, another heuristic algorithm (see Algorithm 1) was developed to maximize the number of serviced vessels and at the same time minimize possible delays. In relation to the previous case (Sect. 3.2) the latest departure time and the selection of the best possible dock for the service of each vessel are additionally taken into account. As mentioned before, up to a point the procedure is the same as in the FCFS heuristic with only some minor changes. This time, vessels are firstly sorted by the order they arrive at the port and secondly by their latest departure time. In cases where two or more vessels arrive at the port of destination at exactly the same time, then priority is given to the vessel that has the soonest latest departure time in order to minimize possible delays. Towards this goal, the proposed algorithm selects the quicker dock in terms of its unloading speed in case restrictions 1 and 2 (Sect. 2) apply to more than one dock for a vessel. If there is only one dock that meets restrictions 1 and 2 for a vessel, then it is automatically chosen.

4   Evaluation

In this section, we evaluate all three algorithms on different sets of vessels and a different number of the ports' docks, to determine their ability to maximize the number of serviced vessels and minimize delays. We examine the average waiting time of all vessels outside the port, the average delay time of vessels according to their latest departure time from the port, and the average unload time of vessels' cargo at the assigned dock. Regarding the time window the algorithms are running, this is set in a range starting from the moment the first vessel arrives at the port until the time corresponding to the latest deadline of all vessels. To this end, we use realistic datasets for vessels retrieved from MarineTraffic[4]. Due to the fact that the complexity of the Optimal algorithm grows exponentially, we divide our experiments into two categories. The first two, include all three algorithms and use small vessels' datasets, while the third uses only the heuristic approaches but larger datasets.

4.1   Algorithms' Performance Evaluation

Experiment 1 (10 Docks, 10 Vessels). The first experiment considers a port having 10 docks and 10 vessels. The fact that the number of port's docks is equal to the number of vessels arriving at the port, means that in the extreme case that all vessels arrive at the port at exactly the same time there will be an available dock for each vessel. The initial date and time of the problem are set to be: date 2022-01-01 and time 00:00:00. The latest departure dates and times (deadlines) of the vessels from the port are set to be until the end of the first ten days of the year, which is: date 2022-01-10 and time 23:59:59. The following Fig. 1 presents the results obtained using all three examined algorithms to calculate

---

[4]   https://www.marinetraffic.com/.

Algorithm 1. "Smart" Heuristic Algorithm

Require: p, A, t_α^{latest} (for each $\alpha \in A$), t
1: Create Lists: , $delays$, $waitTimes$
2: Create Dictionaries: $entryDates, travelTimes, unloadingTimes, assignedVessels$
3: **for** each $\alpha \in A$ **do**
4:     Calculate $travel_{time}$ using distance between α, p and V_α^{aver}
5:     Add $travel_{time}$ and (t_α^{latest}) to $travelTimes$
6: Sort $travelTimes$ ▷ By: 1) Min($travel_{time}$), 2) Min(t_α^{latest})
7: **for** each $\alpha \in A$ **do**
8:     Calculate t_α^{arr}
9: **while** $[size(unloadTimes) = \emptyset]$ or $[size(unloadTimes) \leq size(A)]$ **do**
10:     **for** each $\alpha \in A$ **do**
11:         **if** $unloadTimes(\alpha) \neq \emptyset$ **then**
12:             Calculate t_α^{dep}
13:             **if** $t_\alpha^{dep} = t$ **then**
14:                 Find $wait_{time}(\alpha)$ and add to $waitTimes$
15:                 Find $delay(\alpha)$ and add to $delays$
16:                 Set d assigned to α to "available"
17:         **if** ($t_\alpha^{arr} \leq t$) and (α not in ($assignedVessels$) **then**
18:             **for** each $d \in D$ **do**
19:                 **if** ($\mu_d \geq l_\alpha$) and (d is "available") **then**
20:                     Calculate $unload_{time}$
21:             Select min_d ▷ Criteria: s_d
22:             $min_{time} = unload_{time}(min_d)$
23:             **if** $min_{time} \neq \emptyset$ **then**
24:                 Set d to "Not available"
25:                 Add min_{time} to $unloadingTimes$
26:                 Add t to $entryDates$
27:                 Assign α to min_d
28:                 Set min_d to $\emptyset$
29:                 Set min_{time} to $\emptyset$
30:     Go to the next time point, t_{++}
31:     **if** (each $d \in D$ is "available") and ($size(assignedVessels) = size(A)$) **then**
32:         $break$
    return $waitTimes, delays, unloadTimes$

---

the average wait time, the average delay time and the average unload time of all serviced vessels at the port of reference. The y-axis of the figure is in the form hours:minutes:seconds. According to Fig. 1, both average wait time and average delay time are minimal for all three methods. Regarding average unload time we observe a reduction of about 50 min or 27.78% from FCFS heuristic to "Smart" heuristic and about another 50 min reduction or a percentage of 37.78% from "Smart" heuristic to Optimal algorithm.

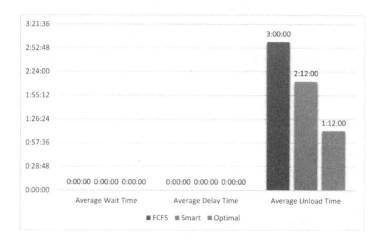

Fig. 1. Average Wait, Delay and Unload Time for Experiment 1

Experiment 2 (10 Docks, 20 Vessels). The second experiment also considers a port having the same 10 docks as in experiment 1, but this time 20 vessels instead of 10 (experiment 1) arrive at the port. Note that based on the data of the vessels and that of the port, some of the vessels will arrive at the port at exactly the same date-time. Also, it is worth mentioning that the number of docks of the port are fewer than the total number of vessels arriving at the port which means that not all vessels will be able to be served at the port at exactly the same time. The starting date and time of the vessels from the port have not changed compared to the first experiment. Figure 2 presents the results obtained for all three algorithms. In this experiment, we observe that

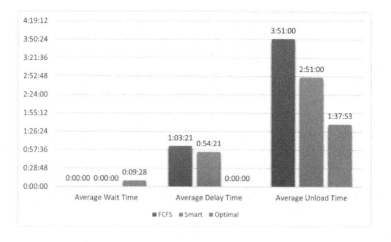

Fig. 2. Average Wait, Delay and Unload Time for Experiment 2

the Optimal algorithm manages to eliminate the average delay time and reduces the average unload time by about 1 and 2 h compared to the FCFS and the "Smart" heuristics respectively. However, the Optimal's average wait time has increased from zero to almost 10 min in relation to the other two algorithms. This occurs because the heuristic algorithms do not examine future arrivals and when a vessel arrives they serve it immediately in most cases. Whereas, the Optimal takes into account all future arrivals, and considers how to minimize all criteria in total, so it may let some vessels wait for some time outside the port in order to maximize the other criteria in the set of requests. Thus we can state that the Optimal algorithm is the best option among the three algorithms.

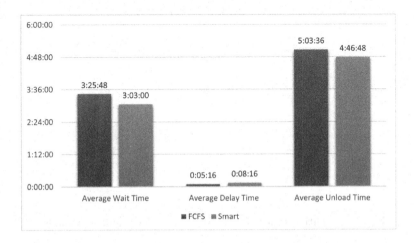

Fig. 3. Average Wait, Delay and Unload Time for Experiment 3

Experiment 3 (20 Docks, 100 Vessels). This final experiment considers 20 docks and 100 vessels and is conducted only for FCFS and "Smart" heuristics. Optimal algorithm is not used because of its high complexity due to the high number of vessels leading to an exponentially increase of the execution time. Similarly to the previous experiments, some of the vessels will arrive at the port at exactly the same date and time (two-two, three-three, etc.). The vessels' data used in this experiment are exactly the same as these of experiment 2. The number of docks at the port is smaller than the total number of vessels arriving at the port, at a ratio of 1 dock to 5 vessels. Again that means that not all vessels will be able to be served at the port at the same time, but this time more vessels arrive simultaneously at the port than in the second experiment. The starting date and time of the vessels from the port have also not changed. Average wait time and average unload time using "Smart" heuristic are lower compared to the FCFS heuristic algorithm (Fig. 3). In contrast, regarding the average delay time we can observe that FCFS is the one with the lower time result. Such a case may occur because "Smart" heuristic algorithm takes into account two different criteria (soonest deadline and quicker dock's crane in terms of unload speed) in the case where two or more vessels arrive at the port at exactly the same time. However, overall the "Smart" heuristic algorithm reduces average wait time by about 10.73% (i.e., 22 min) and average unload time by 5.61% (i.e., 17 min), whereas it is only three minutes lower regarding delay time compared to the FCFS heuristic algorithm. Considering all these findings, it is undeniable that this time the "Smart" heuristic is the best possible option.

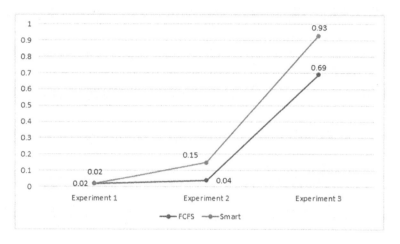

Fig. 4. Execution times of the 2 Heuristic Algorithms in seconds

4.2   Execution Times

Figures 4 and 5 summarize the execution times (E.T), in seconds, of each algorithm for each experiment presented above. Regarding the first experiment, it is clear that the two heuristic procedures solve the problem in just a few fractions of a second, whereas the optimal needs 85 s or 1.5 min to do so. In fact, its execution time is thousand times longer even though it is the most efficient. In the second experiment, again the Optimal algorithm needs a lot more time than the others, especially since the number of vessels has increased and the possible solutions to examine are multiplying. Finally, in the last experiment, the execution time of FCFS heuristic is about 88% smaller than the "Smart" heuristic but still, both execution times are short (under 1 s). Another essential observation is that the execution time of the two heuristic approaches is increasing slightly, while we increase the number of vessels. On the other hand, the execution time of the Optimal algorithm is increasing rapidly, because there are numerous combinations of vessels and docks for the algorithm to consider (to find the optimal solution). Consequently, when we tried to run this algorithm on the data of the third experiment, it was unable to terminate in a reasonable amount of time. In such cases, the "Smart" heuristic algorithm is a very quick and effective way to solve the proposed scheduling problem.

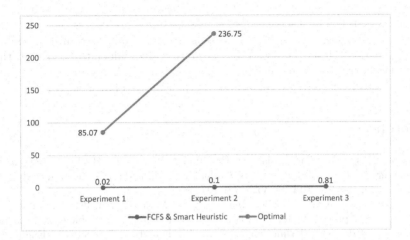

Fig. 5. Execution times of Optimal's and Heuristics' Algorithms in seconds

5   Conclusions and Future Work

The aim of this work was to study the problem of scheduling the service of cargo vessels in a port taking into account spatial and temporal constraints. Toward this goal, two greedy scheduling algorithms and an optimal algorithm were implemented. The first approach is a First Come First Served (FCFS) heuristic algorithm that takes into account only the order in which vessels arrive at the port of reference and assigns a vessel to a random dock of the port for service. The second approach is a so-called "Smart" heuristic algorithm that takes into account not only the order in which they arrive at the port but also the deadline of departure for each ship and chooses the quicker dock in terms of cargo unloading. Last but not least, the optimal algorithm implemented, solves this scheduling problem as a MIP problem and finds the optimal solution. Through an empirical evaluation, we conclude that even though all three algorithms managed to serve all the vessels arriving at the port of reference, the Optimal algorithm fully dominates the heuristic approaches. However its execution time increases rapidly as the number of vessels and docks examined increases, so on large datasets it is not feasible to execute it in a reasonable amount of time. In such cases, "Smart" heuristic algorithm usually leads to considerably better results than the simple FCFS heuristic. However, the factors and constraints considered by the "Smart" algorithm may sometimes not be enough to get good results for all the variables under consideration, although it is still possible to serve all vessels. The latter reveals that there is clearly room for improvement in this algorithm.

Various extensions could be considered as future work of this study: 1) The "Smart" heuristic algorithm that was developed could take into account more factors and constraints such as energy constraints related to vessels and their fuels, but also environmental constraints related to the "Green" scheduling problem, most notably carbon dioxide (CO_2) emissions [8,10]. 2) Another limitation that could be taken into account for vessel scheduling problem is the costs (operating, maintenance, etc. cost) that vessels will have until arriving at the port of reference as well as the cost that the port will shoulder to service all these vessels that arrive at it in a certain period of time. 3) Apply mechanism design techniques to incentivize vessels to report their desired latest departure time.

References

1. Brouer, B.D., Dirksen, J., Pisinger, D., Plum, C.E., Vaaben, B.: The vessel schedule recovery problem (VSRP) - a MIP model for handling disruptions in liner shipping. Eur. J. Oper. Res. **224**(2), 362–374 (2013)
2. Castillo-Villar, K.K., González-Ramírez, R.G., Miranda González, P., Smith, N.R.: A heuristic procedure for a ship routing and scheduling problem with variable speed and discretized time windows. In: Mathematical Problems in Engineering 2014 (2014)
3. Daganzo, C.F.: The crane scheduling problem. Transp. Res. Part B: Methodol. **23**(3), 159–175 (1989)
4. Dulebenets, M.A.: Green vessel scheduling in liner shipping: modeling carbon dioxide emission costs in sea and at ports of call. Int. J. Transp. Sci. Technol. **7**(1), 26–44 (2018)
5. Dulebenets, M.A., Pasha, J., Abioye, O.F., Kavoosi, M.: Vessel scheduling in liner shipping: a critical literature review and future research needs. Flex. Serv. Manuf. J. **33**(1), 43–106 (2021)
6. Fu, Y.M., Diabat, A., Tsai, I.T.: A multi-vessel quay crane assignment and scheduling problem: formulation and heuristic solution approach. Expert Syst. Appl. **41**(15), 6959–6965 (2014)
7. Gatica, R.A., Miranda, P.A.: Special issue on Latin-American research: a time based discretization approach for ship routing and scheduling with variable speed. Netw. Spat. Econ. **11**(3), 465–485 (2011)
8. Golias, M., Boile, M., Theofanis, S., Efstathiou, C.: The berth-scheduling problem: Maximizing berth productivity and minimizing fuel consumption and emissions production. Transp. Res. Rec. **2166**(1), 20–27 (2010)
9. Malliappi, F., Bennell, J.A., Potts, C.N.: A variable neighborhood search heuristic for tramp ship scheduling. In: Böse, J.W., Hu, H., Jahn, C., Shi, X., Stahlbock, R., Voß, S. (eds.) ICCL 2011. LNCS, vol. 6971, pp. 273–285. Springer, Heidelberg (2011). https://doi.org/10.1007/978-3-642-24264-9_21
10. Qi, X., Song, D.P.: Minimizing fuel emissions by optimizing vessel schedules in liner shipping with uncertain port times. Transp. Res. Part E: Logist. Transp. Rev. **48**(4), 863–880 (2012)
11. Ronen, D.: Cargo ships routing and scheduling: Survey of models and problems. Eur. J. Oper. Res. **12**(2), 119–126 (1983)
12. Sluiman, F.: Transit vessel scheduling. Naval Res. Logist. (NRL) **64**(3), 225–248 (2017)

IoT/Fuzzy Modeling/Augmented Reality

Improving Supply Chain Management by Integrating RFID with IoT Shared Database: Proposing a System Architecture

Elena Puica[✉]

Economic Informatics Doctoral School, The Bucharest University of Economic Studies,
Bucharest, Romania
elenaa.puica@gmail.com

Abstract. This scientific research paper proposes a system architecture for integrating Internet of Things (IoT) shared database and Radio Frequency Identification (RFID) in supply chain management (SCM) with self-transactional materials. The architecture aims to improve inventory management, data transparency, resource utilization, and business insight by facilitating efficient information exchange between different layers of the supply chain. The use of self-transactional materials enables automated and seamless execution of transactions, eliminating human errors and delays in the supply chain processes. Furthermore, the IoT and RFID technologies enable real-time monitoring and tracking of inventory, improving accuracy and efficiency in SCM. The results suggest that the proposed architecture has the potential to significantly improve SCM performance. The feasibility and cost-effectiveness of implementing self-transactional materials in the supply chain should also be assessed to determine practicality. Overall, the proposed architecture represents an innovative and promising approach to improving SCM in the modern business landscape.

Keywords: RFID in Supply Chain Management · RFID-IoT in Supply Chain Management · Sel-Transactional Materials

1 Introduction

The increasing complexity and dynamic nature of Supply Chain Management (SCM) has created a need for more efficient and effective solutions. Radio frequency identification (RFID) and the Internet of Things (IoT) are expected to play a significant role in fulfilling customer requirements in the supply chain. The integration of RFID with IoT (RFID-IoT) aims to develop automated sensing, seamless, interoperable and highly secure systems by connecting IoT devices through the internet. The main benefits of RFID are optimizing resources, quality customer service, improved accuracy, and efficient business and healthcare procedures. RFID-IoT offers a new operating solution in the supply chain by focusing on manufacturing, retail shops, inventory, transportation, assembly, asset tracking, location, and even environmental detection. The evolution of

© IFIP International Federation for Information Processing 2023
Published by Springer Nature Switzerland AG 2023
I. Maglogiannis et al. (Eds.): AIAI 2023, IFIP AICT 676, pp. 159–170, 2023.
https://doi.org/10.1007/978-3-031-34107-6_13

RFID-IoT will bring a significant impact to the revolution of SCM [1, 2, 3]. With the ubiquitous interconnectivity offered by RFID-IoT technologies, each stage in SCM can be interconnected to ensure correct processes and products are delivered at the right time, at the right quantity, to the right places. The advent of cloud computing (CC) and IoT adds the relevant information and events capture issue, transfer, storage, processing and sharing. Additionally, for better collaboration and interoperability enhancement in the supply chain, it is interesting to notify automatically each event related to logistic flows to involved actors. RFID technology is one of the key technologies to realize the IoT [4], consisting of tags, readers, and back-end computer systems. The two types of tags, active and passive, have different power sources and transmission distances. The adoption of RFID-IoT technologies improves operational processes and reduces costs, providing information transparency, product traceability, compatibility, scalability, and flexibility in SCM.

Supply chain management has long been plagued by difficulties in identifying, tracing, and tracking goods due to the variety of platforms and technologies used by different actors in the chain. However, the emergence of IoT and cloud computing offers a new approach, enabling better cooperation and interoperability between supply chain partners through the collection, transfer, storage, and sharing of logistics flow information. This issue encompasses the tracking and tracing of goods, data sharing and processing with access and authorization control, management of interactions between actors, and the need for a common policy and communication protocol. Existing platforms have failed to address key challenges such as collecting data directly from sensors on goods for real-time processing, managing interoperability between heterogeneous IT infrastructures, and making information available from mobile devices.

RFID technology offers a wireless communication system for sensing, detecting, identifying, tracking, and monitoring multiple objects, making it an appealing solution for numerous applicative scenarios in SCM [5]. Different types of RFID sensors are proposed, ranging from electronic sensors integrated into the tag to electromagnetic sensors that modify the tag response for sensing. RFID is now a standardized technology, offering decisive practical benefits such as unitary identification, wireless communication, and low cost of tags, driving new developments in concepts and applications [6].

The scientific study aims to propose a system architecture for integrating IoT shared database and RFID with Self-Transactional Materials in SCM. The study begins with an introduction that provides an overview of RFID in SCM, followed by a discussion of the potential benefits of integrating IoT shared database and RFID. The proposed system architecture is evaluated using a case study approach. The results section presents the findings of the study, which demonstrate that the proposed system architecture has the potential to significantly improve supply chain management performance. The architecture facilitates efficient information exchange between different layers of the supply chain and enables real-time monitoring and tracking of inventory. Furthermore, the use of self-transactional materials in the architecture enables the automated and seamless execution of transactions, which eliminates human errors and delays in the supply chain processes. The study concludes by recommending further research and testing to validate the effectiveness of the proposed architecture in real-world scenarios.

2 Radio Frequency Identification (RFID) in Supply Chain Management

Radio Frequency Identification (RFID) is a wireless communication technology that enables automatic identification tasks by using electronic devices with wireless communication capabilities. RFID systems typically consist of one or more readers and multiple RFID tags. During operation, the reader sends requests to the tags, which are affixed to objects. In response, the tags transmit a message containing their unique ID. RFID technology enables data capture that can be associated with various identification attributes such as serial number, position, color, date of purchase, and more. This Automatic Identification and Data Capture (Auto-ID) technology is capable of providing greater granularity in labeling compared to previous Auto-ID technologies, such as barcodes. RFID technology is based on the exchange of electromagnetic waves between RFID tags and readers, and it requires no manual intervention for identification tasks. The technology is highly versatile and can work in a variety of harsh environments. Additionally, RFID technology has relatively low costs and maintenance requirements, making it highly suitable for integration into Supply Chain Management (SCM) systems. By embedding RFID sensors directly into products, it is possible to generate smart objects that can interact with their environment throughout their entire lifecycle, from manufacturing and testing to use and disposal. RFID technology is similar to barcode technology in that it requires specialized tags and reader equipment to monitor objects, but RFID offers the added benefit of wireless identification. Common components of an RFID system include tags, transponders, tag readers, antennas, and interfaces. The versatility and flexibility of RFID technology make it suitable for a wide range of applications, including RFID printers, RFID scanners, RFID readers, and RFID antennas. The three basic components of RFID, are:

1. RFID tag, that is attached to an asset or item. The tag contains information about that asset or item and also may incorporate sensors, embeds specific information of the item on which it is attached.
2. RFID interrogator/reader, which communicates with (also called interrogating) the RFID tags. The reader empowers the tag and reads the information stored within it and a data base that processes the information and performs the global RFID application.
3. The backend system, which links the RFID interrogators to a centralized database. The centralized database contains additional information, such as price, for each RFID tagged item.

In a typical RFID system, an object is equipped with a small, inexpensive tag that contains a digital memory chip with a unique electronic product code. The interrogator, consisting of an antenna packaged with a transceiver and decoder, emits a signal that activates the RFID tag and allows data to be read and written to it. When the RFID tag passes through the electromagnetic zone, it detects the reader's activation signal. The reader then decodes the data encoded in the tag's integrated circuit and passes the data to the host computer, where it is processed by application software.

RFID middleware is used to bridge RFID hardware systems to higher-level enterprise systems, enabling user access, control interface, interaction with enterprise databases and servers, and filtering, aggregation, and routing of captured tag data. The success of

RFID integration in a process is directly related to the associated middleware's features and performance, including user interfaces, security and authentication protocols, and upgradability.

RFID technologies can be classified into three categories:

1. **Passive RFID**: A passive RFID tag is powered by the electromagnetic energy, radiated from RFID reader antennas, based on backscattering. A passive tag can't transmit radio waves of its own, and its information storage capacity and computing capability are limited. It can be read only at short range (0.6 to 3 m). Based on the radio frequency used, the passive RFID technologies are usually categorized into low frequency (LF) RFID, high frequency (HF) RFID, ultra-high frequency (UHF) RFID, and microwave RFID.
2. **Active RFID**: An active tag is powered by an on-board long-life battery that provides sufficient energy to allow independent communication capability within greater range (approximately 90 m). To establish communication between RFID tags and readers, antennas are required. Active tags are fed by batteries, and are able to send data without solicitation from a reader. The active tag typically offers longer reading ranges with a limited lifespan than the passive tag with its built-in power source. The active tag works to track the object by providing real-time data continuously.
3. **Semi-passive RFID**: The semi-active tag uses a hybrid mechanism: self-powered, it is activated at the request of the tag reader, allowing lower power consumption than active tags. The reading distance of RFID chips range from a few centimeters to a few meters (10 m), and can go beyond (200 m) with long range communication technologies.

3 Internet of Things (IoT) Shared Database and Radio Frequency Identification (RFID) in Supply Chain Management

IoT represents a technological advancement in the field of computer and communication that enables the connection of physical objects via the Internet. This connection creates an interwoven web of information and events that can be utilized to facilitate object tracking, management, control, and coordination. One of the key challenges associated with IoT is the integration of diverse technologies and concerns [7]. A network structure that supports heterogeneity, scalability, energy optimization, cost minimization, self-organization, self-adaptation, self-reaction, privacy, security, and quality of service is essential for the realization of this paradigm [8]. RFID technology has been instrumental in inspiring the IoT paradigm, by enabling the integration of physical objects into an informative network. Through IoT, RFID and sensor network technologies can be used to monitor the location, status, movement, and process of objects, thereby enhancing remote access and facilitating decision-making [9]. The interaction and communication among objects and machines enable them to respond autonomously and solve complex problems intelligently. The IoT system comprises of five layers [10]: perception, network, middleware, application, and business layers. This five-layered architecture provides a framework for integrating RFID-IoT with business or management models.

The details of each layer are explained as follows:

- **Perception layer**: Collect and identify information from various IoT devices such as RFID tags that stick on the product and other IoT sensors such as temperature, optical sensors, proximity sensors, accelerometers, and gyroscopes to indicate the product environment.
- **Network layer**: Transmits information generated by IoT sensors into the server by utilizing a Wi-Fi network.
- **Middleware layer**: Ingest, process and store data generated from the network layer according to the data format types.
- **Application layer**: Analyze and visualize the collected data in SCM systems.
- **Business layer**: Understand the data and change the business or management model according to the trend.

RFID technology integrated with the IoT enables the automatic identification of objects, equipment, workers, and stock in SCM through the capture of real-time data. RFID-IoT can detect events, such as the start or finish of a process, using signal arrival and departure from the RFID-IoT covered area. IoT facilitates communication and interaction among different devices through the internet and equips objects with data collection and analysis automation, enabling real-world events to be reacted to, and predictions and decisions to be made without human intervention. This technology provides an opportunity to solve multifaceted problems requiring sophisticated analysis and rapid response in a ubiquitous computing environment, leading to improvements in inventory management, data transparency, resource utilization, and business insight. Combining RFID and other IoT technologies facilitates tracking the product from the manufacturer to the retailer, mitigating time and production costs, enhancing brand protection, quality assurance, and customized client preferences. The integration of different technologies, including RFID, allows for real-time data collection, while RFID tracks and identifies products. IoT optimizes SCM, making the supply chain management visible, effective, and agile through real-time management and complete integration, affecting the manufacturing, warehousing, transportation, and selling links of the supply chain.

As the network expands and becomes less expensive, more devices can be connected to transmit data. However, some devices may not have network connectivity or may not be configured to the network. In such cases, the new technology behind RFID acts as a mechanism for transmitting information, ensuring that up-to-date information is gathered and deployment times are streamlined. Transmitting small amounts of data is not particularly powerful on its own, but RFID offers low-cost and low-power capabilities, enabling devices to invoke data without substantially adding to the device's cost. Additionally, transmitting data can be performed even when the device is off, as RFID can be self-powered.

4 Proposing a System Architecture for Integrating Internet of Things (IoT) Shared Database and Radio Frequency Identification (RFID) in Supply Chain Management

Proposing a System Architecture for integrating Internet of Things (IoT) Shared Database and Radio Frequency Identification (RFID) in Supply Chain Management with five layered architecture that consists of the perception layer, network layer, middleware layer, application layer, and business layer. The purpose is to provides a friendly environment to improve inventory management, data transparency, resource utilization and business insight.

4.1 Problem Faced by Inventory Management

The problem faced by Inventory Management is the inability to handle heavy workloads and constant demand for product diversity. In addition, traditional inventory management systems rely on manual input, which can lead to errors, delays, and discrepancies in inventory records. As a result, it can be difficult to keep track of inventory levels and to know when to reorder or restock items. This can result in stockouts, overstocking, and decreased customer satisfaction. Furthermore, lack of visibility and transparency of inventory data within the supply chain can make it difficult to identify and address issues quickly, leading to inefficiencies and increased costs, all of which can impact the bottom line of a business.

4.2 The Proposed RFID System in Inventory Management, Integration with "Self-Transactional Materials"

RFID technology provides a solution to the challenges faced by traditional inventory management systems. RFID tags can be attached to inventory items, and RFID readers can collect data about the location, status, and movement of these items in real-time. This data can be transmitted wirelessly to a central database, where it can be processed, stored, and analyzed. The proposed system consists of the following components (see Fig. 1):

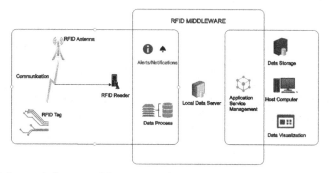

Fig. 1. RFID System in Inventory Management, integration with "Self-Transactional Materials".

RFID Tags: Each inventory item would be tagged with an RFID tag that contains a unique identifier and other relevant information, such as the product name, description, and quantity.

Self-transactional Materials: Self-transactional materials would be used to track inventory. These materials are composed of thin, flexible substrates that contain antennas and microchips, allowing them to communicate with RFID readers.

RFID readers: RFID readers would be placed throughout the inventory management system, including at entry and exit points, on conveyor belts, and in storage areas. The readers would capture the information stored in the self-transactional materials as the items move through the system.

Middleware: The RFID readers would be connected to middleware software, which would collect and process the data captured by the readers. The middleware would also filter and analyze the data, and provide alerts or notifications when necessary.

Database: The RFID system would be integrated with a database that would store the inventory data, including the unique identifier and other relevant information about the product. The database would also provide real-time inventory updates and allow users to search and retrieve inventory data.

Cloud Computing: The inventory database would be stored in the cloud, allowing authorized users to access the data from anywhere and at any time. This would enable remote inventory management and provide greater flexibility and scalability for the system.

Mobile Devices: Authorized users would be able to access the inventory data using mobile devices, such as smartphones and tablets. This would allow them to view inventory data in real-time and make informed decisions about inventory management.

Analytics: The RFID system could be integrated with analytics software, which would provide insights into inventory trends, patterns, and opportunities for improvement. This would enable users to optimize inventory management and reduce waste.

The RFID system for inventory management that uses self-transactional materials would provide real-time visibility into inventory levels, enable remote inventory management, and provide valuable insights into inventory trends and opportunities for improvement. Additionally, using self-transactional materials would provide a more flexible and durable tracking solution, enabling accurate inventory tracking even in challenging environments.

4.3   Data Storage and Real-Time Event Processing with the IoT Shared Database

The middleware layer of the system architecture includes the IoT cloud platform for storing and processing data in real-time. This platform allows for the efficient storage and processing of inventory data, which can be accessed from anywhere and at any time. The IoT cloud platform database is where all inventory data is stored. This database is accessible from anywhere and at any time, which allows for real-time monitoring of inventory data. The middleware layer of the system architecture includes the IoT cloud platform for storing and processing data in real-time. One solution for an IoT shared database for RFID Self-Transactional materials in inventory management would be to use a cloud-based system. This would allow for a centralized database that all parties involved in the inventory management process can access and update in real-time. Each self-transactional material is equipped with an RFID tag that contains information about the material, such as its type and quantity. Each time the material is moved or used, the RFID tag is scanned and the transaction is recorded in the cloud-based database. The database is accessible to all parties involved in the inventory management process, such as suppliers, manufacturers, distributors, and retailers. Each party can access the database to view the current status of the materials, including their location, quantity, and usage history. The database can also include automated notifications or alerts when certain conditions are met, such as when inventory levels fall below a certain threshold. The database can also be used to track the movement of materials throughout the supply chain, allowing for greater visibility and traceability.

All parties involved have access to the same information, which can help reduce errors and miscommunications. In the proposed system architecture, the IoT cloud platform serves as the pillar of the system, providing a centralized location for data storage and processing. The platform should be scalable and able to handle large amounts of data generated by the self-transactional materials. Data/Event Handler is responsible for processing the data and events generated by the self-transactional materials. The shared database should be able to store all the relevant data generated by the Self-Transactional materials. The database should be scalable and able to handle large amounts of data. The system should be able to process events generated by the self-transactional materials in real-time. This would allow for quick response times and better inventory management. Notifications should also be sent to relevant stakeholders in the supply chain, such as suppliers, distributors, and retailers.

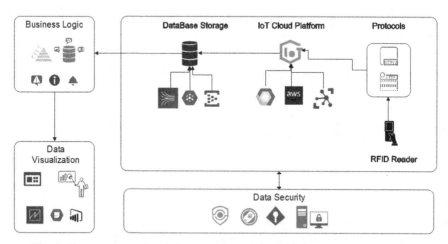

Fig. 2. Data storage and real-time event processing with the IoT Shared Database.

In Fig. 2 is described the solution proposed, an IoT cloud platform is used that provides features like real-time data processing, analytics, and security. The IoT cloud platform is connected with the RFID readers, using protocols, these readers will collect data from the self-transactional materials and send it to the cloud platform. Data processing and data storage will be implemented once the data is received by the IoT Cloud Platform. The business logic is implemented using serverless functions or microservices. These services will analyze the data, trigger actions, and send alerts in real-time based on business rules and events. After that, the data visualization is implemented using tools that provide real-time insights and dashboards that help in making better inventory management decisions. The most important component of the solution is to implement security measures such as encryption, access control, and monitoring to ensure the integrity and confidentiality of the data (see Fig. 2).

Overall, the proposed solution for data storage and real-time event processing with the IoT cloud platform in inventory management using self-transactional materials would provide a more efficient and transparent supply chain management system.

4.4 Communication and Data Transmission

The network layer of the system architecture is responsible for communication and data transmission. It ensures that data collected from the RFID readers and sensors is transmitted to the middleware layer for processing and storage. It also ensures that inventory data is accessible from anywhere and at any time. The cloud-based database stores all data related to the self-transactional materials, including their quantity, prices and usage history. The database can be accessed by all parties involved in the inventory management process, such as suppliers, manufacturers, distributors, and retailers. Each party can access the database to view the current status of the materials, as well as to update information as needed. Automated notifications or alerts can be set up to trigger when certain conditions are met, such as when inventory levels fall below a certain threshold. The system can also be integrated with other software platforms, such as inventory management systems or enterprise resource planning (ERP) systems, to provide real-time inventory data and optimize supply chain processes.

An IoT Shared Database can be especially useful for communication and data transmission between the actors within the SCM when using Self-Transactional Materials. Here are some ways in which an IoT shared database can be used for this purpose:

- Real-time tracking and sharing of Self-Transactional Materials data: track and record data about the movement and status of products within the supply chain in real-time.
- Automated data sharing: An IoT shared database can be used to automate the exchange of data between different systems used by the actors in the SCM (automatically update the with information about the quantity in real-time).
- Improved coordination: An IoT shared database can help to improve coordination between different actors in the SCM by providing a centralized location for storing and sharing data.
- Enhanced security and transparency: Self-Transactional Materials can provide an additional layer of security and transparency within the SCM. This can be especially important when dealing with sensitive or high-value products.

An IoT shared database can be a valuable tool for communication and data transmission between the actors within the SCM when using Self-Transactional Materials.

By providing real-time tracking and sharing data, automated data sharing, improved coordination, and enhanced security and transparency.

4.5 The Proposed Architecture

The proposed system architecture for integrating IoT shared database and RFID in supply chain management consists of five layers:

1. Perception Layer:

To implement this layer, the appropriate RFID tags and readers for the inventory items based on the requirements of the supply chain are used at various points in the supply chain, including warehouses and transportation vehicles. With the RFID readers data about inventory items is collected, that will be transmitted to the middleware layer for processing and storage.

The perception layer includes self-transactional materials that are attached to the products or inventory items. These materials contain RFID tags and sensors that capture real-time data about the product. The RFID readers are installed at different points in the warehouse, such as at the entry point, exit point, and various checkpoints to monitor the movement of the inventory. These RFID readers capture the data from the RFID tags on the self-transactional materials and transmit it to the network layer.

2. Network Layer:

The network layer provides the communication infrastructure for the system, including wired and wireless networks, protocols, and standards. It is responsible for transmitting data between the various components of the system. The appropriate network infrastructure is used to support the transmission of data between the various components of the system. To ensure compatibility between the components of the system, the necessary protocols and standards are implanted.

The network layer consists of RFID readers that capture the data from the self-transactional materials and transmit it to the middleware layer. In this layer, the data transmitted by the RFID readers is collected, processed, and stored in the IoT Shared Database. The data is transferred securely over the internet. The IoT Shared Database stores and manages the inventory data in real-time and allows access to it from anywhere.

3. Middleware Layer:

The middleware layer is responsible for processing and filtering the data captured by the RFID readers. It performs tasks such as data filtering, aggregation, and normalization, and ensures that the data is consistent and accurate. It also includes the IoT Shared Database for storing and processing data in real-time. The appropriate middleware software based on the requirements of the supply chain is used to configure the middleware software to handle data collection, filtering, processing, and storage. To transmit data between the various components of the system, the middleware software is integrated with the network layer, the data is stored and processed in real-time in the IoT Shared Database.

This layer acts as a bridge between the network layer and the application layer. It consists of various software components such as API gateways, data processing engines, and rules engines. The middleware layer filters, cleans, and normalizes the inventory data before sending it to the application layer.

4. Application Layer:
The application layer provides an interface for authorized users to access the data stored in the IoT shared database. This layer includes applications that allow users to view inventory levels, track shipments, and manage orders. The applications can be accessed from any device, such as smartphones, tablets, or computers. The appropriate application software is used to provide real-time visibility and insight into inventory data. A user interface for displaying inventory data in real-time is implemented, equipped with tools for analyzing and managing inventory data. Data visualization tools can be used to create visual representations of the inventory data, enabling users to quickly identify trends and patterns.

5. Business Layer:
The business layer includes the business processes and workflows that govern inventory management, including order processing, dispatching, and resource utilization. The business layer is responsible for the overall management and coordination of the supply chain. The data captured by the RFID system is used to inform decision-making in the business layer, enabling supply chain managers to optimize the supply chain and reduce costs. To implement this layer, the existing business processes and workflows has to be analyzed to identify areas where the proposed system architecture can improve inventory management, data transparency, resource utilization, and business insight. Based on the capabilities of the proposed system architecture, new business processes and workflows are designed.

In this solution, self-transactional materials, such as RFID-tagged items, are used to automate the inventory management process. These materials are equipped with RFID tags that contain information such as product code, batch number, quantity, expiration date. When the materials are moved, the RFID readers installed at various points in the warehouse capture the data and transmit it to the network layer for processing and storage.

Overall, by leveraging the power of IoT shared database and RFID technology with Self-Transactional materials, this solution can enable accurate, real-time inventory tracking, improving inventory management, data transparency, resource utilization, and business insight in Inventory Management.

5 Conclusion

The proposed system architecture for integrating IoT Shared Database and RFID in SCM with Self-Transactional materials offers a promising solution for improving inventory management, data transparency, resource utilization, and business insight. The architecture facilitates efficient information exchange between different layers of the supply chain, which enhances visibility and control over the supply chain processes. The use of self-transactional materials in this architecture enables the automated and seamless execution of transactions, which eliminates human errors and delays in the supply chain processes. Furthermore, the IoT and RFID technologies used in this architecture enable real-time monitoring and tracking of inventory, which improves accuracy and efficiency in supply chain management.

The results indicate that the proposed architecture has the potential to significantly improve the performance of SCM. However, further research and testing are recommended to validate the effectiveness of the proposed architecture in real-world scenarios. Additionally, the feasibility and cost-effectiveness of implementing self-transactional materials in the supply chain should be assessed to determine the practicality of this solution. Overall, the proposed architecture represents an innovative and promising approach to improving SCM in the modern business landscape.

References

Urbano, O., et al.: Cost-effective implementation of a temperature traceability system based on smart RFID tags and IoT services. Sensors **20**(4), 1163 (2020). https://doi.org/10.3390/s20041163

Nabeel, M., Srinivasan, M., Prince, E., Padmanabhan, R.: IoT architecture for advanced manufacturing technologies. Mater. Today Proc. **22**, 2359–2365 (2019). https://doi.org/10.1016/j.matpr.2020.03.358

Fan, K., Luo, Q., Zhang, K., Yang, Y.: Cloud-based lightweight secure RFID mutual authentication protocol in IoT. Inf. Sci. **527**, 329–340 (2020). https://doi.org/10.1016/j.ins.2019.08.006

Finkenzeller, K.: RFID Handbook: Fundamentals and Applications in Contactless Smart Cards, Radio Frequency Identification and Near-Field Communication. Wiley, New York (2010)

Cao, J., Zhang, S.: Research and design of RFID-based equipment incident management system for industry 4.0. In: 4th International Conference on Electrical & Electronics Engineering and Computer Science (ICEEECS 2016), vol. 50, pp. 889–894 (2016). https://doi.org/10.2991/iceeecs-16.2016.172

Tedjini, S., Andia Vera, G., Marcos, Z., Freire, R.C.S., Duroc, Y.: Augmented RFID tags. In: Proceedings of IEEE Radio and Wireless Week, Austin, TX, USA, 23–27 January 2016 (2016)

Benghozi, P.J., Bureau, S., Massit-Folléa, F.: L'Internet des objets: Quels enjeux pour les Européens? Ministère de la recherche, Délégation aux usages de l'Internet, Paris (2008)

Miorandi, D., Sicari, S., De Pellegrini, F., Chlamtac, I.: Internet of things: vision, applications and research challenges. Ad Hoc Netw. **10**(7), 1497–1516 (2012)

dos Santos, Y.L., Canedo, E.D.: On the design and implementation of an IoT based architecture for reading ultra-high frequency tags. Information **10**(2), 41 (2019). https://doi.org/10.3390/info10020041

Khan, R., Khan, S.U., Zaheer, R., Khan, S.: Future internet: the internet of things architecture, possible applications and key challenges. In: Proceedings - 10th International Conference on Frontiers of Information Technology, FIT 2012, pp. 257–260 (2012). https://doi.org/10.1109/FIT.2012.53

Utilizing AR and Hybrid Cloud-Edge Platforms for Improving Accessibility in Exhibition Areas

Dionysios Koulouris[1,2], Filimon Trastelis[1], Andreas Menychtas[1,2],
Dimitrios Kosmopoulos[3], and Ilias Maglogiannis[2(✉)]

[1] BioAssist S.A., Kastritsiou 4, Rion, Greece
{denkoul,ftrastelis,amenychtas}@bioassist.gr
[2] Department of Digital Systems, University of Piraeus, Piraeus, Greece
imaglo@unipi.gr
[3] University of Patras, Patras, Greece
dkosmo@upatras.gr

Abstract. The technological advancements in the areas of mobile and edge computing provide nowadays the required levels of performance to handheld commodity devices to carry out computational intensive tasks which are required for an effective human-computer interaction. This enables advanced Augmented Reality - AR and Computer Vision approaches to operate on edge and mobile devices offering an immersive experience to the users by augmenting the foreground scene without the need of additional and expensive hardware. In this work we demonstrate the capabilities of AR and Computer Vision technologies for object and scene identification when deployed in a hybrid cloud-mobile environment. The prototype addresses the requirements of a real-world usage scenario for improving the accessibility for hearing and mild vision impaired visitors in museums and exhibition areas. This project is part of the implementation of the SignGuide project, an interactive museum guide system for deaf visitors, which can automatically recognize an exhibit, and create an interactive experience including the provision of content in sign language content using an avatar or video. The proposed system introduces a novel Multitenant Cloud AR-based platform and a client library for mobile apps capable of effectively identifying points of interest and creating new opportunities of interactivity between the real and digital worlds.

Keywords: Augmented Reality · Computer Vision · Object Detection · Accessibility

1 Introduction

The mobile device's multitask processing capabilities and graphics hardware facilitate the development of new applications that utilize cutting-edge technologies for interacting both with the users and also the physical world. An application which applies new techniques for acquiring the user's input and improves

© IFIP International Federation for Information Processing 2023
Published by Springer Nature Switzerland AG 2023
I. Maglogiannis et al. (Eds.): AIAI 2023, IFIP AICT 676, pp. 171–182, 2023.
https://doi.org/10.1007/978-3-031-34107-6_14

human-computer interaction, can also mitigate the accessibility issues of persons with impairments [3]. To this direction, state-of-the-art Augmented Reality technologies can utilize a commodity mobile device's hardware to offer real-world interaction to the user.

In recent years, it is a primary concern for many museums to enhance the experience of their visitors, and most importantly of those with accessibility issues like the deaf or vision impaired whose senses are limited for interacting with the exhibits and art objects. Visitors with disabilities can utilize helper applications, like AR assistants, to address accessibility issues and improve their visiting experience. Among other factors, AR uses image feature-points to provide localization functionality [18] which in this work is demonstrated in the case of museum exhibit identification and point-of-interest recognition (e.g. sector entrances, next/previous/related exhibits). Visually impaired persons could use the camera of their mobile device (or a mobile device provided by the museum) to automatically guide them in the exhibition while deaf can utilize the exhibit recognition to limit their interaction with the system and instantly get information of the exhibit in their display.

An important factor for exhibition areas and especially museums, is the static equipment required for installing assistive systems, which hinders and disturbs the visiting experience. Mobile guidance systems often require the use of QR codes [9], Bluetooth [19] or other hardware installations. Our solution offers zero interference with the museum area and the exhibits, allowing thus for optimal design of the exhibition for better experiences. There is no need to adapt the exhibition for vision and hearing impaired persons.

This paper introduces a novel Multitenant Cloud AR-based platform which utilizes a mobile commodity device's localization ability to recognize exhibits for increasing accessibility in a museum environment. The proposed system is a part of the SignGuide project, a prototype solution which offers a tour guide and computer-machine communication in sign language for the deaf visitors of the Archeological Museum of Thessaloniki - AMT [11].

The rest of the paper is structured as follows: Sect. 2 highlights past research at the field and introduces the demonstrated background technologies. System architecture, design and implementation are extensively described in Sect. 3, while Sect. 4 demonstrates the operation of the system at the project location. Section 5 presents results from the system's operation and finally, Sect. 6 concludes our work.

2   Scientific Background

2.1   Related Work

The improvement of a museum's accessibility necessitates the integration of new technologies in this area and, thus, the utilization of mobile museum applications. The identification of the main features for the design of a museum application can give insightful thoughts for both museum managers and application developers [16]. Curiosity, Usability, Interaction, Motivation and Satisfaction are components that need to be taken into consideration when developing such applications [1]. Based on the aforementioned factors and the fact that Mobile AR - MAR has proven to be beneficial for the deaf visitors of a museum during their visit, the MAR for the Hearing Impaired Museum visitors' Engagement - MARHIME conceptual model has been introduced [2]. To overcome the difficulties during the tour of visitors in a museum, a system based on AR is introduced to predict the optimal routes in a museum [23].

A different approach for guidance and exhibition presentations is the combination of wearable technologies and AR [22]. The case of the Literary Museum [8] illustrates the user engagement that AR offers, even when the visitors have minimum experience with mobile applications. AR is integrated in different fields of application, as in the development of exergames for remote patient monitoring [13], in nature based solution utilizing AR Cloud Anchor technique with gamification elements [14] or in healthcare education for pharmaceutical substances recognition [12]. From the integration of AR in a museum for school children with zero experience, research concluded that AR increases the interest of the visitors and the gained knowledge [15].

Computer Vision technology, in general, can be implemented in a museum app to collect visitors data and measure their engagement [4]. Other applications conduct state recognition and then object identification to provide the museum visitors an advanced tour [21]. The implementation of multimedia augmented reality information systems that can display 3D models of museum artifacts and provide multimedia content to the visitors [6] increases the overall experience of the exhibition. Moreover, combination of such content with Virtual Reality - VR and AR shows increase of engagement in exhibitions [25]. Many statistical techniques and methods are utilized to measure the impact of the implementation of AR and VR in the museum service model and their results demonstrate they affect the interaction of users with accessibility issues [24].

Part of the developed application that needs to be briefly mentioned, but is not the key contribution of this work, is the binding of a retrieved exhibit with content for the deaf. For a complete interaction between the visitors and the app, deaf users need to perform questions in Sign Language. A crucial problem that needs to be addressed is the monitoring speed of the gesture hands and the hands flexibility [7]. Most techniques for the modeling of sign language are directly dependent on multidimensional data without considering the innate limitations of the human body's physiology or sign language. Deep learning architectures are proposed to reduce the extent of this issue by modeling the information in separate routes [5]. There are general-purpose museum content management systems or static content systems to locate the data required for processing a query. SQL Language is used to extract videos from a library and specifically the most relevant parts that are essential to present the results [10]. Although an Avatar presentation is challenging, as it is related to various facial and hand gestures [17], the virtual character approach of Ada and Grace has been successfully developed at the Boston Science Museum [20]. Various deep learning methods for sign language recognition, the Virtual Avatar and, most importantly, exhibit recognition are utilized in the SignGuide project to achieve human-computer interaction for the deaf.

2.2 Technological Foundation

Augmented Reality. Augmented Reality's biggest advantage -when running on mobile commodity devices- is hardware independence. Most latest generation mobile phones include the sufficient sensors and processors required to run AR, which are: IMU sensors and HD camera. The phone's camera feed can be augmented resulting in displaying 3D content which is seamlessly integrated to the real world. Digital items attached in the foreground scene are referred as AR **Anchors** due to their ability of remaining static at a surface. Such surfaces, that allow Anchor placements and persistence, are referred as AR **Planes**. Any device movement (even change of rooms) will not affect the AR experience as it relies itself on a Simultaneous Localization and Mapping (SLAM) technique. Attaching an Anchor to a Plane requires software that implements SLAM.

Simultaneous Localization and Mapping. SLAM algorithms achieve surrounding area recognition by utilizing camera feed along with data from device IMU sensors. Feature points from certain and dense segments of each camera frame are extracted while the area is steadily scanned. Raw data from IMU sensors (accelerometer, gyroscope) in combination with the feature points create a 3D representation of the foreground scene allowing, thus, the placement of Anchors relevant to these points. Once an Anchor is attached, nearby feature points are captured and included in the Anchor's metadata. A cloud-enabled Anchor identification process utilizes the aforementioned technique to save these feature points in the cloud, for future use. When another device captures the same area, it will recognize, using AI, patterns referring to the pre-captured feature points. If the confidence is high, which means that the area looks the same, a new Anchor will be placed at the exact same spot. This technique requires some computational power resulting, thus, in a limitation of simultaneous Anchor searches, depending on the Cloud Anchor implementation. In our prototype we use the Google Cloud Anchors library which allows 20 simultaneous Anchor retrieval attempts at the same time.

3 Design and Implementation

3.1 System Overview

The proposed system provides advanced user interaction functionalities for creating rich experiences to the users and addressing accessibility issues in exhibition areas and related environments. The system consists of two main elements:

A. *Multitenant Cloud Platform for AR-based POI Resolution*: a generic AR-based platform which is capable of real-time identification of relevant POIs - Points of Interest in a context-aware manner.

B. *User Application*: a prototype mobile app which is integrated with the cloud platform to provide the aforementioned functionalities to users in the world scenario of a museum.

The mobile app is classified in the category of museum applications that have as main target to provide additional help and ease the accessibility issues, especially of hearing impaired people. Through the integration with the *Multitenant Cloud Platform for AR-based POI Resolution* and the customization of the operational parameters for the particular usage scenario, a set of features for advanced interactivity become available to the User Application.

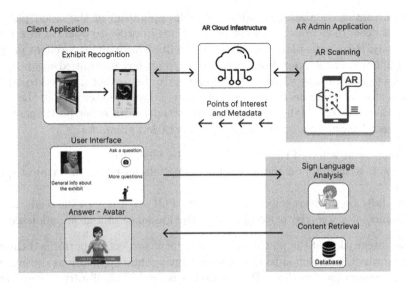

Fig. 1. System Overview and Core Functionalities

Figure 1 presents an overview of the system's design and its core functionalities. The users, as visitors of the exhibition/museum, which are equipped with the app installed in their mobile phones, can open the camera in order to identify exhibits and other points of interest, without the need to use other tools or mechanisms (such as QR codes), and in turn view related rich multimedia for the identified object. The whole process is realized by the AR components which are deployed locally in the app and are configured to identify points of interest in the specific area. The points of interest are preconfigured through the cloud platform for the particular application/scenario and represent specific points in the premises which are considered relevant to the scenario and potentially have interest for the users, such as exhibits, entrances and exits of exhibitions, and other facilities. The real world points of interest, technically defined as anchors, are represented in the digital environment of the mobile app enriched with 3D models, multimedia content and other information providing a unique experience to the users. Besides the metadata attached to each anchor from the cloud platform, additional information for the exhibit is presented within the app. In this scenario, the additional curated content is retrieved from the museum's information systems and consolidated to the digital representation of the POIs. Furthermore, additional services are integrated in the app to provide bi-directional interactivity using sign language in order to facilitate accessibility. The user can ask a unique question in Sign Language which will be analyzed and then, an Avatar will respond using Sign Language.

3.2 Multitenant Cloud Platform for AR-Based POI Resolution

A key advantage of the approach is that the operation of the cloud platform has been decoupled from the client applications in order to operate in a multitenant way. Hence, the platform can serve simultaneously multiple client projects adapting however the operational mode to each project for context-aware identification of anchors. The identification process can be further adapted to address dynamically changing needs during runtime based on the user profile, the condition of the area (e.g. highly crowded), interactivity with other participants and other special requirements. This dynamic operation allows for:

– dynamic allocation of the list of POIs to be identified,
– response with different metadata for each POIs based on the request query, and
– consolidation of alternative content to the POI according to the scenario (e.g. guidance of a sole visitor compared to the guidance of a group adolescents).

The integration of the platform with the client projects is performed through a library which is attached to the related client mobile applications during their implementation (see section AR Integration below). This library is responsible for capturing the video stream from the camera of the mobile device and the identification of the POIs by communicating with the cloud platform. The identification is performed in a hybrid fashion as follows:

– The client library makes a request to the cloud platform for a list of anchors to be identified providing contextual information (e.g. building, floor), the recently identified POIs and optionally user related information.
– The platform processes the request and responds with a list of anchors and their visual features.
– The features are used in the client library to identify locally the specific anchor in real-time from the video stream.
– When an anchor is identified, another request is performed to the platform in order to get the respective POI which is associated with the anchor, its metadata and the related content.

It should be noted that an anchor represents a specific spot in the area, which may represent one or more POIs, and according to the usage scenario and the request that will be performed, a different POI may be attached to this

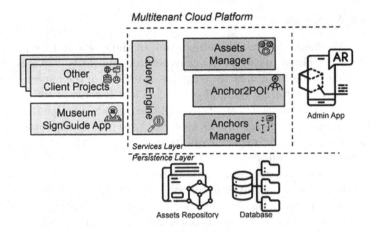

Fig. 2. Cloud Platform Architecture

anchor. Furthermore, the information and the metadata of the POI may also be dynamically produced and updated during runtime. The architecture of the platform is presented in Fig. 2.

In conceptual level, it includes three main elements, a) the *Persistence Layer*, for storing all information regarding anchors and the assets related to them, b) the *Services Layer* where the business logic of the platform is implemented, and c) the *Admin App* for the definition of the anchors. The *Admin App* is used by the managers of the platform and dedicated users (e.g. the museum staff) and its main functionality is the initial identification and definition of the anchors in the area of interest. Through the app which is installed to the managers' mobile device the area is scanned using the camera, and the features of the foreground scene, of the surfaces, and of the objects are recorded in order to place the virtual anchors and store them in the database. The *Anchors Manager* component allows for editing the configuration and the metadata of the anchors as well as their ownership and access parameters so that they are available during runtime only to the specified audience. The *Assets Manager* component undertakes the process for uploading to the system and configuring the assets that will be in turn associated with the POIs. This is carried out through the *Anchor2POI* component where a many-to-many relationship is defined between anchors and POIs. Therefore an anchor may represent different POIs according to the context, or a POI may span across multiple anchors. The *Query Engine* is the interface of the platform towards the client library and is responsible for the analysis of the client requests and for producing the list of anchors and related material (POIs and Assets) which will be used at any time from the mobile app.

3.3 User Application

The user application, through the integration of the client library for communication with the cloud platform, provides several innovative features with the most prominent being the ability to recognize an exhibit of the museum and have instant access to its information. Following the identification of the exhibit, and the presentation of the initial content, a set of questions is displayed, in both text and Sign Language. Furthermore, the user can have a look at photos related to the museum exhibitions or a specific question or answer. All the data is derived from a database of the museum based on the Heurist CMS tool[1].

The client library is responsible for performing the exhibit recognition on the mobile device. Once the appropriate button is selected, feed from the camera of the device pops up and indicates the user to point at an exhibit. At the same time in the background, the feature point recognition subsystem has already downloaded the features of the exhibits and continuously checks the current camera feed for patterns. When a frame contains sufficient features matching an anchor, the related POI content is displayed at the spot of the anchor. If the euclidean distance (in meters) between the Anchor and the device is less than 1.5 m, the user is considered to be close to the Anchor, resulting, thus, in the recognition of the corresponding exhibit.

While all AR related functionalities are exclusively integrated to the system by this work, User Application acts also as the front-end of sign language recognition and Virtual Avatar presentation processes. The user can either select one of the predefined questions or ask a question facing at the device's front camera. Answers are generated either in text or in sign language using prerecorded video or Virtual Avatar illustration. Needs to be mentioned, though, that back-end implementations of the aforementioned processes are developed by the other project partners.

4 The System in Practice

The minimization of user-machine interaction needs is achieved through an efficient exhibit recognition subsystem which is trained to recognize the exhibits and POIs of AMT, where the project takes place. A combination of the two Applications, Client Application and AR Admin Application, is required for the system to work properly. First, the area needs to be scanned, using the AR implementation, and the locations of the affected exhibits must be picked. The scanning process requires a clean-of-presence area allowing for optimal feature-point detection at the point of interest. When an exhibit is scanned, an anchor is placed at its location and feature-points along with related metadata are stored to the cloud. Furthermore, such Anchors are linked using a 1–1 relationship with the affected exhibits and their multimedia assets resulting, thus, in the relation between a location and an exhibit.

---

[1] Heurist CMS tool: https://heuristnetwork.org/.

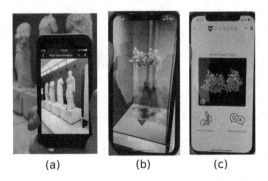

(a)   (b)   (c)

Fig. 3. The system in practice

The client-side application aims at improving the accessibility of impaired people while visiting exhibition sites. When the application is launched, a large distinctive button with an appropriate icon is visible at the center of the screen prompting the visitor to open the camera. Immediately the AR subsystem is initialized and the SLAM procedure recognizes the front view. Once an exhibit is visible on the device, and its feature-points are confidently identified, information about this exhibit is retrieved to the application. Due to the possibility of simultaneous recognition of nearby exhibits, the distance between the device and the affected exhibit's location is required to be less than 1.5 m, however alternative configurations can be set in other scenarios and deployments. Figure 3 demonstrates (a) the Anchor scan and POI definition process, (b) exhibit recognition, and (c) successful exhibit information retrieval.

5   Results and Evaluation

The proposed system has been tested at the exhibition of AMT under real usage scenarios with visitors present. Eight museum exhibits have been selected for the test using four different mobile devices: iPhone 12, iPhone SE 2, Galaxy A52s and Galaxy Tab S8 Ultra. Ten tests were performed for each device, for each exhibit, examining the recognition process. Five of the tests searched for the exhibit in its frontal space while five started the procedure at a 45° angle. Table 1 demonstrates average results from 5 tests conducted on each exhibit, with a total of 40 tests, highlighting the time required for each device to successfully detect the exhibit along with a success rate, when searched from the frontal space. Table 2 demonstrates the same number of tests, but exhibits were scanned from a 45° angle.

Results from the tests show that although there is a slight decrease in recognition duration and success rate when scanned from an angle, overall performance of the system is well accepted, considering that there is no reference point (e.g. QR Code) or other identification intervention.

Table 1. Exhibit scanned from the frontal space

Device	Time(s)	Test success rate (out of 5)
iPhone 12	3.39	96% (4.80)
iPhone SE 2020	4.11	94% (4.70)
Samsung Galaxy A52s	4.43	93% (4.66)
Samsung Galaxy Tab S8 Ultra	4.01	95% (4.74)

Table 2. Exhibit scanned from angle

Device	Time(s)	Test success rate (out of 5)
iPhone 12	3.56	95.2% (4.76)
iPhone SE 2020	4.33	93.6% (4.68)
Samsung Galaxy A52s	5.01	94% (4.70)
Samsung Galaxy Tab S8 Ultra	4.21	94.4% (4.72)

6   Conclusion

Mobile commodity devices already achieve satisfactorily results when they are required to run intensive tasks, such as image processing, data transmission and human-computer interaction. These advantages can be utilized to improving the quality-of-life and accessibility of impaired people while at the same time reducing their social exclusion. The general goal of the SignGuide project is to introduce an interactive museum guide platform for the deaf, with capabilities of capturing and responding to sign language, using only mobile devices provided by the museum or owned by the visitor. In this work a prototype AR solution is introduced and integrated to the project, for increasing system accessibility. It is capable of recognizing and interacting with the exhibition area without the need of preinstalled equipment or any sort of intervention. The Cloud Platform for AR-based POI Resolution achieves efficient object detection and object-exhibit correlation using the Services' Layer Query Engine. Run-time tests from the end-user prototype, which runs on both Android and iOS devices, show that even if the exhibition area is partially crowded, or the exhibit is scanned at an angle, the identification is performing well, while at the same time requiring an almost effortless process of training the system. Additional libraries, such as the Unity Framework, can be utilized to further improve the performance of the solution as well as the experience of the users when utilizing the system. Further extensions to the client library and the cloud platform are also foreseen to enhance the accuracy of the system and the time required to identify the POIs even in highly complex and crowded environments.

Acknowledgements. This work is partially supported by the Greek Secretariat for Research and Innovation and the EU, Project SignGuide: Automated Museum Guidance using Sign Language T2EDK-00982 within the framework of "Competitiveness, Entrepreneurship and Innovation" (EPAnEK) Operational Programme 2014–2020.

References

1. Baker, E.J., Abu Bakar, J.A., Zulkifli, A.N.: Mobile augmented reality elements for museum hearing impaired visitors' engagement. J. Telecommun. Electron. Comput. Eng. (JTEC). **9**(2–12), 171–178 (2017). https://jtec.utem.edu.my/jtec/article/view/2788
2. Baker, E.J., Bakar, J.A.A., Zulkifli, A.N.: Evaluation of mobile augmented reality hearing-impaired museum visitors engagement instrument. Int. J. Interact. Mob. Technol. **16**(12) (2022)
3. Bergman, E., Johnson, E.: Towards accessible human-computer interaction. Adv. Human-Comput. Interact. **5**(1), 208–405 (2001)
4. Budiarto, A., Pardamean, B., Caraka, R.E.: Computer vision-based visitor study as a decision support system for museum. In: 2017 International Conference on Innovative and Creative Information Technology (ICITech), pp. 1–6 (2017). https://doi.org/10.1109/INNOCIT.2017.8319128
5. Camgoz, N.C., Hadfield, S., Koller, O., Bowden, R.: Subunets: end-to-end hand shape and continuous sign language recognition. In: 2017 IEEE International Conference on Computer Vision (ICCV), pp. 3075–3084 (2017). https://doi.org/10.1109/ICCV.2017.332
6. Chen, C.-Y., Chang, B.R., Huang, P.-S.: Multimedia augmented reality information system for museum guidance. Pers. Ubiquit. Comput. **18**(2), 315–322 (2013). https://doi.org/10.1007/s00779-013-0647-1
7. Erol, A., Bebis, G., Nicolescu, M., Boyle, R.D., Twombly, X.: Vision-based hand pose estimation: a review. Comput. Vision Image Underst. **108**(1), 52–73 (2007). https://doi.org/10.1016/j.cviu.2006.10.012
8. Fenu, C., Pittarello, F.: Svevo tour: the design and the experimentation of an augmented reality application for engaging visitors of a literary museum. Int. J. Human-Comput. Stud. **114**, 20–35 (2018)
9. Haworth, A., Williams, P.: Using QR codes to aid accessibility in a museum. J. Assist. Technol. **6**(4), 285–291 (2012)
10. Hwang, E., Subrahmanian, V.: Querying video libraries*. J. Visual Commun. Image Represent. **7**(1), 44–60 (1996). https://doi.org/10.1006/jvci.1996.0005, https://www.sciencedirect.com/science/article/pii/S104732039690005X
11. Kosmopoulos, D., et al.: Museum guidance in sign language: The signguide project. In: Proceedings of the 15th International Conference on PErvasive Technologies Related to Assistive Environments, pp. 646–652 (2022)
12. Koulouris, D., Gallos, P., Menychtas, A., Maglogiannis, I.: Exploiting augmented reality and computer vision for healthcare education: the case of pharmaceutical substances visualization and information retrieval. In: Digital Professionalism in Health and Care: Developing the Workforce, Building the Future, pp. 87–91. IOS Press (2022)
13. Koulouris, D., Menychtas, A., Maglogiannis, I.: An IoT-enabled platform for the assessment of physical and mental activities utilizing augmented reality exergaming. Sensors **22**(9), 3181 (2022)

14. Koulouris, D., Pardos, A., Gallos, P., Menychtas, A., Maglogiannis, I.: Integrating AR and iot services into mhealth applications for promoting wellbeing. In: 2022 18th International Conference on Wireless and Mobile Computing, Networking and Communications (WiMob), pp. 148–153 (2022). https://doi.org/10.1109/WiMob55322.2022.9941578

15. Moorhouse, N., tom Dieck, M.C., Jung, T.: An experiential view to children learning in museums with augmented reality. Museum Manage. Curatorship. **34**(4), 402–418 (2019)

16. Palumbo, F., Dominici, G., Basile, G.: Designing a mobile app for museums according to the drivers of visitor satisfaction. In: Recent Advances in Business Management and Marketing-Proceedings of the 1st International Conference on Management, Marketing, Tourism, Retail, Finance and Computer Applications (MATREFC 2013). Dubrovnik, Croatia, WSEAS Press (2013)

17. Papanikolaou, P., Papagiannakis, G.: Real-time separable subsurface scattering for animated virtual characters. In: GPU Computing and Applications, pp. 53–67 (2015)

18. Reitmayr, G., et al.: Simultaneous localization and mapping for augmented reality. In: 2010 International Symposium on Ubiquitous Virtual Reality, pp. 5–8. IEEE (2010)

19. Sornalatha, K., Kavitha, V.: IoT based smart museum using Bluetooth low energy. In: 2017 Third International Conference on Advances in Electrical, Electronics, Information, Communication and Bio-informatics (AEEICB), pp. 520–523. IEEE (2017)

20. Swartout, W., et al.: Virtual museum guides demonstration. In: 2010 IEEE Spoken Language Technology Workshop, pp. 163–164 (2010). https://doi.org/10.1109/SLT.2010.5700842

21. Taverriti, G., Lombini, S., Seidenari, L., Bertini, M., Del Bimbo, A.: Real-time wearable computer vision system for improved museum experience. In: Proceedings of the 24th ACM International Conference on Multimedia, pp. 703–704 (2016)

22. Tom Dieck, M.C., Jung, T., Han, D.I.: Mapping requirements for the wearable smart glasses augmented reality museum application. J. Hospital. Tour. Technol. **7**, 230–253 (2016)

23. Torres-Ruiz, M., Mata Rivera, M., Zagal, R., Guzmán, G., Quintero, R., Moreno, M.: A recommender system to generate museum itineraries applying augmented reality and social-sensor mining techniques. Virtual Reality. **24** (2020)

24. Trunfio, M., Lucia, M.D., Campana, S., Magnelli, A.: Innovating the cultural heritage museum service model through virtual reality and augmented reality: the effects on the overall visitor experience and satisfaction. J. Herit. Tour. **17**(1), 1–19 (2022). https://doi.org/10.1080/1743873X.2020.1850742

25. Wojciechowski, R., Walczak, K., White, M., Cellary, W.: Building virtual and augmented reality museum exhibitions. In: Proceedings of the Ninth International Conference on 3D Web Technology, pp. 135–144. Web3D 2004, Association for Computing Machinery, New York, NY, USA (2004)

Learning
(Active-AutoEncoders-Federated)

Active Learning Query Strategy Selection Using Dataset Meta-features Extraction

Vangjel Kazllarof$^{(\boxtimes)}$ (iD) and Sotiris Kotsiantis (iD)

Department of Mathematics, University of Patras, 26504 Rio Achaia, Greece
vkazlarof@upatras.gr

Abstract. In the age of information, data abundance has enabled scientists to create models that have great positive impact in our life and society. However, many times the rate of data production is much bigger than the rate of classifying them in the appropriate label due to complexity, personnel or cost of equipment for the labeling task. For this reason, Active Learning techniques have been developed with the Uncertainty Sampling being one of the most popular techniques for querying the unlabeled data. However, selecting the correct Query Strategy for ranking the uncertainty in order to create the best possible model is a time and cost consuming task and most of the times the Active Learning process needs to be repeated multiple times during training. In this work, we exploit the Meta-Features extracted by 123 datasets and select the winning Query Strategy among Least Confidence, Smallest Margin and Entropy for each dataset. In the sequence, we create a dataset with a subset of the extracted Meta-Features and the winning Query Strategy for each dataset and train it in order to create a Decision Tree that can be used in order to select the most suitable Query Strategy.

Keywords: Active Learning · Uncertainty Sampling · Meta-Features

1 Introduction

Active Learning have played a major role in creating performant models when the knowledge of the data labels is limited. Expensive equipment, specialized personnel and limited time have always been a burden in labeling acquired data [1]. For this reason, Active Learning techniques have been developed that help scientists to query and acquire the label only of the most important and informative data in order to achieve a performant model with limited knowledge [2].

On the one hand, the development of Active Learning techniques have helped a lot in acquiring efficiently the most informative instances. On the other hand, selecting the best of these techniques is not something trivial because every technique has its advantages and disadvantages and most of the times their results are dependent to the dataset itself [3]. In this work we take advantage of the Meta-Features extracted by a number of datasets in order to select the most performant Active Learning technique. Meta-Features are measures that are used mainly in the Meta-Learning field in order to characterize datasets along with their relation to algorithm bias [4].

© IFIP International Federation for Information Processing 2023
Published by Springer Nature Switzerland AG 2023
I. Maglogiannis et al. (Eds.): AIAI 2023, IFIP AICT 676, pp. 185–194, 2023.
https://doi.org/10.1007/978-3-031-34107-6_15

The outline of the paper continues with Sect. 2 where we explain the Active Learning techniques used in the work while in Sect. 3 we demonstrate the Meta-Features in more detail. In Sect. 4 we analyze the related works on the subject. Section 5 is dedicated to the experiments and the results and we conclude in Sect. 6 with brief conclusions and the work that we plan to do in the future.

2   Active Learning

Active Learning process starts with a small amount of labeled data (L) and a much bigger amount of unlabeled data (U). In the beginning, a model is trained using the labeled data. Then, in the Pool-based scenario that is used in this work, the trained model is used for ranking the unlabeled instances on the informativeness they provide to it. A number of instances with the highest rank are then provided to an expert in order to label them. After acquiring the label, the instances are added to the labeled pool and the model is trained again, concluding an Active Learning cycle. The Active Learning cycles go on until a stopping criterion is met and the last trained model is the outcome of the whole process [5]. In Fig. 1 a visualization of Active Learning cycle in the Pool-based scenario is demonstrated.

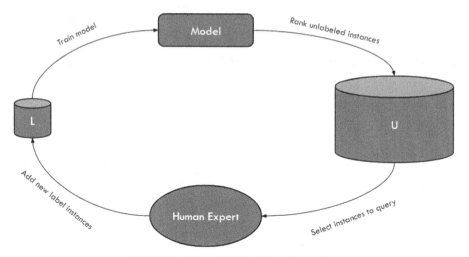

Fig. 1. Pool-based Active Learning cycle

For the sampling process, one of the most popular methods is the Uncertainty Sampling. In this method, the top ranked instances are the one that the model has the lowest confidence for its class. In the work, we used three popular query strategies for measuring the uncertainty, the Least Confidence (LC), the Smallest Margin (SM) and the Entropy (Ent) [5].

In the Least Confidence Query Strategy the active learner selects the instances that has the highest belief that they are misclassified and it is described by Eq. 1.

$$x_{LC} = \underset{x}{argmax}\,1 - P_{model}\left(\hat{y}|x\right) \tag{1}$$

where $\hat{y}$ is the most probable label and equals and it is described by Eq. 2

$$\hat{y} = argmax_y P_{model}(y|x) \tag{2}$$

In the Smallest Margin Query Strategy the active learner also takes under consideration the distribution of the remaining labels. For this reason tries to find the instances that their top two ranked instances has the smallest margin between them and it is described by Eq. 3

$$x_{SM} = \underset{x}{argmin}\,P_{model}\left(\hat{y}_1|x\right) - P_{model}\left(\hat{y}_2|x\right) \tag{3}$$

where $\hat{y}_1$ and $\hat{y}_2$ are the first and second most probable labels respectively.

Entropy Query Strategy seeks to find the instances that increases the overall entropy of the model and it is described by the Eq. 4

$$x_{Ent} = \underset{x}{argmax}\,1 - \sum_i P_{model}(y_i|x)\log P_{model}(y_i|x) \tag{4}$$

where y_i ranges over all labels [5].

3 Meta-features Extraction

Meta-Features extraction is a process of obtaining knowledge of a dataset by measuring value characteristics and use them for data mining tasks. The meta-knowledge, as referred in the literature, is mainly used in Meta-Learning [6] and AutoML [7] fields in order to understand and characterize a dataset along with its learning biases and then provide this information to a learner in order to optimize it.

Generally a Meta-Feature is a function $f : D \rightarrow \mathbb{R}^s$ where D is the dataset space using initially a measure function $m : D \rightarrow \mathbb{R}^m$ and then a summarization function $s : \mathbb{R}^m \rightarrow \mathbb{R}^s$ along with their hyper-parameters h_m and h_s respectively. A Meta-Feature function can be shortly described by Eq. 5 [8].

$$f(D) = s(m(D, h_m), h_s) \tag{5}$$

Meta-Features can be distinguished on their nature of the measurement. This way they can be grouped in the following groups. General is the simplest group of measurements like number of instances, number of attributes or number of classes. Statistical is the group of measurements that describe the numerical attributes of data distribution while Information-theoretic group is the one that describe the categorical attributes and their relationship with the classes. Model-based Meta-Features are measurements that describe characteristics that are extracted by simple models. Landmarking, Relative-Landmarking and Subsampling-Landmarking are a groups of performances, relative-performances and performances of dataset subsamples respectively of simple and efficient learners. Clustering is a group of measurements that describe the information extracted from external validation indexes. Concept measurements estimate the density of the instances along with the variability of the classes. Itemset group is the one that computes the correlation between binary attributes and finally the Complexity group consists of measurements that estimate how difficult the separation of instances into their classes is [9].

4   Related Works

In the literature, Meta-Learning is combined with Active Learning techniques mainly for reducing the meta-examples required to train by selecting the most informative one when trying to construct a reliable meta-learner. Such process has been developed in [10] in which Uncertainty Sampling methods have been combined with Active Meta-Learning in order increase the Meta-Learning performance by generating more relevant meta-examples. Similar approach has been used in [11] in which they managed to achieve similar Meta-Learning performance by selecting only up to 20% of labeled meta-examples using Uncertainty Sampling methods. Moreover, in [12] Outlier Detection techniques were applied along with Active Learning and Meta-learning in order to remove meta-examples that were considered as outliers to the meta-learner resulting to an improved performance. Another similar approach was conducted in [13] where a combination of Meta-Learning and Active Learning has been used in improving the performance of peptide datasets using only few training examples.

Although Meta-Learning has been combined with Active Learning in order to improve the meta-learner, few have been published for improving the active-learner. In [14] Meta-Learning has been used for automatic tuning of the Uncertainty Sampling threshold in stream classification, improving the performance and the cost efficiency of the active-learner. Similarly, in this work we try to improve the cost efficiency of the Active Learning process by taking advantage of the Meta-Features and create a Decision Tree that can be used in order to predict the best Query Strategy for the active-learner.

5   Experiments and Results

5.1   Dataset Construction

For the dataset construction, we use 123 datasets sourced by OpenML [15]. Initially we extract all the Meta-Features listed in the groups mentioned above. For this task we used the Pymfe [9] package written in Python resulting to a dataset of 123 instances and 182 attributes that each one describe an extracted Meta-Feature.

In the sequence, we determine the winning Active Learning Query Strategy between Least Confidence, Smallest margin and Entropy methods for each dataset in order to label each instance. Initially every dataset is splitted into train and test sets. For the train set we use the 80% of instances and for the test set we use 20% of instances of each dataset. Train set will be used for the Active Learning process while test set will be used for evaluating the performance of the trained model obtained after process finishes.

For the Active Learning process, every dataset train set starts with a small pool of initially labeled instances of 5% of the total train set in order simulate more realistically real-world problems. The remaining 95% will be the pool of the unlabeled instances in which the query strategies will search for the most informative one. The stopping criterion for the Active Learning task is the 15 iterations of Active Learning cycles and in every cycle a dynamic batch of top rated instances is selected in order to double the pool of the labeled instances and reach to 10% of the total train set. For the labeling process a simulated oracle is used that always predicts the correct label for the queried instances. For base learner we chose is simple Decision Tree classifier in order to have a fast training process.

The Active Learning task described above classified every instance on the winning Query Strategy resulting to a dataset of 42 instances classified to Least Confidence, 41 instances classified to Smallest Margin and the remaining 40 instances classified to Entropy Query Strategy. For the implementing the Active Learning task we used Libact [16] package along with Scikit-Learn [17] package, both written in Python.

5.2 Decision Tree Creation

For the Decision Tree construction we used a Java implantation of C4.5 [18] algorithm called J48 from the WEKA [19] software. After pruning, the resulted Decision Tree contained only 17 from the 182 Meta-Features meaning that only with a small subset of Meta-Features we can obtain a winning Query Strategy efficiently. Below we list the Meta-Features used by the Decision Tree along with their category group and their description:

- General

  - **NrInst:** Number of instances [20]

- Statistical

  - **Cor(mean):** Mean of absolute values of the correlation of distinct dataset column pairs [21]
  - **MAD(mean):** Mean of the Median Absolute Deviation adjusted by a factor [22]
  - **CanCor(sd):** Standard distribution of canonical correlations of the data [23]
  - **NrNorm:** Number of attributes normally distributed based in a given method [24]

- Model-based

  - **LeavesPerClass(sd):** Standard distribution of proportion of the leaves per class in Decision Tree model [25]
  - **NodesPerAttr:** Ratio of nodes per number of attributes in Decision Tree model [26]
  - **LeavesCorrob(sd):** Standard distribution of leaves corroboration of the Decision Tree model [26]

- Complexity

  - **T1(sd):** Standard distribution of the fraction of hyperspheres covering data [27]
  - **Density:** Average density of the network [27]

- Clustering

  - **PB:** Pearson correlation between class matching and instance distances [28]

- Landmarking

  - **NaiveBayesRel(sd):** Standard distribution of relative performances of the Naive Bayes classifier [29]
  - **EliteNN(mean):** Mean of the performances of Elite Nearest Neighbor [29]
  - **EliteNN(sd):** Standard distribution of performances of Elite Nearest Neighbor classifier [29]
  - **OneNNRel(sd):** Standard distribution of the relative performances of the 1-Nearest Neighbor classifier [29]
  - **RndNodeRel(sd):** Standard distribution of the relative performances of the single Decision Tree node model induced by a random attribute [29]
  - **LinearDiscrRel(sd):** Standard distribution of relative performances of the Linear Discriminant classifier [29]

In the following Rule Set, the rules of the produced Decision Tree are demonstrated. The tree consists of 45 nodes and has a height of 13 branches. From the nodes, 23 are leaves of the tree that describe the classification class along with the classified instances and the wrongly classified instances. The rest of the nodes describe the Meta-Features used and the vertices the value of each Meta-feature for the decision making process.

```
NrInst<=140
  Cor(mean)<=0.130823:LC(8.0)
  Cor(mean)>0.130823
    EliteNN(sd)<=0.184284
      PB<=-0.082785:LC(7.0/1.0)
      PB>-0.082785:SM(5.0/1.0)
    EliteNN(sd)>0.184284:SM(6.0)
NrInst>140
  NaiveBayesRel(sd)<=2.5
    LeavesPerClass(sd)<=0.117851:SM(3.0)
    LeavesPerClass(sd)>0.117851
      EliteNN(sd)<=0.073421:SM(3.0/1.0)
      EliteNN(sd)>0.073421:LC(8.0/1.0)
  NaiveBayesRel(sd)>2.5
    T1(sd)<=0.047321
      OneNNRel(sd)<=3
        RndNodeRel(sd)<=6:SM(6.0/1.0)
        RndNodeRel(sd)>6:Ent(3.0)
      OneNNRel(sd)>3
        NodesPerAttr<=176.333333
          RndNodeRel(sd)<=3.5
            LeavesCorrob(sd)<=0.003182:Ent(6.0)
            LeavesCorrob(sd)>0.003182
              NaiveBayesRel(sd)<=3:SM(2.0)
              NaiveBayesRel(sd)>3
                LinearDiscrRel(sd)<=3:SM(3.0/1.0)
                LinearDiscrRel(sd)>3
                  CanCor(sd)<=0.309755
                    NrNorm<=0
                      LinearDiscrRel(sd)<=5
                        MAD(mean)<=245.13684:LC(9.0/1.0)
                        MAD(mean)>245.13684:Ent(2.0)
                      LinearDiscrRel(sd)>5:LC(7.0/1.0)
                    NrNorm>0:Ent(3.0/1.0)
                  CanCor(sd)>0.309755:Ent(11.0/3.0)
          RndNodeRel(sd)>3.5:LC(3.0)
        NodesPerAttr>176.333333:SM(3.0)
    T1(sd)>0.047321
      MAD(mean)<=0.320958
        Density<=0.998825:SM(8.0)
        Density>0.998825:Ent(2.0)
      MAD(mean)>0.320958
        EliteNN(mean)<=0.75:Ent(13.0)
        EliteNN(mean)>0.75:SM(2.0)
```

Decision Tree (Rule Set). Produced Decision Tree as a set of rules for selecting a winning Query Strategy using Meta-Features.

In order to evaluate the produced Decision Tree, we used the constructed dataset as the test set. In the Table 1 we demonstrate the confusion matrix of the tree.

Table 1. Confusion matrix of the produced Decision Tree

Query Strategy	Least Confidence	Smallest Margin	Entropy
Least Confidence	38	2	2
Smallest Margin	2	37	2
Entropy	2	2	36

From the results, it is shown that 111 instances are classified correctly and 12 incorrectly with each class having 4 incorrectly classified instances resulting to a classification accuracy of 90.24%.

In the Table 2, Precision, Recall and F-Measure of the produced Decision Tree are demonstrated.

Table 2. Precision, Recall and F-Measure of the produced Decision Tree

Query Strategy	Precision	Recall	F-Measure
Least Confidence	90.5%	90.5%	90.5%
Smallest Margin	90.2%	90.2%	90.2%
Entropy	90%	90%	90%
Weighted Average	90.2%	90.2%	90.2%

From the performance metrics, it is shown that the Decision Tree produces reliable classification results since both Precision and Recall are over 90% along with the F-Measure.

6 Conclusion and Future Work

In this work we constructed a dataset of Meta-Features and then produced a Decision Tree that can be used for selecting the appropriate Uncertainty Sampling Query Strategy for Active Learning tasks. The classification accuracy of the Decision Tree indicates that calculating a small set of Meta-Features in new datasets can be enough for selecting the appropriate Query Strategy without having to run all of them, saving a lot of time and resources.

In the future we would like to try using a more sophisticated base learner like Random Forest [30] for the Active Learning process and evaluate how the classes change and how biased the produced Decision Tree can be. Moreover, we would like to extend the research to imbalance datasets [31] and to regression problems [32]. Finally, we would like to use a noisy oracle in order to give in the Active Learning process an error rate when evaluating the label of the datasets [33].

References

1. Settles, B., Craven, M., Friedl, L.: Active learning with real annotation costs. In: Proceedings of the NIPS Workshop on Cost-Sensitive Learning, pp. 1–10 (2008)
2. Tharwat, A., Schenck, W.: A survey on active learning: state-of-the-art practical challenges and research directions. Mathematics **11**(4), 820 (2023). https://doi.org/10.3390/MATH11 040820
3. Kazllarof, V., Karlos, S., Kotsiantis, S.: Investigation of combining logitboost (M5P) under active learning classification tasks. Informatics **7**(4), 50 (2020). https://doi.org/10.3390/inf ormatics7040050
4. Brazdil, P., Giraud-Carrier, C., Soares, C., Vilalta, R.: Metalearning (2009). https://doi.org/ 10.1007/978-3-540-73263-1
5. Settles, B.: Active learning. Synth. Lect. Artif. Intell. Mach. Learn. **18**, 1–111 (2012). https:// doi.org/10.2200/S00429ED1V01Y201207AIM018
6. Rivolli, A., Garcia, L.P.F., Soares, C., Vanschoren, J., de Carvalho, A.C.P.L.F.: Meta-features for meta-learning. Knowl.-Based Syst. **240**, 108101 (2022). https://doi.org/10.1016/J.KNO SYS.2021.108101
7. Rakotoarison, H., Milijaona, L., Rasoanaivo, A., Sebag, M., Schoenauer, M.: Learning Meta-features for AutoML (2022). https://hal.inria.fr/hal-03583789v2. Accessed 07 Mar 2023
8. Rivolli, A., Garcia, L.P.F., Soares, C., Vanschoren, J., de Carvalho, A.C.P.L.F.: Characterizing classification datasets: a study of meta-features for meta-learning (2018). https://doi.org/10. 48550/arxiv.1808.10406
9. Alcobaça, E., Siqueira, F., Rivolli, A., Garcia, L.P.F., Oliva, J.T., de Carvalho, A.C.P.L.F.: MFE: towards reproducible meta-feature extraction. J. Mach. Learn. Res. **21**(111), 1–5 (2020). http://jmlr.org/papers/v21/19-348.html. Accessed 07 Mar 2023
10. Prudêncio, R.B.C., Ludermir, T.B.: Combining uncertainty sampling methods for active meta-learning. In: ISDA 2009 - 9th International Conference on Intelligent Systems Design and Applications, pp. 220–225 (2009). https://doi.org/10.1109/ISDA.2009.160
11. Prudêncio, R.B.C., Soares, C., Ludermir, T.B.: Uncertainty sampling-based active selection of datasetoids for meta-learning. In: Honkela, T., Duch, W., Girolami, M., Kaski, S. (eds.) ICANN 2011. LNCS, vol. 6792, pp. 454–461. Springer, Heidelberg (2011). https://doi.org/ 10.1007/978-3-642-21738-8_58
12. Prudêncio, R.B.C., Ludermir, T.B.: Active meta-learning with uncertainty sampling and outlier detection. In: Proceedings of International Joint Conference on Neural Networks, pp. 346–351 (2008). https://doi.org/10.1109/IJCNN.2008.4633815
13. Barrett, R., White, A.D.: Investigating active learning and meta-learning for iterative peptide design. J. Chem. Inf. Model. **61**(1), 95–105 (2021). https://doi.org/10.1021/ACS.JCIM.0C0 0946/ASSET/IMAGES/LARGE/CI0C00946_0006.JPEG
14. Martins, V.E., Cano, A., Junior, S.B.: Meta-learning for dynamic tuning of active learning on stream classification. Pattern Recognit. **138**, 109359 (2023). https://doi.org/10.1016/J.PAT COG.2023.109359
15. Vanschoren, J., van Rijn, J.N., Bischl, B., Torgo, L.: OpenML: networked science in machine learning. ACM SIGKDD Explor. Newsl. **15**(2), 49–60 (2014). https://doi.org/10.1145/264 1190.2641198

16. Yang, Y.-Y., Lee, S.-C., Chung, Y.-A., Wu, T.-E., Chen, S.-A., Lin, H.-T.: libact: Pool-based Active Learning in Python (2017). https://doi.org/10.48550/arxiv.1710.00379
17. Pedregosa, F., et al.: Scikit-learn: machine learning in python. J. Mach. Learn. Res. **12**, 2825–2830 (2012). https://doi.org/10.48550/arxiv.1201.0490
18. Salzberg, S.L.: C4.5: programs for machine learning by J. Ross Quinlan. Morgan Kaufmann Publishers, Inc., 1993. Mach. Learn. **16**(3), 235–240 (1994). https://doi.org/10.1007/BF0099 3309
19. Hall, M., Frank, E., Holmes, G., Pfahringer, B., Reutemann, P., Witten, I.H.: The WEKA data mining software: an update. SIGKDD Explor. **11**(1) (2009). https://citeseerx.ist.psu.edu/vie wdoc/summary?doi=10.1.1.148.3671. Accessed 07 Mar 2021
20. Fulkerson, B., Michie, D., Spiegelhalter, D.J., Taylor, C.C.: Machine learning, neural and statistical classification. Technometrics **37**(4), 459 (1995). https://doi.org/10.2307/1269742
21. Castiello, C., Castellano, G., Fanelli, A.M.: Meta-data: characterization of input features for meta-learning. In: Torra, V., Narukawa, Y., Miyamoto, S. (eds.) MDAI 2005. LNCS (LNAI), vol. 3558, pp. 457–468. Springer, Heidelberg (2005). https://doi.org/10.1007/11526018_45
22. Ali, S., Smith, K.A.: On learning algorithm selection for classification. Appl. Soft Comput. **6**(2), 119–138 (2006). https://doi.org/10.1016/J.ASOC.2004.12.002
23. Kalousis, A.: Algorithm selection via meta-learning (2002). https://doi.org/10.13097/ARC HIVE-OUVERTE/UNIGE:104435
24. Kopf, C., Taylor, C.: Meta-Analysis: From Data Characterisation for Meta-Learning to Meta-Regression (2000)
25. Filchenkov, A., Pendryak, A.: Datasets meta-feature description for recommending feature selection algorithm. In: Proceedings of Artificial Intelligence and Natural Language and Information Extraction, Social Media and Web Search FRUCT Conference AINL-ISMW FRUCT 2015, pp. 11–18 (2016). https://doi.org/10.1109/AINL-ISMW-FRUCT.2015.7382962
26. Bensusan, H., Giraud-Carrier, C., Kennedy, C.: A higher-order approach to meta-learning, pp. 109–117 (2000). https://research-information.bris.ac.uk/en/publications/a-higher-order-approach-to-meta-learning. Accessed 07 Mar 2023
27. Lorena, A.C., Garcia, L.P.F., Lehmann, J., Souto, M.C.P., Ho, T.K.A.M.: How complex is your classification problem? ACM Comput. Surv. **52**(5), 1–34 (2019). https://doi.org/10.1145/334 7711
28. Gupta, S.D.: Point biserial correlation coefficient and its generalization. Psychometrika **25**(4), 393–408 (1960). https://doi.org/10.1007/BF02289756/METRICS
29. Bensusan, H., Giraud-Carrier, C.: Discovering task neighbourhoods through landmark learning performances. In: Zighed, D.A., Komorowski, J., Żytkow, J. (eds.) PKDD 2000. LNCS (LNAI), vol. 1910, pp. 325–330. Springer, Heidelberg (2000). https://doi.org/10.1007/3-540-45372-5_32
30. Breiman, L.: Random forests. Mach. Learn. **45**(1), 5–32 (2001). https://doi.org/10.1023/A: 1010933404324/METRICS
31. Aggarwal, U., Popescu, A., Hudelot, C.: Active Learning for Imbalanced Datasets, pp. 1428–1437 (2020)
32. Wu, D., Lin, C.T., Huang, J.: Active learning for regression using greedy sampling. Inf. Sci. **474**, 90–105 (2018). https://doi.org/10.1016/j.ins.2018.09.060
33. Gupta, G., Sahu, A.K., Lin, W.Y.: Noisy Batch Active Learning with Deterministic Annealing (2019). http://arxiv.org/abs/1909.12473. Accessed 13 Mar 2021

Maritime Federated Learning for Decentralized On-Ship Intelligence

Anastasios Giannopoulos[1(✉)], Nikolaos Nomikos[1], Georgios Ntroulias[2], Theodoros Syriopoulos[1], and Panagiotis Trakadas[1]

[1] National and Kapodistrian University of Athens, 34400 Psachna, Evia, Greece
{angianno,ptrakadas}@uoa.gr, {nomikosn,tsiriop}@pms.uoa.gr
[2] Hydrus Engineering S.A, Agia Paraskevi, 15343 Athens, Greece
g.ntroulias@hydrus-eng.com

Abstract. Maritime trade unavoidably influences the economy, transportation and market worldwide. Deploying efficient, privacy-preserving and environmental-friendly solutions in maritime environments requires a continuous global effort. There are many obstacles associated with the centralized optimization for on-sail ships, including data security violation, signaling overhead and high-latency response. Contradictorily, the emerging Federated Learning (FL) paradigm has been proposed as an efficient solution for promoting data privacy, low latency and high communication efficiency. In this context, this paper proposes a maritime-based FL scheme to ensure distributed, collaborative and secure optimization for enabling predictive on-ship intelligence. A scenario targeting the accurate prediction of the Primary Engine Power (PEP) of large cargo ships is considered, as the output PEP is directly proportional to fuel consumption. Based on real data, several Machine Learning (ML) models were tested and validated, in terms of their PEP prediction accuracy, with all models exploiting both weather- and ship-related data. Simulation results towards the selection of the PEP predictor, as well as the quantification of the FL scheme efficacy over traditional benchmarks were carried out, achieving a beneficial equilibrium between the prediction accuracy, data privacy and communication efficiency.

Keywords: Distributed Intelligence · Federated Learning · Fuel Consumption · Machine Learning · Maritime Communication Network

1 Introduction

Maritime trade is responsible for carrying out the majority of global trade and a major driver of economic growth. Modern maritime systems necessitate significant improvements in energy efficiency and environmental-awareness with considerable reduction of their CO2 emissions. These requirements become more stringent due to the "Fit for 55" agreement, according to which, 173 countries declare to reduce emissions by 2050 produced by transport, buildings, agriculture and waste by about 55%, relative to the

© IFIP International Federation for Information Processing 2023
Published by Springer Nature Switzerland AG 2023
I. Maglogiannis et al. (Eds.): AIAI 2023, IFIP AICT 676, pp. 195–206, 2023.
https://doi.org/10.1007/978-3-031-34107-6_16

total emissions of 2008 [1]. Taking seriously this agreement and considering the maritime sector as one of the primary sectors being responsible for CO_2 emissions, the maritime industry should be transformed in several cross-coupled domains, including the transportation [2], communication and intelligence layers [3].

A concerted global effort has been observed in developing novel solutions, being required in the domains of communication and intelligence. In this context, the introduction of advanced services and technologies, such as the Internet of Things (IoT), is expected to leverage optimum transportation solutions due to the huge amount of data that are collected, stored, and processed [3]. Hence, real-time monitoring and automated optimization procedures are expected to play a key role in future maritime transportation systems for ship path optimization or energy consumption-dependent and speed optimization purposes [4]. To this end, traditional optimization approaches might not be effective, since in general, they lead to non-convex problems, which are solved via iterative optimization approaches.

IoT solutions in the maritime sector include the transmission and processing of a large amount of heterogeneous data under harsh propagation conditions [5]. Therefore, reliable maritime communication and networking design becomes a critical and challenging task, due to the multiple constraints that need to be taken into consideration. The goal of this design should be the optimization of certain performance metrics (i.e., overall data throughput, network outages) with reduced transmission power and signaling burden [6]. In the vast majority of related works, the initial non-convex problem is decomposed into a discreet number of convex problems and solved via iterative optimization approaches. Still, performance loss is inherently introduced, while the frequent execution of iterative algorithms has a negative impact on the overall system response times [7]. Therefore, relying on conventional optimization to achieve ultra-reliable low latency communications (URLLC), being needed in maritime transportation applications is highly questionable.

Meanwhile, Machine learning (ML) comprises an ever-growing domain, mainly because it provides a powerful solution towards large-scale constrained optimization and predictive capabilities [8]. Most of the ML algorithms typically employed in the maritime sector require huge amounts of historically collected data. In order to ensure proper data processing and analytics, ML models are trained on a dataset to provide alarms, predictions or corrective actions, given a particular optimization task [9]. ML is classified into 3 main categories, namely (i) Supervised Learning (SL) in which labeled data are available as groundtruth to guide the model parameter adjustment during the training. SL algorithms are further divided, based on the type of the labels: classification refers to categorical labels, whereas regression refers to scalar-valued labels; (ii) Unsupervised Learning (UL) in which the goal is to identify hidden clusters with high feature similarity or to reduce the dimensions of the data through the usage of linear combinations of the features (i.e. components); (iii) Reinforcement Learning (RL) algorithms in which a cognitive agent finds an optimal decision-making policy through trial-and-error interactions with the maritime environment, aiming to maximize a reward (e.g., best possible behavior or path) in a specific situation [10].

However, there are several obstacles towards enabling ML functionalities in the maritime sector [3]. ML models require huge amounts of data in order to provide efficient solutions and predictions. From the maritime perspective, since the transmission and exchange of multi-source data in such an environment can be characterized by a high degree of heterogeneity, attributed to the distances that the components of a signal have to cover and the diverse transmission conditions, traditional centralized ML seems quite problematic. Moreover, centralized data collection raises privacy violation issues, considering that the training carries commercial sensitive information that requires protection against malicious attacks. Since the demanding transmissions and exchange of data, as well as privacy violation in such environments are mainly the case in centralized schemes, the solution of distributed cooperative ML is preferred.

Contrary to the aforementioned drawbacks, Federated Learning (FL) has been widely promoted, as an effective collaborative learning scheme [11]. FL training process can ensure fast ML execution, no need for data transmissions and privacy preservation of maritime sensitive data. In FL, maritime nodes exploit shared models trained from excessive amounts of data, without the need to centrally store it. In this context, instead of constantly updating a central node with data, the training of ML models is performed locally, and then, the global model is periodically updated. Therefore, this method can lead to four very important advantages: (i) reduction of the signaling load, (ii) reduction of the wireless transmission power, (iii) protection of security and privacy and (iv) enhanced model sharing abilities between maritime nodes, given the global observability of the FL-constructed global model that is finally deployed.

The present paper outlines the implementation and comparison of FL methodology against various ML benchmark schemes. Using a labeled commercial dataset from a maritime enterprise, a scenario focusing on the prediction of the Primary Engine Power (PEP) of large cargo ships is considered. As PEP is proportional to the fuel oil consumption, we target to demonstrate the potency of FL-assisted methods towards collaborative PEP prediction. Noteworthy, weather-related and on-sail ship-related features were used to accurately estimate the PEP required for the ship propulsion. To obtain optimal performance of FL, multiple SL ship-specific models were compared in the single-ship datasets, for the purpose of finding the best PEP regressor. The advantages and disadvantages of using FL against baseline methods are also identified. In summary, the contributions of this work can be identified as:

(i) The exploitation of historical knowledge of both weather- and ship-related features, extracted by real data from a maritime enterprise, to obtain accurate and ship-specific supervised learning models,

(ii) The proposition of a general-purpose FL-based architecture to enable privacy-preserving and low-latency predictive abilities for on-sail cargo ships.

(iii) The adoption of an end-to-end processing pipeline to implement FL in the maritime sector, including the training, testing and comparison of multiple regression models to properly find the best regressor for each ship.

(iv) The quantitative comparison of FL against centralized and decentralized team learning methods in maritime setups.

(v) The limitations of centralized ML solutions are tackled, facilitating the integration of ML in the maritime industry by addressing the privacy concerns of the involved stakeholders while avoiding excessive transmission overheads in the operation of the FL solution.

2   Architectural and Technical Methodology

2.1   Maritime Federated Learning

In this section, a three-tier Maritime Federated Learning (MFL) architecture is proposed (see Fig. 1). MFL is an adaptation of FL principles, properly embodied within a maritime setup, so as to provide an efficient handling of distributed ship-dependent datasets and to decouple model training from excessive transmissions to the central server. In the considered MFL scenario, local ship clients can be seen as common-goal agents, aiming to converge in an adequate solution of a given learning task. This process takes place with the supervision and collaboration of the central server, which is responsible for aggregating knowledge from all agents. Ship-specific data remain localized; hence, any data privacy issue can be met only in isolated ship sites, not affecting the federation.

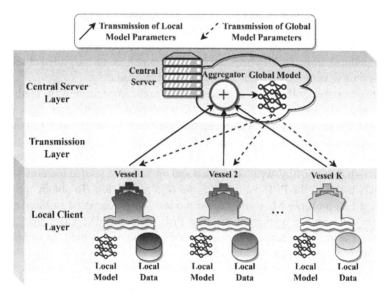

Fig. 1. Three-tier Federated Learning Architecture for on-sail maritime intelligence. Local Models are trained in a decentralized manned, based on local ship-specific data. Only model parameters are exchanged through the Transmission layer. The Central Server layer aggregates the local models before sending the averaged global model back to the local ship agents.

Driven by the aforementioned process, MFL can offer a unified distributed ML platform, allowing local models to exploit information observed and processed by other learners using the global model. Moreover, incoming new models can directly grasp the knowledge obtained by the global model, after long-term federated training among existing clients. MFL can also enable learning, based on non-independent and identical distributed (non-i.i.d) sets of data [11]. This attribute can be extremely beneficial in on-sail multi-ship collaborative learning, since different types of ships with diverse sizes of available datasets can also be harmonized according to MFL. Note that, although here, we illustrate only neural networks as local/global models, MFL models can be of any type, spanning from decision tree, logistic regression and ensemble models to recurrent and convolutional neural networks.

2.2 Cargo Ship Dataset

To train the ML schemes deployed in this study, a 1-year duration dataset of two twin cargo ships was available. For each cargo, ten time-varying variables are captured with a sampling frequency of 1 sample per minute. The temporal course of the variables refers to multiple voyages of the ships. The data were sampled from 01-07-2021 to 30-06-2022, resulting in 514,525 (for ship 1) and 525,005 (for ship 2) total instances per variable. Specifically, the dataset contained measures about both ship"s on-sail features and wind characteristics which are detailed below:

i. *Speed over ground (SOG):* It quantifies the ship"s speed in relation to the surface of the earth and is measured in knots.
ii. *Speed through water (STW):* Different from SOG, STW represents the ship"s speed in relation to the water currents and is measured in knots.
iii. *Heading:* It denotes the actual on-sail direction in which the ship is pointing and it is expressed, as the angular distance relative to north ($0°$), clockwise through $359°$.
iv. *Continuous wind speed (CWS):* It is the wind strength expressed in m/s.
v. *Discretized wind speed (DWS):* It is the discretized version of CWS, quantized according to the Beaufort scale (bft). DWS can be considered as a categorical variable ranging from 0 to 12 in steps of 1 and mapping with the 13 wind classes or weather flags (from "calm" to "hurricane-force").
vi. *Wind direction (WD):* It represents the true wind direction in relation to the ship"s on-board heading. Thus, WD is expressed in degrees and varies between $0°$-$360°$ (wind on the bow at $0°$, wind on the beam at $90°$, wind on the stern at $180°$).
vii. *Draft forward (DF):* The draft forward (bow) is the ship"s depth in meters measured at the perpendicular of the bow based on predefined depth levels.
viii. *Draft aft (DA):* The draft aft (stern) is the ship"s depth in meters, measured at the perpendicular of the stern, based on predefined depth levels.
ix. *Trim:* The trim is simply the difference between the DF and DA (depth in meters), relative to the designed waterline located at the middle of the ship. It determines the minimum depth of water a ship can safely navigate.
x. *Primary engine power (PEP):* It is the aggregated power supplied by the prime mover(s) which are responsible to provide useful propulsion to the ship and is expressed in kW. Obviously, PEP is positively correlated with the electricity require-ments of the ship"s diesel engine, therefore being directly proportional to the fuel oil consumption. Additionally, PEP has also bi-directional causal relationship with the ship"s SOG and STW, as well as it is strongly affected by wind conditions, sea currents and ship"s drafts.

The ML methodology presented below exploits the labelled dataset, considering the PEP as the target variable (model output) and the rest of the measures as potential predictors (or model inputs). This will allow the adoption of an accurate training and verification process of the developed ML model by measuring the error between the model-predicted outputs and the actual historical values of the target variable.

2.3 Machine Learning-Based Pipeline for PEP Prediction

To ensure high signal-to-noise ratio and sufficient performance of the final-stage collaborative learning schemes, a gradual 3-phase pipeline was adopted, including the data preparation, the ship-specific local model selection and the comparison among collaborative methods for multi-ship PEP prediction (see Fig. 2).

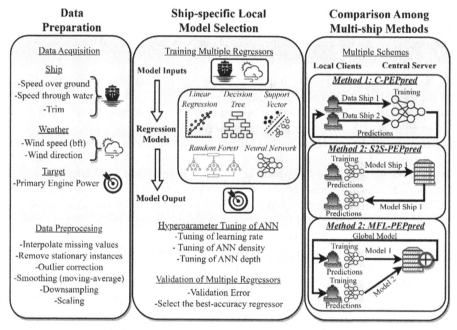

Fig. 2. Proposed pipeline for Collaborative Learning of ship's Primary Engine Power.

1. *Data Preparation:* In this phase, all the preliminary steps required to reduce the model dimensionality and mitigate the data size and noise were performed. Initially, a set of multi-collinearity criteria were investigated towards avoiding feature redundancy and mitigating the model input dimensions. As an independent factor of the ship"s fuel consumption, Heading parameter was avoided from the regression inputs. In addition, both types of vessel drafts (DF and DA) were also ignored, given that retaining only their difference (Trim parameter) does not imply any information loss. Moreover, only one version of the wind speed was selected (i.e. DWS in bft) to reflect the wind strength. Noteworthy, since STW indirectly carries information about sea currents (whereas SOG is the ground-referenced speed), both types of speed

(SOG and STW) were kept as model inputs. Then, the missing values were replaced, following an average-interpolation calculation, based on the previous and the next available samples. The final number of interpolated values was not more than 8% of the total samples per variable. Instances corresponding to near-zero vessel speed (SOG < 0.2 knots) were also ditched. Afterwards, the moving-average filter was applied to slightly smooth the data and eliminate the aliasing-caused distortion that will follow upon downsampling. Given the slow variations observed in all time-series, a downsampling operation was applied to ensure a sampling frequency of 1 sample per 15 min. Finally, the values of each variable were scaled in the range [0,1] using a Min-Max scaling operation.

2. *Ship-specific local model selection:* In principle, the relationship between the ship"s PEP and the model inputs (SOG, STW, DWS, WD and Trim) is unknown and it can be either linear or non-linear. ML algorithms can be employed to create a local regression model, using historical instance-specific features as inputs and the respective PEP values as labels. To reveal the best ship-specific regressor, several ML (linear and non-linear) regression algorithms were trained and tested, namely:

   i. *Multiple Linear Regression (MLR)* assumes that a weighted linear combination of N independent features can predict the target. The resulting model is linear with coefficients w_i ($i = 1, 2, \ldots N$), graphically demonstrated by the best-fitting straight line, showing the minimum mean squared error between the real and MLR-predicted values (calculated over validation samples).

   ii. *Decision Tree Regression (DTR)* is a non-parametric ML model which produces a rule-based tree by splitting the feature space properly, so as to guarantee low information entropy in each decision area. Then, using the separated decision areas as tree leafs, it constructs several rule paths, arriving at terminal leafs according to the prior feature space splitting rules. Each leaf predicts the average target value, computed across the target values of all samples, included in the respective decision area.

   iii. *Support Vector Regression (SVR)* uses an ε-insensitive tube to allow for more flexibility in errors. Unlike *Linear Regression*, *SVR* penalizes only the data points that have at least ε distance from the fitting curve. The target of the SVR is to fit the best line within a threshold value (ε), reflecting the distance between the hyperplane and boundary line.

   iv. *Random Forest Regression (RFR)* is an ensemble learning version of DTR. By splitting the dataset in N segments, multiple segment-specific DTRs are constructed. Given a new sample, the RFR predicts the average prediction, computed across all the individual trees.

   v. *Artificial Neural Network (ANN)* is a supervised non-linear learning scheme of sequentially-stacked and fully-connected layers. Each layer consists of multiple units, each one calculating the weighted sum of all the previous-layer outputs and then applying an activation function (e.g. ReLu, SoftMax). ANN properly tunes the connections between units (i.e. weights), so as to minimize the prediction error (or loss function).

3. *Collaborative methods for multi-ship PEP prediction:* Three schemes were contrasted in terms of the provided PEP prediction accuracy preparation, including one
   centralized and two decentralized collaborative schemes, namely:

   i. *Centralized PEP prediction (C-PEPpred)* is the traditional method to deploy ML
      models. Being sensitive to malicious attacks, C-PEPpred simply collects all the
      data in the central server, before building a powerful heavy model. Both ships can
      predict future PEP values upon request on the central model. Note that, this method
      can have near-optimal PEP estimation error, since the central model has been
      trained on the multi-ship dataset, thus obtaining global environment observability.

   ii. *Ship-to-ship model transfer for PEP prediction (S2S-PEPpred)* is based on trans-
      ferring a ship-specific already trained model to the rest of the ships, thus dras-
      tically reducing the training effort. Given adequate similarities across ships and
      their respective feature distributions, this method can have beneficial outcomes,
      leading both to extremely fast training and privacy-preservation, since the central
      server is used only for exchanging the models between local agents.

   iii. *Maritime Federated Learning for PEP prediction (MFL-PEPpred)* is based on
      transmitting only the pretrained model parameters to the central server, where the
      conventional FedAvg [11] algorithm is running. Periodically, local model weights
      are replaced with a weighted average model derived by aggregation at the server
      site (usually located in ports). Apart from data privacy protection and low model
      dimensionality compared to C-PEPpred, MFL-based local models have finally
      a global knowledge and can be proactive in predicting previously-unseen PEP
      conditions, as they indirectly exchange information between each other.

3   Simulation Results

For each of the following training setups, single-ship datasets were separated in training
and testing sets after a 90/10 split ratio. All algorithmic implementations were conducted
in Python 3.0, using the Tensorflow (v2.4) and Scikit-learn libraries [12].

3.1 Optimization of ML Model Hyperparameters

To ensure optimal configuration of the collaborative methods presented in Subsect. 3.3,
a careful hyperparameter tuning is required for ANN and RFR. The former"s convergence performance is considerably affected by the network depth and the learning rate
parameters, whereas the latter is strongly influenced by the number of individual tree
estimators that are deployed to comprise the forest. Extensive simulations with varying learning rates ($\alpha = 0.1, 0.01, 0.001, 0.0001, 0.00001$) and number of hidden layers
($H = 1, 2, 3, 4, 5$) were conducted to optimize the ANN performance. The ith hidden
layer density was (6-i)$\times$ 200 (where i = 1, 2, ...,5). For each (α, H) pair, the validation metric was the mean squared error (MSE) between the actual and predicted PEP,
computed over the testing set. Figure 3 shows the validation MSE for different values
of (α, H), as well as the loss curve for the optimal (α, H) configuration. The impact of
the different number of estimators in the RFR is also depicted.

Evidently, both ship-specific ANN models are optimally trained for H = 4 hidden
layers and $a = 10^{-3}$ learning rate. In addition, the RFR algorithm showed the best

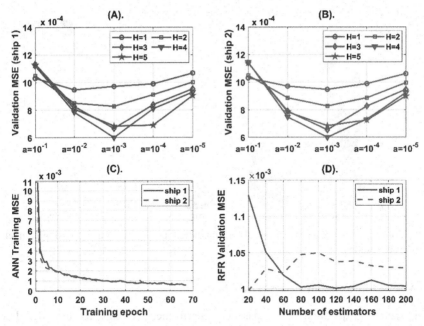

Fig. 3. Hyperparameter tuning of ANN and RFR models. **A – B.** Validation MSE for varying values of learning rate and number of hidden layers, for ship 1 and 2, separately. **C.** ANN training loss curves for ships 1 and 2 using the optimal hyperparameters. **D.** Validation MSE of RFR model, as a function of the number of estimators.

outcomes for 120 (ship1) and 20 (ship 2) number of tree estimators, comprising the forest.

3.2 Ship-Specific Model Selection

Using the optimally configured RFR and ANN models for both ships, this section presents the performance comparisons between five ML model regressors, namely MLR, DTR, SVR, RFR and ANN. To decide which model is the best PEP predictor for representing the local models in an FL setup, all models were compared, in terms of their resulting validation error, calculated over the testing set (see Fig. 4).

As shown in Fig. 4, all models show a validation MSE constantly below 0.018. Given the presence of non-linearities in the PEP prediction, MLR showed the highest prediction error. Allowing non-linear mapping between the features and the target, SVR and DTR exhibited improved error performance (in the order of 10^{-3}). The ensemble version of DTR (i.e. RFR) improved further the MSE outcomes, being very close to the best regressor, which was the ANN models. Since ANN regressors outperform the rest of models, exhibiting an MSE of 0.0006 for both ships, they were finally selected to represent the local models of the subsequent analyses.

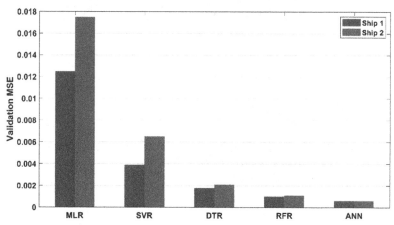

Fig. 4. Comparison among different local PEP prediction models for ship 1 and ship 2, in terms of the validation MSE.

3.3 Multi-ship Collaborative ML Methods

In this section, a quantitative comparison is performed, amongst the considered collaborative between-ships learning schemes, namely the C-PEPpred, S2S-PEPpred and MFL-PEPpred (see Sect. 2.3). Based on an evaluation set of 100 data samples drawn from both ship 1 and ship 2 testing sets, the three collaborative methods were compared, in terms of their goodness of fit, based on normalized root MSE (NRMSE, degree of fitness between actual and predicted PEP values). To visually illustrate the fitting strength of all methods, Fig. 5 (panels A-C) depicts the actual PEP curve and the corresponding method-predicted series with all samples representing the evaluation set.

Evidently, C-PEPpred shows the best accuracy, as the large ANN used (5 hidden layers) has been trained on the datasets of both ships (global observability). Contrary to the high demands of C-PEPpred to acquire the training data (massive data transmission to/from central server, privacy violation), S2S-PEPpred method shows the most relaxed requirement of having finally a model at each ship site, however providing multiple selfish models. This is attributed to the fact that the transferred model has been only trained on the source model data (low global observability). Towards achieving a reasonable trade-off between the accuracy of C-PEPpred and the flexibility of S2S-PEPpred, the MFL-PEPpred model showed a goodness of fit very close to that of C-PEPpred, offering also low-dimensionality and privacy-preserving benefits. The adequate performance of MFL-PEPpred relies on the ability to obtain general observability for all the ship agents, given the aggregation operation at the central server, across all individual FL contributors.

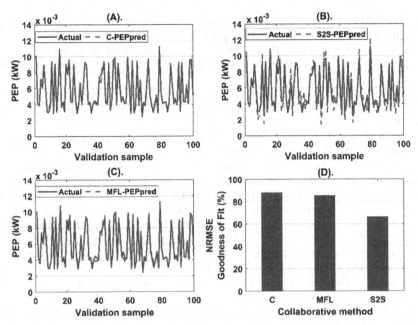

Fig. 5. Performance comparison between different collaborative PEP learning methods. **A – C.** Actual versus method-predicted PEP curves for C-, S2S- and MFL-PEPpred, respectively. **D.** Normalized Root MSE-base Goodness of Fit (%) for the three methods.

4 Conclusions

In this paper, a Maritime Federated Learning scheme for decentralized on-ship learning is proposed, targeting to overcome the limits of the current centralized approaches. Considering a fuel consumption prediction use case, several models are compared, as local ship learners, with ANNs outperforming the benchmark ML algorithms. Using a real dataset that includes both on-sail ship features and wind information, multiple simulations were conducted for the optimal configuration of the ML models. The Federated Learning method was compared against a centralized and a decentralized transfer learning-based method, in terms of the collaborative performance of multi-ship prediction. Results showed that Federated Learning comprises a promising solution for enabling accurate, collaborative and team learning abilities in maritime setups, overcoming the obstacles faced by centralized schemes.

Acknowledgment. This work was partially supported by the TARDIS Project, funded by EU HORIZON EUROPE program, under grant agreement No 101093006.

References

1. Bagoulla, C., Guillotreau, P.: Maritime transport in the French economy and its impact on air pollution: an input-output analysis. Mar. Policy **116**, 103818 (2020)

2. Lister, J., Poulsen, R.T., Ponte, S.: Orchestrating transnational environmental governance in maritime shipping. Glob. Environ. Chang. **34**, 185–195 (2015)
3. Nomikos, N., Gkonis, P.K., Bithas, P.S., Trakadas, P.: A survey on UAV-aided maritime communications: deployment considerations, applications, and future challenges. IEEE Open J. Commun. Soc. (2022)
4. Jimenez, V.J., Kim, H., Munim, Z.H.: A review of ship energy efficiency research and directions towards emission reduction in the maritime industry. J. Cleaner Prod. 132888 (2022)
5. Zhang, J., Wang, M.M., Xia, T., Wang, L.: Maritime IoT: An architectural and radio spectrum perspective. IEEE Access **8**, 93109–93122 (2020)
6. Giannopoulos, A., Spantideas, S., Tsinos, C., Trakadas, P.: Power control in 5G heterogeneous cells considering user demands using deep reinforcement learning. In: Maglogiannis, I., Macintyre, J., Iliadis, L. (eds.) AIAI 2021. IAICT, vol. 628, pp. 95–105. Springer, Cham (2021). https://doi.org/10.1007/978-3-030-79157-5_9
7. Spantideas, S.T., Giannopoulos, A.E., Kapsalis, N.C., Kalafatelis, A., Capsalis, C.N., Trakadas, P.: Joint energy-efficient and throughput-sufficient transmissions in 5G cells with deep Q-learning. In: 2021 IEEE International Mediterranean Conference on Communications and Networking (MeditCom), pp. 265–250. IEEE (2021)
8. Kaloxylos, A., Gavras, A., Camps Mur, D., Ghoraishi, M., Hrasnica, H.: AI and ML—Enablers for beyond 5G networks. Zenodo, Honolulu, HI, USA, Technical report (2020)
9. Angelopoulos, A., et al.: Allocating orders to printing machines for defect minimization: a comparative machine learning approach. In: Artificial Intelligence Applications and Innovations: 18th IFIP WG 12.5 International Conference, AIAI 2022, vol. 647, pp. 79–88. Springer, Cham (2022). https://doi.org/10.1007/978-3-031-08337-2_7
10. Giannopoulos, A., Spantideas, S., Kapsalis, N., Karkazis, P., Trakadas, P.: Deep reinforcement learning for energy-efficient multi-channel transmissions in 5G cognitive hetnets: centralized, decentralized and transfer learning based solutions. IEEE Access **9**, 129358–129374 (2021)
11. McMahan, B., Moore, E., Ramage, D., Hampson, S., y Arcas, B.A.: Communication-efficient learning of deep networks from decentralized data. In: Artificial Intelligence and Statistics, pp. 1273–1282. PMLR (2017)

OF-AE: Oblique Forest AutoEncoders

Cristian Daniel Alecsa[1,2]([✉]) [iD]

[1] Romanian Institute of Science and Technology, Cluj-Napoca, Romania
`alecsa@rist.ro`
[2] Technical University of Cluj-Napoca, Cluj-Napoca, Romania

Abstract. We propose an unsupervised ensemble method consisting of oblique trees that can address the task of auto-encoding, which is an extension of the *eForest* encoder introduced in [14]. By employing oblique splits, we will devise an auto-encoder method through the computation of a sparse solution of a set of linear inequalities consisting of feature values constraints. The code for reproducing our results is available at https://github.com/CDAlecsa/Oblique-Forest-AutoEncoders.

Keywords: Autoencoder · Oblique Decision Tree · Random Forest · Image reconstruction · Optimization problems

1 Introduction

The original CART algorithm [10] partitions the feature space using axis-parallel splits. The training of a classical *Decision Tree* $\mathcal{T}$ (denoted as DT) relies on *greedy optimization*, i.e. the root of the tree is the whole input space $\mathcal{X}$ which is split into two disjoint regions, and this process continues in a recursive manner. There are numerous extensions to classical CART methods. As an example, the extremely randomized trees (briefly ERT) [16] is implemented in SKLearn as *ExtraTreeRegressor* and induces randomization into the optimization of the trees by selecting the threshold fully at random for each candidate feature.

A popular extension of CART is the *Random Forest* algorithm, briefly RF, introduced by Leo Breiman in [9] (see also [8]). The RF method consists of different randomized decision trees $\mathcal{T}_1, \ldots, \mathcal{T}_N$ which are trained independently and which are finally aggregated all together with the average of the underlying individual scores. CART and RF methods can also be perceived as clustering methods. Some examples are the works of Lin and Jeon [21] which shows a connection between RF and nearest neighbor predictors, and the Extremely Randomized Clustering Forest (ERCForest) of Moosmann et. al. [24] (see also [22,25]) which is an ensemble of clustering trees based on spatial partitioning.

This work was supported by a grant of the Romanian Ministry of Research and Innovation, CCCDI – UEFISCDI, project number 178PCE/2021, PN-III-P4-ID-PCE-2020-0788, *Object PErception and Reconstruction with deep neural Architectures* (*OPERA*), within PNCDI III.

© IFIP International Federation for Information Processing 2023
Published by Springer Nature Switzerland AG 2023
I. Maglogiannis et al. (Eds.): AIAI 2023, IFIP AICT 676, pp. 207–219, 2023.
https://doi.org/10.1007/978-3-031-34107-6_17

A different extension to classical CART methods represent the so-called *Soft Decision Trees* (SDT) considered in [15,18] that can be considered as the probabilistic variants of CART, which are based upon the idea of splitting the parameters of the tree via gradient descent-type methods. A similar idea was developed for the so-called *Probabilistic Random Forest* (PRF) introduced in [30] where the underlying algorithm takes into account the uncertainty in both features and labels. Some extensions are represented by the *Deep Neural Decision Forest* (DNDF) introduced in [20] where each node is represented by a neural network layer and where the backpropagation algorithm is used in the training process, and the *Adaptive Neural Trees* (ANT) from the work [32]. These types of trees are optimized with respect to a global loss function and the nodes in the DNDF and ANT uses the same input x belonging to the dataset. At the same time, SDT and its variants rely on hierarchical decisions, instead of hierarchical features.

2   Related Work

An improvement over CART are the *Oblique Decision Trees* (briefly ODT) which partitions the input space $\mathcal{X}$ using multivariate tests. These trees test at each internal node several attributes by utilising linear combinations of features, and it is well known that training ODT is in general associated with a high training run-time cost (see Murthy et. al. [26]).

The pioneering work on oblique trees began with the work of Bremain et. al. [10] which introduced the so-called *Classification and Regression Trees - Linear Combination*, in a nutshell CART-LC. There are multiple extensions of the classical Oblique Tree CART-LC. One of them is the recent CO2 algorithm (*Continuous Optimization of Oblique Splits*) from [28], which focuses on optimizing an objective function through gradient-based methods. A different methodology is considered in [33] where the authors introduced the so-called *HHCART* oblique decision method. The underlying approach is that the original space where the dataset belongs to is transformed into a feature space. Then, one finds an axis-parallel split in the feature space which corresponds to a multivariate oblique split in the original space. The reflected training samples are given by $\hat{\mathcal{D}} = \mathcal{D}\mathcal{H}$, where $\mathcal{D}$ represents the original training data and the Householder matrix is $\mathcal{H} = \mathcal{I} - 2uu^T$, where $u = \dfrac{e - d}{\|e - d\|_2}$. Here, d represents the dominant eigenvector of the estimated covariance matrix corresponding of a class (suggesting the orientation of that class), and e is the standard basis vector corresponding to a chosen feature. Since the Householder matrix $\mathcal{H}$ is symmetric and orthogonal, a sample point in the transformed space can be mapped with a minimal cost to the original space, due to the fact that $\mathcal{H}\mathcal{H} = \mathcal{I}$. The last Oblique Tree we recall is the *RandCART* algorithm (see [6]) where, as in the case of *HHCART*, an oblique decision split in the original space corresponds to an axis-parallel split in a feature transformed space. The training samples $\mathcal{D}$ are converted into a new feature space $\mathcal{D}'$ of the same dimension as $\mathcal{D}$, for which one generates randomly and independently p^2 terms $m_{ij} \sim \mathcal{N}(0, 1)$ which defines a square matrix $\mathcal{M}$, the latter being decomposed using QR decomposition as $\mathcal{M} = QR$, where Q is orthogonal and R is upper triangular. After that, the new feature space is obtained as $\hat{\mathcal{D}} = \mathcal{D}Q$.

We end the present section by turning our focus to the idea of autoencoders which dates back to [7]. Despite the fact that most autoencoder models are, in general, neural networks (as an example, see [3,19]), only recently autoencoders based upon DT gained significant attention from the Machine Learning community. Irsoy and Alpaydin in [17] introduced an SDT-type method where a sigmoid gating function is used at every internal node, and where the final structure is based on stacking two SDTs with a layer-by-layer training. On the other hand, the interpretable autoencoder introduced in the paper of Aguilar et. al. [2] is based on multiple DT, where the ith tree is trained with all of the features except the ith attribute where this attribute is considered the target class. A different type of model are the Generative Trees (GT) recently introduced in [27] which are generative-like autoencoder models. The last model that we recall is the *eForest* encoder method from [14] in which the encoding is done by making the input samples go through all of the RF estimators in order to find the path from each tree where every sample goes to. Then, for each sample which will be decoded, it builds up the estimator spaces which represents the restriction on all the features. For decoding, the *eForest* encoder gathers up the attributes restrictions from all the subspaces and then uses the Maximum Compatibility Rule (MCR) in order to find the lower and upper values of the features.

3 Proposed Methodology

In this section we shall present the technique that will aid us extending the *eForest* encoder to ODT. In what follows, we shall employ different types of ODT coupled simultaneously into a Bagging Regressor which will form an unsupervised encoding-decoding method that will be called **Oblique Forest AutoEncoder**, namely *OF-AE*. For the *eForest*, the decoder part consists in taking, for a given sample, the feature restrictions from the right branches of the trees paths, while the final application of the MCR is related to taking the maximum bound of the feature values from these features subspaces. On the other hand, for our ODT we can gather, for a given sample which need to be decoded, all of the feature restrictions from the underlying path (by taking into account also the sign of the branches) and form an optimization problem with constraints. Additionally, for the image reconstruction cases we shall add auxilliary constraints such that the feature values belong to the closed interval $[0, 255]$, and we will employ the same technique as in *eForest* by training a different encoder-decoder pair for every channel. In what follows we shall propose our encoding-decoding method for a given ensemble of ODT $\mathcal{T}_1, \ldots, \mathcal{T}_N$. For every tree of this ensemble that is already trained, the forward encoding process consists in sending an input vector through each individual tree and to retain the weights and the tresholds for every internal node from the path the samples passes through. For some index $i \in \{1, \ldots, N\}$, we consider a tree $\mathcal{T}_i$ (depicted in Fig. 1). For a sample $x \in \mathcal{X}$, the path traversed by the input vector x is highlighted with blue while the other internal nodes not used in the current path are denoted with light green.

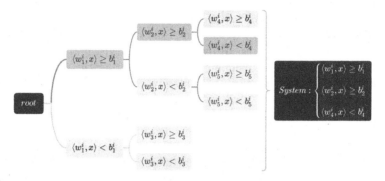

Fig. 1. A system of constraints obtained from a sample path.

For the tree depicted in Fig. 1 we observe that the first oblique condition on the root is $\langle w_1^i, x \rangle \geq b_1^i$ for the right branch, and $\langle w_1^i, x \rangle < b_1^i$ for the left branch. Furthermore, for the internal node from the right branch of the sample path, the right branch condition is $\langle w_2^i, x \rangle \geq b_2^i$ while the left branch inequality is $\langle w_2^i, x \rangle < b_2^i$. Finally, for the last internal node of the sample path of x, the conditions are $\langle w_4^i, x \rangle \geq b_4^i$ for the right branch and $\langle w_4^i, x \rangle < b_4^i$ for the left branch. In order to simplify our analysis and from our preliminary simulations we observed that for the system of equations we can use non-strict inequalities thus, for the tree $\mathcal{T}_i$ we get the system based on the weights and the tresholds from the path of x:

$$\begin{cases} \langle w_1^i, x \rangle \geq b_1^i \\ \langle w_2^i, x \rangle \geq b_2^i \\ \langle -w_4^i, x \rangle \geq -b_4^i \end{cases}$$

For the entire ODT ensemble $\mathcal{T}_1, \ldots, \mathcal{T}_N$, we consider a generic tree $\mathcal{T}_i$ of a given index $i \in \{1, \ldots, N\}$. If $\mathcal{T}_i$ has the depth d_i then the maximum number of nodes is $2^{d_i} - 1$. For the first node (root) we have the right and left branch conditions $\langle w_1^i, x \rangle \geq b_1^i$ and $\langle -w_1^i, x \rangle \geq -b_1^i$, respectively. For the second node, we obtain the inequalities $\langle w_2^i, x \rangle \geq b_2^i$ and $\langle -w_2^i, x \rangle \geq -b_2^i$. By continuing the argument for the maximum depth, we will have the general form of the right and left inequalities $\langle w_j^i, x \rangle \geq b_j^i$ and $\langle -w_j^i, x \rangle \geq -b_j^i$ for $j \in \{1, \ldots, n_i\}$, where $n_i \leq 2^{d_i} - 1$ is the number of nodes in the ODT $\mathcal{T}_i$. For a sample $x \in \mathcal{X}$, the path of x denoted as $\mathcal{P}_i = \{k_1^i, \ldots, k_{m_i}^i\}$, contains the indices of the nodes in the path: x traverses m_i nodes defined by the permutation $\{k_1^i, \ldots, k_{m_i}^i\}$. A sample x is encoded through the system of inequalities $\left(sign(j)\langle w_j^i, x \rangle \geq sign(j)b_j^i \right)_{j \in \mathcal{P}_i}$, i.e.

$$\begin{cases} sign(k_1^i)\langle w_{k_1}^i, x \rangle \geq sign(k_1^i)b_{k_1}^i \\ sign(k_2^i)\langle w_{k_2}^i, x \rangle \geq sign(k_2^i)b_{k_2}^i \\ \dotfill \\ sign(k_{m_i}^i)\langle w_{k_{m_i}}^i, x \rangle \geq sign(k_{m_i}^i)b_{k_{m_i}}^i \end{cases} \qquad \text{where } sign(j) = \begin{cases} 1; & j \text{ goes right} \\ -1; & j \text{ goes left} \end{cases}$$

Now, if we put together all of the sample paths of x from the tree ensemble, and denoting p as the number of features, we obtain the system $Ax \geq b$, with

$$
b = \begin{bmatrix} sign(k_1^1)b_{k_1}^1 \\ \cdots \\ sign(k_{m_1}^1)b_{k_{m_1}}^1 \\ \cdots \\ sign(k_1^N)b_{k_1}^N \\ \cdots \\ sign(k_{m_N}^N)b_{k_{m_N}}^N \end{bmatrix} \quad \text{and} \quad A = \begin{bmatrix} sign(k_1^1)w_{k_1}^1 \\ \cdots \\ sign(k_{m_1}^1)w_{k_{m_1}}^1 \\ \cdots \\ sign(k_1^N)w_{k_1}^N \\ \cdots \\ sign(k_{m_N}^N)w_{k_{m_N}}^N \end{bmatrix},
$$

where $b \in \mathbb{R}^{m_1 \times m_2 \times \cdots m_N}$ and $A \in \mathbb{R}^{m_1 \times m_2 \times \cdots m_N \times p}$. Furthermore, for the decoding of a sample $x \in \mathcal{X}$ we consider the optimization problem

$$
\begin{cases} minimize \; \|x\|_1 \\ subject \; to \; Ax \geq b \end{cases}
$$

For our codes we made the computing of a sparse solution of the set of the linear inequalities given by the weights and thresholds with the help of the CVXPY package ([1,12]). Also, we have considered only the *HHCART* and the *RandCART* as the choices of ODT since they are faster than other types of ODT. Furthermore, we have implemented a unsupervised version of the *Bagging Regressor* from SKLearn ([29]) by employing another technique from the SKLearn's implementation of *RandomTreesEmbedding* (which was used in the original version of the *eForest* encoder) where a one-dimensional target is uniformly generated for the tree ensemble. Our codes are based upon the implementations from [13] and https://github.com/valevalerio/Ensemble_Of_Oblique_ Decision_Trees related to [23] (where *HHCART* was adapted for regression problems using *MSE* criterion). The original *HHCART* implementations use the *PCA* method for transforming the original space to the feature space, but we have utilized the *PCA* method along with other alternatives: *Truncated-SVD*, *FastICA* and *Gaussian Random Projection* (briefly *GRP*), with a one-dimensional feature space.

4 Experiments

In this section we shall present the results of our approach for various tabular and image datasets.

4.1 Datasets and Experimental Setup

Concerning tabular datasets, we consider the following: from SKLearn we will employ the *Diabetes* dataset (442 samples / 10 features), and from the UCI ML repository we shall use *Seeds* (210 samples / 7 features) and *HTRU2* (17898 samples / 8 features), and also *Compas* (6172 samples /

13 features) from https://github.com/tunguz/TabularBenchmarks/tree/main/ datasets, respectively. On the other hand, for image-related datasets, we will consider as baseline datasets *MNIST* (60000 samples / 28 × 28) and *CIFAR10* (60000 samples / 32 × 32), and the *Oxford Flowers* dataset (8189 samples / various sizes) from https://www.robots.ox.ac.uk/~vgg/data/flowers/102/.

Furthermore, we will also utilize the image dataset used in [31] (which we will succinctly call it *CHD2R - Cultural Heritage Dataset for Digital Reconstruction*) which is comprised of cultural heritage assets and textile artefacts with traditional motifs (732 samples / 256 × 256). For RGB-type images, similar to *eForest* encoder, we will consider for each channel a different **OF-AE** model and then stack the results in order to fully decode an image.

In what follows, the parameters which will be used in our experiments are the following: `max_features` denotes the number of features drawn from the training dataset that are used to train each estimator, `max_samples` is the number of samples which are drawn with replacement from the same training dataset for each base estimator, `max_depth` will denote the maximum depth of each tree, `n_estimators` are the number of estimators (represented as oblique trees) which form the entire ensemble. For the datasets where we utilize the train-test splitting procedure, `test_size` represents the size percentage of the test dataset, while `n_train` and `n_test` will denote the explicit train and test number of samples if these integer values are given.

4.2 Tabular Data Reconstruction

In the present subsection we shall consider some basic experiments for the reconstruction of features from various tabular datasets. Our first experiment is related to the *Diabetes* dataset for which we have set `test_size` to 0.25, `n_estimators` to 200, `max_features` to 0.75, `max_samples` 0.5, and `max_depth` is set to 3.

From Fig. (2a) one observes that we obtain almost perfect reconstruction for the chosen numerical features even though we have chosen a moderate number of estimators and a low maximum depth value. Our second experiment relies on the reconstruction of some categorical features from the *Compas* dataset. We have considered the same parameters as in the previous experiment, but the train and test datasets were given indepedently. The results presented in Fig. (2b) reveals the fact that even categorical features can be reconstructed with the appropriate number of estimators. In the previous experiments, we have used the *HHCART* method. For the *Compas* dataset, we have utilized the *PCA* method, while for the feature transformation for *HHCART* on *Diabetes* dataset we used the *GRP*.

Now we will analyze the impact of various parameters of the oblique trees ensemble. In Fig. 3 we have the variation of the `max_depth`, `max_features`, `max_samples` and `n_train` parameters with respect to the *MSE* values of the decoded test samples reconstruction on the *Diabetes* dataset. Despite the fact that we have not chosen the best values that will give us the lowest *MSE*, Fig. 3 highlights the importance of the parameters underpinning these methods. For the plot concerning the `max_depth` parameter, we have chosen (`n_estimators`, `max_samples`, `max_features`) = $(50, 0.5, 0.75)$, while for the

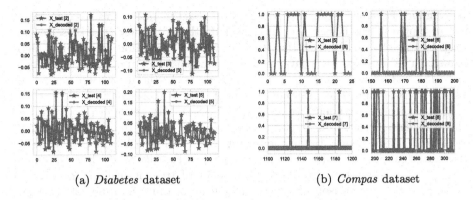

(a) *Diabetes* dataset   (b) *Compas* dataset

Fig. 2. Feature reconstruction

`max_features` plot, we have taken (`n_estimators`, `max_samples`, `max_depth`) = $(100, 0.5, 3)$. For `max_samples` plot we chose (`n_estimators`, `max_features`, `max_depth`) equal to $(100, 0.75, 3)$, while for the `n_train` plot we used the fixed parameters (`n_estimators`, `max_samples`, `max_features`, `max_depth`) = $(50, 0.5, 0.75, 3)$.

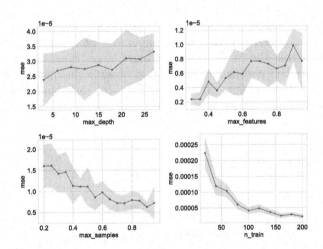

Fig. 3. Ablation study for the ***OF-AE*** method on *Diabetes* dataset

For each plot we have made 10 simulation runs, while the `test_size` was set to 0.25, and the *GRP* was used for *HHCART*.

From Fig. 3 one can easily see that the maximum depth has little influence on the reconstruction error in the situation when the number of estimators is set to a moderate value of 50. Moreover, the maximum number of features seems to slightly increase the *MSE* values. An explanation for this may be that a large percentage of the maximum features used reduces the inherent randomization of the ensemble methods, but one can't exclude the possibility that these results may appear due to the fact that the number of simulation runs is not large enough. The most decisive parameters are `max_samples` and `n_train`, namely the *MSE* values are monotonically decreasing when the maximum number of samples or the number of training data points are increased.

For the next experiment, we have used the *Seeds* dataset in order to compare the train and decode time values of the *HHCART* and *RandCART* oblique-type trees, respectively. Here, `n_estimators` are set to 200, `max_samples` to 0.5, `max_features` to 0.75 and `max_depth` to 3. For the *Seeds* dataset (where `test_size` was set to 0.25) the high number of trees is utilized in order to emphasize the comparison of the running time of different types of ODT. In Fig. (4a) the line of the categories presented in the barplots represent the variation of 10 simulation runs. We observe that *HHCART* is slower than *RandCART* at training and also at decoding. The major difference lies in the training time where there exists a large variation for the running time of *HHCART*. As noticed before, there are some differences between the fit time of the *HHCART* method in comparison with the training time of the *RandCART* method. Despite this fact, we are interested not only in how fast our ensemble methods are, but how precise they are with respect to reconstruction errors. We investigate the differences in the *MSE* values for the aforementioned oblique-type methods. In Fig. (4b) we have used the *HTRU2* dataset and we considered again 10 runs, 50 sample points for training, 10 test sample points for decoding, along with the following choices: (`max_samples`, `max_features`, `max_depth`) = (0.5, 0.75, 3). Despite the fact that the *MSE* values are quite large (since we have chosen the previously mentioned parameters in order to observe the qualitative behaviour of our methods), the boxplots presented in Fig. (4b) show that *HHCART* using *PCA* gives better results than *RandCART*.

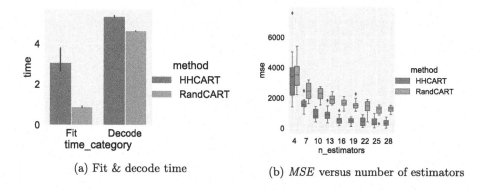

(a) Fit & decode time

(b) *MSE* versus number of estimators

Fig. 4. Methods comparison for tabular datasets

4.3   Image Reconstruction

In this subsection, we shall study the case of image reconstruction. As for the case of the *eForest* encoder [14], the **OF-AE** method is suitable also for the reconstruction of images belonging to various datasets. In what follows, for the image reconstruction plots, the first row will represent the chosen test samples, while in the second row we will always plot the reconstructed images.

For our first experiment, we consider the *MNIST* dataset, where n_estimators is 300, n_train is 100, max_samples is 1.0, max_features is 0.75, and max_depth was set to 3. After the training, we have applied the usual encoding-decoding technique of **OF-AE** on 10 test samples.

Fig. 5. Image reconstruction of *MNIST* images

From the depiction of Fig. 5 we observe that we obtain a good representation of the test images even though we have used only 100 training samples, similar to *eForest* encoder. We have used lower values for n_estimators and max_depth than the ones from [14]. For a better decoding quality we can increase the number of trees, but our results suggest that the oblique splits can retain a compact representation of the features. In the previous image reconstruction experiment we have used the *PCA* method, while in our second simulation we will compare the *SSIM* values (also on the *MNIST* dataset) for different methods for transforming the original space. In (Fig. 6a) we observe the *SSIM* values of *PCA* (*eig*), alongside various implementations from SKLearn: *Truncated-SVD* (*svd*), *FastICA* (*fast_ica*), *FactorAnalysis* (*factor*) and *GRP* (*proj*), respectively. In this simulation, n_estimators and n_train are set to 50, while (max_samples, max_features, max_depth) = $(0.75, 0.75, 3)$.

We observe that the variation in the 10 simulation runs is almost the same for every type of feature transformation method, while the *GRP* seems to have the lowest impact on the reconstruction values.

For our third experiment, we plan to evaluate the *SSIM* values obtained from the decoded samples on the test dataset for the *HHCART* (using *GRP*) and *RandCART*. In Fig. (6b) we have utilized our custom *CHD2R* dataset where all the images are resized to 28×28. We took 10 simulation runs and we set (max_samples, max_features, max_depth) = $(0.25, 0.5, 30)$. We observe that we get better results (in the case of *SSIM* values) for the *HHCART* method, and even though we can improve the results by increasing the number of estimators (or modifying other parameters), the results from (Fig. 6b) represent the main aspect of the difference between the aforementioned oblique methods.

We will continue our ablation study with the investigation of the training time of **OF-AE** with respect to the number of estimators, along with the width and the height values of the images, respectively. For the case when we make the comparison of the image resize values versus the training time, we took (n_estimators, max_samples, max_features, max_depth) = (30, 0.25, 1.0, 10). On the other hand, for the comparison between the number of estimators versus the training time, we chose (resize_value, max_samples, max_features, max_depth) = (28, 0.25, 1.0, 10). For both situations, we used the *HHCART* oblique trees with the *GRP*, along with n_train set to 50 and 10 test samples, on the *Oxford Flowers* dataset. The results depicted in sub-figures (Fig. 6c) and (Fig, 6d) suggest a disadvantage our method: the training time grows quickly if we increase the number of trees or the size of the images. The qualitative decoding of the autoencoder deeply depends on the number of ODT (this effectively represents that by increasing the number of estimators, we increase the number of constraints on the features through the weights equations). On the other hand, by increasing the size of the images, we observe that our method suffers from a "curse of dimensionality" problem, which is also present for the *eForest* encoder (where, for the same reconstruction quality of the decoded images, the number of axis-parallel trees is much larger) and for the tree-type encoder presented in [2] (where for each feature we must construct a DT with the labels as possible pixel values).

For the next experiment we consider some simulations on *CIFAR10* using ensemble of *RandCART* ODT with max_depth = 3. In Fig. 7 we have 6 versions, where, from left to right: on the first row v3 and v1, in the second row v2 and v4, while in the last row v5 and v6. Under each subfigure from Fig. 7 we

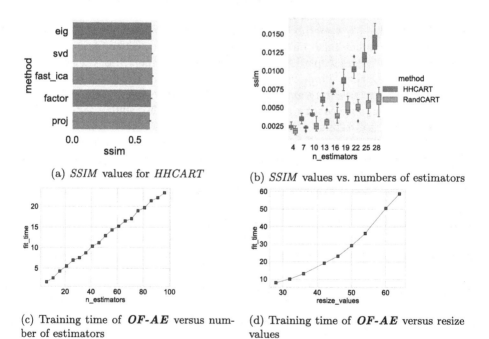

(a) *SSIM* values for *HHCART*

(b) *SSIM* values vs. numbers of estimators

(c) Training time of ***OF-AE*** versus number of estimators

(d) Training time of ***OF-AE*** versus resize values

Fig. 6. Methods comparison for image datasets

have the parameters (`n_train`, `n_estimators`, `max_samples`, `max_features`). From the first row we see that, for a low number of estimators, the results are unsatisfactory. In addition, for the transition between v3 and v1 we get some decoding improvements by increasing the number of trees.

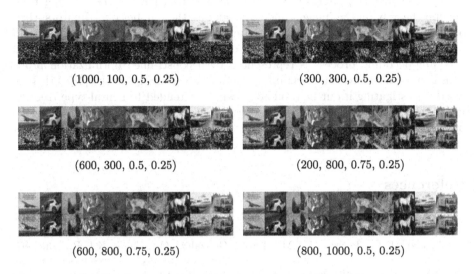

(1000, 100, 0.5, 0.25)   (300, 300, 0.5, 0.25)

(600, 300, 0.5, 0.25)   (200, 800, 0.75, 0.25)

(600, 800, 0.75, 0.25)   (800, 1000, 0.5, 0.25)

Fig. 7. Ablation study on *CIFAR10*

For the second row results we have the transition between v2 and v4 them which is given by decreasing the number of training samples and increasing the number of estimators, which suggest that `n_estimators` have a larger influence over the decoding process than `n_train`. In the last row, the transition between v5 and v6 is given by increasing `n_estimators` and `n_train` which leads to even better results. But, increasing the quality of the reconstructed images, in this transition we have decreased also the `max_samples` parameter.

Our last experiment is the same as the one from [14] regarding model reuse. We have trained **OF-AE** with `n_train` equal to 1000 on *CIFAR10*, and we have decoded 10 test samples (resized to *CIFAR10* dimensions 32×32) belonging to *Oxford Flowers* and *CHD2R*. By setting (`n_estimators`, `max_samples`, `max_features`, `max_depth`) = $(1000, 0.5, 0.25, 3)$ and using the *HHCART* with the *GRP*, we get the results from Fig. 8. Quite interestingly, our method trained on a small number of images is able to reproduce almost exactly images from different datasets.

Fig. 8. Model reuse on the *Oxford Flowers* & *CHD2R* datasets

5   Conclusions and Discussions

In this paper we have extended the *eForest* encoder to unsupervised ensembles of oblique trees. Our method ***OF-AE*** has the same limitations as the *eForest* encoder and the interpretable autoencoder from [2], i.e. the training time depends heavily on the image dimensions and on the number of estimators, thus our method becomes unfeasible for large datasets. Up to our knowledge, the method introduced in this paper is the only forest-type autoencoder where the encoding-decoding process is represented by a constrained optimization problem, hence this represents a significant departure from the works [4,5,11]. It is worth investigating if our methodology can be extended to neural-type trees as in [20,32], respectively. In addition, a possibility would be to expand our work by drawing upon the methods used in [34] where the discrete tree parameters are learned using a global loss function.

References

1. Agrawal, A., Verschueren, R., Diamond, S., Boyd, S.: A rewriting system for convex optimization problems. J. Control Decis. **5**(1), 42–60 (2018)
2. Aguilar, D.L., Perez, M.A.M., Loyola-Gonzalez, O., Choo, K.K.R., Bucheli-Susarrey, E.: Towards an interpretable autoencoder: a decision tree-based autoencoder and its application in anomaly detection. IEEE Trans. Dependabl. Secur. Comput. (2022)
3. Bengio, Y., Yao, L., Alain, G., Vincent, P.: Generalized denoising auto-encoders as generative models. In: Advances in Neural Information Processing Systems, vol. 26 (2013)
4. Bennett, K.P.: Decision tree construction via linear programming. University of Wisconsin-Madison Department of Computer Sciences, Technical report (1992)
5. Bennett, K.P., Blue, J.A.: Optimal decision trees. Rensselaer Polytechn. Inst. Math Rep. **214**, 24 (1996)
6. Blaser, R., Fryzlewicz, P.: Random rotation ensembles. J. Mach. Learn. Res. **17**(1), 126–151 (2016)
7. Bourlard, H., Kamp, Y.: Auto-association by multilayer perceptrons and singular value decomposition. Biol. Cybern. **59**(4), 291–294 (1988)
8. Breiman, L.: Bagging predictors. Mach. Learn. **24**(2), 123–140 (1996)
9. Breiman, L.: Random forests. Mach. Learn. **45**(1), 5–32 (2001)
10. Breiman, L., Friedman, J., Stone, C.J., Olshen, R.: Classification and Regression Trees. CRC Press (1984)
11. Brown, D.E., Pittard, C.L., Park, H.: Classification trees with optimal multivariate decision nodes. Pattern Recogn. Lett. **17**(7), 699–703 (1996)
12. Diamond, S., Boyd, S.: CVXPY: a python-embedded modeling language for convex optimization. J. Mach. Learn. Res. **17**(83), 1–5 (2016)
13. ECNU: Oblique decision tree in python (2021). https://github.com/zhenlingcn/scikit-obliquetree
14. Feng, J., Zhou, Z.H.: Autoencoder by forest. In: Thirty-Second AAAI Conference on Artificial Intelligence (2018)
15. Frosst, N., Hinton, G.: Distilling a neural network into a soft decision tree. arXiv preprint arXiv:1711.09784 (2017)

16. Geurts, P., Ernst, D., Wehenkel, L.: Extremely randomized trees. Mach. Learn. **63**(1), 3–42 (2006)
17. Irsoy, O., Alpaydin, E.: Autoencoder trees. In: Asian conference on machine learning, pp. 378–390. PMLR (2016)
18. Irsoy, O., Yıldız, O.T., Alpaydın, E.: Soft decision trees. In: Proceedings of the 21st International Conference on Pattern Recognition (ICPR2012), pp. 1819–1822. IEEE (2012)
19. Kingma, D.P., Welling, M.: Auto-encoding variational bayes. arXiv preprint arXiv:1312.6114 (2013)
20. Kontschieder, P., Fiterau, M., Criminisi, A., Bulo, S.R.: Deep neural decision forests. In: Proceedings of the IEEE International Conference on Computer Vision, pp. 1467–1475 (2015)
21. Lin, Y., Jeon, Y.: Random forests and adaptive nearest neighbors. J. Am. Stat. Assoc. **101**(474), 578–590 (2006)
22. Liu, B., Xia, Y., Yu, P.S.: Clustering through decision tree construction. In: Proceedings of the Ninth International Conference on Information and Knowledge Management, pp. 20–29 (2000)
23. Majumder, T.: Ensembles of Oblique Decision Trees. The University of Texas at Dallas (2020)
24. Moosmann, F., Nowak, E., Jurie, F.: Randomized clustering forests for image classification. IEEE Trans. Pattern Anal. Mach. Intell. **30**(9), 1632–1646 (2008)
25. Moosmann, F., Triggs, B., Jurie, F.: Fast discriminative visual codebooks using randomized clustering forests. In: Advances in Neural Information Processing Systems, vol. 19 (2006)
26. Murthy, S.K., Kasif, S., Salzberg, S.: A system for induction of oblique decision trees. J. Artif. Intell. Res. **2**, 1–32 (1994)
27. Nock, R., Guillame-Bert, M.: Generative trees: Adversarial and copycat. arXiv preprint arXiv:2201.11205 (2022)
28. Norouzi, M., Collins, M.D., Fleet, D.J., Kohli, P.: Co2 forest: Improved random forest by continuous optimization of oblique splits. arXiv preprint arXiv:1506.06155 (2015)
29. Pedregosa, F., et al.: Scikit-learn: machine learning in Python. J. Mach. Learn. Res. **12**, 2825–2830 (2011)
30. Reis, I., Baron, D., Shahaf, S.: Probabilistic random forest: a machine learning algorithm for noisy data sets. Astron. J. **157**(1), 16 (2018)
31. Stoean, C., et al.: On using perceptual loss within the u-net architecture for the semantic inpainting of textile artefacts with traditional motifs. In: SYNACS Conference Publishing Service (CPS) (2022)
32. Tanno, R., Arulkumaran, K., Alexander, D., Criminisi, A., Nori, A.: Adaptive neural trees. In: International Conference on Machine Learning, pp. 6166–6175. PMLR (2019)
33. Wickramarachchi, D.C., Robertson, B.L., Reale, M., Price, C.J., Brown, J.: HHCART: an oblique decision tree. Comput. Statist. Data Anal. **96**, 12–23 (2016)
34. Zantedeschi, V., Kusner, M., Niculae, V.: Learning binary decision trees by argmin differentiation. In: International Conference on Machine Learning, pp. 12298–12309. PMLR (2021)

VAE-Based Generic Decoding via Subspace Partition and Priori Utilization

Mingyang Sheng, Yongqiang Ma, Kai Chen, and Nanning Zheng[✉]

Institute of Artificial Intelligence and Robotics, Xi'an Jiaotong University,
Xi'an 710049, Shaanxi, China
smysmy2016@stu.xjtu.edu.cn, nnzheng@mail.xjtu.edu.cn

Abstract. Generic decoding is a challenging problem in visual neural decoding. The existing methods based on generative models ignore the application of prior knowledge, which leads to poor interpretability, and few pay attention to fMRI (functional Magnetic Resonance Imaging) processing. To tackle these problems, a novel framework for generic decoding has been proposed named GD-VAE. GD-VAE is based on Variational Auto-Encoder (VAE) which is capable of meaningful latent space, and contains four modules: feature extractor, feature VAE, Prior Knowledge Network (PKN) and Latent Space Disentangling Network (LSDN). The feature extractors extract features of raw visual and cognitive data, and feature VAE implements decoding with a shared latent space for both modalities. The PKN and LSDN constrain the latent space of VAE with delicate structure, in order to apparently reveal the information in the subspace. Benefiting from these modules, the alignment between visual and cognitive modality can be achieved, and greater interpretability can be acquired. Experiments on Generic Decoding Dataset validate the effectiveness and interpretability of the proposed method.

Keywords: Generic decoding · Variational Auto-Encoder · Subspace disentanglement

1 Introduction

One of the most important challenges in the field of neuroscience and artificial intelligence is to understand how the brain works, which is inseparable from "neural decoding". Visual brain decoding is an important branch of neural decoding, aiming to extract information of visual tasks from brain activities in visual cortices, of which signal contains useful message highly related with visual perception [10]. With the development of neuroimaging technology such as fMRI (functional magnetic resonance imaging), we can obtain enough indirect or direct reflection of brain activity.

According to the granularity of decoding, visual brain decoding can be divided into visual reconstruction and visual identification [14]. The former one

© IFIP International Federation for Information Processing 2023
Published by Springer Nature Switzerland AG 2023
I. Maglogiannis et al. (Eds.): AIAI 2023, IFIP AICT 676, pp. 220–232, 2023.
https://doi.org/10.1007/978-3-031-34107-6_18

implements on the image reconstruction from pixel to pixel, while the latter one focuses on image classification or identification based on decoding features. Compared with visual reconstruction, the advantage of visual identification lies in a better understanding about how the brain generates object-based information, which is usually more directly related to our visual guidance behavior than raw images in the real world. This paper is based on an extended paradigm of visual identification, namely the generic decoding paradigm [9], which requires decoding the corresponding image representation from the given fMRI data, comparing the similarity with the image features of all categories in the candidate set, and selecting the most similar category as the classification result. The categories in training set and those in test set do not intersect at all, which is also known as zero-shot learning.

Currently, generic decoding is still in its infancy. This paradigm was first proposed by Horikawa et al. [9]. It uses sparse linear regression model to learn the mapping from selected fMRI voxels to image features. Recently, some methods have applied the generation model to this problem, using probability graph model to model the data generation process with the assistance of semantic information [1,3,7]. In addition, DGMM combines probability graph model with neural network [5]. There are still a few literatures regarding it as multi-view learning, learning the linear or nonlinear mapping of two modality data to the shared feature space.

These methods ignore the processing of fMRI data and feature extraction. The high dimensional and strong noise characteristics of fMRI data make it necessary to extract useful information for decoding. Besides, insufficient interpretability of the model remains further consideration. The trivial latent space in generative model does not completely disentangle different information. We still know little about the information encoded in the latent space.

In this paper, we design a VAE-based visual decoding framework, which consists of four modules: visual and cognitive feature extractors, feature VAEs, prior knowledge network (PKN) and Latent Space Disentangling Network (LSDN). Feature extractors extract features of input images and raw fMRI data, and feature VAEs are used to create a meaningful latent space. In order to generate a more interpretable latent space, latent space is divided into two subspaces and default prior distribution (normal distribution) is substituted by the distribution encoded by PKN from prior knowledge. Meanwhile, latent space disentangling network helps regularize the two subspace to be disentangled. Our main contributions are as follows:

· A VAE based decoding framework is proposed, which is the first deep learning based framework for generic decoding.
· The designed fMRI feature extractor incorporates prior knowledge about brain connections and data, and is more general and reasonable for decoding.
· We propose prior knowledge network and latent space disentangling network for a more interpretable latent space. Experiments verify the effectiveness of the method.

Other sections are organized as follows. Section 2 summarizes related work about generic decoding, zero shot learning and VAE. The proposed framework and method are explained in Sect. 3. Experiment results are shown in Sect. 4. Section 5 concludes our contribution and prospect for future work.

2 Related Work

2.1 Generic Decoding

Generic decoding was formally proposed by Horikawa et al. [9], who used sparse linear regression model, to extend visual identification to unseen classes in training phase. MVBGM [1] proposes to solve this problem from the perspective of multi-view learning, introducing probability graph model, which used shared hidden variables to explain the data generation process. On this basis, MS-MVBGM [3] was proposed to solve the function alignment problem of multiple subjects. Semi-MVBGM [2] used semi-supervised learning to utilize unpaired images to increase the scale of dataset. Some methods related to generic decoding are summarized in [14]. The current methods lack the interpretability of decoding process due to the lack of prior knowledge. Injecting prior knowledge into current model is promising.

2.2 Zero-Shot Learning (ZSL)

ZSL is proposed to solve the dilemma that traditional classification can only classify limited categories in training set, expecting knowledge transfer from visual to semantic and from seen to unseen. ZSL can be divided into embedding model [6] and generative model [17]. The embedding model learns a mapping function to transform visual features and semantics into the shared embedded space, while the generative model generates image features for unseen classes using semantic attributes. Our approach combines embedding and generative model. To be more specific, our approach learns the projections of visual and cognitive spaces to a shared latent space and knowledge transfer from cognitive to visual features by generation process of data.

2.3 Variational Auto-Encoders (VAE)

VAE has emerged as a effective method for modeling the generation process of data [12]. The prior in KL divergence was modified to capture complicated structure of latent space [19]. In order to achieve disentanglement, some methods deformed KL divergence into different forms [8,16]. AAE [13] and WAE [18] substituted KL divergence with adversarial learning or Wasserstein distance to achieve better compactness in latent space. As for more than one modality input, [20] built paralleled single-modality VAE with strong correlation regularization between corresponding layers. However, few consider disentanglement performance on complex datasets. We aim to address this issue.

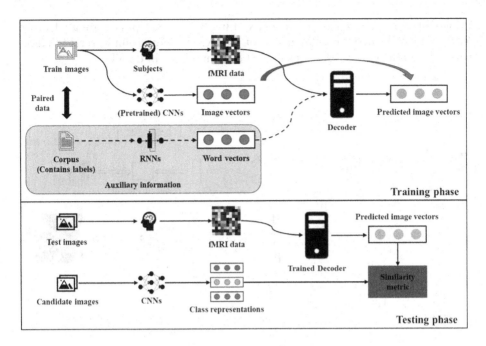

Fig. 1. Generic decoding framework.

3 Method

Problem Settings. Suppose we have N_{tr} training and N_{te} testing image-fMRI pairs and N_{ca} candidate images. For training pairs, semantic vectors (usually word embeddings corresponding to the image label) are also available. Denote $\mathcal{V}$ as visual space constructed by visual images, $\mathcal{C}$ and $\mathcal{S}$ as cognitive space (constructed by fMRI) and semantic space (constructed by semantic vectors) respectively. Let $D_{tr} = \{(v_i, c_i, s_i)|v_i \in \mathcal{V}, c_i \in \mathcal{C}, s_i \in \mathcal{S}\}_{i=1}^{N_{tr}}$ be the training set, and $D_{te} = \{(v_i, c_i)|v_i \in \mathcal{V}, c_i \in \mathcal{C}\}_{i=1}^{N_{te}}$, $D_{ca} = \{v_i|v_i \in \mathcal{V}\}_{i=1}^{N_{ca}}$ be the test set and the candidate set respectively. The aim of generic decoding is to learn a mapping (decoder) from space $\mathcal{C}$ to $\mathcal{V}$, and then decodes c in the test set into $\hat{v}$, finally classified by nearest neighbour searching in the candidate set under certain similarity metric. The training and testing phase of generic decoding can be summarized as Fig. 1.

3.1 Overall Model Architecture

The overall architecture is shown as Fig. 2. The framework mainly consists of four modules: visual and cognitive feature extractors (EXT), feature VAEs, PKN and LSDN. In training phase, given an image-fMRI pair (v, c), firstly the pair is fed into feature extractors to obtain features (x_v, x_c). Secondly, prior knowledge about the image v can be obtained by pretrained models, and the corresponding prior distribution is encoded by PKN. Finally, (x_v, x_c) pass through feature VAEs jointly with the regularization of LSDN, forming an interpretable latent space. The following subsections describe the modules in detail.

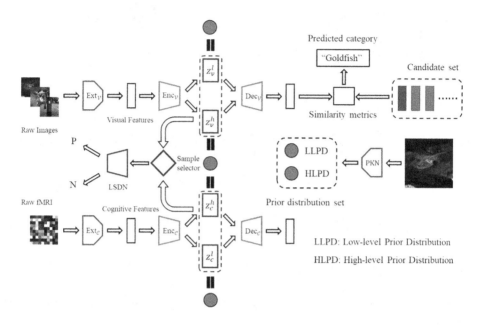

Fig. 2. The overall architecture.

3.2   Feature Extractor

The first step of framework is feature extraction. As mentioned before, the reason for using extracted features instead of raw data is to filter out useless information in raw data. For visual and cognitive data, two different extractors should be applied.

Visual Feature Extractor: A large number of studies have shown that VGG19 is more consistent with the working process of human visual pathway. Therefore, the pretrained VGG19 is used as the visual feature extractor.

Cognitive Feature Extractor: There is no widely recognized feature extractor in terms of fMRI feature extraction. Although simple MLP with shallow layers (or linear model) as the extractor is effective, we expect a feature extractor that combines the fitting ability of nonlinear model. In addition, we have prior knowledge about fMRI and brain structure. The fMRI data is high-dimensional and noisy. In addition, the cortices in the visual pathway are bidirectional connected

[11,15], and there is also a direct pathway from lower cortices to higher cortices. Therefore, this work proposes a feature extractor that combines our prior knowledge of fMRI data and brain connection, as shown in Fig. 3.

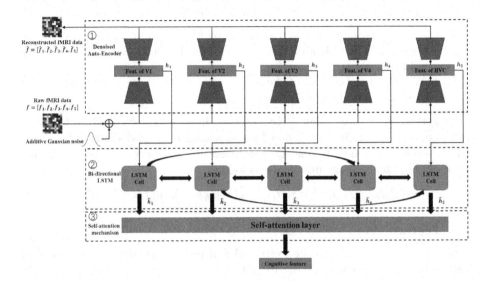

Fig. 3. The fMRI feature extractor. We divide the whole visual cortices into five regions of interest (ROI), V1, V2, V3, V4 and HVC (Higher visual cortices). Firstly, $\{f_i\}_{i=1}^5$ pass through DAEs and hidden states of DAEs $\{h_i\}_{i=1}^5$ can be obtained. Secondly, $\{h_i\}_{i=1}^5$ are fed into modified Bi-LSTM. Finally, hidden states of Bi-LSTM $\{\hat{h}_i\}_{i=1}^5$ are averaged by self-attention mechanism and the averaged vector as the extracted features.

The extractor consists of three parts: denoised auto-encoder (DAE), modified bidirectional LSTM (Bi-LSTM) and self-attention mechanism (SA). Hidden states of DAEs are dimension-reduced and noise-free. Modified Bi-LSTM adds connections cross cells, aiming to simulate the direct pathway and bidirectional connection in the brain as well. Self-attention can dynamically adjust the average weights according to different cognitive tasks. The fMRI extractor loss $\mathcal{L}_{\text{EXT}}$ is:

$$\mathcal{L}_{\text{EXT}} = \sum_{i=1}^{5} \| \hat{f}_i - f_i \|_2^2 \tag{1}$$

3.3 Subspace Partition and Prior Knowledge Network (PKN)

Images contain low-level information (LLI) and high-level information (HLI). LLI generally refers to edges, colors, textures, etc.; while HLI is mainly semantic. The two kinds of information are intrinsically different, and should not be blended and represented by the same whole latent space, which is a common setting in VAEs.

Inspired by the different level of information in images, latent space should be carefully designed, where we introduce subspace partition, dividing the original whole latent space z into two subspaces z^l and z^h, each representing only one kind of information. Accordingly, it is necessary to generate reliable prior distribution specific to the subspaces, where prior knowledge should be introduced.

· LLI: An image maintains the main color by blurring, and preserves edges by edge detector. Thus blending the two processed images can retain LLI. We denote LLI as I_l.
· HLI: Word2vec embedding of the image label is used here as HLI, which is a usually choice. We denote HLI as I_h.

After getting prior knowledge, PKN encodes the prior knowledge into low-level and high-level prior distribution, which is assumed normal distribution. Two MLP encoders $\mu()$ and $\sigma()$ encode the mean and variance. The encoded low-level and high-level distributions are as follows:

$$p_l(z^l|I_l) = \mathcal{N}(\mu_l(I_l), \sigma_l(I_l)), \quad p_h(z^h|I_h) = \mathcal{N}(\mu_h(I_h), \sigma_h(I_h)) \tag{2}$$

3.4 Feature VAE

Denote x_m ($m \in \{v, c\}$) as the extracted features of modality m. The goal of feature VAE_m is to maximize the ELBO:

$$\begin{aligned}
\log p(x_m) &\geq \mathbb{E}_{\mathbf{z_m} \sim q_\phi(\mathbf{z_m}|x_m)}[\log p_\theta(x_m|\mathbf{z_m})] - \text{KLD}(q_\phi(\mathbf{z_m}|x_m) \parallel p(\mathbf{z_m})) \\
&= \mathbb{E}_{\mathbf{z_m}}[\log p_\theta(x_m|\mathbf{z_m})] - \text{KLD}(q_\phi(\mathbf{z_m}|x_m) \parallel p(\mathbf{I}))
\end{aligned} \tag{3}$$

where $\mathbf{z_m} = [z_m^l; z_m^h]$ is the concatenated latent variables, $\mathbf{I} = [I_l, I_h]$ is the prior knowledge and $q_\phi(\mathbf{z_m}|x_m)$ is the encoder parametrized by ϕ, and $p_\theta(x_m|\mathbf{z_m})$ is the decoder parametrized by θ. The first term is the reconstruction loss of features of modality m. The second term is the KL-divergence loss regularizing the latent space $\mathbf{z_m}$. By adopting the assumption that z^l and z^h are independent, the second term can be rewritten as follows:

$$\begin{aligned}
\text{KLD}(q_\phi(\mathbf{z_m}|x_m) \parallel p(\mathbf{I})) &= \text{KLD}(q(z_m^l|x_m) \parallel p(I_l)) \\
&\quad + \text{KLD}(q(z_m^h|x_m) \parallel p(I_h))
\end{aligned} \tag{4}$$

In order to alleviate posterior collapse, unlike traditional VAEs, VAE_m adopts skip connection [4] from hidden layer to layers in decoder, avoiding mode collapse by maximizing mutual information between latent variable and output. Also the raw KL loss is substituted by free-bit KL loss. The final loss of feature VAE_m is:

$$\begin{aligned}
\mathcal{L}_{\text{VAE}_m} &= \mathcal{L}_{\text{rec}_m} + \alpha \mathcal{L}_{\text{KLD}_m} \\
&= -\mathbb{E}_{\mathbf{z_m}}[\log p_\theta(x_m|\mathbf{z_m})] + \alpha \text{KLD}(q_\phi(\mathbf{z_m}|x_m) \parallel p(\mathbf{I}))
\end{aligned} \tag{5}$$

Visual and cognitive feature VAEs are jointly learned, maximizing the joint log-likelihood:

$$\begin{aligned}
\log p(\mathbf{x}) &= \log p(x_v) + \log p(x_c) \\
&\approx \log p(x_v) + \mathbb{E}_{\mathbf{z_c}}[\log p_\theta(x_c|\mathbf{z_c})] - \alpha \text{KLD}(q_\phi(\mathbf{z_c}|x_c) \parallel q_\phi(\mathbf{z_v}|x_v))
\end{aligned} \tag{6}$$

where $\mathbf{x} = [x_v, x_c]$. By revising the term $\log p(x_c)$ (or $\log p(x_v)$), a strong connection is established between VAE_v and VAE_c.

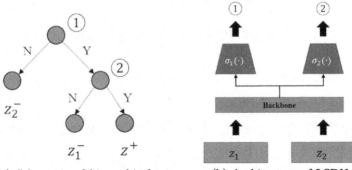

(a) Schematic of hierarchical classification.

(b) Architecture of LSDN.

Fig. 4. (a): The first step of hierarchical classification is to discriminate whether two set of variables are from different subspace, if they are from different subspace, then the second step is to discriminate whether two set of variables are from different labels. (b): LSDN receives two set of variables z_1 and z_2, and has a shared backbone and two prediction branches $\sigma_1()$ and $\sigma_2()$ for predicting the probability of different subspace and labels, respectively. ①: whether the two set are from different subspace, ②: whether the two set are from different sample.

3.5 Latent Space Disentangling Network

Although PKN is proposed to generate different subspace, there is no explicit regularization to disentangle the two subspace. LSDN is an explicit constraint to force the subspaces to be discriminative. Because the two subspaces may overlap, our aim is to discriminate subspaces between samples within the same label rather than across labels. Our sample selection strategy is: given one pair (v_i, c_i) with label y_i and z_i the corresponding latent variables, $\{(z_i^l, z_j^h) \mid y_j = y_i\}$ is seen as positive pairs z^+ and $\{(z_i^l, z_j^h) \mid y_j \neq y_i\}$ are negative pairs z_1^-. Also $\{(z_i^l, z_j^l) \mid y_j = y_i\}$ are negative pairs z_2^-. The reason for introducing z_2^- is to avoid LSDN discriminating according to labels only rather than subspaces. The difficulty of distinguishing different labels and subspaces are not equal. Thus, we proposed hierarchical classification, which convert one-step classification of positive and negative samples to two-step classification. The schematic is shown in Fig. 4(a).

The architecture of LSDN is shown in Fig. 4(b). Assuming there are P_i positive samples z^+ and M_i negative samples z_1^- and N_i negative samples z_2^-, the loss of LSDN is:

$$\mathcal{L}_{\mathrm{LSDN}} = \sum_{i=1}^{P_i} \log(\sigma_1(z^+)\sigma_2(z^+))$$
$$+ \sum_{j=1}^{M_i} \log(\sigma_1(z_1^-)[1 - \sigma_2(z_1^-)]) + \sum_{j=1}^{N_i} \log(1 - \sigma_1(z_2^-)) \tag{7}$$

3.6 Training and Inference

Training. The proposed method includes EXT loss, VAE loss and LSDN loss. The total loss is as follows:

$$\mathcal{L} \doteq \mathcal{L}_{\mathrm{EXT}} + \alpha\mathcal{L}_{\mathrm{VAE}_v} + \beta\mathcal{L}_{\mathrm{VAE}_c} + \gamma\mathcal{L}_{\mathrm{LSDN}} \tag{8}$$

where α, β and λ are hyper-parameters adjusting the weights of each loss term. All of the modules with parameters except visual feature extractor are trained together.

Inference. A cascaded encoder of VAE_c and decoder of VAE_v is used as the decoder of visual decoding. Given a piece of fMRI c, the corresponding visual feature vector $\hat{v}$ is computed, then the identified category $\hat{y}$ is retrieved by $\arg\max_i \{sim(\hat{v}, v_i)\}_{i=1}^{N_{ca}}$ where $sim(\bullet, \bullet)$ is some kind of similarity metric.

4 Experiments

4.1 Experimental Settings

Dataset. The method is evaluated on GD dataset [9] which collects data of five subjects, each containing 1200 image-fMRI pairs with 150 classes for training and 50 pairs with 50 classes for testing. As for semantic vectors, we use 300-dimensional word2vec embeddings corresponding to image labels. We select several images for each of 10000 categories from ImageNet as the candidate set. Images features within the same category in the candidate set are used as category features.

Evaluation Metrics. We choose mean rank as the metric which is a common metric in other works. The mean rank is computed as follows: First sort similarity scores in descending order for each test image, and then fetch the rank of correct category, finally average across all images. Also, we use T-SNE to visualize the clustering of latent space.

Implementation Details. Visual feature extractor is a pretrained VGG19 network, and auto encoders in cognitive feature extractor is one-layer MLP with hidden dimension 512. The PKN consists of two MLPs with one fully-connected layer. The backbone of LSDN is a two-layer MLP and the two branches is one fully-connected layer. Both of the encoders of feature VAEs are two fully-connected layer with hidden dimension [300, 200], and the structure of decoders are symmetric with skip connection. Dimension of z^l and z^h are set to be equal. The proposed model is trained using Adam with default settings in Pytorch. α, β and γ are set to $1e^{-4}$, $1e^{-3}$ and $1e^{-3}$. The learning rate $1e^{-3}$ is controlled by cosine annealing with $T_0 = 5$ and $T_{mult} = 2$. $sim(\bullet, \bullet)$ is cosine distance. The model is trained 175 epochs.

Table 1. Comparison of different methods.

	Ref. [9]	BCCA-V	BCCA-C	MVBGM	MS-MVBGM	GD-VAE
Subject 1	867.38	988.76	1883.9	731.88	672.82	**650.32**
Subject 2	646.16	586.46	1496.2	436.84	420.92	**415.44**
Subject 3	406.78	421.84	1484.2	373.90	**351.56**	370.11
Subject 4	464.94	515.92	1545.1	451.26	392.02	**390.94**
Subject 5	625.28	585.22	1692.0	448.34	**410.36**	418.21

Table 2. Effectiveness of prior distribution ($p_{\mathcal{N}}$ means standard normal distribution).

p_l	p_h	$p_{\mathcal{N}}$	Mean rank
✓	✓		370.11
	✓	✓	1284.28
✓		✓	1530.46
		✓	2521.42

4.2 Results

We compare our proposed GD-VAE with the methods in Refs. [1,3,9] and BCCA-V and BCCA-C. In those methods, sparse linear regression (SLR) and probability graph model (PGM) are applied to map fMRI activity into visual features. BCCA-V and BCCA-C translate fMRI into visual and category features respectively. As shown in Table 1, the mean rank of our method improves in subject 1, 2 and 4, which shows the superiority of our method.

4.3 Ablation Study

The Effect of Prior Distribution. From Table 2, it can be observed that standard normal distribution will cause severe mode collapse, which is the joint effect of strong expression ability of VAE and scarce data pairs. Only applying both low-level and high-level prior distribution can achieve better performance, which implies the disentanglement of latent subspaces. T-SNE of latent subspace z^h (Fig. 5) has also shown that high-level prior distribution helps form compact latent space (we don't observe the same obvious compactness with low-level prior distribution).

The Effect of LSDN. By setting λ to 0 during training, we can verify the impact of LSDN. It can be observed that mean rank of four of five subjects (except subject 2) drops and the cross entropy loss (Eq. 7) increase about 0.05, indicating the effectiveness of LSDN for subspace disentanglement.

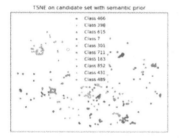   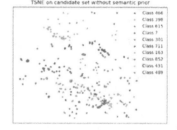

(a) T-SNE with high-level prior dis-   (b) T-SNE without high-level prior
tribution.   distribution.

Fig. 5. Visualization of latent space z^h (Image categories randomly from ILSVRC-2012 dataset).

5 Conclusion

In this paper, we propose a generic decoding framework named GD-VAE, aiming to achieve mapping from fMRI activity to visual features based on VAE. fMRI feature extractor is designed to purify fMRI activity from noise and simulate brain connections. We introduce prior knowledge and corresponding distribution to substitute the original standard normal distribution to get greater interpretability of latent space, with the regularization of LSDN. Experiments and ablation studies validate the effectiveness of the proposed method. We will continue to analyze the effect of nonlinear model in fMRI feature extractor and improve the interpretability of decoding process in the future.

Acknowledgements. This work is supported by the National Science Foundation of China (No. 62088102), China National Postdoctoral Program for Innovative Talents from China Postdoctoral Science Foundation (No. BX2021239).

References

1. Akamatsu, Y., Harakawa, R., Ogawa, T., Haseyama, M.: Estimating viewed image categories from fMRI activity via multi-view Bayesian generative model. In: 2019 IEEE 8th Global Conference on Consumer Electronics (GCCE), pp. 127–128. IEEE (2019)
2. Akamatsu, Y., Harakawa, R., Ogawa, T., Haseyama, M.: Brain decoding of viewed image categories via semi-supervised multi-view Bayesian generative model. IEEE Trans. Sig. Process. **68**, 5769–5781 (2020)
3. Akamatsu, Y., Harakawa, R., Ogawa, T., Haseyama, M.: Multi-view Bayesian generative model for multi-subject fMRI data on brain decoding of viewed image categories. In: ICASSP 2020–2020 IEEE International Conference on Acoustics, Speech and Signal Processing (ICASSP), pp. 1215–1219. IEEE (2020)
4. Dieng, A.B., Kim, Y., Rush, A.M., Blei, D.M.: Avoiding latent variable collapse with generative skip models. In: The 22nd International Conference on Artificial Intelligence and Statistics, pp. 2397–2405. PMLR (2019)
5. Du, C., Du, C., Huang, L., He, H.: Reconstructing perceived images from human brain activities with Bayesian deep multiview learning. IEEE Trans. Neural Netw. Learn. Syst. **30**(8), 2310–2323 (2018)
6. Frome, A., Corrado, G., Shlens, J., et al.: A deep visual-semantic embedding model. In: Proceedings of the Advances in Neural Information Processing Systems, pp. 2121–2129 (2013)
7. Higashi, T., Maeda, K., Ogawa, T., Haseyama, M.: Estimation of visual features of viewed image from individual and shared brain information based on fMRI data using probabilistic generative model. In: ICASSP 2021–2021 IEEE International Conference on Acoustics, Speech and Signal Processing (ICASSP), pp. 1335–1339. IEEE (2021)
8. Higgins, I., et al.: β-VAE: learning basic visual concepts with a constrained variational framework. In: International Conference on Learning Representations (2017)
9. Horikawa, T., Kamitani, Y.: Generic decoding of seen and imagined objects using hierarchical visual features. Nat. Commun. **8**(1), 15037 (2017)
10. Huang, S., Shao, W., Wang, M.L., Zhang, D.Q.: fMRI-based decoding of visual information from human brain activity: a brief review. Int. J. Autom. Comput. **18**(2), 170–184 (2021). https://doi.org/10.1007/s11633-020-1263-y
11. Huang, W., et al.: Long short-term memory-based neural decoding of object categories evoked by natural images. Hum. Brain Mapp. **41**(15), 4442–4453 (2020)
12. Kingma, D.P., Welling, M.: Auto-encoding variational bayes. arXiv preprint arXiv:1312.6114 (2013)
13. Makhzani, A., Shlens, J., Jaitly, N., Goodfellow, I., Frey, B.: Adversarial autoencoders. arXiv preprint arXiv:1511.05644 (2015)
14. Papadimitriou, A., Passalis, N., Tefas, A.: Visual representation decoding from human brain activity using machine learning: a baseline study. Pattern Recogn. Lett. **128**, 38–44 (2019)
15. Qiao, K., et al.: Category decoding of visual stimuli from human brain activity using a bidirectional recurrent neural network to simulate bidirectional information flows in human visual cortices. Front. Neurosci. **13**, 692 (2019)

16. Rodriguez, E.G.: On disentanglement and mutual information in semi-supervised variational auto-encoders. In: Proceedings of the IEEE/CVF Conference on Computer Vision and Pattern Recognition, pp. 1257–1262 (2021)

17. Schonfeld, E., Ebrahimi, S., Sinha, S., Darrell, T., Akata, Z.: Generalized zero- and few-shot learning via aligned variational autoencoders. In: Proceedings of the IEEE/CVF Conference on Computer Vision and Pattern Recognition, pp. 8247–8255 (2019)

18. Tolstikhin, I., Bousquet, O., Gelly, S., Schoelkopf, B.: Wasserstein auto-encoders. arXiv preprint arXiv:1711.01558 (2017)

19. Tomczak, J., Welling, M.: VAE with a VampPrior. In: International Conference on Artificial Intelligence and Statistics, pp. 1214–1223. PMLR (2018)

20. Wang, X., Peng, D., Hu, P., Sang, Y.: Adversarial correlated autoencoder for unsupervised multi-view representation learning. Knowl.-Based Syst. **168**, 109–120 (2019)

Machine Learning

A Difference Measuring Network
for Few-Shot Learning

Yu Wang[1], Junpeng Bao[1(✉)], Yanhua Li[2], and Zhonghui Feng[1]

[1] Xi'an Jiaotong University, Xi'an 710049, China
wangy032@stu.xjtu.edu.cn, {baojp,fzh}@mail.xjtu.edu.cn
[2] Beijing Institute of Control Engineering, Beijing 100190, China

Abstract. Few-Shot Learning (FSL) aims to distinguish novel categories for which only a few labeled samples are accessible. Due to significant advances in metric learning over the past decade, several metric-based approaches have been investigated for FSL to classify unseen categories with the k-nearest neighbor strategy. However, the existing metric-based FSL methods are typically based on the instance-level or class-level representations that might suffer from the adaptation problem because of the gap between seen and unseen classes. A fact is that human beings can quickly acquire new concepts by comparing similarities and differences between instances. Inspired by this fact, we explore a novel idea that learns difference-level representations instead of instance-level representations. This paper proposes a Difference Measuring Network (DMNet) that learns the patterns of difference from input paires of query-support. The DMNet converts both seen and unseen categories into a binary space that only contains the *Same* and the *Different* categories. Therefore, it concentrates on mining the patterns of differences between any two samples rather than the patterns of an individual instance. Finally, the DMNet distinguish whether a pair of inputs belongs to the same category or not. Experiments on five benchmark datasets demonstrate that the proposed DMNet is conducive to generalization ability of FSL.

Keywords: Few-shot Learning · Image Classification · Difference Measuring · Metric Method

1 Introduction

Few-Shot Learning (FSL) [2,16,24] has gained considerable attention in recent years with the aim of recognizing novel visual categories by accessing only a few labeled samples like human beings. Recently, a surge of FSL research has focused on metric methods as distance metric learning [6] has been successfully applied to recognition systems such as image classification, object detection, and semantic segmentation [5,12,23]. However, due to the gap between the seen and

Supported by CAAI-Huawei MindSpore Open Fund.

© IFIP International Federation for Information Processing 2023
Published by Springer Nature Switzerland AG 2023
I. Maglogiannis et al. (Eds.): AIAI 2023, IFIP AICT 676, pp. 235–249, 2023.
https://doi.org/10.1007/978-3-031-34107-6_19

the unseen categories, metric-based FSL faces new challenges. A vast majority of existing metric-based FSL methods [1,9,18,20,21] follow the paradigm that the model first extracts instance-level representations and then calculates the distance between them, which makes FSL heavily rely on the learned feature space. If the feature space fails to adapt the trained instance-level representations to the unseen categories, the distance metric might face substantial measuring errors caused by these incorrect representations.

In this work, we explore metric-based FSL from a new perspective that we call **difference-level representations** to transform samples into a more compact binary space. It is motivated by the fact that human beings can easily acquire new concepts through capturing the same and the difference between instances. For example, a child has no problem recognizing that an image drawing a *cat* and an image drawing a *bird* belong to different categories, even if he knows nothing about what a *cat* and what a *bird* are. People have a super-strong ability to tell what is the *same* and what is the *difference*. Thus, they can easily distinguish various examples either of the seen or the unseen categories. This paper mimics this fast-learning skill of humans and proposes a Difference Measuring Network (DMNet) to exploit the patterns of difference between two samples. Learning on the feature of difference rather than feature of individuals, the DMNet can achieve a good generalization capability on the novel categories. The main contributions of our work are as follows:

1) This paper presents a new perspective of few-shot learning that we call difference-level representations based FSL, which learns the patterns of difference between a query-support pair, rather than patterns of individuals.
2) We propose a simple effective Difference Measuring Network (DMNet) model that captures the patterns of difference from multi scales through a sequence of convolutional modules.
3) The experiments show that the different-level representations based FSL achieves a good generalization capability. We evaluate the performance of the proposed model on five popular datasets from two typical scenarios. The results demonstrate that our model favorably outperforms the competitors.

The remainder of the paper is organized as follows. Section 2 reviews the metric-based few-shot learning models from two typical views: feature-wise and metric-wise. Section 3 briefly introduces the target problem and proposes the Difference Measuring Network. Section 4 shows the experimental results of the proposed model. Section 5 states our conclusions.

2   Related Work

The metric-based FSL models among the recent literature target 1) learning the representations of every single class, 2) then comparing the examples based on these representations. Therefore, we review these metric-based models from two views: feature-wise methods and metric-wise methods.

2.1   Feature-Wise Methods

The feature-wise methods mainly focus on learning a good representation. We summarize them into two directions: class representations and relationship combined features.

Class Representations. Several methods aim to gain strengthen class representations from a few samples. The Prototypical Network [18] firstly adopted the mean vector of the embedded supports as the class prototype. Allen et al. [1] then proposed the Infinite Mixture Prototypes that represented each class by a set of clusters, unlike a single cluster in [18]. Li et al. [9] presented the Global Class Representations by registering every episodic class mean together. Karlinsky et al. [5] give a multi-model distribution method. It represented each class by a mixture model with multiple modes and considered the centres of these modes as the class representations. Recently, Simon et al. [17] produced the Adaptive Subspaces model, which introduced a subspace method to describe classes rather than the vector representations mentioned above.

Relationship Combined Features. The relationship between support-query image pairs is vital to few-shot recognition, thus gaining significant concerns recently. Unlike the methods that compute the distance after feature representations, some approaches arise with the relationship combined during feature extracting. Hou et al. [4] introduced the attention mechanism to model the semantic relevance between the class feature and query feature. They adopt the generated cross attention map to weigh the original features of the support and the query. Whereafter, Liu et al. [13] described a Cross-Reference Network for few-shot segmentation. They combined the co-occurrent features with the original features to generate the updated feature representations. Fan et al. [3] promoted a Fully Guided Network, which extracted the attention map from the support and enhanced the query features with the map. Very recently, Xiao [25] acquired the support and the query feature via a more complex aggregation scheme (not only the multiplicated operation but also the subtraction). They finally fused these relationship maps with the query features to gain an aggregated representation for object detection.

Compared to the existing feature-wise methods, this paper emphasizes that the difference among samples is more crucial than the sample. Therefore, we resort to learning the difference-level representations between two classes rather than the common instance-level representations.

2.2   Metric-Wise Methods

Unlike the aforementioned feature-wise methods, the metric-wise methods care more about designing a fixed or a learnable metric module to classify the query samples. Vinyals et al. [21] firstly proposed the Matching Networks (MN) to perform one-shot classification. They adopted the cosine similarity to compare the learned representations of query samples with that of the support samples. Snell et al. [18] then promoted the Prototypical Networks (PN) by comparing query samples with the mean of all support samples in the class. It provided significant improvements over [21] by using Euclidean distance instead of cosine. After that, Li et al. [11] presented a Deep Nearest Neighbor Neural Network, which only considered the k-nearest support samples for distance measuring. Zhang et al. [26] introduced the Earth Mover's Distance as a metric to compute the distance. It produced significant improvements by considering local features and image structures. Different from the above fixed metric methods, Sung et al. [20] provide adaptive metrics by setting learnable neural networks. They proposed the Relation Networks to train a metric module via convolution networks. Recently, some studies designed metric approaches from the distribution level. Li et al. [10] combined the KL divergence measure with the k-nearest neighbour's measure and proposed an Asymmetric Distribution Measure network.

In contrast to these metric-wise methods that execute the metrics on a multi-class feature space, this paper performs metric and classification with a more compact binary space.

3   Methods

This section declares the problem definition and introduces the proposed DMNet in detail.

3.1   Problem Definition

Given a set of input images X, the set Y is the corresponding category. We describe them as Eq. (1).

$$X = X_{train} \cup X_{test} = \{x^{(1)}, x^{(2)}, ..., x^{(m)}\}, \quad X_{train} \cap X_{test} = \emptyset$$
$$Y = \mathcal{B}(X) = Y_{train} \cup Y_{test} = \{c_1, c_2, ..., c_z\}, \quad Y_{train} \cap Y_{test} = \emptyset \tag{1}$$

where $\mathcal{B}()$ represents the label of the corresponding category for each input image. For few-shot classification, the class set of the training data is disjoint with that of the test data, and they are called the *Seen Categories* and the *Unseen Categories* separately in this paper. Equation (2) shows the whole dataset in this work.

$$D = <X, Y> = \{(x^{(1)}, y^{(1)}), (x^{(2)}, y^{(2)}), ..., (x^{(m)}, y^{(m)})\},$$
$$x^{(i)} \in X, \quad y^{(i)} = \mathcal{B}(x^{(i)}) \in Y \tag{2}$$

This work follows the form of the episodic training strategy [21]. It considers both the training set (X_{train}, Y_{train}) and the test set (X_{test}, Y_{test}) as a distribution of tasks $P(\mathcal{T}) = \{\tau_1, \tau_2, ..., \tau_n\}$. Here, we take the training stage as an example to illustrate. Each N-way K-shot task τ_i is called an *episode* and is composed of a support subset and a query subset:

$$\tau_i = (Q_i, S_i) \tag{3}$$

We randomly sample these two subsets from N categories of the training set, where N is much less than the number of classes in the training set. And a category in the support subset only contains a few images (typically, $K \leq 5$). Equation (4) shows these two subsets in detail.

$$
\begin{aligned}
& S_i = <X_i, Y_i>, \quad Q_i = <X_j, Y_i>, \\
& X_i, X_j \in X_{train}, \quad Y_i \in Y_{train}, \quad X_i \cap X_j = \emptyset, \\
& |X_i| = N \times K, \quad |X_j| = M \\
& |Y_i| = N \ll |Y_{train}|
\end{aligned}
\tag{4}
$$

The existing methods of metric-based FSL project the samples into a feature space $\mathcal{F}$ and execute the metric with instance-level representations in the space $\mathcal{F}$. Equation (5) describes the training objective of the existing models.

$$
\begin{aligned}
& \min_{\psi} \mathbb{E}_{(Q,S) \sim P(\mathcal{T})}[\mathcal{L}(\mathcal{F}_\psi(Q), \mathcal{F}_\psi(S))], \\
& \mathcal{L}(\mathcal{F}_\psi(Q), \mathcal{F}_\psi(S)) = \mathbb{E}_{\mathbf{x}_q \in \mathcal{Q}, \mathbf{x}_s \in \mathcal{S}}[-logP(\hat{y}_q | d(\mathcal{F}_\psi(\mathbf{x}_q), \mathcal{F}_\psi(\mathbf{x}_s)))]
\end{aligned}
\tag{5}
$$

where d means the metric methods, such as the Cosine distance in [21], or the Euclidean distance in [18]. For contrastive learning methods, its key point is the contrastive loss function which pursues the object that the distance from query to the same category is much smaller than that to the others category. Equation (6) shows the general training objective of contrastive learning methods.

$$
\begin{aligned}
& \min_{\psi} \mathbb{E}_{(Q,S) \sim P(\mathcal{T})}[\mathcal{L}(\mathcal{F}_\psi(Q), \mathcal{F}_\psi(S))], \mathcal{L}(\mathcal{F}_\psi(Q), \mathcal{F}_\psi(S)) \\
& = \mathbb{E}_{\mathbf{x}_q \in \mathcal{Q}, \mathbf{x}_s \in \mathcal{S}}[\frac{d(\mathcal{F}_\psi(\mathbf{x}_q i), \mathcal{F}_\psi(\mathbf{x}_s i))}{\sum d(\mathcal{F}_\psi(\mathbf{x}_q i), \mathcal{F}_\psi(\mathbf{x}_s j))}]
\end{aligned}
\tag{6}
$$

This paper proposes to learn the difference-level representations instead of the instance-level ones. We exploit the metric-based FSL by extracting the difference-level patterns between two samples rather than the pattern of one single sample. Equation (7) shows the training objective of this paper.

$$
\begin{aligned}
& \min_{\phi} \mathbb{E}_{(Q,S) \sim P(\mathcal{T})}[\mathcal{L}(\mathcal{M}_\phi(Q \ominus S))], \\
& \mathcal{L}(\mathcal{M}_\phi(Q \ominus S)) = \mathbb{E}_{\mathbf{x}_q \in \mathcal{Q}, \mathbf{x}_s \in \mathcal{S}}[-logP(\hat{y}_q == y_s | \mathcal{M}_\phi(\mathbf{x}_q \ominus \mathbf{x}_s))]
\end{aligned}
\tag{7}
$$

where $\mathcal{M}_\phi$ represents the learner of difference-level patterns and $\mathbf{x}_q \ominus \mathbf{x}_s$ denotes the basic difference between query and support samples (Sect. 3.2 shows the detailed description). Thus, the objective of our model is to distinguish if the two samples $\mathbf{x}_q$ and $\mathbf{x}_s$ belong to the same category or not by exploiting the difference-level feature space $\mathcal{M}_\phi$ between them.

3.2   DMNet Model

Overall. This work proposes a Difference Measuring Network (DMNet) for few-shot learning. It extracts the patterns of difference for each query-support pair

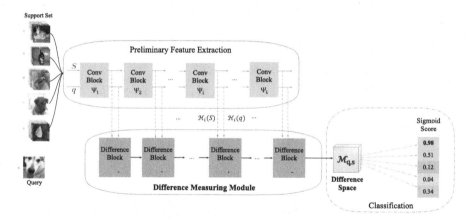

Fig. 1. The Framework of the DMNet. The Preliminary Feature Extraction component gives original representations of support and query samples. The Difference Measuring Module extracts the features of difference for each query-support pair and produces a difference space for classification.

and transforms all sample pairs into a compact difference-level space $\mathcal{M}$ for classification. Equation (8) presents the main idea of the DMNet.

$$\Phi(Q \ominus S) \rightarrow \Theta \tag{8}$$

where Q and S denote query data and support data. $\ominus$ denotes a kind of difference operation. Φ denotes a neural network component, and Θ denotes a classification component. Figure 1 illustrates the overall architecture of the proposed DMNet, which mainly consists of three components: the preliminary feature extraction component Ψ, the parallel difference measuring component Φ, and the classification component Θ. Equation (9) describes the function of each component in detail.

$$\begin{aligned}
\Psi &: (x_q, x_s) \rightarrow \mathcal{H}_{x_q, x_s} \\
\Phi &: \mathcal{H}_{x_q \ominus x_s} \rightarrow \mathcal{M}_{x_q \ominus x_s} \\
\Theta &: \mathcal{M} \rightarrow C
\end{aligned} \tag{9}$$

where $\mathcal{H}$ is the preliminary features, $\mathcal{M}$ is the difference-level space, and C is the predicted classes. The following subsections will introduce them separately.

Preliminary Feature Extraction. We first design a feature encoder module Ψ to extract preliminary feature representations for query and support samples. Here, the module Ψ can be any proper CNN. It consists of several convolutional blocks Ψ_i. Given a support image $\mathbf{x}_s$ and a query image $\mathbf{x}_q$, module Ψ produces multi-scaled preliminary features for $\mathbf{x}_s$ and $\mathbf{x}_q$ via Eq. (10)

$$\begin{aligned}
\Psi &= \{\Psi_i\}_{i=1}^{L}, \\
\Psi_i &= \mathcal{F}_{enc}^i(\mathbf{x}_q, \mathbf{x}_s) \in \mathbb{R}^{2c_i \times h_i \times w_i}
\end{aligned} \tag{10}$$

where L stands for the number of convolutional blocks. $\mathcal{F}_{enc}$ stands for the convolutional operation with the ReLU activation function. (c_i, h_i, w_i) represents the shape of the features. For a N-way K-shot task τ, the support set is $S_\tau^{N \times K}$ and the query set is Q_τ^M. Thus, the output of module Ψ is shown as Eq. (11).

$$\mathcal{H}_\psi(Q_\tau, S_\tau) = \{\mathcal{F}_{enc}^i(Q_\tau, S_\tau)\}_{i=1}^L = \{\mathcal{F}_{enc}^i(\mathbf{x}_q, \mathbf{x}_s)\}^{L \times N'} \tag{11}$$

where $N' = M \times N$ is the number of query-support pairs.

Difference Measuring Module. Then we promote a difference measuring module Φ that is a parallel structure to the feature encoder module Ψ. It takes the features $\mathcal{H}^{L \times N'}$ from the module Ψ as the input and calculates multi-scale difference for query-support pairs. Finally, module Φ transforms all pairs into a difference-level pattern space $\mathcal{M}$, which produces the pattern of difference for each query-support pair. Equation (12) illustrates the output of module Φ.

$$\Phi(\mathcal{H}_\psi(Q_\tau, S_\tau)) \in \mathcal{M}^{N'} \tag{12}$$

Correlating with the feature encoder, the difference measuring module Φ contains several blocks. Each block Φ_i (shown as Fig. 2) contains two main parts that we describe in detail as follows.

Difference Maps. For a query-support pair $(\mathbf{x}_q, \mathbf{x}_s)$, the block Φ_i first generates the difference feature map $\delta \in \mathbb{R}^{c \times h \times w}$ via Eq. (13).

$$\delta_i(\mathbf{x}_q, \mathbf{x}_s) = |\mathcal{H}_{\mathbf{x}_q}^i \ominus \mathcal{H}_{\mathbf{x}_s}^i| \tag{13}$$

where $|\cdot|$ is the symbol of absolute value and $\ominus$ can be any proper operators. We take the operator SUBTRACTION as an example in the following paper for easy understanding. Thus, the multi-scale difference feature maps for all query-support pairs are:

$$\Delta = \{\Delta_1, ..., \Delta_i, ..., \Delta_L\}$$
$$\Delta_i = \begin{bmatrix} \delta_i(\mathbf{x}_{q_1}, \mathbf{x}_{\bar{s}_1}) & ... & \delta_i(\mathbf{x}_{q_1}, \mathbf{x}_{\bar{s}_N}) \\ ... & ... & ... \\ \delta_i(\mathbf{x}_{q_M}, \mathbf{x}_{\bar{s}_1}) & ... & \delta_i(\mathbf{x}_{q_M}, \mathbf{x}_{\bar{s}_N}) \end{bmatrix} \tag{14}$$

Difference Fusion. We fuse the multi-scale difference maps $\{\Delta_1, ..., \Delta_L\}$ via convolutional layers g in order to extract high-level difference patterns. Each fusion layer g_i concatenates the current difference map Δ_i with the last obtained difference-level patterns $\Phi_{i-1}(\Delta_{i-1})$ to form the new difference maps, which is

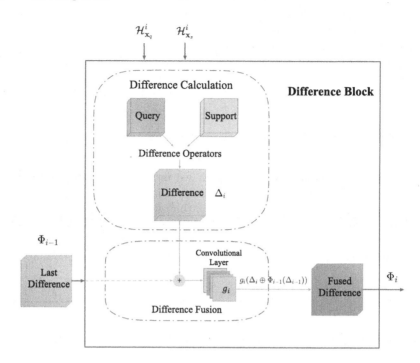

Fig. 2. The Difference Block. It first calculates a preliminary difference for each query-support pair through optional operators. Then, the following convolutional layer extracts the features of difference and fuses multi-scale difference maps.

then fed into a convolutional layer to extract the higher-level difference-level patterns. Equation (15) illustrates this difference fusion function.

$$\Phi_i(\Delta_i) = g_i(\Delta_i \oplus \Phi_{i-1}(\Delta_{i-1})) \tag{15}$$

where $\oplus$ denotes the concatenate operation via the channel axis, and the $\Phi_i(\Delta_i)$ means the higher-level difference patterns. Finally, the difference block transforms all query-support pairs into a difference-level feature space $\mathcal{M}$, described as Eq. (16).

$$\Phi_L(\Delta_L) \in \mathcal{M}^{N'} \tag{16}$$

Classification. This work performs the classification in the difference-level feature space $\mathcal{M}$ with the extracted patterns of difference. We project the difference-level representations in Eq. (16) into a set of difference scores $\mathcal{A} \in \mathbb{R}^{M \times N}$ via two fully connected layers with the Sigmoid function.

$$\mathcal{A} = \begin{bmatrix} \sigma(\mathcal{M}_{q_1,s_1}) & \cdots & \sigma(\mathcal{M}_{q_1,s_N}) \\ \cdots & \cdots & \cdots \\ \sigma(\mathcal{M}_{q_M,s_1}) & \cdots & \sigma(\mathcal{M}_{q_M,s_N}) \end{bmatrix} \tag{17}$$

where σ presents the fully connected layers with the Sigmoid activation function, and each element $\sigma()$ represents the difference score for each query-support pair. As a result, the index of the minimum score along axis N is the predicted class of the query instance $\mathbf{x}_q$. Equation (18) shows the classification target.

$$\hat{y}_q = \arg\min_{c}\{\mathcal{A}\,[q, s_c]\}_{c=1}^{N} \tag{18}$$

Equation (19) shows the training goal.

$$\psi, \phi \leftarrow \arg\min_{\psi,\phi} \sum_{q=1}^{M} \sum_{s=1}^{N} \mathcal{L}(\mathcal{M}_\phi(\mathbf{x}_q \ominus \mathbf{x}_s), \mathbf{1}(\hat{y}_q == y_s)) \tag{19}$$

This paper adopts the original binary cross-entropy loss function to train the DMNet end-to-end.

4 Experiments

In this section, we first introduce the data sets and experimental settings. Then we present results on the five data sets from two scenarios. Finally, we evaluate the effectiveness of the proposed DMNet.

4.1 Datasets

Table 1. Experimental data statistic.

DATASETS	#SAMPLES	#CLASS	TRAIN/VAL/TEST
mini-ImageNet	60,000	100	64/16/20
tiered-ImageNet	778,848	608	351/97/160
Standford Dogs	20,580	120	70/20/30
Stanford Cars	16,185	196	130/17/49
CUB-200-2011	11,788	200	100/50/50

We conduct the experiments from two scenarios: the generic scenario and the fine-grained scenario. The data on fine-grained scenario has lower inter-class variance. For the generic scenario, we execute the experiments on *mini-ImageNet* [21] and *tiered-ImageNet* [15] Datasets. For the fine-grained scenario, we evaluate the proposed models on *Standford Dogs* [7], *Standford Cars* [8] and *CUB-200-2011* [22] Datasets. Table 1 shows the statistic information of these datasets. We resize all images of the three data sets to 84×84 pixels to facilitate a fair comparison with the baselines for few-shot classification.

4.2 Experimental Settings

This paper implements the experiments on two backbones: a shallow CNN and the deeper ResNet. Considering the fairness of the comparison experiments, we adopt the commonly used four convolution blocks in [18,20] as the shallow backbone. Each block consists of a 3×3 convolutional layer with 64 channels, a batch normalization layer, a ReLU layer, and a max-pooling layer. Notably, we extend the four-layer CNN to a deeper ResNet backbone with 12 convolutional layers to show the proposed model's effectiveness when the network goes deeper. We set the same ResNet backbone as in [14], which contains four residual blocks of three stacked 3×3 convolutional layers, each block followed by a 2×2 max-pooling layer. We follow a general practice to evaluate the model with N-way K-shot and 15 query images. We randomly sample and construct 500,000 episodes for the training set, and we adopt the early stop scheme to alleviate overfitting. All models are trained using Adam optimizer with the initial learning rate of 10^{-3} and reduced by half for every 100,000 episodes.

4.3 Experimental Results

This subsection presents the mean accuracy rates (average scores of 600 test episodes) of DMNet on the above five datasets from the generic and fine-grained scenarios.

Results on Generic Scenario. We conduct the experiments on the *mini-ImageNet* and *tiered-ImageNet* datasets to evaluate the performance of the proposed DMNet on generic scenario. Our DMNet transforms all samples into a difference-level pattern space via a difference measuring module parallel to the feature encoder, thus obtaining superior results.

As shown in Table 2, the proposed DMNet offers significant improvements over the baselines. Compared to the three typical metric-based models (MatchingNet [21], ProtoNet [18] and RelationNet [20]), our DMNet gains 7.75%, 1.89%, 0.87% improvements and 5.68%, 4.04%, 2.87% improvements in 1-shot settings on the two datasets respectively. It proves that the Difference Patterns between two samples are more effective and more crucial than the original patterns of the samples.

Typically, our DMNet model outperforms the RelationNet on mini-ImageNet and gains more significant improvements (2.87% in 1-shot settings and 1.73% in 5-shot settings) on tiered-ImageNet. It further indicates that learning the patterns of difference during feature extracting can be a more effective method for few-shot learning, especially for datasets with more categories.

Table 2. 5-way few-shot classification results on mini-ImageNet and tiered-ImageNet datasets. We report the average accuracy (%) across 600 test episodes.

Methods	Backbone	Type	mini-ImageNet		tiered-ImageNet	
			1-shot	5-shot	1-shot	5-shot
OptimiLSTM	Conv-4	Meta	43.44	60.60	–	–
MAML	Conv-4	Meta	48.70	63.11	51.67	70.30
R2-D2	Conv-4	Meta	49.50	65.40	–	–
SNAIL	Conv-4	Meta	45.10	55.20	–	–
MatchingNet	Conv-4	Metric	43.56	55.31	–	–
ProtoNet	Conv-4	Metric	49.42	68.20	53.31	72.69
RelationNet	Conv-4	Metric	50.44	65.32	54.48	71.32
IMP	Conv-4	Metric	49.60	68.10	–	–
CovaMNet	Conv-4	Metric	51.19	67.65	54.98	71.51
DN4	Conv-4	Metric	51.24	**71.02**	53.37	**74.45**
DMNet (Ours)	Conv-4	Metric	**51.31**	65.56	**57.35**	73.05
ProtoNet	ResNet-12	Metric	59.25	75.60	61.74	80.55
TADAM	ResNet-12	Metric	58.50	76.70	–	–
DN4	ResNet-12	Metric	54.37	74.44	–	–
DSN	ResNet-12	Metric	62.64	**78.83**	66.22	82.79
DMNet (Ours)	ResNet-12	Metric	**62.76**	78.38	**68.04**	**82.93**

For the comparison results in 5-shot settings, the improvements of the DMNet are not as significant as it in 1-shot settings. It is probably because of the inaccurate class prototypes. The shallow backbone (for example, the Conv-4 in the experiments) can not extract the exact sample features, which causes the class prototypes to be far from the actual one. These poor class prototypes will cause the degradation of learning the accurate difference patterns. When the embedding backbone goes deeper (for example, the ResNet-12 in the experiments), the class prototypes are more accurate, and the performance of the DMNet goes much better.

Results on Fine-Grained Scenario. We conduct the experiments on three fine-grained datasets, i.e., CUB, Standford Dogs, Standford Cars. Our model achieves competitive results.

As shown in Table 3, the proposed DMNet is 5.29%, 3.38%, 4.22% higher than the state-of-the-art models on each of the three fine-grained datasets in 1-shot settings. Compared to the MatchingNet and the ProtoNet, which calculate the difference after extracting the instance-level features, our DMNet achieves over 10% improvements on all the three fine-grained datasets.

For the comparison results with the DN4, the DMNet outperforms it in 1-shot settings on all three datasets (improves 5.29%, 6.65%, 4.22%, respectively). However, the 5-shot results are not ideal. The reason is that DN4 adopted k-nearest neighbours to calculate the distance, which needs no class prototypes, as we analyse in the last paragraph.

Table 3. 5-way few-shot classification results on three fine-grained datasets, i.e., CUB, StandfordDogs, and StandfordCars. We report the average accuracy (%) across 600 test episodes.

Methods	CUB		Standford Dogs		Standford Cars	
	1-shot	5-shot	1-shot	5-shot	1-shot	5-shot
K-NN	38.85	55.58	24.53	40.30	26.99	43.40
SVM	34.47	59.19	23.37	39.50	25.66	51.07
SiameseNet	37.38	57.73	23.99	39.69	25.81	48.95
MatchingNet	45.30	59.50	35.80	47.50	34.80	44.70
ProtoNet	37.36	45.28	37.59	48.19	40.90	52.93
CovaMNet	52.42	63.76	49.10	63.04	56.65	71.33
DN4	53.15	**81.90**	45.73	66.33	61.51	**89.60**
DMNet (Ours)	**58.44**	73.33	**52.38**	**67.91**	**65.73**	81.64

4.4 Visualization

We visualize the gradients of the raw query-support pairs using the Guided Back-propagation technique [19] to understand the proposed DMNet's improvement further. Figure 3 shows the visualization on *mini-ImageNet* and *CUB* datasets. The two images in one green rectangular box represent a support-query pair. The pairs in the first two boxes are from the same class, while those in the last two boxes belong to two different classes. This work proposes the DMNet model that recognizes the difference patterns directly from the support-query pairs. The idea is distinctive from most metric-based approaches that focus on learning instance-level representations. For comparison, we also visualize the gradients of the Relation Network [20], which is a very typical study of the existing metric-based models.

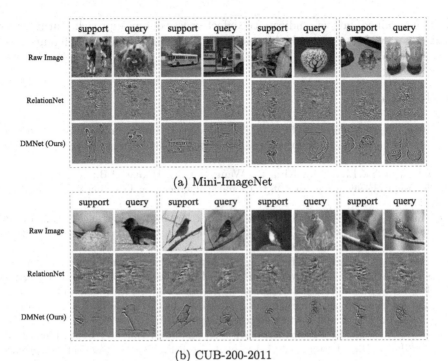

(a) Mini-ImageNet

(b) CUB-200-2011

Fig. 3. The visualization of the gradients for the test samples using the Guided Back-propagation method. The higher gradient value (the brighter colored area) represents the more important area. (a) The visualization on the mini-ImageNet dataset. (b) The visualization on the CUB dataset.

From Fig. 3, the proposed DMNet shows a more vital ability to concentrate on the essential areas of the corresponding classes. For example, the second box in Fig. 3a shows that the DMNet cares more about the *school bus* but not the *kid* because the support instance is a *school bus* and the query instance is from the same class. Furthermore, the first box in Fig. 3b also indicates the DMNet can easily find the actual objects, even if part of them are sheltered. For the pairs from the different classes, the DMNet can recognize the typical features of each instance and distinguish them correctly. For example, the key distinction between the images in the third box in Fig. 3b is the *feather*. For the images in the fourth box, the main difference lies in the *neck*.

5   Conclusions

This paper proposes a Difference Measuring Network for FSL from a novel perspective called difference-level representations, which mimics the fast learning ability of humans to mine the patterns of difference between instances with the result of converting FSL into a more compact binary space helps alleviate adaptation problems in general multi-class recognition. Experiments on both generic and fine-grained datasets indicate the effectiveness of our approach. Future work will explore various practical schemes for capturing more accurate difference-level representations.

References

1. Allen, K., Shelhamer, E., Shin, H., Tenenbaum, J.: Infinite mixture prototypes for few-shot learning. In: International Conference on Machine Learning, pp. 232–241. PMLR (2019)
2. Chen, W.Y., Liu, Y.C., Kira, Z., Wang, Y.C.F., Huang, J.B.: A closer look at few-shot classification. In: International Conference on Learning Representations (2019)
3. Fan, Z., et al.: FGN: fully guided network for few-shot instance segmentation. In: Proceedings of the IEEE/CVF Conference on Computer Vision and Pattern Recognition, pp. 9172–9181 (2020)
4. Hou, R., Chang, H., Ma, B., Shan, S., Chen, X.: Cross attention network for few-shot classification. In: Advances in Neural Information Processing Systems (2019)
5. Karlinsky, L., et al.: RepMet: representative-based metric learning for classification and few-shot object detection. In: Proceedings of the IEEE/CVF Conference on Computer Vision and Pattern Recognition, pp. 5197–5206 (2019)
6. Kaya, M., Bilge, H.Ş: Deep metric learning: a survey. Symmetry **11**(9), 1066 (2019)
7. Khosla, A., Jayadevaprakash, N., Yao, B., Li, F.F.: Novel dataset for fine-grained image categorization: stanford dogs. In: Proceedings of CVPR Workshop on Fine-Grained Visual Categorization (FGVC), vol. 2. Citeseer (2011)
8. Krause, J., Stark, M., Deng, J., Fei-Fei, L.: 3D object representations for fine-grained categorization. In: Proceedings of the IEEE/CVF International Conference on Computer Vision Workshops, pp. 554–561 (2013)
9. Li, A., Luo, T., Xiang, T., Huang, W., Wang, L.: Few-shot learning with global class representations. In: Proceedings of the IEEE/CVF International Conference on Computer Vision, pp. 9715–9724 (2019)
10. Li, W., Wang, L., Huo, J., Shi, Y., Gao, Y., Luo, J.: Asymmetric distribution measure for few-shot learning. In: International Joint Conference on Artificial Intelligence (2020)
11. Li, W., Wang, L., Xu, J., Huo, J., Gao, Y., Luo, J.: Revisiting local descriptor based image-to-class measure for few-shot learning. In: Proceedings of the IEEE/CVF Conference on Computer Vision and Pattern Recognition, pp. 7260–7268 (2019)
12. Li, X., Yu, L., Fu, C.W., Fang, M., Heng, P.A.: Revisiting metric learning for few-shot image classification. Neurocomputing **406**, 49–58 (2020)
13. Liu, W., Zhang, C., Lin, G., Liu, F.: CRNet: cross-reference networks for few-shot segmentation. In: Proceedings of the IEEE/CVF Conference on Computer Vision and Pattern Recognition, pp. 4165–4173 (2020)
14. Oreshkin, B.N., Rodriguez, P., Lacoste, A.: TADAM: task dependent adaptive metric for improved few-shot learning. In: Advances in Neural Information Processing Systems (2018)
15. Ren, M., et al.: Meta-learning for semi-supervised few-shot classification. In: International Conference on Learning Representations (2018)
16. Shu, J., Xu, Z., Meng, D.: Small sample learning in big data era. arXiv preprint arXiv:1808.04572 (2018)

17. Simon, C., Koniusz, P., Nock, R., Harandi, M.: Adaptive subspaces for few-shot learning. In: Proceedings of the IEEE/CVF Conference on Computer Vision and Pattern Recognition, pp. 4136–4145 (2020)
18. Snell, J., Swersky, K., Zemel, R.S.: Prototypical networks for few-shot learning. In: Advances in Neural Information Processing Systems (2017)
19. Springenberg, J.T., Dosovitskiy, A., Brox, T., Riedmiller, M.: Striving for simplicity: the all convolutional net. arXiv preprint arXiv:1412.6806 (2014)
20. Sung, F., Yang, Y., Zhang, L., Xiang, T., Torr, P.H., Hospedales, T.M.: Learning to compare: relation network for few-shot learning. In: Proceedings of the IEEE/CVF Conference on Computer Vision and Pattern Recognition, pp. 1199–1208 (2018)
21. Vinyals, O., Blundell, C., Lillicrap, T., Wierstra, D., et al.: Matching networks for one shot learning. In: Advances in Neural Information Processing Systems, vol. 29, pp. 3630–3638 (2016)
22. Wah, C., Branson, S., Welinder, P., Perona, P., Belongie, S.: The Caltech-UCSD Birds-200-2011 dataset. Technical report CNS-TR-2011-001, California Institute of Technology (2011)
23. Wang, K., Liew, J.H., Zou, Y., Zhou, D., Feng, J.: PANet: few-shot image semantic segmentation with prototype alignment. In: Proceedings of the IEEE/CVF International Conference on Computer Vision, pp. 9197–9206 (2019)
24. Wang, Y., Yao, Q., Kwok, J.T., Ni, L.M.: Generalizing from a few examples: a survey on few-shot learning. ACM Comput. Surv. (CSUR) **53**(3), 1–34 (2020)
25. Xiao, Y., Marlet, R.: Few-shot object detection and viewpoint estimation for objects in the wild. In: Vedaldi, A., Bischof, H., Brox, T., Frahm, J.-M. (eds.) ECCV 2020. LNCS, vol. 12362, pp. 192–210. Springer, Cham (2020). https://doi.org/10.1007/978-3-030-58520-4_12
26. Zhang, C., Cai, Y., Lin, G., Shen, C.: DeepEMD: few-shot image classification with differentiable earth mover's distance and structured classifiers. In: Proceedings of the IEEE/CVF Conference on Computer Vision and Pattern Recognition, pp. 12203–12213 (2020)

Accelerated Monitoring of Powder Bed Fusion Additive Manufacturing via High-Throughput Imaging and Low-Latency Machine Learning

Ayyoub Ahar$^{(\boxtimes)}$ ⓘ, Rob Heylen ⓘ, Dries Verhees ⓘ, Cyril Blanc ⓘ,
and Abdellatif Bey-Temsamani ⓘ

Flanders Make, 3920 Lommel, Belgium
ayyoub.ahar@flandersmake.be

Abstract. Metal 3D printing in particular laser powder bed fusion is in the forefront of product manufacturing with complex geometries. However, these printed products are susceptible to several printing defects mainly due to complexities of utilizing high-power, ultra-fast laser for melting the metal powder. Accurate defect prediction methods to monitor the printing process are of high demand. More critically, such solutions must maintain a very low computational cost to enable feedback control signals for future low-latency laser parameter correction loops, preventing creation of defects in the first place. In this research, first we design an experiment to explore impact of several laser settings on creation of the most common defect called "keyhole porosity". We print an object while recording the laser meltpool with an externally installed high-speed visual camera. After extracting keyhole pore densities, we annotate the meltpool recordings and use it to evaluate performance of a simple but fast CNN model as a low-latency defect detector.

Keywords: pore density · melt-pool monitoring · keyhole pores · defect detection · additive manufacturing · laser powder bed fusion

1 Introduction

Layer by layer 3D printing of objects with high-complex geometries has been possible in a process called Additive Manufacturing (AM) [12]. Its advantages over other traditional manufacturing methods among others are: on-demand production of uniquely designed objects in limited quantities, substantial cost reduction via shorter supply chain and less storage [3], reduced parts counts, faster and less complicated assembling and decreased time and complexity for replacing the used parts [10]. Various printing materials like polymers and metals can be utilized mainly via an AM method called laser powder bed fusion (LPBF). In this method the powder of chosen material is melted with a moving laser beam. The laser melting patterns are adjustable and derived from the 3D model

© IFIP International Federation for Information Processing 2023
Published by Springer Nature Switzerland AG 2023
I. Maglogiannis et al. (Eds.): AIAI 2023, IFIP AICT 676, pp. 250–265, 2023.
https://doi.org/10.1007/978-3-031-34107-6_20

of the object to be printed. Industries such as dental [4], construction [5], and aerospace [7] are especially interested in utilizing such production method.

Nevertheless, LPBF is yet to displace conventional manufacturing due to its sensitive nature which depends on many factors to achieve a high-quality defect-free product. Multiple microstructural defects and anomalies can occur during the printing that can significantly degrade the structural integrity and quality of the build [9]. Among others, creation of tiny voids and pores inside the product is a common defect that can occur mainly due to unstable printing conditions and variations in laser power and speed [1]. Current solutions to reduce such defects are mostly heuristic and mainly involve costly post-production testing via both destructive and non-destructive approaches which thereafter will guide the readjustment of the printing parameters. However, following such approaches requires several repeated printings which impose high cost to the final product.

Ideally, an automated monitoring system embedded in a low-latency feedback control loop can provide on-the-fly correction commands during the print process to prevent generation of defects in the first place or compensate for it by remelting the faulty region. The first building block toward such solution is creating an efficient monitoring system to not only analyze the printing process in a close to real time manner but also be able to predict whether the ongoing print is going to create any defects or not. This requires more than just detecting anomalies in printing parameters. Because not all deviations from the nominal print settings are going to end up creating defects. From another point of view, being able to provide more detail on the spatial location of defect in the product being printed is desired for creating more accurate controlling signals as well. As a result, utilizing visual cameras over photodiodes as the input sensors are justified. Although, to be able to cope with the fast movements of the laser beam i.e. laser speeds up to 1500 mm mm/s, using high speed video cameras with sampling rates up to 20000 frames per second are proposed [1]. Nevertheless, in the same research authors emphasized that using deep learning prediction approaches imposes high computational cost beyond the requirements of an integrated monitoring system in a low-latency control feedback loop. To further clarify this, let us approximate printing one layer of a small 5×5 mm square object. To print 1 layer of this object with ≈ 50 scan lines and fixed laser speed of 1000 mm/s it will take quarter of a second to print a full layer and 5 ms per line. A high speed camera of $20K\,fps$ will produce 100 images of $\approx 14K$ pixels per print line which means to have at least one control feedback signal after printing each 20 lines, the full monitoring pipeline should process ≈ 1000 frames in ≈ 100 ms! This time slot includes capturing, writing/reading into memory, feature extraction, and finally defect prediction step. Even with best hardware integration and optimization solutions, the allocated time slot for the prediction model currently remain well below anything but the most simplistic regression techniques. Consequently, to alleviate this issue with a more practical solution, Booth et al. [1] proposed a simplified fully-connected network with couple of hidden layers combined with a heavier pre-process on the input data to engineer multiple features, extracted from the captured raw videos.

In this research, our main objective is to further decrease the computational cost of the full monitoring pipeline by dropping the costly feature extraction steps and analyzing the raw video inputs instead. We focus on the most common porosity defect called "keyhole pore". We design a specific specimen in such a way that let us exhaustively investigate state of keyhole pore generation for several variations of off-nominal laser power (P) and speed (V). We then print it with 316L stainless steel powder using LPBF while recording the laser meltpool with an externally installed high speed visual camera. Next, we extract the keyhole pore densities from the X-ray computed tomography imaging (xCT) of the printed specimen to conduct a laser PV-space keyhole pore analysis of which to the best of our knowledge, provides the most detailed analysis of its kind at least for the case of the stainless steel LPBF. We prepare the ground-truth data to train our prediction models using those CT extracted pore densities and then use them to annotate each and every captured video frame. Finally, we propose clipping a region of interest (ROI) from each video frame to use it as input to a simple but fast Convolutional Neural Network (CNN). We then provide its performance analysis across entire tested PV space, to directly predict the laser power and speeds as well as keyhole pore occurrence. Additionally, We test a deeper CNN architecture on full (un-cropped) video frames as anchor to highlight the difference between model performances. We report that our fully-annotated dataset of this experiment is also available to download upon request.

2   Materials and Methods

2.1   Specimen Description

A test specimen was 3D printed on a 3D Systems ProX DMP320 laser powder bed fusion (LPBF) machine in 316L stainless steel. This machine employs a 500W power-adjustable IPG fiber laser to melt metal powder layers with configurable thickness between 30 and 60 μm. Each of these print layers are created by several laser scan lines. For our specimen, layer thickness was set at 30 μm, with a laser focal spot of 75 μm and hatching distance 100 μm. Powder particle size distribution is between 20–50 μm. The build chamber is vacuum-cycled and filled with an argon over-pressure before commencing the LPBF process.

The specimen (see Fig. 1a) is bar-shaped, with a 9×9 mm square in the horizontal plane, and an object height of 18 mm in total. A 10×9 mm base plate and a $1 \times 1 \times 1$ mm cube were added at the bottom and top respectively to allow easy orientation of the object. The base plate was printed on 8 mm offsets and removed from the printer bed mechanically with a cutting disk after completion.

The machine is equipped with the Materialise Control Platform (MCP), which allows us to alter the print parameters for every line. The bulk of the material is printed with nominal settings, i.e., laser power $P = 215$ W and laser speed $V = 900$ mm/s. Hatching rotates with $90°$ between layers. A set of three subsequent layers is printed with nominal speed but low laser power (60 W) near the bottom and top of the object (layers 400–402 and 800–802). These print settings are in the lack-of-fusion (LoF) regime, inducing thin flat layers of unfused material in the object. These LoF regions are easy to locate on CT scans, and allow accurate alignment of the post-process CT scan.

(a) printed specimen objX

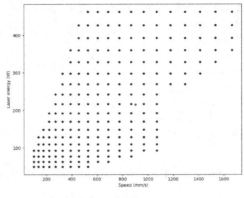

(b) laser PV space.

Fig. 1. (a) An image of the specimen after printing, before detachment from the print bed. (b) The sampled settings in laser PV space. Each black star corresponds with a single error line printed in the sample. Nominal laser power and speed settings are indicated with a red star. (Color figure online)

Error layers (i.e. layers printed with off-nominal laser speed and power) are introduced in the object every 30th print layer, with 29 nominal layers (i.e. layers printed with nominal print settings) in between. For each error layer, most lines are also printed with nominal settings, except lines 10, 15, 20, ..., 80 that are printed with a unique off-nominal laser setting pair. The interline distance is the hatching distance, 100 μm. This spacing between error lines in two dimensions in our experimental setup allows us to identify each introduced porosity with the error line that caused it, with the assumption that nominal settings do not introduce porosities.

We aim to investigate the creation of keyhole porosities in our system, to construct a power/velocity (PV) diagram that identifies the keyhole regime, to obtain statistical information on these keyhole porosities, and to predict keyhole creation events and system setting deviations from high-speed video measurements of the process. The focus therefore lies on system settings that potentially create keyhole errors, while at the same time sampling a wide enough area in PV space to cover settings around nominal as well.

The system settings from the error lines were chosen from the diagram shown in Fig. 1b. This distribution was inspired by results from literature [8,13], where PV diagrams of similar LPBF setups were experimentally derived or simulated. We employed the following reasoning:

- 215 error settings in total (15 error layers with 15 error lines each)
- Reasonable minimal and maximal values: $P \in [50\text{--}500]$ and $V \in [100\text{--}1800]$. Values outside this range are incompatible with the machine, or are highly unrealistic.

- A larger PV space sampling density for lower speed and energy values to obtain better understanding of the expected shape of the keyhole border in this region.
- The energy density E should remain within realistic values, we chose energy densities between 25% and 400% of nominal. As $E \sim P/V$, these restrictions denote two lines with different slopes in the PV diagram.
- We are less interested in values where we know a priori that the chance on keyhole pores is very low. Therefore, we cut off a part of the PV space with high V and low P.

2.2 Printing Process Monitoring Setup

The meltpool was monitored during the printing using a custom setup explained in [11]. This setup utilizes an off-axis high-speed camera (Mikrotron Eosens 3CL) placed with an inclination angle of about 25° with respect to the normal of the build plate. This off-axis monitoring setup is particularly advantageous for recording the spatter signature in the vertical direction and being in a stationary position independent from the movements in optical path of the laser beam. The video stream is recorded at 20,000 frames per second, with each frame having 120×120 pixels. Consequently, each pixel corresponds to approximately $100 \ \mu m \times 100 \ \mu m$ over a total field of view of $12\,mm \times 12\,mm$. To protect the sensor from the excessive brightness of laser, a short-wavelength pass filter with a cut-off value of 975 nm was placed before the camera. The monitoring system was capable to record wavelength range between 350 nm and 975 nm which corresponds to the visible to near infrared range of the spectrum. The exposure time of the camera was set at 30 μs, combined with a 50 mm lens with an aperture of f/16. The aperture and shutter time are set manually to optimize the visibility of the spatters while recording the meltpool.

The video recording was accompanied with the metadata provided by the MCP which was collected at 100 kHz. The metadata included the x, y coordinates of the laser on the build area, the laser on/off signal, the laser power, the laser speed, and timestamps. The high-speed camera was connected via Camera Link to NI PXI. Data was stored to an NI SSD drive with a high-speed data transfer rate of around 1.5 GB/s.

2.3 Prediction Methodology

In this section first we explain the prediction model input, their format, their structure and utilized preprocessing steps. Then, structure of the utilized neural networks and their characteristics are discussed.

Structure of the Input Data
Initially we synchronize and annotate each of the captured images with their corresponding metadata collected from the MCP controller. Next, they are associated to the extracted pore densities from the CT scan data. Then, we randomize their capture order and for each experiment, two separate subsets of

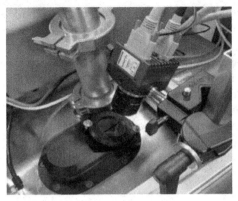

(a) Off-axis camera setup   (b) sample image captured at 20KHz

Fig. 2. (a) Position of the installed monitoring camera and **(b)** a sample image captured from the meltpool

the images for training and testing are selected from the total image pool. The default training subset selected in the way that includes 100 images from each one of 225 printed lines with specified system settings shown in Fig. 1b, yielding a total of 22500 images. After subtracting the training set, the testing subset is selected from the remaining pool in the way that includes 10 images from each one of 225 printed lines with specified system settings shown, yielding a total of 2250 images. For certain experiments we use only the part of each image that shows the close region around the meltpool. To do so, a 21×21 ROI around the brightest point is extracted from each image which we assume it contains the most important information of the captured scene. No other image processing is applied on the images at this point.

Prediction Models
As it was emphasized in the introduction section, in these experiments complex models and deep neural networks are categorically ignored mainly due to strict runtime limitations of the problem. Additionally, a quick scan through the captured video frames indicates that our input data is mainly consists of a small bright spot representing the laser melt pool in the presence of large dark background (See Fig. 2b) with occasional exceptions due to arbitrary appearance of spatters and noise. Therefore, for such simple scenes content-wise, deep model architectures commonly overfit which potentially lead those models to quickly memorize the patterns, the noise and random fluctuations present in the training set all together. Instead, in this experiment we utilize straightforward CNN structures. The number of hidden layers and trainable network parameters are empirically chosen for this experiment.

The *Model-A* is a CNN with more hidden layers is used only for the full-size video frame data in order to better capture the underlying patterns of the whole scene. It has 8 hidden layers and 4 pooling layers, connected to a final dense layer for regression. To predict the laser settings, We utilize the results of this model as a point of reference to evaluate the performance of the faster but shallower proposed model-B.

The *Model-B*, has only 4 hidden layers and 2 pooling layers, connected to a final dense layer for regression. This model is mainly intended to be used for the 21×21 pixels ROI inputs extracted from video frames, but we also test it on the full-frame videos to compare the impact of the ROI extractions on its performance. Both models are implemented in python language using Keras neural-network library [2] and simply reproducible. To facilitate better comparison conditions, all models are trained with 100 epochs.

3 Experimental Results

In this section first we explain the results of post-print scanning of the test object and analysis of the created pores in response to the tested laser settings. This analysis effectively generates the ground-truth data for evaluation of prediction models. Prediction model performance analysis is presented separately for predicting the laser parameter settings and pore density respectively.

3.1 CT Segmentation

After printing, detachment from the printer bed, and grinding and polishing to remove the supports, the object was CT scanned with a FleXCT micro CT imaging system, resulting in a CT reconstruction with 10 μm square voxels. The CT scan was denoised with a total variation denoising method and thresholded to create a pore segmentation following the procedure described in [6].

Registration of the CT reconstruction with the experiment's coordinate system was performed by minimizing the deviation of several features from their theoretical values with respect to translation and rotation degrees of freedom: The locations of the LoF layers, and the alignment of top and bottom horizontal cuts with squares.

The aligned pore segmentation is shown in Fig. 3 in a 3D view and a side view. The error lines that created these pores are indicated as well. It is clear that the majority of *PV* setpoints do not create keyhole pores. When pores are created, significant differences can be observed on the number and depth of the pores. This is to be expected: The penetration depth of the laser and the subsequent keyhole pore creation processes show a complex dependence on the laser parameters [13].

To quantify these qualitative observations, two measures were calculated from each error track and the observed pores below (track and pore identifications are shown by red/green boxes in Fig. 3):

– The total number of segmented voxels in box beneath the line track. This is a measure for the total pore volume

- The weighted depth of the pores, calculated by averaging the distances of each segmented voxel with the green line, which corresponds to the print layer (or Z-coordinate) where the error line was introduced.

These measures are shown in Fig. 4 as contour graphs over the PV space. Only parts that effectively contain pores are color coded. These graphs show a clearly delineated area in PV space where keyhole pores will be present.

We observe that keyhole pores are formed when laser speed V is low and laser power P is high. This is inline with the reports from other independent experiments like those reported in [8,13]. But the exact relation between these two settings and keyhole pore formation is complex and nonlinear, which is also confirmed by our experimental results. Furthermore, our experiment results indicates that there is a strong dependence of the volume of pores and the depth where these pores occur on both system parameters: Lower speeds induce a large pore volume, while the depth of the pores correlates better with increasing the laser power.

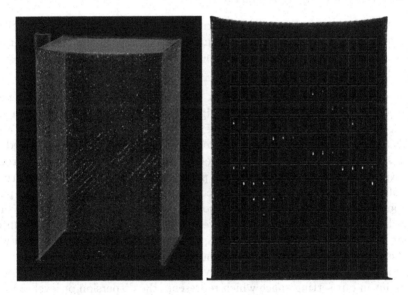

Fig. 3. Segmentation of the pores inside the object, where pores are denoted as transparent white voxels. (a) A 3D view with the borders of the object in gray. (b) A side view with the total number of segmented voxels in grayscale. Error lines are printed perpendicular to the screen/paper. The box around each group of pores is used to identify pores with the error line that created them. The middle of each green line is where the error line was printed, with the created pores below. (Color figure online)

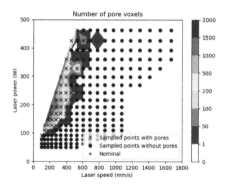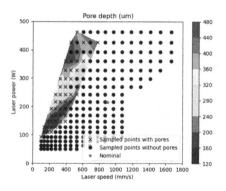

Fig. 4. (a) The number of pore voxels found below each error line, visualized as a contour graph in the *PV* diagram. Note the nonlinear color coding. (b) The average depth in μm of the pore voxels in an analogous visualization.

3.2   System Settings Prediction

In this section, we investigate the performance of the tested CNNs for prediction of two prominent system parameters namely the laser speed and laser power from the off-axis camera images capturing the object printing process.

Model-A Trained on Full-Frame Raw Video Recordings
As We explained in Sect. 2.3, Model-A is utilized to predict the laser settings from the raw captured video frames. Figure 5(a), (b) show the prediction error maps for the laser power and speed respectively. The error in the maps corresponds to the Mean of Absolute Difference (MAD) between the predicted and target settings. Results demonstrate reliable laser power predictions throughout majority of the setting space with prediction errors $\leq 50w$ particularly for large off-nominal settings. The best accuracy also belongs to low laser power and speeds. Laser speed predictions though prove to be more tricky especially for the high-laser speed regime where prediction errors can scale up to 300 mm/s. Similar to the Power predictions, best speed prediction accuracy achieved when both laser power and speed are substantially lower than nominal value.

Also, Fig. 5c shows the standard deviation of the prediction distribution for each point in our setting space which represents the dispersion or level of uncertainty for predictions per tested laser setting. The blue and red circles represent values for the laser speed and power respectively. It can be observed that the speed predictions are generally more dispersed than the power predictions. This dispersion is also more significant for large off-nominal speed settings on both high and low speed regimes.

Model-B Trained on Extracted ROI from Raw Video Recording
Next, we would like to repeat the laser setting prediction experiment this time using Model-B with raw images redacted into only extracted ROIs. Figure 6(a), (b) show the corresponding prediction error maps where their colormap ranges has been kept equal to the ones of Fig. 5 for easier comparison. Here, in Fig. 6(a),

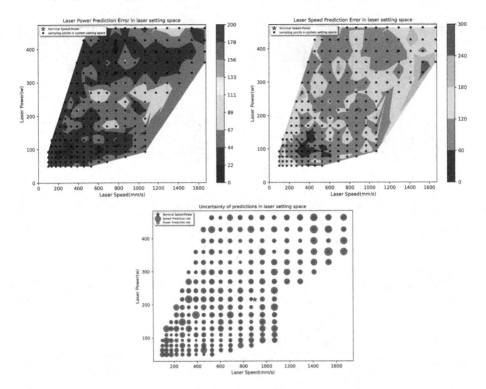

Fig. 5. Prediction errormap for (**a**) laser power and (**b**) for the laser speed for CNN trained on full-size image. The error corresponds to the mean absolute difference. The nominal setting is indicated by a red star. (**c**) Dispersion of predicted settings per sampling point demonstrated by the size of the red and blue circles for the laser power and speed respectively. The radius of each circle corresponds to the standard deviation of the prediction value distribution for the corresponding point in PV space. (Color figure online)

a clear improvement on laser power predictions can be observed compared to the previous case. In Fig. 6(**b**) though, the laser speed prediction accuracy got poorer in general. However, compared to Fig. 5, here a rather distinct color gradient can be observed. In the error map of Fig. 6(**a**) highest and lowest accuracy indicated with light and dark blue respectively appear to be inversely related to the low and high laser power regimes. In the speed prediction error map (Fig. 6(**b**)) though, the direction of color gradient seems to be horizontal and again inversely related to the low and high laser speed regimes. From another perspective, Fig. 6c demonstrates large dispersion for speed predictions especially in low power regions.

Comparison of the results for these two experiments demonstrates that utilizing a low-complexity shallow CNN model (Model-B) combined with significantly reducing the model input size (by choosing only a small region of interest), not only improves the prediction runtime of our monitoring system effectively, but

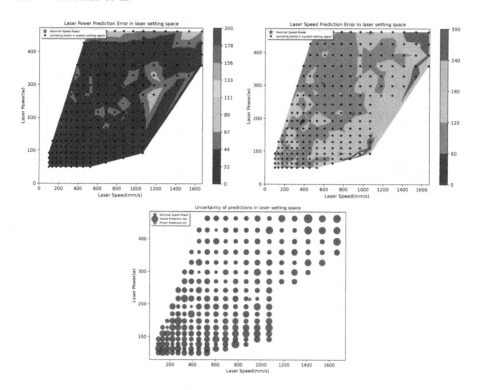

Fig. 6. Prediction errormap for (**a**) laser power and (**b**) for the laser speed for CNN trained on ROI. The error corresponds to the mean absolute difference. The nominal setting is indicated by a red star. (**c**) Dispersion of predicted settings per sampling point demonstrated by the size of the red and blue circles for the laser power and speed respectively. The radius of each circle corresponds to the standard deviation of the prediction value distribution for the corresponding point in PV space. (Color figure online)

also lead to better prediction results for laser power while retaining acceptable margin of error for the laser speed predictions across the whole laser setting space. Our further experiments demonstrated similar performance of Model-A when compared to Model-B. To avoid cluttering, in the following section we only present the analysis of the Model-B performance which is the main focus of the experiment due to faster run-time overall.

3.3 Pore Density Prediction

In the final part of our experiments, we would like to utilize the keyhole pore density information that we extracted from our CT scan data analysis to identify the performance of Model-B for direct prediction of keyhole pore density from the captured video. Apart from the ROI extracted input, we conduct an additional test for Model-B this time using the raw video inputs. This way we can identify impact of proposed ROI extraction to the keyhole pore density prediction performance of same model compared to using full-frame videos.

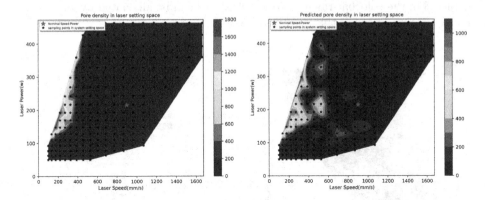

Fig. 7. Contour map of pore density (**a**) reference values extracted from the CT of the object and (**b**) corresponding predicted values with Model-B trained on full-frame raw video. The nominal setting is indicated by a red star. (Color figure online)

Model-B Trained on Full-Frame Video

Figure. 7(**a**) demonstrates the contour map for the detected pore densities in the CT scan of the object which we call them as the "target pores" hereafter. Figure 7(**b**) shows the prediction results of Model-B. While the pore prone region has been identified by the model, it is observed that amount of false positives in the non-porous regions of the PV space is significant. Also the scale of the predictions are not the same as the target pore densities as depicted in the colorbar ranges.

To better observe the difference between the target and predicted pore densities, we have calculated the error map as well, which can be seen in the Fig. 8(**a**). The dispersion of the predictions per laser setting point is demonstrated in Fig. 8(**b**). In both cases it is clear that the accuracy of the predictions and the dispersion of their distributions don't demonstrate a reliable performance. One particular point of attention is the area around the nominal settings (depicted with an star in the center of PV space). The prediction model is particularly expected to identify this region as the pore free setting area, but this is clearly not the case here.

Model-B Trained on Extracted ROI from Raw Video Recording

Figure 9(**a**) shows the contour map of the target pores. Figure 9(**b**) shows the prediction results of Model-B. It is obvious that the general trend and pore prone region has been nicely detected by the model. Although, two points are important to notice here. First, despite being much less than the case of training with full-frame video, there are still some false positive regions in the predictions close to the pore prone region. Second, similar to the full-size video input case, the scale of the predictions are not the same as the target pore densities as depicted in the colorbar ranges. Nonetheless this can be alleviated by a constant multiplication knowing that such issue exists.

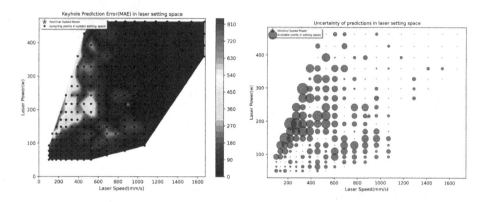

Fig. 8. (**a**) Prediction errormap for pore prediction using Model-B trained on full-frame raw video. The error corresponds to the mean absolute difference. (**b**) Dispersion of predicted pore density per sampling point in the PV space demonstrated by the size of the blue circles. The radius of each circle corresponds to the standard deviation of the prediction distribution for the corresponding point in setting space. (Color figure online)

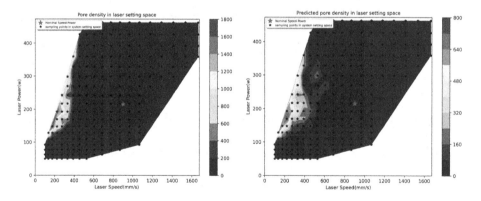

Fig. 9. Contour map of keyhole pore density (**a**) reference values extracted from the CT of the object and (**b**) corresponding predicted values from Model-B trained on ROI. The nominal setting is indicated by a red star. (Color figure online)

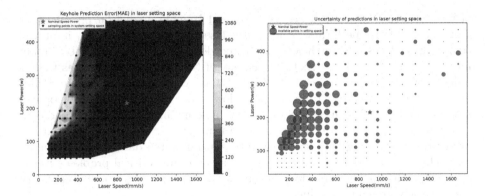

Fig. 10. (a) Prediction errormap for pore prediction using Model-B trained on ROI. The error corresponds to the mean absolute difference. (b) Dispersion of predicted pore density per sampling point in the PV space demonstrated by the size of the blue circles. The radius of each circle corresponds to the standard deviation of the prediction distribution for the corresponding point in setting space. (Color figure online)

The error map however, represents a much improved prediction accuracy which can be seen in the Fig. 10(a). The dispersion of the predictions demonstrated in Fig. 10(b) also shows improved dispersion for the prediction distributions.

Considering the fact that we used both full-frame video and the proposed ROI as the inputs for the same prediction model, it is demonstrated that utilizing the proposed ROI extraction clearly improves the prediction performance while it will provide a significant advantage on the prediction runtime of the monitoring system via substantial reduction of the input data.

4 Conclusions

In this paper we present an industrial machine learning usecase for the defect detection problem where highly pragmatic solutions are of the main interest. In this context, we utilized our LPBF machine to 3D print a metal object with a wide range of laser settings variations. Utilizing post-print CT scan of the print, we identified the boundaries of the keyhole pore subspace within the practical bounds of the laser PV space. Together with the high-framerate video clips captured from the printing process, we generated an extensive annotated dataset which is also publicly available upon request. To further ease the computational load of the prediction process, we propose using only a small region of interest from the full-size video frames which effectively redact each frame to slightly more than 3 percent of its original pixel count. Having much smaller input, we then opt for a compact CNN with only 4 hidden layers to further reduce the overall computational cost. Our results reveal that using proposed ROI instead of full-frame video, will improve the keyhole pore prediction by removing the redundant and noisy information which clutter and destabilize the prediction of the network. We report that our proposed keyhole prediction pipeline provides a competitive performance across the laser PV space with highly improved computational cost. Nevertheless, we acknowledge that there is a lot of room for improvement on the prediction accuracy of the proposed pipeline as well as reducing the false positive cases. Also, the final verdict in terms of suitability of the proposed monitoring pipeline for a low-latency control feedback loop can only be achieved after fully integrating the pipeline into the hardware and control unit of the printer which remains for future works. We are hoping that the presented analysis together with access to our annotated dataset attracts more researches to address this and many other similar time-critical problems in the industry with more pragmatic solutions where low computational complexity and accuracy are equally valued.

Acknowledgment. This research is supported by the Flemish Innovation and Entrepreneurship Agency through the research project 'VIL_ICON' (project NO: HBC.2019.2808) and by Flanders Make (the strategic research center for the manufacturing industry & imec (the international research & development organization, active in the fields of nanoelectronics and digital technologies). The research is also supported by AI Flanders that is financed by Economie Wetenschap & Innovatie (https://flandersairesearch.be/en). and the CoE RAISE project (https://coe-raise.eu), which has received funding from the European Union's Horizon 2020 - Research and Innovation Framework Program H2020-INFRAEDI-2019-1 under grant agreement no. 951733.

References

1. Booth, B.G., Heylen, R., Nourazar, M., Verhees, D., Philips, W., Bey-Temsamani, A.: Encoding stability into laser powder bed fusion monitoring using temporal features and pore density modelling. Sensors **22**(10), 3740 (2022)
2. Chollet, F., et al.: Keras (2015). https://github.com/fchollet/keras
3. Debnath, B., Shakur, M.S., Tanjum, F., Rahman, M.A., Adnan, Z.H.: Impact of additive manufacturing on the supply chain of aerospace spare parts industry–a review. Logistics **6**(2), 28 (2022)
4. Galante, R., Figueiredo-Pina, C.G., Serro, A.P.: Additive manufacturing of ceramics for dental applications: a review. Dent. Mater. **35**(6), 825–846 (2019)
5. Gardner, L.: Metal additive manufacturing in structural engineering-review, advances, opportunities and outlook. Structures **47**, 2178–2193 (2023)
6. Heylen, R., et al.: 3D total variation denoising in X-CT imaging applied to pore extraction in additively manufactured parts. Meas. Sci. Technol. **33**(4), 045602 (2022)
7. Kumar, S.A., Pathania, A., Shrivastava, A., Rajkumar, V., Raghupatruni, P.: Applications of additive manufacturing techniques in aerospace industry. Nanotechnol.-Based Addit. Manuf. Prod. Des. Prop. Appl. **2**, 561–578 (2023)
8. Lo, Y.L., Liu, B.Y., Tran, H.C.: Optimized hatch space selection in double-scanning track selective laser melting process. Int. J. Adv. Manuf. Technol. **105**(7), 2989–3006 (2019). https://doi.org/10.1007/s00170-019-04456-w
9. Mostafaei, A., et al.: Defects and anomalies in powder bed fusion metal additive manufacturing. Curr. Opin. Solid State Mater. Sci. **26**(2), 100974 (2022)

10. Sepasgozar, S.M.E., Shi, A., Yang, L., Shirowzhan, S., Edwards, D.J.: Additive manufacturing applications for industry 4.0: a systematic critical review. Buildings **10**(12), 231 (2020)
11. Thanki, A., et al.: Off-axis high-speed camera-based real-time monitoring and simulation study for laser powder bed fusion of 316L stainless steel. Int. J. Adv. Manuf. Technol. **125**, 4909–4924 (2023). https://doi.org/10.1007/s00170-023-11075-z
12. Vafadar, A., Guzzomi, F., Rassau, A., Hayward, K.: Advances in metal additive manufacturing: a review of common processes, industrial applications, and current challenges. Appl. Sci. **11**(3), 1213 (2021)
13. Zhao, C., et al.: Critical instability at moving keyhole tip generates porosity in laser melting. Science **370**(6520), 1080–1086 (2020)

AutoTiM - An Open-Source Service for Automated Provisioning and Operation of Time Series Based Machine Learning Models

Andre Ebert$^{(\boxtimes)}$ 🆔, Jakob Kempter🆔, Marina Siebold🆔, Robert Pesch, Tetyana Turiy🆔, Tevin Tchuinkam🆔, and Thomas Caffin Sune🆔

inovex, Karlsruher Straße 71, 75179 Pforzheim, Germany
{andre.ebert,jakob.kempter,marina.siebold,robert.pesch,tetyana.turiy,
tevin.tchuinkam,thomas.caffin-sune}@inovex.de
https://www.inovex.de/

Abstract. The ubiquitous availability of heterogeneous sensor data created by *Internet-of-Things* (IoT) technologies and *Industry 4.0* trends drastically accelerated the development of machine learning applications. *AutoML* services enable users with sparse machine learning knowledge to develop AI-based applications and rapidly evaluate the feasibility of data-driven ideas. Therefore, there exists a demand for holistic, low-code, end-to-end *AutoML* systems, which cover all stages of the machine learning lifecycle (i.e., feature engineering, model training, evaluation, versioning, provisioning, etc.). Although there are proprietary, cost-intensive platforms addressing these issues, no open-source solutions covering these aspects are known to us. In this paper we present *Auto-TiM*, an open-source service capable of creating and operating highly performant machine learning models without requiring domain expertise or machine learning knowledge.

Keywords: AutoML · Democratization · Automated Machine Learning

1 Introduction

IoT technologies offer vast opportunities to gather information from various data sources and to aggregate it within data lakes or lakehouses [8]. This accelerates the adoption of data-driven applications for consumer use as well as for industrial purposes, such as predictive maintenance, context-aware services, energy consumption forecasts, etc. Machine learning models are usually at the core of such applications, therefore, *Automated Machine Learning* (AutoML) libraries and tools have received a lot of attention lately. *AutoML* enables automated

Supported by *Service-Meister*, a research project funded by the german *Federal Ministry for Economics and Climate Action* (BMWK), https://www.servicemeister.org/.

© IFIP International Federation for Information Processing 2023
Published by Springer Nature Switzerland AG 2023
I. Maglogiannis et al. (Eds.): AIAI 2023, IFIP AICT 676, pp. 266–278, 2023.
https://doi.org/10.1007/978-3-031-34107-6_21

model training and evaluation without requiring domain expertise; it is also a critical component of holistic *Machine Learning Operations* (MLOps) architecture [18]. While big companies like *Google* already provide comparatively mature *AutoML* solutions, the number of such holistic, end-to-end systems available as open-source software is rather sparse. Most of free-of-charge libraries focus on specific aspects of machine learning like feature engineering or model training individually, rather than combining all necessary steps to create and operate machine learning models within one system. Hence, a holistic and publicly available end-to-end *AutoML* service would offer great value for various stakeholders, be it machine learning experts or novice users. Furthermore, it would eliminate the need to transfer complex domain expertise through a time-consuming process of data exploration, feature engineering, model training and evaluation. Small and medium-sized companies with limited machine learning expertise would be empowered to independently deploy intelligent applications. Thus, the holistic approach to *AutoML* encompassing all of these aspects is a crucial precondition for the democratization of machine learning.

In the following, we provide an overview of related work in Sect. 2. Afterwards, we present *AutoTiM*, an end-to-end and easy-to-use *AutoML* open-source service in Sect. 3. The evaluation in Sect. 4 demonstrates *AutoTiM*'s capabilities to provide highly competitive machine learning models without undertaking any manual steps and without the inclusion of domain expertise. Finally, we summarize our findings and outline future work in Sect. 5.

2 Related Work

AutoTiM is a low-code, end-to-end *AutoML* service focused on time series classification. In the following, we define time series classification and look at specific application fields in industry, namely, predictive maintenance or anomaly detection. Moreover, we provide an overview of the existing *AutoML* approaches.

2.1 Time Series Classification and Its Application

Time series are collections of chronologically organized data obtained from sequential measurements [6], whereby data sources can be industrial sensors, medical monitoring devices, and others. A decade ago, its analysis with algorithms of supervised classification was perceived to be a challenging task, while today there are numerous productive applications in the areas of *IoT* and *Industry 4.0* as well as in the consumer market [13,14].

A characteristic example for the application of time series classification in production is *Predictive Maintenance* (PdM), which is a maintenance management strategy resulting from its predecessor strategies *1) Reactive Maintenance* and *2) Preventive Maintenance*. By employing predictive tools as well as algorithms of machine learning, continuous monitoring of production processes and machinery is implemented. Goals are the optimization of maintenance costs, the minimization of downtimes, and increasing productivity [3]. Naturally, the effectiveness of any *Predictive Maintenance* concept relies on the algorithmic approach it is based on, i.e., machine learning models, statistical approaches, or mathematical models [9]. Currently and especially when not automated, the efficient creation of prediction models by manual integration of algorithms requires a lot of domain expertise for feature engineering, selection of algorithms, training of models, etc. [10]. An example illustrating these challenges during segmentation, classification, and anomaly detection with sensor data is given by Coelho et al. [4]. Other examples within the automotive and the railway industry are given by the authors of [5].

Anomaly Detection is an important field for *Predictive Maintenance* as it deals with identifying outliers that deviate from an expected distribution [16]. Though it could be interpreted as a binary supervised classification problem (*anomaly* vs. *no anomaly*) the sheer application of supervised algorithms is not sufficient in reality. Reasons among others are labor-intensive labeling and common strong class imbalances in datasets [16]. Hence, the application of unsupervised, self- and semi-supervised toolkits for *Anomaly Detection* covering conventional as well as *Deep Learning* based concepts gains attention [2,12].

Table 1. Machine learning automation levels as presented in [10].

		Systems	TF	PE	FE	ML	ATV	RSR
Level 6	Fully automated ML agent	?	✓	✓	✓	✓	✓	✓
Level 5		ComposeML + Level 4 systems	✓	✓	✓	✓		
Level 4		IBM AutoAI, AutoBazaar, RapidMiner, **AutoTiM**		✓	✓	✓		
Level 3	ML + ATV combined	Rafiki, Amazon SageMaker, H2O, ATM, AUTO-WEKA				✓	✓	
Level 2	ML + ATV separate	scikit-learn, Keras, ORANGE, Tensorflow, Pytorch, WEKA				✓	✓	
Level 1		Implementation of Decision Tree, KMeans, SVM, etc.				✓		
Level 0	No automation	Programming languages (python, C++, etc.)						

2.2 Automated Machine Learning

Commonly, *AutoML* deals with the automation of one or more steps of the *Machine Learning Lifecycle* due to its iterative, labor-intensive nature. Karmaker et al. define 6 levels of maturity for *AutoML* systems based on the number of tasks handled without user interaction [10]. These are *Task Formulation (TF), Data Visualization, Cleaning, and Curation (DCC), Prediction Engineering (PE), Feature Engineering (FE), Machine Learning Model Development (ML), Alternative Model Exploration, Testing, and Validation (ATV),* and *Result Summary and Recommendation (RSR)* (see Table 1). Within this taxonomy, *AutoTiM* is classified as Level 4, which includes automated feature engineering, model development, ATV, model provisioning, and operation.

In contrast to the above-named proprietary and potentially costly services by *IBM*[1], *Amazon*[2], and *Google*[3], *AutoTiM* is fully open-source. The partially open-source platform RapidMiner[4] and the fully open-source framework *Auto-Bazaar* support a wider range of data inputs and machine learning subtasks [17]. Other than *AutoTiM*, no other Level 4 system available as open-source software provides comparable capabilities of automated versioning, evaluation, and deployment of machine learning models.

3   Concept

This Section examines core requirements for *AutoTiM* and provides an overview of its architecture. Extensive documentation of all functionalities is also provided at the official *Github* repository: https://github.com/inovex/AutoTiM.

3.1   Requirements

We define the following requirements for holistic ready-to-use *AutoML* services:

1. **End-to-End** Provide all functionality necessary to train, evaluate, version, and serve machine learning models for a generic, time-series-based use-case.
2. Environment **Independence** Local operation for rapid prototyping as well as operation in a cloud-based production infrastructure is supported.
3. **Simplicity** Interfaces are standardized and easy to understand.
4. **No domain knowledge** is needed for feature extraction and model training.
5. **Adaptability** to various domains, data sources, and use-cases without restrictions as long as the input data is time-series-based.
6. **Model Quality** Performance has to be competitive in comparison to manual machine learning approaches.

3.2   Technical Notes

AutoTiM is built with the use of several open-source technologies; in the following, specific design choices are illustrated. All service components depicted in Fig. 1 are deployed as multi-container *Docker* applications that communicate via REST APIs. For feature engineering, model exploration, training, and evaluation, existing libraries including *tsfresh, H2O AutoML*, and *scikit-learn* were applied. Recent evaluations show that none of the currently existing *AutoML* libraries significantly outperforms the others [7,19]. *AutoTiM* makes use of *H2O*'s model training and exploration capabilities, which provide a wide range of algorithms including *Deep Learning*. These are neither present for *auto-sklearn* nor for *mljar-supervised* while for *TPOT* support of *Deep Learning* is only experimental. *Auto-Keras*, on the

---

[1] https://www.ibm.com/cloud/watson-studio/autoai.
[2] https://aws.amazon.com/machine-learning/automl/.
[3] https://cloud.google.com/automl.
[4] https://rapidminer.com/platform/.

other hand, only supports *Deep Learning*. Furthermore, compared to frameworks like *Auto-Gluon* or *MLBox*, *H2O* can be considered a mature framework with an active community of users and developers [7].

For automated extraction of expressive features, *AutoTiM* employs *tsfresh*. Unlike comparable solutions like *featurewiz, autofeat*, or *featuretools*, it is explicitly designed for the analysis of time series. Other time series focused frameworks like *tsflex* and *tsfel* do not offer important functionalities like relevance-based feature selection for classification tasks and are generally considered less mature than *tsfresh*.

3.3   Architectural Overview

Subsequently, the four key components of *AutoTiM*'s architecture are presented. Namely, these are the *Filesystem*, the *Training* and *Prediction Services*, and the *MLflow* instance for persisting models and related parameters (see Fig. 1).

Endpoints. The complete *AutoTiM* workflow is accessible through three REST endpoints:

- /store is used to persist a dataset in the *Filesystem* and to tag it with a use-case name and a unique dataset identifier. Depending on the user configuration, a cloud storage or a (local) *Docker* volume can be used.
- /train starts an automated feature extraction followed by model training and evaluation (see 3.3 *Training Service*); models are versioned in *MLflow*.
- /predict generates predictions for a set of raw data points using a previously trained model (see 3.3 *Prediction Service*).

Training Service. The *Training Service* as depicted in Fig. 1 is responsible for automated feature engineering, model training, model evaluation, and model preservation in *MLflow* (see 3.3 *Tracking and Versioning*). To trigger training for a specific use-case, there are two mandatory parameters needed: 1) the use-case identifier, used for tagging and allocating data for a specific use-case, and 2) the dataset identifier. Optional parameters allow the definition of an upper limit for the feature set size, of the duration of training and model exploration as well as of a custom metric to evaluate a model's performance (see also Sect. 4.2). The logical flow within the *Training Service* is depicted in Fig. 2. The first step is automated feature extraction with *tsfresh*. Once extracted, features are selected based on their statistical significance for the classification task at hand. The settings used for extracting features also need to be persisted as a model artifact, in order to reuse them for extraction during prediction (see 3.3 *Prediction Service*). Output of this step is a feature set, which is used to train several prediction models by utilizing *H2O AutoML*. Thereby, a diversity of base models, including *GBMs, Random Forests, Deep Neural Networks*, and *GLMs* are trained, cross-validated, and subjected to hyperparameter tuning [11]. Two additional stacked ensemble models are formed from the base models to obtain the best classification performance. All learners are evaluated further based on their accuracy.

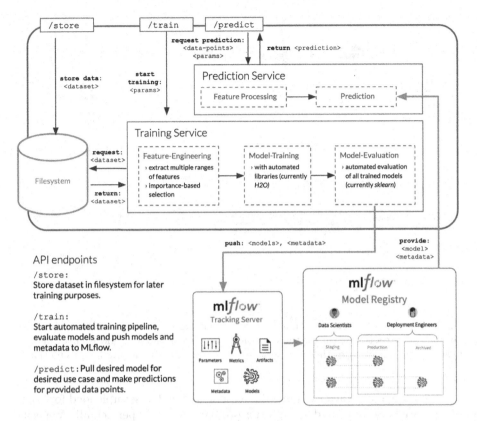

Fig. 1. Overview of the *AutoTiM* architecture, encompassing the **/store**, **/train**, and **/predict** endpoints as well as the *Filesystem*, the *Training* and *Prediction Services* and an *MLflow* instance.

The best-performing model is versioned in *MLflow* and made available for live predictions. Along with the model, all performance metrics, a confusion matrix, feature settings, and additional metadata are stored. The last step is benchmarking against previously trained models for the actual use-case and dataset combination. Several metrics are calculated using *scikit-learn*, including, *Accuracy*, *Balanced Accuracy*, *Recall*, *Precision*, and *F1-score*. Thereby, the performance of a new model is compared to the performances of existing models in *MLflow*. The best model is tagged for production and deployed to be used for prediction generation.

Prediction Service. Once a model for the desired use-case has been generated by the *Training Service*, a prediction can be made for new instances by querying the *Prediction Service*. Three parameters are required: 1) the use-case identifier used for tagging and allocating a set of datasets for a specific use-case, 2) the dataset identifier itself, and 3) one or more time series instances to be classified.

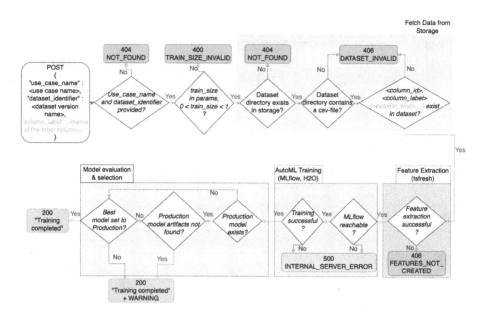

Fig. 2. Flow chart of the *Training Service*, encompassing the acquisition of data, the automated extraction features, the training of prediction models, and their evaluation including the selection of the best-performing model and its tagging for production.

The instances must have the same dimensions as the dataset uploaded for training. For prediction the model tagged for production is used per default. A specific version can be requested explicitly by providing an optional /predict endpoint parameter. When triggering the *Prediction Service*, suitable feature settings and the model itself are retrieved from *MLflow*. The feature settings are used to calculate a feature set with the same specifications from the given time series instances as it was calculated during the prior training. The *Prediction Service* is capable of classifying single as well as multiple instances and returns a list with predicted labels.

Result Tracking and Model Versioning. Versioning and benchmarking of machine learning models, persisting their corresponding parameters and metrics as well as the provision of models for production can be organized by different platforms, such as *MLflow*, *Weights & Biases*, or *Neptune*. Due to its widespread community support, its free availability, and its matured condition, *MLflow* is used to fulfill these requirements for *AutoTiM*. Upon the first launch of *AutoTiM*, a local *MLflow* instance is created and made accessible for the service in order to log experiments, models, and their parameters for each use-case, respectively. For each combination of use-case and dataset, multiple models can be stored. Logged parameters encompass 1) training parameters, 2) performance metrics (see 3.3 *Training Service*), and 3) further artifacts: a confusion matrix, feature settings, model weights, etc.

4   Evaluation

To demonstrate *AutoTiM*'s capabilities regarding the classification of time series as well as regarding the ability to generalize across heterogeneous use-cases and domains of application, it was evaluated on the *UEA MTSC* archive [1]. To verify the quality of models generated with *AutoTiM*, we compared its results to 20 other recent approaches examined in the *Great multivariate time series classification bake off* [15]. In the following, we first introduce the datasets as well as the methodology used for evaluation. Secondly, we present and discuss the evaluated results for *AutoTiM*.

4.1   Datasets

The *UEA MTSC* archive used for evaluation consists of 30 datasets covering a variety of domains [1]. Thereof, 26 datasets contain time series instances of equal length: 8 datasets of electrical biosignals (electrocardiograms, electroencephalogram, and magnetoencephalography), 7 of accelerometer data, 3 of coordinates in Cartesian space, 3 of audio data in spectrogram format, and 5 containing miscellaneous data sources (see Table 2). Besides the data itself, benchmarkable results and documentation are available at the corresponding website[5]. Table 2 provides an overview of the archive datasets and their specifications. Varying dataset attributes, i.e. dimensions, time series length, etc., are indicating the holistic approach *AutoTiM* was aiming for. Out of 26 datasets in Table 2, 20 were included in the evaluation. Reasons for leaving out six sets were: 1) the maximum time given for feature engineering was exceeded (4 sets), and 2) deviating data format (2 sets).

4.2   Methodology

In order to simplify dataset preprocessing, missing values are filled with a built-in naïve data imputation strategy: backward fill followed by forward fill, whereby each dimension is handled independently from others. For evaluation, the number of extracted features is limited to 1000 in order to address technical preconditions such as limited resources (memory, processing power). Three experiments were conducted with fixed training times of 2, 10, and 30 min for each dataset in Table 2, respectively. During the 2 min of training time, 10 models are generated for each dataset; for all other time spans, 5 models were generated. The automated feature extraction and selection as well as model training and tuning are performed for each run. A fourth experiment was conducted with a fixed maximum number of models to train $n_m = 10$ and a training time t_{train} which was calculated dynamically with respect to the number of features f and dataset size d: $t_{train} = \min(\sqrt{f \cdot d} + 120, 1800)$. For comparability, the definition of the dynamic timeframe within a range from 120 s until 1800 s is derived from the static experiments minimum and maximum times (2 and 30 min). Subsequently, the *Stopping Tolerance S* can be determined based on t_{train} and n_m: $S = \frac{1}{t_{train}} * \sqrt{\frac{1}{n_m}}$.

---

[5] https://www.timeseriesclassification.com.

Table 2. Summary of datasets used for evaluation as presented by Bagnall et al. [1].

Dataset	Source	Train	Test	Dims	Length	Classes	Included	Comments
AWR	coordinates	175	300	9	144	25	✓	
AF	electrical biosignal	15	15	2	640	3	✓	
BM	accelerometer	40	40	6	100	4	✓	
CR	accelerometer	108	72	6	1197	12	✓	
DDG	audio	50	50	1345	270	5	✗	deviating data format
EW	others	128	131	6	17984	5	✗	maximum time exceeded
EP	accelerometer	137	138	3	206	4	✓	
EC	others	261	263	3	1751	4	✓	
ER	others	30	270	4	65	6	✗	deviating data format
FD	electrical biosignal	5890	3524	144	62	2	✗	maximum time exceeded
FM	electrical biosignal	316	100	28	50	2	✓	
HMD	electrical biosignal	160	74	10	400	4	✓	
HW	accelerometer	150	850	3	152	26	✓	
HB	audio	204	205	61	405	2	✓	
LIB	coordinates	180	180	2	45	15	✓	
LSST	others	2459	2466	6	36	14	✓	
MI	electrical biosignal	278	100	64	3000	2	✗	maximum time exceeded
NATO	accelerometer	180	180	24	51	6	✓	
PD	coordinates	7494	3498	2	8	10	✓	
PEMS	others	267	173	963	144	7	✗	maximum time exceeded
PS	audio	3315	3353	11	217	39	✓	
RS	accelerometer	151	152	6	30	4	✓	
SRS1	electrical biosignal	268	293	6	896	2	✓	
SRS2	electrical biosignal	200	180	7	1152	2	✓	
SWJ	electrical biosignal	12	15	4	2500	3	✓	
UW	accelerometer	120	320	3	315	8	✓	

Experiments were run on consumer-grade hardware (e.g., Lenovo ThinkPad T14s laptop) without dedicated GPUs, in order to simulate real world working conditions and demonstrate the low barrier to entry of the *AutoTiM* service.

4.3   Results and Benchmark Comparison

A comparison of the achieved model performances and the benchmark results taken from [15] is presented in Table 3, whereby models were trained for all selected datasets from Table 2. The results show that *AutoTiM* delivers a strong performance for most of the tested datasets without using any kind of expert or domain knowledge. All in all, the results were better or on par with the respective benchmark results for 7 out of 20 datasets: *BM, EC, FM, LIB, LSST, SRS2,* and *SWJ*. For 7 datasets, the results are still very competitive (maximum deviation 3%): *AWR, CR, EP, HB, PD, RS,* and *SRS1* (4.2%). The results for 2 datasets are clearly poorer but still usable for classification: *NATO* and *PS*. Finally, the models of 4 datasets are significantly worse and do not appear useful for a production use-case: *AF, HMD, HW,* and *UW*.

Table 3. Classification accuracies (ACC) achieved with *AutoTiM* compared to the benchmark results presented in [15]. For the benchmark results, the average accuracy of 30 runs for the best-performing classification algorithm (Alg.) and the average accuracy of all trained algorithms per dataset are given. For *AutoTiM*, we provide the best accuracy and the average accuracy of multiple runs for each of the four experiments (see Subsect. 4.2).

| | Benchmark results [15] | | *AutoTiM* results | | | | | | | |
| | ∅ Best Alg. | ∅ All Algs. | 2 min | | 10 min | | 30 min | | dynamic limit | |
			Best ACC	∅ ACC	Best ACC	∅ ACC	Best ACC	∅ ACC	Best ACC	∅ ACC
AWR	0.996	0.979	0.957	0.856	0.907	0.897	0.920	0.873	0.967	0.967
AF	0.740	0.305	0.333	0.260	0.333	0.293	0.333	0.240	0.267	0.227
BM	1.0	0.977	1.0	0.985	1.0	0.98	1.0	0.975	1.0	0.98
CR	1.0	0.986	0.986	0.962	0.986	0.975	0.986	0.978	0.986	0.947
EP	1.0	0.970	0.993	0.98	0.978	0.970	0.964	0.949	0.986	0.984
EC	0.824	0.490	0.981	0.701	0.981	**0.835**	0.981	**0.835**	0.441	0.416
FM	0.561	0.542	0.620	0.536	0.600	**0.566**	0.580	0.508	0.570	0.540
HMD	0.522	0.373	0.243	0.243	0.243	0.243	0.257	0.254	0.365	0.365
HW	0.657	0.467	0.118	0.090	0.124	0.104	0.126	0.099	0.111	0.098
HB	0.765	0.719	0.761	0.730	0.766	0.684	0.761	0.718	0.741	0.735
LIB	0.941	0.868	0.983	**0.968**	0.972	0.863	0.922	0.813	0.856	0.839
LSST	0.637	0.532	0.982	**0.980**	0.985	**0.982**	0.981	**0.740**	0.695	**0.690**
NATO	0.971	0.852	0.739	0.705	0.739	0.666	0.739	0.713	0.739	0.711
PD	0.997	0.974	0.975	0.960	0.973	0.925	0.975	0.944	0.975	0.974
PS	0.329	0.241	0.245	0.234	0.258	0.250	0.265	0.238	0.259	0.257
RS	0.930	0.887	0.914	0.863	0.908	0.895	0.875	0.836	0.868	0.868
SRS1	0.957	0.832	0.901	0.881	0.915	0.888	0.894	0.870	0.908	0.887
SRS2	0.536	0.508	0.456	0.456	0.456	0.456	0.456	0.456	0.578	**0.537**
SWJ	0.464	0.377	0.733	**0.513**	0.467	0.347	0.533	0.427	0.467	0.400
UW	0.949	0.896	0.219	0.192	0.216	0.191	0.209	0.194	0.681	0.679

4.4 Discussion

Overall, the results of *AutoTiM* proved to be better or at least highly competitive for 14 out of 20 datasets. Concerning the poor performance of *AutoTiM* for *AF*, *HMD*, *HW*, and *UW*: except for *UW* with an accuracy of more than 94%, the average benchmark performance for the other 3 datasets is also significantly low. This indicates that the underlying data is complex and not easy to classify without domain-specific tailoring, wich is out of scope for *AutoTiM*. The data sources for both *AF* and *HMD* are electrical biosignals, while *HW* as well as *UW* encompass accelerometer data. However, both groups of data are also covered by other datasets for which *AutoTiM* trained highly performant models. This implies that trained models are not dependent on underlying categories or types of data.

A qualitative evaluation as well as a more critical look at the service is possible if the requirements from Sect. 3.1 are taken into consideration. Regarding points 1 to 4, *AutoTiM* meets all requirements as it is an end-to-end service for automated training, evaluation, versioning, and deployment of machine learning models for time-series-based data, available both locally and in cloud-based environments. Moreover, it is manageable via three standardized and parameterized REST interfaces; no domain expertise is required to build highly capable prediction models within minutes. In contrast and as discussed above, the requirements of points 5 and 6 from Sect. 3.1 regarding *Adaptability* and *Model Quality* are not fully met yet.

5   Summary and Future Work

Within this paper, we presented *AutoTiM*, a hollistic end-to-end automated machine learning service that includes all necessary technical components and logical steps for training, evaluation, and provisioning of supervised classification models for time series data. In addition, the service is available as an environment-independent open-source application, which makes it particularly interesting for small and medium-sized enterprises, as it enables a low-cost entry to the development and operation of machine learning applications. As such, it can be used in local environments for rapid prototyping as well as in productive, cloud-based machine learning applications, e.g., as an automated retraining component in complex *MLOps* architectures. Section 4 shows that the performance of *AutoTiM* is mostly competitive and sometimes even outperforming other approaches, which conduct steps like feature engineering, training, and tuning in a manual fashion. Not only is this time-consuming, but also requires lots of domain expertise. In contrast to that, *AutoTiM* only needs a few minutes for training and no domain knowledge.

The release of *AutoTiM* is a first step: there are still open issues that will be addressed by the authors in the upcoming research project *DeKIOps*[6]. Contributions from the open-source community are welcome and encouraged. Currently, the service focuses on time series data, so preprocessing raw data may be challenging. Thereby, the formalization of existing and the standardization of new preprocessing modules would facilitate compatibility with heterogeneous data sources. Additionally, the number of supported algorithms must be extended to broaden the range of applications of *AutoTiM* in productive scenarios. Another area of improvement lies within the classification performance itself. The results in Sect. 4 illustrate that competitive results can be achieved without domain knowledge, but also showcase use-cases where meaningful data patterns could not be detected automatically. Therefore, it is reasonable to explore ways to facilitate (but not require) injection of existing knowledge into an automated service such as *AutoTiM*. Bringing these unresolved issues into the open-source community and thus promoting the creation of a mature generic service available to everyone with no restrictions is one of the authors' main concerns within the upcoming *DeKIOps* research project.

---

[6] *DeKIOps - Democratization of AI With Explainable and Easily Accessible Machine Learning Operations.*

References

1. Bagnall, A., et al.: The UEA multivariate time series classification archive. arXiv preprint (2018). https://doi.org/10.48550/arXiv.1811.00075
2. Carmona, C.U., Aubet, F.X., Flunkert, V., Gasthaus, J.: Neural contextual anomaly detection for time series. In: IJCAI-2022, pp. 2843–2851 (2022). https://doi.org/10.24963/ijcai.2022/394
3. Carvalho, T.P., Soares, F.A., Vita, R., Francisco, R.P., Basto, J.P., Alcalá, S.G.: A systematic literature review of machine learning methods applied to predictive maintenance. CAIE **137**, 106024 (2019). https://doi.org/10.1016/j.cie.2019.106024
4. Coelho, D., Costa, D., Rocha, E.M., Almeida, D., Santos, J.P.: Predictive maintenance on sensorized stamping presses by time series segmentation, anomaly detection, and classification algorithms. Procedia Comput. Sci. **200**, 1184–1193 (2022). https://doi.org/10.1016/j.procs.2022.01.318
5. Davari, N., Veloso, B., de Assis Costa, G., Pereira, P.M., Ribeiro, R.P., Gama, J.: A survey on data-driven predictive maintenance for the railway industry. Sensors **21**(17), 5739 (2021). https://doi.org/10.3390/s21175739
6. Esling, P., Agon, C.: Time-series data mining. ACM Comput. Surv. **45**(1), 1–34 (2012). https://doi.org/10.1145/2379776.2379788
7. Ferreira, L., Pilastri, A., Martins, C.M., Pires, P.M., Cortez, P.: A comparison of AutoML tools for machine learning, deep learning and XGBoost, pp. 1–8. IEEE (2021). https://doi.org/10.1109/IJCNN52387.2021.9534091
8. Giebler, C., Gröger, C., Hoos, E., Schwarz, H., Mitschang, B.: Leveraging the data lake: current state and challenges. In: Ordonez, C., Song, I.-Y., Anderst-Kotsis, G., Tjoa, A.M., Khalil, I. (eds.) DaWaK 2019. LNCS, vol. 11708, pp. 179–188. Springer, Cham (2019). https://doi.org/10.1007/978-3-030-27520-4_13
9. Jardine, A.K., Lin, D., Banjevic, D.: A review on machinery diagnostics and prognostics implementing condition-based maintenance. MSSP **20**(7), 1483–1510 (2006). https://doi.org/10.1016/j.ymssp.2005.09.012
10. Karmaker ("Santu"), S.K., Hassan, M.M., Smith, M.J., Xu, L., Zhai, C., Veeramachaneni, K.: AutoML to date and beyond: challenges and opportunities. ACM Comput. Surv. **54**(8), 1–36 (2021). https://doi.org/10.1145/3470918
11. LeDell, E., Poirier, S.: H2O AutoML: scalable automatic machine learning. In: 7th ICML Workshop on Automated Machine Learning (AutoML) (2020)
12. Patel, D., Ganapavarapu, G., Jayaraman, S., Lin, S., Bhamidipaty, A., Kalagnanam, J.: AnomalyKiTS: anomaly detection toolkit for time series, vol. 36, pp. 13209–13211 (2022)
13. Polge, J., Robert, J., Le Traon, Y.: A case driven study of the use of time series classification for flexibility in industry 4.0. Sensors **20**(24), 7273 (2020). https://doi.org/10.3390/s20247273
14. Roblek, V., Meško, M., Krapež, A.: A complex view of industry 4.0. SAGE Open **6**(2), 2158244016653987 (2016). https://doi.org/10.1177/2158244016653987
15. Ruiz, A.P., Flynn, M., Large, J., Middlehurst, M., Bagnall, A.: The great multivariate time series classification bake off: a review and experimental evaluation of recent algorithmic advances. Data Min. Knowl. Disc. **35**(2), 401–449 (2020). https://doi.org/10.1007/s10618-020-00727-3
16. Shaukat, K., et al.: A review of time-series anomaly detection techniques: a step to future perspectives. In: Arai, K. (ed.) FICC 2021. AISC, vol. 1363, pp. 865–877. Springer, Cham (2021). https://doi.org/10.1007/978-3-030-73100-7_60

17. Smith, M.J., Sala, C., Kanter, J.M., Veeramachaneni, K.: The machine learning bazaar: harnessing the ML ecosystem for effective system development, pp. 785–800 (2020). https://doi.org/10.1145/3318464.3386146
18. Zaharia, M., et al.: Accelerating the machine learning lifecycle with MLflow. IEEE Data Eng. Bull. **41**(4), 39–45 (2018)
19. Zöller, M.A., Huber, M.F.: Benchmark and survey of automated machine learning frameworks. JAIR **70**, 409–472 (2021). https://doi.org/10.1613/jair.1.11854

Characterization of an Absorption Machine Using Artificial Neural Networks

A. Ferre[1], M. Castilla[1], J. A. Carballo[2], and J. D. Álvarez[1]([envelope])

[1] CIESOL Joint Centre University of Almería-CIEMAT, University of Almería,
Almería, Spain
{mcastilla,jhervas}@ual.es
[2] Plataforma Solar de Almería, Almería, Spain
joseantonio.carballo@psa.es

Abstract. To fulfil current energy objectives established by governments and public institutions is mandatory to develop zero-emission buildings or refurbish existing ones using, to this aim, systems based on renewable energy sources. Absorption machines are becoming an increasingly important alternative to conventional vapour-compression chillers due to the possibility of being powered with heat from renewable energy sources, such as solar energy, biomass or others. Thus, this kind of system can be the keystone of the air-conditioning system in residential, public or commercial buildings. Most current approaches to model absorption machines are made on stationary conditions, with less attention paid to the dynamic phenomena inherent to renewable energy sources. Besides that, the lack of internal measures in this kind of plant makes the development of a dynamic model a challenging task. This work presents a dynamic model of a LiBr Absorption Machine developed through Artificial Neural Networks. Comparison with real data shows an appropriate behaviour of the obtained model. Simulations were done to evaluate the performance of external temperatures and mass flow rates; moreover, the Coefficient Of Performance (COP) is also included in the model predictions.

Keywords: Artificial Neural Network · Absorption machine · Time series forecasting model

1 Introduction

In the European markets reference indices, the rise of certain fossil fuels, such as gas and oil, is pushing on the price of electricity. This increase in the cost at the continental level is due to various factors that do not have to be mutually exclusive: i) the fact that it has been possible to reach the production peak of the leading gas suppliers at the European level, ii) to various geopolitical tensions that affect supply, the war in Ukraine, and, iii) logistics and transportation

Grant TED2021-131655B-I00 funded by AEI/10.13039/501100011033 and by the "European Union Next GenerationEU".

© IFIP International Federation for Information Processing 2023
Published by Springer Nature Switzerland AG 2023
I. Maglogiannis et al. (Eds.): AIAI 2023, IFIP AICT 676, pp. 279–291, 2023.
https://doi.org/10.1007/978-3-031-34107-6_22

problems due to the energy demand rebound once the pandemic caused by Covid-19 has been left behind.

The main sectors causing energy consumption at a global level are the industrial, transport and residential sectors [9]. In developed countries, also known as first-world countries, the energy consumption associated with residential buildings and the tertiary sector is approximately one-third of the total energy consumed [9]. The building sector is crucial for achieving the EU's energy and environmental goals. At the same time, better and more energy-efficient buildings improve the quality of citizens' life while bringing additional benefits to the economy and society. To boost the energy performance of buildings, the EU has established a legislative framework that includes the Energy Performance of Buildings Directive 2010/31/EU (EPBD) and the Energy Efficiency Directive 2012/27/EU. Therefore, the European Climate, Infrastructure and Environment Executive Agency (CINEA) is running parts of Horizon 2020 and Horizon Europe (HORIZON) Programme in transport and energy, as well as innovation of energy-efficient technologies and solutions for buildings, heating and cooling, etc.

In buildings, the Heating, Ventilation and Air-Conditioning (HVAC) system can account for 38% of buildings consumption, equivalent to 12% of final energy [6]. Thus, as for new buildings or older ones that will be refurbished is worth keeping in mind this fact if the building's CO_2 emissions want to be reduced, become it in a Zero-Emission Building (ZEB). Absorption machines arise as an alternative to traditional HVAC with the main advantage that they can be fed by heat from renewable energy sources, such as solar energy, biomass or others. On the other hand, their main disadvantages are: i) the complexity of this kind of system versus traditional HVAC and ii) it needs advanced control systems to manage it [3,16]. Advanced control systems are needed since the absorption machine has, besides that renewable energy sources, other conventional sources, such as a gas heater, to support its operation when the renewable source is unavailable. Thus, during the operation of the plant is necessary to switch among energy sources depending on the weather conditions, so the control problem becomes a challenging task.

These advanced control systems are based on dynamic models of the system. Thus, through these models is possible to forecast the dynamic behaviour of the plant under certain situations. Most current approaches to model absorption machines are made on stationary conditions [17], with less attention paid to the dynamic phenomena inherent to renewable energy sources. On the other hand, recent works have developed models based on thermodynamic equations [12]. The lack of internal measures in this kind of system makes necessary the use of state predictors to complete the dynamic model and set it to adjust its predictions to the real values of the plant outputs.

This work proposes a black-box model of an absorption machine where no physical equations are needed nor any physical knowledge about the machine's working. The black-box model is an artificial neural network (ANN) that has been set through a large amount of data from a real absorption machine placed at a bioclimatic building. Validation results show that the ANN model can forecast the absorption machine's behaviour under several operation situations. Thus, it can be used later for the development of control systems.

The rest of the paper is structured as follows: Sect. 2 describes both the working of the absorption machine and the framework in which this system is used, that is, the bioclimatic building at which it is placed. Section 3.1 introduces the time forecasting models and, more specifically, the ANN and its structures. Section 4 presents the main results obtained through the training and validation of the ANN model and, finally, in Sect. 5, the main conclusions of this work are drawn, and future works are listed.

2   Scope of the Research: CIESOL Building

The CIESOL building (https://ciesol.com/) is a solar energy research centre located within the campus of the University of Almería, in the southeast of Spain. One of the main features of this building is that it has been built according to bioclimatic architecture criteria. Therefore, it has some passive characteristics that allow it to take advantage of the typical climate of its location in order to reduce energy consumption, such as the use of different enclosures based on its orientation or the setback of the windows facing east and south. In addition, the CIESOL building also has some active strategies which make use of solar energy, such as the Heating, Ventilation and Air Conditioning (HVAC) system based on solar cooling. This system is composed of a flat-plate solar collectors field, two hot-water storage tanks, a gas boiler, an absorption machine with its refrigeration tower, etc.

The HVAC system based on solar cooling has two operation modes: winter and summer. In winter mode, a heat-exchanger is used to transfer the energy produced in the heat production circuit to the building's consumption circuit, and thus, the energy is distributed among all the buildings' enclosures through a set of fan-coil units. On the contrary, in summer mode, the heat-exchanger is replaced by an absorption machine, see Fig. 1.

2.1   Description of the Absorption Machine

Generally, within residential and commercial building sectors is very common the use of air-to-air heat pumps instead of absorption machines. In broad terms, the main objective of both of them is to transfer heat from one place to another but they operate in different ways. More in detail, air-to-air heat pumps use electricity to transfer heat from one environment to another through a process of compression and expansion of a refrigerant. They can extract heat from the outside air and transfer it to the inside of a building (heating) or vice-versa (cooling). On the contrary, absorption machines use a chemical process to absorb or release heat. Absorption machines are more common in industrial and large building HVAC applications, as they can take advantage of other heat sources, such as waste heat or solar thermal energy.

Concretely, in the CIESOL building, a *Yazaki WFC SC20* model [1] absorption machine is being used. In this case, it uses as a source energy the heat

282   A. Ferre et al.

produced by a hot water circuit from a solar collectors field. Moreover, the fluid used in the refrigeration cycle is a solution of water and lithium bromide ($LiBr$) where the water is the refrigerant and the $LiBr$ represents the absorbent. The main characteristics of the *Yazaki WFC SC20* model are summarized in Table 1.

Table 1. Main characteristics of the *Yazaki WFC SC20* absorption machine model. Source: [1].

Description	Unit	Value
Cooling capacity	kW	70.3
Chilled water circuit - Water flow rate	m³/h	11.0
Chilled water circuit - Inlet/outlet temperature	°C	12.5/7.0
Hot water circuit - Inlet cooling capacity	kW	100.0
Hot water circuit Water flow rate	m³/h	17.28
Hot water circuit - Inlet/outlet temperature	°C	88.0/83.0

The absorption cycle that takes place in that machine is composed of four stages [15], see Fig. 2. In the first stage, named *generation*, hot-water from the flat-plate solar collectors field enters the generator where it increases the temperature of a dilute solution producing steam from the water in this solution. Then, water vapour passes to the condenser while the concentrate solution obtained in the previous phase is moved to the absorber. Afterwards, in the second stage, denoted as *condensation*, water vapour is condensed in the condenser, precipitating into the evaporator where the pressure is lower. As a result of this stage, a certain amount of heat is released, and thus, it is necessary the use of an additional cooling system, as a refrigeration tower or buried wells. These additional systems do not require a considerable energy input since their operation temperature range is usually very close to ambient temperature. In the third stage,

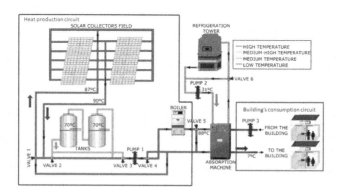

Fig. 1. Operation scheme of the HVAC system based on solar cooling. Source: [4]

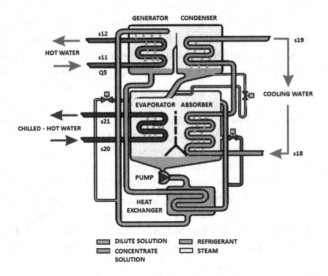

Fig. 2. Operation scheme of the *Yazaki WFC SC20* absorption machine

evaporation, the fluid obtained from the condensation stage absorbs the heat of
the fluid to be cooled in the evaporator. Finally, the evaporator fluid enters into
the absorber and, in the fourth stage, named *absorption*, the concentrate solution coming from the generator absorbs the fluid from the evaporator, becoming
a dilute solution which is sent back to the generator by means of a pump that
increases its pressure, closing the cycle. Therefore, for a correct operation of the
absorption machine, it can be seen that the main energy input is required by
the generation stage, where it is necessary both to increase and to maintain the
temperature of the solution within a certain range. From an optimal management point of view, one of the main problems is the lack of internal sensors in
the absorption machine. Hence, it is very difficult to predict its behaviour, and
thus, to optimize its operation. For this reason, this paper presents a black-box
model based on Artificial Neural Networks (ANNs) of the absorption machine.

3   Time-Series Forecasting Models

In the simulation field, the process of predicting future events based on past and
present data is known as forecasting. Specifically, forecasting based on a suc-
cession of data measured at certain times and ordered chronologically is called
time-series forecasting. In other words, time-series forecasting is a modeling technique that uses historical and current data to predict values over a period of
time. A time series forecasting model is usually modeled like a sequence of time-
dependent random variables. Due to the temporal dependencies in time series
data, different validation techniques are needed than traditional modeling, for
example, cross-validation, time series split cross-validation and blocked cross-
validation.

Nevertheless, the most relevant aspect of times series modeling is understanding your data model and knowing which process needs to be modeled using this data. For that, common problems in time series forecasting include generalizing from a single data source and difficulty in obtaining appropriate measurements and accurately identifying the correct model to represent the data. Currently exist many different types of time-series models (Autoregressive (AR), Moving average (MA), Autoregressive moving average (ARMA), Autoregressive integrated moving average (ARIMA) model, Seasonal autoregressive integrated moving average (SARIMA), Vector autoregressive (VAR), Vector error correction (VECM), Vector Autoregression Moving-Average (VARMA), Vector Autoregression Moving-Average with Exogenous Regressors (VARMAX), Simple Exponential Smoothing (SES), Holt Winter's Exponential Smoothing (HWES) [7]. Time series forecasting is a scientific simulation field that is attracting great interest as a result of the great number of possible applications and thanks to the increasing amount of data available due to the improvement of data acquisition and storage technologies.

3.1   Artificial Neural Networks

Currently, thanks to advances in computing, apart from the above modeling techniques, time series forecasting modeling based on machine learning is taking on great relevance. Among the best-known machine learning techniques that can be used to extrapolate time-series data, it can be found random forest, gradient-boosting regressor, and neural networks. Neural network or artificial neural network is one of the most interesting techniques due to it has proved to be suitable for handling such complex problems, particularly when the physical phenomena inside the system are difficult to model [11,14], for example, the absorption process that could be very complex and unpredictable when the boundary conditions are variable.

For all that, models based on neural networks are well suited for time series forecasting of chiller operation, as the scientific literature shows. For example, in [10] a novel, the model-based control strategy for absorption cooling systems was based on a chiller model that used artificial neural networks. This model takes into account inlet and outlet temperatures as well as the flow rates of the external water circuits. The configuration showed excellent agreement between the prediction and the experimental data. Later, was published a methodology to model and evaluate the energy performance and outlet temperatures of absorption chillers [11]. The methodology can be applied to systems that can be found on the market and there is no need to create a physical model of the system.

Recently, it has been published a comparative that aims to predict the coefficient of performance and thermal energy consumption of an absorption chiller network using three widely-used machine learning methods of the artificial neural network, support vector machine, and genetic programming, [14]. The highest prediction accuracy among the mentioned methods was obtained by the artificial neural network.

A successful neural network modeling application is described in [5], in where a steady state modeling based on the artificial neural network of a double effect absorption chiller using steam as the heat input is developed. The model predicts the chiller performance based on the chilled water inlet and outlet temperatures, cooling water inlet and outlet temperatures, and steam pressure. Another successful neural network modeling application is presented in [8]. In this paper, it was simulated with good results a dual-effect absorption chiller in MATLAB using a neural network. The neural network was used to convert a dual-effect absorption chiller model that is in TESS library of the TRNSYS software into a function in MATLAB software.

4   Results and Discussion

4.1   Inputs, Outputs and Training for the ANN

As commented before, the first step before calculating the ANN model is to understand the process and decide which signals will be the inputs and outputs of the model. Thus, after several analyses and model tests, the list of inputs is: i) the inlet flow to the generator: Q5 signal, ii) the inlet water temperature from the solar field or gas heater to the absorption machine: s11 signal, iii) the inlet water temperature to the absorption machine from the building: s18 signal and, iv) the inlet water temperature from the additional cooling system, that is, the refrigeration tower: s20 signal.

On the other hand, the chosen outputs are: i) the return temperature from the absorption machine to the solar field: s12 signal, ii) the outlet chilled water temperature from the absorption machine to the different building rooms: s19 signal, and iii) the outlet water temperature from the absorption machine to the refrigeration tower: s21 signal.

Besides that, the outputs are fed back as inputs delayed one or two samples to test if better predictions are obtained from the model. The location of the selected inputs and outputs regarding the absorption machine can be observed in Fig. 2.

The training parameters are also crucial for achieving high accuracy in learning and prediction. One popular training algorithm for neural networks is the Levenberg-Marquardt algorithm [13], its implementation in MATLAB has been used in this work. This algorithm combines the advantages of the Gauss-Newton and steepest descent methods to achieve fast convergence with high accuracy.

The training has been configured with 1000 epochs of training and a learning rate of 10^{-3}. The number of epochs determines the number of times the entire dataset is used to update the network weights, while the learning rate controls the size of the weight updates at each iteration.

4.2   Datasets Construction

To develop an appropriate ANN model, a key point is the availability of suitable datasets. In this case, historic data from the CIESOL building has been used. In addition, it should be noted that the absorption machine is only used during the summer season, but the building is closed due to summer vacation during the month of August. Hence, the data from the month of June has been chosen for training purposes; specifically, the data available from June 2014 has been selected. This dataset has a sample time equal to 1 min. This dataset has been split into three subsets to train, validate and test the ANN model with a proportion of 70%, 15% and 15% of the data, respectively.

Furthermore, a second dataset corresponding to June 2015 has been prepared and used as an independent dataset for testing purposes. The results obtained with this second dataset are included and discussed in Sect. 4.4.

4.3   Architecture and Structure Selection

To select an appropriate architecture for the ANN model it is necessary to take into account that, for the system presented in this paper, it should be able to learn long temporal dependencies among the involved variables. Hence, a recurrent architecture denoted as Nonlinear Autoregressive with eXogenous input (NARX) have been chosen [2]. This type of ANN architecture has as inputs two tapped delay lines: one for the input signals and the other for the outputs signals. Besides, it also has a hidden layer with a certain number of neurons which should be carefully chosen. To do that, an analysis of the performance of ANN models obtained while increasing the number of neurons in the hidden layer has been done based on Mean Squared Error (MSE). Equation 1 shows how the MSE is calculated, whereas Fig. 3 depicts how this index changes, Y axis in logarithm scale, with the number of neurons in the ANN hidden layer, X axis.

$$MSE = \frac{1}{n} \sum_{i=1}^{n} \left(Y_i - \hat{Y}_i \right)^2 \tag{1}$$

Before the calculation of the ANN model, the datasets were preprocessed: a low-pass filter was applied, and the gaps in the data were filled. The MSE value falls down drastically until three neurons, see Fig. 3. From this number of neurons, the MSE value keeps almost constant. However, with the second testing dataset belonging to June 2015, the MSE value is higher than with the June 2014 dataset. For this reason, looking for a trade-off between simplicity and performance of the model, the number of neurons has been set to six.

It is worth mentioning that although the internal structure of an absorption machine does not differ so much from one model to another, see Fig. 2, the ANN model must be recalculated if the absorption machine would be another commercial model or proceed from another manufacturer. The ANN structure may be the same, but the weights must be set with new data.

4.4   Results Obtained from the Second Testing Dataset

Firstly, an evaluation of the results provided for each output by the absorption machine ANN model using the testing portion of the first dataset (June 2014)

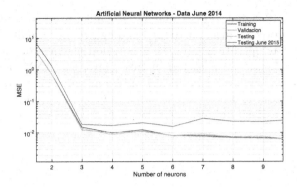

Fig. 3. MSE per number of neurons in the ANN

has been done. Then, the proposed model has also been tested using the second dataset (June 2015). For goodness-of-fit evaluation, an analysis based on some statistical indexes has been performed. More specifically, the following indexes have been considered: Rng (range of the dataset), N (number of samples), MAE (Mean Absolute Error), MRE (Mean Relative Error), S_n (Standard deviation) and $NMAE$ (Normalized Mean Absolute Error). The formulas associated with these indexes have not been included in this paper mainly due to the lack of space. In Table 2, a summary of the quantitative analysis is shown:

Table 2. Summary results obtained for both datasets.

Parameter	1st Dataset: June 2014			2nd Dataset: June 2015		
	s12 [°C]	s19 [°C]	s21 [°C]	s12 [°C]	s19 [°C]	s21 [°C]
Rng	52.87	25.70	9.71	55.33	25.06	9.15
N	31396	31396	31396	30194	30194	30194
MAE	0.042	0.043	0.043	0.091	0.040	0.039
MRE	$6.51 \cdot 10^{-4}$	0.004	0.002	0.0014	0.0032	0.0013
S_n	7.70	7.31	1.54	7.84	8.50	2.02
$NMAE$	0.08%	0.17%	0.44%	0.17%	0.16%	0.42%

Furthermore, Fig. 4 depicts the results obtained from the ANN absorption machine prediction model for each one of the three outputs using the second testing dataset from June 2015. The upper graph in Fig. 4 shows the evolution of the return temperature to the heat production circuit for both real data gathered at the CIESOL building (in blue) and the results provided by the absorption machine ANN model (in orange). Besides, the middle graph depicts

288   A. Ferre et al.

the evolution of s19 signal, that is, the outlet chilled water temperature, which
flows from the absorption machine to the building's rooms. Finally, in the bottom
graph, the outlet temperature from the absorption machine to the refrigeration
tower is shown. As can be observed in this figure, the ANN model is able to
perfectly capture the dynamics of the absorption machine in all the cases. On the
other hand, as it can be observed in Table 2, the results obtained are acceptable
since the NMAE is less than 1% in all cases.

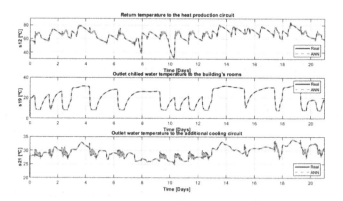

Fig. 4. Results obtained from the second testing dataset, June 2015 (Color figure
online)

Finally, the last graph shows a comparison of the Coefficient Of Performance
(*COP*) between the one calculated through the real measurements from the
absorption machine and the other calculated through the values predicted by
these variables with the ANN model. The COP is defined as the relationship
between the power (*kW*) that is drawn out of the absorption machine, as cooling
or heat, and the power (*kW*) that is supplied to it. It can be calculated with the
following equation:

$$COP = \frac{Q4 \cdot C_p \cdot (s18 - s19)}{Q5 \cdot C_p \cdot (s11 - s12)} \quad (2)$$

where Q4 is the outlet flow from the generator and C_p is the water specific heat
which value has been set to 4.18 J/(kg · K). The comparison results are showed
in Fig. 5 where zoom-in has been made to appreciate better the accuracy of the
predicted COP.

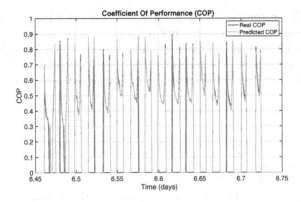

Fig. 5. Coefficient OF Performance (COP) results, June 2015

5 Conclusions and Future Works

As commented before, the behavior of an absorption machine is complex, with long temporal dependencies among the involved variable. In addition, it should be considered that the absorption machine, which is the object of this work, is a commercial machine with a lack of internal sensors. For all that, it is very difficult to predict its behavior, and thus, control its operation from an optimal management point of view. However, thanks to the existence of a time series data set and the capabilities of the neural networks for handling complex problems when the physical phenomena inside the system are difficult, it has been decided to develop a black-box model based on ANNs of the absorption machine that allows optimizing the control of the absorption machine. ANN architecture called NARX has been chosen due to its ability to learn long temporal dependencies among variables.

After carrying out tasks to understand the process to be modeled and different studies about the influence of the available variables on the data set, a list of inputs and outputs of the model is defined. These variables allow to achieve the main objective of developing a black box model for optimization tasks of the operation based on the installation state. With the data set divided for training, validation, and test tasks and with the model structure defined, the next step consists of the optimization of the model hyper-parameters, which are the number of neurons in the hidden layer. The analysis of the performance of ANN models obtained while increasing the number of neurons in the hidden layer revealed that six neurons are a good trade-off between the simplicity and performance of the model. Finally, the validation and testing process of the model with the second testing dataset revealed that the ANN model is able to perfectly capture the dynamics of the absorption machine with acceptable results.

Future works include increase and analyze in depth the data set to improve its variability, analyze the use of other ANN structures, sensitivity study of the input variables with the aim of using less and improve the training configuration. Finally, the most important future work: develop a optimal controller based on the black box model developed in this work and measure its performance.

References

1. Absorsistem: Enfriadoras de absorción accionadas por agua caliente - Serie WFC SC. Technical report (2023). https://www.absorsistem.com/brands/yazaki/. Accessed 9 Mar 2023
2. Boussaada, Z., Curea, O., Remaci, A., Camblong, H., Bellaaj, N.M.: A nonlinear autoregressive exogenous (NARX) neural network model for the prediction of the daily direct solar radiation. Energies 11(3), 620 (2018)
3. Camacho, E.F., Gallego, A.J., Escaño, J.M., Sánchez, A.J.: Hybrid nonlinear MPC of a solar cooling plant. Energies 12(14), 2723 (2019)
4. Castilla, M., Álvarez, J.D., Rodríguez, F., Berenguel, M.: Comfort Control in Buildings. Springer, London (2014). https://doi.org/10.1007/978-1-4471-6347-3
5. Chan, W.M., Le, D.V.K., Chen, Z., Tan, J., Chew, I.M.L.: Resource allocation in multiple energy-integrated biorefinery using neuroevolution and mathematical optimization. Process Integr. Optim. Sustain. 5, 383–416 (2021). https://doi.org/10.1007/s41660-020-00151-6
6. González-Torres, M., Pérez-Lombard, L., Coronel, J.F., Maestre, I.R., Yan, D.: A review on buildings energy information: trends, end-uses, fuels and drivers. Energy Rep. 8, 626–637 (2022). https://doi.org/10.1016/j.egyr.2021.11.280
7. Hajirahimi, Z., Khashei, M.: Hybrid structures in time series modeling and forecasting: a review. Eng. Appl. Artif. Intell. 86, 83–106 (2019). https://doi.org/10.1016/j.engappai.2019.08.018
8. Hosseini, P.: Deep-learning neural network prediction of a solar-based absorption chiller cooling system performance using waste heat. Sustain. Energy Technol. Assess. 53, 102683 (2022)
9. IEA: International Energy Agency - key world energy statistics 2021. Technical report (2022). https://www.iea.org/reports/key-world-energy-statistics-2021. Accessed 9 Mar 2023
10. Labus, J., Hernández, J., Bruno, J., Coronas, A.: Inverse neural network based control strategy for absorption chillers. Renew. Energy 39(1), 471–482 (2012)
11. Lazrak, A., et al.: Development of a dynamic artificial neural network model of an absorption chiller and its experimental validation. Renew. Energy 86, 1009–1022 (2016)
12. Liu, M., Cheng, Y., Cheng, W., Zhan, C.: Dynamic performance analysis of a solar driving absorption chiller integrated with absorption thermal energy storage. Energy Convers. Manag. 247, 114769 (2021)
13. Marquardt, D.W.: An algorithm for least-squares estimation of nonlinear parameters. J. Soc. Ind. Appl. Math. 11(2), 431–441 (1963)
14. Panahizadeh, F., Hamzehei, M., Farzaneh-Gord, M., Villa, A.A.O.: Evaluation of machine learning-based applications in forecasting the performance of single effect absorption chiller network. Therm. Sci. Eng. Prog. 26, 101087 (2021)
15. Pasamontes, M.: Estrategias de control avanzadas aplicadas a un sistema de climatización basado en energía solar. Ph.D. thesis, Universidad de Almería (2013)

16. Pataro, I.M., Gil, J.D., Guzmán, J.L., Berenguel, M., Lemos, J.M.: Hierarchical control based on a hybrid nonlinear predictive strategy for a solar-powered absorption machine facility. Energy **271**, 126964 (2023). https://doi.org/10.1016/j.energy.2023.126964
17. Zhao, T., Chen, X., Chen, Q.: Heat current method-based modeling and optimization of the single effect lithium bromide absorption chiller. Appl. Therm. Eng. **175**, 115345 (2020)

Comparing Machine Learning Techniques for House Price Prediction

Konstantinos Panagiotis Fourkiotis$^{(\boxtimes)}$ and Athanasios Tsadiras

Aristotle University of Thessaloniki, Thessaloniki, Greece
kfourkio@csd.auth.gr, tsadiras@econ.auth.gr

Abstract. One sector that already is feeling the impact of Artificial Intelligence (AI) is the real estate industry. AI is being used in the real estate sector to improve various aspects of the industry such as property search, pricing, marketing, and risk management. There are various techniques used for predicting house prices, including linear regression, decision tree and random forest. These algorithms can take into account factors such as location, square footage, number of bedrooms and bathrooms, and other relevant characteristics of the property. Predicting house prices with AI has many advantages over traditional methods, such as the ability a) to handle large amounts of data and b) to identify patterns and trends that might be overlooked by humans. It can also help us understand why housing prices are changing, and what factors are driving these changes. This information can be invaluable for real estate agents, investors, and homeowners who need to make informed decisions regarding the market. This paper provides a comparison of the performance of various Machine Learning algorithms in their attempt to predict the price of houses. The regression methods that are compared include Support Vector Machine, Kernel Ridge, Gradient Boosting, Lasso, Random Forest, XGB, LGBM, Average and Voting Regressor. The comparison shows that the best algorithm was Voting Regressor for R Squared metric and for RMSLE metric was the Average model. In conclusion, AI has the potential to bring new levels of accuracy and insight into the real estate industry.

Keywords: Machine Learning · Real Estate · House Prices · Regression

1 Introduction

Machine Learning (ML) is a subfield of Artificial Intelligence (AI), that utilizes algorithms and statistical models to enable computers to learn and improve by using data without human intervention. It's a crucial aspect of AI and is used to educate AI systems to carry out various functions such as image identification, natural language understanding and decision-making [1].

In this paper an analysis of the use of ML in house price prediction is presented. House price predictions can be beneficial for various parties involved in the real estate market. For buyers, predictions can assist in making informed decisions during purchasing a property, determining if a property is over or underpriced and negotiating better deals.

© IFIP International Federation for Information Processing 2023
Published by Springer Nature Switzerland AG 2023
I. Maglogiannis et al. (Eds.): AIAI 2023, IFIP AICT 676, pp. 292–303, 2023.
https://doi.org/10.1007/978-3-031-34107-6_23

Sellers can use predictions to price their properties correctly and avoid pricing errors. Investors can use predictions to identify properties that are likely to increase in value and make better investment decisions. Real estate agents can use predictions to provide accurate property valuations and to find potential buyers, while banks and lenders can use predictions to evaluate the risk of loan defaults and make more informed loaning decisions. Additionally, government can use predictions to create policies, taxations and regulations. Overall, predictions of house prices can be a valuable tool for anyone involved in the real estate market as they can assist in making informed decisions and identifying growth opportunities [2].

When it comes to predicting house prices, there is no one-size-fits-all algorithm. It is crucial to recognize that there is no single algorithm that can be applied to all cases. The selection of an appropriate algorithm depends on several factors, including the data quality, the complexity of the problem, and the choice of evaluation metrics.

The best algorithm to use depends on factors such as the size and complexity of the dataset, the level of accuracy needed, and the resources available for computation. Candidate algorithms are for example Support Vector Machine, Kernel Ridge, Gradient Boosting, Lasso, Random Forest, XGB, LGBM, Averaged models and Voting Regressor. These techniques are commonly used in machine learning for regression problems. By applying these methods to housing price data, a better understanding of trends and patterns in the housing market can be identified.

The current state of housing prices reflects the overall economic climate and is of concern to both buyers and sellers. Factors that affect housing prices include the number of bedrooms and bathrooms, as well as location and accessibility to amenities such as highways, schools, malls, and job opportunities [3].

This paper is organized into seven sections. After the introduction in Sect. 1, Sect. 2 provides a literature review of relevant studies and practices in this field. Section 3 outlines the dataset and the problem definition of this paper. Section 4 presents the preprocess and the Data Analysis of the Dataset. In Sect. 5 is being depicted the implementation of the ML models and in Sect. 6 has been illustrated the results and the model evaluation. Finally, Sect. 7 summarizes the key conclusions of the study and gives some suggestions for future research which indicate regional differences in housing prices and shifts in consumer preferences towards less densely populated areas.

2 Literature Review

This is a review of current literature on the prediction of housing prices that analyzes the existing research on the topic, including the methods and techniques used to predict house prices, evaluating their effectiveness, and identifying their strengths and limitations. There are many relevant studies, with the most important be the following:

Bahia [4] independently forecasts home prices in the real estate market using data mining techniques. To arrive at the most accurate prediction, the authors estimate the median home value in Boston suburbs based on 13 neighborhood attributes and a sample size of 506. Using SVM, LSSVM which is a variant of the Support Vector Machine (SVM) algorithm that solves for both the decision boundary and the regression function simultaneously[5], and PLS which is a statistical method used for analyzing relationships between multiple latent variables[6], algorithms, Mu et al. [7] found that SVM and LSSVM were superior in dealing with nonlinearity, predicting Boston housing values with the goal of aiding real estate developers in making better decisions. In their study, Banerjee et al. [8] found that the RF technique was the most accurate for predicting house prices, although it had the most overfitting, while the SVM technique proved to be the most consistent and reliable. Park et al. [9], using a sample of 5359 row houses in Virginia, researched the accuracy of ML models in determining house prices and found that the RIPPER algorithm significantly improved price prediction compared to the RF and Naive Bayesian algorithms. In the Netherlands, Voutas Chatzidis [3] used different regression-based machine algorithms to predict house prices and found that CatBoost obtained the best results with an accuracy rate of 90% among LGBM, XGBM, CatBoost, and RF algorithms. XGBM was found to perform the best among various machine learning techniques by Kok et al. [10] in their analysis of real estate appraisals based on 84,305 observations from three states in the US from 2011 to 2016. In the Czech Republic, Hromada [11] presents software for real estate evaluation and analysis of advertisements by collecting and analyzing over 650,000 price quotations every 6 months and storing all advertisements in a database for credibility analysis. Hong [12] compared the performance of three machine learning algorithms (XGBM, LGBM, CatBoost) with the traditional hedonic price model (HPM) in predicting transaction prices of apartments in Seoul. The results showed that machine learning algorithms have better predictive power than OLS, a statistical method for estimating the parameters of a linear regression model to minimize the sum of the squared differences between the observed and predicted values [13], with CatBoost being the most effective in predicting prices even with the presence of outliers. The ensemble model, consisting of the three algorithms, was also found to have higher accuracy compared to the individual algorithms.

In comparison with the Boston house prices dataset, in which has been represented a challenging task of predicting the median value of owner-occupied homes in the city. A plethora of machine learning algorithms have been employed, including Random Forest, Support Vector Machine, XGBoost, LightGBM, and CatBoost, and their performances were measured using the mean squared error. The findings indicate that the choice of the right machine learning algorithm is crucial for accurate prediction of house prices. Further research is needed to determine the best performing algorithm for different data sets and evaluation criteria, and to improve the accuracy of house price prediction models.

In this study, we have thoroughly evaluated a variety of widely utilized techniques to provide a comprehensive understanding of their efficacy and strengths. The methods we have analyzed have been carefully selected based on their prevalence and proven track record in the field, ensuring that our findings are reliable and relevant to the current state of the industry.

3 Dataset and Problem Definition

The dataset we used in this study is the Ames Iowa House Price dataset provided on Kaggle [14]. The problem statement of the dataset was to predict the sale price of houses in Ames, Iowa based on the containing 79 explanatory variables describing almost every aspect of residential homes in Ames, Iowa. The data set contains 1458 house-cases and included information such as the number of bedrooms and bathrooms, square footage, and various features of the property like the type of roof, heating, and cooling system, etc.

It's important to evaluate the performance of different applied algorithms by using suitable evaluation metric such as RMSLE and R-Squared. RMSLE measures the error between the predicted and actual values, while R squared measures how well the model fits the data. The RMSLE metric was chosen because it computes the proportional error between the predicted and true values, while also being resilient to outliers. R-Squared is an intuitive and widely used standardized metric that works well for simple regression models and can be used with other metrics for a more complete picture of model performance [15]. The evaluation of models in house price prediction is based on two metrics: RMSLE and R-squared. The determination of a suitable threshold value for distinguishing between good and bad models depends on various factors. An RMSLE score of 0 to 0.5 is considered excellent, while an R-squared score between 0.7 and 0.9 is generally viewed as good. Equation (1) represents the RMSLE formula, while Eq. (2) represents the R-Squared formula. RMSLE is an extension of the Mean Squared Error (MSE) that is used primarily when predictions have large variances, as is the case in our dataset. The house price values range from 34,900 to 755,000 and so we don't want to penalize deviations in the forecast as much as we do with the MSE.

$$RMSLE = \sqrt{\frac{1}{n}\sum_{i=1}^{n}(log(pi+1) - log(a_i+1))^2} \tag{1}$$

$$R^2 = 1 - \frac{sum\ squared\ regression(SSR)}{total\ sum\ of\ squares(SST)} = 1 - \frac{\sum (yi - {}^{\wedge}yi)^2}{\sum (yi - {}^{-}yi)^2} \tag{2}$$

4 Preprocessing the Dataset and Data Analysis

In this study, 9 different machine learning algorithms were used to develop house price prediction models for the data set described in Sect. 3. In order to achieve this, the standard machine learning workflow presented in Fig. 1 has been followed, covering all crucial steps such as pre-processing, data analysis, algorithm implementation, and model evaluation.

Fig. 1. Machine Learning Workflow.

The dataset is split into a train set and a test set with the training set to have 1166 observations, and the test set to contain 292 observations. The data processing begins by identifying and removing outliers in the dataset. Outliers since they are values that fall outside of the typical range of values, they can skew the results of the analysis. By removing outliers, the analysis is more likely to be accurate and representative of the data.

An analysis of the Sale Price variable is conducted, as it is the target variable that we want to predict. The target variable is skewed to the right, which is a problem for linear models that require normally distributed data. To fix this, we need to transform the variable to make it more normal. The SalePrice distribution is depicted in Fig. 2. With population mean = 180932.92 and standard deviation = 79467.79. A distribution plot for the variable "SalePrice" is also depicted in Fig. 3. With the log-transformation of the target variable is performed to make the distribution more normal. In the study, we log-transformed the sale price target variable and the skewed numerical features to normalize their distributions. The output of this transformation is a more symmetrical distribution, which lessens the impact of outliers and boosts the performance of the prediction model.

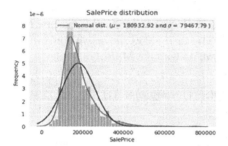

Fig. 2. SalePrice Distribution.   **Fig. 3.** SalePrice Distribution log1p.

The next step in our workflow is Feature Engineering, where new features are created, or existing features are transformed to improve the performance of the model. This process starts by concatenating the training and testing data into the same dataframe, making it easier to work with the data. Missing values in the data are identified, and variables with high missing ratios such as PoolQC, Misc Feature and Alley are examined in more detail in Table 1. The approach to impute missing values in a dataset using Python code is to fill in missing values with appropriate values based on the nature of the feature. In this case, it is filling in missing values with "None", "0", or the most frequent value, depending on the feature. In the case of "PoolQC" and "Misc Feature", it makes sense to replace missing values with "None" to reflect the absence of the feature. For other Features, for example "LotFrontage", is a common approach to dealing with missing data, as it allows the data to be used in statistical analyses and machine learning models. Imputing missing values with the most frequent value may be appropriate for categorical features such as "MasVnrType", which describes the type of masonry veneer on the house. The goal is to prepare data for predictive modeling.

Data Correlation is also examined, with a Correlation map in Fig. 4. to see how features are correlated with SalePrice. Missing values are then input by proceeding sequentially through features with missing values. Additional feature engineering is performed

Table 1. Percent missing data by feature

Percent missing data by feature	
PoolQC	99.691464
MiscFeature	96.400411
Alley	93.212204
Fence	80.425094
FireplaceQu	48.680151
LotFrontage	16.660953
GarageFinish	5.450806
GarageQual	5.450806

by transforming some numerical variables that are categorical, such as MSSubClass, OverallCond, YrSold and label encoding categorical variables that may contain information in their ordering set. A new feature, TotalAreaSquareFeet, has also been added. To better determine house prices based on important area features, a new feature TotalAreaSquareFeet has been added, which sums up the area of basement, first and second floor of each house. The final number of variables in the dataset is 79, including the TotalAreaSquareFeet feature. The dummy categorical features are then obtained because most machine learning algorithms cannot work with categorical data directly. In the "Data Processing" section of the notebook, utilizes the Pandas corr() method to compute the pairwise correlation among all the numerical features. Such an approach is crucial for detecting possible relationships and patterns between the variables.

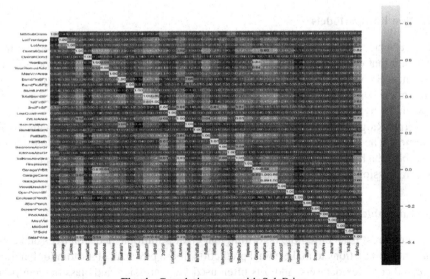

Fig. 4. Correlation map with SalePrice.

In order to get the best results of the RMSLE and R-squared metrics we will try to find the best parameters with the best measurements. Essentially, we will find the optimal parameters. We will not achieve this manually, using the test and repeat method, but it will be done automatically using the GridSearch method.

In the following section, a comprehensive overview of the algorithms employed in this paper will be represented, highlighting their key contributions and significance to the research findings.

5   Application of Algorithms

The next step in the workflow is the application of the algorithms. The algorithms that were examined in our study were classified in categories and they are presented below. To get the most of each of these, various values for their hypermeters were examined and they are presented in Table 2. The values of the hyperparameters that achieve the best performance in our experiments are shown in bold. A 5-fold cross validation strategy was followed with the train/test split rule to follow the 80/20 strategy in the train set.

5.1   Linear Models

Elastic Net regression is a hybrid algorithm between LASSO and Ridge regression. ElasticNet regression is used to regularize and select the important predictor variables to obtain a simple model with the most significant predictor variables despite high multicollinearity between the predictors [16].

Lasso is a regularization technique that is used to prevent overfitting in linear regression models. It adds a penalty term to the linear regression objective function, which encourages the model to use only a subset of the input features [17].

5.2   Non-linear Models

Support Vector Machines are commonly used methods which is a supervised learning algorithm that can be used for classification and regression problems. Support Vector Machines (SVM) works by finding the hyperplane that best separates data points into different classes, using a mathematical optimization process that maximizes the margin between the hyperplane and the closest data points [18].

Kernel Ridge Regression is an algorithm that merges Ridge Regression with the use of kernels. The application of kernels makes it possible for KRR to handle non-linearly separable data by transforming the input into a higher-dimensional feature space where linear regression can be carried out [19].

5.3   Ensemble Models

Random Forest is an ensemble algorithm that creates multiple decision trees and combines their predictions to make a final prediction. It is a powerful algorithm for handling large and complex datasets, and it is often used for regression and classification problems [20]. A machine learning algorithm that utilizes multiple decision trees to make predictions by aggregating the results from individual trees. It works by randomly selecting subsets of features and data points, which helps to prevent overfitting and increase accuracy [21].

Gradient Boosting is another ensemble algorithm that creates multiple decision trees and combines their predictions to make a final prediction. The algorithm is known for its ability to handle large and complex datasets, and it is often used for regression and classification problems [22].

XGBoost (eXtreme Gradient Boosting) is a scalable tree boosting system that is designed for speed and performance and is particularly effective for large datasets with complex features. It is an ensemble learning technique that combines the predictions of several decision trees to improve the accuracy and robustness of the model [23].

LightGBM (Light Gradient Boosting Machine) is a highly efficient gradient boosting decision tree model that is designed for large-scale datasets and high-dimensional features. It uses a novel tree-growing algorithm and several other techniques to achieve faster training speed, lower memory usage, and higher accuracy compared to other gradient boosting models [24].

XGB (XGBoost) and LGBM (Light GBM) are two popular gradient boosting libraries that are widely used in machine learning and industry projects [25, 26].

An Average Model is a technique where multiple models are trained on the same dataset and their predictions are averaged to obtain a final prediction. This technique is often used in ensemble methods like the Bagging Regressor [27]. In our case, we used an average of all 6 models created by the application of the algorithms presented above and in Table 2.

Voting Regressor is an ensemble meta-estimator that combines multiple machine learning regression models to improve the overall performance and accuracy of the predictions [28]. Each of the created base models gets a vote on what the final prediction should be, and the voting regressor considers all the votes to make its final prediction. In our case a Voting Regressor was examined, using the methods Support Vector Machine, XGB and LGBM.

As shown in the table below, we have passed the values of the most influential hyperparameters for each of the algorithms used in our research.

Table 2. Optimized Hyperparameter Values for Regression Algorithms

Algorithm	Hyper Parameter	Values
ElasticNet	alpha L1_ratio random_state	[0.0004,**0.004**, 0.04] [0.1,0.2,0.3,0.4,0.5,0.6,0.7,0.8,**0.9**] [**1**,2,3,4,5,6,7,8,9]
Lasso	Alpha random_state	[**0.000391**,0.001,0.01,0.1,1] [**1**,5,10]
Support Vector Machine	C gamma epsilon	[**100**,50,25] [0.0003,0.0004,0.0005,**0.0006**] [**0.0001**,0.0002,0.0003]

(continued)

Table 2. (*continued*)

Algorithm	Hyper Parameter	Values
Kernel Ridge Regression	Alpha coef0 degree kernel	[**0.5**,0.6,0.7,0.9,] [**5**,6,7] [**3**,4,5,6] polynomial
Random Forest	max_depth max_features min_samples_leaf min_samples_split n_estimators	[16,**17**,18] None [**5**,10,15] [5,**10**,15] [**1300**,1500,1600]
Gradient Boosting	learning_rate loss max_depth subsample	[**0.01**,1,10] Huber [**2**,20] [**0.8**,0.9,1.0]
XGB	gamma learning_rate max_depth min_child_weight n_estimators	[0.005, **0.0045**,0.35,0.5] [0.01,**0.1**,0.001] [**3**,0.3,0.003] [**1.7817**,0.178,0.0178] [**2200**,220,22]
LGBM	bagging_fraction feature_fraction learning_rate min_data_in_leaf n_estimators num_leaves objective	[0.7,**0.8**] [**0.7**,0.8] [**0.05**,0.06] [**6**,7] [**5**,6] regression
Voting	Weights: [SVR, XGB, LGBM]	[0.2,0.6,0.2], [0.6,0.2,0.2], [**0.40,0.40,0.20**], [0.20,0.40,0.40]

6   Results and Models Evaluation

Using the optimized values of hyperparameters of Table 2, the models created were tested on the test data. Table 3 presents the results of the metrics for each model, where the best value to be in bold. The number in parentheses after the name of the algorithm presents its rank according to the RMSLE metric. This metric is the most important for our case, as discussed in Sect. 3. Furthermore, it was proposed by the definition of the problem in Kaggle.

Our analysis of various techniques shows that the method which obtains the highest score using the Root Mean Squared Logarithmic Error metric, is the Average method, with a score of 0.1071 and for the R Square metric is the Voting method, with a score of 0.9193. The Average method combines the next six algorithms such as Support Vector Machine, Random Forest, ElasticNet, Gradient Boosting, Kernel Ridge Regression and

Table 3. Comparison of Regression Algorithm Performance on Test Set

Methods	Test Set Metrics	
	RMSLE	R^2
Linear Methods		
ElasticNet (5)	0.1146	0.9082
Lasso (4)	0.1145	0.9084
Non-Linear Methods		
Support Vector Machine (7)	0.1200	0.8993
Kernel Ridge Regression (8)	0.1200	0.4369
Ensemble Methods		
Random Forest (9)	0.1325	0.8768
Gradient Boosting (2)	0.1087	0.9175
XGB (6)	0.1155	0.9067
LGBM (10)	0.1348	0.9157
Average (1)	0.1071	0.9010
Voting (3)	0.1093	0.9193

Lasso methods. The Voting method combines the SVR, XGB and LGBM algorithms with respectively weights of 0.4, 0.4 and 0.2 per cent.

Since both Average method and Voting method achieve high performances (1st and 3rd positions in the rank), it can be concluded that the specific problem of the house price prediction is quite complicated and ensemble methods can be useful because they can combine and aggregate the advantages of various algorithms.

7   Conclusion and Future Work

In this paper several linear, non-linear and ensemble algorithms were applied in the problem of predicting house prices and their performance was measured. The dataset used contains a number of house attributes that were preprocessed to improve the prediction accuracy. The root mean square logarithmic error (RMSLE) and R-Squared metrics were used in this study. In the field of house price prediction, it is crucial to recognize that there is no single algorithm that can be applied to all cases. The selection of an appropriate algorithm depends on several factors, including the data quality, the complexity of the problem, and the choice of evaluation metrics. After extended experiments (grid search) on different hypermeters of the applied algorithms, the best examined hypermeters were used while evaluating their performance in the test set. It was found that the Average model method achieves the best RMSLE score, followed by Gradient Boosting and the Voting method. Also, it was found that the Voting method achieves the best R Squared score, followed by XGB and LGBM method. Ensemble methods were found to be valuable in our case because they can accumulate the advantages of various individual algorithms.

It would be interesting for the conclusions of this study to be examined in other data sets that regards house price prediction. Furthermore, other methods can be examined to identify if they are beneficial. Such methods could be neural networks and deep learning, that were not examined mainly because of the not big enough size of the data set. Moreover, various preprocessing techniques can be examined in order to see their contribution towards the precision of the house price predictions.

References

1. Chattu, V.K.: A review of artificial intelligence, big data, and blockchain technology applications in medicine and global health. Big Data Cognit. Comput. **5**(3), 41 (2021). https://doi.org/10.3390/bdcc5030041
2. Kirkeby, S.J., Larsen, V.H.: House Price Prediction Using Daily News Data
3. Voutas Chatzidis, I.: Prediction of housing prices based on spatial & social parameters using regression & deep learning methods. Aristotle University of Thessaloniki (2019)
4. Bahia, I.S.H.: A data mining model by using ANN for predicting real estate market: comparative study. Int. J. Intell. Sci. **03**, 162–169 (2013). https://doi.org/10.4236/ijis.2013.34017
5. Suykens, J.A.K., Lukas, L.: Least Squares Support Vector Machine Classifiers: a Large Scale Algorithm Least Squares SVM View project LS-SVM Applications View project (2000). https://www.researchgate.net/publication/2626391
6. Sarstedt, M., Ringle, C.M., Hair, J.F.: Partial least squares structural equation modeling. In: Handbook of Market Research, pp. 1–47. Springer, Cham (2021). https://doi.org/10.1007/978-3-319-05542-8_15-2
7. Mu, J., Wu, F., Zhang, A.: Housing value forecasting based on machine learning methods. Abstr. Appl. Anal. **2014**, 1–7 (2014). https://doi.org/10.1155/2014/648047
8. Banerjee, D., Dutta, S.: Predicting the housing price direction using machine learning techniques. In: 2017 IEEE International Conference on Power, Control, Signals and Instrumentation Engineering (ICPCSI), pp. 2998–3000. IEEE (2017). https://doi.org/10.1109/ICPCSI.2017.8392275
9. Park, B., Bae, J.K.: Using machine learning algorithms for housing price prediction: the case of Fairfax County, Virginia housing data. Exp. Syst. Appl. **42**(6), 2928–2934 (2015)
10. Kok, N., Koponen, E.-L., Martínez-Barbosa, C.A.: Big data in real estate? from manual appraisal to automated valuation. J. Portfolio Manage. **43**, 202–211 (2017). https://doi.org/10.3905/jpm.2017.43.6.202
11. Hromada, E.: Real estate valuation using data mining software. Procedia Eng. **164**, 284–291 (2016). https://doi.org/10.1016/j.proeng.2016.11.621
12. Hong, J.: An application of XGBoost, LightGBM, CatBoost algorithms on house price appraisal system. Hous. Financ. Res. **4**, 33–64 (2020). https://doi.org/10.52344/hfr.2020.4.0.33
13. Fu, C., Miller, C.: Using Google trends as a proxy for occupant behavior to predict building energy consumption. Appl. Energy **310**, 118343 (2022). https://doi.org/10.1016/j.apenergy.2021.118343
14. Kaggle. House Prices: Advanced Regression Techniques. https://www.kaggle.com/competitions/house-prices-advanced-regression-techniques. Accessed 2 Feb 2023
15. Figueiredo Filho, D.B., Júnior, J.A.S., Rocha, E.C.: What is R2 all about?. Leviathan (São Paulo) (3), 60–68 (2011). https://doi.org/10.11606/issn.2237-4485.lev.2011.132282
16. Zou, H., Hastie, T.: Regularization and variable selection via the elastic net. J. R. Stat. Soc.: Ser. B (Statistical Methodology) **67**(2), 301–320 (2005)

17. Tibshirani, R.: Regression shrinkage and selection via the lasso. J. R. Stat. Soc.: Ser. B (Methodological) **58**(1), 267–288 (1996)
18. Evgeniou, T., Pontil, M.: Support vector machines: theory and applications. In: Paliouras, G., Karkaletsis, V., Spyropoulos, C.D. (eds.) ACAI 1999. LNCS (LNAI), vol. 2049, pp. 249–257. Springer, Heidelberg (2001). https://doi.org/10.1007/3-540-44673-7_12
19. You, Y., Demmel, J., Hsieh, C.J., Vuduc, R.: Accurate, fast and scalable kernel ridge regression on parallel and distributed systems. In: Proceedings of the International Conference on Supercomputing, Association for Computing Machinery, pp. 307–317 (2018). https://doi.org/10.1145/3205289.3205290
20. Louppe, G.: Understanding Random Forests: From Theory to Practice (2014). http://arxiv.org/abs/1407.7502
21. Cutler, A., Cutler, D.R., Stevens, J.R.: Random Forests. In: Ensemble Machine Learning, pp. 157–175. Springer, Cham (2012).https://doi.org/10.1007/978-1-4419-9326-7_5
22. Natekin, A., Knoll, A.: Gradient boosting machines, a tutorial. Front. Neurorobot. **7**, 21 (2013). https://doi.org/10.3389/fnbot.2013.00021
23. Chen, T., Guestrin, C.: XGBoost: a scalable tree boosting system. In: Proceedings of the ACM SIGKDD International Conference on Knowledge Discovery and Data Mining, 13–17 August 2016, pp. 785–794 (2016). https://doi.org/10.1145/2939672.2939785
24. Ke, G., et al.: LightGBM: A Highly Efficient Gradient Boosting Decision Tree. https://github.com/Microsoft/LightGBM
25. Gan, M., Pan, S., Chen, Y., Cheng, C., Pan, H., Zhu, X.: Application of the machine learning lightgbm model to the prediction of the water levels of the lower columbia river. J. Mar. Sci. Eng. **9**, 496 (2021). https://doi.org/10.3390/jmse9050496
26. Yoshizoe, K., Sakamoto, K.: Ensemble of regressors by averaging their predictions and its relationship to StackNet. In: Proceedings of the Thirteenth International Conference on Machine Learning and Applications (2014). https://doi.org/10.1109/ICMLA.2014.80
27. Erdebilli, B., Devrim-Ictenbas, B.: Ensemble voting regression based on machine learning for predicting medical waste: a case from Turkey. Int. J. Environ. Res. Public Health **18**(13), 6947 (2021)

Forecasting Goal Performance for Top League Football Players: A Comparative Study

Nikolaos Giannakoulas[ID], George Papageorgiou[ID], and Christos Tjortjis[(✉)][ID]

The Data Mining and Analytics Research Group, School of Science and Technology,
International Hellenic University, Thessaloniki, Greece
c.tjortjis@ihu.edu.gr

Abstract. In this paper, we review the literature on Sports Analytics (SA) and predict football players' scoring performance. Based on previous years' performance, we predict the number of goals that players scored during the 2021–22 season. To achieve this, we collected advanced statistics for players from five major European Leagues: the English Premier League, the Spanish La Liga, the German Bundesliga, the French Ligue1 and the Italian Serie A, for seasons from 2017–18 up to 2021–22. Additionally, we used one-season lag features, and three supervised Machine Learning (ML) algorithms for experimental benchmarking: Linear Regression (LR), Random Forest (RF) and Multilayer Perceptron (MLP). Furthermore, we compared these models based on their performance. All models' results are auspicious and comparable to each other. LR was the best performing model with Mean Absolute Error (MAE) 1.60, Mean Squared Error (MSE) 7.06 and Root Mean Square Error (RMSE) 2.66. Based on feature importance analysis, we established that every player's upcoming scoring performance is strongly associated with previous season's goals (Gls) and expected goals (xG).

Keywords: Sports Analytics (SA) · Performance Prediction · Machine Learning (ML)

1 Introduction

Sports Analytics (SA) is a rapidly growing field, and its applications are very useful to sports clubs. This paper focuses on football, and it aims to investigate which Machine Learning (ML) approach performs better in seasonal performance forecasting for top League football players' goals, which predictors are most significant for enhancing model predictive performance and finally, if performance prediction using just open data can be valid and accurate.

Currently, many football games take place every week and they produce numerous statistics. SA is used for collecting these statistics, analyzing them, and providing conclusions to sports clubs about their players' performance. Over the last few years, SA has become a vital part of sports. Football is the most famous sport with millions of fans worldwide, and it produces numerous statistics including goals, assists and cards. Such

© IFIP International Federation for Information Processing 2023
Published by Springer Nature Switzerland AG 2023
I. Maglogiannis et al. (Eds.): AIAI 2023, IFIP AICT 676, pp. 304–315, 2023.
https://doi.org/10.1007/978-3-031-34107-6_24

data about football generate interest for scientists who are keen on understanding this domain.

SA provides useful information that can be used by coaches and managers to better understand their teams. Sports organizations collect this information and make the appropriate decisions about their players and related tactics. Moreover, SA has many applications such as performance prediction, ticket prizes, betting, and a team's strategy planning. One of the most important applications is the ability to predict player injuries and the time required for cure. All these applications are very important for clubs because they can improve their performance year by year and consequently increase their value [22].

This research aims to predict player performance in terms of goals scored by utilizing their statistics from previous years. Data validity is one of the most important issues in SA, especially in football, because there are numerous sources with statistics that are invalid, and therefore could introduce errors and bias into results. For this purpose, we collected advanced football statistics from the Sports Reference organization, for seasons 2017–18 up to 2021–22 for players from all positions on the field [24]. The initial database created regards over 2.500 football players from five major leagues in the world, namely the English Premier League, the Spanish LaLiga, the German Bundesliga, the French Ligue1 and the Italian Serie A. Moreover, the database includes over 30 features about them.

The next step after data collection was cleansing, to remove data that do not add value for the purpose of this research [10]. Then, during feature engineering, we transformed the data into historical by creating one season's-lag features. After that, we used three different types of ML algorithms for the research's last but most significant stage, which was prediction. Linear Regression (LR), Random Forest (RF) and Multilayer Perceptron (MLP) were selected. Finally, we evaluated the models and the predictions they generated using Mean Absolute Error (MAE), Mean Squares Error (MSE) and Root Mean Square Error (RMSE) [6, 28]. Additionally, we investigated feature importance for each model, aiming to determine the most important factors that lead the forecasting, and draw conclusions based on our results.

The structure of the remainder of this paper follows. Background reviews SA background and previous work in football performance prediction. The Methodology section presents the problem and the methodology we followed. In the Findings, we illustrate results and compare algorithmic performance. The Discussion section discusses our findings. In the Conclusion, we conclude and propose future work, and lastly, in the Appendix, we illustrate the advanced football statistics we used.

2 Background

Nowadays, researchers are more likely to conduct research on football than in previous years, because of the numerous statistics in this field. More and more clubs worldwide hire data scientists to collect statistics and extract valuable information about their performance, because this abundance of statistics helps coaches and managers to improve their decision-making [4]. We live in an era with many available sources with regards to previous research in the field of football performance prediction, so we can take advantage of them to expand our knowledge.

In 2018, Pariath et al. predicted a player's overall performance and market value. For this purpose, they created two LR models for both cases. Using data from a famous video game, FIFA, they achieved good accuracy for both experiments. The first model, regarding general performance, achieved 84% accuracy, 2.67 RMSE and 2.01 MAE. The second model regarding market value achieved 91% accuracy, 0.41 RMSE and 0.30 MAE. Moreover, they concluded that the best performance indicator is the player's overall value [21].

Apostolou and Tjortjis, in 2018, conducted research in football with three experiments. In the first one, they predicted a player's position on the field based on his characteristics, and they achieved 81.5% accuracy using RF and Sequential Minimal Optimization. In the second one, they predicted the number of goals that Lionel Messi and Luis Suarez scored. RF, Logistic Regression, MLP and Linear Support Vector Classification were used, with RF being the most accurate. The last experiment focused on predicting the number of shots by a player during a match. Again, RF was the algorithm with the highest accuracy [3].

In 2017, Shrinivasan predicted the number of passes among players in a football match, using networks. He created passing networks for teams, based on their passing distributions, which measure how well the players pass the ball among them before a goal. Players are nodes and passes among them are edges in the networks created. He used Support Vector Machine, RF and Gradient Boosting (GB), and achieved MSE of around 6.88 [25].

Further research in this field was conducted by Manish et al. in 2021. In their research, they used different algorithms to predict football player statistics based on their position on the field in previous seasons. They found that the position of a player has a high dependence on his performance. Finally, the Multiple Regression algorithm was the most efficient one, with 0.88 MAE, 1.16 MSE and 1.077 RMSE [19].

Moreover, in 2019, Pantzalis and Tjortjis conducted two experiments. The first was team performance prediction, while the second was player performance prediction. During the first experiment, they used two different approaches. The former separated football teams into those whose final position was better than the previous year and these whose final position was worse than the previous year, achieving 70% accuracy. The latter simulates every match and classifies it based on the result as home/away win and draw. In that case, the accuracy was higher than that of the former approach. During the second experiment, they examined which attributes can influence a defender's rating during a game. They used Multiple LR, and the results were very good as the R-squared was 0.9 and the adjusted R-squared was 0.88. Finally, they found that 30 features can influence a defender's performance, including clearances and interceptions [20].

Moreover, in 2022 Al-Asadi and Tasdemir estimated players' market value through four different ML algorithms and identified the most significant features that determine this value. These algorithms were LR, Multiple LR, RFs and Decision Trees. RF had the best performance with 1.64 RMSE and 0.95 R2. Finally, they concluded that many factors could affect player value, like potential and international reputation [1].

Currently, more and more clubs use wearable devices, cameras, and magnetic jackets to collect statistics that can provide valuable information about their players [7]. For example, these statistics include heart condition, player movements, shooting habits and general player's physique. All these statistics are considered confidential, and gaining access is challenging [11]. Therefore, there is limited research involving statistics from these devices regarding football players' physique.

Finally, in 2019, Frey et al. predicted the player's position on the field with the use of three different ML algorithms, RF, GB and Convolutional Neural Network. In this research, they collected data from wearable devices. They achieved accuracy around 80% for all models, and they found that there was limited misclassification in positions like wingers and midfielders, in which players share common characteristics [8].

3   Methodology

This section presents our Research Questions and elaborates on our data preparation and modeling approach.

3.1   Research Questions

As motivated by the literature review presented in Sect. 2, we attempted to address two key research questions, presented here.

1. Which ML approach performs best for football players' goals forecasting, and which predictors are significant for enhancing model predictive performance?
2. Could football players' performance forecasting be valid and accurate using just open data?

3.2   Data Preparation and Modeling

The process we followed was divided into six phases. These phases are data collection, in which data was scraped, pre-processing to remove noise as well as errors, feature engineering, in which data were transformed to historical data, modeling, and evaluation, in which we compared the results to find the best performing model.

First, the appropriate dataset should be collected. The dataset was scraped from the Sports Reference organization [24]. We extracted statistics for football players for the last five seasons, from season 2017–18 up to season 2021–22. We ended up with a database with almost 2.500 football players from five major leagues in the world, which are Premier League, LaLiga, Bundesliga, Ligue1 and Serie A. Moreover, the database included 32 features in total, including more than 15 advanced features, listed in the Appendix.

The next phase was pre-processing which is divided into data cleaning, player removal, feature removal and feature encoding. Starting with null and missing values removal, we then removed features that do not add value to our forecasting approach, such as nationality, competition, and squad. Then, we implemented feature encoding [14] transforming string values into numerical. Finally, we filtered the players who started their career after 2017–18 or finished their career before 2021–22. We ended up with a database of over 800 football players.

After that, the feature engineering phase follows. We used four out of five seasons of statistics (from 2017–18 up to 2020–21) for training and the last season (2021–22) for testing. Next, we converted data to historical by creating season's lag-features. Season's lag-features are variables that contain data from prior time steps. In our approach, we transformed our initial dataset's features to one-season-lag-features for each player's record containing data from his last season's performance.

The algorithms used were LR, RF and MLP. Their selection was targeted, as all three models are fundamentally different. LR is the basic linear based algorithm, RF is tree based and MLP is a type of Artificial Neural Network (ANN) [27, 17]. In more detail:

LR: is a supervised ML algorithm and one of the most common models for predictions. LR models the relationship between dependent and independent variables. Moreover, it produces a straight line, known as regression line, which depicts the relationship among variables. This line can be positive or negative [2]. Generally, LR is a good tool for predictions because it is simple and easy to understand. On the other hand, it is very sensitive to outliers and missing values, which means that it can deteriorate performance [13].

RF: is a supervised ML algorithm that constructs different decision trees to solve a problem. RF creates decision trees based on the dataset, it aggregates every tree's prediction, and outputs the optimal result. This technique of using different models to achieve better performance is called model ensembling. Generally, it is very good at handling numerical data and capturing non-linear interactions between features and the target [2]. RF is robust to outliers and can handle many input variables. On the other hand, it can be slow to train and make predictions on large datasets [23].

MLP: is a feed forward ANN, consisting of at least three layers of nodes. These layers are known as the input, hidden and output layers. Each node in every layer is connected with a specific weight with all the nodes from the next layer. Besides the input node, the others are neurons that use a non-linear activation function, which defines the output of that node [26]. MLP can capture complex non-linear relationships among input and output variables. However, it requires an extensive dataset for good performance [12].

Finally, we evaluated our results with MAE, MSE and RMSE. These were selected for this purpose because the nature of our experiment and the specific dataset allow the use of them. Additionally, we investigated the more crucial factors that determine our forecasting by analyzing the weights assigned to each feature in the LR model and using feature importance scores from RF and MLP.

4 Findings

In this section, the algorithms' results, the use case of two football players, and the more important predictors for this experiment are presented. Generally, all algorithms performed well as their metric values are low, but LR performed better than the other two algorithms followed by MLP which in turn was closely followed by RF. The results are shown in Table 1.

LR resulted in the lowest MAE, MSE and RMSE. Then MLP follows, while RF's performance is the worst. MAE for all algorithms is between 1.60 and 1.69. Correspondingly, MSE ranges from 7.06 to 7.75, while RMSE ranges from 2.66 to 2.78. Generally, it is noticeable that all three models demonstrated good results with slight differences in their performances, with MAE from 1.60 to 1.69, when the Standard Deviation (SD) of Season's 2021–22 true Goals was four. This addresses our first Research Question.

Table 1. Results.

Metrics	LR	MLP	RF
MAE	1.60	1.63	1.69
MSE	7.06	7.68	7.75
RMSE	2.66	2.77	2.78

The predictions for two football players are presented next, in order to better understand the differences among models. Figure 1 illustrates the predictions for two football players, David Silva and Danny Welbeck. During season 2021–22, they scored 2 and 6 goals, respectively. Their selection is not random, as they are both midfielders and strikers. The results confirm that LR performs better, as it predicts that David Silva and Danny Welbeck would score 3 and 6 goals respectively. Then, MLP's predictions follow predicting 3 and 7 goals respectively and finally the RF's predictions for the two players are 4 and 7 goals, respectively.

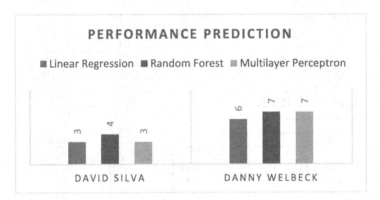

Fig. 1. Performance Prediction Example.

However, many players' goals predictions were inaccurate. For instance, Lionel Messi used to score 30 goals in any average season, but in the season 2021–22 that we made the predictions for, he scored just six goals. However, the algorithms identified and followed the earlier trend and predicted that he would score at least 20 goals.

We then produced coefficients for the LR model, features importance for RF, and weighted coefficients for MLP to determine the relative importance of each feature and the most important factors in predicting the performance of football players who belong to the selected pool [18, 29]. Table 2 shows the results of these identifications for each model.

Based on these results, the top three features for LR, that have the highest positive impact on predicting future goals for our pool of players are the previous season's non-penalty expected goals per 90 min (npxG per 90), the previous season's expected goals per 90 min (xG per 90), and previous season's goals plus assists per 90 min (G + A per 90).

Additionally, the RF model indicates that the previous season's expected goals (xG) is the most important predictor, followed by previous season's non-penalty expected goals (npxG) and previous season's expected goals per 90 min (xG per 90).

Finally, the MLP model shows that the top four features that contribute significantly to our predictions are previous season's goals per 90 min (Gls per 90), previous season's expected goals plus expected assisted goals per 90 min (xG + xAG per 90), previous season's goals plus Assists per 90 min (G + A per 90), and previous season's non-penalty expected goals plus expected assisted goals per 90 min (npxG + xAG per 90). This addresses our first Research Question.

Table 2. Feature importance and coefficients (Top 3 Highlighted per Model).

Features	LR (Coefficient)	RF	MLP (Weights Coefficient)
npxG per 90:	33.4578	0.0148	11.3758
xG per 90:	28.1599	0.0571	11.0137
G+A per 90:	23.7282	0.0160	11.3785
G-PK per 90:	19.7128	0.0187	10.9199
Ast per 90:	12.4782	0.0197	10.4302
xG+xAG per 90:	11.3893	0.0414	11.4351
G+A-PKper 90:	11.0409	0.0167	11.1907
Gls per 90:	7.5871	0.0186	11.7314
xAG per 90:	4.9581	0.0185	10.1835
npxG+xAG per 90:	4.3857	0.0166	11.8397
PKatt:	2.8251	0.0049	10.0188
PK:	2.3797	0.0060	9.4945
npxG:	1.9374	0.1302	9.6061
xG:	1.5504	0.4370	10.3756
npxG+xAG:	1.1518	0.0504	11.2250
xAG:	1.0387	0.0225	10.2168
CrdR:	0.2143	0.0044	9.8497
90s:	0.1642	0.0239	10.2893
Starts:	0.1618	0.0144	9.7125
G-PK:	0.0872	0.0182	9.4400
Ast:	0.0521	0.0093	9.3500
MP:	0.0255	0.0215	10.6533
CrdY:	0.0185	0.0194	11.1278

5 Discussion

In this section, we discuss and evaluate our results in the light of the Research Questions stated in Sect. 3. Generally, the results were good for all 3 algorithms particularly given that we used only open data for our experiments. Comparing algorithmic performance, we observe that LR is the best, with MAE 1.60, MSE 7.06 and RMSE 2.66. LR can accurately predict players' scoring capability with a slight deviation of almost two goals, while the SD for Goals during the 2021–22 season was four.

The other two algorithms, MLP and RF, are also reliable for prediction, given their corresponding very low MAE, MSE and RMSE. Moreover, their results are very similar. For instance, their MAE is 1.63 and 1.69, respectively. However, we observe from the results that MLP performs better than RF, because its metrics are lower than those of RF. Their MSE is 7.68 and 7.75, respectively, while their RMSE is 2.77 and 2.78 respectively. This addresses our first Research Question.

Furthermore, with regards to our first Research Question, we investigated the predictors that are most important for enhancing model predictive performance. Each feature related to the previous season's expected goals (xG) is a consistently important feature in forecasting player performance across all three models. Additionally, statistics related to the previous season's goals are also crucial for prediction-making. These imply that a player's ability to create high-quality goal-scoring opportunities and opportunities for teammates is critical to their overall performance. In contrast, some features, such as the previous season's Minutes Played (MP), Yellow Cards (CrdY), and Red Cards (CrdR), appear to have relatively little impact on predicting future goals based on these models.

Regardless of the positive results obtained, it is important to consider threats to the validity of research findings. Players' performance deviation across their carriers is affected by multiple factors. Factors contributing to players' performance are injuries sustained during a specific period, the "chemistry" among team players and squad, transfers, and conditions in different countries that are transferred; each psychological state could be a daunting experience for a player [5].

Every profound change in a player's state of mind, physical health, and teamwork with coaches and other players could affect the next season's performance and produce anomalies in his enduring performance momentum. Moreover, Messi's use case for season 2021–22, which we presented, provides valuable insights based on the earlier assumptions; Messi in Barcelona from seasons 2017–18 to 2020–21 scored 30 to 35 goals having a specific scoring momentum with slight deviations while transferring in the summer of 2021 to Paris Saint-Germain, resulting in his declining scoring performance with 6 season's 2021–22 goals. This also partly addresses our second Research Question.

6 Conclusions

6.1 Conclusion

In this paper, we aimed to predict the performance of football players who are currently active in the best European leagues. We predicted how many goals a player would achieve in season 2021–22 based on his previous years' performance, from season 2017–18 up to 2020–21. To achieve this, we implemented three ML algorithms: LR, RF and MLP. The models were evaluated with the use of MAE, MSE and RMSE. We found that LR performs better than the other two algorithms. The results are good for all models, as the predictions were very close to the goals actually scored by the players. LR's performance was MAE 1.60, MSE 7.06 and RMSE 2.66. MLP's performance was MAE 1.63, MSE 7.68, and RMSE 2.77. Lastly, RF's performance was MAE 1.69, MSE 7.75 and RMSE 2.78.

Additionally, based on feature importance analysis of these models, we concluded that specific advanced performance statistics from the previous season are strongly associated with predicting the future goals of our selected football players' pool. The most important features identified across all models include the previous season's xG and Gls. These findings provide valuable insights for teams and coaches, as they can use this information to identify and recruit players with high goal-scoring potential and develop existing players' skills in key areas to improve their performance.

In order to excel in forecasting goal scoring performance, the changes in a player's state of mind, physical health, and teamwork with coaches and other players should also be considered, and their effect evaluated. Considering only open advanced football statistics provide us with a good overview of each player's upcoming performance, however, the performance momentum, if any of the above changes are applied, should be detected with external transfer data, data associated with performance based on synergies and different tactics for each player's or next season's team.

Furthermore, because of this research findings, while xG is the most critical statistic for predicting upcoming scoring performance, data from wearable devices and cameras for identifying physical players' health movements on the field are considered essential, capturing each player's performance momentum and ability to create and finish scoring chances.

6.2 Future Work

The results from our research indicate that we can predict a player's performance for the next season with sufficient accuracy, based on historical open data. However, further work in this field could yield further improvements. Obviously, results may improve with the addition of more features. Players' physical characteristics like height and weight, number of successful passes and minutes with ball possession during a game, are some examples of such features. Moreover, using different ML techniques could improve performance.

Furthermore, it would be very helpful to take advantage of statistics from wearable devices, magnetic jackets, and cameras. Also, future research can focus on strikers. As mentioned earlier, it is more challenging for the algorithms to predict the goals of a center forward whose scoring capability presents fluctuations. Lastly, future work with different techniques can be done to expand this research. For instance, association rules and sentiment analysis can be utilized. Association rules' implementation will help to find patterns and correlations in the database that are probably undiscovered, while applying sentiment analysis can be very helpful to consider for instance the players' feelings, information that will be useful to our predictions [9, 15, 16].

Acknowledgments. This research is co-financed by Greece and the European Union (European Social Fund-SF) through the Operational Programme «Human Resources Development, Education and Lifelong Learning 2014–2020» in the context of the project "Support for International Actions of the International Hellenic University", (MIS 5154651).

Appendix

We include here both basic and advanced features for forecasting experiments.

Basic and Advanced Features Dataset Glossary

Term	Meaning
npxG	Non-penalty expected goals
npxG per 90	Non-penalty expected goals per 90 min
xG	Expected goals
xG per 90	Expected goals per 90 min
G-PK	Non-penalty goals
G-PK per 90	Goals minus penalty kicks per 90 min
Ast	Assists
Ast per 90	Assists per 90 min
npxG + xAG	Non-penalty expected goals plus expected assisted goals
npxG + xAG per 90	Non-penalty expected goals plus expected assisted goals per 90 min
xAG	Expected assisted goals
xAG per 90	Expected assisted goals per 90 min
xG + xAG per 90	Expected goals plus expected assisted goals per 90 min
G + A-PK per 90	Goals plus assists minus penalty kicks per 90 min
G + A per 90	Goals plus assists per 90 min
Gls per 90	Goals per 90 min
PKatt	Penalty kicks attempted
PK	Penalty kicks made
CrdR	Red cards
90s	Minutes played divided by 90
Starts	Games started
MP	Games played
CrdY	Yellow cards

References

1. Al-Asadi, M.A., Tasdemir, S.: Predict the value of football players using FIFA video game data and machine learning techniques. IEEE Access **10**, 22631–22645 (2022). https://doi.org/10.1109/ACCESS.2022.3154767
2. Acharya, M.S., Armaan, A., Antony, A.S.: A comparison of regression models for prediction of graduate admissions. In: 2019 International Conference on Computational Intelligence in Data Science (ICCIDS) (2019). https://doi.org/10.1109/iccids.2019.8862140

3. Apostolou, K., Tjortjis, C.: Sports analytics algorithms for performance prediction. In: 2019 10th International Conference on Information, Intelligence, Systems and Applications (IISA), pp. 1–4 (2018). https://doi.org/10.1109/IISA.2019.8900754

4. Babbar, M., Rakshit, S.K.: A systematic review of sports analytics. Int. Conf. Bus. Manage. (2019)

5. Calleja, P., Muscat, A., Decelis, A.: The effects of audience behaviour on football players' performance. J. New Stud. Sport Manage. **3**(1), 336–353 (2022). https://doi.org/10.22103/JNSSM.2022.18890.1055

6. Chai, T., Draxler, R.R.: Root mean square error (RMSE) or mean absolute error (MAE)?-arguments against avoiding RMSE in the literature. Geoscientific Model Dev. **7**, 1247–1250 (2014). https://doi.org/10.5194/gmd-7-1247-2014

7. Cintia, P., Pappalardo, L., Rinzivillo, S.: A network-based approach to evaluate the performance of football teams. In: Machine Learning and Data Mining for Sports Analytics Workshop (MLSA 2015) (2015)

8. Frey, M., Murina, E., Rohrabach, J., Walser, M., Haas, P., Dettling, M.: Machine learning for position detection in football. In: 2019 6th Swiss Conference on Data Science (SDS), pp. 111–112 (2019). https://doi.org/10.1109/SDS.2019.00009

9. Ghafari, S.M., Tjortjis, C.: A survey on association rules mining using heuristics. Wiley Interdisc. Rev.: Data Min Knowl. Disc. **9**(4), (2019). https://doi.org/10.1002/widm.1307

10. Gupta, S., Gupta, A.: Dealing with noise problem in machine learning datasets: a systematic review. Procedia Comput. Sci. **161**, 466–474 (2019)

11. Gyarmati, L., Hefeeda, M.: Competition-wide evaluation of individual and team movements in soccer. In: 2016 IEEE 16th International Conference on Data Mining Workshops (ICDMW), pp. 144–151 (2016). https://doi.org/10.1109/icdmw.2016.0028

12. Hinton, G.E.: How neural networks learn from experience. Sci. Am. **267**(3), 144–151 (1992). https://doi.org/10.1038/scientificamerican0992-144

13. Iqbal, M.A.: Application of regression techniques with their advantages and disadvantages. Elektron Magazine **4**, 11–17 (2021)

14. Jackson, E., Agrawal, R.: Performance evaluation of different feature encoding schemes on cybersecurity logs. In: 2019 SoutheastCon (2019). https://doi.org/10.1109/SoutheastCon 42311.2019.9020560

15. Kapoteli, E., Koukaras, P., Tjortjis, C.: Social media sentiment analysis related to COVID-19 vaccines: case studies in English and Greek language. Artif. Intell. Appl. Innov. (2022). https://doi.org/10.1007/978-3-031-08337-2_30

16. Koukaras, P., Tjortjis, C., Rousidis, D.: Mining association rules from COVID-19 related twitter data to discover word patterns, topics and inferences. Inf. Syst. **109**, 1–21 (2022). https://doi.org/10.1016/j.is.2022.102054

17. Krogh, A.: What are artificial neural networks? Nat. Biotechnol. **26**(2), 195–197 (2008). https://doi.org/10.1038/nbt1386

18. Kursa, M., Rudnicki, W.: The all relevant feature selection using random forest (2011)

19. Manish, S., Bhagat, V., Pramila, R.: Prediction of football players performance using machine learning and deep learning algorithms. In: 2021 2nd International Conference for Emerging Technology (INCET). pp. 1–5 (2021). https://doi.org/10.1109/INCET51464.2021.9456424

20. Pantzalis, V.C., Tjortjis, C.: Sports analytics for football league table and player performance prediction. In: 2020 11th International Conference on Information, Intelligence, Systems and Applications (IISA) (2020). https://doi.org/10.1109/iisa50023.2020.9284352

21. Pariath, R., Shah, S., Surve, A., Mittal, J.: Player performance prediction in football game. In: Second International Conference on Electronics, Communication and Aerospace Technology (ICECA), pp. 1148–1153 (2018). https://doi.org/10.1109/ICECA.2018.8474750

22. Sarlis, V., Chatziilias, V., Tjortjis, C., Mandalidis, D.: A data science approach analyzing the impact of injuries on basketball player and team performance. Inf. Syst. **99**, 101750 (2021). https://doi.org/10.1016/j.is.2021.101750

23. Singh, J.: Random Forest: Pros and Cons. Medium (2020). https://medium.datadriveninves tor.com/random-forest-pros-and-cons-c1c42fb64f04

24. Sports Reference, https://www.sports-reference.com/. Accessed 1 Sept 2022

25. Srinivasan, B.: A social network analysis of football – evaluating player and team performance. In: 2017 Ninth International Conference on Advanced Computing (ICoAC), pp. 242–246 (2017). https://doi.org/10.1109/ICoAC.2017.8441301

26. Subramanya, T., Harutyunyan, D., Riggio, R.: Machine learning-driven service function chain placement and scaling in MEC-enabled 5G networks. Comput. Netw. 1–20 (2019). https://doi.org/10.1016/j.comnet.2019.106980

27. Tzirakis, P., Tjortjis, C.: T3C: improving a decision tree classification algorithm's interval splits on continuous attributes. Adv. Data Anal. Classif. **11**(2), 353–370 (2016). https://doi.org/10.1007/s11634-016-0246-x

28. Willmott, C., Matsuura, K.: Advantages of the mean absolute error (MAE) over the root mean square error (RMSE) in assessing average model performance. Climate Res. **30**, 79–82 (2005). https://doi.org/10.3354/cr030079

29. Yang, J.B., Shen, K.Q., Ong, C.J., Li, X.P.: Feature selection for MLP neural network: the use of random permutation of probabilistic outputs. IEEE Trans. Neural Netw. **20**(12), 1911–1922 (2009). https://doi.org/10.1109/tnn.2009.2032543

Forecasting of Wind Turbine Synthetic Signals Based on Nonlinear Autoregressive Networks

Cristian Blanco[1]([✉]), J. Enrique Sierra-García[2], and Matilde Santos[3]

[1] ETSI Informática, UNED, Madrid, Spain
cblanco177@alumno.uned
[2] Department of Electromechanical Engineering, University of Burgos, Burgos, Spain
jesierra@ubu.es
[3] Institute of Knowledge Technology, Complutense University of Madrid, Madrid, Spain
msantos@ucm.es

Abstract. The importance and future prospects of offshore wind power generation invite great efforts and investments to make it an efficient technology. A crucial aspect is the development of efficient control strategies, which in many cases require models to identify time accurately the state of the turbine at a given. These models must be simple enough not to increase the computational complexity of the control algorithm while being able to capture the nonlinearity and coupling of the wind devices. In this work, we exploit the possibility of using neural networks to identify a wind turbine control-oriented model to predict its power output. Two nonlinear autoregressive with exogenous inputs models, with different input variables, have been proposed, based on feedforward neural networks. Results are satisfactory in terms of model accuracy of an offshore 5MW WT even ruling out relevant variables.

Keywords: NARX neural networks · system identification · control-oriented model · forecasting · offshore wind turbine

1 Introduction

Offshore wind energy is experiencing an important growth with an increase of this kind of installation, up to 21% in 2021 [1]. Most of these offshore wind turbines are built in shallow water with fixed foundations, while floating turbines present significant challenges due to their greater complexity [2]. This complexity requires the use of models and control algorithms able to capture all dynamic effects to design and operate optimally the turbines. Besides, these controllers must be computationally cost efficient to operate in real time [3]. The main objectives of wind turbine control are to maintain safe operation, maximize power generation, mitigate fatigue loads on the structure, and avoid fault conditions [2].

Commercial wind turbines typically operate at variable speed, and use different control strategies depending on the operating regime [3]. The use of classical control

© IFIP International Federation for Information Processing 2023
Published by Springer Nature Switzerland AG 2023
I. Maglogiannis et al. (Eds.): AIAI 2023, IFIP AICT 676, pp. 316–324, 2023.
https://doi.org/10.1007/978-3-031-34107-6_25

technics like PID (Proportional-Integral-Derivative) regulators based on a single input single output (SISO) scheme require multiple control loops to stabilize the structure. For more complex turbines, multiple-input multiple-output (MIMO) strategies that are able to capture the most critical dynamics are a must. It is in this context where the identification of the most important features of the turbine system is an important step, in order to design effective control strategies such as MPC (Model Predictive Control) or State Space based control.

Some researchers have worked on this approach. In [4], a MPC based control strategy to stabilize the power generation and reduce the dynamic loads in the structure of the 5-MW floating turbine [5], in the constant speed operation regime, is proposed. An internal linear model, identified from the results of a highly complex non lineal model, is used to predict the system behavior and optimize the control signals. Another approach is to design a digital twin of a 1.5-MW turbine to monitor the state of the structure from the loads estimated with the twin [6]. The authors use a Kalman filter based linear model designed with operational data complemented by nonlinear simulations. This model allows estimating the state of the system at an instant of time with limited information about it. In a similar way, in [7] a monitoring system of a gear box based on data obtained from different wind farms is presented. Different machine learning (ML) and deep learning (DL) methods are used to design predictive models. The model based on deep neural networks performs the best. The use of neural networks to estimate turbine power generation is an interesting topic. In [8] an artificial neural network (ANN) is used to estimate the power generated by a five-turbines wind farm, and to propose optimized angles to reduce the wake effect on the turbines. Long short term memory (LSTM) neural networks have been shown as an effective tool to predict the power generation of the turbines in a wind farm [9]. The training of the networks is done using historical wind data and turbine power generation. In [10] and [11], an effective wind speed estimator based on neural networks is successfully used to improve the performance of a classical controller. These types of networks have also been used in the design of controllers as substitutes of complex and computationally costly strategies [12]. In [13] a blade pitch controller for a 7-MW turbine based on neural networks and reinforcement learning is design, showcasing the potential of the neural network to both substitute other control strategies, and complement and improve their performance. An example of a MIMO that uses a complex autoregressive model based on simple neural networks is presented in [14], the autoregressive model is used to estimate important state-space variables of the system.

In this paper, the use of nonlinear autoregressive with exogenous input models (NARX) based on artificial neural networks (ANN) to identify nonlinear systems is studied using simulated data of a 5-MW turbine [5]. Two models with different input signals are compared. In the first model, the power generated is estimated at t instant using several key signals, including the wind speed, in past instants. For the second model, the wind speed signal is ruled out. It is considered interesting to compare the performance of both models given that the simulated wind speed data coming from Openfast [15] is usually not available in the typical commercial wind turbine, or the sensor measurement may present uncertainties or faulty behaviour. Therefore, having a model that does not rely on this information is interesting.

The paper is structured with a first section in which the turbine, the software, and the models used in the study are described. The data used to train the neural networks, as well as its structure, are also presented. Next, the tests performed to study the performance of the models and results comparison are presented and discussed. Lastly, the conclusions and possible future lines of study are set out.

2   System and Models Description

2.1   Wind Turbine Description

The wind turbine used is described in [16]. It is an offshore 5-MW wind turbine with a fixed pillar as support. – shows a summary of the key characteristics of the turbine (Table 1).

Table 1. Wind Turbine Characteristics

Rating	5 MW
Rotor orientation, Configuration	Upwind, 3 Blades
Control	Variable Speed, Collective Pitch
Drivetrain	High Speed, Multiple-Stage Gearbox
Rotor, Hub Diameter	126 m, 3 m
Hub Height	90 m
Cut-In, Rated, Cut-Out Wind Speed	3 m/s, 11.4 m/s, 25 m/s
Cut-In, Rated Rotor Speed	6.9 rpm, 12.1 rpm
Rated Tip Speed	80 m/s

This choice is particularly convenient since reliable simulation data for this turbine can be generated with Openfast software [15] in the validation tests, Test 19 in particular. Openfast is a software developed by NREL (National Renewable Energy Laboratory), formerly known as FAST (Fatigue, Aerodynamics, Structures, and Turbulence), used for wind turbine nonlinear simulation and multidisciplinary analysis.

This study uses data generated by Openfast to train the neural networks. Data of the wind speed is generated using the Turbsim [16], with an average speed of 12 m/s.

2.2   Neural Network Models Signals Description

The objective of this work is to study the possibility of modeling the power generation in the wind turbine using neural networks. An analysis of the correlation between the Openfast output channels is carried out and the most representative signals for the case study are selected.

The wind turbines variables considered for the neural model are presented in Table 2. They include the output power as the target, and as possible inputs, we will work with

Table 2. Key Signals for the Networks

SIGNAL	UNITS	OPENFAST CHANNEL	INPUT/OUTPUT (MODEL)
Wind Speed x component	[m/s]	Wind1VelX	Input (1)
Wind Speed y component	[m/s]	Wind1VelY	Input (1)
Wind Speed z component	[m/s]	Wind1VelZ	Input (1)
Blade Pitch	[°]	BldPitch1	Input (1 and 2)
Rotor Speed	[rpm]	RotSpeed	Input (1 and 2)
Rotor Torque	[kNm]	RotTorq	Input (1 and 2)
Generator Power	[KW]	GenPwr	Input/Output (1 and 2)

the wind speed Cartesian components, the angle of the blades (pitch), the rotor speed and its torque.

The output of the networks is the ouput power. Model 1 uses all the signals to train the networks, whereas in model 2 the wind speed signals are ruled out. The data are generated with an Openfast simulation for 3000 s, with time increments of 50 ms. In the rest of the article the models, for the shake of clarity, will be called model 7-signals, the first model, and model 4-signal the second one.

2.3 Neural Networks Description

The networks are feedback neural networks used to create the nonlinear autoregressive with exogenous input model. Figure 1 shows a typical NARX network. In this figure, $x(t)$ is the exogenous input, $y(t)$ is the autoregressive variable, W is the matrix of weights, and b the bias introduced.

The neural networks are generated with Tensorflow [17]. Both neural networks have the same macro structure. It has not been thoroughly optimized, but parameters that yield acceptable results from a set of values tested have been selected. The networks have one input layer of 10 artificial neuron units and an output layer with 1 standard unit, with a ReLu activation function.

The input data for the networks are the state vectors with the selected signals with a time window of a second, i.e. 20 temporal increments of 50 ms each. Thus the input has 20 state vectors. The network output is the estimated generator power.

Figure 2 shows a summary of the networks. The number of parameters of the input layer is the number of state vectors (20), times the number of signals (4/7), times the number of neurons (10), plus the number of outputs of each neuron to the next layer (10), for a total of 810 (4-signals model) and 1410 (7-signals model) parmeters. The number of parameters of the output layer is the number of inputs from the previous layer (10), plus the output (1), for a total of 11 parameters.

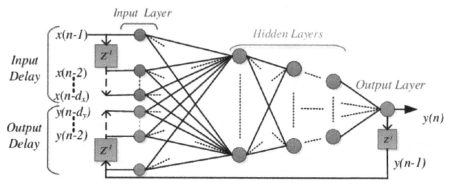

Fig. 1. NARX Network Scheme [18]

Layer (type)	Output Shape	Param #
dense (Dense)	(None, 10)	1410
dense_1 (Dense)	(None, 1)	11

Total params: 1,421
Trainable params: 1,421
Non-trainable params: 0

Layer (type)	Output Shape	Param #
dense (Dense)	(None, 10)	810
dense_1 (Dense)	(None, 1)	11

Total params: 821
Trainable params: 821
Non-trainable params: 0

Fig. 2. Networks Structure Summary (Top – 7-signals, bottom – 4-signals)

2.4 System Identification

To perform the system identification, the neural networks have to be trained. It is done using the Openfast generated data over 3000 s, with time increments of 50 ms. That is, there are 60,000 data points for each selected signal. A 60%, 20%, 20% split is performed for training, validation, and test sets. Since it is a time series, this division is done in chronological order. The performance over the test data set is shown in Fig. 3 and Fig. 4.

In Table 3 the values of the MAE (mean absolute error) and RMSE (root mean square error) that have been used as metrics are presented.

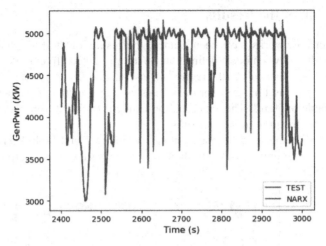

Fig. 3. Training Results 7-signals

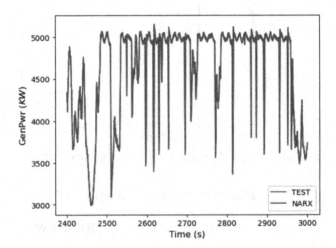

Fig. 4. Training Results 4-signals

Table 3. Training Performance Summary

MODEL	MAE [KW]	RMSE [KW]
7-SIGNALS	8.94	11.77
4-SIGNALS	4.23	7.81

As can be seen, both networks show good performance on the training data. Nevertheless, the second model stands out for the smaller errors it presents, even with fewer signals.

3   Discussion of the Results

Once the neural networks have been trained, the results of the tests that have been carried out with the two models defined above are presented. To compare the models performance with reliable data, the regression test data no. 19 of the Openfast software is used. This test dataset has data for the signals used in this study for a period of 60 s, with time sample of 50 ms. The data used for testing is different from the training data used during the validation of the networks.

The results of both models test are summarized in Fig. 5 and Table 4. The results are consistent with the training results. Both networks types show good performance.

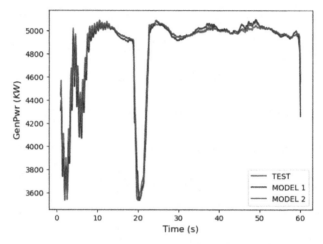

Fig. 5. Predicted generated power with the two models

Table 4. Model 1 Results Summary

MODEL	MAE [KW]	RMSE [KW]
7-SIGNALS	39.76	67.60
4-SIGNALS	**21.93**	**40.99**

It is worth it to remark that the model with less exogenous inputs shows the best performance. Results are good and errors are within acceptable limits, although bigger than the ones obtained in the training process.

4   Conclusions and Future Works

The suitability of nonlinear autoregressive with exogenous inputs models based on feed-forward neural networks to estimate the generator power of a wind turbine is studied. Two models with different input signals are trained and used to compare their performance. The second model, with fewer inputs given that the wind speed is not used, performs similarly compared to the first model. Both models give good results regarding the prediction of the output power. However, it is an interesting exercise given that the wind speed is a variable that might not be available or may be not reliable.

Even though the results when an abrupt variation of the signal is not desirable, this performance can be improved optimizing the hyper-parameters of the networks or even implementing different mechanisms as a function of these changes [19]. The number of state vectors considered as input to the networks is possibly one of such parameters that might be sensitive to the mentioned behaviour. Moreover, it could be interesting to modify or increase the Openfast signals used as inputs to improve the predictions. Lastly, a future line of study could also be to design a similar model specifically tailored to use as part of a model predictive controller.

Acknowledgement. This work was partially supported by the Spanish Ministry of Science, Innovation and Universities under MCI/AEI/FEDER Project no. PID2021-123543OB-C21.

References

1. Council, G.W.E.: Global Wind Report 2022. GWEC, Brussels (2022)
2. Hu, R., Conghuan, L., Ding, H., Zhang, P.: Implementation and evaluation of control strategies based on an open controller for a 10 MW floating wind turbine. Renew. Energy **179**, 1751–1766 (2021)
3. Wright, A.D., Fingersh, L.J.: Advanced control design for wind turbines Part I: control design, implementation, and initial tests. NREL, Golden (2008)
4. Wakui, T., Nagamura, A., Yokoyama, R.: Stabilization of power output and platform motion of a floating offshore wind turbine-generator system using model predictive control based on previewed disturbances. Renew. Energy **173**, 105–127 (2021)
5. Jonkman, J., Butterfield, S., Musial, W., Scott, G.: Definition of a 5-MW reference wind turbine for offshore system development. NREL (2009)
6. Branlard, E., Jonkman, J., Dana, S., Doubrawa, P.: A digital twin based on OpenFAST linearizations for real-time load and fatigue estimation of land-based turbines. In: Journal of Physics: Conference Series, vol. 1618 (2020)
7. Wang, L., Zhang, Z., Long, H., Xu, J., Liu, R.: Wind turbine gearbox failure identification with deep neural networks. IEEE Trans. Industr. Inf. **13**(3), 1360–1368 (2017)
8. Sun, H., Qiu, C., Lu, L., Gao, X., Chen, J., Yang, H.: Wind turbine power modelling and optimization using artificial neural network with wind field experimental data. Appl. Energy **280**, 115880 (2020)
9. Zhang, J., Yan, J., Infield, D., Liu, Y., Lien, F.-S.: Short-term forecasting and uncertainty analysis of wind turbine power based on long short-term memory network and Gaussian mixture model. Appl. Energy **241**, 229–244 (2019)
10. Sierra-García, J.E., Santos, M.: Improving wind turbine pitch control by effective wind neuro-estimators. IEEE Access **9**, 10413–10425 (2021)
11. Sierra-Garcia, J.E., Santos, M.: Deep learning and fuzzy logic to implement a hybrid wind turbine pitch control. Neural Comput. Appl. **34**(13), 1–15 (2021). https://doi.org/10.1007/s00521-021-06323-w
12. Blanco Fernández, C., Sierra García, J.E., Santos, M.: Control de un laboratorio de control de temperatura mediante redes neuronales recurrentes. XLIII Jornadas de Automática 193–200 (2022)

13. Sierra-García, J.E., Santos, M.: Redes neuronales y aprendizaje por refuerzo en el control de turbinas eólicas. Rev. Iberoamericana de Automática e Informática Ind. **18**(4), 327–335 (2021)
14. Alonso, A., Zabaljauregi, A., Larrea, M., Irigoyen, E., Sanchís, J.: Studying the use of ANN to estimate state-space variables for MIMO systems in a NMPC strategy. In: 17th International Conference on Soft Computing Models in Industrial and Environmental Applications (SOCO 2022). SOCO 2022. Lecture Notes in Networks and Systems, vol. 531, pp. 464–473 (2022). https://doi.org/10.1007/978-3-031-18050-7_45
15. Jonkman, J., Musial, W.: Offshore Code Comparison Collaboration (OC3) for IEA Task 23 Offshore Wind Technology and Deployment. NREL, Golden (2010)
16. https://github.com/OpenFAST/openfast. National Renewable Energy Laboratory, https://github.com/OpenFAST/openfast. Accessed 1 Sept 2022
17. Abadi, M., et al.: Tensorflow: a system for large scale machine learning. In: OSDI, vol. 16, pp. 265–283 (2016)
18. Habibi, M.R., Hamid, B., Dragicevic, T.: Detection of false data injection cyber-attacks in DC microgrids based on recurrent neural networks. IEEE J. Emerg. Sel. Top. Power Electron. **9**, 5294–5310 (2010)
19. Sierra-García, J., Santos, M.: Switched learning adaptive neuro-control strategy. Neurocomputing **452**, 450–464 (2021)

Hybrid Machine Learning and Autonomous Control Assisted Framework for Fault Diagnostics and Mitigation in Diesel Engines

Raman Goyal[1]($\boxtimes$), Dhrubajit Chowdhury[1], Subhashis Hazarika[1],
Raj Pradip Khawale[2], Shubhendu Kumar Singh[2], Lara Crawford[1],
and Rahul Rai[2]

[1] Palo Alto Research Center, Palo Alto, CA, USA
{rgoyal,chowdhury,shazarika,lcrawford}@parc.com
[2] Department of Automotive Engineering, Clemson University, Clemson, SC, USA
{rkhawal,shubhes,rrai}@clemson.edu

Abstract. The paper proposes a hybrid machine learning framework along with a hierarchical control module for fault diagnosis, isolation, and mitigation to develop a resilient diesel engine system. The hybrid diagnostics system combines experimental data with physics-based simulation data to improve fault diagnosis, isolation, and severity prediction. The hybrid architecture consists of a denoising autoencoder to transform the engine data to a fixed lower-dimension latent space representation. The combined data is then passed to a Twin-Deep Neural Network (DNN) framework to detect and predict fault severity. The hierarchical control module consists of control calibration maps generated offline using Bayesian optimization to maintain the desired engine torque while minimizing fuel consumption. The module also uses proportional-integral (PI) and extremum seeking (ES) controllers on top of the offline map to compensate for engine faults and modeling errors. The simulation results show the efficacy of the proposed architecture to maintain the desired performance for different fault scenarios.

Keywords: Machine Learning · Neural Network · Engine Diagnostics · Fault mitigation · Bayesian Optimization · Autoencoder · Engine Control

1 Introduction

The concept of full autonomy is still a major challenge, especially in the realm of autonomous vessels. The US Navy aspires to create self-sufficient ships that are capable of resolving faults without human intervention. This requirement extends to other autonomous vehicles and systems that must make decisions on their own to achieve specific goals. However, there still exists a gap in the ability

© IFIP International Federation for Information Processing 2023
Published by Springer Nature Switzerland AG 2023
I. Maglogiannis et al. (Eds.): AIAI 2023, IFIP AICT 676, pp. 325–339, 2023.
https://doi.org/10.1007/978-3-031-34107-6_26

of autonomous systems to respond and adapt to faults, as they lack the necessary models and decision-making processes. The driving force behind this research is the necessity to autonomously address engine faults to ensure mission completion [15]. The paper aims to develop a comprehensive online fault detection and mitigation framework for marine engines. The comprehensive online framework would help in the successful completion of the mission in adverse environments.

Despite diesel engines being a popular choice for maritime vessels because of their dependability and efficiency, they are still prone to faults resulting in reduced performance, increased emissions, and even catastrophic failure. Fault diagnosis is critical to ensure the safe and efficient operation of diesel engines. Traditional diagnostic methods rely on expert knowledge and manual inspection, which are time-consuming, costly, and limited in their accuracy. Various advanced fault diagnosis techniques, such as model-based and data-driven approaches, have emerged in recent years. Model-based approaches rely on mathematical models that describe the physical behavior of the diesel engine under normal and faulty conditions. These models are based on fundamental principles and are used to simulate the engine's response to different operating conditions and detect faults by analyzing the deviation of residuals from a pre-defined threshold [1]. Nohra et al. [8] suggested a linearized linear time-invariant model based on mu-analysis control theory, which effectively detects and isolates faults in turbocharged diesel engines, even in the presence of noise and uncertainties. These models are developed using analytical or numerical methods and can provide insights into the underlying mechanisms of fault propagation. However, they require detailed knowledge of the engine's structure and parameters and may only be accurate under some operating conditions and fault types.

Contrary to the model-based approach, data-driven models are based on the statistical analysis of the data collected from the engine under normal and faulty conditions. These models can capture the complex and nonlinear relationships between the diagnostic signals and the fault. Rahimi et al. [11] devised an SVM and RBF-based approach to explore the impact of oil metal contamination on the operational conditions of diesel engines using extensive datasets. Guoqiang et al. [2] introduced a deep belief network technique for intelligent fault diagnosis of marine diesel engines. However, data-driven approaches usually need more interpretability and generalizability and require a large amount of training data.

To overcome the limitations faced by the traditional model-based and data-driven approaches, researchers are resorting to a new class of methods termed Physics-Informed Machine Learning (PIML) [5]. PIML aims to enhance ML models' accuracy, interpretability, and generalizability by incorporating domain-specific knowledge and constraints into the learning process. In the context of diesel engine fault diagnosis, PIML can leverage the physical laws governing the engine's operation to guide the feature extraction, model selection, and decision-making steps of the ML pipeline. PIML can also provide insight into the underlying mechanisms of fault propagation and enable the design of more effective diagnostic strategies. In this research, we propose a hybrid physics-informed twin neural network framework for fault detection and severity prediction in a diesel engine system.

Once the faults are identified, the engine needs to autonomously mitigate the effect of faults. One aspect of these faults can be decreased generation of torque that can be compensated by controlling the fuel quantity and timing in the combustion phase. The fuel injection system uses electronic control to change the fuel quantity and timing based on a calibrated lookup table. The lookup table stores the values of engine control parameters, which are optimized to achieve maximum fuel efficiency for different engine operating conditions. This control structure is open-loop in nature as the engine control parameters are optimized offline [14]. This structure suffers in practice due to differences in engine modeling errors, non-calibrated operating points, and faults, which necessitates the need for online feedback control [14]. Extremum seeking (ES) controllers have been used for online calibration of the engine control parameters due to their model-free nature [7]. Some of the implementations of ES controller for engine optimization include [3,6,10], and a comprehensive review of the optimization algorithms used for engine calibration can be found in [17]. This paper will develop a hierarchical control framework that will pool offline and online controllers to mitigate the effect of faults and modeling errors while optimizing for fuel consumption.

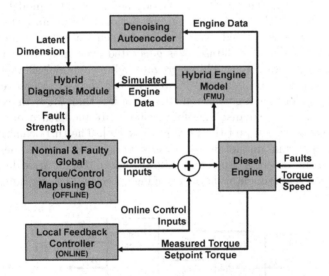

Fig. 1. The complete framework for fault detection and mitigation.

Main Contribution: The paper provides a comprehensive framework for autonomous fault detection and mitigation in a diesel engine system as shown in Fig. 1. The paper first develops a hybrid (analytical and ML-based) engine model tuned using experimental data. Then, a Denoising Autoencoder (DAE) is developed to remove the noise and to represent the system in a fixed-dimension latent representation. A machine learning based hybrid Twin-Deep Neural Network (DNN) framework is developed to diagnose faults and predict fault severity.

The paper further develops a hierarchical control module that provides setpoint control parameters and an online feedback controller to mitigate faults. The setpoint control parameters are obtained offline using Bayesian Optimization (BO) to minimize fuel consumption and the online feedback control is based on proportional-integral (PI) and Extremum seeking (ES) controllers. The paper finally shows the full integration results of fault mitigation for the fuel injector and intake manifold leak faults.

2   Hybrid Engine and Fault Model

The paper develops a high-fidelity hybrid engine model for a 7.6-liter 6-cylinder Navistar diesel engine installed at Clemson University. There exist multiple mean value models with various complexities and states in the literature [4,13]. The paper uses Wahlström and Eriksson [16] as the baseline model and improves the fidelity of the model by replacing and adding various components. We started with a detailed thermodynamic cylinder model that simulates the in-cylinder processes and their thermodynamic states but the detailed model was computationally expensive. Thus, to improve the computational speed of the overall physics-based model, the detailed thermodynamic cylinder model is replaced with a NN reducing the computational simulation time by an order of magnitude. This network is trained over the dataset generated from the thermodynamic cylinder model. The dataset was generated over an entire feasible range of input cylinder parameters. This surrogate cylinder model showed the Mean Squared Error (MSE) of 3.42×10^{-4} over the test dataset. Moreover, the outputs of the cylinder model give us a difference of less than 5% with experimental data. The intake and exhaust manifold systems are modeled using the principle of mass conservation and the ideal-gas law [16]. The turbocharger model is composed of a turbine model, a compressor model, and a turbo inertia model. Finally, the entire model is depicted in Fig. 2 (refer to [16] for more details) and is calibrated using experimental data for engine speed and torque ranges between

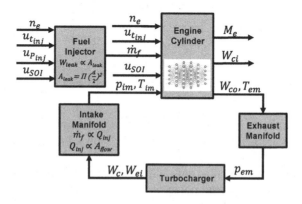

Fig. 2. Hybrid engine model structural diagram

800–2000 RPM and 100–600 Nm, respectively. The control input parameters are : engine speed (n_e), injection pressure (u_{Pinj}), injection duration (u_{tinj}), and start of injection (u_{SOI}).

2.1 Different Fault Models

This subsection provides a brief description of intake manifold faults modeled using a pinhole leak and fuel injection system faults like fuel injector nozzle erosion due to cavitation and fuel injector nozzle clogging, which can be simulated by increasing and decreasing the area of the injector nozzle, respectively.

Intake Manifold Leak Model: The intake manifold is connected to the cylinder head using a seal to keep it airtight. However, over time these seals might wear off which introduces a leak in the intake manifold and as a result decreases the engine efficiency. The leak is modeled as a flow through a restriction and has been validated in [9] with good accuracy. The leakage mass flow rate from the intake manifold is:

$$W_{\text{leak}} = \frac{A_{\text{leak}}p_{im}}{\sqrt{R_{im}T_{im}}}\psi_\kappa \left(\frac{p_{\text{atm}}}{p_{im}}\right) \tag{1}$$

where R_{im} is the gas constant of air in the intake manifold, T_{im} is the temperature in the intake manifold, p_{im} is pressure in the intake manifold, A_{leak} is the area of the hole given by $\pi(d/2)^2$ with d as leak diameter, and the function ψ_κ is a complex function given in [9].

Fuel Injector Area Erosion/Clogging Model: The Navistar engine has a high-pressure common-rail fuel injection system and the corresponding injection flow rate is modeled as follows:

$$Q_{inj} = \text{sign}(u_{Pinj} - P_{cyl})\alpha c_d A_{ff}A_{fl}\sqrt{\frac{2}{\rho}|u_{Pinj} - P_{cyl}|}, \tag{2}$$

where α is a binary value used to incorporate injection duration, P_{cyl} is the cylinder pressure, C_d is the discharge coefficient for injector, A_{fl} is the injector nozzle area, and ρ is the fuel density. The fuel injector erosion and clogging are modeled using the area fault factor parameter A_{ff}, where $A_{ff} > 1$ corresponds to erosion and $A_{ff} < 1$ corresponds to clogging.

3 Online Hybrid Diagnostics Module for Fault Prediction

3.1 Denoising Autoencoder

The sensor readings collected from an engine can be a challenging dataset to directly ingest into a machine learning pipeline. The engine data needs to be checked for data consistency, in terms of missing or corrupted values and different noise levels. We address such issues through our data assimilation step which pre-processes the data and makes it ready for downstream hybrid machine learning models. A key component of the data assimilation stage is a denoising Autoencoder (DAE) model. Autoencoders (AE) are neural network models commonly

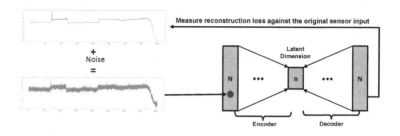

Fig. 3. Overview of the Denoising Autoencoder model.

used to model high-dimensional multivariate data signals. They learn the inter-variable relationships and project them to representative low-dimensional latent spaces. Compared to popular dimensionality reduction methods like principal component analysis (PCA), which are linear models, AE's can capture non-linear multivariate relationships. AE models comprise of an *encoder* and a *decoder* network. They are trained in such a way that the encoder takes in an input high-dimensional vector and produces a low-dimensional latent representation, whereas, the decoder takes in the latent vector and tries to reconstruct the original high-dimensional vector back. DAE's are a popular variant of AE, which take in high-dimensional noisy signals and reconstruct the original signal back as illustrated in Fig. 3. DAE learns to map the high-dimensional data space to latent space in the presence of noise. We utilize this property of DAE to learn the simplified latent representation of the multivariate engine data in the presence of noise. The mean squared error of reconstruction was used as the standard loss function to train our model. We trained the DAE to a maximum noise level of 30%. The generated latent representation capturing the important multivariate relationships is then used in the hybrid model development phase. The DAE training plot is given in Fig. 4(a) and the reconstruction of the torque variable is shown in Fig. 4(b).

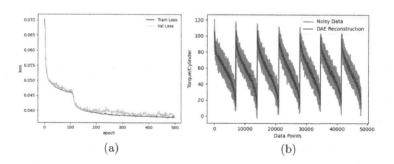

(a)   (b)

Fig. 4. (a) Training and validation loss for the training of the DAE. (b) The plot shows the noisy data and the reconstructed data for the cylinder torque for all the training data. The plot repeats itself for different values of RPMs.

3.2   Twin-Neural Network Framework for Fault Diagnosis

The proposed hybrid diagnosis framework, as shown in Fig. 5, is based on a twin neural network structure, where one deep neural network (DNN) based sub-model classifies fault while the other DNN-based regression model was used to estimate the severity of the fault. The input to both the DNN-based sub-models is a 42-dimensional feature vector obtained by concatenating a 4-dimensional latent variables vector from the denoising autoencoder and 38-dimensional data from the multi-physics simulation model of the diesel engine. The influx of physics into the neural network-based sub-models ensures that their solutions are physically meaningful and consistent with the underlying physical phenomena. Additionally, the physics of the system helps to regularize the DNN models, thus reducing overfitting, improving generalization, and ultimately enhancing the overall accuracy of the fault diagnosis framework. And the data-driven DNN models help to extract patterns and relationships from the dataset that may not be immediately apparent from the underlying physics. Besides, the DNN models help to identify outliers in the data that may indicate a fault or anomaly in the system. Combining this information with the physical constraints of physics-based models enables the hybrid model to diagnose faults accurately.

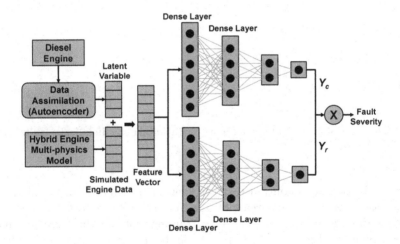

Fig. 5. Architecture for the hybrid diagnosis module.

As evident from Fig. 5, the top DNN model is the classification model whose output is Y_c, and the bottom model is the regression model with Y_r as its output. The two DNN models are trained separately with the output of the classification model as $Y_c = \{0, 1\}$, where $Y_c = 0$ represents the nominal condition and $Y_c = 1$ represents the fault condition. Fig. 6 shows the confusion matrix for the classification of intake manifold leaks and fuel injector faults. Notice that the intake leak fault is harder to detect and has higher false positives compared to the fuel injector faults, which have a direct effect on the amount of fuel injected and thus generated torque.

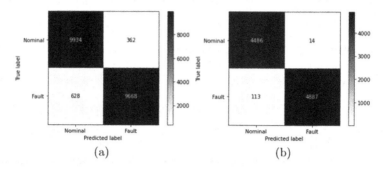

Fig. 6. (a) The confusion matrix for classification of intake manifold leaks faults. (b) The confusion matrix for classification of fuel injector faults.

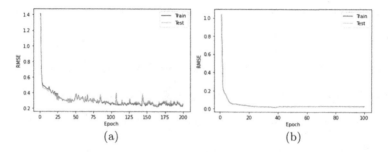

Fig. 7. The regression model training plots for (a) intake manifold leaks faults and (b) fuel injector faults.

The regression model output takes on continuous values from $Y_r = [0.5 - 1.5]$ for the case of fuel injector area clogging and $Y_r = [0 - 0.012]$ for the case of intake manifold leak. Figure 7 shows the training plots for the regression model of intake manifold leaks and fuel injector faults. The final output of the hybrid diagnosis module is the fault severity $Y_c \times Y_r$.

The reason for training the two models separately and using the multiplication of the two outputs is to reduce the chances of incorrect fault prediction for the nominal operating condition, as the regression model can have an incorrect small fault severity prediction due to overfitting. The twin neural network structure of the diagnostics framework helps in achieving higher accuracy and faster convergence compared to a single large neural network as each individual network in the framework can specialize in learning different features or patterns, allowing for more efficient and accurate learning.

4 Hierarchical Control Module for Fault Mitigation

The paper uses two model-free controllers as part of the hierarchical control module for fault mitigation. The first controller uses the Bayesian optimization (BO) algorithm to generate offline control calibration maps that minimize fuel consumption and obtain the desired engine torque. The second is the online extremum seeking (ES) feedback controller that is used on top of the nominal optimal engine control parameters found using BO to compensate for modeling errors and engine faults. This section provides a description of these two algorithms.

4.1 Control Calibration Maps for Different Fault Strength Using Bayesian Optimization

We used the BO algorithm to generate the control calibration maps for both nominal and faulty operating conditions. The BO is generally used to find the global optimum of a computationally expensive objective function $f(\mathbf{x})$ without a closed form expression [12]. The problem can be defined as: $\mathbf{x}^* = \arg \max_{\mathbf{x} \in \mathcal{X}} f(\mathbf{x})$, where $\mathcal{X}$ is the design space of interest. The BO develops a Gaussian Process based surrogate model which is initialized with a prior belief about the behavior of the unknown objective function. The model is then sequentially refined with new data when the function is evaluated at new query points using a Bayesian posterior update. Acquisitions functions are used in the BO framework to provide a trade-off between exploration and exploitation and thus provide the next query point for function evaluation $f(\mathbf{x})$.

We used BO to generate the control calibration maps by optimizing the fuel efficiency $\dot{m}_f$ for a combination of different engine operating points with engine speeds ranging from 1000 to 1600 RPM with a step of 1000 RPM and torque values ranging from 100 to 500 Nm with a step of 50 Nm. The maps are also generated for the fuel injector area faults ranging from $A_{ff} = 0.5$ to $A_{ff} = 1.5$ with a step of 0.1 and for the intake manifold leak with the leak diameter varying from $d = 2$mm to $d = 12$mm with a step of 2mm. The optimization problem for engine calibration can be described as:

$$\min_{u_1, u_2, u_3} \quad \dot{m}_f(u_1, u_2, u_3, n_e, M_e) \quad \text{s.t. } M_e = M_e^s, \ n_e = n_e^s, \ \underline{u}_i \le u_i \le \bar{u}_i, \quad (3)$$

where $i = 1, 2, 3$ and $u_1 = u_{Pinj}$, $u_2 = u_{tinj}$, $u_3 = u_{SOI}$, are controllable engine parameters. The variables n_e^s, and M_e^s are the setpoint speed and torque. In the actual implementation, the torque constraint is relaxed to inequality constraints with a small number $\delta = 0.3$ Nm. The ranges for control calibration variables used in the simulation setup are as follows: $u_{Pinj} \in [4 - 25]$MPa, $u_{tinj} \in [0.3 - 3]$ms, and $u_{SOI} \in [345 - 380]$CAD. Figure 8(a) illustrates the estimated objective function $(\dot{m}_f)$ obtained by running the BO algorithm for 150 iterations by varying the injection pressure and SOI.

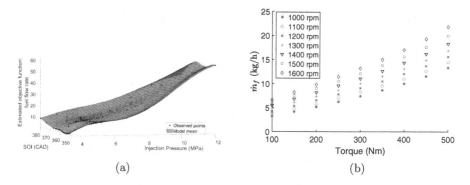

(a)   (b)

Fig. 8. (a) Objective function mean estimated by Bayesian optimization. (b) Optimized fuel vs torque map generated using BO for a range of torque and engine RPM.

Figure 8(b) illustrates the optimized fuel consumption rate for all the operating points. Notice that the fuel consumption rate increases with the increase in torque and engine speed. Figure 9(a) compares the obtained injection pressures for the nominal case with the area clogging in the fuel injector. As seen from the figure, with an increase in area clogging the optimized injection pressure increases as higher injection pressures are required to generate the same fuel flow rate as in the nominal case. Figure 9(b) compares the optimized fuel flow rate for the nominal case with the presence of a leak in the intake manifold. Notice that the fuel flow rate increases with an increase in speed and with an increase in leak diameter. This is because larger leaks result in a higher drop in torque value and as a result, a higher fuel flow rate is required to achieve the same torque as in the nominal case.

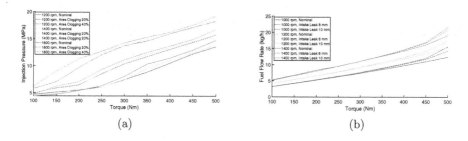

(a)   (b)

Fig. 9. (a) Comparison of optimized injection pressure vs torque map in the presence/absence of area clogging. (b) Comparison of optimized fuel vs torque map in the presence/absence of intake manifold leaks.

4.2   Online Feedback Controller for Fault Mitigation

This subsection describes a PI+ES online feedback controller for optimization of the engine control parameters in cases of modeling errors and engine faults.

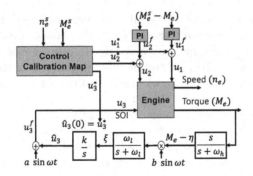

Fig. 10. Control architecture for online engine calibration

The ES controller [7] is a model-free approach for adaptive control, which is used for systems where the input-to-output map $f(\mathbf{x})$ is unknown but is known to have an extremum. This online feedback controller is used in conjunction with the calibration maps as the optimized control inputs might not achieve the desired torque setpoint M_e^s due to modeling errors and uncalibrated engine faults. The overall control architecture is shown in Fig. 10. The PI controller uses the tracking error $M_e^s - M_e$ to change the injection duration and pressure to maintain the desired setpoint torque and the ES controller to change the SOI to minimize the fuel consumption rate by maximizing the torque M_e. The PI controllers for injection pressure and duration are described as u_1^f and u_2^f and the ES controller can be described as: $u_3^f = \hat{u}_3 + a\sin\omega t$, $\dot{\eta} = -\omega_h\eta + \omega_h M_e$, $\dot{\xi} = -\omega_l\xi + \omega_l(M_e - \eta)b\sin\omega t$, $\dot{\hat{u}}_3 = k\xi$, where ω_h, ω_l, and ω are the frequencies of the high-pass filter, low-pass filter, and perturbation signal. The modulation amplitude is given by a, and the demodulation amplitude is given by b. The adaptation gain is given by k, and the low-pass and high-pass filter states are given by ξ and η. Finally, $\hat{u}_3$ represents the mean perturbation. The initial condition of the integrator is chosen as $\hat{u}_3(0) = u_3^*$. The final engine control parameters then fed to the engine are given as: $u_1 = u_1^f + u_1^*$, $u_2 = u_2^f + u_2^*$, $u_3 = u_3^f$, where u_1^*, u_2^*, and u_3^* represent the engine control parameters generated from the engine control map.

5 Integrated Simulation Results

This section shows the results of the complete framework of fault detection and mitigation for the case of two kinds of faults considered in the paper.

5.1 Fuel Injector Clogging

The simulation results were generated for the setpoint torque of 300 Nm and speed of 1400 RPM with injection area fault of value $A_{ff} = [1, 1, 0.6, 1, 1, 0.8]$ introduced at time $t = 8$ second. The diagnosis module is run every 5 secs.

Figure 11 shows the torque, fuel flow rate, and control injection parameters plot where the engine takes around 2 secs to reach the steady state value and then a sudden decrease in torque value is observed due to injector clogging in cylinders 3 and 6 at time $t = 8$ sec. When the torque value deviates from the setpoint torque value of 300 Nm, the online feedback control adjusts the control parameters to obtain the desired torque. Notice that at $t = 5$ secs, there is no fault and hence no change in injection parameters or torque, but at time $t = 10$ secs, the diagnosis module detects the fault and updates the control parameters based on the offline maps corresponding to the estimated fault strength. At $t = 15$ sec, no further degradation in engine health (constant clogging) does not alarm the diagnosis module further and the system steadily maintains the same control configuration and system state. Notice that there is no considerable change in fuel efficiency from the locally optimal feedback controller to the globally optimal fuel map generated using BO. This is due to the nature of the fault as erosion or clogging in the fuel injector has a minimal effect on the amount of fuel required to obtain the same setpoint torque. Also, notice that the local feedback controller increases the value of the injection pressure and injection duration for both cylinders 3 and 6 (higher for cylinder 3 due to 40% clogging compared to cylinder 6 with 20% clogging), but the global control maps shift the injection pressure even higher while bringing back the duration to the original value of 1.2 ms. This is due to the control input maps being generated for the fixed value of injection duration as explained in the previous section. The small perturbations in cylinders 3 and 6 are visible due to the excitation present as part of the ESC. The area fault factor parameters predicted at each diagnosis time point of 5, 10, and 15 secs are $A_{ff} = [1.02, 1.02, 1.02, 1.02, 1.02, 1.02]$, $A_{ff} = [1.02, 1.02, 0.61, 1.02, 1.02, 0.82]$, and $A_{ff} = [1.02, 1.02, 0.62, 1.02, 1.02, 0.81]$, respectively.

5.2   Intake Manifold Leak

This subsection shows the results for the case of intake manifold leak with the leak diameter of $d = 12$mm introduced at time $t = 8$ second. The simulation results were generated for the setpoint torque of 300 Nm with a value of 1200 RPM and the diagnosis module is run every 5 secs. Figure 12(a) shows the torque and fuel flow rate and Fig. 12(b) shows the control injection parameters required to maintain the desired setpoint torque in the presence of a leak. The engine reaches the steady state in 2 secs, and then the torque drops due to the leak at time $t = 8$ second. When the torque value deviates from the setpoint torque, the online feedback control adjusts the control parameters to obtain the desired torque. Notice that at time $t = 10$ secs, the diagnosis module detects the leak in the intake manifold and updates the control parameters based on the offline maps corresponding to the estimated fault strength of diameter $d = 12$mm. Notice that there is small chattering observed due to added perturbations as a part of a local PI + ESC controller, but at $t = 10$ second, the control values are replaced with the globally optimal control injection parameters generated for a particular fault strength. This results in a slightly lower fuel consumption to obtain the same desired torque. Also, notice that the local feedback controller increases the value

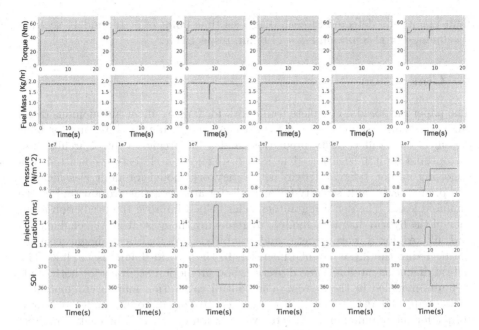

Fig. 11. The torque, fuel mass flow rate, and control input parameters (pressure, duration, and SOI) obtained for the six cylinders in the case of fuel injector clogging.

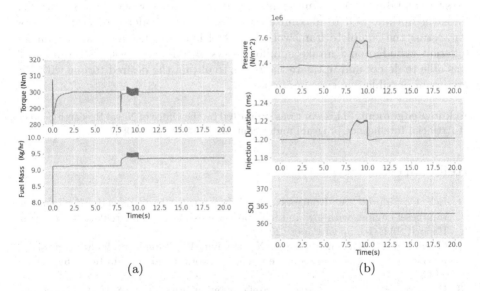

(a)   (b)

Fig. 12. (a) The total torque and fuel mass flow rate. (b) The control input parameters (pressure, duration, and SOI) for the case of intake manifold leak.

of the injection pressure and injection duration with no change in the value of SOI, but the global control map shifts the injection pressure and injection duration to a lower value and thus resulting in a more fuel-efficient result. The fault magnitude detected at each diagnosis time point of 5, 10, and 15 secs are $d = 0$mm, $d = 11.8$mm, and $d = 11.6$mm, respectively.

6 Conclusion

The paper proposed a complete framework for fault-resilient autonomous diesel engine systems. We developed a hybrid machine learning architecture for fault classification, fault severity prediction, and a hierarchical control architecture for optimal fault mitigation. The hybrid diagnosis architecture consisted of a denoising autoencoder and twin neural network model for fault classification and prediction of fault severity for fuel injector area clogging/erosion, and intake manifold leaks. The denoising autoencoder helped improve the prediction accuracy of the hybrid diagnosis module by removing the noise from the engine data and allowed for a more general and computationally efficient diagnosis module by fixing the input latent dimension to the hybrid diagnosis module. The hybrid diagnosis module showed overall good prediction accuracy for both kinds of faults modeled in the system. The control calibration maps were generated offline using BO and provided the optimal control inputs to maintain the desired torque for the nominal and predicted value of fault severity. The control module further used an online PI and ES controller to compensate for modeling errors and inaccurate engine fault predictions. The PI controller controls the injection pressure and duration and maintains the desired torque, while the ES controller finds the optimal SOI to maximize the torque. We considered several scenarios for testing the complete framework with fuel injector clogging and erosion for different cylinders and intake manifold leaks of different sizes. The framework was able to detect and mitigate the faults to obtain the desired torque with the minimum possible fuel consumption.

Acknowledgement. This work was supported by the Office of Naval Research Science of Artificial Intelligence program under contract N00014-20-C-1065.

References

1. Eck, C., Sidorow, A., Konigorski, U., Isermann, R.: Fault detection for common rail diesel engines with low and high pressure exhaust gas recirculation. Technical Report, SAE Technical Paper (2011)
2. Guoqiang, Z., Baozhu, J., Feng, X., Huaiyu, W.: Intelligent fault diagnosis of marine diesel engine based on deep belief network. Chin. J. Ship Res. **15**(3), 136–142 (2020)
3. Hellstrom, E., Lee, D., Jiang, L., Stefanopoulou, A.G., Yilmaz, H.: On-board calibration of spark timing by extremum seeking for flex-fuel engines. IEEE Trans. control Syst. Technol. **6**(21), 2273–2279 (2013)
4. Heywood, J.B.: Internal Combustion Engine Fundamentals. McGraw-Hill Education, New York (2018)
5. Karniadakis, G.E., Kevrekidis, I.G., Lu, L., Perdikaris, P., Wang, S., Yang, L.: Physics-informed machine learning. Nat. Rev. Phys. **3**(6), 422–440 (2021)

6. Kitazono, S., Sugihira, S., Ohmori, H.: Starting speed control of SI engine based on extremum seeking control. IFAC Proc. Volumes **41**(2), 1036–1041 (2008)
7. Krstić, M., Wang, H.H.: Stability of extremum seeking feedback for general nonlinear dynamic systems. Automatica **36**(4), 595–601 (2000)
8. Nohra, C., Noura, H., Younes, R.: A linear approach with μ-analysis control adaptation for a complete-model diesel-engine diagnosis. In: 2009 Chinese Control and Decision Conference, pp. 5415–5420. IEEE (2009)
9. Nyberg, M., Perkovic, A., Nielsen, L.: Model based diagnosis of leaks in the air-intake system of an SI-engine. SAE SPEC PUBL, SAE, WARRENDALE, PA, (USA), Feb 1998, vol. 1357, pp. 25–31 (1998)
10. Popovic, D., Jankovic, M., Magner, S., Teel, A.R.: Extremum seeking methods for optimization of variable cam timing engine operation. IEEE Trans. Control Syst. Technol. **14**(3), 398–407 (2006)
11. Rahimi, M., Pourramezan, M.R., Rohani, A.: Modeling and classifying the in-operando effects of wear and metal contaminations of lubricating oil on diesel engine: a machine learning approach. Expert Syst. Appl. **203**, 117494 (2022)
12. Shahriari, B., Swersky, K., Wang, Z., Adams, R.P., De Freitas, N.: Taking the human out of the loop: a review of bayesian optimization. Proc. IEEE **104**(1), 148–175 (2015)
13. Stefanopoulou, A.G., Kolmanovsky, I., Freudenberg, J.S.: Control of variable geometry turbocharged diesel engines for reduced emissions. IEEE Trans. Control Syst. Technol. **8**(4), 733–745 (2000)
14. Tan, Q., Divekar, P.S., Tan, Y., Chen, X., Zheng, M.: Pressure sensor data-driven optimization of combustion phase in a diesel engine. IEEE/ASME Trans. Mech. **25**(2), 694–704 (2020)
15. Vachtsevanos, G., Lee, B., Oh, S., Balchanos, M.: Resilient design and operation of cyber physical systems with emphasis on unmanned autonomous systems. J. Intell. Robot. Syst. **91**(1), 59–83 (2018)
16. Wahlström, J., Eriksson, L.: Modelling diesel engines with a variable-geometry turbocharger and exhaust gas recirculation by optimization of model parameters for capturing non-linear system dynamics. Proc. Inst. Mech. Eng. Part D: J. Autom. Eng. **225**(7), 960–986 (2011)
17. Yu, X., Zhu, L., Wang, Y., Filev, D., Yao, X.: Internal combustion engine calibration using optimization algorithms. Appl. Energy **305**, 117894 (2022)

Machine Learning for Predicting Production Disruptions in the Wood-Based Panels Industry: A Demonstration Case

Cláudia Afonso[1,2] , Arthur Matta[1,2] , Luís Miguel Matos[2] ,
Miguel Bastos Gomes[3], Antonina Santos[3] , André Pilastri[1] ,
and Paulo Cortez[2(✉)]

[1] EPMQ, CCG/ZGDV Institute, Guimarães, Portugal
{claudia.afonso,arthur.matta,andre.pilastri}@ccg.pt
[2] ALGORITMI/LASI, Department Information Systems, University of Minho,
Guimarães, Portugal
{luis.matos,pcortez}@dsi.uminho.pt
[3] SONAE Arauco Portugal, S.A.,, Oliveira do Hospital, Portugal
{miguel.gomes,antonina.santos}@sonaearauco.com

Abstract. In this paper, we study the application of Machine Learning (ML) in detecting and predicting Ahead-of-Time (AoT) production disruptions in a Portuguese Wood-Based Panels Industry. Assuming an Industry 4.0 concept, the analyzed ML classification task presents several challenges, such as a high number of Internet of Things (IoT) sensors, high-velocity data generation and extremely imbalanced data. To solve these issues, we adapt and compare five state-of-the-art ML algorithms for anomaly detection. Moreover, we preprocess the big data and employ a Selective Sampling (SS) technique to train and test computationally efficient ML models. Overall, high-quality results were obtained by an eXtreme Gradient Boosting (XGBoost) model, both in terms of detection and AoT prediction of production stoppages. Finally, we applied an eXplainable AI (XAI) technique based on sensitivity analysis to the XGBoost model, enabling the understanding of the impact of the sensor inputs on the disruption condition.

Keywords: Anomaly Detection · Industry 4.0 · Machine Learning · Ahead-of-Time Prediction

1 Introduction

The Industry 4.0 paradigm is causing a transformation in diverse industries. Advanced Information Technologies (IT), such as the Internet of Things (IoT), Big Data, Artificial Intelligence (AI) and Machine Learning (ML), can enable more efficient and intelligent manufacturing [7,15]. In particular, ML has emerged as a powerful tool in several Industry 4.0 applications, such as Product

© IFIP International Federation for Information Processing 2023
Published by Springer Nature Switzerland AG 2023
I. Maglogiannis et al. (Eds.): AIAI 2023, IFIP AICT 676, pp. 340–351, 2023.
https://doi.org/10.1007/978-3-031-34107-6_27

Quality Assessment, Predictive Maintenance (PdM) and Detection of Production Anomalies [14].

In this paper, we demonstrate the usefulness of an ML approach to detect and even predict Ahead-of-Time (AoT) Production Disruptions related to a Portuguese Wood-Based Panels Industry. The final goal is to create a digital twin to simulate the stoppages conditions and ultimately prevent their occurrence by employing a prior intelligent control of some relevant production variables (e.g., top and bottom plate temperatures of the press operation). The analyzed AoT binary classification task ("normal production", "stoppage") corresponds to an instance of the Machine Learning based Early Decision Making (ML-EDM) general problem, which is considered challenging [1]. Indeed, the Wood-Based Panels AoT production disruption task is nontrivial for three main reasons. Firstly, it involves a large number of IoT sensors, resulting in hundreds of potential inputs. Second, the sensors generate data at a high velocity, creating big data that requires a prohibitive ML computational effort. For instance, the analyzed period of nine months corresponds to around 360 Gb of raw production data. Thirdly, the data is extremely imbalanced, with only a small fraction of the data records corresponding to stoppages (around 2%).

To handle the AoT stoppage detection task, we adapt and compare five state-of-the-art anomaly detection ML algorithms: unsupervised – Isolation Forest (IF) and deep Autoencoder (AE); and supervised – Random Forest (RF), eXtreme Gradient Boosting (XGBoost), and a Deep FeedForward Neural network (DFFN). The five algorithms are compared regarding their computational effort and AoT predictive performance. For the ML experimentation, we create two production stoppage datasets: **Full2d** – corresponding to two days of full data and used in preliminary ML experiments; and **SS9m** – which assumes a novel Selective Sampling (SS) that is executed over the full nine-month big data, resulting in a much smaller dataset that allows to adequately train and test the ML algorithms while making a reasonable usage of computational resources. Within our knowledge, our approach is novel when compared with state-of-the-art works. For instance, some of the explored ML algorithms have been applied to predict production machine failures in the wood industry, such as executed in [3] (XGBoost and RF) and [16] (IF and AE). However, none of these works studied AoT stoppage prediction or employed a SS to handle big data. Moreover, we employ an eXplainable AI (XAI) technique based on sensitivity analysis [6] to the best AoT predictive model, which allows for demonstrating the impact of the adopted sensor inputs in the stoppage condition.

2   Materials and Methods

2.1   Industrial Data

The collected raw data assumed 221 IoT sensors installed on distinct wood-based panels' production line machines, recorded from May 2021 to February 2022. These sensors provide a continuous data stream on diverse aspects of the production line, including machine conditions, the goods being produced and the materials being used. To facilitate the analysis of the sensor data, we categorized them into 7 distinct groups based on their similarities, as shown in Table 1.

Table 1. Groups of IoT sensors with similar characteristics

Group	Description	# sensors	# records
Infeed	Board and paper infeed area (e.g., active station)	46	4,514,999
Press	Press area (e.g., temperature)	53	65,392,678
Cut	Cut area (e.g., intensity)	13	7,653,753
Edge Cleaner	Edge cleaner area (e.g., trimmer speed)	25	22,739,428
Stacking	Stacking area (e.g., elevation speed)	36	2,777,763
General	General information of the production order (e.g., shift)	48	15,510,539
Materials	Raw materials used (e.g., melamine code)	42	28,322,721

To differentiate between sensor readings captured during regular production and those captured during disruptions, we relied on previous disruptions' start and end timestamps in the production line. The database accessed contained also a distinctive identifier for the specific area of the production line where the reading took place. It should be noted that distinct sensors have different data generation frequencies. For instance, some sensors produce multiple readings per minute while others only produce one value every 10 min. Thus, the raw data records are not produced at regular time intervals but only when there is at least one sensor reading. When such a reading occurs with a timestamp t, all previous unchanged sensor values are repeated, thus each data record contains all received sensor values at time t. On average, 3 records are produced for each second.

For ML experimentation purposes, we created two datasets: Full2d and SS9m. The first Full2d was aimed at a preliminary ML proof-of-concept, to test if the ML stoppage detection was possible and a computationally feasible task. Given the sheer volume of data, it only includes the first two days of raw production data, which corresponds to 448,058 records related to 5 production stoppages. In the preprocessing stage, all empty, constant, or categorical input variables that directly signaled a stoppage condition were removed, resulting in a total of 95 variables. Then, the remaining categorical inputs were transformed into numeric values by assuming a simple label encoding.

As for the second dataset (SS9m), it assumes a Selective Sampling (SS) that covers with more detail all stoppages and normal conditions rear these stoppages while retaining a realistic imbalanced disruption ratio of examples (Fig. 1). The rationale is to allow an AoT analysis closer to and during stoppage events rather than prolonged normal production stages. The SS method is applied for all production segments, where each segment is made of a normal working cycle that is ended by a disruption. In this work, we assume a total of $N = 5$ consecutive records that occur at the beginning of a stoppage. Since the ratio of non-disruption to disruption records is $R=49{:}1$, we sample a total of $49 \times N = 245$

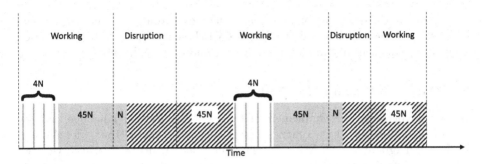

Fig. 1. Schematic of the proposed Selective Sampling (SS) approach.

normal production examples that occur before a stoppage. Around $45 \times N = 225$ of these examples occur sequentially before the disruption event, thus resulting in a denser sampling that allows an AoT prediction analysis (shown as a gray area in Fig. 1). The other $4 \times N = 20$ normal instances (area with vertical gray lines) are sampled at larger and equally spaced intervals within the previous normal working zone of the production segment, with exception of the initial segment records (stripped area) that are ignored (total of $45 \times N$ instances). The excluded area (stripped zone in Fig. 1) includes a stoppage staled status (uninteresting data), a manual production reboot (which is not predictable), and its subsequent initial machine rebooting readings. We note that the adopted N=5 value allowed to create a reasonable sized SS dataset related with the whole nine month raw data.

After consulting the wood-based panel production experts, the SS9m dataset was filtered to only include disruptions up to the press stage, since these correspond to the stoppages that have more impact on the well-functioning of the production process and some disruptions after the press stage are not even predictable. Thus, all data features related to sensors after the press area were excluded, which includes those in the "edge cleaner", "cut", and "stacking" groups. Also, all data records that occur after the press area were removed. Furthermore, a more in-depth data quality feature selection preprocessing was conducted by employing an exploratory data analysis. As the result of this analysis, features that met at least one of the following criteria were removed: contain reading interruptions over time (missing data); represent a theoretical or a predefined value, not a real measured one; describe another feature; remain nearly constant throughout the entire period; has no relevance to the study; have timestamps that do not accurately reflect the actual time of the readings; Or are highly correlated with another feature (correlation coefficient higher than 0.95). The final set of input variables included a total of 68 distinct sensor readings. Then, the known One-Hot (OH) encoding technique was applied to the categorical attributes, transforming each categorical level into a numeric input that represents a boolean value (0 or 1) by using the Python package CANE[1] [12]. After

---

[1] https://pypi.org/project/cane/.

preprocessing the data, the SS9m dataset includes a total of 984 numeric inputs and 649,161 records that are related to 68 IoT sensors and 1,107 production segments (sequences of sampled normal and stoppage conditions).

2.2   Machine Learning Methods

All ML algorithms were implemented by using the Python language and the following modules: scikit-learn[2] – for IF and RF; TensorFlow[3] – for AE and DFFN; and Xgboost[4] – for XGBoost classifier model. Unless stated otherwise, we adopt the default Python implementation values for the ML hyperparameters.

RF is a supervised ML algorithm that utilizes an ensemble of individual decision trees to form a prediction. Each decision tree is built using a random selection of input variables and a subset of training samples, known as bagging [2]. The RF algorithm is used to predict anomaly class probabilities, where the resulting values ($d_i \in [0.0, 1.0]$) represent the degree of anomaly present in the input data instance.

XGBoost is another ML tree ensemble that employs gradient boosting, assuming a loss function to evaluate the accuracy of the predictions made by each tree base learner. XGBoost has been demonstrated to outperform several other ML algorithms in diverse predictive modeling tasks [4].

The DFFN model is a deep learning architecture that includes several hyperparameters that are often set using heuristics and trial-and-error experiments [10]. In this paper, we adopt the dense network structure presented [13], which assumes a triangular-shaped multilayer perceptron, in which each subsequent layer size is smaller. The DFFN hyperparameters were tunned using preliminary experiments that were conducted using only the training data, from which 30% of the most recent values were used as the validation set. For both datasets, the DFFN includes a fixed structure with 8 hidden layers, with the following number of nodes: (I, 1024, 512, 256, 128, 64, 32, 16, 8, 1), where I denotes the number of inputs. The hidden nodes use the linear (Full2d) and Leaky ReLu (SS9m) activation functions, while the output node of both DFFNs computes the logistic function, to output the abnormal class probability. The popular Adam optimizer, with a batch size of 1024 and a binary cross-entropy loss function, was used to train the DFFNs. The training algorithm was stopped when the validation error does not improve or after a maximum of 100 epochs.

The Isolation Forest (IF) is a one-class ML algorithm, that utilizes the concept of isolation, where an anomaly is expected to be more isolated compared to normal data points [11]. The algorithm constructs a forest of decision trees. Each tree is grown by recursively partitioning the dataset into two random parts until the anomalies are isolated in their tree branches. The anomalies are isolated due to their inherent rarity and a high degree of difference from standard data points. The scikit-learn IF implementation provides a decision score that

---

[2] https://scikit-learn.org/stable/.
[3] https://www.tensorflow.org/.
[4] https://xgboost.readthedocs.io/.

ranges from $\hat{y}_i = -1$ (highest abnormal score) to $\hat{y}_i = 1$ (highest normal score). This score was normalized such that the final disruption probability is set within the [0,1] range.

Autoencoders (AEs) use an unsupervised learning method that can efficiently compress data into a lower-dimensional representation [10]. In this paper, we assume the AE proposed in [9], which uses a deep dense multilayer perceptron with a bottleneck layer of L_b hidden nodes and that includes two components. The first component is a triangular-shaped encoder that starts with I inputs. Then, the number of hidden layer units decreases by half in each subsequent hidden layer, until three hidden layers are defined. For instance, for the SS9m dataset, the encoder includes the following number of layer nodes: ($I = 984$, 492, 246, $L_b = 123$). The second decoder component shape is symmetric to the encoder, ending up with I output nodes. When adapted for anomaly detection, the AE training algorithm is only fed with normal instances and the goal is to generate output values identical to the inputs. The same Adam optimizer used to train the supervised DFFN model is adopted to train the AE, with the exception that the Mean Absolute Error (MAE) is used as the loss function. The same MAE value is used as the reconstruction error. The higher the reconstruction score, the higher the anomaly class probability, thus the predictive MAE error for a new instance was normalized (using training data) within the [0,1] range. In preliminary experiments (using only training data), we compared two AE hidden function activations (ReLU and linear). The best results were obtained by the linear activation AEs, which were used in the ML comparison experiments.

To extract XAI knowledge from a trained ML model we adopt the computationally efficient one-Dimensional Sensitivity Analysis (1D-SA) method proposed in [6]. The method involves fixing all ML inputs at their average values, except for a target input that is ranged with $L=7$ distinct levels. The ML responses are stored and then the overall input relevance is computed based on the Average Absolute Deviation (AAD) measure applied to the sensitivity responses. The Variable Effect Characteristic (VEC) curves can also be produced, plotting the overall sensitivity analysis effect of an input response on the target output. This XAI method was implemented by using the `rminer` package of the R tool[5][5].

2.3   Evaluation

The predictive anomaly detection performance is based on the Receiver Operating Characteristic curve [8]. When a classifier outputs a decision score d_t at time t, the class can be interpreted as positive if $d_t > K$, where K is a fixed decision threshold, otherwise it is considered negative. With the class predictions, there will be True Positives (TP), True Negatives (TP), False Positives (FP) and False Negatives (FN). The ROC curve shows the performance of a two-class classifier across all $K \in [0,1]$ values, plotting one minus the specificity (x-axis), or False Positive Rate (FPR), versus the sensitivity (y-axis), or True Positive Rate (TPR). The discrimination performance is given by the Area Under the

---

[5] https://CRAN.R-project.org/package=rminer.

Curve (AUC): $AUC = \int_0^1 ROCdK$. It is common to interpret the quality of the AUC values as: 0.5 – equal to a random classifier; 0.6 – reasonable; 0.7 – good; 0.8 – very good; 0.9 – excellent; and 1 – perfect. We also record the computational effort, in terms of the total training time (in s) and prediction response time for all test instances (in s) when using a 2.4 GHz i9 Intel processor. Given that both datasets (Full2d and SS9m) are quite large, in all ML experiments we assume one execution of a time-ordered holdout split, where the oldest 70% records were used as the training set and the more recent 30% of the examples were used as the test set.

For the 9th month data (SS9m), we also perform an AoT analysis, where a distinct ROC curve is computed for different AoT prediction time values ($A \in \{0, 1, ..., A_{max}\}$). Let y_t denote the target output values at time t, where t is a time-ordered example from the analyzed data (e.g., test set). The AoT analysis is performed for each production segment, by considering the target output values from the first normal event ($y_{t_n} = 0$ at time t_n) of the segment until the last stoppage event ($y_{t_s} = 1$ at time t_s). The goal is to only analyze sensor-based predictable normal or stoppage events since a production reboot (the return of a normal condition) is executed manually. When $A = 0$, a strict stoppage detection is performed, by comparing all predicted anomaly scores d_t from the production segment with the target output values (y_t). An AoT prediction occurs when $A > 0$, where the ROC curve is built by matching the d_{t-A} predictions with the same target output values (y_t). In this work, the AoT analysis is achieved by computing a proposed AoT Stoppage Prediction Graph (ASG). The ASG plot shows the evolution of the AUC values (y-axis) for the ROC curves associated with an increasing A value (x-axis). As mentioned in Sect. 2.1, on average there are around 3 data records per second. For the AoT analysis, we set $A_{max} = 15$, which corresponds to an average maximum AoT prediction of 5 s.

3   Results

Table 2 summarizes the results obtained by five ML algorithms on the two analyzed datasets, namely Full2d and SS9m. The stoppage detection (thus $A = 0$) metric is the AUC of the ROC curve, while the full training and test computational effort times are shown in seconds.

In terms of the Full2d data, the best detection was obtained by the supervised deep learning model (DFFN, with an AUC of 99%), followed by the unsupervised IF (94%) and then RF and AE (91%). However, these preliminary results should be analyzed with some caution, since the Full2d dataset only covers two days of data, with the training set containing only 3 stoppages and the test set 2 production disruption events. Thus, rather than ranking the ML algorithm results for this dataset, the obtained AUC values do show that there is a potential to detect wood-based panel production disruptions since they were substantially higher than a random classifier (AUC of 50%). As for the computational effort, the lighter training algorithm was the RF (2 s), while the faster prediction time was obtained by XGBoost (0.1 s). And as expected, the deep learning algorithms (DFFN and AE) required substantially higher training times.

After obtaining the promising but initial Full2d results, we designed the SS and created the more representative SS9m, which covers all 1,107 stoppages that occur during nine months. When using this dataset, the AUC results favor the supervised learning methods, with the best result achieved by XGBoost (97%), followed by DFFN (94%) and RF (92%). In contrast, the unsupervised methods produce much worse results, closer to the random classifier performance (AE – 59%; IF – 48%). Regarding the computational effort, the ML training times are very reasonable. For instance, XGBoost requires only five minutes to fit a model when using around 454 thousand training samples that cover around 6 months of production time. As for the test time, it is much faster, only requiring around 2.5 s to produce around 195,000 predictions. This clearly attests to the usefulness of the proposed SS, which allows training some lightweight ML models that achieve a high-quality detection performance, with the test set including a realistic sample with around 330 stoppages.

Table 2. Stoppage detection results (best values in **bold**).

Dataset	Method	Model	Train Time (s)	Test Time (s)	AUC
Full2d	Supervised Learning	XGBoost	18.19	**0.10**	0.72
		RF	**2.02**	0.35	0.91
		DFFN	406.57	16.02	**0.99**
	Unsupervised Learning	AE	43.65	**4.46**	0.91
		IF	**5.04**	6.22	**0.94**
SS9m	Supervised Learning	XGBoost	315.55	**2.58**	**0.97**
		RF	**61.56**	3.28	0.92
		DFFN	266.55	26.71	0.94
	Unsupervised Learning	AE	**238.78**	**45.29**	**0.59**
		IF	355.63	55.31	0.48

Given the SS9m AUC results, an AoT analysis was further executed using only the supervised ML algorithms, which is shown by the ASG plotted in Fig. 2. For the full AoT time (around 5 s on average), all three ML algorithms are capable of producing interesting AoT AUC values. In particular, the XGBoost results are highlighted (blue curve), since it always produces the highest AUC values when compared with DFFN (second best model) and RF. Moreover, the XGBoost AUC values are of excellent quality, higher than 90% for most of the A range of values (e.g., up to $A=10$).

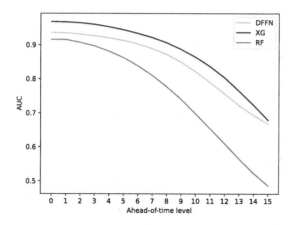

Fig. 2. AoT Stoppage Prediction Graph (ASG) for the supervised ML models.

For demonstration purposes, Fig. 3 shows the individual ROC curves for the selected XGBoost model that were computed for pure detection ($A = 0$) and a large AoT prediction ($A = 15$).

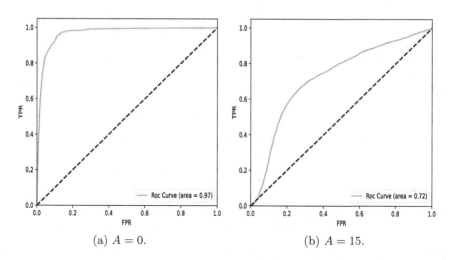

(a) $A = 0$.   (b) $A = 15$.

Fig. 3. ROC curves for the XGBoost model and the two ASG extreme A values.

To further demonstrate the application domain value of the XGBoost AoT prediction model, we applied the SA XAI approach described in Sect. 2.2. Figure 4(a) plots the obtained input importance for the five most relevant input features. For instance, the most influential input is related to the number of press cycles (total relevance of 19%). As for Fig. 4(b), it shows the Variable Effect Characteristic (VEC) curves for the same five top relevant inputs (the x-axis denotes the full range of input domain values, while the y-axis denotes the overall obtained prediction output). The plot reveals that the most influential input (Number of Press Cycles) produces the largest XGBoost output response change (thus impacting more on the model). It also confirms that some types of materials (melamine code) are more prone to produce stoppages. In general, an increase in the numeric input also produces an increase in the production line stoppage probability. The obtained XAI knowledge was also provided to the production experts, which confirmed that both input influence and input effects were interesting.

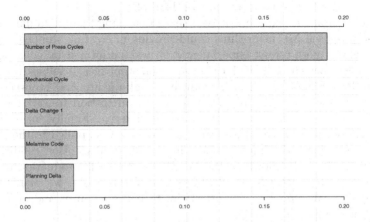

(a) Importance values (in %) for the top five relevant inputs.

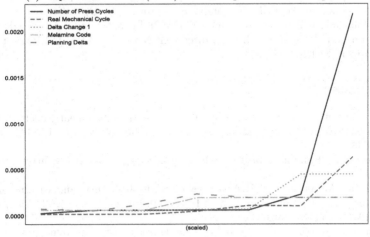

(b) Top 5 input VEC curves.

Fig. 4. Extracted XAI knowledge from the XGBoost model.

4   Conclusions

In this paper, we demonstrate the usefulness of using a Machine Learning (ML) approach to detect and predict Ahead-of-Time (AoT) production disruptions related to a Portuguese Wood-Based Panels Industry. We adapt and compare five state-of-the-art anomaly detection ML algorithms: unsupervised - Isolation Forest and deep Autoencoder; and supervised - Random Forest, XGBoost, and a Deep FeedForward Neural network. From the collected raw big data, we create and preprocess two production stoppage datasets: a shorter dataset including two days of full data (Full2d) and a Selective Sampling (SS) dataset comprising all interesting events during a nine months (SS9m).

First, preliminary experiments were executed using the Full2d data, showing that the proposed ML algorithms could provide interesting stoppage detection results. Then, more robust experimentation was performed by considering the SS9m dataset, which includes 1,107 production stoppages. The best results were obtained by the XGBoost, which produces a high-quality AoT stoppage prediction performance (ranging from 97% for a pure detection to 72% for an AoT of 5 s) under a reasonable computational effort usage. Finally, an eXplainable AI (XAI) approach based on a sensitivity analysis was applied to the XGBoost model, presenting the influence of the inputs in the disruption condition. The obtained results were shown to the Wood-Based Panels production managers, which provided positive feedback. Indeed, in future work, we plan to deploy the proposed ML model as a digital twin, to better monitor and even prevent production stoppages.

Acknowledgements. This work was supported by the European Structural and Investment Funds in the FEDER Component through the Operational Competitiveness and Internationalization Programme (COMPETE 2020) under Advanced Decision Making in productive systems through Intelligent Networks (ADM.IN) Project 055087 (POCI-01-0247-FEDER-055087).

References

1. Bondu, A., et al.: Open challenges for machine learning based early decision-making research. SIGKDD Explor. **24**(2), 12–31 (2022). https://doi.org/10.1145/3575637.3575643
2. Breiman, L.: Random forests. Mach. Learn. **45**(1), 5–32 (2001). https://doi.org/10.1023/A:1010933404324
3. Calabrese, M., et al.: SOPHIA: an event-based iot and machine learning architecture for predictive maintenance in industry 4.0. Inf. **11**(4), 202 (2020). https://doi.org/10.3390/info11040202
4. Chen, T., Guestrin, C.: XGBoost: A scalable tree boosting system. In: Proceedings of the 22nd acm sigkdd International Conference on Knowledge Discovery and Data Mining, pp. 785–794 (2016). https://doi.org/10.1145/2939672.2939785
5. Cortez, P.: Data mining with neural networks and support vector machines using the R/rminer tool. In: Perner, P. (ed.) ICDM 2010. LNCS (LNAI), vol. 6171, pp. 572–583. Springer, Heidelberg (2010). https://doi.org/10.1007/978-3-642-14400-4_44

6. Cortez, P., Embrechts, M.J.: Using sensitivity analysis and visualization techniques to open black box data mining models. Inf. Sci. **225**, 1–17 (2013). https://doi.org/10.1016/j.ins.2012.10.039

7. Dalzochio, J., et al.: Machine learning and reasoning for predictive maintenance in industry 4.0: current status and challenges. Comput. Ind. **123**, 103298 (2020). https://doi.org/10.1016/j.compind.2020.103298

8. Fawcett, T.: An introduction to ROC analysis. Pattern Recogn. Lett. **27**, 861–874 (2006). https://doi.org/10.1016/j.patrec.2005.10.010

9. Fontes, G., Matos, L.M., Matta, A., Pilastri, A.L., Cortez, P.: An empirical study on anomaly detection algorithms for extremely imbalanced datasets. In: Artificial Intelligence Applications and Innovations - 18th IFIP WG 12.5 International Conference, AIAI 2022, Hersonissos, Crete, Greece, June 17–20, 2022, Proceedings, Part I. IFIP Advances in Information and Communication Technology, vol. 646, pp. 85–95. Springer, Cham (2022). https://doi.org/10.1007/978-3-031-08333-4_7

10. Goodfellow, I., Bengio, Y., Courville, A.: Deep Learning. MIT Press, Cambridge (2016). http://www.deeplearningbook.org

11. Liu, F.T., Ting, K.M., Zhou, Z.: Isolation Forest. In: Proceedings of of the 8th IEEE International Conference on Data Mining (ICDM), Pisa, Italy. pp. 413–422. IEEE (2008). https://doi.org/10.1109/ICDM.2008.17

12. Matos, L.M., Azevedo, J., Matta, A., Pilastri, A., Cortez, P., Mendes, R.: Categorical attribute traNsformation environment (CANE): a python module for categorical to numeric data preprocessing. Softw. Impacts 100359 (2022). https://doi.org/10.1016/j.simpa.2022.100359

13. Matos, L.M., Cortez, P., Mendes, R., Moreau, A.: A deep learning-based decision support system for mobile performance marketing. Int. J. Inf. Technol. Decis. Making (IJITDM) **22**(02), 679–703 (2023). https://doi.org/10.1142/S021962202250047X

14. Silva, A.J., Cortez, P., Pereira, C., Pilastri, A.L.: Business analytics in/industry 4.0: a systematic review. Expert Syst. **38**(7) (2021). https://doi.org/10.1111/exsy.12741

15. Singh, H.: Big data, industry 4.0 and cyber-physical systems integration: a smart industry context. Mater. Today: Proc. **46**, 157–162 (2021). https://doi.org/10.1016/j.matpr.2020.07.170

16. Özgün, K., Aklan, S., Tekin, A., Cebi, F.: Malfunction detection on production line using machine learning: case study in wood industry, pp. 1116–1124 (2021). https://doi.org/10.1007/978-3-030-51156-2_130

ML-Based Prediction of Carbon Emissions for Potato Farms in Iran

Seyedeh Razieh Ehsani Amrei$^{(\boxtimes)}$ [iD], Lakshmi Babu-Saheer[iD],
and Cristina Luca[iD]

School of Computing and Information Sciences, Anglia Ruskin University,
Cambridge, UK
se573@pgr.aru.ac.uk, {lakshmi.babu-saheer,cristina.luca}@aru.ac.uk

Abstract. Agriculture is one of the main contributors to carbon emissions. Understanding different processes involved in farming and estimating the carbon emissions in each step can help in accurately calculating the carbon factor and support in optimizing and reducing the carbon emissions. Potato is a popular food product cultivated across the world. Potato farming involves several processes such as preparing the land, using fertilizers and manures, irrigation, and plowing, and all these steps have been contemplated to generate carbon emissions. This article investigates the steps involved in potato cultivation as a case study and generates standardized features related to carbon emissions in each step. Different machine learning and deep learning algorithms are used to model these standard features. This research predicts the carbon emission using different regression models such as random Forest, multiple linear regression, lasso regression, K-Nearest Neighbour, and neural network regression and finally compares them based on the metrics of root-mean-square error (RMSE) and R^2. The results show that all the models have comparable performance with a R^2 score very close to 1 and very low RMSE. The novelty of the work is in introducing standard features for modeling carbon emissions in agriculture which help to streamline different farming datasets even across different crops.

Keywords: Carbon factor · Farming · Feature Standarisation ·
Regression models · Machine Learning · Deep Learning

1 Introduction

The world population is currently approximately 7.9 billion, which is estimated to reach 9.7 billion by 2050, and may even reach 11.2 billion by 2100 [20]. The need for food in the world is expected to increase due to this growing population which calls for a rapid increase in food production, both in agriculture and factory-processed food products. Some studies have also reported a sudden surge in the amount of food intake by individuals [19]. Potato is one of the popular food among people and paying attention to its production process will be beneficial both in terms of climate and economy. Agricultural crops including

© IFIP International Federation for Information Processing 2023
Published by Springer Nature Switzerland AG 2023
I. Maglogiannis et al. (Eds.): AIAI 2023, IFIP AICT 676, pp. 352–361, 2023.
https://doi.org/10.1007/978-3-031-34107-6_28

potatoes have the potential to play an important role in reducing climate change. Farming processes can be optimized to reduce greenhouse gas (GHG) emissions and hence, support climate action. Potato often has lower GHG emissions and water needs than other staple products (maize, rice, and wheat) on a per-calorie basis [12]. A comparative study on potatoes, pasta, and basmati rice using the life cycle assessment (LCA) approach showed that potato production and distribution generated less carbon than pasta and basmati rice [7]. But any amount of carbon emission optimization can support climate action and can be easily translated and generalized to other food products. Research on four types of potato production in Zimbabwe showed that the use of fertilizers and emissions from soil contributed to the largest proportion of carbon emissions [18]. Common features like energy and fuel consumption can be identified for each stage of farming and can be translated into carbon equivalent which in total will help in the prediction of carbon emissions across all farming processes. Similar studies on potato farms have proved that GHG emissions can be reduced by cutting down the energy usage [4]. LCA has been used traditionally to estimate energy consumption but, recently, Machine Learning algorithms have been proven to be more powerful.

This paper presents a novel approach for predicting the carbon factor in potato farming by using standardized features. The farming-related information from the dataset considered in this research is transformed into standard features that represent the carbon factors in each step of the entire farming process. Such efforts of standardization of features can help to align different datasets and streamline features used for carbon emission modeling without having to deal with the intricate details or differences in farming conditions even across different crops. The potato farming dataset is used as a case study here. This technique can be easily scaled to other crops or farms. Five Machine Learning models have been evaluated and their results compared using two different metrics.

This paper is organized as follows. Section 2 presents the related work; Sect. 3 describes the methods used in this research; Sect. 4 discusses the results and presents the evaluation done. Finally, the conclusions are drawn in Sect. 5 where future work is also presented.

2   Related Work

Environmental degradation and climate crisis are among the most complex issues in the world today that require creative solutions to improve the situation. In total, about 65% of GHG emissions are generated by the energy sector, while about 15% is from agriculture [11,16]. Farmers are often concerned about crop protection, weather forecasting, proper irrigation management, site nutrient management, and crop yield as well as harvesting prediction [3], while most of the time, GHG emissions and their impact on the environment are neglected. In this regard, research performed in Slovenia developed a model to calculate the total greenhouse gas emission of agricultural products including grains and fruit as an entire integrated process. Results showed energy consumption and productivity have an influence on the amount of carbon footprint [2].

A comprehensive discussion about the role of artificial intelligence (AI) and Internet of Things (IoT) analysis in agri-food systems including greenhouse monitoring has been presented by Misra et al. [14]. AI can be used in validating food production processes and predicting parameters such as carbon footprint [13]. In [15], an artificial neural network (ANN) was selected as the best model to predict the output of energy including carbon emission. The findings showed in rice production that farm emissions have an important influence on global warming and acidification. A long short-term memory (LSTM) method is used as a deep learning approach for forecasting time-series carbon dioxide emission in [5]. [17] shows that the Support Vector Machine (SVM) has been successfully used to predict carbon emission in the alcohol industry and had the smallest Root Mean Square Error (RMSE).

Our study follows the research of [9], which investigated the GHG emission and energy output in potato farming using an ANN model. Other reviewed studies have not fully considered the characteristics of crop cultivation or have not used machine learning algorithms to improve the results. This paper attempts to consider both neglected characteristics and various Machine Learning models. [9] shows that the important factors in emitting carbon for potato cultivation are electricity, fertilizer and seeds, and the total amount of carbon released was calculated as 116.4 kg for every ton of potatoes produced. The authors used an artificial neural network, and the coefficient of determination (R^2) was reported to be 0.98 for energy and 0.99 for greenhouse gas emissions [9]. Also, in the previous study, the standardization of the features was not done. In addition, work has been done on bespoke data and only one model of artificial intelligence was used to carry out. These gaps have strengthened the need for more research in the field of investigating the carbon factor in potato cultivation.

In our proposed research, more generic novel features are taken into account to achieve a more realistic result that can be translated and generalized to other farms and products around the world. The carbon emission is calculated more accurately for each step, compared to the previous study. A comprehensive range of algorithms is investigated in this study to obtain more precise and reliable results.

3   Methodology

3.1   Potato Farm Dataset

The potato farm dataset used in this study was collected in 2013 in Fereydounshahr, Isfahan province, Iran. This dataset has information on 266 potato farms, collected through face-to-face questionnaires, and has been used to estimate energy consumption and carbon emissions [9]. This dataset contains a set of field information including land area, type of irrigation, tools of plowing, application of different fertilizers, and diesel and electricity consumption. Figure 1 highlights the percentage of energy consumption in different parts of farm operation in potato prediction.

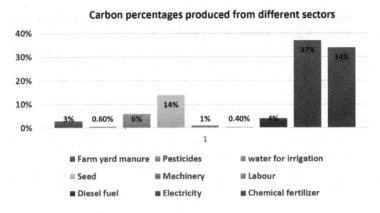

Fig. 1. Carbon produced from different sectors of potato farms [9]

3.2 Feature Standardisation and Engineering

There is a common set of operations for the production of potatoes, which are often used across all parts of the world. These stages and operations of potato cultivation require different resources of energy as highlighted in Fig. 2.

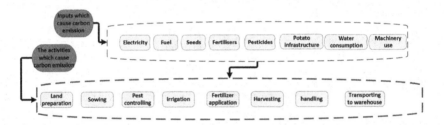

Fig. 2. Inputs and activities which cause carbon emission in potato production

Following a detailed analysis of the dataset, the following features have been selected to be considered in this study as inputs for carbon emission prediction: the cultivated area, the total amount of product harvested from the unit area, the total amount of seed required per unit area, soil texture, the amount of phosphate, potassium, and nitrogen fertilizer per unit surface, the amount of animal manure per unit area, the quantity of vinegar per unit land surface, amount of toxins needed for the production, irrigation type, irrigation frequency, amount of time spent for each irrigation, the total amount of water, fuel, and electricity consumption.

This research proposes a novel set of features, listed din Table 1, to estimate carbon emissions on the basis of the standardization of features identified for farming. Table 1 also shows the carbon emission coefficient values for each of these input features along with related references that were identified for calculating the corresponding carbon coefficients.

Equation 1 calculates PCE, the total carbon emission in the potato farming process.

$$PCE = \sum_{i=1}^{k} I_i * CE_i \tag{1}$$

where I_i is the amount of input for step i; CE_i is the carbon coefficient of step i as displayed in Table 1; i refers to each separate process related to planting, growing and harvesting potatoes for which the carbon emissions are calculated; k is the total number of features.

Table 1. Carbon emission coefficients in potato farm

Input Features	Unit for Coefficients	Carbon coefficient ($kgCO2eq/unit$)
Diesel fuel	L	2.76 [10]
Nitrogen	Kg	1.3 [10]
Phosphate	Kg	0.2 [10]
Potassium	Kg	0.2 [10]
Electricity	Kwh	0.608 [8]
Herbicides	Kg	6.3 [10]
Insecticide	Kg	5.1 [10]
Seed	Ton	115 [6]
Soil	Ha	437 [6]
Farm Yard Manure	Kg	81.2 [1]

3.3   The Regression Models

Four Machine Learning regression models - Random Forest, Multiple Linear Regression, Lasso Regression, K-Nearest Neighbour, and Neural network regression have been used and evaluated in this research. General data cleanup and pre-processing are carried out by removing the missing values in the dataset. The dataset is split into train and test sets with an 80–20% ratio and training data are further divided into validation sets for performing k-fold validation. The models are trained with appropriate hyperparameter optimization in each case. Finally, each model is evaluated with the root mean square error (RMSE) and R^2 metrics.

4   Results and Evaluation

The coefficient of determination(R^2 score) has been used to validate the model predictability, and the performance of applied machine learning models is compared against the feed-forward neural network results presented in an earlier work [9]. To benchmark the ML models, 5-fold cross-validation was utilized along with grid search to find the best hyperparameters on a train-test split of 80–20%. Both R-squared, a relative measure of fit, and RMSE an absolute measure of fit have been used to validate the models. As the square root of the variance, RMSE can be interpreted as the standard deviation of the unexplained variance. It has the useful property of being in the same units as the response variable. Lower values of RMSE indicate a better fit. Notably, all models show comparable performance, and none of them performs significantly better than others as demonstrated in Table 2.

Table 2. ML models performance

Models	R^2	RMSE
Multiple Linear Regression	0.9642	0.0447
Lasso Regression	0.9999	0.0006
Random Forest Regression	0.9862	0.0242
KNN Regression	0.9556	0.0436
Neural Network Regression	0.9996	0.0039
Feed Forward Neural Network [9]	0.9989	0.0273

The strength and direction coefficients of the relationship between two variables can be estimated using the regression coefficient formula. In the current research, a 5-fold cross-validation grid search is used to fine-tune the hyperparameters. For example, in the Multi Linear Regression (MLR) model, the results can be seen in Fig. 3a. It is clearly visible that the efficiency of this model is significantly improved by increasing the number of features. However, as soon as the number of features exceeds 17, the model saturates and becomes overfitted. Therefore, we determined through empirical experiments that the optimal number of features for the MLR model is 17. The performance of the model as measured by the R^2 score is equal to 0.96 in the most optimal state before saturation. The plot of the MLR features' coefficients is displayed in Fig. 4.

Figure 3b illustrates that by implementing the same method for the Lasso Regression model and running a grid search on the Alpha hyperparameter, the best performance is achieved when the Alpha is equal to 0.0 where the R^2 score of the model reaches 0.99. The results obtained indicate that with the increase of alpha, the performance of the model decreases. The best alpha obtained is equal to 0.0, which means that the Lasso model will behave similarly to an Ordinary Least Squares Regression model. The Lasso features coefficients chart

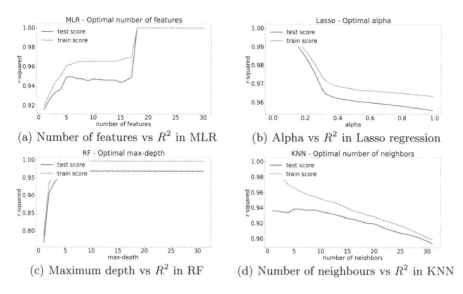

(a) Number of features vs R^2 in MLR   (b) Alpha vs R^2 in Lasso regression

(c) Maximum depth vs R^2 in RF   (d) Number of neighbours vs R^2 in KNN

Fig. 3. Results of a grid search using 5-fold cross-validation to find the best hyperparameters for each model.

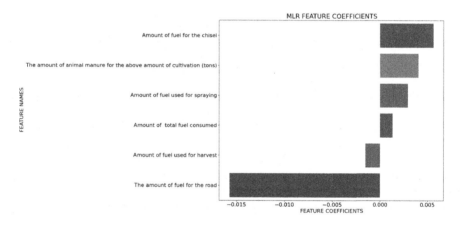

Fig. 4. MLR Coefficients

is displayed in Fig. 5. The performance obtained using a grid search on hyperparameters with cross-validation for the Random Forest model is shown in Fig. 3c. The best result is achieved for depth 8, where R^2 of the model reaches 0.98. The plot of Random Forest feature importance can be found in Fig. 6. In the KNN model, the most important hyperparameter is the number of neighbours. By applying grid a search on hyperparameter values using cross-validation for this model, the best result is obtained for k = 6, where the R^2 of the model is equal to 0.95 which can be seen in Fig. 3d. It can be concluded that simple models can perform this task as effectively as or sometimes even better than neural networks with better explainability.

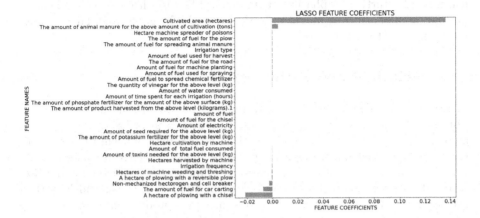

Fig. 5. Lasso Coefficients

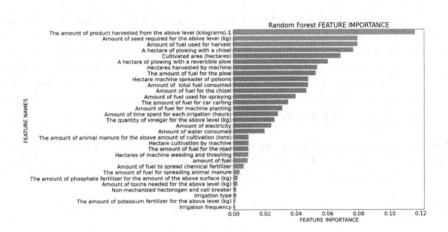

Fig. 6. Feature Importance of the Random Forest Model

The effectiveness of the features being used in our models is also analyzed through feature importance visualizations as presented in this section. It can be noted that different models emphasize a different set of features but give comparable results. Figure 4 shows the coefficients of the multi-linear regression model. MLR performs feature selection and it seems like fuel used especially for transport and other process plays a major role. Figure 5 shows coefficients of the Lasso regression model. Apart from the fuel, this model also gives importance to the size of the farms. Figure 6 shows the feature importance of the Random Forest regression model which also identifies the fuel and farm size as important features, but also relates to the amount of product harvested as one of the main features. This further emphasizes that standard features like the fuel and energy per unit area or per unit weight of the product can be good candidates to unify the farming features and modeling.

5   Conclusions and Future Work

In recent years, researchers have investigated the amount of energy consumption in both agricultural production and industries in order to minimize the amount of carbon emissions. However, there is a scarcity of accurate, clean data that could be used for training artificial intelligence algorithms effectively in this domain. In this study, we demonstrate how features can be standardised across different farms to build simple ML models for this task and how these frameworks can predict carbon emissions in potato production as a case study. This paper presents the results of multiple ML models that were investigated with these novel features representing the farming processes, and it is observed that all ML models achieve comparable results with almost the same amount of computational resources and data samples. In this research, potato agricultural land is only considered as a case study, this means that these models and approaches can be used for similar crop cultivations if sufficient data is available. Simpler ML models can further provide better insights into the features being modeled through the feature importance visualizations. In the current research, prediction for the amount of carbon released was applied to only one product with a selected range of machine learning models. There is great potential for the proposed features and models to be scaled and generalized to other products and regions investigating more models using reliable datasets.

Acknowledgement. We thank the data providers of this work. Datasets were collected by the authors of [9] from the Faculty of Agricultural Engineering and Technology, University of Tehran, Karaj, Iran.

References

1. Aguirre-Villegas, H.A., Larson, R.A.: Evaluating greenhouse gas emissions from dairy manure management practices using survey data and lifecycle tools. J. Clean. Prod. **143**, 169–179 (2017)
2. Al-Mansour, F., Jejcic, V.: A model calculation of the carbon footprint of agricultural products: The case of slovenia. Energy **136**, 7–15 (2017)
3. Angarita-Zapata, J.S., Alonso-Vicario, A., Masegosa, A.D., Legarda, J.: A taxonomy of food supply chain problems from a computational intelligence perspective. Sensors **21**(20), 6910 (2021)
4. Bakhtiari, A.A., Hematian, A., Moradipour, M., et al.: Energy, economic and GHG emissions analysis of potato production. J. Biodivers Environ. Sci. **6**(2), 398–406 (2015)

5. Chen, C.Y., Chai, K.K., Lau, E.: Ai-assisted approach for building energy and carbon footprint modeling. Energy AI **5**, 100091 (2021)
6. Haverkort, A., Hillier, J.G.: Cool farm tool-potato: model description and performance of four production systems. Potato Res. **54**, 355–369 (2011)
7. Hess, T., Chatterton, J., Daccache, A., Williams, A.: The impact of changing food choices on the blue water scarcity footprint and greenhouse gas emissions of the British diet: the example of potato, pasta and rice. J. Clean. Prod. **112**, 4558–4568 (2016)
8. Khodi, M., Mousavi, S.: Life cycle assessment of power generation technology using GHG emissions reduction approach. In: 7th National Energy Congress, pp. 22–23 (2009)
9. Khoshnevisan, B., Rafiee, S., Omid, M., Mousazadeh, H., Rajaeifar, M.A.: Application of artificial neural networks for prediction of output energy and GHG emissions in potato production in Iran. Agric. Syst. **123**, 120–127 (2014)
10. Lal, R.: Carbon emission from farm operations. Environ. Int. **30**, 981–990 (2004)
11. Li, Y., Han, M., Liu, S., Chen, G.: Energy consumption and greenhouse gas emissions by buildings: a multi-scale perspective. Build. Environ. **151**, 240–250 (2019)
12. Liu, B., et al.: Promoting potato as staple food can reduce the carbon-land-water impacts of crops in china. Nature Food **2**(8), 570–577 (2021)
13. Milczarski, P., Zieliński, B., Stawska, Z., Hłobaż, A., Maślanka, P., Kosiński, P.: Machine learning application in energy consumption calculation and assessment in food processing industry. In: Rutkowski, L., Scherer, R., Korytkowski, M., Pedrycz, W., Tadeusiewicz, R., Zurada, J.M. (eds.) ICAISC 2020. LNCS (LNAI), vol. 12416, pp. 369–379. Springer, Cham (2020). https://doi.org/10.1007/978-3-030-61534-5_33
14. Misra, N., Dixit, Y., Al-Mallahi, A., Bhullar, M.S., Upadhyay, R., Martynenko, A.: IoT, big data, and artificial intelligence in agriculture and food industry. IEEE Internet Things J. **9**(9), 6305–6324 (2020)
15. Nabavi-Pelesaraei, A., Rafiee, S., Mohtasebi, S.S., Hosseinzadeh-Bandbafha, H., Chau, K.W.: Integration of artificial intelligence methods and life cycle assessment to predict energy output and environmental impacts of paddy production. Sci. Total Environ. **631**, 1279–1294 (2018)
16. Röck, M., Saade, M.R.M., Balouktsi, M., Rasmussen, F.N., Birgisdottir, H., Frischknecht, R., Habert, G., Lützkendorf, T., Passer, A.: Embodied GHG emissions of buildings-the hidden challenge for effective climate change mitigation. Appl. Energy **258**, 114107 (2020)
17. Saleh, C., Dzakiyullah, N.R., Nugroho, J.B.: Carbon dioxide emission prediction using support vector machine. In: IOP Conference Series: Materials Science and Engineering. vol. 114, p. 012148. IOP Publishing (2016)
18. Svubure, O., Struik, P., Haverkort, A., Steyn, J.M.: Carbon footprinting of potato (solanum tuberosum l.) production systems in Zimbabwe. Outlook Agric. **47**(1), 3–10 (2018)
19. Tilman, D., Balzer, C., Hill, J., Befort, B.L.: Global food demand and the sustainable intensification of agriculture. In: Proceedings of the National Academy of Sciences of the United States of America, vol. 108, pp. 20260–20264 (2011). https://doi.org/10.1073/pnas.1116437108
20. UN Desa: https://www.un.org/development/desa/en/news/population/world-population-prospects-2017.html (2017)

Pre-launch Fashion Product Demand Forecasting Using Machine Learning Algorithms

Marios Arampatzis[✉], G eorgios Theodoridis, and Athanasios Tsadiras

Aristotle University of Thessaloniki, Thessaloniki, Greece
{agmarios,tsadiras}@econ.auth.gr, ttgeorgios@csd.auth.gr

Abstract. The importance of sales forecasting is undeniable. Predicting the sales of the businesses' products have impact in more than one department of a company. In most cases successful forecasting is a complicated issue especially when the product has not or has just been released to the market hence there are no historical data of sales of that exact product. The current research focuses on addressing a problem that bibliographically is not widely researched, that is forecasting the sales of new fashion products before their market release via analyzing their fundamental features and the historical sales data of other, previously released products. To generate accurate results and present a complete strategy various Machine Learning algorithms are modeled, trained, and compared to solve the above mentioned problem. The algorithms examined are categorized as non-linear, ensemble and neural networks methods, and the hyperparameters of non-linear and ensemble algorithms are optimized via Grid Search and the hyperparameters of neural networks are optimized via Bayesian optimization. The results reveal that the Convolutional Neural Network (CNN) method is outperforming all the examined algorithms according to Weighted Absolute Percentage Error (WAPE) and Mean Absolute Error (MAE) metrics. No specific category of methods among non-linear, ensemble and neural networks, was found to perform better.

Keywords: Machine Learning · Sales Forecasting · New Product · Pre-Launch · Non-Linear Methods · Ensemble Methods · Neural Networks

1 Introduction

It has been noticed that sales forecasting undoubtedly plays a vital role in decision making, particularly in relation to manufacturing scheduling, and inventory replenishment. Inaccuracies in forecasting could cause excess inventories or lost sales [12].

Both the designers and retailers of clothing products need to face the inherent problem of short product life cycles therefore it is necessary for businesses to timely forecast the demand of these goods [21]. An accurate demand forecasting is vital for clothing industry because of problems such as a) inadequate inventory level, b) inferior customer service, and c) substantial number of lost sales [9].

One of the factors that makes the forecasting of clothes' demand difficult is the lack of historical sales (or demand) data for every new collection of fashion items that the

© IFIP International Federation for Information Processing 2023
Published by Springer Nature Switzerland AG 2023
I. Maglogiannis et al. (Eds.): AIAI 2023, IFIP AICT 676, pp. 362–372, 2023.
https://doi.org/10.1007/978-3-031-34107-6_29

designers and retailers introduce. Since there is no historical data for these new products, the researchers or managers must rely on sales of previous collections taking into account the characteristics of previous similar fashion clothes. Additionally, the high degree of uncertainty involved when introducing new products increase even more the difficulty of new product sales forecasting [3].

However, the importance of accurate forecasting is unquestionable. By predicting the demand of their products, companies will assist their business planning, budgeting, and risk management. Moreover, it offers them the chance to optimally allocate their resources and estimate their costs and revenue.

The importance of the connection between forecasts and resource decisions cannot be underrated by manufacturing organizations. Additionally, without sales forecasting there could be no long-term production planning of future sales that allows sufficient capacity and labor needs [22].

Considering the facts that have been mentioned above the current work attempts to successfully forecast the sales of newly released fashion products. The dataset that is being used in this study contains 5,577 new clothing products and their sales in the first 12 weeks after their initial release to the market. Ensemble Machine Learning algorithms and Neural Networks are extensively trained, optimized, and applied to accurately predict sales. The use of Ensemble Machine learning algorithms and Neural Networks for that kind of problem is the innovation of the present research. Additionally, have been applied Non-Linear algorithms with the same aim.

The structure of the work is as follows. In Sect. 2, a literature review is presented where related work is being discussed. The description of the dataset with details regarding the structure of our experiments (the inputs, the algorithms that are being used and the outputs) are given in Sect. 3. Section 4 presents the main characteristics of the algorithms that are applied, while Sect. 5 presents the utilized-evaluation metric. Finally, in Sect. 6 the results of the algorithms are being presented, commented, and discussed, with Sect. 7 to conclude the study with the synopsis, the findings and proposals for future research.

2 Literature Review

Introducing new products can provide a competitive advantage as well as a long-term financial return on investment. On the other hand, new product development is also a lengthy process with a high risk of failure but absolutely necessary because in this way companies are able to expand their market share with new buyers [19]. The development of a new product allows each company to become competitive, but many of them consider new product sales forecasting as one of the most difficult forecasting problems they encounter [3]. A small number of publications have dealt with this problem, and they are discussed below.

One of the main retailers' challenges is pricing and predicting demand for products that have never been sold before, especially in the case of retailers where these products correspond for the majority of sales and revenue. To tackle this challenge, in [8], a plethora of machine learning techniques has been utilized to estimate historical lost sales and predict future demand of new products.

Other researchers have focused on forecasting the sales of new products using time series. More specifically, in [7], multiple time-series have been analyzed and grouped together to create a model that is able to predict the sales of a new product. The goal was to forecast the sales of a new product using the sales history of other products. In order to achieve this task, the k-nearest Neighbor (KNN) algorithm and different Encoder-Decoder Sequence models have been used.

In another project, presented in [16], the researchers used the Visuelle dataset which provides the sales of the first 12 week of clothing products, the images of these clothes, textual data like category, color, fabric and release date of the goods and google-trends relating to these cloths. Their task was, to predict the first 6 weeks sales of the clothes, by using various combinations of inputs. The algorithms they used are kNN, GBoosting, MultiModal-RNN and a custom novel "GTM-transformer". One conclusion that could be drawn was that the more features of the products have been considered the better results the algorithms give us.

Similarly, in [17], the researchers had at their disposal the Visuelle 2.0 which includes the sales of the twelve first weeks of 5,355 different new released fashion products. In their first attempt to predict the sales of these new products, they assumed that they knew the first two weeks of these products' sales and they had to forecast the sales of the other ten weeks. In their second attempt they assumed that they know they know the sales of two continuous weeks and each time they predict the sales of the following week. The algorithms that they used are the k-Nearest Neighbors and an Attention-based RNN.

Finally with the same Visuelle there was an attempt to create and introduce time series data that the authors call Potential Performance [10]. These time series show the "potential" sales of new products for many weeks before their release. Afterwards, by inputting these time series to their models, they forecast the sales of the first weeks of the aforementioned products by using Gradient Boosting, RNN and the "GTM-transformer" algorithms.

3 Dataset

The problem in our study, as has been mentioned above has as aim the forecast of the sales of new released products, particularly of new clothes. The VISUELLE dataset is used [16] which includes two pre-defined datasets with the training and testing sets. The dataset consists of a total of 5,577 new clothing products. Additionally, generic categorical information is given for each one of these clothes, like their color (grey, red, etc.), fabric (georgette, fries, etc.), category (short sleeves, long sleeve, etc.), season of their collection (Spring-Summer 2019, Autumn-Winter 2019, etc.) and finally one more supplementary category, named "extra" that declares one more attribute for each product of our dataset. All these nominal variables have been converted into numerical form with Categorical Boosting (CatBoost) Encoder [14]. CatBoost implements several ways to deal with categorical features. Uses a more efficient strategy which reduces overfitting and allows to use the whole dataset for training [6].

Furthermore, aforementioned "Potential Performance (POP)" [10] is also available and utilized within the current study. The POP is the potential sales, of 52 weeks, that the products would have if they have been released 52 weeks before the date that they have been, actually, released to the market.

All these features are used as model inputs to train and optimize the algorithms. The outputs of our dataset are the forecasted sales of the first 6 weeks after the date that the clothes have been released to the market by the designers. The training set consists of 5,080 products and the testing set consists of 497. In conclusion, with the help of the POP timeseries and the other features of the dataset, the sales of the 6 first weeks of the products must be forecasted. The inputs and outputs are being described in the Fig. 1.

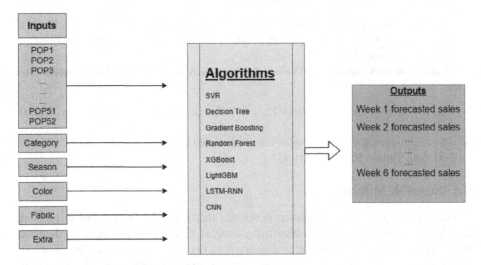

Fig. 1. Inputs, Processing and Outputs.

4 Categories of Predictive Methods

The solution of our problem requires, among others, non-linear regression models. Furthermore, Ensemble Methods and Neural Networks will be used to potentially increase the prediction accuracy of products' sales. Taking the above into account, the algorithms presented in paragraphs 4.1, 4.2 and 4.3 are considered as viable options. Additionally, the results of non-linear and ensemble algorithms via grid search and 10-fold Cross Validation (CV) have been optimized and the results of Neural Networks algorithms have been optimized via Bayesian optimization, so the Mean Absolute Error is minimized. The final hyperparameters searched and selected (bold) are also presented.

4.1 Non-linear Methods

Support Vector Machines (SVMs) are a set of supervised learning methods used for classification, regression (Support Vector Regression, SVR), and outlier detection [5]. The SVM algorithm was developed in 1995 and is based on statistical learning theory [4]. In the case of regression, the goal is to construct a hyperplane that lies "close" to as many of the data points as possible. Therefore, the objective is to choose a hyperplane with small norm while simultaneously minimizing the sum of the distances from the data points to the hyperplane.

The parameters and searched values that have been used for our experiments are the following:

- Regularization parameter C: **0.1**, 1, 10, 100, 200, 500, 600, 1000
- Kernel coefficient gamma: 0.001, 0.01, 0.1, **1**
- Kernel type: **'rbf'**, 'poly', 'sigmoid'

Decision Tree is a tree data structure that consists of an arbitrary number of nodes and branches at each node. The values of the input variable(s) consider a particular function in the training stage [13].

The parameters and searched values that have been used for our experiments are the following:

- The maximum depth of the tree: 1, 2, **3**, 4, 5, 10, 15, 20, 50, 70, 80, 90, 100, 110, 200, 300
- The minimum number of samples required to split an internal node: 35, 45, 55, 100, 300, 500, **1000**, 1500, 2500, 4000.

4.2 Ensemble Methods

Random Forest (RF) is an algorithm developed in 2001 and it is appropriate for both classification and regression problems. It functions by constructing multiple decision trees while training and outputting a value or a class in case of regression or classification, respectively. Additionally, Random Forest can handle up to thousands of explanatory variables and it is suitable for demonstrating the nonlinear effect of input variables, and it can model complex, non-linear interactions among variables [1].

The parameters and searched values that have been used for our experiments are the following:

- The maximum depth of the tree: 1, 2, **3**, 4, 8, 10, 12, None
- The number of trees in the forest: 10, 25, **50**, 100, 200, 300, 600, 800, 1000, 1200, 1400, 1600
- The maximum number of features used: square root of features, log2 of features, **None**

The Gradient Boosting method strategically resamples the training data to provide the most useful information for each consecutive model and is more accurate in predictions because it develops multiple models in sequence by putting emphasis on the training cases that are difficult to estimate [23]. This is the reason it is included in the ensemble methods.

The parameters and searched values, that have been used for our experiments are the following:

- Maximum depth of the individual regression estimators: **1**, 2, 3, 4, 8, 10, 12, None
- The number of boosting stages to perform: 10, 20, 30, 40, 50, 70, **100**, 200, 300, 600, 800, 1000

- The maximum number of features used: square root of features, log2 of features, **None**

XGBoost has been described as a scalable end-to-end tree boosting system. This method, is widely used by data scientists and analysts to achieve results in many machine learning challenges. It has been proved that this method gives state-of-art results on a wide range of problems. The most important factor behind the success of XGBoost is that it can cope with multiple different scenarios hence being robust [2].

The parameters and searched values that have been used for our experiments are the following:

- Maximum depth of the tree: **1**, 2, 3, 4, 8, 10, 12, None
- Maximum number of leaves: **1**, 5, 10, 15, 20, 25, 30, 50, 100, 150
- The number of boosting stages to perform: 10, 25, **50**, 75, 100, 200, 300, 600, 800, 1000
- L1 regularization term weights: 0.1, **0.5**, 0.8
- L2 regularization term of weights: 0, 1, **1.5**, 2
- Booster used: **GBTree**, DART

LightGBM is a gradient boosting decision tree (GBDT) [11]. This method contains two novel techniques: Gradient-based One-Side Sampling and Exclusive Feature Bundling to deal with large number of data instances and large number of features respectively. Previous experiments on multiple datasets show that, LightGBM is twenty times faster during training procedure than the conventional GBDT and at the same time achieves similar accuracy in the results.

The parameters and searched values that have been used for our experiments are the following:

- The maximum depth of the tree: 1, 2, **3**, 4, 8, 10, 12, None
- Maximum number of leaves: 5, 10, 15, **20**, 50, 100, 150
- The number of boosting stages to perform: 1, 5, 10, **20**, 50, 70, 100, 200, 300, 600, 800, 1000
- L1 regularization term on weights: 0.001, 0.01, 0.1, **0.5**, 0.6, 0.7, 0.8
- L2 regularization term on weights: 0, 1, 1.5, 2, 2.5, **3**, 3.5, 4
- Minimum number of data needed in a child (leaf): 1, 5, **10**, 20, 40, 80
- Booster used: GBTree, **DART.**

4.3 Neural Networks

Neural Networks are algorithms that are patterned after the structure of the human brain. They contain several mathematical equations that are used to simulate humans' brain processes such as learning and memory. Many different types of neural network training algorithms have been developed. Two of them are the Long Short-Term Memory-Recurrent Neural Network (LSTM-RNN) and the Convolutional Neural Network (CNN) [20].

RNNs may alleviate potential problems by using recursive structures between the previous frame and the current frame to capture the long-term contextual information to make a better prediction and, Long Short-Term Memory-Recurrent Neural Network (LSTM-RNN) introduces the concepts of memory cell and a series of gates to dynamically control information flow, which well solves the vanishing gradient problem [18].

The architecture of the network is the following:

- Number layers: 5
- Number of epochs: 100
- Batch size: 32

To optimize the parameters of the LSTM-RNN, a Bayesian Optimization is used, instead of grid search.

- The units, the number of neurons connected to the layer holding the concatenated vector of hidden state and input. Values: 16–128, step 16. **Optimal**: layer 1 set to 128 units, 2 to 112, 3 to 80, 4 to 16 and 5 to 16.
- LSTM Activation function. Values: "relu", "tanh", "sigmoid". **Optimal**: for 1 set to "tanh", for 2 to "sigmoid", for 3 to "tanh", for 4 to "tanh" and for 5 to "tanh".
- The dropout rate of every dropout layer. Values: from 0 to 0.5, step 0.1. **Optimal**: layer 1 set to 0.4 units, 2 to 0.2, 3 to 0.2, 4 to 0 and 5 to 0.
- The recurrent dropout. Values: from 0 to 0.5, step 0.1. **Optimal**: layer 1 set to 0.1, 2 to 0.1, 3 to 0.0, 4 to 0.0 and 5 to 0.0

Convolutional Neural Network (CNN), auto-encoders, and deep belief network are widely known models in deep learning. The CNN are deep learning model mainly applied in image classification problems. Recently, different CNN architectures are applied on multi-channel time series data for activity recognition problems [15].

The architecture of the network is the following:

- Convolutional layer: Conv1D
- Number of epochs: 100
- Batch size: 32

To optimize the parameters of the CNN, a Bayesian Optimization is used.

- Dropout rate. Values: from 0.1 to 0.5. **Optimal**: 0.156954
- Learning rate. Values: from 0.001 to 0.01. **Optimal**: 0.00457.

5   Description of the Metrics

A set of evaluation metrics, including Weighted Absolute Percentage Error (WAPE), Mean Absolute Error (MAE), Symmetric Mean Absolute Percentage Error (sMAPE), and Root Mean Square Error (RMSE) are used to compare the forecasted values with the real actual values. Their formulas are presented in Table 1.

WAPE is more effective when it is important to prioritize popular items and reduce the error effect of non-popular items over the evaluation period. It is a more accurate evaluation metric as it would calculate the percentage error over the total item sales across 6 weeks.

Table 1. The metrics' formulas and descriptions (n = the total number of observations)

Metrics' Formulas	Description
$WAPE = \dfrac{\sum_{t=1}^{n}\lvert Actual\ Value_t - Forecasted\ Value_t\rvert}{\sum_{t=1}^{n}\lvert Actual\ Value_t\rvert}$	It is the sum of the absolute error between the actual and forecasted value normalized by the total demand or sales of all products or items
$MAE = \dfrac{\sum_{t=1}^{n}\lvert Actual\ Value_t - Forecasted\ Value_t\rvert}{n}$	Represent the average magnitude of the errors in a set of predicts, without considering their direction
$sMAPE = \dfrac{1}{n}\sum_{t=1}^{n}\dfrac{\lvert Forecasted\ Value_t - Actual\ Value_t\rvert}{\frac{\lvert Actual\ Value_t\rvert + \lvert Forecasted\ Value_t\rvert}{2}}$	Is an accuracy measure based on relative errors
$RMSE = \sqrt{\dfrac{\sum_{t=1}^{n}(Actual\ Value_t - Forecasted\ Value_t)^2}{n}}$	Is a quadratic scoring metric which represent the average magnitude of the error

6 Results

After the optimization of the hyperparameters via Grid Search and Bayesian optimization the models could now be tested using the test data.

Table 2 presents the results of the metrics that the algorithms calculated after rounding of the model outputs, as sales of fashion product can only have integer values. The best value for each metric is in bold.

Table 2. The results of the metrics by considering the exact results of the algorithms.

Algorithms	WAPE	MAE	sMAPE	RMSE
Non-Linear methods				
SVR (8)	2.229	55.872	0.843	64.384
Decision Tree (2)	0.898	32.107	0.634	37.884
Ensemble Methods				
GBR (7)	0.948	31.974	0.628	37.349
Random Forest (3)	0.913	31.823	0.628	37.279
XGBoost (5)	0.942	32.016	0.628	37.422
LightGBM (4)	0.934	31.547	**0.620**	**36.903**
Neural Networks				
LSTM-RNN (6)	0.947	32.056	0.634	37.284
CNN (1)	**0.783**	**31.224**	0.649	38.851

In this study, WAPE is considered the primary evaluation metric, as it common in studies regarding forecasting sales of new fashion products [10, 16]. The rank of each algorithm based on the WAPE metric is being denoted in Table 2, with the number into the parenthesis next to the name of the method.

The results in Table 2 and Fig. 2, denote that the best algorithm, according the WAPE and MAE, is the CNN followed by the Decision Tree method according to WAPE and by LightGBM according to MAE. The best algorithm according to the sMAPE and RMSE metrics is LightGBM. The other examined algorithms perform relatively similarly well, with the exemption of SVR that performs poor.

A conclusion that can be drawn is that there is not a specific category of algorithms that seems to perform better in our study, since the best algorithm according to WAPE (CNN) belongs to Neural Networks, the second best (Decision Tree) belongs to non-linear methods, while two Ensemble methods (Random Forest and LightGBM) have the third and fourth position. This means that in forecasting sales of new fashion products, all kinds of algorithms should be examined, regardless of the categories that they belong, since the complex nature of the specific problem can make any of them a potential good solution.

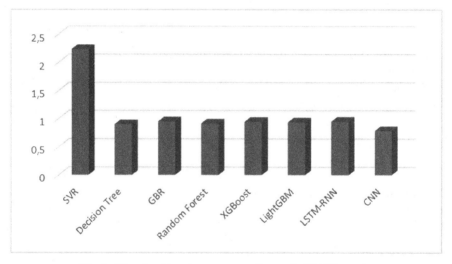

Fig. 2. The algorithms' scores according to the WAPE metric.

7   Conclusions and Suggestions for Future Research

This research has as aim to forecast the sales of new fashion products before the company release them to the market. For that reason, eight different Machine Learning algorithms separated in the three categories (non-linear, ensemble and Neural Networks) have been used. The results show that the best machine learning method based on the metrics WAPE and MAE is the CNN algorithm followed by the Decision Tree method according to WAPE. No specific category of methods among non-linear, ensemble and neural networks, was found to perform better in our study. This leads us to the conclusion that regardless the category that an algorithm belongs, it should be carefully examined, because the complexity of the particular problem may make any of them a candidate for a good solution.

In the future, we plan to verify the results that were drawn from this study, on other similar datasets. Furthermore, it would be interesting to study new ways to create timeseries of hypothetical demand of new fashion products, that exist even before the release of the products (similar to the POP timeseries that were used in this paper) and use them for forecasting the actual demand. Moreover, a study regarding the estimation of the importance of each fashion product characteristic towards its sales, could be of great importance for fashion companies.

References

1. Breiman, L., Cutler, A.: Random forest, machine learning. Stat. Dept. Univ. Calif. **1**, 33 (2001)
2. Chen, T., Guestrin, C.: XGBoost: a scalable tree boosting system. In: Proceedings of the 22nd ACM SIGKDD International Conference on Knowledge Discovery and Data Mining, pp. 785–794 (2016)
3. Ching-Chin, C., Ieng, A.I.K., Ling-Ling, W., Ling-Chieh, K.: Designing a decision-support system for new product sales forecasting. Expert Syst. Appl. **37**(2), 1654–1665 (2010)
4. Cortes, C., Vapnik, V.: Support-vector networks. Mach. Learn. **20**, 273–297 (1995)
5. Coussement, K., Van den Poel, D.: Churn prediction in subscription services: an application of support vector machines while comparing two parameter-selection techniques. Expert Syst. Appl. **34**(1), 313–327 (2008)
6. Dorogush, A.V., Ershov, V., Gulin, A.: CatBoost: gradient boosting with categorical features support (2018). arXiv preprint arXiv:1810.11363
7. Ekambaram, V., Manglik, K., Mukherjee, S., Sajja, S.S.K., Dwivedi, S., Raykar, V.: Attention based multi-modal new product sales time-series forecasting. In: Proceedings of the 26th ACM SIGKDD International Conference on Knowledge Discovery & Data Mining, pp. 3110–3118 (2020)
8. Ferreira, K.J., Lee, B.H.A., Simchi-Levi, D.: Analytics for an online retailer: demand forecasting and price optimization. Manuf. Serv. Oper. Manag. **18**(1), 69–88 (2016)
9. Huang, H., Liu, Q.: Intelligent retail forecasting system for new clothing products considering stock-out. Fibres Text. Eastern Eur. **1**(121), 10–16 (2017)
10. Joppi, C., Skenderi, G., Cristani, M.: POP: mining potential performance of new fashion products via webly cross-modal query expansion. In: Avidan, S., Brostow, G., Cissé, M., Farinella, G.M., Hassner, T. (eds.) Computer Vision–ECCV 2022, ECVV 2022. LNCS: 17th European Conference, Tel Aviv, Israel, October 23–27, 2022, Proceedings, Part XXXVIII, vol. 13698, pp. 34–50. Springer: Cham (2022). https://doi.org/10.1007/978-3-031-19839-7_3
11. Ke, G., et al.: LightGBM: a highly efficient gradient boosting decision tree. In: Advances in Neural Information Processing Systems, vol. 30 (2017)
12. Lawrence, M., O'Connor, M., Edmundson, B.: A field study of sales forecasting accuracy and processes. Eur. J. Oper. Res. **122**(1), 151–160 (2000)
13. Loh, W.Y.: Classification and regression trees. Wiley Interdiscip. Rev. Data Min. Knowl. Discov. **1**(1), 14–23 (2011)
14. Prokhorenkova, L., Gusev, G., Vorobev, A., Dorogush, A.V., Gulin, A.: CatBoost: unbiased boosting with categorical features. In: Advances in Neural Information Processing Systems, vol. 31 (2018)

15. Sateesh Babu, G., Zhao, P., Li, X.-L.: Deep convolutional neural network based regression approach for estimation of remaining useful life. In: Navathe, S.B., Wu, W., Shekhar, S., Du, X., Wang, X.S., Xiong, H. (eds.) DASFAA 2016. LNCS, vol. 9642, pp. 214–228. Springer, Cham (2016). https://doi.org/10.1007/978-3-319-32025-0_14

16. Skenderi, G., Joppi, C., Denitto, M., Cristani, M.: Well googled is half done: multimodal forecasting of new fashion product sales with image-based google trends (2021). arXiv preprint arXiv:2109.09824

17. Skenderi, G., Joppi, C., Denitto, M., Scarpa, B., Cristani, M.: The multi-modal universe of fast-fashion: the Visuelle 2.0 benchmark. In: Proceedings of the IEEE/CVF Conference on Computer Vision and Pattern Recognition, pp. 2241–2246 (2022)

18. Sun, L., Du, J., Dai, L.R., Lee, C.H.: Multiple-target deep learning for LSTM-RNN based speech enhancement. In: 2017 Hands-free Speech Communications and Microphone Arrays (HSCMA), pp. 136–140. IEEE (2017)

19. Thomas, R.J.: New product development: managing and forecasting for strategic success. University of Texas Press (1993)

20. Tu, J.V.: Advantages and disadvantages of using artificial neural networks versus logistic regression for predicting medical outcomes. J. Clin. Epidemiol. **49**(11), 1225–1231 (1996)

21. Van Steenbergen, R.M., Mes, M.R.: Forecasting demand profiles of new products. Decis. Support Syst. **139**, 113401 (2020)

22. Wacker, J.G., Lummus, R.R.: Sales forecasting for strategic resource planning. Int. J. Oper. Prod. Manag. **22**, 1014–1031 (2002)

23. Zhang, Y., Haghani, A.: A gradient boosting method to improve travel time prediction. Transp. Res. **58**, 308–324 (2015)

Rapid Thrombogenesis Prediction in Covid-19 Patients Using Machine Learning

Joong-Lyul Lee[1]([envelope]) [iD], Safaa Alwajidi[2], Mike Tree[3], Angelo Cristobal[4],
and Haitao Zhao[1]

[1] The University of North Carolina at Pembroke, Pembroke, NC 28372, USA
{joonglyul.lee,haitao.zhao}@uncp.edu
[2] The University of Baghdad, Baghdad, Iraq
safaa.alwajidi@sc.uobaghdad.edu.iq
[3] Corvid Technologies, Mooresville, NC 28117, USA
mike.tree@corvidtec.com
[4] Institute of Digital Engineering USA, Mooresville, NC 28117, USA
angelo.cristobal@ideusa.org

Abstract. Machine Learning (ML) algorithms are increasingly being utilized in the medical field to manage and diagnose diseases, leading to improved patient treatment and disease management. Several recent studies have found that Covid-19 patients have a higher incidence of blood clots, and understanding the pathological pathways that lead to blood clot formation (thrombogenesis) is critical. Current methods of reporting thrombogenesis-related fluid dynamic metrics for patient-specific anatomies are based on computational fluid dynamics (CFD) analysis, which can take weeks to months for a single patient. In this paper, we propose a ML-based method for rapid thrombogenesis prediction in the carotid artery of Covid-19 patients. Our proposed system aims to decrease the waiting time for clinicians to receive this information, leading to quicker treatment plans and improved patient outcomes. And we trained and tested several ML algorithms and found the optimal training data size while maintaining high accuracy. The dataset for this study was collected from previous studies and was pre-processed to ensure that the data was reliable and accurate. The proposed system's main contribution is the ability to quickly predict thrombogenesis in Covid-19 patients using ML models, which can help in preventive medicine by detecting serious diseases in advance.

Keywords: Thrombogenesis · Machine Learning · Covid-19 ·
Computational Fluid Dynamics

1 Introduction

Advances in medical technology and engineering have introduced the concept of patient-specific medical treatments, particularly in cardiovascular applications [1]. The importance of fluid mechanics within the cardiovascular system

© IFIP International Federation for Information Processing 2023
Published by Springer Nature Switzerland AG 2023
I. Maglogiannis et al. (Eds.): AIAI 2023, IFIP AICT 676, pp. 373–384, 2023.
https://doi.org/10.1007/978-3-031-34107-6_30

has resulted in an entire industry surrounding its understanding and treatment. However, the time required to setup, execute, and analyze cardiovascular computational models precludes their general use [2]. High fidelity models of complex patient-specific anatomical systems require significant computational time and expertise which results in limiting the positive impact of these technological advances. Current methods for reporting thrombogenesis-related fluid dynamic metrics on patient-specific anatomies are based on computational fluid dynamics (CFD) analysis, and require weeks to months for a single patient. While the information is still valuable at this time interval, decreased wait time for the clinician to receive this information will naturally lead to quicker treatment plans and improved patient outcomes. Machine Learning (ML) may be able to reduce both the time and technical expertise required to model patient-specific cardiovascular flows enough to result in a bed-side clinical tool. To be clinically useful, a non-expert in fluid mechanics modeling must be able to acquire the additional information that patient-specific cardiovascular flow modeling can provide within a couple of hours. This can help clinicians predict disease progression, fill existing gaps in medical imaging, and aid clinical decision-making processes on a patient-by-patient basis [3]. In this paper, we investigate the use of ML approaches to predict blood clot formation (thrombogenesis). This problem was chosen due to many recent studies finding that Covid-19 patients experience a drastically increased incidence of blood clots [4–9]. Specifically, we investigate variations in the anatomy of the carotid artery aiming to derive patient-specific risk of developing potentially dangerous blood clots. The risk is measured through the prediction of carotid artery wall shear stress levels, which have been shown to be correlated with blood clot formation that may result in a stroke [10,11].

Contribution of this paper: the main contributions can be summarized as follows:

1. We proposed a framework that utilizes machine learning models to enable rapid predictions of thrombogenesis. Our proposed framework represents a significant improvement over current methods for reporting thrombogenesis related computational fluid dynamics (CFD) analyses, which typically require weeks to months for a single patient. By using ML-based approach, we have dramatically reduced the time required to obtain results, enabling clinicians to receive predictions in a matter of minutes rather than weeks
2. Several ML algorithms were investigated to predict risk metrics for rapid thrombogenesis in the carotid artery and the optimal training data size was determined that would result in acceptable metric prediction in an effort to reduce future data synthesis requirements from expensive CFD simulation.

The rest of the paper is organized as follows: Sect. 2 discusses a literature review on the related work. Section 3 describes the ML models and the dataset used in theses experiments. Section 4 discusses simulation results. Finally, we summarize our work and outline future work in Sect. 5.

2   Related Work

In the medical field, ML algorithms are used in various fields to manage and diagnose diseases, helping to improve patient treatment and disease management. A blood clot in the carotid artery can interrupt blood flow to the brain, leading to a stroke. In [12], the authors demonstrate the use of Support Vector Machine (SVM) and Decision Tree (DT) methods in identifying vulnerable plaque progression in mice. In [13], the authors researched the current state of the detection and management of atrial fibrillation using ML algorithms. Since a stroke is a medical emergency that can cause lasting brain damage, long-term disability, or even death, [14] investigated the mechanical retrieval of thrombotic material from acute ischemic stroke. In [15], the authors compared multiple ML algorithms and logistic regression models with multiple variable selection methods to predict radiological and clinical outcomes after Endovascular treatment (EVT) in stroke patients. This paper showed no difference in the performance results between the best-performing ML algorithms and the best-performing logistic regression models in predicting radiological or clinical outcome. Carotid artery stenting (CAS) can be used in a timely manner to help prevent such strokes, reducing the risk of stroke in [16,17]. It is essential to anticipate readmission within 30 days of the CAS procedure. By creating a model using ML algorithms to predict initial readmission, the authors in [18] can classify patients with a high readmission potential and focus on high-risk patients. Similar to this study, Feiger et al. used neural networks to predict pressure drop and time-averaged wall shear stress values in coarcted aorta geometries based of CFD simulations [1]. The authors also included an exercise based on design of experiments principles to evaluate the training data requirements for their neural network model to provide an arbitrary accuracy level.

3   Methods

3.1   Dataset and Data Preprocessing

The machine learning training data was composed of 384 transient CFD simulations consisting of 3 cardiac cycles worth of physical time. The 384 CFD simulations were created by varying fluid parameters for 3 different patient-specific geometries. Thus, the training data should be considered simulated, synthetic data based on real-world geometry. The varied parameters in the training dataset were related to specified flow through the geometry for each CFD simulation. The CFD simulation required specifying flow rate through the geometry as a function of time, static pressure at the geometry inlets and outlets as a function of time, and fluid viscosity. The flow rate was defined via a transient curve deconstructed using a fast Fourier transform (FFT) algorithm to include its most influential frequencies. Table 1 summarizes the parameters modified to create the 384 sets of CFD simulation training data.

The CFD simulations conducted consumed between 5,000 and 38,500 cpu-hours of resources and were post-processed to produce two key metrics related

Table 1. CFD Simulation Features

Feature	Description
nu_0	Maximum fluid viscosity (Pa·s)
Q_mean_cca	Mean volumetric inflow rate (into the common carotid artery, m^3/sec)
T_cc	Cardiac cycle period length (sec)
area_cca	Cross sectional area (m^2)
normal_cca	Unit vector normal to the inflow plane
fft_array_size	xfft array size; used to reconstruct the inflow waveform
fft_data	List of 10 tuples describing the fft solution of the inflow waveform (the top 10 frequency contributions to the curve)
Rp_ica	Internal carotid artery proximal resistance
C_ica	Internal carotid artery capacitance
Rd_ica	Internal carotid artery distal resistance
Pi_ica	Internal carotid artery initial Pressure (Pa)
Rp_eca	External carotid artery proximal resistance
C_eca	External carotid artery capacitance
Rd_eca	External carotid artery distal resistance
Pi_eca	External carotid artery initial Pressure (Pa)

*Rp, C, and Rd values are used to compute pressure at each outlet (internal and external carotid arteries) given the inflow waveform using a 1D

Table 2. CFD Target Risk Metrics

Feature	Description
washout	Percent of Lagrangian particles that washout in one cardiac cycle when the velocity field is seeded with particles at a consistent location
mean_tawss	Spatial mean of the time-averaged wall shear stress

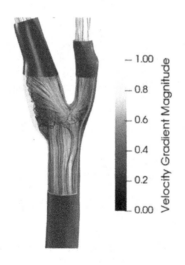

Fig. 1. CFD Particle Traces

to blood clots: mean time-averaged wall shear stress and fluid washout. The mean time-averaged wall shear stress is a measure of the friction force existing between the fluid and the artery wall. The fluid washout metric was represented as a percentage of neutrally-buoyant Lagrangian particles present in the fluid domain after a set amount of time. Table 2 lists the blood clot risk metrics to be predicted using the machine learning algorithm.

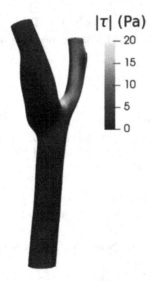

Fig. 2. Time-Averaged Wall Shear Stress (TAWSS) contours on the patient-specific anatomy

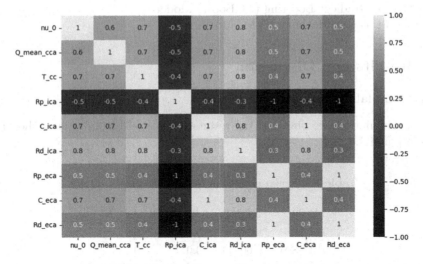

Fig. 3. Correlation analysis in features

Figure 1 shows CFD particle trace image and Fig. 2 shows Time-Averaged Wall Shear Stress (TAWSS) contours on the patient-specific anatomy. We show the correlation analysis to understand which features influence the data in the Fig. 3. From this result, we can see that there is a positive relationship between all variables except Rp_ica, which has a negative relationship with all other variables. Additionally, there is a strong correlation higher than 0.7 between almost all variables. Rp_eca and Rd_eca have a weak relationship of 0.3 or 0.4.

We re-processed the data values described in Table 1 in re-scaling the range of features to scale the range in [0, 1] by using the Min-Max Normalization method.

3.2   Machine Learning Algorithms

The ML algorithms used in our study were several regression models and Support Vector Machine(SVM), which has been demonstrated to achieve good generalization performance on clinical data. We implemented the following ML models with cross-validation using Sklearn libraries and Keras libraries with Tensorflow in Python.

- Linear Regression (LR) Model
- Random Sample Consensus (RANSAC) Model
- Ridge Regression Model
- Least Absolute Shrinkage and Selection Operator (LASSO) Regression Model
- Elastic Net Regression Model
- k-Nearest Neighbor (k-NN) Model
- Decision Tree (DT) Model
- Polynomial Regression Model
- eXtreme Gradient Boosting (XGBoost) Model
- Support Vector Machine (SVM) Model.

4   Results and Discussion

4.1   Simulation Results

In this simulation, we obtained the results for several ML models as shown in Table 3, and 4.

Table 3. Simulation results using different ML models

Model	Avg MSE	Avg MAE	Avg R^2
LR	0.00343	0.047	0.955
RANSAC	0.00343	0.047	0.955
Ridge	0.966	0.243	−0.285
Lasso	0.829	0.217	−0.103
ElasticNet	0.0766	0.211	−0.0187
k-NN	0.0814	0.223	−0.0841
DT	0.00385	0.0489	0.949
SVM	0.00364	0.0483	0.952
XGBoost	0.0957	0.0143	0.9852

Table 4. Polynomial Regression model results

Model	Avg MSE	Avg MAE	Avg R^2
Degree-1	0.00345	0.0471	0.955
Degree-2	0.00757	0.0728	0.899
Degree-3	4.04e + 24	1.33e + 12	−5.42e + 25
Degree-4	6.82e + 23	5.61e + 11	−9.07e + 24
Degree-5	0.0188	0.112	0.75

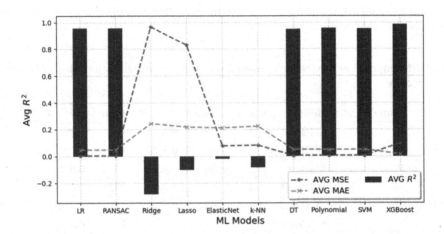

Fig. 4. Simulation results of average accuracy (R^2), average MAE, and average MSE using different ML models

The LR, RANSAC, DT, SVM, XGBoost, and Polynomial Regression models showed high accuracy levels of 0.955, 0.955, 0.949, 0.952, 0.9852, and 0.955, respectively, with XGBoost exhibiting the highest accuracy where accuracy is measured using the R^2 score. On the other hand, Ridge, Lasso, ElasticNet and k-NN models produced negative accuracy results. The R^2 score is a measure of how well a regression model fits the data. A high R^2 score indicates that the model explains a large proportion of the variance in the dependent variables, while a low R^2 score indicates that the model does not explain much of the variance in the dependent variables. The R^2 score ranges from 0 to 1, with 1 indicating a perfect fit between the predicted values and the actual values, and 0 indicating no relationship between the independent and dependent variables. Regarding the Polynomial Regression model, we observed the highest accuracy of 0.955 in the first degree, slightly lower in the second degree and fifth degree, and negative values in the third and fourth degree, as shown in Table 4.

Figure 4 shows the average mean absolute error (MAE), average mean squared error (MSE), and R^2 score in average accuracy. The graph indicates that high accuracy is associated with relatively low error rates, while low accuracy is associated with relatively high error rates. The average MSE results, which are presented in Fig. 4, are consistent with the average MAE results in showing low error values relative to the high accuracy levels.

4.2   Dataset Quantity Study

Typically, more data is better. However, when the cost of generating the dataset is significant, determining the quantity of data needed for acceptable accuracy is desired. In order to obtain the optimal number of training dataset and testing dataset, we conducted experiments by dividing several data sets as shown in Table 5 to train XGBoost, DT, and LR models that had previously shown high accuracy results in simulations.

Table 5. Simulation results for optimal data quantity using ML models that showed high accuracy

Num of Data	Model	Avg. R^2	Model	Avg. R^2	Model	Avg. R^2
10	XGBoost	0.72	DT	0.54	LR	0.728
20	XGBoost	0.87	DT	0.873	LR	0.908
30	XGBoost	0.92	DT	0.829	LR	0.912
40	XGBoost	0.93	DT	0.881	LR	0.919
51	XGBoost	0.95	DT	0.875	LR	0.912
61	XGBoost	0.95	DT	0.872	LR	0.905
71	XGBoost	0.96	DT	0.873	LR	0.957
81	XGBoost	0.97	DT	0.864	LR	0.957
92	XGBoost	0.97	DT	0.847	LR	0.952
101	XGBoost	0.99	DT	0.954	LR	0.96

Figure 5 displays the average accuracy (R^2) of the XGBoost, LR, and DT models as the number of training data increase, as shown in Table 5. The graph shows that the R^2 score increases with an increase in the number of data.

We confirm that the XGBoost model performed best for this type of data in this simulation. Therefore, we select this type of model for additional study. In this additional experiment, we checked the R^2 score, MAE, and MSE values while increasing the data size. As shown in Fig. 6, 7 and 8, random repeated sampling from the data were taken for each quantity (total 126 data items) and statistics were derived to observe trends. Additionally, hyperparameters for all XGBoost models were optimized.

Based on this study, acceptable simulation results required at least 30 data items in training dataset. Beyond 30 data items, the accuracy shows improvement with less variance across the sampling permutations. However, the inflection point is at approximately 30 data items. This is the requisite quantity of data for modeling the three anatomies currently in our dataset. It is expected that

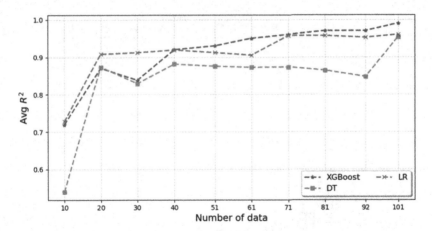

Fig. 5. Simulation results of average accuracy (R^2) to find a optimal number of training data size using ML models

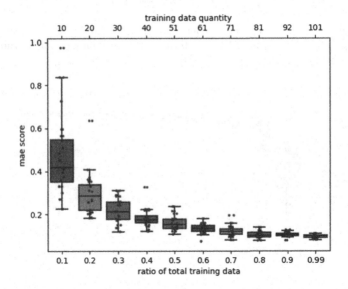

Fig. 6. Simulation results for the XGBoost model, showing the MAE as a function of the training data quantity, in order to determine the optimal amount of training data

more data would be required as additional geometries are inspected. In practice, optimized XGBoost models should be generated as training data results become available, where simulation features are determined using design of experiments methods such as the Latin Hypercube method or Adaptive Sampling. Once the model behavior shows diminishing returns, generation of new data can be stopped.

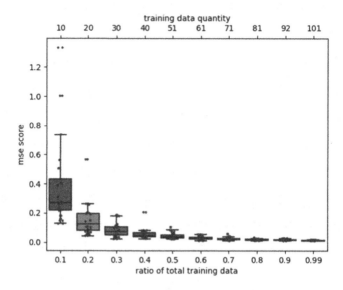

Fig. 7. Simulation results for the XGBoost model, showing the MSE as a function of the training data quantity, in order to determine the optimal amount of training data

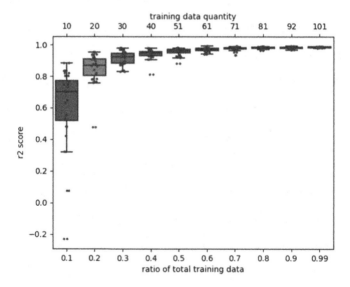

Fig. 8. Simulation results of R^2 score for determining optimal training data quantity using XGBoost model

5   Conclusions

Blood clotting is a common complication among Covid-19 patients, which requires accurate and timely diagnosis. While CFD simulation data has shown promise in predicting blood clots, it can take weeks to complete. To address this issue, we present a framework for predicting blood clots using 10 different ML models on patient MRI data. Our study reveals that XGBoost, LR, and DT models show a high accuracy rate of over 95% in predicting blood clots. Moreover, we conducted simulations to determine the minimum training dataset size necessary to maintain high accuracy, and the results show that the XGBoost model is the most accurate. Importantly, our proposed framework significantly reduces the time required to obtain results from weeks to minutes.

In future studies, we will implement a neural network and deep learning-based model to process more data and achieve better results. Overall, our framework has the potential to assist clinicians in making quick and accurate diagnoses of blood clotting in Covid-19 patients.

Acknowledgements. This project is supported by the North Carolina Collaboratory at the University of North Carolina at Chapel Hill with funding appropriated by the North Carolina General Assembly via the American Rescue Plan Act of 2021 (H.R. 1319) (federal award identification number SLFRP0129).

References

1. Feiger, B., et al.: Accelerating massively parallel hemodynamic models of coarctation of the aorta using neural networks. Sci. Rep. **10**(1), 1–13 (2020)
2. Qin, S., Wu, B., Liu, J., Shiu, W.-S., Yan, Z., Chen, R., Cai, X.-C.: Efficient parallel simulation of hemodynamics in patient-specific abdominal aorta with aneurysm. Comput. Biol. Med. **136**, 104652 (2021)
3. Marsden, A.L., Esmaily-Moghadam, M.: Multiscale modeling of cardiovascular flows for clinical decision support. Appl. Mech. Rev. **67**(3), 030804 (2015)
4. Klok, F., et al.: Incidence of thrombotic complications in critically ill ICU patients with covid-19. Thrombosis Res. **191**, 145–147 (2020)
5. Poissy, J., et al.: Pulmonary embolism in patients with covid-19: awareness of an increased prevalence. Circulation **142**(2), 184–186 (2020)
6. Ramlall, V., et al.: Immune complement and coagulation dysfunction in adverse outcomes of sars-cov-2 infection. Nat. Med. **26**(10), 1609–1615 (2020)
7. Huertas, A., et al.: Endothelial cell dysfunction: a major player in sars-cov-2 infection (covid-19) (2020)
8. Varga, Z., et al.: Endothelial cell infection and endotheliitis in covid-19. Lancet **395**(10234), 1417–1418 (2020)
9. Magro, C., et al.: Complement associated microvascular injury and thrombosis in the pathogenesis of severe covid-19 infection: a report of five cases. Transl. Res. **220**, 1–13 (2020)
10. Wootton, D.M., Ku, D.N.: Fluid mechanics of vascular systems, diseases, and thrombosis. Ann. Rev. Biomed. Eng. **1**(1), 299–329 (1999)

11. Zarins, C.K., Giddens, D.P., Bharadvaj, B., Sottiurai, V.S., Mabon, R.F., Glagov, S.: Carotid bifurcation atherosclerosis. quantitative correlation of plaque localization with flow velocity profiles and wall shear stress. Circ. Res. **53**(4), 502–514 (1983)

12. Li, B., et al.: Contralateral artery enlargement predicts carotid plaque progression based on machine learning algorithm models in apoe-/- mice. Biomed. Eng. Online **15**(2), 233–246 (2016)

13. Wegner, F.K., et al.: Machine learning in the detection and management of atrial fibrillation. Clin. Res. Cardiol. 1–8 (2022). https://doi.org/10.1007/s00392-022-02012-3

14. Dargazanli, C., et al.: Machine learning analysis of the cerebrovascular thrombi proteome in human ischemic stroke: an exploratory study. Front. Neurol. **11**, 575376 (2020)

15. Van Os, H.J., et al.: Predicting outcome of endovascular treatment for acute ischemic stroke: potential value of machine learning algorithms. Front. Neurol. **9**, 784 (2018)

16. Flaherty, M.L., et al.: Carotid artery stenosis as a cause of stroke. Neuroepidemiology **40**(1), 36–41 (2013)

17. Bonati, L.H., Lyrer, P., Ederle, J., Featherstone, R., Brown, M.M.: Percutaneous transluminal balloon angioplasty and stenting for carotid artery stenosis. Cochrane Database Syst. Rev. 9 (2012)

18. Amritphale, A., et al.: Predictors of 30-day unplanned readmission after carotid artery stenting using artificial intelligence. Adv. Therapy **38**(6), 2954–2972 (2021)

Natural Language

Are These Descriptions Referring to the Same Entity or Just to Similar Ones?

Péter Kardos[1(✉)] and Richárd Farkas[1,2]

[1] Institute of Informatics, University of Szeged, Szeged, Hungary
{kardos,rfarkas}@inf.u-szeged.hu
[2] ELKH-SzTE Research Group on Artificial Intelligence, Szeged, Hungary

Abstract. The Knowledge Graph matching task is to identify nodes in the two graphs that refer to the same concept. In this paper, we focus on the analysis of textual descriptions of the concepts. We employ neural language models as they can score well on text content similarity On the other hand, we show that the text similarity of entity descriptions does not equal to referring to the exact same entity. Our text-based multi-step system was among the top participants at the Knowledge Graph matching track of the Ontology Alignment Evaluation Initiative.

Keywords: NLP · Language Models · Graph matching

1 Introduction

A Knowledge Graph (KG) is a unique data structure for representing entities in a structured and connected fashion. The number of publicly available knowledge graphs is increasing year by year both in the domain-specific and general contexts. These data structures may be used to provide background knowledge in order to solve a problem or used as a source to support the interpretation of an AI algorithm [1]. The most commonly used general KGs are YAGO [15], DBPedia [14] or WikiData [18] to name a few.

As more and more companies see the benefits of representing their data in a structured way they create KGs independently from any other publicly available KG. It is possible for there to be multiple KGs that share some of the same information. The focus of this research is to align these different KGs in a way where each entity shall be represented only once so that there are no duplicates. In these cases, the pairable nodes are just a fraction of all of the nodes as it is very unlikely that the information of the two graphs is completely overlapping. The names or labels of real-world entities in KGs are usually a good indicator of node matching, but there are several exceptions (e.g. `Darth Vader - Anakin Skywalker`) because the various KGs were created by different editors following different principles.

As most knowledge graphs have textual information about each concept these can give clues or support claims about matching nodes. In this paper, we focus on the analysis of textual descriptions of the concepts.

© IFIP International Federation for Information Processing 2023
Published by Springer Nature Switzerland AG 2023
I. Maglogiannis et al. (Eds.): AIAI 2023, IFIP AICT 676, pp. 387–398, 2023.
https://doi.org/10.1007/978-3-031-34107-6_31

In recent years the usage of pre-trained neural language models has dominated the field of Natural Language Processing (NLP). When approaching a new task it is now a standard to take a pre-trained neural language model, like BERT [2] or any variant of it [9,10], and fine-tune it for the particular new task using a classification layer or prompt a generative model for the task [13]. Our proposal to solve the graph matching is a multi-step system starting with simple exact string matching steps, followed by a BERT-based step that filters upon the textual description similarity of nodes and ending with a bit more complex BERT-based classifier step that exploits an automatic training example generation method in order to discriminate similar descriptions from descriptions referring to the exact same entity.

We introduce empirical results achieved by various modules of our system on the Knowledge Graph matching track of the Ontology Alignment Evaluation Initiative in 2022. As a summary our contributions are the following:

- A novel multi-step system to find node pairs in the Graph Matching task
- An automatic training example generation process
- State of the Art results on the Ontology Alignment Evaluation Initiative 2022 - Graph matching track.

2   Dataset

2.1   Ontology Alignment Evaluation Initiative

The Ontology Alignment Evaluation Initiative (OAEI) [7] is a campaign organized annually in the field of ontology matching where given multiple ontologies the task is to find the nodes that represent the same concept between these ontologies. The campaign consists of multiple tracks where the most complex one is the Knowledge Graph track. Here we are given pairs of KGs from different fandom wiki sites (Start Trek, Star Wars, Marvel) and a gold set of correct matching pairs referring to the same concept. The OAEI organizers created a collection of 5 KG pairs and gold standard pairings in 2022. The task is to find all the matching pairs in the two given KGs without any supervision. The prediction is evaluated only on the gold set.

The graph is separated into instances, properties and classes. The instances are actual entities that exist in the universe for example `Anakin Skywalker`. The classes represent some grouping terms in which an instance can belong to, for example weapon or character. The properties represent some information about an instance for example name or gender. More information about the dataset sizes can be found in Table 1 and Table 2. The gold sets are somewhat special because all of the pairs are 1:1 (No 1:N pairs) and consequently as these graphs differ in size, not every node is pairable. Later on, we are going to focus on the description of the nodes, so we report what percentage of the nodes have this information in the last column.

Table 1. OAEI - Knowledge Graph track dataset sizes. The Desc. column shows what % of nodes have a description.

Source URL	Instances	Properties	Classes	Desc.
http://starwars.wikia.com	145 033	700	269	82%
http://swtor.wikia.com	4 180	368	101	88%
http://swg.wikia.com	9 634	148	67	70%
http://marvel.wikia.com	210 996	139	186	1%
http://marvelcinematicuniverse.wikia.com	17 187	147	55	90%
http://memory-alpha.wikia.com	45 828	325	181	89%
http://stexpanded.wikia.com	13 426	202	283	83%
http://memory-beta.wikia.com	51 323	423	240	83%

Table 2. OAEI - Knowledge Graph track gold pair sizes.

starwars-swg	starwars-swtor	malpha-mbeta	malpha-stexp	mcu-marvel
1 121	1 429	9 364	1 779	1 666

2.2 Evaluation

As the input KG sizes are quite large it would require a lot of manual effort to find all of the pairs with the same meaning. The given gold sets were constructed by manual annotation, but it is not guaranteed that all of the pairs have been found. However, it is guaranteed if one node is in this gold set then all of its pairs have been found. The official OAEI evaluation metrics are Precision, Recall and F1 Score with an extra step. Considering a competing system that predicts pairs we have 3 possibilities:

1. The pair is in the gold set, hence it is correct.
2. One of the elements of the pair can be found in the gold set but connected to a wrong element, then the pair is incorrect.
3. If none of the elements from the pair can be found in the gold set, we discard the pair as we cannot decide if the annotators didn't find it or if it is incorrect.

For the OAEI KG matching track, a whole framework is available for evaluating predictions called MELT [6]. We've evaluated all of our results using this official evaluation software.

3   Methods and Results

Based on the input data we have two types of information we can use, the graph structure and the textual information. In this paper, we focus on using only the latter to solve the graph matching problem.

In our previous work [8], we experimented with using the graph's structural information through RDF2VEC vectors [12], however the mapping of graph nodes to a common vector space for the entity matching problem achieved poor performance.

Our solution is a multi-step system. We started out with the most basic exact string similarity measures and worked our way to more complicated semantics-based steps involving language models. In the following sections, we describe this approach in detail.

3.1 Exact Matching

A first assumption would be if two nodes have the same name we can consider them to refer to the same entity as it is rare to have multiple entities in a universe, especially in a special domain, with the same name. Our baseline solution finds these so-called trivial pairs. To find matching pairs the step receives one or more textual properties and scans for nodes with the same textual value over them. If our assumption is correct then the resulting pair set should have very high precision. In the case of multiple given properties, the OR operator is applied so any match between the properties counts as a good pair.

Table 3. Exact matching results over the Label and Label+AltLabel properties. A Label can be interpreted as the name of the entity. The AltLabel is an additional name such as a nickname or a shortened form.

	mcu marvel			memoryalpha memorybeta			memoryalpha stexpanded			starwars swg			starwars swtor		
	P	R	F-m	P	R	F-m	P	R	F-m	P	R	F-m	P	R	F-m.
Label	89.7	56.6	69.4	94.7	77.4	85.2	98.3	84.3	90.7	93.9	63.2	75.5	94.6	86.2	90.2
Label + AltLabel	88.7	66.6	76.1	94.1	88.6	91.3	96.7	91.8	94.2	92.8	72.1	81.1	93.9	89.8	91.8

We also tried replacing the exact similarity with fuzzy similarity matching while also adding a threshold value to filter the pairs. Even though the recall would increase the new pairs were too noisy resulting in a decrease of the overall F-score.

3.2 The SentenceBERT Step

Table 3 shows that exact label matching achieves high precision, but lower recall. This can be attributed to the gold pairs having Labels/AltLabels of different text values. We aimed to increase the recall by comparing the textual description of KG nodes. Our assumption here is that textual descriptions of entities have to reveal their equality even in cases when the labels of two entities do not have any string similarity. The best case scenario would be to increase the recall to 100% while also not degrading the precision too far so that we get an F score increase.

We utilize BERT-type neural language models for measuring content similarity between a pair of texts. BERT [2] is a transformer-based language model pre-trained on a large amount of text. It can be used to solve several tasks along with fine-tuning.

At first glance, we could approach the issue by comparing the descriptions of all pairs of texts and fine-tuning a BERT to classify whether these descriptions talk about the same entity or not. However, the sheer number of comparisons required for this approach may exceed our computing capability due to the computationally intensive nature of BERT. We follow a computationally lighter approach. First, we generate pairs that do not necessarily refer to the same entity but do have similar textual descriptions. This is computationally efficient and we can find top K similar texts easily and restrict computationally heavy special classification only to these top K candidates.

We employ SentenceBERT [11], which is an extension of BERT where given a document the model can convert it into a vector representing the meaning of the whole sentence. BERT assigns a vector for words aiming for a useful representation for a classification task, while SentenceBERT aims to provide a good sentence representation for similarity analysis. Between two SentenceBERT vectors, cosine similarity can be calculated to get a metric of how similar the documents really are.

We embedded all nodes of all KGs textual descriptions by a pre-trained English SentenceBERT model into a vector space. As all of the nodes have been granted a vector, we can select the most similar pair for each node using the cosine similarity measure. Then we also apply a threshold value and only predict pairs with SentenceBERT similarity over the threshold. We look for SentenceBERT pair only for nodes that the exact matching step has already not found any match, making it an extension set over the exact matching pairs.

To evaluate this step's results we used the Abstract property.

Table 4. SentenceBert (SB) results over the Abstract property. SB-2 means the abstracts are trimmed after the first 2 sentences

	mcu marvel			memoryalpha memorybeta			memoryalpha stexpanded			starwars swg			starwars swtor		
	P	R	F-m	P	R	F-m	P	R	F-m	P	R	F-m	P	R	F-m.
Label +AltLabel	88.7	66.6	76.1	94.1	88.6	91.3	96.7	91.8	94.2	92.8	72.1	81.1	93.9	89.8	91.8
SB	88.0	66.7	75.9	91.1	90.4	90.8	94.1	93.8	94.0	88.3	78.9	83.3	91.9	90.9	91.4
SB-2	88.0	66.7	75.9	91.2	90.7	91.0	94.1	94.3	94.2	87.8	78.1	82.6	92.1	91.0	91.6

To better understand the behavior of SentenceBERT similarity, we calculated the top 10 similar pairs of the gold standard set. Fig. 1 depicts the frequency of position of gold pairs in the SentenceBERT ranking over the memoryalpha-stexpanded dataset. We noticed that the abstract texts contain more important information at the beginning - the quasi-definition of the concept - and not so much towards the end. Therefore we introduced a trimming of the abstract texts to the first 2 sentences. We can say that over 90% of the gold pairs are located at the first place and we can increase this percentage with trimming.

Based on the results in Table 4, taking only the first two sentences can give a slight boost confirming our observation that the main information is at the beginning.

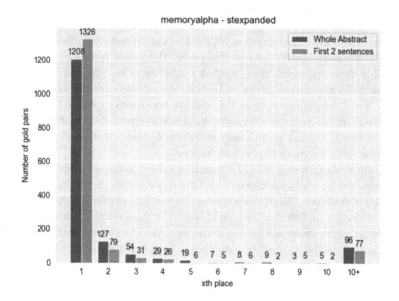

Fig. 1. Based on the SentenceBert vector similarities at which rank gold pairs are located. The two different bars mean if the abstracts have been trimmed or not.

3.3   The Same vs Similar (SvS) Step

Figure 1 shows that sometimes the correct pair is not the most similar text by SentenceBERT scores. Recall has been increased with the SentenceBERT step, however, it brings noise with itself degrading the F-score metric below the exact match baselines. These issues raise the need for an additional correction step.

We created a self-supervised approach for this correction step. As all of the provided pairs by the SentenceBERT step should be at least similar to each other, we can build a classifier over SentenceBERT top K candidates making a decision whether the pair represents the exact same concept or not. As the candidate set has been reduced to a reasonable size thanks to the previous step, it is now computationally feasible even employing a BERT model fine-tuned to our specific task.

We generate a training dataset automatically for a binary classifier with `positive=same` and `negative=similar` target classes. We consider the Label+AltLabel exactly match pairs as `same` since they already have high precision. We automatically generate negative (i.e. `similar`) training samples for each of the exact matching pairs. We pick one of the elements from a `positive` pair so that we can use the SentenceBERT step to get a similarity ranking to that node. A negative sample is going to be the pair with the highest similarity that is not the `positive` exact match pair itself. In the OAEI datasets, we can safely do this as only 1:1 gold pairs exist in the evaluation set, so by excluding the exact matching pair we cannot have false negatives. Additionally more than 1 negative sample can be generated if the second-highest probability pair is included as well.

In Table 5. We demonstrate how we construct the positive and negative pairs over the Senator node of the memoryalpha graph and its SentenceBert Top 3 pairs from the stexpanded graph. Here the correct match would be the Senator-Senator found by the exact match step as their labels are the same so by looking at the SentenceBert similarity scores the third pair is the positive. From this ranking, we would exclude this positive pair and any other pair can be picked to be a negative pair, but we always choose the one with the highest score. If needed, more negative examples can be picked out from the list in descending order. Based on this the classifier that we train should be able to identify these clues where the SentenceBert similarities were not perfect.

Based on these positive and negative training examples we can fine-tune a pre-trained English BERT model to separate the two classes. The trained classifier can make a prediction for all of the candidate pairs we obtained from the SentenceBERT step and keep only pairs with **same** prediction. In case there are multiple **same** predictions in a candidate list, or a node appears in more than one list we can take the highest posterior probability pair to get 1:1 matches only.

Table 5. Same vs Similar positive-negative generation example. Most similar pairs to Senator with scores and the first sentence of their abstracts in the memoryalpha-stexpanded datasets.

Pairs	SentenceBert Score	Abstract
Senator		A senator was a member of a legislative or deliberative body known as a senate
Romulan_Senate ⊖	0.696855	The Romulan Senate was the governing body of the Romulan Star Empire and headed by the Praetor
Lyran_Senate ⊖	0.647295	The Lyran Senate was an executive body of the Lyran Star Empire, tasked with the day-to-day administration of the Empire
Senator ⊕	0.643694	A senator is an official who sits in a senate

Note that this step could also work without using the SentenceBERT step's output as candidates, but a prediction should be made for all of the possible node pairs between the two graphs, which would require a lot more computation power.

3.4   Pipeline

In this section, we describe how we use each of the steps in our pipeline. We start out by getting exact matches over the `Label` property and extend this set with the `AltLabel` property exact matches over the nodes where no pairs were found previously. This set can be considered the final alignment which we will

Table 6. SvS results over the Abstract property. SvS uses the whole abstract, SvS-2 uses only the first two sentences

	mcu marvel			memoryalpha memorybeta			memoryalpha stexpanded			starwars swg			starwars swtor		
	P	R	F-m	P	R	F-m	P	R	F-m	P	R	F-m	P	R	F-m
SB-2	88.0	66.7	75.9	91.2	90.7	91.0	94.1	94.3	94.2	87.8	78.1	82.6	92.1	91.0	91.6
SvS	87.7	66.3	75.5	93.6	89.5	91.5	96.0	93.7	94.8	92.6	72.1	81.0	93.4	90.6	92.0
SvS-2	87.7	66.3	75.5	93.2	89.9	91.5	96.8	94.0	95.4	87.2	77.5	82.1	93.0	90.6	91.8

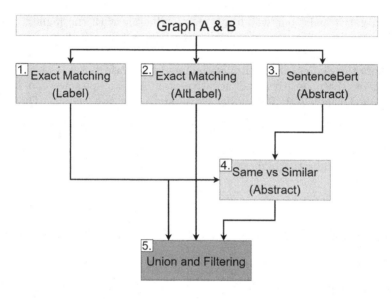

Fig. 2. Pipeline's dataflow. The brackets indicate which property was used.

extend in the next steps to improve the recall. Next up is the SentenceBERT step where we select the `Abstract` property's first two sentences. We select the X most similar pairs to each node based on the abstract property's embedding vector using cosine similarity and filtered further by a threshold value. We pass this set to the Same vs Similar (SvS) step as a candidate pool, still using the Abstracts as text. To train the model we use the pairs of the Exact match over the Labels. As a last step, we discard the 1:N pairs leaving only the ones with the highest confidence and add them to the final alignment, discarding any overlapping nodes with the exact matches. To simply put, if two nodes have been paired in previous steps, they cannot be paired anymore. In Fig. 2 we visualized the pipeline's dataflow. The code is available the github repository: https://github.com/kiscsonti/GraphMatching_SameVsSimilar.

3.5   Parameters

The selected SentenceBERT model was the *all-MiniLM-L6-v2* [11] model. At maximum, the top 6 pairs were selected for each node and discarded all pairs below 0.6 cosine similarity threshold. For the SvS step the selected Language Model was *albert-base* [9] pre-trained on the MRPC [3] task which is a sentence similarity task. As for the training process a batch size of 1 (due to GPU memory capacity) and a learning rate of 10^{-5} were used. The training process was allowed to run for 100 epochs, but an EarlyStop with 5 patience could shut it down before, which means that we split the generated dataset to train and evaluation sets.

4 Discussion

In this section, we analyze how well our pipeline's steps perform and discuss how the results deviate from our expectations.

4.1 Exact Match

The best case scenario of the exact matching would be if all the pairs represent the same entity resulting in a 100% precision, completing the goal of the exact matching step's purpose. However, the results show otherwise. This would mean that there are multiple nodes in a single KG with the same labels. We found that there are disambiguation pages that have the same Label property while the gold standard pair is the disambiguated actual node. Also, there are so-called "Legends" nodes which would be the correct pair based on the annotations. For example, swg/Chef - starwars/Chef is an incorrect pair, because starwars/Chef/Legends would be the correct one.

4.2 Language Model Steps

We noticed on the marvel dataset that the language model-based steps cannot increase the recall. This is due to the dataset having abstracts in only 1% of the nodes in the marvel KG, consequently these steps very rarely find any pairs. The recall increases at other datasets.

By looking at the false positives of the SentenceBERT step we could outline the main reason for the mistakes, which is wrong node type detection, such as confusion between race and a character or location and race. For actual examples for the starwars graph, it connected starwars/Borgle_bat - swg/Borgle_Bat_Cave or starwars/Sayormi - swg/Sayormi_Queen, but there are a lot more difficult pairs starwars/Tortur - swg/Torton where in one of the abstracts you can find *'Torturs were a close genetic cousin of the Torton.'* which can give a false clue to the Language Model of these being the same.

Activating the SvS step can successfully filter out the similar pairs resulting in a better F-score than the exact match baselines. Same as before, cutting the abstracts at the first 2 sentences gives a slight boost. We manually investigated some of the new matches introduced by the SvS step. For example, Anakin Skywalker could be correctly matched to Darth Vader which is supported by Anakin's abstract where we can find the information "he was known as Darth

Vader" which should be enough to consider them the same. The question is whether the fine-tuned language model can recognize these clues correctly in general.

The number of false negative matches of the Exact Matching steps is low. To get a better insight into the performance of the SvS approach and how well the fine-tuned model can differentiate between the same and similar descriptions, we also generated a dataset using all gold standard pairs' abstract text. We used the same negative generation process as before. We split it into train and test sets for this evaluation exercise, just for getting a basic understanding of how hard this particular task is. The trained classifier could achieve a 97%¡ accuracy on the test sets.

Investigating the incorrect pairs of the SvS step, we can conclude that the main sources of errors are the same as in the SentenceBERT step, i.e. different types of entities getting paired together. Some examples such as starwars/High_Inquisitor - swg/Inquisitor_Fa'Zoll which is a rank-character pair, but we can find confusion between the same type of entities as well such as starwars/Old_war_bunker - swg/Naboo_Pirate_Bunker, both being on the same planet making them even more similar. All in all, thanks to the high precision of the learned model it can discard enough of these incorrect pairs so that the overall F-score increases.

5   Related Work

5.1   OAEI Competition

Each year the OAEI competition is held where several systems were submitted. We compared our results to the top 5 best performing systems on the OAEI KG track. You can see the results in Table 7. Overall our system performed the best on 2 out of 5 datasets and was close to the TOP 1 in other datasets as well considering the F-score. The ATMatcher [5] was the competitor who could perform the best on the other 3 datasets. This competitive system works in two steps. First, it tries to match the classes and properties based on their name/label information with synonym detection. It is just like our exact matching but extended with synonyms. As a second step, it moves onto the instances where only the instances with the same class/properties would be matched together based on string matching and similar neighbor filtering. On the OAEI 22 track the Graph-Matcher [4] was proposed which tried to solve the graph matching problem with the use of Graph Attention networks in a siamese network style, however, the system was not submitted on the Knowledge Graph track, therefore we cannot compare to its performance.

5.2   Complete Alignment

Another group of the graph-matching tasks is the one where a complete alignment of all nodes between the two graphs is expected. Not to be confused

Table 7. OAEI22 Knowledge Graph Track competing systems.

	mcu marvel			memoryalpha memorybeta			memoryalpha stexpanded			starwars swg			starwars swtor		
	P	R	F-m	P	R	F-m	P	R	F-m	P	R	F-m	P	R	F-m
Ours	87.7	**66.3**	**75.5**	93.2	89.9	91.5	96.8	**94**	**95.4**	87.2	77.5	82.1	93	90.6	91.8
ATMatcher	67	52	59	**96**	**91**	**93**	96	92	94	93	76	**84**	**95**	**91**	**93**
KGMatcher	**89**	56	69	94	77	85	**98**	82	89	**94**	62	75	94	83	88
LogMap	84	46	59	89	76	82	88	75	81	**94**	68	79	94	75	84
LSMatch	63	42	50	59	75	66	53	79	63	76	24	37	81	82	82
Matcha	0	0	0	56	90	69	67	93	78	70	**80**	74	73	89	80

with our main task, these are mainly graphs in different languages therefore the assumption that the same entity can be expressed in both languages [17] mainly holds. This variant of the graph matching can be considered as a multi-linguality challenge where the focus is on how well you can translate a node to other languages based on their properties. There have been attempts to create so-called dangling cases in [16], resulting in a partial alignment, but the task is still different from our original.

6   Conclusion

This paper proposes a multi-step solution for the KG matching problem. It uses only the textual information of the graph by first focusing on the trivial pairs as an exact matching search is applied between the two KGs to produce high-precision pairs. Next, with the help of neural language models, a pool of similar textual descriptions are gathered. In the last phase, we automatically construct a training set and fine-tune a language model to differentiate the same and similar descriptions. Based upon our error analysis the analysis of descriptions are useful tools to find very similar descriptions, but can easily get confused about the entity types.

Our approach performed the best on 2 out of 5 tasks in the 2022 OAEI KG matching track. As other top systems put a special focus on aligning the classes first, in the future we would focus on adding this information to the language models as well.

Acknowledgements. This research has been supported by the European Union project RRF-2.3.1-21-2022-00004 within the framework of the Artificial Intelligence National Laboratory.

References

1. Balogh, V., Berend, G., Diochnos, D.I., Turán, G.: Understanding the semantic content of sparse word embeddings using a commonsense knowledge base. In: Proceedings of the AAAI Conference on Artificial Intelligence, vol. 34, no. 05, pp. 7399–7406, April 2020. https://doi.org/10.1609/aaai.v34i05.6235, https://ojs.aaai.org/index.php/AAAI/article/view/6235

2. Devlin, J., Chang, M., Lee, K., Toutanova, K.: BERT: pre-training of deep bidirectional transformers for language understanding. CoRR abs/1810.04805 (2018). http://arxiv.org/abs/1810.04805

3. Dolan, W.B., Brockett, C.: Automatically constructing a corpus of sentential paraphrases. In: Proceedings of the Third International Workshop on Paraphrasing (IWP2005) (2005). https://aclanthology.org/I05-5002

4. Efeoglu, S.: Graphmatcher: a graph representation learning approach for ontology matching (2022)

5. Hertling, S., Paulheim, H.: Atbox results for oaei 2021. In: CEUR Workshop Proceedings, vol. 3063, pp. 137–143. RWTH Aachen (2021)

6. Hertling, S., Portisch, J., Paulheim, H.: MELT - matching evaluation toolkit. In: Acosta, M., Cudré-Mauroux, P., Maleshkova, M., Pellegrini, T., Sack, H., Sure-Vetter, Y. (eds.) SEMANTiCS 2019. LNCS, vol. 11702, pp. 231–245. Springer, Cham (2019). https://doi.org/10.1007/978-3-030-33220-4_17

7. Euzenat, J., Meilicke, C., Stuckenschmidt, H., Shvaiko, P., Trojahn, C.: Ontology alignment evaluation initiative: six years of experience. In: Spaccapietra, S. (ed.) Journal on Data Semantics XV. LNCS, vol. 6720, pp. 158–192. Springer, Heidelberg (2011). https://doi.org/10.1007/978-3-642-22630-4_6

8. Kardos, P., Szántó, Z., Farkas, R.: Rdf2vec in the knowledge graph matching task. CSCS (2022). https://www.inf.u-szeged.hu/cscs/pdf/cscs2022.pdf

9. Lan, Z., Chen, M., Goodman, S., Gimpel, K., Sharma, P., Soricut, R.: ALBERT: a lite BERT for self-supervised learning of language representations. CoRR abs/1909.11942 (2019). http://arxiv.org/abs/1909.11942

10. Liu, Y., et al.: Roberta: a robustly optimized BERT pretraining approach. CoRR abs/1907.11692 (2019). http://arxiv.org/abs/1907.11692

11. Reimers, N., Gurevych, I.: Sentence-bert: Sentence embeddings using siamese bert-networks. CoRR abs/1908.10084 (2019). http://arxiv.org/abs/1908.10084

12. Ristoski, P., Rosati, J., Di Noia, T., De Leone, R., Paulheim, H.: Rdf2vec: Rdf graph embeddings and their applications. Semantic Web 10(4), 721–752 (2019)

13. Schick, T., Schütze, H.: Exploiting cloze questions for few-shot text classification and natural language inference. CoRR abs/2001.07676 (2020). https://arxiv.org/abs/2001.07676

14. Auer, S., Bizer, C., Kobilarov, G., Lehmann, J., Cyganiak, R., Ives, Z.: DBpedia: a nucleus for a web of open data. In: Aberer, K., Choi, K.-S., Noy, N., Allemang, D., Lee, K.-I., Nixon, L., Golbeck, J., Mika, P., Maynard, D., Mizoguchi, R., Schreiber, G., Cudré-Mauroux, P. (eds.) ASWC/ISWC -2007. LNCS, vol. 4825, pp. 722–735. Springer, Heidelberg (2007). https://doi.org/10.1007/978-3-540-76298-0_52

15. Suchanek, F.M., Kasneci, G., Weikum, G.: Yago: a core of semantic knowledge. In: Proceedings of the 16th International Conference on World Wide Web, pp. 697–706 (2007)

16. Sun, Z., Chen, M., Hu, W.: Knowing the no-match: entity alignment with dangling cases. CoRR abs/2106.02248 (2021). https://arxiv.org/abs/2106.02248

17. Sun, Z., Hu, W., Li, C.: Cross-lingual entity alignment via joint attribute-preserving embedding. CoRR abs/1708.05045 (2017). http://arxiv.org/abs/1708.05045

18. Vrandečić, D., Krötzsch, M.: Wikidata: a free collaborative knowledgebase. Commun. ACM 57(10), 78–85 (2014). https://doi.org/10.1145/2629489

Efficient Approaches for the Discovery of Sensitive Information by Using Natural Language Processing Techniques

Kushal Shree Dhani, Benedikt Zundel, and Doina Logofătu[✉]

Frankfurt University of Applied Sciences, Frankfurt am Main, Germany
benedikt.zundel@stud.fra-uas.de, logofatu@fb2.fra-uas.de

Abstract. The quantity of data and documents created on a huge scale has recently increased. This signifies a rise in unstructured textual information. Extracting sensitive data is usually done manually, following certain rules, which means additional time costs and elevated chances of errors and non-performance. There is a growing need to automatically solve these types of problems, leading to the need of utilizing methodologies that are more intelligent than those previously used. The likelihood of automating this kind of assignment might significantly facilitate compliance with safety policies and imposed regulations. This work aims to highlight the status of Named Entity Recognition (NER) by evaluating models and presenting their overall presentation. It also describes the conflicts and factors that affect the perception of a given entity.

Keywords: Named Entity Recognition · spaCy NER Model · Flair NER Model · Comparison of NER models

1 Problem Description

The Named Entity Recognition (NER) process is used to recognize specific groups of words that have common semantic characteristics [8]. In reality, NER interacts with a large number of names and signifiers. The task of full named object recognition can often be split into two parts: identifying names and names being classified according to the sort of entity they relate to, such as people, organizations, or locations. Ambiguity and abbreviations as well as identifying phrases that can have more than one meaning are major challenges in recognizing named entities in language. NER is challenging because the target phrases are mainly nouns or unregistered phrases. To train the NER engine, suitable and annotated data is required. Producing training sets is the high-priced part of developing a NER engine. Annotated refers back to the reality that named entities need to be recognized within the training set, and those annotations need to be dependable to supply a well-acting engine. Therefore, we're dealing with information challenges as opposed to algorithm challenges. Algorithms will evolve and enhance over time. However, they may usually depend upon exceptional training material which is difficult and high priced to supply.

© IFIP International Federation for Information Processing 2023
Published by Springer Nature Switzerland AG 2023
I. Maglogiannis et al. (Eds.): AIAI 2023, IFIP AICT 676, pp. 399–410, 2023.
https://doi.org/10.1007/978-3-031-34107-6_32

2   Introduction

Private Identifiable Information (PII) being derived from unstructured text is an important task in many fields. For instance, the collected information can be used for document indexing, classification, and other applications. Identifying PII items is time-consuming work that can be automated by using a NER model. The goal is to develop a NER model that reduces the cost of this task by preprocessing documents before extracting information manually. Training a NER model to extract PII requires a lot of privacy-rich text, which creates privacy issues during data annotation and model training. Named entity recognition comprises of natural language processing (NLP), which is the process by which researchers use computer systems to analyze human language and extract important metadata from the text.

To conduct reproducible research, the feasibility is presented of the suggested method on a dataset generated with a library for artificial data generation in python. Following contributions are made:

1. The comprised labeled dataset is annotated in 4 classes of personal information.
2. Creating a training set and later training a NER Model with the libraries spaCy and Flair.
3. Applying the model to new sentences and therefore testing the model on the test data.

3   PII Dataset

Personal Identification Information datasets are those datasets that consist of personal information of people which can be categorized by a name, address, identification number, etc. Private Identifiable Information (PII) is retrieved from unstructured text which is a critical task in many areas such as medicine [6], legal documents [11] data mining of user-generated content [7], and publication processes [2]. Our objective in this study is to put confidentiality at the forefront of building a PII extractor, from dataset development to model training [4]. There is a need to build a tool to reduce the expense of manual PII retrieval.

In this study, the focus lies more on medical data, e.g. health insurance numbers, email addresses, names, phone numbers. To create an artificial PII dataset for training a NER model, a data frame containing information about a patient and their medical record is generated and saved for later reference. It is guaranteed that each field which is created in the data frame has some unique element. The aforementioned fields are then used to generate textual data on which the model can be trained and tested. To generate textual data for the model, the unique fields from the data frame are extracted and substituted into a randomly chosen text from a collection of pre-written phrases. Those are then written to a file, which results in paragraphs of medical information for artificial patients.

4   NER Algorithm

The algorithm for preparing the dataset and developing the model is provided in this section. Names, email addresses, phone numbers, and health insurance numbers were all included in the new dictionaries [13]. These dictionaries are used to annotate the extracted sentences, which are then separated into training and testing datasets. The flow diagram (Fig. 1) shows the process of using the PII dataset to create the NER model and extracting the labels from the trained model.

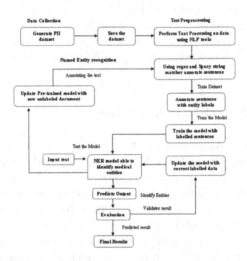

Fig. 1. Flow Diagram of NER algorithm

The method of creating the PII datasets is illustrated in preceding section. After generating the required PII dataset, the dataset is pre-processed using NLP tools. After applying pre-processing to the dataset, annotation is being created in which the annotated text with each entity label present in the text is represented. After generating the annotated text the goal is to train the model using a library that will create a model for our custom entities [13]. In this study, two libraries were used to create a NER model, namely Flair and spaCy. After building a model, the labels are predicted for the new sequence of texts to validate the result. In case the model fails to predict the required labeled entities, the model needs to be updated with correct labeled data and the model is rebuilt. To add new custom entities to the model, the pre-trained model needs to be updated with a new dataset that includes a new entity and the process repeats from creating annotations and training the model. This is the complete process to create the NER model.

4.1   Algorithm: NER [9]

Input: Preprocessed text documents.
Output: Labelled entities **Collections:** **D**– Corpus, **S**– collection of phrases, **A**– collection of annotated phrases, **E**– collection of entities, **W**– collection of words, **CD**– created dataset.

4.2   Generating Dataset [9]

The resulting dataset is saved in JSON format. The saved data is put into the main python script to train the model. The suggested method has been tested with both a blank model and an existing model [5]. Using the Transfer learning principle, the current model is retrained. CNN plays a significant part in training the model. The model trained is subsequently stored with a unique name on a disk.

5   Building the NER Framework

The system requires two inputs from the user. Location of configuration files and training data. In JSON format, the former includes model size, model language, and model training hyperparameters. "Model size" and "Model language" indicate pre-trained spaCy models where users train their data to generate new fitted models, and "Hyperparameters" include those values. It will be used during the development of hyperparameters. This framework is generalized, because choices can be made for both the spaCy model which is trained and the hyperparameter settings which is trained, and each dataset which is generated is unique based on the configuration data provided to the framework [5]. It will be a compliant model. The main features of the framework are:

1. Loading the configuration file
2. Getting the spaCy model
3. Conversion of JSON data to spaCy training data format
4. Creating training data
5. Model Training Function
6. Model saving.

6   Implementation of SpaCy

6.1   Introduction to SpaCy Training Sets

This section details the training sets and how to use spaCy's entity ruler to automatically generate training datasets that require manual validation. The data used to train machine learning models were provided in three formats: data for training, assessment data, and test data. All this data is in the same format. This is a list data structure where each index contains text (sentence, paragraph, or full text). The length of this paragraph is determined by your goals for using machine learning named entity recognition. The only other components needed to train the data are the list of entities in this text and their start, end, and labels. These annotations enable the convolutional neural network (spaCy's machine learning architecture) to learn from the data and accurately identify the entity throughout the training phase. SpaCy requires training data to be in a very special format.

Since JSON training data is in list dictionary format, we will convert it using a function that converts JSON data to spaCy training data format. SpaCy, on the other hand, provides data for training in the style of string-formatted text. This annotated data consists of a start index, end index, and entity label. Therefore, it is necessary to convert the annotated JSON text file to the required spaCy format.

6.2   Using SpaCy to Create a NER Training Set

To produce a spaCy machine learning training dataset through entity ruler, a rule-based technique is first used to automatically generate a baseline training set. This model will be used only temporarily, so create an English model. Then all the patterns of the corresponding labels are added in this entity ruler by passing patterns to the add patterns function. Then it is going to load these patterns into the ruler which is also loaded into our NLP. The entity ruler is built and linked to the spaCy model's network, but by convention spaCy introduces a different pipe all the way to the network's ending. Using spaCy analyze pipe, the pipeline can be viewed.

In this study, the implementation is done with 4 patterns, and therefore when it finds these patterns and the tokens it is automatically going to assign the corresponding label to it. A doc object is being created with the NLP, with the entity ruler loaded in it and it also goes over the whole text and then is iterated over all of those entities as they were just a regular output from the NER. All the entities in the doc object has been taken and printed in all the text with the label in it. In this way, it is checked whether the custom entity that has been loaded in the entity ruler has been activated or not.

6.3   Adding a Custom NER Pipeline and Label in SpaCy

To add custom entities to the model, a custom pipeline is created into it, and thus by using a NER, a custom label is identified.

In this study, custom labels are added such as personal names, phone numbers, health insurance numbers, and email addresses. The patterns for the custom labels have been defined with the help of Regex features. The language model is created and saved on a disk. The standard things that would appear in a blank spaCy model are vocab, meta and tokenizer so that it can do some basic parsing. To add any NER pipelines, the pipes need to be added in the spaCy model. With the help of the NLP object, the NER pipeline is created. After the creation of the NER pipeline, it usually goes to factories and its NER and tries to load the corresponding classes and functions in the pipeline. When any pipe is added with any specific name, it goes to differentiate it from other elements in the pipeline. After adding a pipe, a spaCy model will be replaced with a new spaCy model which will have a new entity added to it. The new pipeline can be found in the meta-JSON file under the new spaCy model. Each of the pipes as NER will have a customs value which will be the name of the pipe and its values will be the list of labels corresponding to that pipe. Then custom labels are added to the path. This is how the spaCy model and a blank NER pipeline are created, then a custom label is added to it and that NLP model is saved.

6.4   Training Custom Entities into SpaCy Models

To get a model into the custom NER, the model must be trained. The dictionary with a key, that corresponds to a value is a list that contains the start and end of an entity and the corresponding label. A function is used to load the JSON data which will allow to import the training data. Once the training data gets imported, the function for training our spaCy model is created.

This function takes two arguments: one being the training data, and the other being the iteration. If there are multiple pipes in a NER Model, then the iteration is achieved as per the requirement to train the model. This is the general process to create a model for custom entities.

6.5   Convert the Training Data to SpaCy Binary Files

By generating the spaCy binary object from the training data, a machine learning model is trained. The comprehensive goal is to convert spaCy2 train data to binary spaCy3 training data.

To achieve this,three parameters are sent to the function:

1. Language: An empty model language.
2. Train Data: A list of lists forming of training data.
3. Output Path: The location of the spaCy binary files in the output directory.

DocBin object was built and stored to make the functionality work. After that, they are transformed into binary objects, and files are saved to a disk.

6.6   Testing Our NER Model

After creating a model, the trained model is used to test the model which demonstrates how well it has performed with some new testing data. The custom-trained spaCy model can extract all the entities as per the requirement. Figure 2 shows the results of a NER model on a sequence of text. The model can extract the name of a person, health insurance number, email address, and phone number.

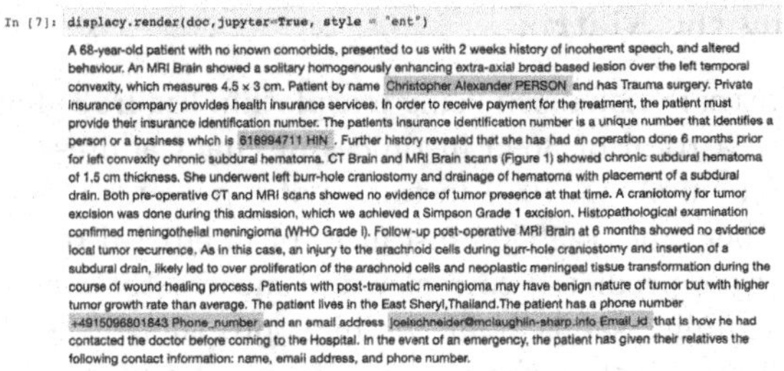

```
In (7): displacy.render(doc,jupyter=True, style = "ent")
```

A 68-year-old patient with no known comorbids, presented to us with 2 weeks history of incoherent speech, and altered behaviour. An MRI Brain showed a solitary homogenously enhancing extra-axial broad based lesion over the left temporal convexity, which measures 4.5 x 3 cm. Patient by name Christopher Alexander PERSON and has Trauma surgery. Private insurance company provides health insurance services. In order to receive payment for the treatment, the patient must provide their insurance identification number. The patients insurance identification number is a unique number that identifies a person or a business which is 618994711 HIN . Further history revealed that she has had an operation done 6 months prior for left convexity chronic subdural hematoma. CT Brain and MRI Brain scans (Figure 1) showed chronic subdural hematoma of 1.5 cm thickness. She underwent left burr-hole craniostomy and drainage of hematoma with placement of a subdural drain. Both pre-operative CT and MRI scans showed no evidence of tumor presence at that time. A craniotomy for tumor excision was done during this admission, which we achieved a Simpson Grade 1 excision. Histopathological examination confirmed meningothelial meningioma (WHO Grade I). Follow-up post-operative MRI Brain at 6 months showed no evidence local tumor recurrence. As in this case, an injury to the arachnoid cells during burr-hole craniostomy and insertion of a subdural drain, likely led to over proliferation of the arachnoid cells and neoplastic meningeal tissue transformation during the course of wound healing process. Patients with post-traumatic meningioma may have benign nature of tumor but with higher tumor growth rate than average. The patient lives in the East Sheryl,Thailand.The patient has a phone number +4915096801843 Phone_number and an email address joelschneider@mclaughlin-sharp.info Email_id that is how he had contacted the doctor before coming to the Hospital. In the event of an emergency, the patient has given their relatives the following contact information: name, email address, and phone number.

Fig. 2. Results Of a spaCy NER model

7   Confusion Matrix for NER Models

A confusion matrix outlines a classifier's classification work concerning test inputs. This is a two-dimensional matrix indexed in the first dimension by the actual class and in the second dimension by the class assigned by the classifier [12].

The following describes a confusion matrix with given descriptions for its values.

1. Amount of correctly predicted negative outcomes
2. Amount of incorrectly predicted positive outcomes
3. Amount of incorrectly predicted negative outcomes
4. Amount of correctly predicted positive outcomes.

7.1   Create Target Vector

The requirement is to create two vectors: The target value, and the predicted value. In tuple lines, the first element is text. Therefore, this text can be used to get a named entity using a trained model. The second element is a list of tuples that represent named entity tags. This allows generating an expected value vector. A target class vector is created using the labeled data.

7.2   Generating the Confusion Matrix

The Confusion matrix is generated using the sklearn library. The parameters to generate the confusion matrix are as follows:

1. *ytrue*: These are the target values. For the NER model, this parameter is being calculated in the method create total target vector.
2. *ypred*: These are the estimated targets values. For the NER model, this parameter is being calculated in the method create total prediction vector.

The *ytrue* and *ypred* parameters are passed in the confusion matrix function.

7.3 Visualizing the Matrix

The confusion matrix is visualized using matplotlib. Figure 3 shows the confusion matrix. There are a total of 3699 instances of email addresses, 3898 instances of health insurance numbers, 7034 instances of a person's name, 3011 instances of the phone number, and 1239508 instances of unlabeled tokens.The degree to which the labels were predicted correctly and incorrectly can also be read from the figure. The training set is built for high precision. The desire is to have the model be able to identify the true positives, at the expense of not having incorrect entities labeled as false positives. The confusion matrix explains the correctly predicted email addresses, health insurance numbers, person names, and phone numbers.

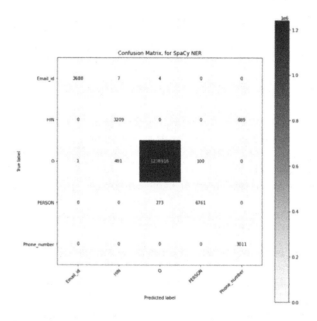

Fig. 3. Confusion Matrix plot with X-axis representing predicted label and Y-axis representing true label. Diagonal elements are correctly predicted and off diagonal elements are incorrectly predicted. Sum of the instances of each row is the total instance of a respective entity.

8   Implementation of Flair

8.1 Introduction to Flair

Flair is an NLP platform designed to simplify training and deployment of language models, text categorization, and sequence labeling. The main goal is to provide a simple and consistent interface for completely embedding many forms of words and text in theory [1]. This is unique to integrations, successfully masking all the technical complexities, allowing researchers to combine different integrations with minimal effort. In addition to traditional model training and hyperparameter selection methods, the platform includes a data acquisition module for loading and converting published NLP datasets into data structures and setting up experiments easily.

8.2   Using Flair to Train a Custom NER Model

The model is trained with flair to identify customized entities from the input text. Data preparation of the data provided for model training is not as easy as spaCy. By creating a training corpus first, the model can be created to find these entities in the given piece of text. In this thesis, the training for custom entities and the dataset is prepared by ourselves. The training dataset should follow the following structure.

1. A blank line divides the sentences in the corpus.
2. There are two-column: The first column contains the text and the second must have the BIO-annotated NER tag.

Data Creation of the Flair Model. To create corpus objects, there is a class called column corpus. The data in the three text files that belong to the train, test, and validation corpus should be in the structure discussed in the preceding section.

1. In the first step the data frame is being preprocessed where special characters are escaped, a space before the punctuation marks is being added, and white space is removed.
2. To create an annotation, the sequence matcher method is imported from difflib and is used to create the start and end index of each pattern present in the text.
3. According to the BIO Scheme, all entities in the phrase are tagged after extracting all the entities from the text. The final data would look like as shown in the Fig. 4.

After getting the data in the desired format, the data is ready to load and start the training. The tag needs to be defined and the model should be capable to anticipate and construct the tag dictionary. To create embeddings, a bunch of pre-trained models needs to be chosen. The following step was to set up the Sequence Tagger and the output of the tagger. The model is then trained with the help of a model trainer. After training, information like training logs, loss statistics, and estimates with a confidence score on the testing sample, as well as the model itself are stored in the working directory.

```
The O
patient O
had O
contacted O
the O
doctor O
using O
a O
phone O
number O
+49962885 B-Phone_number
and O
an O
email O
address O
ellisdarryl@yahoo.com B-Email_id
before O
coming O
to O
hospital O
```

Fig. 4. Results obtained from creating the data for training the flair model

9   Comparison Between Flair and SpaCy NER Models

Both NER models performed satisfactorily. As per the metrics measured, the Flair model has performed better than spaCy, however, both models have slight advantages and downsides. SpaCy is a free and open-source package for sophisticated NLP in Python. It is intended for production usage and aids with the development of applications that process and "understand" massive quantities of text. Whereas Flair's framework is based directly on PyTorch, a well-known deep-learning library. Flair has given two pre-trained NER models, each of which is a bi-LSTM on top of a word embedding layer. Each classifier is trained using a distinct NER dataset. SpaCy, on the other hand, maybe utilized to create information extraction or natural language processing applications. SpaCy, on the other hand, maybe used to create information retrieval and natural language comprehension systems, as well as to pre-process text in preparation for deep learning. SpaCy's precision was insufficient for their purposes, and Flair was sluggish. As a result, employing spaCy on languages other than English may provide poor results with pre-trained NER models, whereas Flair supports several languages. SpaCy is still faster, but the improvements they describe make Flair a better fit for their use case (Table 1).

Table 1. Experimental result of NER methods

Metrics	Flair	spaCy
Precision score	98.8%	99.6%
Recall score	98.9%	92.4%
F-score	98.8%	95.4%
Accuracy	98.6%	99.8%

10   Summary

Named Entity Recognition (NER) plays an essential part in the detection and classification of entities in NLP applications. In this paper, we contributed a new dataset with 10000 unique entities which included the PII Named Entity Recognition task in the medical domain including 17 fields, and proposed methods for measuring the initial performance in terms of recall, precision, and F1-score.

Initially, the model was built from scratch for custom-named entities using the spaCy library. The model performance was good enough to extract all the entities from a new sequence of text. Overall time to build the spaCy model was roughly half an hour. The F1-score for the spaCy model for overall text is 95.4%. SpaCy deals with computational linguistic tasks very well and spaCy NER methodology is very useful. The second model, built using Flair, contextualized word embeddings with the dataset attaining with competitive outcomes. Judging by the F1-score of 98%, the Flair model achieves state-of-the-art performance in the overall corpus. Time spent to build the Flair model was about three hours, which is more as compared to the spaCy model. By utilizing the information from a massive amount of unlabeled data, with language model pretraining it becomes feasible to design a high-quality NER system even with this minimal quantity of annotations.

11   Conclusion

Natural Language Processing encounters a variety of issues in its applications. This research provided a comprehensive assessment of the NER taking PII into account and also identified a specific set of entities. Using spaCy and Flair, two very robust and popular frameworks, this research provides a machine learning method for Named-Entity Recognition with PII datasets, a highly inflected language.

This study examined a NER approach that can find interconnections between names, health insurance numbers, phone numbers, email addresses, etc. Importantly, recent advances through deep learning in artificial intelligence have opened up a fresh viewpoint on NER. There is a huge scope of development in this area of the field.

References

1. Akbik, A., Bergmann, T., Blythe, D., Rasul, K., Schweter, S., Vollgraf, R.: FLAIR: an easy-to-use framework for state-of-the-art NLP. In: Proceedings of the 2019 Conference of the North American Chapter of the Association for Computational Linguistics (Demonstrations), pp. 54–59. Association for Computational Linguistics, Minneapolis, Minnesota, June 2019. https://doi.org/10.18653/v1/N19-4010, https://aclanthology.org/N19-4010
2. Aura, T., Kuhn, T.A., Roe, M.: Scanning electronic documents for personally identifiable information. In: Proceedings of the 5th ACM Workshop on Privacy in Electronic Society, pp. 41–50. WPES 2006, Association for Computing Machinery, New York (2006). https://doi.org/10.1145/1179601.1179608

3. Ghiasvand, O., Kate, R.J.: Learning for clinical named entity recognition without manual annotations. Inf. Med. Unlocked **13**, 122–127 (2018). https://doi.org/10.1016/j.imu.2018.10.011, https://www.sciencedirect.com/science/article/pii/S2352914818301965

4. Hathurusinghe, R., Nejadgholi, I., Bolic, M.: A privacy-preserving approach to extraction of personal information through automatic annotation and federated learning. In: Proceedings of the Third Workshop on Privacy in Natural Language Processing, pp. 36–45. Association for Computational Linguistics, Online, June 2021. https://doi.org/10.18653/v1/2021.privatenlp-1.5, https://aclanthology.org/2021.privatenlp-1.5

5. Kumar, D., Pandey, S., Patel, P., Choudhari, K., Hajare, A., Jante, S.: Generalized named entity recognition framework. In: 2021 Asian Conference on Innovation in Technology (ASIANCON), pp. 1–4 (2021). https://doi.org/10.1109/ASIANCON51346.2021.9544652

6. Kushida, C., Nichols, D., Jadrnicek, R., Miller, R., Walsh, J., Griffin, K.: Strategies for de-identification and anonymization of electronic health record data for use in multicenter research studies. Med. care **50**(Suppl), S82–S101 (2012). https://doi.org/10.1097/MLR.0b013e3182585355

7. Mosallanezhad, A., Beigi, G., Liu, H.: Deep reinforcement learning-based text anonymization against private-attribute inference. In: Proceedings of the 2019 Conference on Empirical Methods in Natural Language Processing and the 9th International Joint Conference on Natural Language Processing (EMNLP-IJCNLP), pp. 2360–2369. Association for Computational Linguistics, Hong Kong, China, November 2019. https://doi.org/10.18653/v1/D19-1240, https://aclanthology.org/D19-1240

8. Naseer, S., et al.: Named entity recognition (NER) in NLP techniques, tools accuracy and performance (2022)

9. Ramachandran, R., Arutchelvan, K.: Named entity recognition on bio-medical literature documents using hybrid based approach. J. Ambient Intell. Humaniz. Comput., 1–10, March 2021

10. Surabhi, M.: Natural language processing future, pp. 1–3 (2013). https://doi.org/10.1109/ICOISS.2013.6678407

11. Tamper, M., Oksanen, A., Tuominen, J., Hietanen, A., Hyvönen, E.: Automatic annotation service APPI: named entity linking in legal domain. In: Harth, A., et al. (eds.) ESWC 2020. LNCS, vol. 12124, pp. 208–213. Springer, Cham (2020). https://doi.org/10.1007/978-3-030-62327-2_36

12. Ting, K.M.: Confusion Matrix, p. 209. Springer, Boston (2010). https://doi.org/10.1007/978-0-387-30164-8_157

13. Tripathi, S.P., Rai, H.: SimNER - an accurate and faster algorithm for named entity recognition. In: 2018 Second International Conference on Advances in Computing, Control and Communication Technology (IAC3T), pp. 115–119 (2018). https://doi.org/10.1109/IAC3T.2018.8674025

Natural Language Processing for the Turkish Academic Texts in the Engineering Field: Key-Term Extraction, Similarity Detection, Subject/Topic Assignment

Bora Kat[1,2]([✉]) [iD]

[1] Middle East Technical University, Ankara, Turkey
borakat@gmail.com
[2] The Scientific and Technological Research Council of Turkey (TÜBİTAK), Ankara, Turkey

Abstract. The information retrieved from texts plays crucial roles in many aspects. Although there are significant attempts on natural language processing for various types of texts in Turkish, none of them deals with academic texts. This study mainly aims to retrieve precise key terms from Turkish academic texts in the field of engineering and develops algorithms for similarity detection and automatic classification based on these key terms. In the first step of this study: a library and customized templates, that can transform the n-grams into structured forms, are created by considering the features of engineering terminology and the grammar of the Turkish language. Then, a customized similarity detection algorithm is developed. Finally, the Naïve Bayes Classifier is used to assign the documents to the appropriate engineering sub-fields. The project proposals submitted to The Scientific and Technological Research Council of Turkey (TÜBİTAK) Academic Research Funding Program Directorate (ARDEB) are analyzed as a case study. The results indicate that the proposed similarity algorithm correctly detects almost all of the re-submitted proposals while the accuracy of the classifier is 83.3% in the first prediction and reaches up to 96.4% in the first three predictions over a sample of 1255 proposals.

Keywords: Key term extraction · Feature extraction · Natural language processing (NLP) · Supervised machine learning · Naïve Bayes classifier · TÜBİTAK · Conceptual similarity · subject/topic assignment

1 Introduction

The era of rapid digitalization and the concomitant expansion in the size of the data make it essential to develop mechanisms that will support the management of big data and the retrieval of valuable information. At this point, natural language processing (NLP) studies provide support to many processes in different fields and for different languages. Academic texts also take its share from this transformation, e.g., feature extraction from

© IFIP International Federation for Information Processing 2023
Published by Springer Nature Switzerland AG 2023
I. Maglogiannis et al. (Eds.): AIAI 2023, IFIP AICT 676, pp. 411–424, 2023.
https://doi.org/10.1007/978-3-031-34107-6_33

unstructured texts, similarity detection between the documents and automatic classification or clustering of the documents. Especially machine learning-based text classification studies [1] have gained momentum in recent years, e.g., sentiment analysis, indexing news texts, grouping social media posts, classification of legal decisions, etc. In line with the increasing amount of funds allocated to R&D, the number of project proposals and the data related to these applications and outputs of funded research have increased significantly. As a result, the need for effective monitoring of data on proposals and their outputs has emerged. To satisfy this need; TÜBİTAK has developed several business software for different phases of funding, i.e., application, evaluation, and monitoring. On the other hand, the need for decision support systems (DSS) that will help the processes for these applications to be carried out in a more effective, efficient and qualified manner is increasing day by day. An example of such a DSS, PaneLIST, in which the problem of identifying the most appropriate reviewers for a set of proposals, was demonstrated in [2].

Considering the Turkish language, there is an important gap in the classification of academic texts according to their subjects. Current study aims to fill this gap with algorithms developed based on a thorough analysis carried out on the project proposals submitted to TÜBİTAK ARDEB. In the current study, as a complement to PaneLIST, new and customized algorithms have been developed to provide solutions to the following three essential issues:

I) Automatic key term extraction from the proposals
II) Similarity level determination between the proposals
III) Automatic subject/topic assignment to the proposals

The study focuses on the project proposals submitted to ARDEB, however, the proposed algorithms can be used (without an extensive revision) for all Turkish academic texts in closer scientific domains.

The rest of the paper is organized as follows. First, the literature review is presented. Then, the methodology is explained in detail with dedicated sub-sections for each step and each problem. Next come the details related to the case study of ARDEB project proposals. Finally, the paper ends with the conclusion and recommendations for future research.

2 Literature Review

The performance of the first step, (I) key term extraction, is very crucial since its outputs are also inputs to the algorithms those are developed in (II) and (III), i.e., similarity level determination and subject/topic assignment. The most critical issue in key-term extraction is the preprocessing procedures that will help transforming the words and phrases in the proposals into structured forms. At this phase, in addition to the to "noise" cleaning (removing stop words such as conjunctions, prepositions and pronouns, along with punctuation marks), "stemming" to obtain the basic roots of words, and "lemmatization" to make the words simple by considering their morphology, are used. For the Turkish language, there are studies [3, 4] indicating that stemming has a limited effect on the subject classification while root analysis algorithms have a positive effect on information extraction [5]. In the current study, besides the standard preprocessing steps, the main distinguishing contribution is the identification of frequently used terms within the scope of the engineering field and the construction of templates that will transform these terms into common key-term structures.

Investigating the similarity of two texts or vectorial structures obtained from these texts, on the other hand, is another well-known problem in the literature and practice. The topic is studied in two general frameworks: algorithm/software development for plagiarism detection [6–8] and studies for detecting conceptual similarity [9]. Moreover, different metrics have been defined to determine the level of similarity [6–9]. Within the scope of the current study, a customized similarity algorithm has been developed in which both textual and conceptual similarity can be detected. Analyzes have shown that the proposed algorithm provides almost 100% accuracy in detecting re-submissions.

Classification of a text according to its subject (III) emerges as a research area that has been frequently studied in recent years, especially employing machine learning-based algorithms [1, 10–15]. It can be in the form of assignment to a pre-defined set of classes, or it can be in the form of dividing the texts into a certain number of groups without any pre-defined class set. For the latter (also in the current study) generally the supervised machine learning algorithms are used. Classification for the Turkish texts have gained importance in recent years [16–23]. Although, these studies include movie [20–24], hotel [20] and restaurant [25] reviews, website content [23], tweet contents [20–24, 26], e-mail contents [27] and fairy tales [22] etc.; the data sets in the classification studies in Turkish is mostly the news data sets [3, 5, 13, 14, 18, 21, 27–29]. On the other hand, while there are extensive studies on the classification of academic texts in English [11, 30–32], no study has been found for the Turkish academic texts. In the present study, the Naïve Bayes [33, 34] algorithm is used as the classifier. This algorithm is frequently used in the literature for similar purposes and generates successful results. Moreover, it has been extensively examined in many aspects (preprocessing, training set size etc.) and significant inferences have been obtained [35–37].

3 Methodology

This section explains all of the steps followed in the study. First, preprocessing procedure is summarized. Next, the algorithm to retrieve keywords and key-terms is illustrated. Then, the postprocessing procedure is explained. Last two sub-sections are devoted to the similarity detection and subfield classification, respectively. Note that the parameters and sets used in the proposed algorithms are summarized below in Table 1.

Table 1. Sets and parameters.

Symbol	Definition	Symbol	Definition
D, d	Set of proposals & elements of the set	δ	Scaling parameter 2 for n-grams
D_e	Training set	θ	Similarity score threshold 1
S, s	Set of classes and each element of the set	τ	Similarity score threshold 2
K^d, k^d	Set of key-terms and elements of the set	σs	Penalty parameter for lower overlaps
$\widehat{GRAM}_1^d$	Average of frequencies of top five one-grams in proposal d	π, C, μ	Scaling and correction parameters for the similarity score
$GRAM_n^d$	Set of n-grams in proposal d; n = 1,2 3, 4	$sim(x, y)$	Similarity score between x and y - [0,1]
$xGRAM_n^d$	Highest frequency value of n-gram in d	s_{ML}	Class with the highest likelihood
$tf^d(k)$	Term frequency of key-term k in d	$m(s)$	Number of proposals in class s
$atf^d(k)$	Term frequency of key-term k in d – adj	α	Correction parameter
γ_n	Scaling parameter 1 for n-grams	V	Set of all key-terms in the training set

3.1 Preprocessing

Some of the preprocessing stages are carried out with the standard methods, and in some of them specific arrangements are made considering the scope of the documents and the features of the Turkish language, i.e., academic engineering terminology, common words/phrases specific to TÜBİTAK application forms and distinguishing structure of key-terms in Turkish. The preprocessing steps performed are presented below:

– **Punctuation marks removal**
– **Lower casing**
– **Stop-words removal**: In addition to the standard stop-words in Turkish, some common words and terms, e.g., "prof" ("prof"), "profesör" ("professor"), "araştırmacı" ("researcher"), "proje ekibi" ("project team"), "öğrenci" ("student"), "lisansüstü" ("graduate"), "TÜBİTAK", "bursiyer" ("scholar"), etc., used in engineering proposals are appended to the stop-words library.
– **Tokenization**: Vectors of uni-grams, bi-grams, 3-g and 4-g are extracted.
– **Tailored stemming**: The templates that convert n-grams into standard forms considering the fact that the single-word key-terms are in nominative form and the multi-word key-terms are generally in the form of inflexional suffixes in Turkish.

3.2 Keyword and Key-Term Extraction - KeyEx

In order to extract key-terms after the preprocessing stage, the texts must first be separated into its tokens. As a result of this tokenization process, sequential arrays consisting of n (n = 1, 2, 3, ...) elements called grams are obtained. In the present study, after creating single (uni-gram), binary (bi-gram), triple (tri-gram) and quadruple (4-g) sequences, a term-frequency vector is created. In addition, if user-defined keywords exists in the proposal, the developed code can distinguish these terms and assign the highest frequency coming from other n-grams. The terms in the final vector are then converted into a word cloud image for further analysis by an expert's eye (see Fig. 2). At this stage, a scaling was carried out on the frequencies in order to obtain a more understandable structure in the cloud image and to get more meaningful results in the similarity algorithm to be run later. The scaling function (for uni-grams and n-grams, respectively) is as follows:

$$atf^d\left(k^d|k^d \epsilon GRAM_1^d\right) = \left[\frac{tf^d(k^d)}{\widehat{GRAM_1^d}}\right]^{\gamma_1} ; \forall d \in D \tag{1}$$

$$atf^d\left(k^d|k^d \epsilon GRAM_n^d\right) = \left[\frac{tf^d(k^d)}{\max\{xGRAM_n^d, \delta \cdot |GRAM_1^d|\}}\right]^{\gamma_n} ; \forall d \in D, n = 2, 3, 4 \tag{2}$$

The primary purpose in these equations is to normalize the frequency values over 0–1 interval. In the first equation, the frequency values of individual grams are divided by the mean of the top five values. In the second equation, the frequency of multi-grams is divided by the highest frequency in the relevant gram set or a certain ratio of the total number of words in the text (to represent the impact of the proposal length). After this calculation, all values greater than 1 are set to 1. Another purpose is to eliminate the incompatibility caused by the frequency difference of single and multiple strings. Single grams can have high frequency by combining with different words and word groups in expressions written for different purposes in a text. The fact that their frequency is high may not be sufficient to conclude that those words are descriptive or distinctive for the relevant text. However, the repetition of multiple sequences in the text strengthens the possibility that these sequences are certain concepts describing the project.

3.3 Postprocessing

The operations carried out in the preprocessing stage are aimed at bringing the text to a standard structure as much as possible. In the final processing stage, updates are made not only in the text, but also in the term-frequency vector obtained from the text. The purpose of using this postprocessing step, which is not often encountered in NLP studies, is to make the retrieved concepts capable of indexing texts as much as possible without the need for an additional expert evaluation process. Then, as a result of detailed preliminary analysis, the concepts in the following three groups were removed from the term-frequency vector:

– Uni-grams that do not make sense on their own. These words may either represent very general meanings, e.g., "amaç" ("purpose"), "ortak" ("common"), "deney" ("experiment"), etc., or they are often part of multiple sequences, e.g., "kendiliğinden" ("spontaneous"), "etkin" ("efficient"), etc.
– Multi-grams with a first word that does not allow a grammatically correct phrase. They usually have a possessive suffix and are located in the later part of the concept in multi-grams, e.g., "dayalı" ("based"), "yapısı" ("structure of ..."), etc.
– Multi-grams with a last word that does not allow a grammatically correct phrase. These last words are generally adjective or adjective in noun and are expected to take place in different positions in other grammatically correct sequences, e.g., "yeni" ("new"), "bölgesel" ("regional"), etc.

3.4 Similarity Detection - SimDet

Within the scope of the study, a tailored similarity algorithm was developed, in which both conceptual and textual similarity are considered together, taking into account the common definitions of similarity, i.e., cosine similarity and jaccard similarity. Let atf^x and atf^y represent adjusted term-frequency vectors created for document x ($x \in D$) and y ($y \in D$). The similarity calculated over these vectors are shown in eqns. (3)-(9) presented below. First, an intersection set of terms with atf values above a certain threshold level is created in key-term sets, see Eq. (3). In Eq. (4)-(6); the number of terms scoring above the threshold levels and the number of terms in the intersection set are calculated. In Eq. (7), a similarity factor is calculated which takes into account how much of the terms in each document are covered by the intersection set.

$$INT(x, y) = set\left(x|atf^x\left(k^x\right) > \theta\right) \cap set\left(y|atf^y\left(k^y\right) > \theta\right) \tag{3}$$

$$len(x) = \left|set\left(x|atf^x\left(k^x\right) > \theta\right)\right| \tag{4}$$

$$len(y) = \left|set\left(y|atf^y\left(k^y\right) > \theta\right)\right| \tag{5}$$

$$lenINT(x, y) = |INT(x, y)| \tag{6}$$

$$\pi = \left[C \cdot \frac{lenINT(x, y)}{len(x)} \cdot \frac{lenINT(x, y)}{len(y)}\right]^{\mu} \tag{7}$$

To create a score for similarity detection; first, the geometric mean of the atf values in each document was taken for the terms in the intersection set, see Eq. (8). Then, in Eq. (9), the arithmetic mean of the geometric means is found. However, as can be seen in the related equation; when calculating the arithmetic mean, the sum of the geometric mean is divided by a fixed number if the intersection set is below a certain value. This adaptation, based on observations made as a result of preliminary studies, prevents misleading results from very few but high-scoring matches. Similarly, previously calculated π factor is used to reflect the impact of how much the terms in the texts overlap (considering proposal lengths). In addition, the power term added for the calculated arithmetic mean was designed to increase the effect of relatively high frequency overlaps and especially to facilitate the identification of re-submissions. The parameters used in the algorithm were determined as a result of a comprehensive preliminary study and are presented in Table 2..

$$atf^z\left(k^z\right) = \sqrt{atf^x(k^z) \cdot atf^y\ (k^z)}; \forall k^z \in INT\,(x, y) \tag{8}$$

$$sim(x, y) = \pi \cdot \left[\frac{\sum_{\forall k^z \in setU\,(x,y)} atf^z(k^z)}{\max\{\sigma, lenINT\,(x, y)\}} \right]^{\frac{2}{(1+|INT\,(x,y)|atf^z\,(k^z) > \tau|)}} \tag{9}$$

Table 2. Values of parameters in SimDet.

$\theta = 0, 60$	$\sigma = 50$	$C = 100$	$\tau = 0, 65$	$\mu = 0, 50$

3.5 Subfield Classification by Machine Learning – SubCla

Naïve Bayes (NB) classifier is employed for automatic assignment of the proposals into the current classification scheme used in ARDEB (see Table 3.). NB classifier, as a supervised machine learning classifier, calculates the probability that a text whose class is to be predicted belongs to each class, by using the probabilities determined over the texts in the training set. In order to use the NB classifier, first of all, a training set, $D_{training}$, is needed. Equation (10) shows the probability of document d belonging to class s according to Bayes theory. It shows the product of the prior probability and the conditional probability divided by the evidence value. As a result, the relationship given in the intermediate stage, Eq. (11) turns into Eq. (12). This equation identifies the class that maximizes the probability of the class that document d belongs to. In order to determine the target class, the $p(s)$ and $p(k|s)$ values in Eq. (12) must be calculated where the former is obtained by dividing the number of documents belonging to class s in the training set by the total number of training documents as represented in Eq. (13). When a text is known to belong to class s, the probability that the term k is in the related text is presented in Eq. (14) where the expression in the numerator gives the total frequency of term k in all documents in the relevant class, and the denominator gives the total number of all terms in all documents in class s. α values added to the numerator and denominator are for correction to prevent the product in Eq. (12) from being 0 and to improve the estimation performance [33, 34]. When $\alpha = 1$, it is called the Laplace correction, and when it is smaller, the Lidstone correction [34].

$$p(s|d) = \frac{p(d|s) \cdot p(s)}{p(d)} \tag{10}$$

$$s_{ML} = argmax_{s \in S} p(s|d) = argmax_{s \in S} \frac{p(d|s) \cdot p(s)}{p(d)} \tag{11}$$

$$s_{ML} = argmax_{s \in S} \left\{ \prod_{k^d \in K^d} p\left(k^d | s\right) \cdot p(s) \right\} \quad (12)$$

$$p(s) = \frac{m(s)}{|D_e|} \quad (13)$$

$$p(k|s) = \frac{\left[\sum_{d \in s} tf^d(k)\right] + 1}{\sum_{v \in V, d \in s}\left[tf^d(v) + 1\right]} = \frac{\left[\sum_{d \in s} tf^d(k)\right] + 1}{\sum_{v \in V, d \in s}\left[tf^d(v)\right] + |V|} \rightarrow \frac{\left[\sum_{d \in s} tf^d(k)\right] + \alpha}{\sum_{v \in V, d \in s}\left[tf^d(v)\right] + \alpha \cdot |V|}$$
$$(14)$$

Two adaptations have been made to ensure the functioning of the algorithm and increase both speed and prediction performance. First, in Eq. (12), where there are many terms, sum of their natural logarithms instead of the product of these terms, are used to overcome the problem of the product of these terms, which have very small values, converge to 0. Second, the terms with a frequency of 3 or more are taken into account for each text; frequency values are also scaled by taking their natural logarithms.

4 Case Study

4.1 The Data

When submitting a project proposal to ARDEB, the applicants mark the support group and the panel areas under this support group for which their projects are suitable. The engineering fields and subfields in the ARDEB's Engineering Research Grant Committee (MAG) are presented in Table 3..

As can be seen, Industrial Eng., Aviation & Space Eng., Petroleum & Natural Gas Eng. Consist of only one main field, while detailed sub-fields and "other" option are defined for the remaining fields of engineering. The list consists of 45 sub-fields. As a result of expert experiences and preliminary analyzes on the subject; Aviation & Space Eng., Petroleum & Natural Gas Eng., and Architecture, which have only several proposals within the selected time period, together with the "other" options, are excluded from the scope. Textile Eng., on the other hand, is considered as a single field. For convenience, a Turkish abbreviation consisting of 4 letters has been defined for the each sub-field used in the case study, as seen in Table 3.. In the study, 1255 project proposals submitted to MAG within the scope of "1001 Program" between 2015–2021 are analyzed. The break-down of these proposals to sub-fields is presented in Fig. 1.

4.2 Performance of the Algorithms

KeyExt: The performance of the key-term extraction mostly depends on the extent to which the engineering concepts in the texts are standardized. For this reason, a detailed preliminary study is carried out and templates that transform words into similar forms were applied to cover almost all terms in the field as much as possible. In addition, different from the preceding studies, the postprocessing step customized specifically for this study made a significant contribution.

Table 3. Engineering fields and sub-fields in MAG.

Industrial Engineering (ENDU)	Chemical Engineering	Material Sci. & Engineering
Aviation & Space Engineering	Separation Processes (KMAI)	Battery/Storage Technologies (MZBP)
Civil Engineering	Biotech.-Bioeng. (KMBB)	Metallurgy/Met. All. & Comp (MZMM)
Geotechnics (INGE)	Polymers (KMPL)	Polymer Composites (MZPK)
Hydraulics (INHD)	Tissue Engineering (KMDM)	Ceramics/Glass (MZSC)
Hydrology (INHJ)	Energy Technologies (KMET)	Applied Physics (MZUF)
Coastal and Ocean (INKL)	Catalysts (KMKT)	Other
Architecture	Other	Pet. And Nat. Gas Engineering
Transportation (INUL)	**Mechanical Engineering**	**Textile Engineering** (TEKS)
Structures & Earthquake (INYD)	Energy Systems (MEES)	Apparel Technology
Materials of Constriction (INYM)	Manufacturing Tech. (MEIM)	Technical Textiles
Building Mechanics (INYK)	Thermo-Fluid (MEIA)	Textile Machinery
Construction Manag. (INYY)	Mach. Theo., Dyn. & Des (MEMT)	Textile Materials
Other	Mechanics (MEMK)	Textile Technologies
Mining Engineering	Mechatronics-Robotics (MEMR)	Textile Finishing & Chemistry
Mineral Preparation (MDCH)	Combustion (MEYN)	Other
Mining (MDIS)	Other	
Other		

The word clouds showing the high-frequency terms are presented in Fig. 2 for randomly selected projects from two different engineering fields. These key-terms are precise enough to be used without requiring an additional expert examination.

SimDet: Determining the similarity for proposals serves two important purposes: identifying re-submitted (revised) proposals and identifying conceptually similar proposals. A pilot study was conducted in MAG to determine the threshold levels of the similarity scores for a proposal to be attributed as a re-submission or as a conceptually similar one. It is found appropriate to evaluate the proposal pairs with a similarity score above 0.90

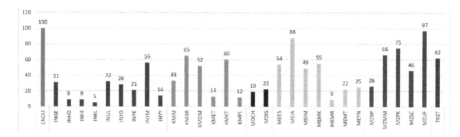

Fig. 1. Break-down of the proposals in the case study by sub-fields: number

Fig. 2. Word cloud representation of key terms for randomly selected project proposals.

as re-submissions, and those with a similarity score between 0.70–0.90 as conceptually close proposals. The re-submission status information (in the ARDEB database) of 1255 proposals covered in the case study was identified and it was determined that there were 148 re-submitted pairs, 12 re-submitted triples and 1 proposal with 4 versions. Considering all pairwise combinations between re-submissions, there is a total of 190 revision pairs, and the number of proposals with any re-submission is 336. In the case study, similarity scores were calculated for pairwise combinations of 1255 proposals $(C(1255,2) = 786,885$ pair-wise comparisons). After running the algorithm, 10 more re-submissions (not marked as re-submission in the database) are identified.

Table 4. Performance indicators of SimDet for identifying revised manuscripts.

Indicator	over proposals	over proposal pairs
Accuracy	97.131%	99.998%
Precision	93.956%	94.146%
Recall	96.067%	96.500%
F1 Score	95.000%	95.309%

The results show that 342 proposals out of 356 re-submissions are correctly predicted. There are 11 pairs that are not actually re-submissions but have a similarity score above 0.90. However, when these proposals are examined in more detail, 7 of these pairs were identified to be submitted by the same research team. Remaining 4 pairs, on the other hand, were found to be very close in terms of subject, content and even the project title. SimDet calculated similarity score below 0.90 for 7 pairs which are originally re-submissions. However, it has been observed that significant changes have been made for these proposals in line with the issues highlighted in the review reports. The performance indicators of the algorithm are presented in Table 4.. As can be seen, the accuracy rate is close to 100% in the analysis performed on pairs.

SubCla: The 1255 proposals used in the case study were allocated 70%-30% to the training and test clusters. As a result, 895 of 1255 project proposals were used in the training set and 360 in the test set. The distribution of the number of proposals and percentages in the training and test sets by sub-field is given in Table 5..

Table 5. Break-down of the training & test data by sub-fields: number of proposals.

	Train	Test		Train	Test		Train	Test		Train	Test
ENDU	70	30	INYM	40	16	MDCH	14	5	MEYN	18	7
INGE	22	9	INYY	10	4	MDIS	16	6	MZBP	19	7
INHD	7	2	KMAI	24	9	MEES	38	16	MZMM	47	19
INHJ	7	2	KMBB	45	19	MEIA	62	26	MZPK	54	21
INKL	4	1	KMDM	38	15	MEIM	35	14	MZSC	33	13
INUL	23	9	KMET	10	2	MEMK	38	17	MZUF	68	31
INYD	20	8	KMKT	42	19	MEMR	7	2	TKST	44	17
INYK	15	6	KMPL	9	2	MEMT	16	6			

Performance indicators of the SubCla algorithm on the first estimates over the all sub-fields can be seen in Table 6.. It shows that the SubCla algorithm is quite successful in estimating such a large number of defined sub-fields. For some of the relatively underperforming sub-fields (INHD, INYK, MEMR), the dataset in the relevant field is limited, for some (MZSC, MZUF), interdisciplinary projects are intense as a subject or actually divided into separate sub-fields. When an evaluation is made on the basis of main areas (see Fig. 3), the performance of the algorithm is significantly higher. The results indicate a perfect performance for the fields with distinct and focused proposals, e.g., industrial/textile/mining eng., while a moderate performance for those with overlapping research avenues, e.g., chemical/civil/mechanical eng. and material science.

5   Results and Discussion

Rapid growth in the R&D funds and the number of stakeholders in the science and technology ecosystem have brought along a significant increase in the total number of applications. TÜBİTAK has developed a number of information management systems in order to manage the increasing workload and effectively meet the needs of all stakehold-ers. However, the significant increase in the volume of transactions makes it essential to

Table 6. Classifier performance of SubCla algorithm.

	Accuracy	Recall	F1		Accuracy	Recall	F1
ENDU	100,0%	96,8%	98,4%	MDCH	100,0%	100,0%	100,0%
INGE	100,0%	90,0%	94,7%	MDIS	100,0%	100,0%	100,0%
INHD	0,0%	-	-	MEES	87,5%	82,4%	84,8%
INHJ	100,0%	66,7%	80,0%	MEIA	92,3%	72,7%	81,4%
INKL	100,0%	100,0%	100,0%	MEIM	78,6%	91,7%	84,6%
INUL	77,8%	100,0%	87,5%	MEMK	88,2%	75,0%	81,1%
INYD	87,5%	77,8%	82,4%	MEMR	50,0%	100,0%	66,7%
INYK	33,3%	50,0%	40,0%	MEMT	50,0%	50,0%	50,0%
INYM	87,5%	100,0%	93,3%	MEYN	71,4%	100,0%	83,3%
INYY	100,0%	100,0%	100,0%	MZBP	71,4%	83,3%	76,9%
KMAI	77,8%	77,8%	77,8%	MZMM	73,7%	73,7%	73,7%
KMBB	78,9%	88,2%	83,3%	MZPK	71,4%	71,4%	71,4%
KMDM	100,0%	71,4%	83,3%	MZSC	69,2%	90,0%	78,3%
KMET	50,0%	100,0%	66,7%	MZUF	74,2%	88,5%	80,7%
KMKT	94,7%	81,8%	87,8%	TKST	100,0%	89,5%	94,4%
KMPL	50,0%	100,0%	66,7%				

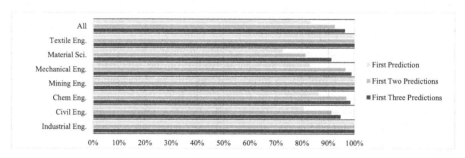

Fig. 3. Classifier performance of SubCla algorithm: over main fields.

develop intelligent DSSs that can assist users and decision makers at every stage. This study, as a continuation of PaneLIST [2], develops NLP-based algorithms for proposals, i.e., extracting key terms, similarity determination, and automatic subject/topic assignment. This study fills an important gap in the literature in the context of these issues for the Turkish academic texts. As mentioned in the literature section; although there are studies on the classification of Turkish texts (comments on movie/hotel/restaurant websites, website/tweet/e-mail contents or news texts), no study has been found on the classification of academic texts. A detailed version of this study is available as a peer-reviewed article in Turkish [38]. In the current study, the proposals submitted to MAG are examined, and a normalization library is created based on the words and terms used in the field of engineering. Then, a data set containing 1255 project proposals is prepared, and in the first stage, key terms are extracted from the proposals and a similarity algorithm was developed over these key-term vectors. Afterwards, the Naïve Bayes classification approach is employed to predict the category that each proposal belongs to. It has been shown that the proposed algorithm fully meets the need in the detection of re-submission or similar proposals. Moreover, for the classification algorithm, a success rate of 83.3% in the first estimation, 92.5% in the first two estimations and 96.4% in the first three estimations is achieved.

References

1. Khan, A., Baharudin, B., Lee, L., Khan, K.: A review of machine learning algorithms for text-documents classification. J. Adv. Inf. Technol. **1**(1), 4–20 (2010)
2. Kat, B.: An algorithm and a decision support system for the Panelist assignment problem: the case of TÜBİTAK. J. Fac. Eng. Archit. Gazi Univ. **36**(1), 69–88 (2021)
3. Çagtayli, M., Çelebi, E.: The effect of stemming and stop-word-removal on automatic text classification in Turkish language. In: Arik, S., Huang, T., Lai, W.K., Liu, Q. (eds.) Neural Information Processing. LNCS, vol. 9489, pp. 168–176. Springer, Cham (2015). https://doi.org/10.1007/978-3-319-26532-2_19
4. Deniz, A., Kiziloz, H.E.: Effects of various preprocessing techniques to Turkish text categorization using n-gram features. UBMK **2017**, 655–660 (2017)
5. Öztürkmenoğlu, O., Alpkoçak, A.: Comparison of different lemmatization approaches for information retrieval on Turkish text collection. INISTA **2012**, 1–5 (2012)
6. Kat, B.: Analysis of the tools used for identifying similarities of scientific texts: addressing the road map and the pertinent approach for ARDEB project proposals. TÜBİTAK (2015)
7. Vrbanec, T., Mestrovic, A.: The struggle with academic plagiarism: approaches based on semantic similarity. MIPRO **2017**, 870–875 (2017)
8. Chong, M., Specia, L., Mitkov, R.: Using natural language processing for automatic detection of plagiarism. In: IPC-2010 (2010)
9. Gomaa, W.H., Fahmy, A.A.: A survey of text similarity approaches. Int. J. Comput. Appl. **68**(13), 975–8887 (2013)
10. Dharmadhikari, S.C., Ingle, M., Kulkarni, P.: Empirical studies on machine learning based text classification algorithms. Adv. Comput. Int. J. **2**(6), 161–169 (2011). https://doi.org/10.5121/acij.2011.2615
11. Kandimalla, B., Rohatgi, S., Wu, J., Giles, C.L.: Large scale subject category classification of scholarly papers with deep attentive neural networks. Front. Res. Metrics Anal. **5**, 600382 (2021)
12. Kadhim, A.I.: Survey on supervised machine learning techniques for automatic text classification. Artif. Intell. Rev. **52**(1), 273–292 (2019). https://doi.org/10.1007/s10462-018-09677-1
13. Gurcan, F.: Multi-class classification of Turkish texts with machine learning algorithms. ISMSIT **2018**, 1–5 (2018)
14. Koksal, O.: Tuning the Turkish Text Classification Process Using Supervised Machine Learning-based Algorithms. INISTA (2020)
15. Küçük, D., Arici, N.: A literature study on deep learning applications in natural language processing. UYBİSBBD **2**(2), 76–86 (2018)
16. Kilimci, Z.H., Akyokus, S.: The evaluation of word embedding models and deep learning algorithms for turkish text classification. UBMK **2019**, 548–553 (2019)

17. Kilimci, Z.H., Akyokus, S.: Deep learning- and word embedding-based heterogeneous classifier ensembles for text classification. Complexity **2018**, 1–10 (2018). https://doi.org/10.1155/2018/7130146

18. Aydin, G., Hallaç, İR.: Automatic topic detection on Turkish text. Firat Univ. J. Eng. Sci. **33**(2), 599–606 (2021)

19. Güran, A., Akyokuş, S., Güler Bayazıt, N., Gürbüz, M.Z.: Turkish Text Categorization Using N-Gram Words. INISTA, pp. 369–373 (2009)

20. Erşahin, B., Aktaş, Ö., Kilinç, D., Erşahin, M.: A hybrid sentiment analysis method for Turkish. Turkish J. Elect. Eng. Comput. Sci. **27**, 1780–1793 (2019)

21. Kaya, M., Fidan, G., Toroslu, I. H.: Sentiment analysis of Turkish political news. In: IEEE/WIC/ACM International Conference on Web Intelligence, pp. 174–180 (2012)

22. Boynukalın, Z.: Emotion Analysis of Turkish texts by using machine learning method. METU (2012)

23. Kaşıkçı, T., Gökçen, H.: Determination of e-Commerce sites by text mining. J. Inf. Technol. **7**(1), 25–32 (2014)

24. Kaynar, O., Görmez, Y., Yildiz, M., Albayrak, A.: Sentiment Analysis with Machine Learning Techniques. IDAP (2016)

25. Salur, M., Aydın, I., Jamous, M.: An ensemble approach for aspect term extraction in Turkish texts. Pamukkale Univ. J. Eng. Sci. **28**(5), 769–776 (2021)

26. Coban, O., Ozyer, B., Ozyer, G.T.: Sentiment analysis for Turkish Twitter feeds. In: SIU, pp. 2388–2391 (2015)

27. Uysal, A.K., Gunal, S.: The impact of preprocessing on text classification. Inf. Process. Manage. **50**(1), 104–112 (2014)

28. Yıldırım, S., Yıldız, T.: A comparative analysis of text classification for Turkish language. Pamukkale Univ. J. Eng. Sci. **24**(5), 879–886 (2018)

29. Aydin, G., Hallac, I.R.: Document Classification Using Distributed Machine Learning. arXiv preprint:1802.03597, 166–169 (2018)

30. Yau, C.-K., Porter, A., Newman, N., Suominen, A.: Clustering scientific documents with topic modeling. Scientometrics **100**(3), 767–786 (2014). https://doi.org/10.1007/s11192-014-1321-8

31. Kim, S.-W., Gil, J.-M.: Research paper classification systems based on TF-IDF and LDA schemes. HCIS **9**(1), 1–21 (2019). https://doi.org/10.1186/s13673-019-0192-7

32. Suominen, A., Toivanen, H.: Map of science with topic modeling: comparison of unsupervised learning and human-assigned subject classification. JASIST **67**(10), 2464–2476 (2016)

33. Kılınç, D., Borandağ, E., Yücalar, F., Tunali, V., Şimşek, M., Özçift, A.: Classification of scientific articles using text mining with KNN algorithm and R language. Marmara J. Pure Appl. Sci. **28**(3), 89–94 (2016)

34. Raschka, S.: Naive Bayes and Text Classification I - Introduction and Theory. arXiv preprint:1410.5329 (2014)

35. Huang, Y., Li, L.: Naive Bayes classification algorithm based on small sample set. In: IEEE CCIS2011, pp. 34–39 (2011)

36. Chandrasekar, P., Qian, K.: The impact of data preprocessing on the performance of a Naïve Bayes classifier. IEEE COMPSAC **2**, 618–619 (2016)

37. Noyan, T., Kuncan, F., Tekin, R., Kaya, Y.: A new content-free approach to identification of document language: angle patterns. J. Fac. Eng. Archit. Gazi Univ. **37**(3), 1277–1292 (2022)

38. Kat, B.: Natural language processing for the Turkish academic texts in the engineering field and development of a decision support system: the case of TUBITAK project proposals. J. Fac. Eng. Archit. Gazi Univ. **38**(3), 1879–1892 (2023)

Towards Automatic Evaluation of NLG Tasks Using Conversational Large Language Models

Md Riyadh[(✉)] and M. Omair Shafiq[(✉)]

Carleton University, Ottawa, ON, Canada
mdriyadh@cmail.carleton.ca1, omair.shafiq@carleton.ca2

Abstract. Evaluating the quality of machine generated open-ended texts is a long-standing challenge in Natural Language Processing (NLP). Even though there have been dramatic advancements in the machine learning technologies that propelled the research work concerning Natural Language Generation (NLG), a subdivision of NLP that focuses on text generation, a promising and widely adopted automatic evaluation technique for NLG tasks is yet to be developed. In this paper, we propose leveraging conversational Large Language Models (LLMs) as automatic evaluators for several open-ended NLG tasks. Our experiments with a recently released conversational LLM named ChatGPT demonstrate the viability of our proposal.

Keywords: NLG · Automatic Evaluator · LLM · ChatGPT

1 Introduction

With the advent of Transformers [1] and large pretrained language models (LLM) (e.g., [2]) in recent years, there have been a plethora of research work in Natural Lan-guage Processing (NLP) that contributed significantly to the advancement of this field. NLP tasks are often broadly categorized into two: Natural Language Understand (NLU) and Natural Language Generation (NLG) [3]. LLMs have dramatically advanced area of NLG, catalyzing development of sophisticated machine learning architectures to execute tasks like paraphrasing, question-answering, machine translation etc. with impressive performance [4]. While there have been rapid advancements in the NLG field, the diffi-culty in evaluating them has become more prominent. Unlike many NLP tasks such as classification tasks like sentiment analysis, NLG tasks cannot be easily evaluated with automatic evaluation techniques. This is due to the nature of the NLG tasks, many of which can be open ended. Some researchers have attempted to develop automatic evalu-ation techniques for NLG tasks [5, 6]. However, none of them have received widespread adoption primarily due to their poor generalizability to evaluate open ended and divserse NLG tasks. As a result, a vast majority of the NLG tasks still require performing tedious and lengthy evaluations by human participants.

A recent addition to the LLM technology is ChatGPT [7], which is closely related to the InstructGPT [8] model and fine-tuned from a GPT-3.5 variant [9]. As the name

© IFIP International Federation for Information Processing 2023
Published by Springer Nature Switzerland AG 2023
I. Maglogiannis et al. (Eds.): AIAI 2023, IFIP AICT 676, pp. 425–437, 2023.
https://doi.org/10.1007/978-3-031-34107-6_34

suggests, ChatGPT is a conversational LLM that can provide detailed answer to a variety of questions. It is trained to understand many simple and complex instructions and execute those instructions effectively. Guo et al. [10] experimented with ChatGPT's capability to perform a variety of NLP tasks. In this study, we tap into the similar capabilities of ChatGPT but with the objective of understanding its ability to be an automatic evaluator for some NLG tasks. In addition to some common NLG tasks, we focus on the domain of Emotion-Cause Analysis (ECS) [11], which consists of several tasks related to the cause of an expressed emotion in a given text. Our experiments cover all the NLG tasks within the ECA domain that are currently available: Emotion-Cause Generation (ECG) [12] and Emotion-Cause mitigating Suggestion Generation (ECSGen) [13]. Through a series of experiments, we attempt to understand if ChatGPT can be an effective automatic evaluator for various NLG tasks, particularly the ones that do not require specific domain knowledge and that typically need to be evaluated by human participants.

The objective of this study is to understand the capability of conversational LLMs as automatic evaluators for open-ended NLG tasks that do not require domain specific information. The main contributions of this study include: (a) We propose leveraging a recently released conversational LLM named ChatGPT as an automatic evaluator for the NLG tasks, especially the open-ended tasks that do not need domain specific knowledge. (b) We perform a series of experiments to understand ChatGPT's ability as an automatic evaluator for three common NLG tasks: Paraphrasing, Question-Answering, Story-cloze test (i.e., evaluates models' commonsense reasoning capability). (c) We also experiment with two ECA related NLG tasks: ECG, ECSGen. These are currently the only two NLG tasks available within the domain of ECA. Consequently, our experiments on the usage of ChatGPT as an automatic evaluator covers all ECA related NLG tasks that exist today. To the best of our knowledge, this is the first attempt to suggest an automatic evaluator for ECA related NLG tasks.

Despite rapid advances in NLG, automatically evaluating the open-ended generated text by machines remains a challenge. We propose using conversational LLMs as automatic evaluators for some common NLG tasks, including for recently introduced ECA related NLG tasks. Our experiments demonstrate the effectiveness of this approach.

2   Related Studies

The evaluation of NLG systems has conventionally been conducted by human eval-uators [14]. In such procedure, human evaluators are presented with generated texts from the NLG systems and written texts from human. The performance of the NLG system is determined by comparing the ratings assigned to each. This evaluation approach, which was first introduced in the mid-90s [15], continues to be utilized in the present day in various forms for the majority of the NLG tasks. Researchers later suggested that evaluating NLG systems by comparing the generated texts to a corpus of human-written texts offers the potential for faster, more cost-effective and scalable evaluation [16–18]. Despite its advantages, this method has faced criticism, with objections such as that the generated texts may differ from corpus texts while still meeting the criteria of successfully completing a NLG task [19].

Some other researchers developed a group of alternative automatic metrics called word-based metrics (WBM). WBMs typically evaluate the similarity between the output text produced by the systems and human-generated reference texts based on various criteria [20]. The closer the similarity between the output and reference texts, the higher the score obtained from the metric. BLEU [21], ROUGE [22] etc. are some common examples of such metrics. However, none of these metrics can perform the tasks typically done by human evaluators due to their limited scope.

In addition to WBM, automatic metrics related to NLG also include readability metrics such as Flesch Reading Ease score [23] that quantifies the "reading ease" of a text based on the number of characters per sentence, words per sentence, and syllables per word. Grammatical correctness is also another automatic metric that some NLG studies tend to use to understand if an output by a machine learning model is grammatically correct [24]. More recently, there has been a growing interest in the use of Transformer-based metrics for evaluating NLG tasks. They can be broadly divided into two categories: reference-based models that require human references (e.g., [27, 28]) and reference-free models that do not (e.g., [25, 26]). The latter category is more cost-effective to implement. However, some researchers pointed out that these metrics are still inadequate for evaluating specific NLG tasks without infusing task specific knowledge in them – which can be burdensome and increase the scope and complexity of any given study [29]. This could be one of the reasons why older and less accurate metrics such as BLEU continue to dominate the field of automatic evaluation of NLG tasks despite their limitations [30, 31].

Due to all these limitations of the existing automatic evaluation techniques for NLG tasks, particularly for tasks that more open ended in nature such as paraphrasing, most researchers still opt for human evaluation in order to conduct more robust and trustworthy analysis.

3 Conversational LLMs as Automatic Evaluators for NLG Tasks

We propose leveraging conversational LLM as an alternative automatic evaluator for many NLG tasks, especially the ones that do not require specific domain knowledge, and that typically require human evaluators. To evaluate our proposal, we use ChatGPT [7], a recently released conversational LLM. Evaluating NLG tasks with human evaluators requires the evaluators to understand the tasks with simple instructions and execute those tasks accordingly. For example, to evaluate the meaningfulness of a summary of a given news article, human evaluators are typically given instructions on how to evaluate the relevance of such summaries in relation to the original news article. Based on that, they may be tasked with ranking the relevancy of those summaries. As we demonstrate in the upcoming sections, ChatGPT is similarly capable of understanding such instructions and complete the given task. This capability, in our opinion, makes ChatGPT a suitable candidate to become an automatic evaluator for many NLG tasks.

To use ChatGPT for such evaluations, the instruction set of each task needs to be designed carefully, ideally through experimenting with ChatGPT and by observing its response. These instruction sets are often called "prompt" in the context of LLMs [32]. After an effective prompt template is determined for set a given NLG task, prompts for each datapoint can be generated automatically by developing simple custom logic in programming languages such as Python [33]. These prompts then can be provided to ChatGPT using the available interface and then its response can be collected subsequently. In the following section, we conduct a series of experiments to understand ChatGPT's capability as an automatic evaluator for some NLG tasks.

4   Evaluation

In this study, we evaluate ChatGPT as an automatic evaluator for the following five NLG tasks: (a) Paraphrasing, (b) Question-Answering, (c) Story-cloze Test [34], (d) ECSGen [13], (e) ECG [12].

4.1   Procedure

We perform five small scale experiments to evaluate ChatGPT for the five selected NLG tasks. Each experiment has some specificities, but they all share some common procedures, which we discuss below:

- We take a small sample of data (i.e., about 100 datapoints) from an existing dataset for each task. This is since we leveraged ChatGPT's Research Preview [7] for this study which (at the time of this study) is accessible through a browser interface requiring tedious manual input. For sampling, we leverage different random sampling techniques including balanced and stratified sampling for different tasks to present diverse data compositions to ChatGPT.
- To use the dataset for our intended evaluation, we preprocess each of them differently depending on their original format and evaluation process. We auto-generate Chat-GPT prompts for each datapoints for all five tasks using Python [33]. We use different prompt formats for each task, which we designed by iteratively experimenting with ChatGPT for the best outcome in terms of aiding ChatGPT to understand the task as well as receiving answer from it in a format that is easy to process for analysis.
- We enter these prompts into ChatGPT's interface and manually collect its response for each of the datapoint. This interaction with ChatGPT Research Preview occurred between Jan 26, 2023, and Feb 16, 2023.
- After that we compare ChatGPT's responses with the ones included in the datasets. To observe how ChatGPT performs as an automatic evaluator for different NLG tasks that can be assessed differently, we leverage diverse techniques such as classification accuracy, multiple choice type questions (MCQ), correlating Likert responses etc. We use Python [33], IBM SPSS [35], and Google Sheet [36] for our analysis. Experiments for each task included some distinct procedures, particularly as it relates to the dataset used for each, how the task is conducted as well as the analysis methods we used for them. We discuss them below.

For the paraphrasing task, we take sample from the GLUE dataset's Quora Question Pairs [37]. The dataset contains two one-sentence long questions. The task is to determine whether the questions are paraphrases of each other. To understand if ChatGPT can automatically evaluate if a paraphrase is correct, we frame this as a binary classification problem for analysis where ChatGPT attempts to determine the correct and incorrect paraphrases. ChatGPT's performance on this would indicate how it can perform as an evaluator for the NLG task when machine learning models generate a paraphrase for a given text (in this case, short text).

For the question-answering task, we utilize the WikiQA dataset [38] where each question has several correct and incorrect answers. The goal is to determine which answers are correct and which ones are not. For the ease of analysis, we randomly sample some questions with one incorrect answer and some with one correct answer. We then frame this task as a binary classification problem for our analysis where ChatGPT's task is to determine which answers are correct for a given question and which are not. We expect this to indicate how ChatGPT can perform as an evaluator to understand a model's performance on generating answer for a given question.

Similarly, we leverage an existing dataset for the Story-cloze test [34] which also evaluate the common-sense reasoning of machine learning models. Each datapoint in this dataset contains a short story consisting of five sentences. For each, the first four sentences are provided in correct order. For the fifth sentence, there are two options, only one of them being correct. The task is to determine which option is the appropriate choice as the fifth or last sentence of the story. ChatGPT's performance in determining the correct fifth sentence in this task would indicate how well it can evaluate the models that are tasked with completing unfinished stories using common-sense reasoning.

The ECSGen dataset [13] contains 5-point Likert responses [39] from human evaluators for each "emotion-cause mitigating suggestion", representing the degree of relevance of the suggestion in relation to the cause of the emotion. The five levels of Likert scale are: 1: Not at all relevant, 2: Slightly relevant, 3: Somewhat relevant, 4: Moderately relevant, and 5: Very relevant. The task for ChatGPT is to rank the sampled suggestions similarly. The dataset contains 3 suggestions for each statement. We sampled 120 datapoints; consequently, our sample contains 360 suggestions. For analysis, we frame this as a multi-category classification problem. Since the human response for each suggestion can be extensively subjective for this type of questions, particularly with 5 intensity levels to choose from, we compare ChatGPT's response with the ones from human evaluators using various techniques such as, correlation testing, classification accuracy at 5-levels, and classifications accuracy at 3 and 2-levels by recoding the Likert labels accordingly. We believe ChatGPT's performance in this experiment can indicate how well it can rank the relevancy of a suggestion that aims to mitigate the cause of an emotion expressed in a short text.

For the ECG task [12], we preprocess a sample from an existing Emotion-stimuli dataset [40] for our study. We replace the "cause-span" for each datapoint with an underscore ("_"). We convert the dataset to a comma-separated values format where the separated cause-span, and the original texts (without the cause-span) are placed into separate columns. Then we create a duplicate column from the "cause-span" column and randomize the order of this new column. Thus, for each datapoint, we have a correct cause and an incorrect cause for the expressed emotion. We remove the datapoints where we found duplicates between these two cause columns and where both causes seemed equally appropriate. We frame it as an MCQ-style binary classification task for ChatGPT where it attempts to pick the correct cause for each statement with an emotional expression. We expect this to indicate ChatGPT's ability to evaluate the meaningfulness or relevance of a generated cause in relation to the emotion expressed in a text. For sample prompts for each task that we explored in this study, please check this repository[1].

In this study, we only evaluate ChatGPT, a recently released conversational LLM, as an automatic evaluator for a set of NLG tasks and report our findings. We do not compare ChatGPT's performance for this with any other LLMs. This is due to the fact our evaluation setting involves providing instructions to ChatGPT in a conversational manner, similar to the ones typically given to human evaluators. To the best of our knowledge, other than ChatGPT, there is no model that is publicly available for inference that can aptly understand these instructions to describe complex tasks and execute the tasks as instructed. Consequently, we only experiment with ChatGPT and report our findings accordingly.

4.2   Results

Paraphrasing: ChatGPT classified the correct and incorrect paraphrases with an accuracy score of 0.81. For the correct ones, precision and recall scores are 0.84 and 0.77 with an F1 score of 0.80 for 60 datapoints, and for the incorrect ones, precision and recall scores are 0.78 and 0.85 with an F1 score of 0.82 for the same amount of datapoints.

Question-Answering: ChatGPT classified the correct and incorrect answers with an accuracy score of 0.89. For the correct answers, precision and recall scores are 0.81 and 0.88 with an F1 score of 0.85 for 34 datapoints, and for the incorrect answers, precision and recall score are 0.94 and 0.89 with an F1 score of 0.91 for 65 datapoints.

Story-cloze Test: For this task, ChatGPT was able to choose the correct fifth sentence with an accuracy score of 0.99 for a total datapoints of 157 short stories. Since it is an MCQ style question that requires identifying only the correct answer between two options, the individual scores (e.g., precision, recall) for each option is not relevant, hence we do not report them.

ECSGen: We conduct a series of analyses to understand ChatGPT's performance on the ECSGen task as the only dataset available for this task is relatively more complicated compared to the other evaluated tasks, which uses 5-point Likert scale representing the degree of relevance of a suggestion to an emotion-cause. As explained in the previous section, 5-point Likert responses can be extremely subjective, particularly between the adjacent levels. Consequently, we analyze this using several techniques to understand ChatGPT's suitability as an automatic evaluator for the ECSGen task. The mean score of 5-point Likert responses from human evaluators and ChatGPT are 2.83 and 2.47 respectively, with a median of 3 and 2, and a standard deviation of 1.451 and 1.117 respectively. For the correlation test, we primarily use Spearman coefficient (0.334) as it fits the data type and distribution used in the study. However, we also report its parametric counterpart: Pearson coefficient (0.33), as an additional correlation measure. Both correlation

---

[1] https://github.com/riyadhctg/ChatGPT-prompts-for-NLG-tasks

tests indicate positive correlation between ChatGPT and human responses and both tests were significant with a p-value < 0.001.

We also report the distance between the Likert responses for each question to understand the percentages of the answers that varied differently. About 26.11% suggestions had the exact same ranking by human evaluators and ChatGPT. ChatGPT and human evaluators' responses varied by only 1 Likert point for 40% of the suggestions. This indicates that more than 65% of the responses are exact match or only varied by 1 Likert-point. For the remainder of the suggestions, 22.50% varied by 2 Likert points, 10.28% varied by 3, and only 1.11% varied by 4 Likert-point.

Additionally, we measure ChatGPT's effectiveness as an automatic evaluator for the ECSGen task by framing this analysis as a classification problem. However, since the responses are in 5-point Likert scale that uses typical labels for intensity measurement, the accuracy score is expectedly low (0.26) for classification with five categories (i.e., 5-point Likert scale). Consequently, we perform further analysis by recoding the Likert scores.

First, we recode this as a 3-category classification problem, where Likert score 1 is recoded as 1, 5 is recoded as 3, and the more ambiguous scores in between are recoded to 2. This expectedly increases the classification accuracy (0.55) compared to the 5-category approach. Next, we recode the original data again in 3-categories. However, this time, we recode 1 and 2 as 1, 4 and 5 as 3, and 3 as 2. This yields a similar classification accuracy (0.48) as the previous 3-category approach although slightly lower. We also analyze this from a binary classification perspective, for which we use two different approaches. First, we remove the datapoints with Likert score 3 from the original 5-point Likert data (i.e., 3 representing the mathematical mid-point in 5-point Likert scale). We recode 1 and 2 as 1, and 4 and 5 as 2. This increases the classification accuracy further to 0.67. Lastly, we look at the agreement of human evaluators and ChatGPT for only the lowest and the highest scores: 1 and 5. This dramatically reduces the datapoints for analysis, but it provides a closer representation of a binary classification problem. The classification accuracy with this approach is significantly higher with a score of 0.91. The confusion matrices in Fig. 1 provides a more detailed view into these various classification results.

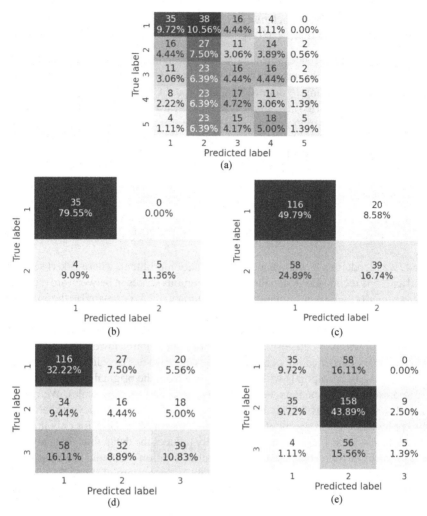

Fig. 1. ECSGen confusion matrices: a) 5-class. b) binary with only label 1 and 5. c) binary with label 3 removed and 1, 2 recoded to 1 and 4, 5 recoded to 2. d) 3-class with label 1 and 2 recoded as 1; 4 and 5 as 3; and 3 as 2. e) 3-class recoded 1 and 2 as 1; 4 and 5 as 3; and 3 as 2.

ECG: Similar to the Story-cloze test, for the ECG task, ChatGPT is tasked with MCQ-style questions where the requirement is to choose an emotion-cause from the two given options that more appropriately explains the emotion expressed in a given statement. ChatGPT achieved an accuracy score of 0.98 for a total datapoints of 120.

Table 1 represents the summary of ChatGPT's performance in evaluating all the NLG tasks considered in this study.

Table 1. Summary of ChatGPT's performance as an evaluator for various NLG tasks. Asterisk (*) indicates alternative recoding technique used (more details above).

Task	Analysis Method(s)	Score(s)
Paraphrasing	Classification Accuracy	0.81
Question Answering	Classification Accuracy	0.89
Story-cloze	Classification Accuracy Score (MCQ)	0.99
ECSGen	Spearman Coefficient, Pearson Coefficient	0.334, 0.33
	Classification Accuracy - Number of classes: 5, 3, 3*, 2, 2*	0.26, 0.55, 0.48*, 0.67, 0.91*
ECG	Classification Accuracy (MCQ)	0.98

5 Discussion

We experimented with five NLG tasks to understand if ChatGPT, a recently released conversational LLM, can be an automatic evaluator for these tasks. Three of them are among the common NLG tasks and the remaining two have been recently introduced within the ECA domain. We observe that ChatGPT can understand all these tasks and conduct the evaluation for them with minimal instructions akin to human evaluators. In addition, we leverage various techniques to evaluate ChatGPT's strength as an automatic evaluator for the given NLG tasks. These include framing the analysis as classification problem with two or more categories, MCQ style questions, and Likert-scale ranking. We observe that ChatGPT is capable of understanding these diverse framings of problems with minimal instructions, which, we believe, reinforce its potential as an automatic evaluator for many NLG tasks.

We observe that ChatGPT achieves almost 100% accuracy for two tasks: ECG and Story-cloze test. For question-answering and para-phrasing it scored 0.89 and 0.81 respectively. We opine that these consistent high scores represent ChatGPT's ability to be an effective evaluator for these NLG tasks. In our analysis, ECSGen task's evaluation is different than the others experimented with in this study given the fact that its dataset comes with a 5-point Likert response from human evaluators which is prone to subjectivity. As explained earlier, we perform more analysis for this task to understand ChatGPT's suitability to be an effective evaluator for this task. Based on the classification accuracy that ChatGPT achieved in our analysis of the ECSGen task, particularly when framed as a binary problem, we suggest that ChatGPT can be considered as a useful evaluator for this task as well. This is also reinforced by the positive score in the correlation tests between ChatGPT and human evaluators' ranking. In addition, we observe that the distance between the Likert responses from ChatGPT and human evaluators indicate high correlation between them. Particularly, more than 65% of the responses having a Likert distance of 1 or 0, while only about 12% of the responses varied widely with Likert distance of 3 or more. However, we believe that for ECSGen, a further study will be beneficial to confirm the findings of our study, especially with binary ranking from human evaluators, which can be then compared against ChatGPT's response with more accuracy.

Based on our overall results, we suggest that ChatGPT can be an effective automatic evaluator for the NLG tasks used in this study. We believe that this statement can potentially be generalized to many other similar NLG tasks. This is because in our observation, ChatGPT is able to understand instructions for evaluating variety of NLG tasks, some of which have been introduced very recently. In our opinion, this ability to understand how to evaluate a new NLG task from simple instructions, and then executing those instructions with decent performance are the two most important features of ChatGPT that can make it an effective automatic evaluator for many NLG tasks in future. However, to use ChatGPT as an automatic evaluator for NLG tasks other than the ones used in this study, we recommend performing a small-scale evaluation with ChatGPT for that task. We expect that the evaluations we performed in this study can be an inspiration for such future experiments.

We observe that designing an appropriate prompt is crucial to help ChatGPT understand the task properly and respond accordingly. We recommend careful considerations while designing these prompts to use ChatGPT as an automatic evaluator for a given NLG task.

Lastly, since this is a newly suggested automatic evaluation technique, we expect this to mature over time with more successive contributions from the researcher community, especially with larger-scale studies. We expect this to initially complement existing evaluation techniques such as human evaluations. This may pave the way for further adoption of this technique in future for many NLG tasks, especially the ones that do not require specific domain knowledge. There is ongoing research to develop more conversational LLMs like ChatGPT [41]. When more such LLMs are available, preferably with enhanced performance, we believe researchers can lever-age multiple conversational LLMs as automatic evaluators and report their finding accordingly for increasing the robustness of their analysis.

5.1 Guidelines for Researchers

We recommend the following general guidelines while using conversational LLMs such as ChatGPT as an automatic evaluator for NLG tasks:

- After the NLG task is complete, researchers can pick a small sample from the output (e.g., 10–20 datapoints, depending on the type of task) and they can use the conversational LLM of choice to evaluate these sampled outputs.
- Optionally, researchers can then provide their own evaluation of these sampled outputs (or they can choose to ask human evaluators to do this).
- Then, these evaluations of the sampled output can be presented to readers in detail including the input text used, and the generated text.

We believe this will provide the readers an understanding of the performance of the automatic evaluator which they can consider when interpreting the findings in a given study that includes automatic evaluation of NLG tasks using conversational LLMs.

6   Limitations and Future Studies

There are several limitations of this study. The chief among them is the fact that we used a small number of samples in our experiments. As described above, this is because ChatGPT Research Preview currently only allows access through a web browser and manually inputting a large amount of datapoint can be tedious and erroneous. It is also because we believe that such sample is sufficient to get an indication on the general efficacy of ChatGPT as an evaluator of the NLG tasks discussed in this study. It is however a noteworthy limitation, and we acknowledge the need of investigating this further with larger samples.

We investigated ChatGPT's effectiveness as an automatic evaluator for several NLG tasks. However, there are many other NLG tasks that we have not experimented with. We constrained this study to a small subset of NLG tasks to keep the experiments within the scope of this study. We acknowledge that our results cannot be generalized all NLG tasks. We encourage researchers to investigate the efficacy of ChatGPT and possible future variants as an automatic evaluator for more NLG tasks.

The current public access of ChatGPT only allows interacting with the model, but not to gain full access to it. In addition, the model is regularly updated with more training data. As a result, its response for one question may change over time. While we expect the response of ChatGPT to become more enhanced over time, we however, suggest that the apparent varying nature of ChatGPT needs to be considered while interpreting the results we publish in this study.

7   Conclusions

We experimented with five NLG tasks to understand the performance of a recently released conversational LLM named ChatGPT as an automatic evaluator for these tasks. We observe that ChatGPT is able to understand how to execute these tasks with simple instructions akin to the ones typically given to the human evaluators. We believe that this capability to understand NLG tasks from simple instructions along with the results from our experiments, suggest that ChatGPT and possible future and more advanced variants of such conversational LLM can be effective automatic evaluators for the NLG tasks explored in this study. We opine that with more experiments, this finding can be potentially generalized to many other similar NLG tasks, especially the tasks that do not require domain specific knowledge.

References

1. Vaswani, A., et al.: Attention is all you need. In: Advances in Neural Information Pro-cessing Systems, Jun. 2017, vol. 2017-December, pp. 5999–6009. Accessed 02 May 2021. https://arxiv.org/abs/1706.03762v5
2. Brown, T.B., et al.: Language Models are Few-Shot Learners (2020). Accessed 12 June 2022. https://commoncrawl.org/the-data/
3. "NLP vs. NLU vs. NLG: the differences between three natural language processing con-cepts - Watson Blog. https://www.ibm.com/blogs/watson/2020/11/nlp-vs-nlu-vs-nlg-the-dif ferences-between-three-natural-language-processing-concepts/. Accessed 20 Jan 2023

4. Subramanyam Kalyan, K., Rajasekharan, A., Sangeetha, S.: AMMUS : A Survey of Transformer-based Pretrained Models in Natural Language Processing (2021). https://mr-nlp.github.io. Accessed 29 Aug 2021

5. Zhao, W., Peyrard, M., Liu, F., Gao, Y., Meyer, C.M., Eger, S.: MoverScore: Text Generation Evaluating with Contextualized Embeddings and Earth Mover Distance (2023). http://tiny.cc/vsqtbz. Accessed 18 Feb 2023

6. Zhang, T., Kishore, V., Wu, F., Weinberger, K.Q., Artzi, Y.: BertScore: evaluating text generation with BERT (2022). https://github.com/Tiiiger/bert_score. Accessed 12 June 2022

7. ChatGPT: Optimizing Language Models for Dialogue (2023). https://openai.com/blog/chatgpt/. Accessed 11 Jan 2023

8. Ouyang, L., et al.: Training language models to follow instructions with human feed-back, March 2022. https://doi.org/10.48550/arxiv.2203.02155

9. Model index for researchers - OpenAI API. https://platform.openai.com/docs/model-index-for-researchers. Accessed 18 Feb 2023

10. Guo, B., et al.: How Close is ChatGPT to Human Experts? Comparison Corpus, Evaluation, and Detection. https://chat.openai.com/chat. Accessed 11 Feb 2023

11. Gao, Q., et al.: Overview of NTCIR-13 ECA Task

12. Riyadh, M., Shafiq, O.: towards emotion cause generation in natural language processing using deep learning. In: ICMLA 2022 (2022)

13. Riyadh, M., Shafiq, M.O.: ECSGen and iZen: a new NLP Task and A Zero-shot Framework to Perform It," Knowledge Based Systems, vol. In Review (2023)

14. Mellish, C., Dale, R.: Evaluation in the context of natural language generation. Comput. Speech Lang. **12**(4), 349–373 (1998). https://doi.org/10.1006/CSLA.1998.0106

15. Coch, J.: Evaluating and comparing three text-production techniques. In: COLING 1996 (1996)

16. Bangalore, S., Rambow, O., Whittaker, S.: Evaluation Metrics for Generation

17. Marciniak, T., Strube, M.: Classification-based generation using TAG. In: Belz, A., Evans, R., Piwek, P. (eds.) Natural Language Generation. LNCS (LNAI), vol. 3123, pp. 100–109. Springer, Heidelberg (2004). https://doi.org/10.1007/978-3-540-27823-8_11

18. Langkilde-Geary, I.: An Empirical Verification of Coverage and Correctness for a General-Purpose Sentence Generator

19. Reiter, E., Sripada, S.: Should Corpora Texts Be Gold Standards for NLG?, pp. 97–104 (2002). https://aclanthology.org/W02-2113. Accessed 18 Feb 2023

20. Belz, A., Reiter, E.: Comparing Automatic and Human Evaluation of NLG Systems

21. Papineni, K., Roukos, S., Ward, T., Zhu, W.-J.: BLEU: a Method for Automatic Evaluation of Machine Translation

22. Lin, C.-Y.: ROUGE: A Package for Automatic Evaluation of Summaries

23. Flesch, R.: A new readability yardstick. J. Appl. Psychol. **32**(3), 221–233 (1948). https://doi.org/10.1037/H0057532

24. Novikova, J., Dušek, O., Curry, A.C., Rieser, V.: Why We Need New Evaluation Metrics for NLG. https://github.com/glampouras/JLOLS_. Accessed 12 Jun 2022

25. Zhao, W., Gao, Y., Eger, S.: Evaluating Machine Translation without Human Refer-ences Using Cross-lingual Encoders"

26. Song, Y., Zhao, J., Specia, L.: SentSim: crosslingual semantic evaluation of machine translation. In: NAACL-HLT 2021 - 2021 Conference of the North American Chapter of the Association for Computational Linguistics: Human Language Technologies, Proceedings of the Conference, pp. 3143–3156 (2021). https://doi.org/10.18653/V1/2021.NAACL-MAIN.252

27. Zhang, T., Kishore, V., Wu, F., Weinberger, K.Q., Artzi, Y.: BERTSCORE: EVALUATING TEXT GENERATION WITH BERT. https://github.com/Tiiiger/bert. Accessed 16 May 2022

28. Colombo, P., Staerman, G., Clavel, C., Piantanida, P.: Automatic text evaluation through the lens of Wasserstein Barycenters. In: EMNLP 2021 - 2021 Conference on Em-pirical Methods in Natural Language Processing, Proceedings, pp. 10450–10466, August 2021. https://doi.org/10.48550/arxiv.2108.12463

29. Leiter, C., Lertvittayakumjorn, P., Fomicheva, M., Zhao, W., Gao, Y., Eger, S.: Towards Explainable Evaluation Metrics for Natural Language Generation. https://github.com/Gringham/explainable-metrics-machine-translation. Accessed 18 Feb 2023

30. Marie, B., Fujita, A., Rubino, R.: Scientific credibility of machine translation research: a meta-evaluation of 769 papers. In: ACL-IJCNLP 2021 - 59th Annual Meeting of the Association for Computational Linguistics and the 11th International Joint Conference on Natural Language Processing, Proceedings of the Conference, pp. 7297–7306, June 2021. https://doi.org/10.48550/arxiv.2106.15195

31. Grünwald, J., Leiter, C., Eger, S.: Can we do that simpler? Simple, Efficient, High-Quality Evaluation Metrics for NLG

32. Yang, K., et al.: Tailor: A Prompt-Based Approach to Attribute-Based Controlled Text Generation

33. About PythonTM | Python.org. https://www.python.org/about/. Accessed 08 Jan 2023

34. Sharma, R., Allen, J.F., Bakhshandeh, O., Mostafazadeh, N.: Tackling the story ending biases in the story cloze test ACL 2018–56th annual meeting of the association for computational linguistics. Proc. Conf. (Long Papers) **2**, 752–757 (2018). https://doi.org/10.18653/V1/P18-2119

35. "SPSS Software | IBM. https://www.ibm.com/spss. Accessed 08 Jan 2023

36. Google Sheets: Online Spreadsheet Editor | Google Workspace. https://www.google.com/sheets/about/. Accessed 18 Feb 2023

37. Wang, A., Singh, A., Michael, J., Hill, F., Levy, O., Bowman, S.R.: GLUE: a multi-task benchmark and analysis platform for natural language understanding

38. Yang, Y., Yih, W.-T., Meek, C.: WIKIQA: A Challenge Dataset for Open-Domain Question Answering, pp. 17–21 (2015). http://aka.ms/WikiQA. Accessed 18 Feb 2023

39. Dobson, K.S., Mothersill, K.J.: Equidistant Categorical Labels For Construc-tion of Likert-type Scales (1979)

40. Ghazi, D., Inkpen, D., Szpakowicz, S.: Detecting Emotion Stimuli in Emotion-Bearing Sentences. In Computational Linguistics and Intelligent Text Processing, pp. 152–165 (2015)

41. Google AI updates: Bard and new AI features in Search. https://blog.google/technology/ai/bard-google-ai-search-updates/. Accessed 18 Feb 2023

Optimization-Genetic Programming

Cognitive Digital Twin in Manufacturing: A Heuristic Optimization Approach

Atiq ur Rehman$^{(\boxtimes)}$ [iD], Mobyen Uddin Ahmed[iD], and Shahina Begum[iD]

Artificial Intelligence and Intelligent Systems Research Group, School of Innovation, Design and Engineering, Mälardalen University, Västerås, Sweden
{atiq.ur.rehman,mobyen.uddin.ahmed,shahina.begum}@mdu.se

Abstract. Complex systems that link virtualization and simulation platforms with actual data from industrial processes are vital for the next generation of production. Digital twins are such systems that have several advantages, notably in manufacturing where they can boost productivity throughout the whole manufacturing life-cycle. Enterprises will be able to creatively, efficiently, and effectively leverage implicit information derived from the experience of current production processes, thanks to cognitive digital twins. The development of numerous technologies has made the digital twin notion more competent and sophisticated throughout time. This article proposes a heuristic approach for cognitive digital twin technology as the next development in a digital twin that will aid in the realization of the goal of Industry 4.0. In creating cognitive digital twins, this article suggests the use of a heuristic approach as a possible route to allowing cognitive functionalities. Here, heuristic optimization is proposed as a feature selection tool to enhance the cognitive capabilities of a digital twin throughout the product design phase of production. The proposed approach is validated using the use-case of Power Transfer Unit (PTU) production, which resulted in an improvement of 8.83% in classification accuracy to predict the faulty PTU in the assembly line. This leads to an improved throughput of the PTU assembly line and also saves the resources utilized by faulty PTUs.

Keywords: Cyber-Physical Systems · Cognitive Digital Twins · Heuristic Optimization · Industrial Manufacturing

1 Introduction

The fourth industrial revolution is referred to mostly as Industry 4.0, connected industries, Smart Manufacturing, Made in China (MIC) 2025, and a few other terms [1]. Utilizing the potential of computation in manufacturing processes is frequently at the core of this wave of future manufacturing visions. The majority of these visions aim to combine cloud computing, cybersecurity, smart sensors, cyber-physical systems, wireless (and wired) communications, advanced robotics,

© IFIP International Federation for Information Processing 2023
Published by Springer Nature Switzerland AG 2023
I. Maglogiannis et al. (Eds.): AIAI 2023, IFIP AICT 676, pp. 441–453, 2023.
https://doi.org/10.1007/978-3-031-34107-6_35

advanced data analytics, simulation and high-performance computing, additive manufacturing, internet of things (IoT), and the machine learning. The fourth industrial revolution aims to produce products and production across decentralized factories and supply networks that are personalized, inexpensive, efficient, resilient, adaptive, and sustainable [2,3].

One of the many technologies that will influence how manufacturing is done in the future is Digital Twins (DTs). Through the integration of the digital and physical worlds, DTs enable seamless communication between digital simulations and real production systems. Manufacturing has been proven to benefit significantly from these DTs [4,5]. Digital twin technology makes use of a variety of auxiliary systems and technologies, including modelling and simulation, IoT sensors, standards for interoperability between digital technologies, computation, and data from various product lifecycle stages. The use of this technology in manufacturing may have an influence on the whole product life cycle, and much like many other contemporary computer research areas, the number of applications for DTs in manufacturing is growing quickly.

Fundamental cognitive processes like perception (having formed useful precepts from raw sensory data), attention, memory, reasoning (drawing inferences from observations, beliefs, and models), problem-solving, and learning (from experiences, and observations) have been incorporated into DTs in order to further their evolution [6]. Cognitive Digital Twins (CDTs) are the result of this evolution through the incorporation of these cognitive processes into the Digital Twin [7–9]. Through the incorporation of cognition-enabling services, CDTs provide the capability to track the present condition of the corresponding manufacturing components, recognise (or even anticipate) production anomalies, investigate their root cause, and then compute, evaluate, and assist in making decisions about potential courses of action for the best (optimised) prevention against the impacts of the associated interruptions [10]. In this article, a CDT based on a heuristic approach is proposed, utilizing a use case from the manufacturing industry. The all-wheel drive (AWD) transfer case used in automobiles and sport utility vehicles is called the Power Transfer Unit (PTU). It enables power to be sent to all four wheels intermittently or continuously, and it also adjusts how much power is sent to the front and back depending on the circumstances of the road. A faulty produced PTU during manufacturing brings a huge economic loss to the manufacturing industry [11]. Prediction of faulty PTUs before the End-of-Line (EOL), during the production phase, can lead to saving resources and helping the manufacturing industry cope with losses incurred due to the production of faulty PTUs. There are certain parameters in the lapping and assembly line which are considered important by human experts to predict faulty PTUs. However, these parameters are manually inspected by the experts in the industry and mostly there is no guarantee to associate the fault with a certain set of parameters. At the same time, the inspection of several parameters through hundreds of sensors manually is not feasible. In order to solve such issues and propose an innovative solution, a heuristic optimization approach is added to the digital twin technology to provide cognitive activities.

Metaheuristic approaches have the capability to solve the NP-hard combinatorial optimization problems [12]. Due to the effective search strategy, these metaheuristics can be utilized to optimize the large feature spaces and increase the prediction accuracy of machine learning algorithms [13]. Moreover, these approaches are computationally more efficient compared to the gradient-based approaches. Therefore, a recently proposed Jumping Particle Swarm Optimization method [14] is incorporated in the Digital twin architecture to optimize its feature space. The proposed approach is validated using a use-case of the PTU manufacturing process to optimize the fault detection process [15]. The proposed architecture is tested on the real data taken from the PTU manufacturing industry and the results show a significant increase in the fault detection accuracy of the system. The rest of the article is organized as follows: Sect. 2 (Methodology) Sect. 3.1 (Results), and Sect. 4 (Conclusion).

2 Methodology

As a use case for this work, the overall PTU manufacturing process is depicted in Fig. 1. Pinion and Ring Gear are the two main components of a PTU. After machining, these two components are passed for lapping and assembly, and from there towards the EOL. The Pinion and Ring Gear are processed as a pair in the lapping and assembly line and during this processing, a lot of data is collected using different sensors. Human experts observe the process closely to avoid any faulty PTU. However, it is not feasible for human experts to monitor a huge amount of data produced by the sensors. To facilitate the prediction of a faulty unit during lapping and assembly lines, this study proposes a CDT based on a heuristic approach. The Pinion and Ring Gear pair is depicted in Fig. 2 (a), whereas, Fig. 2 (b) shows a PTU. The heuristic approach used for the proposed CDT technology is explained next.

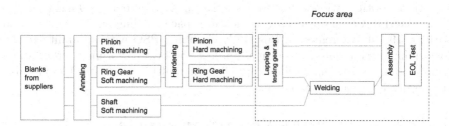

Fig. 1. PTU manufacturing process.

2.1 Metaheuristic for Cognitive Digital Twin

Sophisticated optimization problems are addressed using computational intelligence paradigms such as metaheuristic algorithms. A heuristic method is one that repeatedly tries to make a candidate solution better in terms of a specified quality metric. Without being able to guarantee either feasibility or optimality, or even in many circumstances to indicate how close to optimality a specific

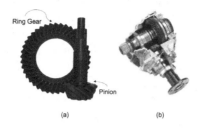

Fig. 2. (a) Pinion and Ring Gear pair, (b) PTU.

viable solution is, heuristics can explore enormous areas of candidate solutions in pursuit of optimal or nearly optimal solutions at a reasonable computing cost. These algorithms have the ability to solve NP-hard optimization problems. Particle Swarm Optimization (PSO) is a metaphor-based metaheuristic optimization algorithm developed initially based on the inspiration from the behaviour of birds and fish folks. During the past few decades, different researchers have worked on the development of PSO, and the algorithm has proved itself as a powerful tool in solving complex optimization problems [16,17]. The main drawback of PSO is its possibility of getting stuck in the local minima while searching in high dimensions. This drawback is solved recently by proposing a Jumping strategy in PSO [14,18]. Complex and large feature spaces are mostly associated with a well-known phenomenon called *curse of dimensionality*. Data produced from the lapping and assembly line during PTU production is usually large in size. Some of these data parameters could predict a faulty PTU in advance. However, if the entire data is used for training machine learning algorithms, the model's performance is not optimum due to redundancy and irrelevance in the feature space. Therefore, to utilize the abilities of machine learning models in an optimum level, optimization of feature space is usually required. PSO has proved to be a powerful tool in optimizing the feature space for different industrial applications [19,20]. Therefore, in this study, Jumping PSO with an ability to skip local minima is adopted to optimally select the best-performing sensor values from lapping and assembly line to predict the faulty PTU units. The proposed framework is explained in the next subsection.

2.2 Cognitive Digital Twin for PTU Manufacturing

The overall concept of the proposed CDT for PTU manufacturing is depicted in Fig. 3. The data from the lapping and assembly lines are utilized to analyze the future prediction of faulty PTUs. The sensor data received from the lapping and assembly lines are quite large in number, and different sensor values define different manufacturing parameters. Most of these parameters have no influence on the prediction of faulty PTUs as described by human experts, while some of these are believed to have an impact on the prediction of faulty PTUs. To analyze all the manufacturing parameters in an optimized way, Jumping PSO is wrapped with machine learning algorithms. The algorithm evolves the feature space in an optimized way to select the best combination of parameters for faulty PTU predictions. The three basic optimization steps carried by PSO are:

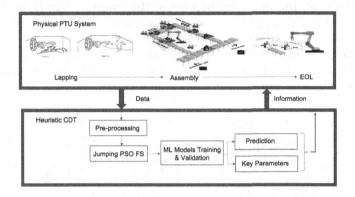

Fig. 3. Overall concept for the proposed CDT for PTU manufacturing.

1. Evaluation of particles against a fitness function.
2. Keeping record of best position and fitness values.
3. Velocity and position update of particles.

The velocity and position update of particles in a classical PSO is done as:

$$v_i(t+1) = wv_i(t) + c_1 rand(g(t) - x_i(t)) + c_2 rand(p_i(t) - x_i(t)) \qquad (1)$$

$$x_i(t+1) = x_i(t) + v_i(t) \qquad (2)$$

here, v_i is the velocity of ith particle, x_i is the position, c_1, c_2 are the exploration and exploitation constants, $p_i(t)$ and $g_i(t)$ are the personal and global best positions at time t. By introducing a jumping strategy, the velocity update equation is modified as [14]:

$$v_i(t+1) = wv_i(t) + c_1 rand(g(t) - x_i(t)) + c_2 rand(p_i(t) - x_i(t)) + J_i(CJ) \qquad (3)$$

where, $J_i(CJ)$ is the jumping value given to i^{th} searching particle. The amount of jump is defined as:

$$J_i(CJ) = (log(\frac{(\frac{CJ}{0.1 \times acceptance})^\alpha}{(\frac{CJ}{0.1 \times acceptance})^\alpha + 1}) + \epsilon) \times rand^N \qquad (4)$$

$$CJ_i = v_i(t) + (g(t) - x_i(t)) + (p_i(t) - x_i(t)) \qquad (5)$$

The whole optimization process is iterative and based on the successive iterations t, the swarm of particles evolves towards convergence. Once the algorithm converges, either by reaching a maximum number of successive iterations or by reaching a certain value of fitness value, the global best position of the algorithm defines the best combination of features (manufacturing parameters) for prediction. The process is explained visually in Fig. 4. The binary numbers in a single row represent the position of a particle, where 0's represent the feature not being selected and 1's show the feature being selected. Combination of particles (rows) form a swarm, and each particle in the swarm is tested for its performance against different machine learning algorithms. The personal best position $p(t)$ of a particle is the combination of features (represented by 1's) at which the machine learning algorithm achieved the highest classification accuracy at particle level. The global best position $g(t)$ is the combination of features in the whole swarm achieving highest classification accuracy.

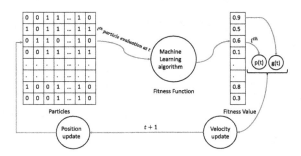

Fig. 4. Proposed process of selecting best manufacturing parameters for the prediction of faulty PTUs.

3   Results and Discussion

The dataset used for the evaluation of the proposed Heuristic Digital Twin is taken from the database of *GKN Automotive*, a global leader in eDrive technologies. The actual data had 41776 observations of PTU manufacturing samples, with 47 important parameters provided by human experts. However, the problem of class imbalance existed in the dataset because there were only 60 observations out of 41776 observed as faulty, the rest of all the observations were standard PTUs. Therefore, to deal with the class imbalance problem in the data, downsampling of the majority class (standard PTU) is done. After the downsampling, the class with Standard PTUs has 72 samples, while the faulty PTUs class has 60 samples.

3.1   Results

To evaluate the power of the proposed heuristic digital twin architecture, some of the standard machine learning algorithms are tested in a wrapper framework. The results are computed for two different scenarios: (i) performance of machine learning algorithms using the important variables identified by human experts, and (ii) performance of machine learning algorithms with optimized feature space using the proposed architecture. All the results are reported after 5-fold cross-validation. The performance of different machine learning algorithms using the

Table 1. Performance of different algorithms with all the parameters.

Model	Accuracy(%)
SVM (RBF)	57.35
Random Forest	55.88
KNN	**66.17**
Nive Bayes	50.00
Discriminant Analysis	53.63
Generalized additive model	58.08
Decision Tree	55.14

important parameters identified by human experts is provided in Table. 1. Here, it can be seen that the performance of different machine learning algorithms in the prediction of faulty PTUs is quite weak using all the features identified by human experts. The best performance achieved is 66.17% using the KNN model with Euclidean distance and 3 nearest neighbours. The results reported in Table. 1 are the best-achieved results after hyperparameter tunning of all the machine learning models. The results achieved using the proposed heuristic digital twin model are reported in Table. 2. From the results in Table. 2, it can be concluded that the proposed framework has the ability to perform better. The best accuracy using an optimized subset of feature space is 75.00%, which is significantly greater than the accuracy achieved by all the features without optimization. It clearly signifies the importance of optimizing the large feature space and identifies the important manufacturing parameters for predicting faulty PTUs in advance. Therefore, the proposed framework has two major advantages: *(i) ability to improve the prediction accuracy*, and *(ii) ability to identify the important prediction parameters*.

There are different subsets of features provided in Table. 2, these subsets are the best-performing combination of features for prediction using the specified model. The experiment is repeated with different swarm sizes of Jumping PSO to see it's influence on the performance. The results with different swarm sizes on two best-performing classifiers are reported in Table. 3. Here, different results reported for the same model indicate the influence of swarm size. The details of different Jumping PSO hyperparameters used for the experimentation are provided in Table. 4, and the details of features taken from the PTU manufacturing are provided in Appendix A, Table. 7.

3.2   Analysis of Results

The results are further analyzed using some of the common evaluation parameters such as Sensitivity, Specificity, Precision, False Positive Rate, F1 score, Matthews Correlation Coefficient, Kappa, and Receiver Operating Characteristic (ROC) curve. The results of these evaluation parameters are reported in Table. 5 and Fig. 5. It can be seen from the results in Table. 5 that the sensitivity

Table 2. Performance of different algorithms with optimized feature space.

Model	#Features	Features	Accuracy(%)
SVM (RBF)	12	**3,4,5,18,26,28,29,30,33,39,43,46**	**75.00**
Random Forest	10	4,7,11,16,20,22,27,45,46,47	72.79
KNN (k=1, cosine)	11	**3,4,9,11,18,29,34,38,39,41,44**	**75.00**
Nive Bayes	6	4,5,9,21,27,45	66.18
Discriminant Analysis	8	4,11,15,18,26,28,36,37,38	68.38
Generalized additive model	12	5,9,11,16,19,20,30,33,40,41,42,43	69.85
Decision Tree	12	3,5,8,11,13,14,16,19,21,29,42,47	73.53

Table 3. Influence of Jumping PSO's swarm size.

Model	swarm size	#Features	Features	Accuracy(%)
SVM	150	12	**3,4,5,18,26,28,29,30,33,39,43,46**	**75.00**
SVM	100	12	4,5,6,12,15,18,21,23,39,43,44,45	71.32
SVM	50	8	5,10,18,22,29,30,39,47	69.85
SVM	150	9	3,5,11,18,23,29,30,41,47	72.05
SVM	100	8	10,11,14,22,23,31,34,39	71.32
KNN	150	11	**3,4,9,11,18,29,34,38,39,41,44**	**75.00**
KNN	100	14	5,10,11,14,18,19,21,27,29,30,31,32,39,41	69.85
KNN	50	2	35,47	66.17
KNN	150	13	3,8,13,18,19,22,27,36,38,39,41,43,44	71.32
KNN	100	13	2,3,4,5,7,18,24,29,30,35,36,39,44	68.38

Table 4. Hyperparameters for Jumping PSO.

Hyperparameter	Value
swarm size	50,100,150
Max. iterations	2000
c_1, c_2	2
α	30
ϵ	0.0001
ω	exponential decrease from 0.9 to 0.1
acceptance	0.1

of the models is low, this shows that the faulty PTU samples are miss-classified as the standard PTU samples. Furthermore, it is also observed that the machine learning models are able to classify the faulty PTUs with a maximum of 75% accuracy. One possibility of these results could be the challenging and complex data that has low discriminatory powers. Secondly, as there are only limited data samples available for faulty PTUs in the real scenarios, therefore, the training samples of faulty PTU's might be limited for sufficient models training. To guar-

Table 5. Performance evaluation on different metrics.

Evaluation	SVM	RF	KNN	NB	DA	GAM	DT
Accuracy	**0.75**	0.72	**0.75**	0.66	0.68	0.69	0.73
Error	**0.25**	0.27	**0.25**	0.33	0.31	0.30	0.26
Sensitivity	0.58	0.65	**0.68**	0.63	0.51	0.66	0.60
Specificity	**0.88**	0.78	0.80	0.68	0.81	0.72	0.84
Precision	**0.79**	0.70	0.73	0.61	0.68	0.65	0.75
False Positive Rate	**0.11**	0.21	0.19	0.31	0.18	0.27	0.15
F1 score	0.67	0.67	**0.70**	0.62	0.59	0.66	0.66
Matthews Correlation Coefficient	**0.49**	0.44	**0.49**	0.31	0.35	0.38	0.45
Kappa	0.47	0.44	**0.48**	0.31	0.34	0.38	0.45

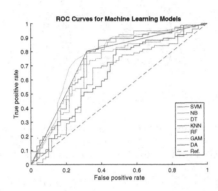

Fig. 5. ROC curves for Machine Learning Models.

antee the best performance, sufficient training samples of faulty PTUs must be provided, and as the current study is based on the limited available data, the performance of the models could be further enhanced after the availability of more training samples. The selected subset of optimized features is also analyzed in terms of the *frequency of selection* of a particular feature in different experiments. The higher frequency of selection shows a higher chance of importance because the feature is selected repeatedly during different experiments. The frequency of selection of features is shown in Fig. 6. It is observed that the feature (i) *Cover Dimension D2 mm* is selected the maximum number of times, followed by (ii) *Press Ball Bering To Housing Force kN*, and (iii) *Press Shim Head Outer Race To Housing Force kN*. Besides these parameters, the frequency of selection of the following parameters is also high: (iv) *Press Shim Outer Race To BPA Force kN*, (v) *Press Inner Ring Upper To Tubular Shaft Length mm*, (vi) *Press Inner Ring Upper To Tubular Shaft Force kN*, (vii) *Housing Dimension H3 mm*, (viii) *Housing Dimension D1 mm*, and (ix) *Press Shim Head Outer Race To Housing Length mm*. Therefore, these features are deemed important to build a CDT model for PTU manufacturing process.

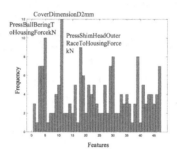

Fig. 6. Feature's selection frequency in different experiments.

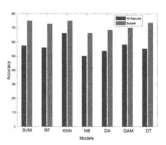

Fig. 7. All features accuracy Vs heuristically selected features.

Table 6. Comparison of proposed heuristic approach with PCA and LDA.

Model	PCA	LDA	Proposed
SVM (RBF)	66.17	63.97	**75.00**
Random Forest	56.61	59.55	**72.79**
KNN (k=1, cosine)	59.55	59.55	**75.00**
Nive Bayes	59.55	58.82	**66.18**
Discriminant Analysis	57.35	60.29	**68.38**
Generalized additive model	59.55	61.76	**69.85**
Decision Tree	64.70	65.44	**73.53**

Furthermore, the importance of adopting a metaheuristic approach for optimizing the feature space in a Digital Twin is shown in Fig. 7. It can be clearly seen from Fig. 7 that the accuracy of selected features is higher than the accuracy of all features for all the tested models. Moreover, the comparison of proposed heuristic approach with PCA and LDA which are conventional feature reduction approaches is provided in Table. 6. The comparison reveals that the proposed approach is better as compared to the state-of-art feature reduction techniques. Furthermore, the use of lesser features makes the model more computationally efficient and less prone to over-fitting. Therefore, a heuristically optimized cognitive digital twin model for PTU manufacturing is recommended.

4 Conclusions

The role of implementing a heuristic approach for designing a CDT in manufacturing is evaluated and recommended in this article. A use case of PTU manufacturing is utilized to evaluate the proposed heuristic CDT model. From the results, it is observed that the use of a heuristic approach for optimizing the feature space is important for CDTs. It not only helps in improving the performance of machine learning models but also provides information about the key parameters. Along with increasing decision-making and control autonomy, the proposed model has the capability to enhance the enterprise's performance (at scale). Therefore, it is recommended to utilize such frameworks while developing the CDT models for the manufacturing industry. Future work involves increasing the availability of a number of faulty PTU samples and improving the classification accuracy of the system.

Acknowledgment. This work was supported in part by the project DIGICOGS project which is financed by Vinnova (Vinnovas Diarienr: 2019-0532) and the innovation program Process Industrial IT and Automation (PiiA) at Mälardalen University.

The authors would like to thank Michael Osbakk, Mikael Eriksson, Jonathan Widén, Jimmy Vesa, and 'GKN Drive line' for all the help and support during this study.

A Details of Features Taken from the PTU Manufacturing Process

Table 7. Features from the PTU manufacturing process utilized for experimentation.

1	Housing Dimension H1 mm	2	Housing Dimension H2 mm
3	Housing Dimension H3 mm	4	Housing Dimension D1 mm
5	Press Ball Bering To Housing Force kN	6	Press Ball Bering To Housing Length mm
7	Press Snappring Length mm	8	Press Input Shaft To Housing Force kN
9	Press Input Shaft To Housing Lenth mm	10	Cover Dimension C1 mm
11	Cover Dimension D2 mm	12	Bearing Plate Adapter Dimension C2 mm
13	Bearing Plate Adapter Dimension D3 mm	14	Pinion Head Bearing Height Dimension mm
15	GMD	16	Shim Pinion Calculated mm
17	Shim Pinion Actual mm	18	Press Shim Head Outer Race To Housing Force kN
19	Press Shim Head Outer Race To Housing Length mm	20	Press Tail Outer Race To Housing Force kN
21	Press Tail Outer Race To Housing Length mm	22	Press Collapsible Spacer Tail Inner Race To Pinion Force kN
23	Press Collapsible Spacer Tail Inner Race To Pinion Length mm	24	Press Companion Flange Force kN
25	Pinion Torque To Turn 80 Nm	26	Pinion Nut Torque 80 Nm
27	Pinion Height mm	28	Pinion Height Real mm
29	Press Inner Ring Upper To Tubular Shaft Force kN	30	Press Inner Ring Upper To Tubular Shaft Length mm
31	Press Inner Ring Lower To Tubular Shaft Force kN	32	Press Inner Ring Lower To Tubular Shaft Length mm
33	Measure Tubular Shaft Dimension R2 mm	34	Measure Tubular Shaft Dimension R3 mm
35	Shim Backlash Calculated mm	36	Shim Back lash Actual mm
37	Shim Preload Calculated mm	38	Shim Preload Actual mm
39	Press Shim Outer Race To BPA Force kN	40	Press Shim Outer Race To BPA Length mm
41	Press Shim Outer Race To Cover Force kN	42	Press Shim Outer Race To Cover Length mm
43	Measure Final Torque To Turn Nm	44	Measure Back lash 180 M1 Degree
45	Measure Backlash 180 M2 Degree	46	Measure Backlash 180 Avarage Degree
47	Serial		

References

1. Rahman, H., D'Cruze, R.S., Ahmed, M.U., Sohlberg, R., Sakao, T., Funk, P.: Artificial intelligence-based life cycle engineering in industrial production: a systematic literature review. IEEE Access **10**, 133001–133015 (2022)
2. Teerasoponpong, S., Sugunnasil, P.: Review on artificial intelligence applications in manufacturing industrial supply chain - industry 4.0's perspective. In: 2022 Joint International Conference on Digital Arts, Media and Technology with ECTI Northern Section Conference on Electrical, Electronics, Computer and Telecommunications Engineering (ECTI DAMT & NCON), pp. 406–411 (2022)
3. Javaid, M., Haleem, A., Singh, R.P., Suman, R., Gonzalez, E.S.: Understanding the adoption of industry 4.0 technologies in improving environmental sustainability. Sustain. Oper. Comput. (2022)
4. Friederich, J., Francis, D.P., Lazarova-Molnar, S., Mohamed, N.: A framework for data-driven digital twins for smart manufacturing. Comput. Ind. **136**, 103586 (2022)
5. Li, L., Lei, B., Mao, C.: Digital twin in smart manufacturing. J. Ind. Inf. Integr. **26**, 100289 (2022)
6. Sheuly, S.S., Ahmed, M.U., Begum, S.: Machine-learning-based digital twin in manufacturing: a bibliometric analysis and evolutionary overview. Appl. Sci. **12**(13) (2022). https://www.mdpi.com/2076-3417/12/13/6512
7. Al Faruque, M.A., Muthirayan, D., Yu, S.Y., Khargonekar, P.P.: Cognitive digital twin for manufacturing systems. In: 2021 Design, Automation & Test in Europe Conference & Exhibition (DATE). IEEE, pp. 440–445 (2021)
8. Abburu, S., Berre, A.J., Jacoby, M., Roman, D., Stojanovic, L., Stojanovic, N.: Cognitwin-hybrid and cognitive digital twins for the process industry. In: 2020 IEEE International Conference on Engineering, Technology and Innovation (ICE/ITMC). IEEE, pp. 1–8 (2020)
9. Li, Y., Chen, J., Hu, Z., Zhang, H., Lu, J., Kiritsis, D.: Co-simulation of complex engineered systems enabled by a cognitive twin architecture. Int. J. Prod. Res. **60**(24), 7588–7609 (2022)
10. Eirinakis, P., et al.: Cognitive digital twins for resilience in production: a conceptual framework. Information **13**(1), 33 (2022)
11. Sheuly, S.S., Ahmed, M.U., Begum, S., Osbakk, M.: Explainable machine learning to improve assembly line automation. In: 2021 4th International Conference on Artificial Intelligence for Industries (AI4I). IEEE, pp. 81–85 (2021)
12. ur Rehman, A., Bermak, A., Hamdi, M.: Shuffled frog-leaping and weighted cosine similarity for drift correction in gas sensors. IEEE Sensors J. **19**(24), 12126–12136 (2019)
13. ur Rehman, A., Bermak, A.: Swarm intelligence and similarity measures for memory efficient electronic nose system. IEEE Sensors J. **18**(6), 2471–2482 (2018)
14. Ur Rehman, A., Islam, A., Azizi, N., Belhaouari, S.B.: Jumping particle swarm optimization. In: Yang, X.-S., Sherratt, S., Dey, N., Joshi, A. (eds.) Proceedings of Sixth International Congress on Information and Communication Technology. LNNS, vol. 236, pp. 743–753. Springer, Singapore (2022). https://doi.org/10.1007/978-981-16-2380-6_65
15. Sheuly, S.S., Barua, S., Begum, S., Ahmed, M.U., Guclu, E., Osbakk, M.: Data analytics using statistical methods and machine learning: a case study of power transfer units. Int. J. Adv. Manuf. Technol. **114**(5), 1859–1870 (2021). https://doi.org/10.1007/s00170-021-06979-7

16. ur Rehman, A., Bermak, A.: Heuristic random forests (HRF) for drift compensation in electronic nose applications. IEEE Sensors J. **19**(4), 1443–1453 (2018)
17. Houssein, E.H., Gad, A.G., Hussain, K., Suganthan, P.N.: Major advances in particle swarm optimization: theory, analysis, and application. Swarm Evol. Comput. **63**, 100868 (2021)
18. Rehman, A.U., Islam, A., Belhaouari, S.B.: Multi-cluster jumping particle swarm optimization for fast convergence. IEEE Access **8**, 189382–189394 (2020)
19. Ahila, R., Sadasivam, V., Manimala, K.: An integrated PSO for parameter determination and feature selection of ELM and its application in classification of power system disturbances. Appl. Soft Comput. **32**, 23–37 (2015)
20. Subramani, S., Selvi, M.: Multi-objective PSO based feature selection for intrusion detection in IoT based wireless sensor networks. Optik **273**, 170419 (2023)

Generation of Optimum Frenet Curves by Genetic Algorithms for AGVs

Eduardo Bayona[1,2]([✉]) [ID], J. Enrique Sierra-Garc[1] [ID], and Matilde Santos[3] [ID]

[1] Department of Electromechanical Engineering, University of Burgos, Burgos, Spain
{ebayona,jesierra}@ubu.es
[2] Michelin España-Portugal, Aranda de Duero, Spain
[3] Institute of Knowledge Technology, Complutense University of Madrid,
Madrid, Spain
msantos@ucm.es

Abstract. This article presents a methodology for the generation of optimized trajectories for Automated Guided Vehicles (AGV) and its implementation. The proposed methodology includes the use of several software tools, such as AutoCAD for defining the occupancy map, MATLAB for mathematical calculations and generating the optimal trajectory, and Unity for visualization. The working process begins with defining the occupancy map using CAD software, selecting waypoints, and generating the optimal trajectory using a genetic algorithm based on the Frenet equations with an optimization parameter. Finally, the generated trajectory is visualized in Unity. The methodology ensures the optimization of the trajectory design process and provides a correct visualization of the results. The proposed approach can be useful in the implementation of AGVs in different fields, such as logistics and manufacturing.

Keywords: Soft computing · Automatic Guided Vehicle · Genetic Algorithms · Industry 4.0 · Trajectories

1 Introduction

The automation of production processes has led to the development of solutions that allow the internal transfer of raw materials, products, and merchandise. One of the most widely used solutions for automating internal logistics is the use of Automated Guided Vehicles (AGV) [4,5]. AGVs are mobile robots capable of self-direction within an environment following physical or virtual paths, and they provide a notable improvement in the production processes, reducing costs, increasing production, and optimizing safety during them [9].

Generating optimized trajectories for AGVs is an essential task to maximize their efficiency and productivity. One of the challenges in generating optimized trajectories for AGVs is to find the best path from a starting point to an end point, avoiding obstacles, and minimizing the travel time [8]. Several methods have been proposed to generate optimized trajectories, including the

© IFIP International Federation for Information Processing 2023
Published by Springer Nature Switzerland AG 2023
I. Maglogiannis et al. (Eds.): AIAI 2023, IFIP AICT 676, pp. 454–464, 2023.
https://doi.org/10.1007/978-3-031-34107-6_36

use of numerical methods based on Frenet-Serret formulas [7], and evolutionary techniques like genetic algorithms [6].

This article presents a methodology for the generation of optimized trajectories for AGVs and its implementation. The proposed methodology includes the use of several software tools, such as AutoCAD for defining the occupancy map, MATLAB for mathematical calculations and generating the optimal trajectory, and Unity for visualization [6]. The working process begins with defining the occupancy map using CAD software, selecting waypoints, and generating the optimal trajectory using a genetic algorithm based on the Frenet equations with an optimization parameter [3]. Finally, the generated trajectory is visualized in Unity.

The proposed approach ensures the optimization of the trajectory design process and provides a correct visualization of the results, making it useful for the implementation of AGVs in different fields, such as logistics and manufacturing. This methodology provides a faster, more efficient, and safer way to generate optimized trajectories for AGVs. By reducing the length of the path, it can significantly reduce the travel time, directly impacting the production time and therefore the productivity of the processes where automated transport solutions are implemented using AGVs.

In conclusion, the use of AGVs has become essential in different business sectors, and the generation of optimized trajectories is a critical aspect of their implementation. The proposed methodology using a genetic algorithm based on the Frenet equations with an optimization parameter and several software tools ensures the optimization of the trajectory design process and provides a correct visualization of the results. Therefore, it can be useful for the implementation of AGVs in different fields, such as logistics and manufacturing.

The paper is structured as follows. Once the motivation of the necessity of generating optimum trajectories for an AGV is presented, in Sect. 2 the flow of the steps to reach the objective is described, including the different tools used. The generation of the occupancy map is developed in Sect. 3. Section 4 explains how the genetic algorithm is applied and the cost function used. Results are shown and discussed in Sect. 5 and 6. The paper ends with the conclusions and future works.

2   Work Methodology

With the need to describe optimized trajectories for the performance and implementation of AGVs, the development of methodologies that automate the trajectory design process and guarantee its optimization and correct visualization of the obtained results for the user, arises.

In this work, the proposed methodology includes the use of several software components. As part of the trajectory generation process, a CAD tool must be used to define an occupancy map. In this work, we will use AutoCAD as computer-aided design software. Mathematical calculation for trajectory generation must be performed by a computer, with Matlab being the mathematical

456 E. Bayona et al.

tool used. Finally, Unity is used as a physical engine and visualization tool for the achieved result. The relationships between the used tools are represented in the component diagram of Fig. 1.

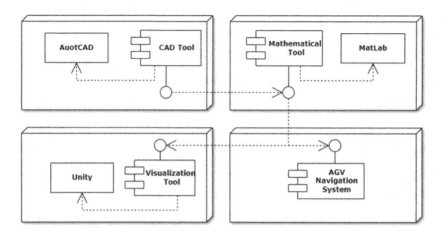

Fig. 1. Component diagram.

The work process begins with the creation of the occupancy map using a CAD tool (AutoCAD in this case) by drawing polylines. Once defined, the points that define each obstacle on the map are exported to a text file, which is then imported into a mathematical tool (Matlab in this case) where they are identified to reconstruct the map geometry.

Within the occupancy map space, minimum waypoints for the trajectory must be selected, including initial and final points as well as intermediate points. Based on these initial conditions, the process of generating the optimal trajectory begins in Matlab. The resulting trajectory is then imported into the simulation tool (Unity) to visualize the AGV's movement on the generated trajectory within the map for discussion (Fig. 2).

3 Occupancy Map

The generation of the occupancy map is carried out with CAD software using polylines. Within the map, fixed and mobile obstacles during the operation of the AGVs and the boundaries of the map itself are delimited by layers.

Using a Lisp macro, all the objects that make up the occupancy map are selected. From the selection, each of the points of the polylines of the objects of the map is exported to a text file with the properties of each one: identity code of the object to which they belong, the layer to which they belong, and their coordinates within the limits of the occupancy map.

From the text file, the points are imported into the mathematical tool based on the properties with which they were exported. The occupancy map is

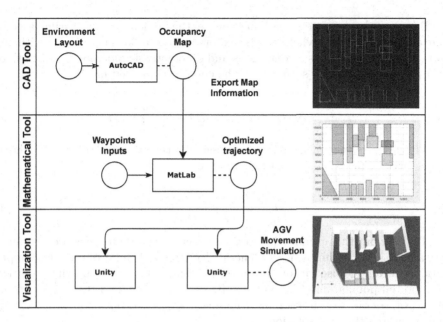

Fig. 2. Methodology process diagram.

constructed from these points, based on the geometric shapes defined in the CAD tool, both the limits and the obstacles.

All the space within the geometric shapes that describe the points of each obstacle is considered an occupied zone, and the space between the geometric shapes and the limits of the map will be free zones of occupancy.

4 Optimization Through Genetic Algorithm

Once the occupancy map in which the AGVs will operate has been generated, the mathematical tool requires the initial conditions to start working on the optimal trajectory. The initial and final points, as well as the intermediate points of passage that the AGV must pass through, must be defined. Based on these conditions, the tool is capable of finding the optimal trajectory that passes through those points according to an optimization parameter.

The generated trajectory is given by the Frenet equations, which represent a flat curve in $\mathbb{R}^2$ where the tangent vector T and the normal vector N satisfy (1). These equations are known as the Frenet equations of a trajectory [2].

$$\left.\begin{array}{l} T's = ksNs \\ N's = -ksTs \end{array}\right\} \tag{1}$$

where s is the distance to the origin of each point, k is the curvature of the trajectory at distance s, T(s) is the tangent vector at distance s, N(s) is the normal vector at distance s, and the symbol '′' denotes the perpendicular vector.

458   E. Bayona et al.

Based on the definition of a Frenet curve, the arc length can be calculated in Cartesian coordinates, where the trajectory will be a flat curve in $\mathbb{R}^2$ with the form $y = f(x)$ where f is a continuous and differentiable function. The length of each of the infinitesimal segments of the curve is expressed in (2).

$$ds = \sqrt{dx^2 + dy^2} = \sqrt{1 + \left(\frac{dy}{dx}\right)^2}\, dx \tag{2}$$

This leads to the mathematical expression of the arc length of the calculated trajectory (s) based on (2) and expressed in (3).

$$s = \int_{(x_i, y_i)}^{(x_f, y_f)} \sqrt{1 + \left(\frac{dy}{dx}\right)^2}\, dx \tag{3}$$

To carry out the optimization of the trajectory based on the chosen parameter, a genetic algorithm is used. Genetic algorithms are an evolutionary computational technique used in optimization problems. It is based on the evolution of an initial population of individuals. Its correct coding and the correct choice of genetic operators (mutation and crossover) are key to the algorithm's convergence towards the best solution [1].

The solutions for this optimization problem are defined as a matrix of 3 elements: $[x, y, \theta]$, where x and y are the coordinates of the intermediate points and θ is the output angle of the trajectory at those intermediate points. Therefore, there will be as many solutions as intermediate points indicated in the tool. The coordinates of the solutions can be any value within the dimensions of the occupancy map and the angles will be any value within the limits of 0 and 2π. These conditions are formally expressed in eqs. (4) to (6).

$$x \in [0, n] \tag{4}$$

$$y \in [0, m] \tag{5}$$

$$\theta \in [0, 2\pi] \tag{6}$$

Being n and m the dimensions on the abscissa and ordinate axis, respectively.

The fitness function of the algorithm will be the inverse of the average of the minimum distances from each point of the trajectory to the occupancy map. Using this fitness function, the genetic algorithm will optimize the generated trajectory in such a way that the points of the trajectory are as far away as possible from the occupancy map on average, ensuring that the selected option is the safest trajectory taking into consideration the distance to obstacles as a parameter.

To calculate the distance from each point to each of the obstacles, the projection of the point onto each of the segments that form each of the obstacles is calculated. If the projection falls on the line on which the segment lies, the minimum distance to the vertices of said segment is used. The value of the distance will be the norm of the vector that joins the point and its projection onto the segment or the nearest vertex. Formally, we can express the projection of a point P onto a line defined by points A and B that describe the segment of the nearest occupancy map vertex as (7).

$$Q = \text{proj}_{\vec{AB}}(\vec{AP}) = \frac{\vec{AB} \cdot \vec{AP}}{|\vec{AB}|^2} \cdot \vec{AB} \qquad (7)$$

Therefore, the value D, as the minimum distance of the points of the trajectory to the occupancy map in case Q will be the norm of $\vec{QP}$ if Q is on $\vec{AB}$ segment as expressed in (8):

$$D = ||\vec{QP}|| = \sqrt{(Q_x - P_x)^2 + (Q_y - P_y)^2} \qquad (8)$$

where Q_x and Q_y are the coordinates of point Q and P_x and P_y are the coordinates of point P.

In case Q is outside the $\vec{AB}$ segment, the value of the minimum distance will be the norm to the nearest vertex A or B. Assuming A is the nearest one it will expressed (9):

$$D = ||\vec{AP}|| = \sqrt{(A_x - P_x)^2 + (A_y - P_y)^2} \qquad (9)$$

where A_x and A_y are the coordinates of point A and P_x and P_y are the coordinates of point P.

The distance D from the point i of the trajectory to the obstacle j is denoted by D_{ij}. Then D_{ij} is computed for all pairs $(i, j) \in N_p \times N_o$, where N_p is the set points in the trajectory and N_o is the set of obstacles in the occupancy map.

The fitness function is thus expressed as the inverse of the average of the distance from each point of the trajectory to nearest obstacle in the occupancy map. This is formalized by (10):

$$f_F = \frac{n}{\sum_{i=1}^{n} \min_{j \in N_o} D_{ij}} \qquad (10)$$

5   Results Visualization

To evaluate the mathematical results within a 3-dimensional environment where the operation of the vehicle can be visualized as expected in the real environment, the optimized trajectory developed in Matlab must be imported into the Unity tool.

The representation of the occupancy map is done using the file created by the CAD tool to generate obstacles in the visualization software. Within the tool, the object representing the AGV vehicle must also be generated based on its real measurements, in order to faithfully represent the expected operation in reality.

From Matlab, the coordinates and output angles of each of the trajectory points are exported to a text file. Within the created occupancy map, the trajectory is reconstructed by importing the coordinates where the vehicle will travel and its orientation at each of those points. Using its graphics engine, Unity renders the movement of the AGV along the trajectory, allowing the evaluation of the result prior to implementation in the real environment.

6   Experiments

In line with the methodology developed previously, two experiments are carried out as a practical demonstration of the methodology. In each experiment, different starting and ending situations are presented, as well as different intermediate points within the same occupancy map, in order to verify the feasibility of the method presented in this work. First, an operating environment for the AGV is generated by simulating an industrial area with various obstacles in the CAD tool used. The different colors correspond to different types of obstacles and the limits of the occupancy map, with yellow representing the fixed obstacle layer, blue representing the mobile obstacle layer, and purple representing the map limits layer. Figure 3a shows the CAD occupancy map.

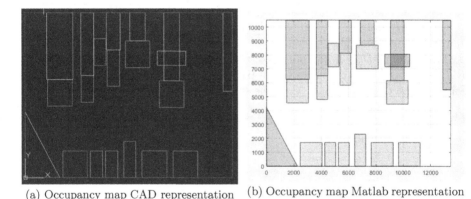

(a) Occupancy map CAD representation   (b) Occupancy map Matlab representation

Fig. 3. Occupancy map in CAD and Matlab.

This map is exported through a macro to obtain the points of the polylines that form the map and be able to work with it in the mathematical tool. Once imported, the occupancy map will have the shape shown in Fig. 3b.

Starting from this map, the initial conditions and intermediate points are selected for the genetic algorithm to operate and optimize the trajectory. In experiment 1, the leftmost point is the initial point and the red point on the right is the final point. In experiment 2, the initial point corresponds to the point at the bottom of the image and the final point is the point at the top. Points within the mobile layer can be selected, which means that the trajectory will start from the central point of that obstacle and, during the development of that trajectory, that obstacle in the mobile layer will not be where it was initially contemplated. Those obstacles where a point has been selected on them disappear, leaving their profile to indicate their existence on the initial map. The initial and final points are represented in red and the intermediate points in blue for each of the experiments. Figure 4a and 4b represent experiment 1 and 2, respectively.

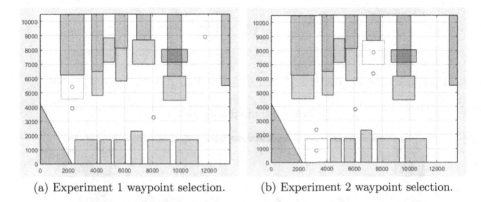

(a) Experiment 1 waypoint selection.   (b) Experiment 2 waypoint selection.

Fig. 4. Selection of waypoints.

With these conditions, the algorithm can now start operating with the output angles of the intermediate points as optimization variables. Figure 5a and 5b show the results of each of the proposed experiments. The trajectory is shown in red, and at each point of it, the profile of the AGV vehicle is shown along its path. The red points on the trajectory are the same points selected earlier as input parameters of the method, and they are also highlighted in the resulting trajectories. The yellow lines represent the minimum distance of each of the points in the optimized trajectory to the occupancy map, so that the average of these distances is maximized.

In both experiments, it is observed that the trajectory does not follow the shortest path to its destination. Instead, the algorithm marks a trajectory whose points remain at the maximum possible average distance from the obstacles in the occupancy map.

The points that make up this trajectory and their respective exit angles are exported to a file to be used by the visualization tool (Unity). Once imported, Unity builds a trajectory from them for the designed vehicle to move within it, maintaining the same exit angle calculated in the mathematical tool. To achieve the simulation of the AGV's movement along the optimized trajectory, an occupancy map analogous to the one used by Matlab must be constructed that uses the same coordinate reference system, so that the coordinates of the points on the trajectory are the same in each of the tools.

Figure 6 shows the occupancy map represented in Unity with the same reference to the origin as the original map. Likewise, it shows the model of the AGV

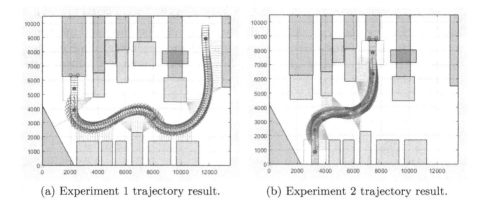

(a) Experiment 1 trajectory result.   (b) Experiment 2 trajectory result.

Fig. 5. Optimized trajectories.

Fig. 6. Visualization software, occupancy map and results representation

vehicle that represents the profile used in the mathematical tool and the trajectory imported from Matlab by which it will move. Based on the represented models and trajectory data, the movement of the vehicle along the trajectory can be visualized as expected to occur in reality, checking for possible situations not contemplated or safety or technical considerations that may arise during operation before the vehicles are deployed in their final location. Therefore, using visualization software allows for a better understanding of the data provided as a result of the mathematical tool, enabling the detection of patterns or trends that may otherwise go unnoticed. Similarly, it allows simulating a multitude of different scenarios and checking how the results affect the operation to help in decision-making when identifying the best solution.

It is also shown the appearance of the Unity representation of the results generated by the mathematical tool for experiment 1. In the image, the shape of the occupancy map and the model of the AGV vehicle can be distinguished. Likewise, the optimized trajectory imported into the tool by which the AGV will move can be distinguished, being able to visualize in real-time how the vehicle's operation will be from the initial point to the end.

7   Conclusions and Future Works

This paper presents a methodology for designing trajectories for AGVs that automates the design process and guarantees optimization of the trajectory based on selected parameters. The methodology combines several software tools such as AutoCAD, Matlab, and Unity for designing and visualizing the optimal trajectory.

Based on the results of the two experiments presented, it is demonstrated that this methodology can be useful for generating trajectories in a real working environment and has been validated through the Unity simulation of the AGV's movement on the generated trajectory.

The generation of the occupancy map using CAD software, in this case Auto-CAD, allows for a detailed definition of the obstacles and boundaries of the map, ensuring high precision in the generation of the trajectory. The process of generating the optimal trajectory through Frenet equations and supported by the use of genetic algorithms also ensures high precision in the generated trajectory.

Simulation in Unity allows for visualization and analysis of the generated trajectory, facilitating validation and adjustment of the trajectory if necessary. In conclusion, the methodology proposed in this paper is a useful tool for designing and generating optimal trajectories for AGVs in industrial working environments and can be adapted and improved for specific applications. The combination of several software tools allows for automation of the design process, reducing the time and effort required to generate an optimal trajectory.

As future works, different fitness functions could be implemented, weighting other factors such as energy saving or the dynamic generations of trajectories in case of pop-up obstacles.

References

1. Abajo, M.R., Sierra-García, J.E., Santos, M.: Evolutive tuning optimization of a PID controller for autonomous path-following robot. In: Sanjurjo González, H., Pastor López, I., García Bringas, P., Quintián, H., Corchado, E. (eds.) SOCO 2021. AISC, vol. 1401, pp. 451–460. Springer, Cham (2022). https://doi.org/10.1007/978-3-030-87869-6_43
2. Alencar, H., Santos, W., Neto, G.: Differential Geometry of Plane Curves. American Mathematical Society, Providence (2022)

3. Bayona, E., Sierra-García, J.E., Santos, M.: Optimization of trajectory generation for automatic guided vehicles by genetic algorithms. In: Bringas, P.G., et al. 17th International Conference on Soft Computing Models in Industrial and Environmental Applications (SOCO 2022). SOCO 2022. Lecture Notes in Networks and Systems, vol. 531, pp. 484–492. Springer, Cham (2023)

4. Berman, S., Schechtman, E., Edan, Y.: Evaluation of automatic guided vehicle systems. Robot. Comput.-Integr. Manuf. **25**(3), 522–528 (2009)

5. Espinosa, F., Santos, C., Sierra-García, J.E.: Transporte multi-agv de una carga: estado del arte y propuesta centralizada. Revista Iberoamericana de Automática e Informática industrial **18**(1), 82–91 (2020)

6. Kim, D.H., Kim, S.B.: Path following control of automated guide vehicle using camera sensor. In: Zelinka, I., Brandstetter, P., Trong Dao, T., Hoang Duy, V., Kim, S.B. (eds.) AETA 2018. LNEE, vol. 554, pp. 932–938. Springer, Cham (2020). https://doi.org/10.1007/978-3-030-14907-9_90

7. Kirsch, C., Künemund, F., Heß, D., Röhrig, C.: Comparison of localization algorithms for AGVs in industrial environments, pp. 183–188 (2012)

8. Yang, Z., Liu, H., Xie, R.: Improved ant colony algorithm based on parameters optimization for AGV path planning. In: 2021 2nd International Symposium on Computer Engineering and Intelligent Communications (ISCEIC), pp. 87–92 (2021)

9. Zamora-Cadenas, L., Velez, I., Sierra-Garcia, J.E.: UWB-based safety system for autonomous guided vehicles without hardware on the infrastructure. IEEE Access **9**, 96430–96443 (2021)

MPPT Control in an Offshore Wind Turbine Optimized with Genetic Algorithms and Unsupervised Neural Networks

Eduardo Muñoz-Palomeque[1]([⊠]) [iD], Jesús Enrique Sierra-García[1] [iD],
and Matilde Santos[2] [iD]

[1] Electromechanical Engineering Department, University of Burgos, Burgos, Spain
emp1016@alu.ubu.es, jesierra@ubu.es
[2] Institute of Knowledge Technology, Complutense University of Madrid, Madrid, Spain
msantos@ucm.es

Abstract. In this work, a control operation of a 1.5 MW offshore wind turbine (WT) for maximum power point tracking (MPPT) when wind speed is below rated, is studied. The implemented controller is designed using the general Direct Speed Control (DSC) scheme in which artificial neural networks (ANN) are incorporated to close the control loop. The neural controller acts in an unsupervised mode updating its weights with the incorporation of a learning algorithm. The optimal configuration parameters of the controller are determined by genetic algorithms. With this intelligent control strategy, the generator speed is regulated by varying the electromagnetic torque while adapting to the external phenomena in real time. Then, the output power, through the power coefficient (C_p), reaches the maximum wind power generation in that region. The offshore WT model is subjected to external loads due to wind and waves, which increase the system complexity and produce tower vibrations, negatively impacting the control efficiency. Despite that, it is shown that the proposed controller is able to operate with satisfactory results in terms of power generation and even reducing vibration, and it has been compared to the OpenFAST embedded torque control for the same WT providing better results.

Keywords: DSC · Neural Networks · Learning Algorithm · MPPT · Offshore Wind Turbine · Genetic Algorithms

1 Introduction

With the increasing energy requirements, renewable sources have been gaining importance. Among them, wind turbine [1] and photovoltaic systems [2] are two promising technologies. Focusing on the wind turbines, the high energy capacity, low environmental impact, affordable cost, and ease of installation have made these systems to be essential in clean energy production. Considering these benefits of the WT, and with the aim of taking advantage of the wider free of obstacles area in coastal and deep waters, offshore wind turbines have become profitable alternatives.

© IFIP International Federation for Information Processing 2023
Published by Springer Nature Switzerland AG 2023
I. Maglogiannis et al. (Eds.): AIAI 2023, IFIP AICT 676, pp. 465–477, 2023.
https://doi.org/10.1007/978-3-031-34107-6_37

To exploit these wind energy converters, the control of offshore wind turbines is a must to guarantee proper operation and efficient power generation. Therefore, some of the common goals in WT control systems are the maximization of the output power, the regulation of the blades angle, reduction of noise and vibration, among others [3, 4], which are of particular importance in the offshore scenarios.

The maximum power point tracking (MPPT) control in wind turbines, when the wind speed is below the nominal conditions, is one of these goals. The system must face the nonlinear loads that directly influence its operation and efficiency. In addition, for offshore WT, these nonlinear effects are increased and the complexity of the optimal control is directly affected by the waves and movement of the structure.

In fact, the mechanical stress and power fluctuations are some of the most negative effects that offshore wind turbines experience due to the harsh conditions to which they may be subjected to [5].

Taking into account all these factors that make the offshore wind turbine control more complex and strongly nonlinear, the importance of effective and more robust controllers is evident. In this context, neural networks have been proved very efficient to deal with these kinds of real systems.

In the MPPT WT operating region, the maximum power extraction is the main target. The power coefficient curve, C_p with which the power is related, must be tracked in order to reach the highest energy level. This is achieved by using a speed controller to regulate the velocity of the generator and thus, the turbine. This assures the largest wind power is captured and converted into electrical energy. In this process, the angle of the blades maintains a specific position that corresponds to the lowest value with which the maximum wind flow is captured.

To address the MPPT problem, conventional as well as intelligent control methods have been studied and applied separately and also complementing each other. For instance, some conventional strategies include the hill-climb searching (HCS) technique, power signal feedback (PSF), tip-speed ratio (TSR), or indirect speed control (ISC) [6–9]. On the other hand, artificial intelligent controllers with different approaches have been also proposed in the literature. In [10] fuzzy logic is applied to enhance the sliding mode control, or in [11, 12] the MPPT problem is faced implementing the fuzzy control under the direct speed control (DSC) scheme. Neural networks (NN) have been also used for the MPPT control [13]. In [14], NN and FLC have been used for maximum voltage estimation and DC-DC boost converter control in a wind turbine. In [15], a backpropagation NN (BPNN) is applied for indirect current control in a wind generator microgrid. In [16], a cascade NN approach is presented for maximum power control.

In this work, the use of an artificial control technique, such as neural networks with learning capability for unsupervised operation, is implemented for the MPPT control of a 1.5 MW offshore wind turbine. The controller is adapted to the DSC control frame to obtain a reference generator speed. Then the NN controller obtains the electromagnetic torque (T_{em}) and the generator speed, tracking the C_p and adapting to the changing environmental conditions that influence its dynamics. The use of genetic algorithms is important in this study to define the optimal configuration of the control scheme, including the neural network and the learning criteria.

As a summary, the main contribution of this article is the use of an online learning control based on neural networks that adapts to disturbances in the MPPT control in an offshore WT, instead of using static offline control algorithm. Also, the use of another artificial intelligent method such as genetic algorithms to enhance the controller finding the best neuro-control configuration shows the efficiency of the hybridization of several techniques.

After this introduction, the model of the WT is described in Sect. 2. Section 3 explains the intelligent neuro-control proposed. Results are discussed in Sect. 4. The paper ends with the conclusions and future works.

2   Wind Turbine Model

2.1   Offshore Wind Turbine

The wind turbine used in this work is a semi-submersible model with 3 blades, adapted from OpenFAST. In this system, the tower height is 92.39 m, and the distance measured from the level sea to the center of mass of the platform is 8.6 m. The platform is anchored to the seabed with a mooring system composed of 3 lines. The WT incorporates a 1.5 MW doubly fed induction generator (DFIG) with a nominal speed of 1200 rpm that is connected to the grid.

2.2   Aerodynamic Model

The wind turbine system captures the energy of the input wind through the blades. This causes the movement of the turbine, and that energy is converted into mechanical energy to move the generator.

In this first stage, the mechanical power that is extracted during the wind turbine operation can be expressed mathematically as [11, 17]:

$$P = \frac{1}{2} C_p A \rho V_w^3 \qquad (1)$$

where V_w is the wind speed (m/s), ρ is the density of the air (Kg/m^3), A is the area covered by the blades (m^2), and C_p is the power coefficient.

The power coefficient is described as a function of two elements: the tip speed ratio (TSR) λ and the blades angle β. The C_p coefficient denotes the efficiency in power extraction and can be approximated by Eq. (2) [18]. As a result, the C_p forms different curves according to the system features reflected in the coefficients $c_1 - c_6$ and the values of TSR and β.

$$C_p = c_1 \left(\frac{c_2}{\lambda_i} - c_3 \beta - c_4 \right) e^{-\frac{c_5}{\lambda_i}} + c_6 \lambda$$
$$\frac{1}{\lambda_i} = \frac{1}{\lambda + 0.08\beta} - \frac{0.035}{\beta^3 + 1} \qquad (2)$$

TSR relates the velocity of the tip blade with the wind speed as expressed in (3).

$$\lambda = \frac{\omega_r R}{V_w} \qquad (3)$$

where ω_r is the turbine rotor speed (rad/s) and R is the blade length (m).

For the wind turbine model used in this work, the maximum C_p is 0.48 and the optimal TSR is 7.1. The blades angle is fixed at 2° in the below rated operating region.

2.3 Mechanical Model

The mechanical process in the wind generator system is given by the gearbox. This mechanism generates the two zones of transmission of speed and torque. They are: the low-speed shaft (LSS) and, after the gearbox, the high-speed shaft (HSS). Expression (4) [19] shows the mathematical relation.

$$T_r = \dot{\omega}_r \left(N^2 J_g + J_r \right) + N T_{em} \tag{4}$$

where $\dot{\omega}_r$ is the rotor angular acceleration (rad/s^2), N is the gearbox ratio, J_g and J_r are the generator and rotor moments of inertia ($Kg \cdot m^2$), respectively, and T_r is the aerodynamic torque (Nm). The rotor acceleration can also be described in terms of the generator acceleration $\dot{\omega}_g$ as: $\dot{\omega}_r = \dot{\omega}_g / N$.

2.4 Electrical Generator Model

The generator type adapted to the wind turbine model for this study corresponds to a DFIG machine. Its representation can be made with the voltages and fluxes using the Park transform, and the expressions are then denoted in the d-q frame [20]. Equations in (5) present this mathematical model. Each term is expressed in the stator (s) or rotor (r) side.

$$\begin{aligned}
V_{ds} &= R_s i_{ds} + \frac{d\psi_{ds}}{dt} - \omega_e \psi_{qs} & \psi_{ds} &= L_s i_{ds} + M \cdot i_{dr} \\
V_{qs} &= R_s i_{qs} + \frac{d\psi_{qs}}{dt} + \omega_e \psi_{ds} & \psi_{qs} &= L_s i_{qs} + M \cdot i_{qr} \\
V_{dr} &= R_r i_{dr} + \frac{d\psi_{dr}}{dt} - \omega_{sl} \psi_{qr} & \psi_{dr} &= L_r i_{dr} + M \cdot i_{ds} \\
V_{qr} &= R_r i_{qr} + \frac{d\psi_{qr}}{dt} + \omega_{sl} \psi_{dr} & \psi_{qr} &= L_r i_{qr} + M \cdot i_{qs}
\end{aligned} \tag{5}$$

where V is the voltage (V); ψ is the flux (Wb); i is the current (A); R is the resistance (Ω); L is the inductance and M is the mutual inductance, both in (H); ω_e is the angular speed (rad/s) and ω_{sl} is the slip angular speed (rad/s).

3 Neural Networks for MPPT Control

Neural networks are applied in the DSC control scheme to address the MPPT problem. Figure 1 illustrates the control strategy that is detailed in this section.

First, the conventional DSC control scheme of a WT consists in obtaining the electromagnetic torque, that is determined from a pre-computed velocity signal, in order to achieve the optimum generator speed so to guarantee the maximum power extraction.

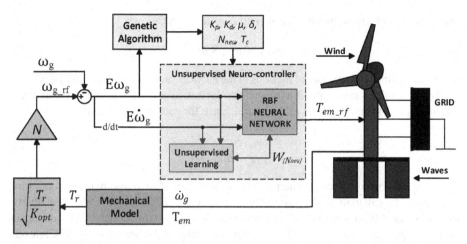

Fig. 1. Control scheme based on DSC and Unsupervised Neural Networks (Color figure online).

According to [21], the reference speed for DSC (7) can be expressed as the relation between the gearbox ratio N, a computed rotor torque T_r obtained from (4), and a constant value K_{opt} (6) calculated in terms of the optimal C_p and TSR.

$$K_{opt} = \frac{\rho \pi}{2} C_{p\_opt} \frac{R^5}{\lambda_{opt}^3} \tag{6}$$

$$\omega_{g\_rf} = N \sqrt{\frac{T_r}{K_{opt}}} \tag{7}$$

Then, the artificial neural network is designed to match the generator speed with the most suitable electromagnetic torque and thus to track the maximum power generation. The network used in this study is a radial basis neural network. In this controller, an unsupervised learning algorithm is used. This way, the neuro-controller updates its weights so to reduce the error speed signal over time.

To complete this process, the generator speed error $E\omega_g$ and the derivative generator speed error $E\dot{\omega}_g$ are calculated using the reference speed (7). These errors are connected to the neural network as inputs. The network produces the electromagnetic torque signal that is used as the reference for the MPPT control.

3.1 Radial Basis Neural Network

Breaking down the neuro-control scheme (yellow square of Fig. 1), it is possible to see two modules, the radial basis neural network and the learning algorithm. The RBNN is defined in a discretized plane whose dimensions are defined by the error speed inputs. This space is equally gridded in both dimensions, creating a dependency between the speed error and its derivative value. The centers of the neurons (o_{ix}, o_{iy}) are located on the vertices of the grid. Thus, the number of neurons that form the neural space is related to the number of divisions on the $E\omega_g$ and $E\dot\omega_g$ axes, as follows:

$$N_{neu} = div_x * div_y \tag{8}$$

where N_{neu} is the total number of neurons in the network and div_x and div_y are the number of divisions of the error speed axis and the derivative error speed axis, respectively. Therefore, the number of cells in the neural space for each dimension is:

$$
\begin{aligned}
N_{cellx} &= div_x - 1 \\
N_{celly} &= div_y - 1
\end{aligned} \tag{9}
$$

Once the control space for the neural network is structured, the mapping operation takes place to calculate an approximate output corresponding to the electromagnetic torque of the MPPT control. The radial basis function is governed by the distances measured at each control instant T_c, between the center of the neurons and the Cartesian point described by the input speed errors ($E\omega_g$, $E\dot\omega_g$). For this purpose, a normalized distance is determined as follows:

$$nrmDst = \sqrt{\frac{(o_{ix} - E\omega_{gen})^2}{E\omega_{g\,max}^2} + \frac{(o_{iy} - E\dot\omega_g)^2}{E\dot\omega_{g\,max}^2}} \tag{10}$$

The radial basis function that represents the output signal of the network is described in (11). This function specifies the neural principle of the applied radial basis neural network in terms of a sum of exponentials.

$$T_{em\_rf} = -\sum_{i=1}^{N_{neu}} W_i \cdot e^{-\left(\frac{nrmDst(o_{ix},o_{iy},E\omega_g,E\dot\omega_g)}{\delta}\right)} \tag{11}$$

where W is the neuron weight and the width of the RBF neuron is δ.

The second module of the intelligent controller is the unsupervised learning algorithm. This function is in charge of modifying the weights of the neurons in order to reach the proper output and reduce the generator speed error. With these variations, the controller automatically adapts to the current conditions of the WT system in real-time.

The updating of weights is managed by the level of impact the errors have on the process. The learning algorithm is also determined by an exponential function and the distance between the neurons and the input errors. This factor is important because the influence of a neuron in the output signal varies in terms of this distance.

The learning operation is described in (12), where K_p and K_d are constants that specify the weight of the speed error and its derivative, respectively, in the learning process, and μ indicates the learning rate.

$$W_j(t_i) = W_j(t_{i-1}) + \mu \cdot \left(K_p E\omega_g(t_i) + K_d E\dot{\omega}_g(t_i)\right) \cdot e^{-\left(\frac{nrmDst}{\delta}\right)} \tag{12}$$

3.2 Control Configuration Parameters

The RBF-NN and the learning algorithm are defined by different parameters, including K_p, K_d, μ, δ, N_{neu} and T_c. The correct definition of these parameters is essential to guarantee the controller operates as desired. In order to determine this set of parameters, genetic algorithms are used. The genetic algorithm works with a population size of 200 individuals randomly initialized. Each individual is composed of 6 chromosomes corresponding to the control parameters. To reduce the speed error, the cost function (13) that is minimized corresponds to the mean squared error metric of the speed (MSE_{vel}):

$$F_{costGA} = MSE_{vel} \tag{13}$$

where the MSE_{vel} is calculated as follows:

$$MSE_{vel} = \frac{1}{n} \sum_{i=1}^{n} \left(E\omega_g\right)^2 \tag{14}$$

And n is the number of elements of the $E\omega_g$ vector.

While the speed error is reduced, the optimal response of the WT for the current conditions is achieved. This means an increment of the power efficiency. The turbine operates at the speed with which the maximum energy of the wind is captured and transformed into electrical energy. Thus, the output power is optimized.

4 Results

Once the controller is designed, it is implemented in Matlab/Simulink, linked to a realistic offshore WT model in OpenFAST. Simulation is performed with random wind speed (Fig. 2) and wave inputs (Fig. 3) that replicate an actual WT system. Wind speed adopts values below the nominal speed 11.5 m/s value to operate in the MPPT region. The proposed control strategy is evaluated in terms of the MSE of the generator speed, output power, power coefficient, structural movement, and comparison with the OpenFAST torque control.

The optimal configuration of the controller is found with the genetic algorithms, obtaining the parameters presented in Table 1.

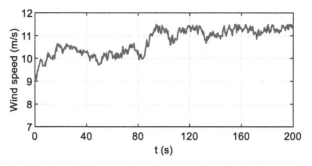

Fig. 2. Wind speed for the MPPT WT operation (Color figure online).

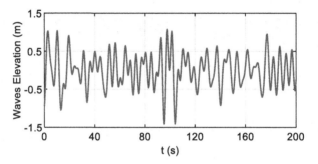

Fig. 3. Waves elevation (Color figure online).

Table 1. Parameters of the controller configuration

Parameter	Value
K_p	4.578686
K_d	0.196675
μ	0.136155
δ	0.446839
N_{neu}	25
T_c	0.098 seg

Each variable of the MPPT process will be analyzed. In Fig. 4, the MSE of the generator speed is presented. It shows the big reduction of the speed error obtained with the neuro-control strategy (red line). That is, the WT speed is closer to the reference than the one obtained with OpenFast (blue line), which allows it the maximum power generation.

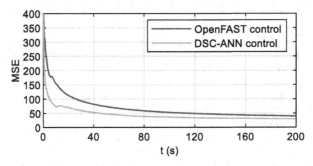

Fig. 4. MSE of the speed in the MPPT WT operation (Color figure online).

In Fig. 5, the output power generated is presented. It experiences quick adjustments in response to the applied torque obtained with the control process, facing the existing nonlinear dynamics. The power level with the neuro-controller achieves higher values, near the nominal value, with an average of 1.1374 MW (red line) in contrast to the average of 1.0488 MW with the OpenFAST controller (blue line). This means an increment of 8.45% in power extraction though it is noisier. These fluctuations result from a quick change in the electromagnetic torque to achieve the optimal relation between torque and speed for maximum energy production. This more oscillatory signal is common during the electric energy generation process. In addition, it can be managed in a later process to balance the power that is introduced in the grid.

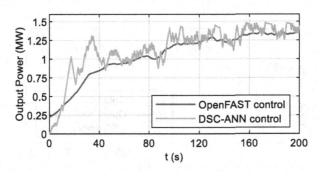

Fig. 5. Output power in the MPPT WT operation (Color figure online).

With the torque regulation, the generator speed (Fig. 6) is controlled. This variable oscillates to keep the speed-torque relation for the best system operation. It can be seen that the speed takes values around the nominal generator velocity during maximum energy conversion.

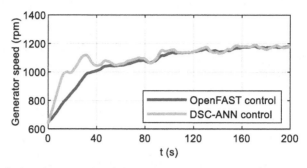

Fig. 6. Generator speed in the MPPT WT operation (Color figure online).

It can be pointed out that the radial basis analysis in the neuro-control space with an even neuron distribution provides a suitable environment to constantly compute a reference torque with quick updates related to the WT dynamics. Thus, the output signal is used to achieve the zero-speed error, resulting in a better speed response, as shown in the figure. The optimized parameters of the network architecture improve the efficiency of the response and the adaptive learning process. At each iteration the electromagnetic torque responds to the rotational speed produced by the variations that the wind, waves, and other involved phenomena cause.

As an indicator of the efficiency of the MPPT control, the power coefficient (Fig. 7) is measured. The tracking of the optimal C_p is more accurate with the neuro-controller and therefore, the maximum power curve, so the optimal power point is successful.

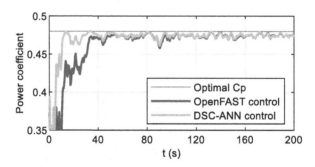

Fig. 7. Power coefficient in the MPPT WT operation (Color figure online).

Finally, it is also important to consider the structural response of the WT. The movement of the tower is shown in Fig. 8. It can be noticed that with the designed control technique, a slightly bigger displacement of the tower top is generated in contrast with the embedded OpenFAST torque control (blue line).

On average, this indicator is 0.24330 m with the DSC-NN controller and 0.23201 m with the OpenFAST control. This may be due to the higher generator speed, that has a bigger effect of the masses of the system, inertia, and faster variations in the variables for tracking better the C_p. Nevertheless, the variations are very small and are justified with the increase in the power extracted.

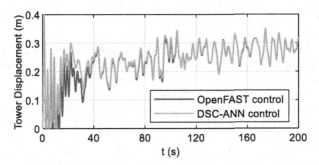

Fig. 8. Tower displacement in the MPPT WT operation (Color figure online).

On the other hand, to relate the effects of vibrations in the WT structure, the acceleration on the tower top is considered. The mean squared acceleration in the wind direction is calculated. A decrement of 0.0045 $(m/s^2)^2$ in the MSE value of the acceleration is finally obtained with the use of the neuro-controller, that is 0.05002 $(m/s^2)^2$ with the intelligent control strategy and 0.054505 $(m/s^2)^2$ with the OpenFAST controller. The small reduction contributes to the decrement of the vibration effects on the wind turbine tower and can be extended to the diverse mechanical elements of the wind turbine, including the platform. Thus, the vibrations in the device floating foundation are also slightly reduced.

5 Conclusions and Future Works

An intelligent control strategy for the MPPT region of an offshore wind turbine system has been developed, based on the conventional DSC control and using an unsupervised neural network with autonomous learning and genetic algorithms.

The incorporation of this control strategy has given positive results in this type of non-linear and complex system. The controller has been able to face and constantly adapt to the nonlinear behaviour of the device and to the external loads that are presented in offshore WTs. The intelligent controller maximizes the output power. In terms of vibrations, a slight increase in the tower movements has been caused, but it can be considered negligible taking into account the efficiency of the energy generation. Despite this condition, the acceleration of the top of the tower has been reduced, decreasing the negative effects of vibrations on the structure.

As future works, this control strategy could be applied to a floating offshore wind turbine, and to a real prototype.

Acknowledgement. This work was partially supported by the Spanish Ministry of Science, Innovation and Universities under MCI/AEI/FEDER Project no. PID2021-123543OB-C21.

References

1. Chaoui, H., Miah, S., Oukaour, A., Gualous, H.: Maximum power point tracking of wind turbines with neural networks and genetic algorithms. In IECON 2014–40th Annual Conference of the IEEE Industrial Electronics Society, pp. 197–201. IEEE (2014)
2. Saxena, V., Kumar, N., Singh, B., Panigrahi, B.K.: A spontaneous control for grid integrated solar photovoltaic energy conversion systems with voltage profile considerations. IEEE Trans. Sustain. Energy **12**(4), 2159–2168 (2021). https://doi.org/10.1109/TSTE.2021.3084103
3. Sierra-García, J.E., Santos, M.: Deep learning and fuzzy logic to implement a hybrid wind turbine pitch control. Neural Comput. Appl. **34**(13), 10503–10517 (2021). https://doi.org/10.1007/s00521-021-06323-w
4. Sierra-García, J.E., Santos, M.: Redes neuronales y aprendizaje por refuerzo en el control de turbinas eólicas. Revista Iberoamericana de Automática e Informática industrial **18**(4), 327–335 (2021)
5. Pustina, L., Lugni, C., Bernardini, G., Serafini, J., Gennaretti, M.: Control of power generated by a floating offshore wind turbine perturbed by sea waves. Renew. Sustain. Energy Rev. **132**, 109984 (2020)
6. Thongam, J.S., Ouhrouche, M.: MPPT control methods in wind energy conversion systems. In: Carriveau, R. (ed.) Fundamental and Advanced Topics in Wind Power. InTech (2011)
7. Pozo, A., Ayala, E., Simani, S., Muñoz, E.: Indirect speed control strategy for maximum power point tracking of the DFIG wind turbine system. Revista Técnica "energía" **17**(2), 92–101 (2021). https://doi.org/10.37116/revistaenergia.v17.n2.2021.426
8. Ayala, E., Simani, S.: Perturb and observe maximum power point tracking algorithm for permanent magnet synchronous generator wind turbine systems. In: Conte, G. (ed.) Proceedings of 15th European workshop on advanced control and diagnosis – ACD. Lecture notes in control and information sciences. Alma Mater Studiorum, University of Bologna, pp. 1–11. Springer, Bologna (2019). https://doi.org/10.1007/978-3-030-85318-1_59
9. Pande, J., Nasikkar, P., Kotecha, K., Varadarajan, V.: A review of maximum power point tracking algorithms for wind energy conversion systems. J. Marine Sci. Eng. **9**(11), 1187 (2021)
10. Malobe, P., Djondine, P., Eloundou, P., Ndongo, H.: A novel hybrid MPPT for wind energy conversion systems operating under low variations in wind speed. Energy Power Eng. **12**(12), 716–728 (2020)
11. Muñoz, E., Ayala, E., Pozo, N., Simani, S.: Fuzzy PID control system analysis for a wind turbine maximum power point tracking using FAST and Matlab Simulink. In: Iano, Y., Saotome, O., Kemper, G., Mendes, A.C., de Seixas, G., de Oliveira, G. (eds.) Proceedings of the 6th Brazilian Technology Symposium (BTSym'20). SIST, vol. 233, pp. 905–917. Springer, Cham (2021). https://doi.org/10.1007/978-3-030-75680-2_100
12. Muñoz, E., Ayala, E., Pozo, N.: Estrategia de Control Fuzzy PI en una Turbina Eólica con Generador de Inducción Doblemente Alimentado para Maximizar la Extracción de Potencia en Presencia de Perturbaciones. Revista Técnica energía **18**(1), 1–10 (2021). https://doi.org/10.37116/revistaenergia.v17.n2.2021.428
13. Muñoz-Palomeque, E., Sierra-García, J.E., Santos, M.: Wind turbine maximum power point tracking control based on unsupervised neural networks. J. Comput. Des. Eng. **10**(1), 108–121 (2023). https://doi.org/10.1093/jcde/qwac132
14. El Aissaoui, H., El Ougli, A., Tidhaf, B.: Neural networks and fuzzy logic based maximum power point tracking control for wind energy conversion system. Adv. Sci. Technol. Eng. Syst. J. **6**(2), 586–592 (2021)
15. Pathak, G., Singh, B., Panigrahi, B.K.: Back-propagation algorithm-based controller for autonomous Wind–DG microgrid. IEEE Trans. Ind. Appl. **52**(5), 4408–4415 (2016)

16. Chandrasekaran, K., Mohanty, M., Mallikarjuna Golla, A., Venkadesan, S.P.: Dynamic MPPT controller using cascade neural network for a wind power conversion system with energy management. IETE J. Res. **68**(5), 3316–3330 (2020). https://doi.org/10.1080/03772063.2020. 1756934

17. Magdi, M., Mojeed, O.: Adaptive and predictive control strategies for wind turbine systems: a survey. IEEE J. Autom SINICA **6**, 364–378 (2019)

18. Yang, B., Zhang, X., Yu, T., Shu, H., Fang, Z.: Grouped grey wolf optimizer for maximum power point tracking of doubly-fed induction generator based wind turbine. Energy Convers. Manage. **133**, 427–443 (2017)

19. Semrau, G., Rimkus, S., Das, T.: Nonlinear systems analysis and control of variable speed wind turbines for multiregime operation. J. Dyn. Syst. Measur. Control **137**(4), 041007 (2015). https://doi.org/10.1115/1.4028775

20. Sahri, Y., Tamalouzt, S., Belaid, S.L.: Direct torque control of DFIG driven by wind turbine system connected to the grid. In: 2018 International Conference on Wind Energy and Applications in Algeria (ICWEAA), pp. 1–6. IEEE (2018)

21. Abad, G., Lopez, J., Rodriguez, M., Marroyo, L., Iwanski, G.: Doubly Fed Induction Machine: Modeling and Control for Wind Energy Generation. John Wiley & Sons (2011)

Predicting Hotel Performance in Oman with AI-Driven Predictive Analytic

R. S. Al Jassim[✉], Karan Jetly, Shqran Al Mansoory, Muna Al-Balushi, and Hilal Al Maqbali

University of Technology and Applied Sciences, Muscat, Oman
rashas.soh@cas.edu.om

Abstract. The primary objective of this study is to assess the performance of hotels in Oman by developing an AI based model using a new approach that we refer to as Linear Genetic Programming for Optimization Decision Tree (LGPDT). The LGPDT algorithm seeks to optimize decision trees, automatically select relevant input attributes, and adjust hyperparameters to improve prediction accuracy. The research findings demonstrate promise after testing the model with datasets from literature and the tourism sector. This approach has the potential to improve the assessment of hotel performance in Oman by providing accurate predictions of customer satisfaction, empowering managers to enhance their services and meet customers' demands more effectively.

Keywords: Genetic Programming · Decision Tree · Tourism

1 Introduction

Tourism is a key driver of economic and social development in many nations worldwide. The industry is closely tied to global geopolitics, societal trends, environmental factors, and technological advancements, all of which have a profound impact on the direction and growth of tourism. By supporting the development of infrastructure, cultural heritage, and the workforce, tourism plays a vital role in the economies of many nations. In recent years, there has been an increasing demand among tourists for personalized experiences, ecotourism, and the incorporation of innovative technologies, all of which have significant implications for the future of the industry.

Extensive research in the field of information technology has explored the tourism industry, utilizing both conventional and unconventional approaches to address various problems in this sector [13]. Artificial intelligence and machine learning techniques have been utilized to tackle diverse tourism related issues, such as William [2] developed a machine learning model to predict hotel occupancy rates, while Nan [15] used a deep learning approach to accurately forecast tourism demand. Furthermore, Rob [10] used deep learning to forecast monthly tourist arrival volume in Macau based on past factors, showing superior accuracy compared to other models. Similarly, Houria [9] presented a deep learning

© IFIP International Federation for Information Processing 2023
Published by Springer Nature Switzerland AG 2023
I. Maglogiannis et al. (Eds.): AIAI 2023, IFIP AICT 676, pp. 478–490, 2023.
https://doi.org/10.1007/978-3-031-34107-6_38

model for forecasting future tourism demand in Morocco. Additionally, Akin [1] compared the accuracy of various models, including SARIMA, support vector machine (SVM), and neural network, for forecasting tourism demand using monthly tourist arrival data from certain countries to Turkey [1]. The application of machine learning and natural language processing has also been employed to enhance the customer experience and gain a competitive advantage such as Wooseok [5] employed these techniques to improve the customer experience, identify areas for improvement, and gain a competitive edge.

Customer satisfaction is a critical factor in the tourism industry, impacting future demand. Extensive research, such as studies by Syjung et al. [3] and others [12], have examined factors affecting customer satisfaction and its implications for airline services. This study aligns with the importance of customer satisfaction in the tourism industry and aims to employ innovative approaches to assess hotel performance in Oman, focusing on service quality, perceived value, and customer satisfaction's impact on intention to revisit an ecotourism destination.

In this paper, we propose Linear Genetic Programming for Optimization Decision Tree (LGPDT), a novel approach for building accurate and interpretable predictive models. LGPDT is a machine learning algorithm specifically designed for optimizing decision trees to check hotel performance in Oman. The approach leverages the strengths of genetic programming [7,14] to enhance overall accuracy and is faster to implement compared to traditional techniques that require manual feature engineering. The algorithm automatically learns the relevant features for tree optimization, reducing overfitting and improving model accuracy. Benefits of this innovative method include automatic selection of relevant input attributes, tuning of decision trees through hyperparameter adjustment, and elimination of manual feature selection, saving time and improving performance.

The objective of this study is to evaluate the effectiveness of a novel learning algorithm in predicting the performance of hotels in Oman. Specifically, the study examines the structure of the data source for hotels in Oman and examines its compatibility with the new learning algorithm. Additionally, the authors aim to provide valuable insights into the modeling of tourism demand in Oman and other regions facing similar challenges by exploring this approach.

The paper consists of six sections: problem statement and study objectives presented in Sect. 2, comprehensive literature review in Sect. 3, framework design and data preparation in Sect. 4, experiment results and comparing the proposed algorithm with other ML algorithms presented in Sect. 5, and conclusion with key findings and future research directions in Sect. 6.

2   Problem Statement and Objectives

Stakeholders in the tourism sector aim to enhance Oman's hotel industry and attract more tourists, but there is a need for an approach to evaluate hotel quality and tourism facilities. Issues such as poor hygiene standards and customer service can negatively impact the tourism industry, leading to negative perceptions and decreased tourist numbers. To enhance Oman's tourism industry, identifying and addressing challenges in the hotel sector is crucial.

Availability of relevant tourism data, particularly publicly accessible sources for analysis, poses a key challenge in this study. Thus, the first research question aims to explore suitable data sources for collecting relevant information on hotel performance in Oman, considering the unavailability and lack of structure in tourism data. To address this, the authors propose collecting data from web-based sources to evaluate the quality of hotels and tourism facilities in Oman. The second research objective is to evaluate the proposed method's effectiveness on preexisting datasets and to assess its efficiency in accurately forecasting hotel performance in Oman. This evaluation will involve comparing the method's performance with other machine learning algorithms commonly used in the field. By achieving these objectives, this study aims to provide insights into the challenges of modeling tourism demand in Oman and to offer a novel approach to addressing these challenges.

3   Literature Review

Many scientific disciplines have successfully applied genetic programming (GP) to their respective fields, including finance and economics. GP has been used in the tourism sector for tasks like predicting tourist demand and simulating the design of unique tourist itineraries. Despite being less researched compared to other evolutionary algorithms, GP's popularity in intelligent tourism is increasing due to its capability for solving complex problems with vague solutions. Its automatic evolution of feasible solutions through evolutionary search makes it well suited for tackling complex tourism challenges [7,8].

Marcos et al. [4] presented a novel two-step approach for predicting tourist arrivals to Spain's Balearic Islands using a genetic programming (GP) algorithm. The results showed that the GP algorithm outperformed traditional statistical methods like ARIMA and exponential smoothing in terms of accuracy and robustness, making it a promising solution for predicting tourist arrivals in the Balearic Islands and other tourist destinations. Similarly, the study by Mie et al. [11] introduced a multitasking GP algorithm for solving the stochastic team orientation problem with time windows (STOPTW) in tourism route planning. The proposed algorithm outperformed other state-of-the-art approaches in benchmark testing, demonstrating its potential for solving combinatorial optimization problems in the tourism industry.

The tourism industry is in need of further research on the full potential of GP as a tool for assessing hotel performance. Therefore, this study aims to explore the potential of using GP, a novel approach that has not been extensively studied in the existing literature, to evaluate hotel performance. Traditional metrics for hotel performance evaluation, such as occupancy rate, average daily rate, revenue per available room, and guest satisfaction scores, are limited in their ability to provide a comprehensive view. GP offers the potential to incorporate multiple variables and complex relationships, providing a more holistic view of hotel performance. Additionally, GP allows for continuous refinement and optimization of the evaluation as new data becomes available, making it a valuable tool for hotel managers and researchers.

4   Framework Designed

The paper's proposed framework comprises three interconnected components for predicting hotel performance in Oman, as depicted in Fig. 1. These components will be elaborated further in subsequent subsections.

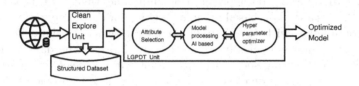

Fig. 1. Overall Framework Designed

4.1   Data Cleaning and Exploration Unit

The proposed framework relies heavily on the data extraction technique, which automatically scrapes web data from Agoda for hotels located in Suhar, Sahalah, and Muscat. This extracted unstructured data offers a wealth of insights into various aspects of our research question. As a result, 17 attributes were included in the dataset. To ensure the proper functioning of the new approach, the data must be structured. However, upon investigation, we found that the data is incomplete, contains missing values, and attributes are not in the correct format. This component plays a significant role in identifying and addressing data quality issues, thereby ensuring that the collected data aligns with the requirements of the new approach.

   In the analysis of the tourism dataset, variables are created and modified using an analysis tool to ensure consistency and uniformity. For instance, a new variable called "city" is derived from the Location attribute to maintain consistency in city names. Hotel ranking is determined by averaging guest evaluations of various features. Variables such as "Great for Walkers", "Number of Restaurants", "Number of Reviews", and "Number of Attractions" are converted into categorical scales with values ranging from 1 to 5. Duplicate hotels are removed, missing values are replaced with zero, and unwanted variables are dropped to create a comprehensive and uniform dataset for analysis. The resulting dataset comprises 376 observations with 15 attributes, including wifi, parking, gym, iron, room service, hotel rank, location rating, cleanliness rating, service rating, value rating, star rating, number of reviews, number of attractions, number of restaurants, and a variable indicating walkability.

4.2   LGPDT Unit

LGPDT is an evolutionary method for developing accurate and intelligible prediction models. LGPDT encodes decision trees using a linear program, with separate genotype and phenotype structures. The genotype represents attributes and hyperparameters, while the phenotype is generated during evaluation. LGPDT aims to create high performing decision trees with minimal complexity by employing fitness functions during the evolutionary process. Benefits of LGPDT include reduced search space, faster convergence, efficient computation of fitness function, flexible encoding of decision trees, automatic feature selection. The LGPDT consists of two primary components: the LGPDT-Prep, which is a genetic programming data preparation unit, and the LGPDT engine. The LGPDT-Prep is a Python-based module designed for data preparation and operates in conjunction with the LGPDT engine. It scans the data file, retrieves feature names, and dynamically adapts to any dataset. The data is then split into training and testing sets, with the target variable selected based on user specifications. The purpose of the LGPDT-Prep unit is to provide high quality input data to the LGPDT engine, ensuring accurate and reliable outputs.

Selection, crossover, and mutation are the three basic operators in most evolutionary algorithms, and LGPDT is no exception. These operators are driven by the fitness function, which chooses which individuals to reward depending on their fitness. However, the way these operators are implemented in LGPDT can significantly impact the quality of the resulting models. Below, we'll discuss the innovative aspects of implementing these operators in further depth.

Individuals Pool Representation. In LGPDT, the population is comprised of chromosomes which contain a set of integer genes. The length of each chromosome varies and is composed of two primary segments. The first segment pertains to the attributes of the dataset, while the second segment represents the hyper parameters of the decision tree. These hyper parameters include the maximum depth of the tree and the minimum number of samples needed to split an internal node. The overall structure of the chromosomes is depicted in Fig. 2.

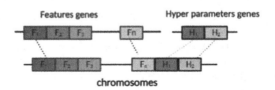

Fig. 2. Structure of Chromosomes in LGPDT.

This method selects genes randomly, subject to two conditions for insertion into the chromosome. First, the number of genes is generated randomly based on the number of features in the dataset. The chromosome length must have at least three genes. The selected genes are represented as integer values that correspond to the index of the selected attributes. These genes do not need to be chosen in any particular order. For instance, if set F is composed of attributes F_i such that $F = F_1, F_2, ...F_n$, then the first part of the chromosome is composed of genes representing any of the features F_i in set F. Given a dataset D with seven features, if the LGPDT algorithm selects three genes at random, the resulting chromosome C may be represented by F_2, F_3, and F_7, where each gene in the chromosome corresponds to a distinct attributes from the set F. The second condition for adding a feature to the chromosome is that it must be unique within the chromosome, implying that the genes within a chromosome are distinct. Suppose chromosome C is composed of the features $F_1, F_2, ...F_7$, and a new gene F_i is added to it, then the intersection of C and F must be an empty set, i.e., $C \cap F = \emptyset$. In other words, the genes within a chromosome are mutually exclusive, and each feature in the dataset can only be represented once within a chromosome. In the second segment of the chromosome, there are only two genes available for depiction. These two genes are utilized to enhance the hyperparameters of the decision tree, specifically the maximum depth value and the minimum samples split value, respectively. Thus, these two genes are critical for determining the efficiency of the decision trees. The minimum samples split and maximum depth value are critical components in controlling the size and depth of the decision tree, and they can have a significant impact on its performance. Let the size of the dataset be denoted by N. The initial value of the min samples split is set to the square root of N, i.e., min samples split$= \sqrt{N}$. This value is then selected randomly to be one of the possible values in the interval $[2, \sqrt{N}]$. On the other hand, the maximum depth value is also randomly chosen from the range specified in the interval $[2, 30]$.

Selection Operator. In genetic programming, new generations are created through parent selection and crossover operations. Parents are carefully chosen using a binary tournament selection operator, which randomly selects individuals from the population and selects the one with the best characteristics as the winner. This approach is simple and effective in maintaining diversity within the population while ensuring successful inheritance of genes [6].

Double Segment Linear Crossover. In the context of LGPDT, a new crossover operator is proposed due to the structure of the chromosome titled Double Segment Linear Crossover. As mentioned previously, the length of the first segment of the chromosome is not uniform. To address this, a random integer within the range of 0 to the length of the two parent individuals is randomly chosen as the crossover point. This ensures that the crossover point is within the boundaries of both parents. Subsequently, the remaining genes from the first parent after the crossover point are copied to one offspring, while the remaining genes from the second parent are copied to the second offspring. Duplicate genes are removed from the resulting offspring to ensure gene uniqueness. To maintain a minimum chromosome length of 2, we calculate the difference $\triangle$ between the length of the parent chromosome and the length of the offspring, i.e., $\triangle = |parent| - |offspring|$, and generate $\triangle$ new genes randomly from the set F to add to the offspring, i.e., $offspring = parent \cup g_1 \cup g_2 \cup ... \cup g_\triangle$, where

$g_i \in F$. This check is performed for the two offspring produced by the two parents (see Algorithm 1). To determine whether to transfer the maximum depth and minimum number of samples from parents to offspring, we set a probability threshold $p = 0.5$. If the probability is greater than p, offspring inherit the values from parents, otherwise, random values are generated.

Algorithm 1. Double Segment Linear Crossover

Require: $F = f_1, f_2, f_3, ..., f_m$
1:   $point \in [0, \min(|parent_1|, |parent_2|)]]$
2:   **for** $i \in [0, point]$ **do**
3:      $(offspring_1, offspring_2) \leftarrow (offspring_2, offspring_1)$
4:   **end for**
5:   $offspring_1 \leftarrow \{gene_i \in offspring_1 : gene_i \notin offspring_2\}$
6:   $offspring_2 \leftarrow \{gene_i \in offspring_2 : gene_i \notin offspring_1\}$
7:   **if** $|offspring1| < 2)$ **then**
8:      $\triangle \Leftarrow |parent1| - |offspring1|$
9:     **for** $i = 1$ **to** $\triangle$ **do**
10:        $gene_i \sim U(F)$
11:       **while** $gene \notin offspring_1$ **do**
12:          $gene_i \sim U(F)$
13:       **end while**
14:        $offspring_1 = offspring_1 \cup gene_i$
15:     **end for**
16: **end if**
17: **if** $|offspring2| < 2)$ **then**
18:      $\triangle \Leftarrow |parent2| - |offspring2|$
19:     **for** $i = 1$ **to** $\triangle$ **do**
20:        $gene_i \sim U(F)$
21:       **while** $gene \notin offspring_2$ **do**
22:          $gene_i \sim U(F)$
23:       **end while**
24:        $offspring_2 = offspring_1 \cup gene_i$
25:     **end for**
26: **end if**

Mutation. After performing crossover operation, the next genetic operator applied is mutation. In this process, a gene is randomly chosen and replaced by another gene based on specific criteria. A new gene is generated within the range of 0 to the number of features in the dataset. To avoid redundancy, it is ensured during the mutation process that the selected gene is not already present in the chromosome. Let r be a random number between 0 and 1. If r is less than or equal to 0.5, the new gene replaces a gene already in the chromosome.

Fitness Function. The fitness function ranks individuals in the LGPDT method and is used for parent selection in crossover and mutation. It promotes survival of the fittest individuals. In LGPDT, the goal of this function is to find the optimal combination of attributes and hyperparameters that results in the best performing decision tree classifier. The fitness function operates on the linear representation of an individual, which consists of genes representing decision tree attributes and hyperparameters. This linear representation is utilized to construct a decision tree model, and its performance is evaluated using a specified metric. The fitness function then assigns a fitness score to the individual based on its model performance, reflecting its effectiveness in addressing the problem under consideration. High fitness individuals become parents for the next generation, undergo crossover and mutation, and repeat until optimal attributes and hyperparameters are found, resulting in the best performing decision tree classifier.

The AUC_Entropy function is the first fitness function that is being tested in LGPDT. It combines two factors, namely the AUC ROC score and entropy, to evaluate the performance of a decision tree. AUC is a commonly used metric in machine learning and measures the quality of a binary classification model. Advantages of this metric include insensitivity to imbalanced class distribution and a single scalar value representing overall model performance. Entropy, on the other hand, measures dataset impurity and aids in decision tree evaluation for identifying high purity splits, improving classification performance. Combining AUC and entropy provides a more balanced evaluation of the model's performance as it considers both aspects of the model's output. The ACU_Entropy function is a useful for developing high performing decision trees that are well suited for a range of classification tasks. An illustration of ACU_Entropy is given in Eq. 1.

$$Fitness(c_i) = 0.8 \times \text{AUC} + 0.2 \times \log_{10}(\text{Entropy}) \tag{1}$$

AUC_Entropy assigns a weight of 0.8 to AUC and 0.2 to entropy, with logarithmic transformation applied to entropy to make entropy values more manageable. It aims to holistically evaluate the model's performance, considering class separation (AUC) and subset purity (entropy). The resulting fitness value reflects the overall performance, with higher values indicating better fitness.

The second fitness function used in LGPDT, known as *AUC_NRules*, considers two factors for evaluation: the AUC ROC score and the number of rules generated by the tree. The number of rules is an indicator of the complexity of the decision tree, with simpler trees preferred for ease of interpretation. The *AUC_NRules* fitness function aims to provide a comprehensive evaluation of the model's performance, considering both class separation ability and complexity, with weights of 0.8 and 0.2, respectively. Taking the reciprocal of the logarithm of the number of rules helps to make the range of values smaller and easier to work with, as well as to amplify the effect of the number of rules on the fitness function. The chromosome c_i is evaluated using the following equation:

$$Fitness(c_i) = 0.8 \times AUC + 0.2 \times \frac{1}{1 + \log_{10}(n\_rules)} \tag{2}$$

The last fitness function in this study is the combination of all three factors (AUC ROC, the number of rules, and entropy) with different weights to evaluate the performance of the decision tree in a more comprehensive way. The weights assigned to the AUC, the number of rules, and entropy are 0.4, 0.2, and 0.5, respectively. The weights were chosen to assign greater importance to the AUC

ROC measure and the entropy measure, while assigning less importance to the number of rules (0.2). This suggests that the model's ability to separate classes and produce pure subsets is more important than the complexity of the decision tree (as measured by the number of rules). An illustration of this function is given in Eq. 3.

$$Fitness(c_i) = 0.4 \times AUC + 0.2 \times \frac{1}{1 + \log_{10}(n_r ules)} + 0.4 \times \frac{1}{1 + \log_{10}(entropy)} \tag{3}$$

All fitness functions will be evaluated to identify the most effective measure of model performance. The best performing fitness function will be determined through experiments and it will be selected for further study. Weights assigned to each factor range from 0 to 1, with the sum of all weights equaling 1. The specific weights for each factor were determined based on experimental results.

5   Experiment

In this section, LGPDT will be applied to predict hotel performance in Oman. Algorithm efficacy will be verified by testing on literature datasets [16], and fitness values of proposed fitness functions will be evaluated on the selected dataset. Findings will be used to establish an appropriate model for the Oman tourism dataset. Implications, study limitations, and future research directions will be discussed.

5.1   Comparative Analysis of LGPDT on Different Datasets

In this research experiment, the Heart Disease, Iris, Pima, and Wine datasets were utilized [16]. The Heart Disease dataset comprises 2 classes, 270 instances, and 13 attributes. In contrast, the Iris dataset consists of 150 instances, 4 attributes, and 3 classes. The Pima dataset is characterized by 8 attributes, 768 instances, and 2 classes. Lastly, the Wine dataset encompasses a total of 178 instances, 14 attributes, and 3 classes.

Table 1 summarizes an empirical study that examined the impact of three fitness functions on multiple datasets. The table presents the results obtained from the experiment, including the number of rules (#Rule), maximum depth (MDepth), selected attributes (SA), minimum sample splits (MSS), and accuracy scores, for various fitness functions and datasets. Accuracy was assessed using hold out testing. We noticed that the AUC_NRule shows that the number of rules obtained from the decision tree and the accuracy score have a negative relationship. A decision tree with fewer rules might not be able to handle the complexity of the dataset, which could make the results less accurate. On the other hand, adding too many rules can result in overfitting, causing the model to fit noise instead of the underlying pattern in the data. This can lead to poor performance on new, unseen data. This explains why this measure was given so little weight in AUC_RE and other fitness function. In the case where entropy is incorporated as a measure within the fitness function, the objective is to minimize entropy

Table 1. Comparison of Fitness Functions on Different Datasets

Fitness	Dataset	#Rules	MDepth	MSS	SA	Accuracy
ACU_Entropy	Heart Disease	27	10	6	10	0.8033
	Iris	14	8	10	4	0.96
	Pima	64	30	13	6	0.785714
	Wine	13	26	4	10	0.9166
AUC_NRules	Heart Disease	18	24	12	11	0.7541
	Iris	10	9	4	4	0.96
	Pima	40	16	26	8	0.7597
	Wine	12	24	11	9	0.9166
AUC_RE	Heart Disease	20	12	10	13	0.7541
	Iris	12	16	5	4	0.9866
	Pima	13	4	18	8	0.7403
	Wine	14	16	8	11	0.9166

for each split in the decision tree. This may result in the generation of complex decision trees with numerous splits and branches, leading to an increased number of rules. Despite this, AUC_Entropy outperforms AUC_NRules in terms of accuracy, even when generating a larger number of rules. Furthermore, it was observed that AUC_RE achieves a favorable trade-off between the number of rules and accuracy, as it minimizes entropy while also considering the number of rules generated. As such, it is advisable to thoroughly evaluate the results obtained from all three functions and select the most appropriate one based on the specific characteristics of the dataset.

The effectiveness of LGPDT assessed through a comparative analysis with another method, specifically C4.5 models. Four distinct datasets were used in this analysis, and a 10 fold cross validation approach was employed for each dataset. Accuracy was used as the evaluation metric to determine the effectiveness of the LGPDT and C4.5 models. Table 2 indicates that LGPDT outperforms C4.5 on all four datasets. LGPDT shows higher mean accuracy (80.86%) with lower standard deviation (3.9%) compared to C4.5 (mean accuracy of 74.5% with standard deviation of 8.2%) on the heart disease dataset. These findings support the use of LGPDT for machine learning tasks, as it demonstrates higher accuracy and consistency in predictions compared to C4.5.

Table 2. Comparison of Accuracy of LGPDT and C4.5.

Dataset	C4.5 Accuracy	LGPDT Accuracy
Heart Disease	$74.5 \pm 8.2\%$	$80.86 \pm 3.9\%$
Iris	$94.1 \pm 4.7\%$	$96.6 \pm 1.79\%$
Pima	$73.9 \pm 5.7\%$	$76.04 \pm 4.3\%$
Wine	$90.9 \pm 7.1\%$	$92.97 \pm 0.4\%$

5.2   Performance of LGPDT on Tourism Dataset

This section applies LGPDT to forecast hotel success in Oman, assessing its efficiency using proposed fitness functions and comparing outcomes to identify the most effective fitness function. Furthermore, the findings of this study will be compared with the outcomes of Weka.

Positive outcomes were seen when the LGPDT algorithm was applied to the tourism dataset, with the AUC_RE fitness function producing the highest accuracy at 73% along with a rule set of 69 rules. Through automated experimentation, we discovered that a maximum depth of 12, a minimum split of 18, and the selection of nine attributes provided the best results for LGPDT. These carefully chosen features constitute a subset that was found to be adequate for precise classification in the current experiment. These results show that LGPDT is a promising tool for tourism data classification because it can produce accurate and interpretable models with a low number of rules (Table 3).

Table 3. Comparison of Fitness Functions on a Tourism Dataset

Fitness	Accuracy	#Rules	MDepth	MSS	#Attributes
AUC_Entropy	0.7173 ± 0.02	73	14	16	6
AUC_NRules	0.7026 ± 0.04	78	12	15	9
AUC_RE	0.7306 ± 0.05	69	12	18	9

Furthermore, a comparison was made between the performance of LGPDT and Weka, utilizing the same dataset and the set of optimized hyperparameters. The results showed that LGPDT outperformed Weka, achieving an accuracy of 73%, compared to Weka's accuracy of 69%. These findings suggest that LGPDT is a more appropriate and effective method for the specific problem domain and dataset at hand. One possible explanation for the superior performance of LGPDT is its unique combination of genetic programming and decision tree learning, which may have enabled it to capture more complex relationships and patterns in the data. Moreover, LGPDT's ability to optimize hyperparameters during the training process could have contributed to its superior performance, as opposed to Weka, which may have relied on a fixed set of hyperparameters. These results highlight the significance of carefully selecting and optimizing the appropriate machine learning algorithm and hyperparameters for a given dataset and problem domain to achieve optimal performance.

6   Conclusion

Managers need to be able to accurately predict how well a hotel will do in order to serve their customers well. In this study, a new method was used to predict how well hotels in Suhar, Sahalah, and Muscat would do. The data for these hotels was scraped from the Agoda website. The study aimed to address two research questions: 1) evaluating the proposed method's performance on collected datasets, and 2) assessing the method's accuracy in predicting hotel performance. The study evaluated LGPDT's performance on existing datasets and compared it to other methods. LGPDT outperformed existing methods, demonstrating its validity and reliability for hotel performance prediction. The study confirmed LGPDT's accuracy in predicting hotel performance, with an average accuracy rate of approximately 73%. In conclusion, this study demonstrated the effectiveness of LGPDT for predicting hotel performance, which has practical implications for managers in the hotel industry. Based on the findings of this study, future work could involve testing LGPDT on a larger and more diverse set of hotel datasets to further validate its effectiveness. Additionally, incorporating additional features such as social media data could potentially improve the accuracy of the predictions. Finally, investigating the impact of hotel performance prediction on business decisions and customer satisfaction could also be a valuable area for future research.

References

1. Akın, M.: A novel approach to model selection in tourism demand modeling. Tour. Manage. **48**, 64–72 (2015)
2. Caicedo-Torres, W., Payares, F.: A machine learning model for occupancy rates and demand forecasting in the hospitality industry. In: Montes-y-Gómez, M., Escalante, H.J., Segura, A., Murillo, J.D. (eds.) IBERAMIA 2016. LNCS (LNAI), vol. 10022, pp. 201–211. Springer, Cham (2016). https://doi.org/10.1007/978-3-319-47955-2_17
3. Hwang, S., Kim, J., Park, E., Kwon, S.J.: Who will be your next customer: a machine learning approach to customer return visits in airline services. J. Bus. Res. **121**, 121–126 (2020)
4. García-Martín, P., Alvarez-Díaz, M., Sanchez-Granero, M.A.: Forecasting tourist arrivals to Balearic Islands using genetic programming. Expert Syst. Appl. **45**, 332–338 (2016)
5. Kwon, W., Lee, M., Back, K.J.: Exploring the underlying factors of customer value in restaurants: a machine learning approach. Int. J. Hosp. Manag. **91**, 102643 (2020)
6. Goldberg, D.E.: Genetic Algorithms in Search, Optimization, and Machine Learning (2013)
7. Koza, J.R.: Genetic Programming: On the Programming of Computers by Means of Natural Selection. The MIT Press, Cambridge (1992)
8. Koza, J.R.: Genetic programming for economic modeling. In: Goonatilake, S., Treleaven, P. (eds.) Intelligent Systems and Business, pp. 251–269. Wiley (1995)
9. Laaroussi, H., Guerouate, F., Sbihi, M.: Deep learning framework for forecasting tourism demand. In: 2020 IEEE International Conference on Technology Management, Operations and Decisions (ICTMOD) (2020)
10. Law, R., Li, G., Fong, D.K.C., Han, X.: Tourism demand forecasting: a deep learning approach. Ann. Tour. Res. **75**, 410–423 (2019)
11. Mei, Y., Zhang, M.: Genetic programming hyper-heuristic for stochastic team orienteering problem with time windows. In: IEEE Congress on Evolutionary Computation (CEC), Brazil, pp. 1–8. IEEE (2018)

12. Park, E., Jang, Y., Kim, J., Jeong, N.J., Bae, K., del Pobil, A.P.: Determinants of customer satisfaction with airline services: an analysis of customer feedback big data. J. Retail. Consum. Serv. **51**, 186–190 (2019)
13. AL Jassim, R.S., Jetly, K., Abushakra, A., Mansori, S.A.: A review of the methods and techniques used in tourism demand forecasting. EAI Endorsed Trans. Creative Technol. **9**(4), e1, (2023)
14. Abdul-Wahhab, R.S.: Gapbnf_Rule: a genetic miner rule. In: Abraham, A.P. (ed.) IADIS European Conference on Data Mining 2008, Amsterdam, The Netherlands, 24–26 July Proceedings, pp. 107–112. IADIS (2008)
15. Yu, N., Chen, J.: Design of machine learning algorithm for tourism demand prediction. Comput. Math. Methods Med. **2022**, 1–9 (2022)
16. Pima, Heart Disease, Iris, Wine. In UCI Machine Learning Repository. https://archive.ics.uci.edu/ml/index.php. Accessed 12 Feb 2023

SASHA: Hyperparameter Optimization by Simulated Annealing and Successive Halving

Ron Triepels[(✉)]

Maastricht University, Tongersestraat 53, 6211 LM Maastricht, the Netherlands
r.triepels@maastrichtuniversity.nl

Abstract. Successive halving (SHA) has become popular for hyperparameter optimization since it often yields good results while consuming
a considerably lower training budget than traditional brute-force algorithms. Nevertheless, SHA is known to suffer from the crossing curves
problem. A configuration that performs poorly at the start may perform
very well with more budget in later rounds, causing its loss curve to cross
that of competing configurations. When this happens, there is a risk that
promising configurations are discarded prematurely. In this paper, we
propose a new variant of SHA which we name SASHA, that combines
Simulated Annealing (SA) with SHA. SASHA discards configurations
stochastically based on their performance relative to the best-performing
configuration. This property allows the algorithm to make more informed
decisions about the configurations to be discarded each round. We study
the behavior of SASHA when optimizing a simple test function and a
logistic regression model. Our results indicate that SASHA can effectively
deal with the crossing curves problem.

Keywords: Hyperparameter Optimization · Simulated Annealing ·
Successive Halving · Machine Learning · Artificial Intelligence

1 Introduction

Hyperparameter optimization has become a critical part of the machine learning
workflow. Modern machine learning models come with an array of hyperparameters that must be carefully tuned to the problem at hand. For example, when
constructing a neural network, one has to make many decisions regarding the
network architecture (e.g., the number of layers and activation functions), regularization (e.g., the use of weight decay or dropout), and optimization (e.g., the
optimizer and learning rate). Inadequate optimization of these parameters may
result in a model that does not generalize well to new and unseen data.

Many algorithms have been proposed to aid machine learning practitioners
in this task. Recently, multi-armed bandit algorithms have become popular with
the introduction of Successive Halving (SHA) [6]. In SHA, multiple instances of
a model with different hyperparameter configurations are iteratively fitted for

© IFIP International Federation for Information Processing 2023
Published by Springer Nature Switzerland AG 2023
I. Maglogiannis et al. (Eds.): AIAI 2023, IFIP AICT 676, pp. 491–502, 2023.
https://doi.org/10.1007/978-3-031-34107-6_39

some budget (e.g., number of epochs) over a series of rounds. In each round, a fixed ratio of the worst-performing configurations is discarded until the best configuration remains. The advantage of SHA over a traditional grid search or random search [1], in which all configurations are fitted with the same budget, is that it avoids spending much budget on unpromising configurations.

Nevertheless, SHA is known to suffer from the crossing curves problem. Configurations are discarded under the assumption that they will not outperform competing configurations with more budget. In practice, however, a configuration that performs poorly at the start may perform very well in later rounds, causing its loss curve to cross that of competing configurations. This behavior occurs, for example, when optimizing the learning rate of a neural network. A high learning rate causes the loss to decrease fast initially but diverge later on, whereas a low learning rate causes the loss to decrease slowly initially but converge to a low loss in the end. When this happens, there is a risk that SHA discards promising configurations prematurely.

Several extensions of SHA have been proposed to mitigate this risk. Hyperband [9] performs multiple runs of SHA, whereby each run optimizes over a smaller set of randomly sampled configurations. The motivation for this strategy is that if the overall budget is fixed, the budget spent on exploring promising configurations depends on the number of configurations under consideration. By performing a grid search over this number, the explorative nature of SHA can be adapted to the problem at hand. BOHB [3] applies a similar strategy. However, instead of randomly sampling configurations, BOHB uses Bayesian optimization to sample promising configurations for each run.

In this paper, we propose a new algorithm for hyperparameter optimization that combines Simulated Annealing (SA) [7] with SHA. We name the algorithm SASHA. The main innovation of SASHA is that it does not discard configurations based on a fixed ratio each round. Instead, configurations are discarded according to a stochastic process based on how much their performance deviates from the best-performing configuration. We study the behavior of SASHA when optimizing the hyperparameters of a simple test function and a logistic regression model. Our experimental results show that SASHA requires a considerably lower overall budget than SHA to obtain similar performance when hyperparameter optimization is subject to the crossing curves problem.

2 Hyperparameter Optimization

2.1 Problem Definition

We study hyperparameter optimization in a traditional framework with a single training and validation set [4]. Let $\mathcal{D}$ be a dataset split into a training set $\mathcal{D}_{\text{train}}$ and validation set $\mathcal{D}_{\text{val}}$. Moreover, let f_θ be a model parameterized by a set of hyperparameters θ, where θ is an element of hyperparameter space Θ. Without loss of generability, we assume that Θ is a discrete space (i.e., a grid of hyperparameters). The performance of f_θ is measured by loss function $\mathcal{L}$. Typically, $\mathcal{L}$ is the error rate in classification tasks or the mean squared error in regressions tasks. The goal of hyperparameter optimization is to find the optimal θ after fitting f_θ on $\mathcal{D}_{\text{train}}$ such that $\mathcal{L}$ on $\mathcal{D}_{\text{val}}$ is minimized. Solving this optimization task is challenging because f_θ has to be fitted on $\mathcal{D}_{\text{train}}$ before $\mathcal{L}$ can be estimated on $\mathcal{D}_{\text{val}}$, and this fitting procedure is generally expensive. It is, therefore, desirable to solve the optimization problem with the least possible budget (e.g., training time or the number of epochs).

Early stopping is a strategy to solve hyperparameter optimization tasks with a minimal budget. In early stopping, it is assumed that f_θ can be fitted iteratively on $\mathcal{D}_{\text{train}}$ and $\mathcal{L}$ on $\mathcal{D}_{\text{val}}$ can be monitored between iterations. Configurations that perform poorly are terminated prematurely under the assumption that they will not outperform competing configurations. This allows more budget to be allocated to promising configurations. In the remainder of this section, we discuss hyperparameter optimization algorithms that are based on such a strategy.

2.2 Successive Halving

Successive Halving (SHA) solves hyperparameter optimization as a best-arm identification problem in a multi-armed bandit setting [6]. In this setting, an arm corresponds to a model with a particular hyperparameter configuration. Pulling an arm corresponds to fitting a model on the training set for some additional budget and measuring its loss on the validation set. SHA aims to find the best arm that yields the lowest loss when there is only a fixed overall budget to pull arms. This is done by repeatedly pulling arms and discarding a fraction of the worst-performing ones until the best arm remains.

Let $\mathcal{A}$ be a set of arms and B the overall budget. Initially, $\mathcal{A}$ contains an arm corresponding to f_θ for each $\theta \in \Theta$ or a (random) subset of Θ. SHA proceeds over several rounds. We denote the number of arms at round i by k_i. At round i, all arms in $\mathcal{A}$ are pulled with additional budget b_i, and the worst-performing arms are discarded according to discard rate $r \in (0, 1)$. This means that there are k_1 arms in round 1, $k_2 = \lfloor rk_1 \rfloor$ arms in round 2, $k_3 = \lfloor rk_2 \rfloor$ arms in round 3, and so on. If follows that the total number of rounds after which $\mathcal{A}$ contains less than $1/r$ arms is:

$$n = \left\lfloor \log_{1/r}(k_1) \right\rfloor \tag{1}$$

After n rounds, the algorithm terminates and the arm in $\mathcal{A}$ with the lowest loss is returned. Algorithm 1 summarizes the SHA algorithm.

Input: Initial arms $\mathcal{A}$, total budget B, discard rate r
for $i = 1$ to n **by** 1 **do**
  Pull each arm in $\mathcal{A}$ with addtional budget b_i;
  Discard worst performing arms based on rate r;
end
Output: Best arm in $\mathcal{A}$

Algorithm 1: SHA [6].

There are many ways to distribute B across the arms and rounds. A common strategy is to fix the total budget per round. This means that the budget per arm at round i is:

$$b_i = \left\lfloor \frac{B}{k_i n} \right\rfloor \tag{2}$$

We will refer to this budget scheme as a geometric budget because b_i follows a geometric series. A nice property of this budget scheme is that it assigns few budget to bad performing arms that are discarded early on and much budget to promising arms that survive many rounds.

However, a disadvantage of a geometric budget is that it requires a relatively high minimum budget for SHA to work properly. If there is an insufficient budget, arms are not fitted and discarded based on how well they perform by their initial (random) parameters. Given Eq. 1 and 2, we have that $b_1 \geq 1$ when:

$$B \geq k_1 \log_{1/r}(k_1) \tag{3}$$

The minimum budget is a linearithmic function of k_1. Furthermore, this budget scheme is prone to the crossing cuves problem because a relatively small portion of the overall budget is allocated to early rounds. Promising arms that require more budget to perform well are discarded prematurely. This risk can be mitigated by increasing r at the expense of a higher minimum budget (Eq. 3) such that more budget is spent on the exploration of good arms in early rounds.

An alternative strategy is to fix the budget per arm at each round:

$$b_i = \left\lfloor \frac{B(1-r)}{k_1(1-r^n)} \right\rfloor \tag{4}$$

We will refer to this budget scheme as a constant budget as b_i is constant across rounds. A constant budget scheme has a lower minimum budget requirement. It follows from Eq. 1 and 4 that $b_1 \geq 1$ when:

$$B \geq \frac{1 - k_1}{r - 1} \tag{5}$$

The minimum budget is a linear function of k_1. Moreover, this budget scheme is less prone to the crossing curves problem because a larger portion of the overall budget is allocated to early rounds. Table 1 provides an example of how the same overall budget is distributed according to a geometric and constant budget. In the remainder of this paper, we will refer to SHA with a geometric and constant budget as SHA-G and SHA-C, respectively.

A drawback of SHA is that the budget, budget scheme, and discard rate must be properly chosen to obtain good results. Finding optimal values for these parameters is challenging as this depends on many factors, including the type of model to be optimized, the nature of hyperparameters considered during the optimization, and the budget available for exploring promising arms. SHA can run for a long time on complex models with many initial arms, often leaving only a small budget for tuning these parameters. Furthermore, there may be better

Table 1. The distribution of budget to arms across rounds according to a geometric and constant budget. Note that the overall budget of the constant budget is slightly lower than the overall budget of the geometric budget due to rounding.

		Geometric Budget		Constant Budget	
Round	Arms	Budget Per Arm	Budget Per Round	Budget Per Arm	Budget Per Round
i	k_i	b_i	$k_i \cdot b_i$	b_i	$k_i \cdot b_i$
1	64	1	64	3	192
2	32	2	64	3	96
3	16	4	64	3	48
4	8	8	64	3	24
5	4	16	64	3	12
6	2	32	64	3	6

strategies than discarding arms based on a fixed discard rate. If the loss of all arms is very close, we should pull arms for a few more rounds to see whether a clear winner emerges with more budget. Likewise, if there is a large discrepancy in the loss of the arms, we should discard bad-performing arms prematurely to avoid wasting budget on these arms later on. It is unlikely that this should always be done based on the same discard rate across rounds. In the next section, we discuss how these issues can be addressed.

2.3 SASHA

SASHA is a combination of Simulated Annealing (SA) and SHA. In contrast to SHA, it does not use a pre-determined budget and fixed discard rate. Instead, arms are pulled for a fixed budget per arm b each round and discarded according to a stochastic process until only a single arm remains.

The probability of an arm being accepted to the next round depends on its performance and the current temperature. The gap in loss of arm a relative to the best-performing arm at round i is:

$$\Delta_a^{(i)} = \mathcal{L}_a^{(i)} - \mathcal{L}_{min}^{(i)} \tag{6}$$

where $\mathcal{L}_{min}^{(i)}$ is the lowest loss observed across all arms at round i. The probability of a being accepted to the next round is:

$$p_a^{(i)} = \exp\left(-\frac{\Delta_a^{(i)}}{t^{(i)}} \right) \tag{7}$$

where $t^{(i)}$ is the temperature at round i. The larger the gap $\Delta_a^{(i)}$, the less likely it is that a is accepted to the next round. Whether a is discarded is determined by random chance according to probability $p_a^{(i)}$. This can be implemented by generating a random number between zero and one. If the number is larger than $p_a^{(i)}$, then a is discarded. It follows from Eq. 6 and 7 that the best-performing arm has zero gap and, hence, is never discarded.

The temperature is annealed over the rounds to ensure the algorithm converges to a single arm. Initially, the temperature will be high, and arms are unlikely to be discarded, even when they perform relatively poorly. However, the temperature will decrease as the optimization progresses, and unpromising arms are more likely to be discarded. The algorithm keeps iterating until the temperature becomes so low that all arms except the best-performing arm are discarded. Algorithm 2 summarizes the proposed algorithm.

Input: Initial arms $\mathcal{A}$, initial temperature $t^{(0)}$, budget per arm b
$i = 1$;
while $|\mathcal{A}| > 1$ **do**
    Update temperature $t^{(i)}$;
    Pull all arms in $\mathcal{A}$ with additional budget b;
    foreach $a \in \mathcal{A}$ **do**
        Calculate acceptance probability $p_a^{(i)}$;
        if $RAND(0,1) > p_a^{(i)}$ **then**
            Discard arm $\mathcal{A} = \mathcal{A} \setminus a$;
        end
    end
    $i = i + 1$;
end
Output: Best arm in $\mathcal{A}$

Algorithm 2: SASHA.

There are many ways to anneal the temperature. Ideally, we want the temperature to decrease fast to avoid spending much budget on unpromising arms, but not too fast to avoid promising arms being discarded prematurely. We use the fast annealing schedule proposed by [10]. The schedule can be defined as:

$$t^{(i)} = \frac{t^{(0)}}{i} \qquad \text{for } i \geq 1 \tag{8}$$

where $t^{(0)}$ is the initial temperature. Our experimental results show that this schedule works well for hyperparameter optimization.

Two parameters control the behavior of SASHA: $t^{(0)}$ and b. $t^{(0)}$ controls the explorative nature of the algorithm. If $t^{(0)}$ is close to zero, the algorithm quickly converges by immediately discarding arms when they fall behind the best-performing arm. In contrast, if $t^{(0)}$ is high, the algorithm converges more slowly by pulling bad-performing arms for more rounds to see whether they recover in the long run. b is the fixed budget for which each arm is additionally pulled each round. It controls how often the optimization progress is checked and changes to the current set of arms are made. In many applications, measuring the loss of an arm is expensive. Hence, b should not be too low to avoid the algorithm spending a large portion of its run-time on progress checks. It is recommended to fix b to a reasonable value and only tune $t^{(0)}$. In this way, the algorithm effectively has only a single parameter that requires fine-tuning.

An advantage of SASHA over SHA is that it can make more informed decisions about the arms to be discarded. It can discard arms early when a clear winner emerges or keep pulling arms when there is strong competition. Our results show that this property reduces the overall budget required to solve optimization problems subject to the crossing curves problem. Furthermore, the behavior of SASHA can be controlled more easily by effectively only a single parameter (the initial temperature) compared to three parameters (the overall budget, budget scheme, and discard rate) in SHA. It is, therefore, more likely SASHA is better tuned to the problem at hand.

However, a limitation of SASHA is that it is not known in advance how much overall budget the algorithm is going to consume. This can be problematic in applications where a model must be optimized under a strict budget. In such a case, an additional stopping criterium can be implemented that terminates the algorithm when a given overall budget is consumed.

3   Experiments

3.1   Test Function

We conducted an experiment to study the behavior of SASHA on a simple test function. The function simulates the loss of a model fitted by an iterative fitting procedure (like gradient descent). It is defined as:

$$\mathcal{L} = -\beta \log(x/\gamma) \qquad \text{for } \beta > 0, \gamma > 0 \qquad (9)$$

where, x can be interpreted as the total number of epochs for which the model has been fitted, β is a hyperparameter to be optimized, and γ is a parameter that controls the difficulty of the optimization. In the experiment, we optimized β over a space of 100 values $\beta \in \{0.01, 0.02, \ldots, 1.00\}$ and fixed $\gamma = 100$. The motivation for this setup is that $\mathcal{L}$ can be evaluated cheaply and the behavior of SHA on this function can be studied analytically. Moreover, $\mathcal{L}$ is of interest because it simulates the crossing curves problem. $\mathcal{L}$ is a monotonic decreasing function whose rate of decrease depends on β and always crosses the point $(\gamma, 0)$, see Fig. 1. If $x < \gamma$, $\mathcal{L}$ is minimized when β is as small as possible, whereas, if $x > \gamma$, $\mathcal{L}$ is minimized when β is as large as possible.

The optimal β found by SHA depends on the round at which the cumulative budget spend on each arm crosses the critical value γ. The cumulative budget spend on each arm after n rounds is:

$$c_n = \sum_{i=1}^{n} b_i \qquad (10)$$

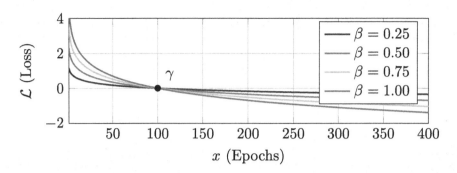

Fig. 1. Plot of $\mathcal{L}$ for different values of β. (Color figure online)

Let $\beta_1 = 0.01$, $\beta_2 = 0.02$, and so on. The optimal β found by SHA when using a discard rate of $r = 0.5$ can be defined as:

$$\hat{\beta} = \begin{cases} \beta_{100}, & \text{if } c_1 \geq \gamma \\ \beta_{50}, & \text{if } c_2 \geq \gamma \\ \beta_{25}, & \text{if } c_3 \geq \gamma \\ \beta_{12}, & \text{if } c_4 \geq \gamma \\ \beta_6, & \text{if } c_5 \geq \gamma \\ \beta_3, & \text{if } c_6 \geq \gamma \\ \beta_1, & \text{otherwise} \end{cases} \tag{11}$$

$\mathcal{L}$ is problematic for SHA to optimize properly. SHA keeps discarding the highest β values each round until the cumulative budget spent on each arm exceeds γ, after which the lowest β values are discarded each round. If the overall budget is too small, such that arms are pulled for a budget less than γ in the first round, promising arms will be discarded prematurely. Moreover, it follows from Eq. 11 that γ controls the difficulty of the optimization. Increasing γ requires a higher overall budget to find the best solution β_{100}.

The goal of the experiment is to determine whether SASHA is less susceptible to the crossing curves problem than SHA when optimizing $\mathcal{L}$. We did this by optimizing $\mathcal{L}$ using SASHA based on 100 different values for the initial temperature $t^{(0)} \in \{100, 200, \ldots, 10000\}$. We ran the algorithm ten times for each temperature, yielding a total of 1000 runs. Accordingly, we compared the optimal β found by SASHA in each run to the solutions found by SHA-G and SHA-C when consuming the same overall budget.

Figure 2 shows the results of the experiment. The figure reveals that SASHA requires a considerable lower overall budget to find the best solution than SHA-G and SHA-C. SASHA finds the best solution when using a budget of approximately 10000 epochs. In contrast, SHA-G and SHA-C require an overall budget of at least 60000 and 19688 epochs respectively to find the same solution.

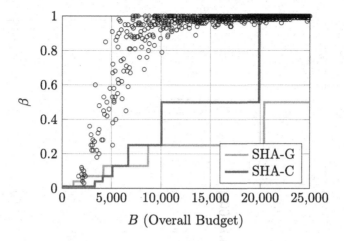

Fig. 2. The results of the experiment on the test function. Each circle corresponds to a value of β found by SASHA in a run. The red and blue lines depict the β found by SHA-G and SHA-C respectively according to Eq. 11. (Color figure online)

3.2 MNIST

We also conducted an experiment to study how well SASHA optimizes the learning rate of a logistic regression model fitted on MNIST [8]. A standard logistic regression model optimized by stochastic gradient descent [2] with mini-batches of 128 images was used in the experiment. The weights of the model were initialized by the heuristic of [5], and its bias term was initially set to zero. The learning rate was optimized over a space of 16 possible rates $(0.10, 0.12, \ldots, 0.40)$.

The goal of the experiment is to compare the efficiency of SASHA and SHA at different performance levels. This was done by randomly partitioning the MNIST training set into a training and validation set based on a 80%-20% split, respectively. Accordingly, we performed 100 runs of SASHA with different initial temperatures $t^{(0)} \in \{0.02, 0.04, \ldots, 2.00\}$. For each run, a logistic regression model was fitted on the entire original MNIST training set based on the optimal learning rate found in the run, and the error rate of the model was measured on the MNIST test set. In a similar way, 100 runs of SHA-G and SHA-C were performed while making sure the algorithms consumed the same overall budgets as SASHA in each run. Finally, we compared the overall budget required by the algorithms to achieve different error rates.

Figure 3 shows the results of the experiment. The figure shows that SASHA requires a considerably lower overall budget than SHA-G and SHA-C to achieve the same level of performance. SASHA achieves an average error rate of 7.76% with an overall budget of approximately 500 epochs. To obtain the same error rate, we need an overall budget of at least 1200 epochs for SHA-G and 800 epochs for SHA-C. Figure 4 reveals that this inefficiency of SHA-G and SHA-C is due to the crossing curves problem. Lower error rates are obtained by lowering the learning rate. However, arms corresponding to low learning rates require more

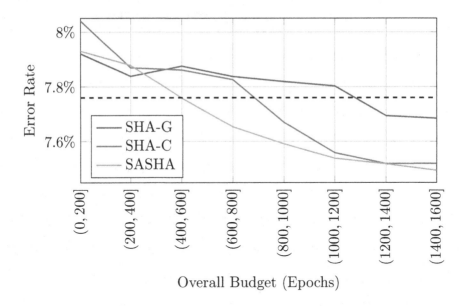

Fig. 3. Average error rate of the logistic regression model fitted on MNIST as a function of the overall budget consumed by SHA-G, SHA-C, and SASHA. Note that the overall budget is grouped by bins of 200 epochs for readability. The dashed line corresponds to an average error rate of 7.76%. (Color figure online)

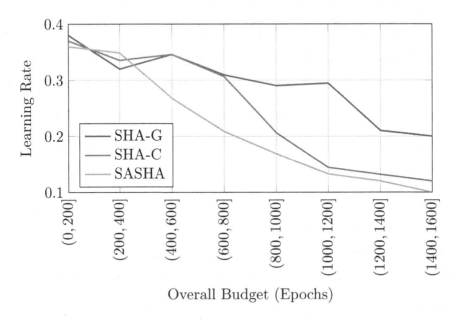

Fig. 4. Average learning rate found by SHA-G, SHA-C, and SASHA as a function of the overall budget consumed. (Color figure online)

epochs to outperform arms with high learning rates and are, therefore, likely to be discarded prematurely by SHA. A higher overall budget is required to ensure these arms perform better in early rounds. SASHA is less susceptible to this problem because of the way the temperature is annealed over the rounds, which allows the algorithm to keep sub-optimal arms in early rounds.

4   Conclusion

We conclude that SASHA can be a good alternative to SHA for hyperparameter optimization problems that are subject to the crossing curves problem. The main innovation of SASHA is that arms are discarded by a stochastic process based on how well they perform relative to the best-performing arm. This property enables the algorithm to make more informed decisions about the arms to be discarded than SHA and better adapt to the problem at hand.

Our work can be improved in several ways. We only experimentally studied the behavior of SHA when optimizing a simple test function and a logistic regression model. Future research could focus on the theoretical properties of the algorithm or study its behavior on more complex models with many hyperparameters. Moreover, we only compared the performance of SASHA to SHA under different budget schemes. An interesting experiment would be to test whether SASHA also performs favorably against variants of SHA including Hyperband and MOHB. We leave this open to future research.

References

1. Bergstra, J., Bengio, Y.: Random search for hyper-parameter optimization. J. Mach. Learn. Res. **13**(2) (2012)
2. Bottou, L.: Stochastic gradient descent tricks. In: Montavon, G., Orr, G.B., Müller, K.-R. (eds.) Neural Networks: Tricks of the Trade. LNCS, vol. 7700, pp. 421–436. Springer, Heidelberg (2012). https://doi.org/10.1007/978-3-642-35289-8_25
3. Falkner, S., Klein, A., Hutter, F.: BOHB: robust and efficient hyperparameter optimization at scale. In: International Conference on Machine Learning, pp. 1437–1446. PMLR (2018)
4. Feurer, M., Hutter, F.: Hyperparameter optimization. Autom. Mach. Learn.: Methods, Syst. Challenges, 3–33 (2019)
5. Glorot, X., Bengio, Y.: Understanding the difficulty of training deep feedforward neural networks. In: Proceedings of the Thirteenth International Conference on Artificial Intelligence and Statistics, pp. 249–256 (2010)
6. Jamieson, K., Talwalkar, A.: Non-stochastic best arm identification and hyperparameter optimization. In: Artificial Intelligence and Statistics, pp. 240–248. PMLR (2016)
7. Kirkpatrick, S., Gelatt Jr, C.D., Vecchi, M.P.: Optimization by simulated annealing. Science **220**(4598), 671–680 (1983)

8. LeCun, Y., Cortes, C., Burges, C. J.: MNIST handwritten digit database (2010)
9. Li, L., Jamieson, K., DeSalvo, G., Rostamizadeh, A., Talwalkar, A.: Hyperband: a novel bandit-based approach to hyperparameter optimization. J. Mach. Learn. Res. **18**(1), 6765–6816 (2017)
10. Szu, H., Hartley, R.: Fast simulated annealing. Phys. Lett. A **122**(3–4), 157–162 (1987)

Robotics

Data Collection Automation in Machine Learning Process Using Robotic Manipulator

Piotr Reczek[1]([✉]) [iD], Jakub Panczyk[3], Andrzej Wetula[2] [iD], and Andrzej Młyniec[1] [iD]

[1] Department of Robotics and Mechatronics, AGH University of Science and Technology,
30-059 Kraków, Poland
reczek@agh.edu.pl

[2] Department of Measurement and Electronics, AGH University of Science and Technology,
30-059 Kraków, Poland

[3] Merit Poland Sp.z o. o., Podole 60, 30-394 Kraków, Poland

Abstract. Collecting data for machine learning algorithms is an important part of the learning process. Moreover, human-machine interface systems operate with the user's physical movements, and recording these gestures is a standard method for creating datasets. However, this process is time-consuming and many people are required due to the risk of model overfitting. In this paper, we present a new method for automatizing data collection. The volunteers were replaced by a robotic arm with a mounted electric circuit to simulate the impedance of the human hand. Data recording and labeling were performed by a dedicated application that controlled the manipulator kinematics. The application generated randomized paths for the effector, with the purpose of collecting data similar to those collected from people. The gestures were recognized by a system based on capacitive sensors and a neural network algorithm executed on a microcontroller received data from the sensor signals. The system was taught with data collected from using the manipulator and tested with physical users. We describe the benefits of the proposed method, with the most significant advantage being that data collection was three times faster than using manual methods.

Keywords: Machine Learning · Automated Data Collection · Robotic Arm · 3D Gesture Recognition · Capacitive Gesture Recognition System · Human-Machine Interface · Embedded Systems

1 Introduction

Machine learning has gained great popularity in recent years, and the models are learned with a high number of accurate training data that must be labeled and recorded. In general, data collection is a crucial aspect of the final operation of a machine learning system. However, this step is considered a major bottleneck [1] in the machine-learning process. In addition, more complex models require more labeled data, resulting in increased effort. Moreover, some ML applications (such as gesture recognition) require collecting data from scratch due to a lack of available datasets, which significantly slows the learning process.

© IFIP International Federation for Information Processing 2023
Published by Springer Nature Switzerland AG 2023
I. Maglogiannis et al. (Eds.): AIAI 2023, IFIP AICT 676, pp. 505–514, 2023.
https://doi.org/10.1007/978-3-031-34107-6_40

Examples from the latest papers related to gesture recognition systems [2–6] indicate that the most popular approach for data collection is to obtain records from physical users (volunteers). However, apart from the effort required to manually collect and label a large amount of data, there are other inconveniences. For example, collecting data from people sometimes causes personal information issues. In [7], the authors created a dataset for gender and smile recognition. Although they had to obtain permission from all volunteers, they could withdraw their authorization within 50 days.

Working with large datasets is both demanding and important because more training data can have a positive impact on the accuracy of the trained models. According to the literature, augmentation is the most common approach for extending the collected dataset. Here, distorting parts of the data and adding them to the original dataset is one of the methods [8]. Another solution, in relation to image classification, was implemented in [9], where additional artificial data were generated by horizontally or vertically reflecting images from the base set. In [10], the authors proposed the generation of completely new data by creating captcha images using random generators. This concept produced training data from the scrap. Another example of generating synthetic data is by combining real pictures with 3D-rendered models as the source data [11]. Moreover, the research presented in [12] about eliminating data collection to learn the Wake Word recognition system was another example in which the researchers faced issues with collecting data. They used synthetic and ready recordings from the Internet and combined them with some noisy sounds, and then made some transformations. All these examples demonstrate that data-gathering issues are not only a matter of HMIs.

In this paper, we propose to use a robotic arm as the only source for generating a training dataset for gesture recognition. This is a novel approach to collecting data for machine learning algorithms for 3D gesture recognition. In this solution, trajectories of a robotic arm are generated that are then used as the input to the whole system. Here, the data goes through the same path as in the system target application, which eliminates any potential data deviations. As the created dataset was fully synthetic, it was interesting to determine how closely it approximated human inputs in the learning application. We verified our concept on an example capacitive gesture recognition system, where the hardware severely limited both the types of gesture and the detection range. This often results in hardware changes (tuning) in development. As a result, the learning process must be repeated many times, making automation more suitable for this application; hence, we termed this approach an automated method.

2 Realization of Gestures and Autmatised Dataset Generation

The proposed excitation system consisted of a 4-axis robotic arm equipped with an effector containing a CR circuit that simulated human hand impedance to ground (Fig. 1). The gesture recognition sensing panel was installed horizontally on the desk, above which the robotic arm performed gestures. This mounting position corresponded to the target application conditions, and the complete setup is presented in Fig. 2. We used the uArm device from UFactory.

We observed that maneuvering the effector over the electrodes resulted in the same signal output as in data collected from humans, which resulted in the idea of using only

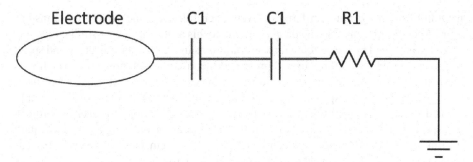

Fig. 1. Circuit for simulating a human hand impedance to ground. $C_1 = 20$ nF, $R_1 = 1500$ Ω

Fig. 2. Experimental setup. Note that a conductive pad is located under a whole setup.

data collected with the manipulator in the learning process. In the automated method, instead of performing gestures and labeling them manually, this was accomplished using a PC application, which was responsible for generating paths, sending commands to the manipulator, gesture data collection, and labeling. The main doubt regarding this approach was the low data diversity compared to human-generated datasets, as people naturally perform gestures differently, even when following the same precise instructions. Accordingly, any training data must imitate this aspect by having similar diversity. This was achieved by introducing random variations in the effector trajectory and speed. A list of coordinates in three axes represented the effector path positions, which were sequentially achieved by the robotic arm with a specified speed. Each gesture had a specified base path and speed, which was then modified before every move. We implemented these variations by generating pseudorandom deviations for every coordinate and speed in a range of −5% to + 5% of the base value. This range was experimentally determined to cover practically the entire range of the system. Generation of the pseudorandom numbers was achieved using the Mersenne Twister generator [13] with a period of 2^{19937}, guaranteeing that the values were not repeated.

3   Gesture Recognition System Used for Verification

To verify the concept, we used a prototype capacitive gesture recognition system designed for the automotive market. This consisted of input circuitry formed from a set of capacitive electrodes, a Microchip MGC3140 capacitive system controller, and an STM32H745ZI Nucleo development board to execute the machine learning algorithm. The predictions were then sent to a PC via UART. A block diagram of the complete system is presented in Fig. 3.

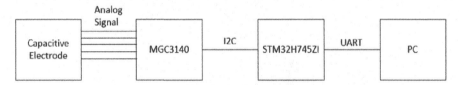

Fig. 3. Block diagram of a gesture recognition system used in experiments.

3.1   Input Circuitry of the Gesture Recognition System

The input circuitry of the system contained five electrodes that were located on a flat surface, as presented in Fig. 4. It should be noted that despite using the terms "Top" and "Bottom" for the electrodes, the actual device was located horizontally.

Two approaches are used for capacitive systems [14]: self and mutual capacitance. In the self-capacitance approach, a change of capacitance between each electrode and ground is used to detect the distance between an electrode and a disturbing object (hand). By comparison, in a mutual capacitance approach, changes in capacitance between a pair of electrodes in the presence of a disturbing object are detected. This approach requires one transmitter (Tx) electrode and one (or more) receiver (Rx) electrodes. The described solution uses a mixed approach, where boundary electrodes (left, right, top, and bottom) are used as Rx, while the central electrode is used as both a Tx and Rx one. Firstly, the central electrode operates as Tx and charged with an excitation voltage, while the boundary electrodes were scanned sequentially. The central electrode worked as an

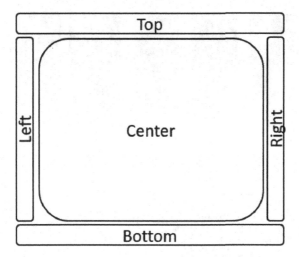

Fig. 4. Arrangement of capacitive electrodes of input circuitry.

Rx for a self-capacitance approach. The MGC3410 chip repeated the cycle with a 5 ms period, which was the system sampling rate. The collected digital data corresponding to the capacitances were sent via the I2C protocol to the STM32H745ZI microcontroller. The microcontroller software then implemented simple level gating by only triggering data acquisition when any detected signal exceeded a predefined limit value, which indicated the presence of the hand in a detection zone. After each trigger event, a constant number of 240 data samples were collected, even when the hand was withdrawn from the detection area earlier.

3.2 Machine Learning Algorithm

The main part of the algorithm for gesture recognition was a 3-phase convolutional neural network, as displayed in Fig. 5. The bottom part of the picture presents the detailed structure of a single layer. Layers 2 and 3 were identical. Although Layer 1 had the same structure, its components (A and B) were of different sizes (A = $1 \times 64 \times 32$, B = $1 \times 64 \times 16$).

The model was trained with both datasets (one collected manually and one automatically). After the training process, we deployed an artificial neural network model for the microcontroller in three steps, as presented in Fig. 6. This starts by converting the.hdf5 model to the.tflite format using the TensorFlow framework. In Step 2, we transform the model to.c and.h files using the MXCUBE AI tool. In the final step, the built model and the embedded application source files result in a binary file in the.elf format. During program execution data from the sensor are normalized and then passed to methods generated by MXCUBE AI, that returns number assigned to predicted gesture.

Due to the lack of a criterium for feature vector creation, this could be considered a deep learning approach, although with a relatively short input vector. The output of the neural network is a five-element vector of probabilities, with each element corresponding to one of the following defined gestures: swipe left, swipe right, swipe up, swipe down,

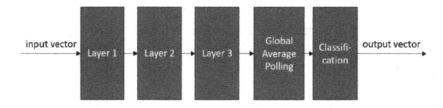

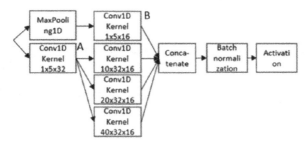

Fig. 5. Neural network model used for gesture recognition.

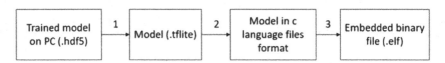

Fig. 6. Embedded system deployment process.

and single tap. The gestures were classified if a calculated probability exceeded 50%. This model is based on the inception architecture in [15].

4   Data Collection

The typical approach to data collection and labeling requires a group of volunteers who physically perform gestures, implying that more diverse data requires a larger group. Each recorded data sample must be labeled, with a certain probability of mislabeling that we estimated to be between 1% and 2%. In our research, this procedure was previously managed by the host engineer who supervised the learning process. This involved inviting dozens of volunteers, who were then asked to perform specified gestures, which was a tedious and time-consuming job. Usually, the volunteers were random people who did not know how the system worked, meaning they had to be instructed where and when to perform the gestures. Fortuitously, because the participants did not understand the technology, this provided the benefit of producing more real-life input data. However, considering all the required stages, this approach was painstaking. Data collection and labeling in gesture recognition systems is particularly time consuming, compared to systems where collecting data does not require any human interaction. We attempted to improve the process by creating a dedicated user interface that eased the data labeling process, although the improvement was relatively insignificant. In contrast to the data collected from volunteers, the automatically collected data had no mislabeling errors. In this research, we developed an approach that shortened and improved the data collection and labeling processes. To collect data in an automated and organized way, a PC application was designed to control the robotic arm described in Sect. 2 and to receive, save, and label the data received from the STM32H745ZI. The input circuitry remained the same as in regular operation. The application executed on the STM32H745ZI detected hand presence and collected 240 samples for a single trigger. The collected data were then sent directly to the PC instead of being processed on the microcontroller. In total, 8780 gestures were collected in this way. To address any errors that occurred during collection, the dataset was then processed to find and remove outliers from each class using a cross-similarity matrix with dynamic time warping [16]. Table 1 presents a comparison of the data collection rates of the tested methods.

Table 1. Comparison data collection rate

Manual	Automated
123 gestures/h	427 gestures/h

Manual - The supervisor manually started and stopped recording the sequence of gestures. Volunteers were asked to perform all five specified gestures in sequence. Labeling was manual.

Automated – Program generates trajectories and controls robotic arm. Program automatically started and stopped the data recording. Labeling was conducted by the application.

5 Training

The collected data was then used to train the neural network. Usually, the data is split into three parts: training, validation, and testing. However, since we wanted to check how well the model was trained on automatically generated data, we split the model into two parts in the following proportions: 80% training and 20% validation. Test data was not required because we tested the model on the target system with gestures performed by volunteers. The training was conducted in Python script using the TensorFlow library.

6 Testing

The quality of the trained model was evaluated realistically by using new data collected through recording gestures made by humans. We invited 10 volunteers who were selected randomly from a group of over 200 colleagues. Each user was requested to perform 10 gestures of each type handled by the system (swipe left, swipe right, swipe up, swipe down, and tap). The values in Table 2 correspond to the number of these gestures that were correctly performed and recognized.

Table 2. Summary of the verification results (percentage of properly recognized gestures)

	swipe left	swipe right	swipe up	swipe down	tap	overall
user1	100	100	80	100	100	96
user2	90	80	90	90	90	88
user3	90	100	50	100	100	88
user4	100	90	70	70	80	82
user5	100	100	40	50	100	78
user6	100	80	100	60	50	78
user7	100	90	60	40	70	72
user8	90	90	0	80	100	72
user9	90	80	50	100	20	68
user10	100	100	60	70	70	80
ALL	96	91	60	76	78	80.2

As depicted in Table 2, the overall accuracy was 80.2%, which is a promising result for using this method. The worst results were obtained for the swipe-up gesture. This was because the flat location of the sensor caused the swipe-up gesture to be performed away from the user, which was the least comfortable movement. It was also observed that after performing the swipe-up gesture (unlike the other gestures), the users behaved in two different ways: some kept their hand over the system, while others took it away from the system immediately. This behavior resulted in different signals at the end of the acquisition window. In automated learning, an effector was always stopped above an electrode after finishing this gesture. The gestures were detected correctly for users who kept their hands in place. For users who removed their hands immediately, the gestures were mislabeled. This result can inform the next stage of automated testing, where a robotic arm could be programmed to perform both types of swipe-up gestures.

7 Summary and Discussion

The proposed solution was deemed promising for teaching a gesture detection system. During the development of such systems, frequent changes require the reacquisition of data, which could prove troublesome with human volunteers. One great advantage of an automated gesture system is speed, due to there being no need to manually tag gestures. For comparison, taking 857 gestures with humans took 6.45 h, while taking 1173 gestures with an automated system took 2.45 h, indicating that the automated system operated approximately three times faster than the manual method. Additionally, the automated system could be left to operate overnight, utilizing the available time more effectively. We analyzed the collected dataset using both methods and concluded that the automatically collected dataset did not contain any mislabeled samples. In comparison, the manual approach always produced at least 1%–2% of data that were mislabeled, which is a natural consequence of simple human mistakes during the process.

Although the calculated precision of verification (80.2% on average) was not very high, there are many areas that could be improved. For example, an outlying "up" gesture was only performed by the automated system in one way, whereas the volunteers performed it in two ways. This result indicated that the automated system could not fully replace human testing. Accordingly, modifying the automated gesture set to mimic human behavior more accurately (and obtain better efficiency), would be a further research topic on the described system. In addition, the system could be expanded by recognizing more complex types of gestures. The idea of using data set collected both manually and automatically could be a good compromise and might eliminate the disadvantages of both approaches. This will be tested in our future development of 3D gesture recognition systems. It is also a wide research area for other machine-learning applications. Finally, a comparison of the automated and manual methods of data collection is presented in Table 3.

Table 3. Comparison between data collection methods

	Manual	Automated
Time	Time-consuming	Shortens time
Supervisor engagement	Supervised continuously	Supervisor must only start the process
Dataset similarity to target application	Very high	High
Environment preparation effort	Moderate	High
Number of volunteers	High	None
Dataset diversity	Depends on volunteers	Depends on randomization

Two most important advantages of Automated method are shorter time and significantly smaller human effort. Lower data diversity, as it was proven, does not disqualify this method. It can be compensated by appropriate manipulator path randomization. Similarity of collected data are slightly lower compared to Manual method, but differences did not impact on gesture prediction accuracy. Higher environment preparation time will save more and more effort with every performed training loop. Automated approach make the development team completely independent from volunteers availability.

References

1. Roh, Y., Heo, G., Whang, S.E.: A survey on data collection for machine learning: a big data - AI integration perspective. IEEE Trans. Knowl. Data Eng. **33**, 1328–1347 (2021). https://doi.org/10.1109/TKDE.2019.2946162
2. Wang, Y., Jiang, H.: Digital gesture recognition based on deep capsule network. In: 2022 IEEE 2nd International Conference on Electronic Technology, Communication and Information (ICETCI), Changchun, China, pp. 1076–1079 (2022). https://doi.org/10.1109/ICETCI55101.2022.9832206

3. Zhang, Z., Wu, B., Jiang, Y.: Gesture recognition system based on improved YOLO v3. In: 7th International Conference on Intelligent Computing and Signal Processing (ICSP), Xi'an, China, pp. 1540–1543 (2022). https://doi.org/10.1109/ICSP54964.2022.9778394

4. Wang, P., Jiang, R., Liu, C.: Amaging: acoustic hand imaging for self-adaptive gesture recognition. In: IEEE INFOCOM 2022 - IEEE Conference on Computer Communications, London, United Kingdom, pp. 80–89 (2022). https://doi.org/10.1109/INFOCOM48880.2022.9796906

5. Qi, R., Zhang, Q.Z., Jing X.: Towards device-free cross-scene gesture recognition from limited samples in integrated sensing and communication. In: 2022 IEEE Wireless Communications and Networking Conference (WCNC), Austin, TX, USA, 2022, pp. 195-198 (2022). https://doi.org/10.1109/WCNC51071.2022.9771992

6. Pan, T.-Y., Tsai, W.-L., Chang, C.-Y., Yeh, C.-W., Hu, M.-C.: A hierarchical hand gesture recognition framework for sports referee training-based EMG and accelerometer sensors. IEEE Trans. Cybern. **52**(5), 3172–3183 (2022). https://doi.org/10.1109/TCYB.2020.3007173

7. Aoto, S.: Collection of 2429 constrained headshots of 277 volunteers for deep learning. Sci. Rep. **12**(1), 12 (2022). https://doi.org/10.1038/s41598-022-07560-2

8. Simard, P.Y., Steinkraus, D., Platt, J.C.: Best practices for convolutional neural networks applied to visual document analysis. In: Seventh International Conference on Document Analysis and Recognition. Proceedings, Edinburgh, UK, 2003, pp. 958–963 (2003). https://doi.org/10.1109/ICDAR.2003.1227801

9. Krizhevsky, A., Sutskever, I., Hinton, G.E.: ImageNet classification with deep convolutional neural networks. Commun. ACM **60**(6), 84–90 (2017). https://doi.org/10.1145/3065386

10. Le, T.A., Baydin, A.G., Zinkov, R., Wood, F.: Using synthetic data to train neural networks is model-based reasoning. In: Proceedings of the International Joint Conference on Neural Networks, vol. 2017-May, pp. 3514–3521 (2017). https://doi.org/10.48550/arXiv.1703.00868

11. Josifovski, J., Kerzel, M., Pregizer, C., Posniak, L., Wermter, S.: Object detection and pose estimation based on convolutional neural networks trained with synthetic data. In: 2018 IEEE/RSJ International Conference on Intelligent Robots and Systems (IROS), Madrid, Spain, pp. 6269–6276 (2018). https://doi.org/10.1109/IROS.2018.8594379

12. Ramanan, B., Drabeck, L., Woo, T., Cauble, T., Rana, A.: Eliminating data collection bottleneck for wake word engine training using found and synthetic data. In: 2019 IEEE International Conference on Big Data (Big Data), Los Angeles, CA, USA, 2019, pp. 2447–2456 (2019). https://doi.org/10.1109/BigData47090.2019.9006601

13. Matsumoto, M., Nishimura, T.: Mersenne twister: a 623-dimensionally equidistributed uniform pseudo-random number generator. ACM Trans. Model. Comput. Simul. **8**(1), 3–30 (1998). https://doi.org/10.1145/272991.272995

14. Reczek, P., Wetula, A., Młyniec, A.: Review and perspective on 3D gesture recognition technologies for automotive industry. Int. J. Autom. Eng. **12**(4), 150–154 (2021). https://doi.org/10.20485/jsaeijae.12.4_150

15. RubinBose, S., SathieshKumar, V.: Efficient inception V2 based deep convolutional neural network for real-time hand action recognition. IET Image Process. **14**(4), 688–696 (2020). https://doi.org/10.1049/iet-ipr.2019.0985

16. Sakoe, H., Chiba, S.: Dynamic programming algorithm optimization for spoken word recognition. IEEE Trans. Acoust. Speech Signal Process. **26**(1), 43–49 (1978). https://doi.org/10.1109/TASSP.1978.1163055

Emergence of Communication Through Artificial Evolution in an Orientation Consensus Task in Swarm Robotics

Rafael Sendra-Arranz[✉] and Álvaro Gutiérrez

E.T.S. Ingenieros de Telecomunicación, Universidad Politécnica de Madrid,
28040 Madrid, Spain
{r.sendra,a.gutierrez}@upm.es
https://www.robolabo.etsit.upm.es/

Abstract. The emergence of communication through evolutionary computation in a swarm of initially non-communicative robots is a highly complex research topic that has vastly captured the attention in the swarm robotics field. In this paper, we empirically study the emergence of communication as a result of an evolutionary algorithm in a swarm of simulated robots with the objective of solving an orientation consensus problem. Specifically, the consensus is reached provided that the heading orientations of the robots point into the same direction. The robots are controlled by Continuous-Time Recurrent Neural Networks whose parameters are evolved using a genetic algorithm. Once evolution is concluded, we assess the performance and scalability of the swarm behavior and the type of communication that emerged. The study is accomplished by means of an statistical analysis of the communication variables produced in a sample of 50 independent simulations. The conducted analysis suggests that the emerged communication is situated, meaning that both the message content and its associated context about the environment are informative and useful in the communication. Very interestingly, the environment context is the only piece of information actually relevant for reaching the consensus. On the contrary, the abstract message content is crucial for drastically reducing the rotation speed of the robots after the orientation consensus is achieved.

Keywords: Swarm Robotics · Orientation Consensus · Evolutionary Robotics · Emergence of Communication

1 Introduction

In Swarm Robotics (SR) [15], multiple simple and homogeneous robots interact and coordinate locally to solve cooperative problems. From the simple behaviors of each robot and their local and decentralized interactions can emerge utterly complex collective behaviors. A great exponent is the emergence of communication in a swarm of initially non-communicative agents. Generally, the emergence of communication in swarm robotics is explored along with the field of

© IFIP International Federation for Information Processing 2023
Published by Springer Nature Switzerland AG 2023
I. Maglogiannis et al. (Eds.): AIAI 2023, IFIP AICT 676, pp. 515–526, 2023.
https://doi.org/10.1007/978-3-031-34107-6_41

Evolutionary Robotics [11]. Multiple studies have investigated from an empirical perspective the emergence and origins of communication in swarm robotics using evolutionary algorithms (see e.g. [2,12,20]). According to [18], there are two main types of emergent communication. *Abstract Communication* [2,9,20] is a type of communication in which only the message content carries information. The environmental context associated to the message is either not processed or not relevant in the emerged communication. In contrast, *Situated Communication* [7,8,17] refers to communication scenarios in which both the message content and its corresponding environmental context carry information within the communication. Environmental context can be, for instance, the signal strength or the direction from where the message was received.

In this paper, we study the emergence of communication in simulated swarms of robots in an orientation consensus problem, in which all the robots in the swarm have to point to the same direction. The robot's controller is a Continuous-Time Recurrent Neural Network whose parameters are evolved using a genetic algorithm. We use the minimal IR-based communication system proposed in [17] as the communication system that the agents can use to complete the task. At the beginning of the evolution, the behavior of the robots is non-communicative. At some point in evolution, the semantics of the communication and their respective processing should emerge as a useful aspect of the robot's behavior for reaching the orientation consensus. An exhaustive post-evolution statistical analysis is accomplished using multiple independent simulations, with the aim of discovering the type of semantics that emerged as a result of the artificial evolution.

The structure of this document is as follows. Section 2 provides an overview of previous works available in the literature related to the orientation consensus task. Section 3 describes the main building blocks used in the experiment. Additionally, Sect. 4 presents the orientation consensus experiment and Sect. 5 shows the results and the emerged communication once evolution is ended. Finally, Sect. 6 concludes the paper.

2   Related Work

Orientation consensus is an important cooperative task as it is one of the pillars of flocking behaviors according to Reynolds' rules [14]. Therefore, the problem of heading alignment has been principally studied and assessed in the context of flocking experiments. Heading alignment is addressed in [21] for a self-organized flocking in swarms of mobile robots using a virtual heading sensor. Each robot senses its own orientation with respect to the North reference, using a digital compass, and broadcasts it to its neighborhood. In [5], the authors propose heading alignment behavior in which a only subset of robots, called informed, are aware of a common objective direction. Informed agents communicate the goal direction to its neighboring robots while uninformed agents relay the average incoming message from its vicinity. Robots correctly achieve alignment with their heading pointing to the goal direction. The swarm members know an absolute reference throughout measuring the light intensity emitted by a light source. In a more recent work, the authors of [13] successfully evolve neural controllers for flocking behaviors. Their fitness is composed by cohesion, separation and alignment terms. Focusing on alignment, robots have an alignment sensor that measures its orientation relative to the average orientation of its neighborhood. In [8], an evolutionary algorithm optimizes the parameters of a recurrent neural network. The emerged behavior was a situated communication because it did not harness the message information itself but the physical conditions of the communication. The orientation consensus is not only a highly relevant behavior in terrestrial swarms of robots but also in underwater environments (see e.g. [16, 19]), where the coordinated navigation must be precise and robust.

3   Materials and Methods

3.1   The Robots and the Communication System

In this paper, we solve the orientation consensus problem using a simulated swarm of static robots placed in a flat square arena. The set of robots is denoted as $\mathcal{R}$. As navigation is not required, robots are seen as static point particles, represented by a position $\mathbf{x}_r$ and a heading orientation θ_r. Even though robots cannot move, they are able to rotate along their center of mass in order to alter their heading orientation.

The robots can communicate and cooperate among them to solve the proposed task by using the communication system proposed in [17]. It is an IR-based minimal communication system with a local and constrained communication range of 80 cm. Using this system, the robots can only perceive a single message at each time step of the simulations from one of four possible discretized orientations. The received information not only comprises the abstract message content but also the relevant context information about the environment (e.g. the signal strength of the received signal or the orientation from where it was sensed). The robot's controller, which is fed by both the received message and its associated context, elaborates a new two-dimensional message to be broadcasted using the communication transmitter. Before sending the message, it is subject to a quantization mapping that converts the raw message into one symbol in the set $\mathcal{C}$ defined in Eq. 1.

$$\mathcal{C} = \left\{ 0, \frac{1}{K-1}, \ldots, \frac{K-2}{K-1}, 1 \right\}^M \tag{1}$$

where M is the dimension of the transmitted message. In this paper, we fix the values of $M = 2$ and $K = 4$, leading to 16 possible two-dimensional symbols.

At the reception side, a message from another robot can be perceived from one of 4 possible IR receivers located at different orientations of the robot perimeter. Thus, the robot can know the relative orientation from where the message was received among the discretized values in the set $\{\theta_r, \theta_r + \pi/2, \theta_r + \pi, \theta_r + 3\pi/2\}$. The communication system of the robots can be either in *send mode*, transmitting their own created message, or in *relay mode*, by emitting a copy of the message received from other robots. This communication state can be controlled by the robot through the binary signal $MODE$. If this signal is 1 then the robots enters the *send mode*. Otherwise, the robot is in *relay mode* provided that $MODE$ is zero.

3.2   Continuous-Time Recurrent Neural Networks

We use a Continuous-Time Recurrent Neural Network (CTRNN) [1] as the model to control the robot actions. CTRNNs are artificial neural networks with feedback connections that operate in continuous time. The employed neuron model is the rate model [3] whose single neuron dynamics are defined in Eqs. 2 and 3.

$$\left. \begin{aligned} \tau_m \frac{\partial v_k(t)}{\partial t} &= -v_k(t) + I_k(t) \\ u_k(t) &= f_k\left(v_k(t) + \beta_k\right) \end{aligned} \right\} \tag{2}$$

Equation 2 depicts the single neuron's voltage $(v_k(t))$ and activation $(u_k(t))$ dynamics. β_k and $f_k(\cdot)$ are the neuron's bias and activation function, respectively. In addition, τ_m is the neurons time constant. $I_k(t)$ is the total current fed to the neuron's soma which is calculated as in Eq. 3,

$$I_k(t) = \sum_{i \in \mathcal{N}_k} w_{ki} u_i(t) + \sum_{j \in \mathcal{N}_k^\phi} w_{kj}^\phi \phi_j(t) \tag{3}$$

where w_{ki} is the weight of the synapse connecting pre-synaptic neuron i with post-synaptic neuron k and w_{kj}^ϕ denotes the weight of the synapse between the j-th input and neuron k. $\phi_j(t)$ is the j-th input signal being fed to the CTRNN and $\mathcal{N}_k$ and $\mathcal{N}_k^\phi$ are the sets respectively comprising the pre-synaptic neurons and pre-synaptic inputs to neuron k.

3.3   Genetic Algorithm

A Genetic Algorithm (GA) [6] is used to evolve the parameters of the CTRNN models that define the behavior of the agents. GA is a biologically inspired population based optimization algorithm that mimics how natural selection and survival of the fittest processes work in nature. A population of candidate solutions, namely individuals, genotypes or chromosomes, are updated with the aim of maximizing some performance score defined by a fitness function. Using the evaluated fitness value associated to each genotype, a set of genetic operators are sequentially applied to the overall population in order to generate the population of the next generation or iteration of the GA. In this paper, we use a Gaussian mutation operator that applies a Gaussian noise with a given standard deviation to the real-valued genes with a small probability of mutation. Additionally, the tournament selection [10] is used as the operator to choose which genotypes are used as parents to create the new generation. Finally, the BLX-α operator [4] is the crossover method.

4   The Experiment

4.1   Description of the Experiment

We address the problem of orientation consensus in swarms of robots. By orientation consensus we refer to the task in which all the robots in the swarm have to point to the same direction. Thereafter, the orientations of all robots $\theta_r(t)$ must converge to the same value for reaching the best performance. For this aim, the swarm of robots is static, so that the positions of the agents are fixed during the simulations. The robots can only modify their heading orientations by means of rotation movements, either clockwise or counterclockwise, at an angular speed modulated by their corresponding neural controller. Robots do not have access to any absolute sensing reference, such a light source or a compass, that would utterly ease the orientation consensus achievement. Agents must infer the orientation of their neighbors relative to its own orientation merely using the minimal communication system exposed in Sect. 3.1, which makes it a challenging experiment.

At the beginning of each simulation, the positions x_r are randomly sampled with a random spatial graph initialization that guarantees that there are no isolated nodes. Heading orientations are also randomly initialized. During evolution, every simulation is executed 600 time steps with swarms of 10 robots.

4.2   Fitness Function

The fitness function is composed by two terms that are merged in a multiplicative way. The fitness score of a single agent r at time step t is shown in Eq. 4.

$$f(t, r) = \left(1 - \frac{\min\{2\pi - |\theta_r(t) - \bar{\theta}(t)|, |\theta_r(t) - \bar{\theta}(t)|\}}{\pi}\right) \cdot (1 - |a_{wr}(t)|) \quad (4)$$

where the first term measures the orientation deviation or misalignment of the robot with respect to the mean orientation of the swarm formulated in Eq. 5.

$$\bar{\theta}(t) = \arg\left(\sum_{r \in \mathcal{R}} e^{j\theta_r(t)}\right) \quad (5)$$

Thereafter, the first term in the product of Eq. 4 will linearly increase as the orientation of the robot r tends to the mean orientation of the swarm. The maximum value of this term corresponds to the scenario in which the orientation consensus is reached. The second part of the fitness function rewards robots for reducing their rotation velocity. The partial fitness of this term will rise as the absolute value a_{wr}, which is the signal that controls the speed and sense of rotation, is diminished.

The function $f(t, r)$ computes the fitness for one robot and at an specific time instant. Therefore, to obtain the total fitness score resulting from an evaluation of T time steps and a swarm of R robots, Eq. 6 is applied.

$$F_{tot} = \frac{1}{RT} \sum_{t=1}^{T} \sum_{r \in \mathcal{R}} f(t, r) \qquad (6)$$

4.3 Neural Controller

Figure 1 shows the CTRNN architecture that defines the behavior of the robots. It is composed by the input layer of dimension 7, two hidden layers, called H_1 and H_2, of 10 neurons and the output ensemble with 4 neurons. Even though it is not shown in the figure for the sake of simplifying the diagram, there are some synapses joining the output layer with H_1. These feedback connections are chosen randomly only once at the beginning of evolution and are the same for all the population genotypes. The total amount of these backward connections is 12, which is a 30% of the maximum number of connections between these two layers.

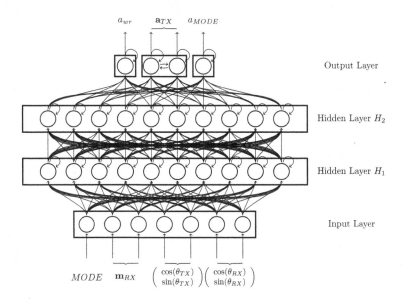

Fig. 1. CTRNN architecture used for controlling the robots. Even though it is not shown in the figure for the sake of simplifying the diagram, there are some synapses joining the output layer with H_1. These feedback connections are chosen randomly only once at the beginning of evolution and are the same for all the population genotypes.

The input layer comprises the relevant signals from the communication receiver of the robot. $\mathbf{m}_{RX}$ is the two-dimensional vector that contains the received message from the agent's neighborhood at the current time step. Additionally, $MODE$ is the binary signal, described in Sect. 3.1, that decides the operation mode of the communication system of the robot. θ_{TX} and θ_{RX} are the discretized orientations from where the message was transmitted and received, respectively, which are relative to the corresponding heading orientations of the sender and the listener robots. The output neurons are split into three layers. Firstly, $a_{MODE} \in [0,1]$ is the signal used to generate the new state of $MODE$. It is subject to a post-processing step that converts it to a value of 0 or 1 by using a Heaviside or step function. Additionally, $\mathbf{a}_{TX} \in [0,1]^2$ is the new message to be broadcasted if $MODE = 1$. $a_{wr} \in [-1,1]$ is the signal that directly controls the speed and sense of the rotation of the robots. The activation function of all the neurons is the sigmoid function, except for the output neuron generating the signal a_{wr}, that employs the hyperbolic tangent function.

The genetic algorithm evolution lasts 1000 generations and the population is composed of 100 individuals. Among these 100 individuals, the 2 best performing genotypes are directly selected as elites every generation. It evaluates in 5 independent trials or simulations the fitness of each individual in order to slightly reduce the variance of the estimation. The probability of mutating a CTRNN parameter is 0.05 while the probability of recombining two genotypes to produce two children individuals is 0.9. A tournament selection is used with a tournament size of 3 and a value of $\alpha = 0.5$ is used in the BLX-α crossover. The genetic algorithm evolves the weights, neuron biases and membrane time constants of the CTRNN. These parameters are bounded as follows: $w_{ij} \in [-5, 5]$, $\beta_i \in [-2, 2]$ and $\tau_i \in [0.3, 32]$, for any neurons i and j.

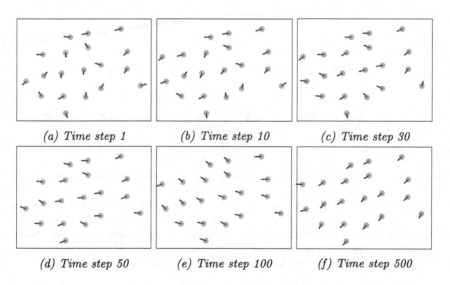

(a) Time step 1   (b) Time step 10   (c) Time step 30

(d) Time step 50   (e) Time step 100   (f) Time step 500

Fig. 2. Frames of a simulation of the orientation consensus experiment. Blue dots depict the robots in the swarm and red arrows show the orientations of the agents. (Color figure online)

5   Results

The evolved agents successfully solve the task of orientation consensus as it can be observed in Fig. 2, where snapshots of the simulation at different time steps are sketched. Blue balls represent the robots in the swarm and red arrows illustrate their heading orientations. The swarm of robots successfully reaches the orientation consensus at time step 100. For further time instants the consensus is correctly maintained, albeit some slight variations of the consensus value can be noticed.

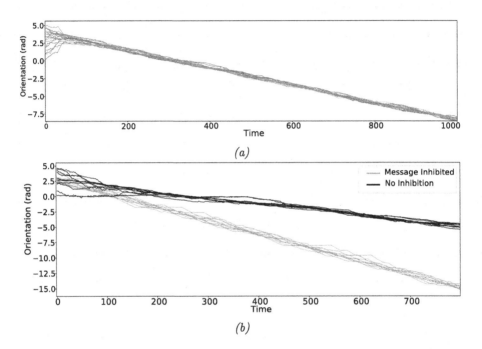

Fig. 3. (a) Temporal evolution of the orientation of the robots in a simulation with swarm size of 20. Each curve corresponds to the orientation of one of the agents. (b) Temporal evolution of the orientation of the robots in a simulation with any communication variable inhibited (black) and with the message content inhibited (red). Curves in each color represent the orientations of the robots in the swarm in the corresponding simulation conditions. In both figures, the orientation range of $[0, 2\pi)$ is extended to the set of real numbers merely for visualization purposes. (Color figure online)

Figure 3a displays an example of the results in a simulation with 20 robots. Each curve represents the evolution of the orientation of the robots. After a transient period of about 100 time steps, the robots tend to reach the orientation consensus by matching their heading direction with the orientation of its neighborhood. Even though consensus is approximately fulfilled, robots still rotate with very low angular speed in order to preserve orientation agreement. This residual rotation can be observed in the figure as the slope in the orientations of the robots, albeit this slope is merely about 0.01 radians per time step.

We now assess the scalability of the evolved system. For this aim, we introduce the misalignment metric defined as in Eq. 7,

$$M_\theta(t) = \frac{1}{R} \sum_{r \in \mathcal{R}} \min \left\{ |\theta_r(t) - \overline{\theta}(t)|, 2\pi - |\theta_r(t) - \overline{\theta}(t)| \right\} \qquad (7)$$

which essentially measures the mean orientation deviation of each robot with respect to the mean orientation of the swarm. The optimal value of this metric is zero, corresponding to a perfect heading orientation consensus. The mean orientation $\overline{\theta}$ was already formulated in Eq. 5.

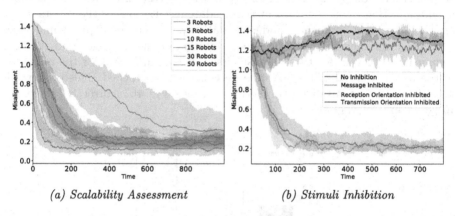

(a) Scalability Assessment   (b) Stimuli Inhibition

Fig. 4. Temporal evolution of the misalignment metric (see Eq. 7) distribution using 50 simulation trials and diverse swarm sizes. The darker curves represent the median of the misalignment using all 50 collected samples. Alternatively, the clearer areas indicate, at each time instant, the first and third and quantiles. In (a), the scalability of the system is assessed by increasing the swarm from 3 robots up to 50 robots. On the contrary, (b) studies the relevance of each controller input related to the communication. Each curve represents the evolution of the orientation misalignment when a different signal inhibited or nullified.

Unlike the results shown in Fig. 3a, that uniquely represent one sample that could be biased, for the scalability evaluation we use a sample of 50 independent simulations. Thereafter, Fig. 4a illustrates the performance with diverse swarm sizes and using the 50 samples to build each curve. At each time instant, the darker curves denote the median value of the misalignment metric across the 50 simulations. Moreover, the shadow areas are delimited by the first and third quantiles. As the swarm size increases, the time elapsed before convergence to the consensus is increased. Additionally, the convergence value or steady state misalignment slightly grows as the swarm size scales. However, the consensus is approximately fulfilled even in the worst case scenario of 50 robots and considering the sparsity and low connectivity degree of the swarm due to the local and constrained IR communication.

The emerged communication semantics are also analysed. Figure 4b shows the misalignment evolution when different variables are inhibited or nullified. The deletion of $\mathbf{m}_{RX}$, θ_{RX} and θ_{TX} are considered and compared to the results without inhibition. The state of the communication (variable $MODE$) was not studied because we observed that all the robots remain always in the *send mode*. The curves in the figure indicate that θ_{RX} and θ_{TX} are both crucial for solving the problem. On the contrary, the inhibition of $\mathbf{m}_{RX}$ leads to an equivalent misalignment evolution compared to the normal conditions. Therefore, apparently, this fact suggests that the message content by itself is not relevant for reaching the orientation consensus.

However, Fig. 3b provides a different perspective that refutes the previous statement. It compares the temporal evolution of the orientation for a single simulation. Black curves represent the heading orientations of the robots in the trial with normal conditions and, alternatively, red curves depict simulations with $\mathbf{m}_{RX}$ nullified. Even though the inhibition of the message content is not significantly relevant for the consensus itself, it is clearly used for the reduction of the rotation speed of the robots once consensus is reached. This property is not reflected in the misalignment metric and, thus, Fig. 4b incorrectly categorizes $\mathbf{m}_{RX}$ as an irrelevant signal.

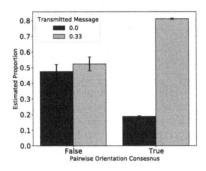

Fig. 5. Proportion estimates and 95% confidence intervals of the times each symbol is transmitted conditioned to the status of pairwise communication.

To conclude the post-analysis of the emerged communication, Fig. 5 deepens into the semantics or meanings of the transmitted symbols. It depicts the estimate of the proportion of times that a robot sends each symbol message when pairwise orientation consensus between sender and listener robots is fulfilled. The CTRNN only generates the symbols $(0, 0)$ and $(0.33, 0.33)$ among the 16 available symbols and, thus, only those symbols are shown in the figure. In addition to the point estimates, the plot additionally illustrates the confidence intervals with 95% of confidence level and using the results from 50 independent trials. When pairwise orientation consensus is reached, the symbol 0.33 is mostly generated. Alternatively, when robots are not aligned, there is not a statistically significant difference in the proportion of times that each symbol is generated. This information matches with the observations of Fig. 3b, indicating the relevance of the message once the consensus is achieved.

6 Conclusions

In this paper we studied the emergence of communication in swarm robotics in an orientation consensus problem. The simulated static robots, that are controlled by CTRNN neural networks evolved using a genetic algorithm, must coordinate with the goal of pointing into the same direction. The simulated robots can use the minimal IR-based communication system previously proposed in [17] for solving the proposed task. After the artificial evolution, a statistical analysis was carried out to assess the performance, scalability and emergent communication of the swarm of robots. The results demonstrate that the robots correctly reach the desired orientation consensus with low error and good scalability. Moreover, the assessment suggests that the emergent communication is a situated communication in which both the pure message and the environmental context are highly relevant. Specifically, the context is the only critical information for reaching the consensus itself. Nonetheless, even though the message seems to be irrelevant for the consensus achievement, it is highly important for the reduction of the rotation speed once the consensus is fulfilled.

Acknowledgements. This work has been supported by Grant PID2020-112502RB-C41 funded by MCIN/AEI/10.13039/501100011033. R. Sendra-Arranz's acknowledges support from the predoctoral grant from the "Programa Propio I+D+i" financed by the Universidad Politécnica de Madrid. The authors gratefully acknowledge the Universidad Politécnica de Madrid (www.upm.es) for providing computing resources on Magerit Supercomputer.

References

1. Beer, R.D., Gallagher, J.C.: Evolving dynamical neural networks for adaptive behavior. Adapt. Behav. **1**(1), 91–122 (1992)
2. de Greeff, J., Nolfi, S.: Evolution of implicit and explicit communication in mobile robots. In: Nolfi, S., Mirolli, M. (eds.) Evolution of Communication and Language in Embodied Agents, pp. 179–214. Springer, Heidelberg (2010). https://doi.org/10.1007/978-3-642-01250-1_11
3. Ermentrout, G.B., Terman, D.H.: Firing rate models. In: Ermentrout, G.B., Terman, D.H. (eds.) Mathematical Foundations of Neuroscience, pp. 331–367. Springer, New York (2010). https://doi.org/10.1007/978-0-387-87708-2_11
4. Eshelman, L.J., Schaffer, J.D.: Real-coded genetic algorithms and interval-schemata. In: Foundations of Genetic Algorithms, Foundations of Genetic Algorithms, vol. 2, pp. 187–202. Elsevier (1993)
5. Ferrante, E., Turgut, A.E., Mathews, N., Birattari, M., Dorigo, M.: Flocking in stationary and non-stationary environments: a novel communication strategy for heading alignment. In: Schaefer, R., Cotta, C., Kołodziej, J., Rudolph, G. (eds.) PPSN 2010. LNCS, vol. 6239, pp. 331–340. Springer, Heidelberg (2010). https://doi.org/10.1007/978-3-642-15871-1_34

6. Goldberg, D.E.: Genetic Algorithms in Search, Optimization and Machine Learning, 1st edn. Addison-Wesley Longman Publishing Co., Inc, USA (1989)
7. Gutierrez, A., Campo, A., Dorigo, M., Donate, J., Monasterio-Huelin, F., Magdalena, L.: Open E-puck range & bearing miniaturized board for local communication in swarm robotics. In: 2009 IEEE International Conference on Robotics and Automation, pp. 3111–3116 (2009)
8. Gutiérrez, Á., Tuci, E., Campo, A.: Evolution of neuro-controllers for robots' alignment using local communication. Int. J. Adv. Rob. Syst. **6**(1), 6 (2009)
9. Hasselmann, K., Robert, F., Birattari, M.: Automatic design of communication-based behaviors for robot swarms. In: Dorigo, M., Birattari, M., Blum, C., Christensen, A.L., Reina, A., Trianni, V. (eds.) ANTS 2018. LNCS, vol. 11172, pp. 16–29. Springer, Cham (2018). https://doi.org/10.1007/978-3-030-00533-7_2
10. Miller, B.L., Goldberg, D.E., et al.: Genetic algorithms, tournament selection, and the effects of noise. Complex Syst. **9**(3), 193–212 (1995)
11. Nolfi, S., Floreano, D.: Evolutionary Robotics: The Biology, Intelligence, and Technology of Self-organizing Machines. MIT Press, Cambridge (2000)
12. Quinn, M.: Evolving communication without dedicated communication channels. In: Kelemen, J., Sosík, P. (eds.) ECAL 2001. LNCS (LNAI), vol. 2159, pp. 357–366. Springer, Heidelberg (2001). https://doi.org/10.1007/3-540-44811-X_38
13. Ramos, R.P., Oliveira, S.M., Vieira, S.M., Christensen, A.L.: Evolving flocking in embodied agents based on local and global application of Reynolds' rules. PLoS ONE **14**(10), 1–16 (2019)
14. Reynolds, C.W.: Flocks, herds and schools: a distributed behavioral model. In: Proceedings of the 14th Annual Conference on Computer Graphics and Interactive Techniques, SIGGRAPH 1987, pp. 25–34. Association for Computing Machinery, New York (1987)
15. Şahin, E.: Swarm robotics: from sources of inspiration to domains of application. In: Şahin, E., Spears, W.M. (eds.) SR 2004. LNCS, vol. 3342, pp. 10–20. Springer, Heidelberg (2005). https://doi.org/10.1007/978-3-540-30552-1_2
16. Sahu, B.K., Subudhi, B., Dash, B.K.: Flocking control of multiple autonomous underwater vehicles. In: 2012 Annual IEEE India Conference (INDICON), pp. 257–262 (2012)
17. Sendra-Arranz, R., Gutiérrez, Á.: Evolution of situated and abstract communication in leader selection and borderline identification swarm robotics problems. Appl. Sci. **11**(8), 3516 (2021)
18. Støy, K., et al.: Using situated communication in distributed autonomous mobile robotics. In: SCAI, vol. 1, pp. 44–52. Citeseer (2001)
19. Tolba, S., Ammar, R., Rajasekaran, S.: Taking swarms to the field: constrained spiral flocking for underwater search. In: 2016 IEEE Symposium on Computers and Communication (ISCC), pp. 1177–1184 (2016)
20. Tuci, E., Ampatzis, C.: Evolution of acoustic communication between two cooperating robots. In: Almeida e Costa, F., Rocha, L.M., Costa, E., Harvey, I., Coutinho, A. (eds.) ECAL 2007. LNCS (LNAI), vol. 4648, pp. 395–404. Springer, Heidelberg (2007). https://doi.org/10.1007/978-3-540-74913-4_40
21. Turgut, A.E., Çelikkanat, H., Gökçe, F., Şahin, E.: Self-organized flocking in mobile robot swarms. Swarm Intell. **2**(2), 97–120 (2008)

Spiking NN

Lossless Method of Constraining Membrane Potential in Deep Spiking Neural Networks

Yijie Miao$^{(\boxtimes)}$ and Makoto Ikeda$^{(\boxtimes)}$

EEIS, Graduate School of Engineering, The University of Tokyo, Tokyo 113-0032, Japan
{miao,ikeda}@silicon.u-tokyo.ac.jp

Abstract. Biologically inspired Spiking Neural Networks (SNNs) offer a promising path toward achieving energy-efficient artificial intelligence systems. However, in the hardware field, the deployment of deep SNNs has been stagnant, where the wide range of membrane potential of spiking neuron poses a significant challenge to hardware efficiency. To address this issue, this work proposes a guideline and a novel hardware-friendly method to constrain the membrane potential, reducing the associated hardware overhead while fully maintaining the inference accuracy. Experiments demonstrate that the proposed method is effective and achieves substantial memory usage reduction for a 20-layer ResNet model. This work paves the way toward the efficient hardware implementation of even deeper SNNs.

Keywords: Spiking neural networks · Membrane potential ·
ANN-SNN conversion · Deep networks · Hardware implementations

1 Introduction

Spiking Neural Networks (SNNs) are novel Artificial Neural Networks (ANNs) that mimic the biological neural system, which uses discrete and sparse spike trains to convey information. Whereas SNNs have received considerable attention for many years due to their potential for energy efficiency benefits, compared to traditional ANNs, training and implementing SNNs are more challenging since they use non-differentiable neuron models with complex internal dynamics [1].

In the software field, converting pre-trained ANNs into SNNs, known as the ANN-SNN conversion method, has emerged as a successful alternative method to overcome the difficulty of directly training SNNs [2–6]. Despite the minor accuracy degradation, converting the state-of-the-art deep ANNs to SNNs has enabled competitive SNN inference performance across various image classification benchmarks from simple MNIST to challenging CIFAR-100 or ImageNet.

If only deployed on general computation hardware like CPUs or GPUs, SNNs would have no opportunity to compete with other state-of-the-art hardware ANNs in terms of energy efficiency and speed. However, the development of dedicated SNN hardware notably lags behind the software. Until recently, the

© IFIP International Federation for Information Processing 2023
Published by Springer Nature Switzerland AG 2023
I. Maglogiannis et al. (Eds.): AIAI 2023, IFIP AICT 676, pp. 529–540, 2023.
https://doi.org/10.1007/978-3-031-34107-6_42

majority of SNN hardware has only been capable of handling simple tasks like MNIST dataset [7–11], with only a few designs having implemented deeper SNN models and supporting tasks of higher complexity [10,12,13].

Considering the overall structural similarities between converted SNNs and source ANNs, the introduction of additional membrane potential by spiking neurons constitutes a significant negative factor, if not the only one, in hardware implementation. Prior work has recognized the crucial role of the wide dynamic range of membrane potential in accurate SNN inference, especially when the network deepens [14]. In software SNNs, the high-precision floating-point format is available, and the value range is generally not a concern. However, in hardware, the wide range of membrane potential can result in excessive computational and storage overhead. To date, no method has been reported to accommodate the impact of membrane potential on inference capability and hardware efficiency in deep SNN scenarios, which limits the further development of SNN hardware.

To address this, we, for the first time, propose a lossless method to constrain the dynamic range of membrane potential in deep SNNs, which can bridge the gap between software and hardware. The contribution of this work could be summarized as follows:

- We examine the mechanism underlying the degradation of SNNs inference capability when constraining the negative membrane potential. Our analysis and observations suggest that the fluctuations in the membrane potential are the primary factor contributing to the degradation. Based on this insight, we derive a guideline for constraining the value range of membrane potential in a lossless manner.
- We propose a hardware-friendly method that utilizes a novel packed spike format, enforcing the above-mentioned lossless constraint on the membrane potential. Our method allows deeper SNNs to employ the same hardware-friendly reduced-precision quantization for membrane potential as used in weights to reduce storage overhead and thereby enable the extension of efficient hardware SNNs to higher layers in the future.

2   Background and Related Work

2.1   Membrane Potential of Spiking Neuron

We start with the Integrate-and-Fire (IF) neuron model, a popular choice for converted SNNs due to its low computational cost. Mathematical details will be presented in the section to follow later, and here we provide a brief overview of its principles. In this model, the input spike trains are multiplied by the weights to form the input potential (Fig. 1a). When positive weights dominate, the input potential integrates to the membrane potential and is released when it exceeds the threshold, firing spikes backward. Consequently, the output spike rate positively correlates with the input spike rates. On the other hand, in cases where negative weights dominate and the input potential is negative, the IF neuron generates no output spike. These principles align well with the ANN

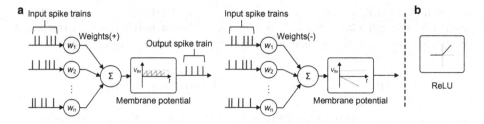

Fig. 1. a. The dynamics of IF spiking neuron in the cases where positive and negative weights dominate. **b.** Rectified Linear Unit (ReLU) activation function in ANNs.

neurons' Rectified Linear Unit (ReLU) activation function (Fig. 1b), thereby enabling the conversion between ANNs and SNNs.

Prior works have recognized the importance of the membrane potential for accurate SNN inference [4,6]. Any changes in membrane potential can cause neurons to fire more or less rapidly, which can significantly impact the network's performance. What is concerning is that the negative membrane potential cannot be released and instead accumulated during inference. Consequently, a much more extensive value range compared to positive membrane potential is necessary, especially when the inference lasts for an extended duration.

Storing such a large negative membrane potential can present a major challenge to SNN hardware. To this end, Hwang et al. [14] were the first to investigate the possibility of constraining negative membrane potential on various network models and tasks. They found that disabling negative membrane potential had little impact on a shallow 4-layer SNN on the MNIST classification task but led to significant accuracy loss for a deeper 10-layer SNN on the CIFAR-10 task. They also assessed the safe lower bounds of the membrane potential for each case, below which there would be no significant accuracy degradation. Unfortunately, they did not offer a method to really alleviate the impact of negative membrane potential. As the networks deepen, the safe lower bound of membrane potential will eventually become impractical.

2.2   Hardware Implementations

There is a surprising lack of information in SNN hardware regarding the handling of membrane potential, particularly for negative membrane potential. Designs in [8,9] have employed reduced-precision fixed-point formats for membrane potential while disabling negative membrane potential. However, both designs were limited to shallow SNNs and tasks with low complexity where the disabling of negative membrane potential is not significantly detrimental.

Even less information is available regarding deeper SNNs. Designs in [10] employed a 32-bit fixed-point format for membrane potential. They implemented a custom and a VGG-16 convolutional neural network (CNN) model, achieving 81.80% and 91.46% CIFAR-10 accuracies, respectively. However, the 32-bit fixed-point format for membrane potential is a step backward compared to the low-bit format used in shallower networks, which can lead to significant hardware overhead. Overall, efficient SNN hardware implementations are largely restricted to shallow layers, limiting their applicability across various applications.

3   Guideline for Constraining Membrane Potential

In this section, we derive a guideline for constraining negative membrane potential in a lossless manner. Contrary to prior research, we demonstrate that disabling negative membrane potential does not necessarily result in accuracy degradation in deep SNNs. Instead, fluctuations in membrane potential are primarily responsible for this outcome, which is alleviable.

3.1   Error Analysis

We start with a theoretical analysis. We follow the IF neuron model described in prior work [3]. The total input potential integrated to the i-th neuron in l-th layer at time step t is defined as:

$$z_i^l(t) = \sum_{j=1}^{M^{l-1}} W_{ij}^l \Theta_j^{l-1}(t) + b_i^l , \tag{1}$$

where M^{l-1} is the number of pre-synaptic neurons, W_{ij}^l is the synaptic weight, b_i^l is the bias and $\Theta_j^{l-1}(t)$ is the step function indicating the spike generation:

$$\Theta_i^l(t) = \Theta(V_i^l(t-1) + z_i^l(t) - V_{thr}), \text{ with } \Theta(x) = \begin{cases} 1, & \text{if } x \geq 0 \\ 0, & \text{else} \end{cases} \tag{2}$$

Meanwhile, at each time step, the input potential z_i^l is integrated to the neuron's membrane potential V_i^l:

$$V_i^l(t) = V_i^l(t-1) + z_i^l(t) - V_{thr}\Theta_i^l(t) + \epsilon_i^l(t, V_{lb}) , \tag{3}$$

where $\epsilon_i^l(t, V_{lb})$ is the error term that appears when a lower bound V_{lb} is imposed on the negative membrane potential. The value of this error term is equal to the discrepancy between the membrane potential that would have been attained in the absence of V_{lb} and the actual value hindered by V_{lb}.

The threshold potential V_{thr} is normally equal to one. By summing and averaging Eq. 3 over the entire inference duration T and rearranging it, we obtain:

$$r_i^l(T) = \frac{1}{T}\sum_{t=1}^T \Theta_i^l(t) = \frac{1}{T}\sum_{t=1}^T z_i^l(t) - \frac{V_i^l(T) - V_i^l(0)}{T} + \frac{1}{T}\sum_{t=1}^T \epsilon_i^l(t, V_{lb}) , \tag{4}$$

where r_i^l is the average output spike rate during T. It may seem that the neuron tends to exhibit abnormally higher firing rates due to the presence of the error

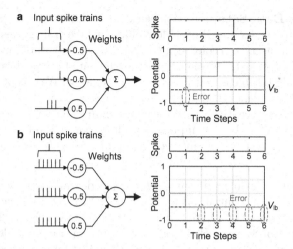

Fig. 2. Two handcrafted examples demonstrate the errors in the membrane potential and their impact on the output spike.

term in comparison to the case where no lower bound is imposed [14]. However, this is not necessarily the case. To explain that, we handcraft two examples under non-monotonic and monotonic input potentials.

Example 1 (Non-monotonic potential). As shown in Fig. 2a, the membrane potential descends to the lower bound V_{lb} at $t = 1$, resulting in an error of $\epsilon = 0.5$. During the subsequent period, the membrane potential ascends to positive, and the error term causes the membrane potential to reach the threshold at $t = 4$, resulting in one unanticipated spike.

Example 2 (Monotonic potential). As shown in Fig. 2b, the membrane potential descends to the lower bound five times at $t = 2, 3, 4, 5$ and 6 during the inference, resulting in a greater cumulative error of $\epsilon = -2.5$ than in Ex. 1. Nevertheless, unlike in Ex. 1, the error does not lead to any unanticipated spike.

Both examples satisfy Eq. 4 and present errors. However, we find that the occurrence of the unanticipated spike actually depends more on the short-term behavior of the membrane potential. In the ideal scenario, for monotonically decreasing membrane potential, errors will accumulate continuously, but no spike will be generated as long as it does not return to the positive value. And for a spiking neural network, as long as the neurons do not release unanticipated spikes, errors in membrane potential will remain localized and not propagate to affect inference capability, regardless of their magnitude.

3.2 Underlying Cause of Accuracy Degradation

The discrepancy between the theory and the conclusions drawn by prior work [14] prompted us to conduct experiments to investigate what exactly happens within the deep SNNs when the negative membrane potential is constrained.

Network and Data Setup. In this work, we conduct all experiments using a custom simulator under the TensorFlow platform. We train a ResNet-20 [15] on the CIFAR-10 datasets and convert it to SNN using the method introduced in [3]. This network is deeper than other SNNs implemented on hardware to date [10, 12,13] and should be able to reflect deep SNN scenarios. We do not use additional techniques such as membrane potential pre-charging [5], as they can also increase hardware overhead, even though they may enhance the inference capability at low time steps. As for the test inputs, we follow the method described in [2] to convert CIFAR-10 test images into corresponding poisson spike trains.

Results. We do confirm significant performance degradation when constraining negative membrane potential. As shown in Fig. 3, in the absence of the lower bound on the membrane potential, the converted spiking ResNet-20 achieves the highest accuracy of 87.80%. However, after applying a uniform lower bound to all neurons' membrane potential, we observe a reduction in both short-term and peak inference accuracies as the lower bound increased. For our configuration, we recommend $V_{lb} = -16$ as the safe lower bound considering a certain margin, below which there would be no significant accuracy degradation. This value is more conservative than the one reported in [14], possibly because we employ a network that is twice as deep.

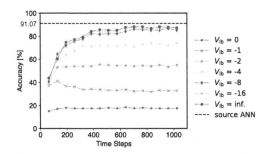

Fig. 3. Influence of membrane potential's lower bound on the SNN inference accuracy on CIFAR-10 dataset.

To pinpoint error occurrences, we directly observe the membrane potential variations during inference. We randomly pick 100 neurons from the first hidden layer and present the behavior of their membrane potentials in Fig. 4a. As expected, in the absence of a lower bound, the negative membrane potentials accumulated during inference.

However, upon closer inspection, we find that negative membrane potentials do not monotonically decrease but exhibit positive fluctuations (Fig. 4b) like the case demonstrated in the handcraft Ex. 1. This phenomenon is attributed to the discrete and unstable nature of poisson spike trains. If only synapses with positive weights receive spikes at specific time steps, the total input potential

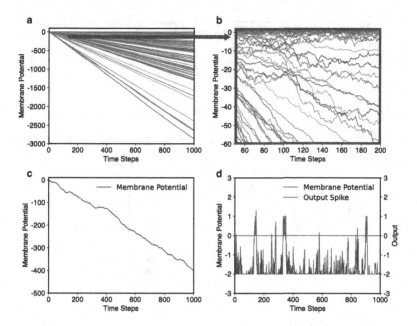

Fig. 4. a,b. Variations in neurons' membrane potentials during inference at the global and local scales. **c,d**. An example to demonstrate that neurons with fluctuating negative membrane potentials can generate unanticipated spikes when $V_{lb} = -2$ is imposed.

can be positive in the short term. When we set a lower bound of V_{lb}, any positive fluctuations greater than $(V_{thr} - V_{lb})$ could cause unanticipated spike firing by exceeding the threshold. Figure 4c,d provide an example where a neuron is not supposed to release backward spikes in the absence of the lower bound. However, with a lower bound of $V_{lb} = -2$, the membrane potential surpasses the threshold and leads to unanticipated firing multiple times, which hurts accurate SNN inference.

Referring to our handcraft examples, we regard such fluctuations in membrane potential resulting from the instability in the poisson spike trains as a major factor that contributes to the degradation of inference accuracy when constraining negative membrane potential.

3.3 Guideline and Validation

Based on the theory and the observations, we establish the following practical guideline for constraining negative membrane potential in deep SNNs.

Guideline: If the non-monotonic fluctuations in the membrane potential can be eliminated, it will be possible to constrain or even disable negative membrane potential without negatively affecting SNN inference accuracy.

We design a demonstration experiment to validate the guideline. To reduce the fluctuations in the membrane potential, we aim to ensure that all synapses

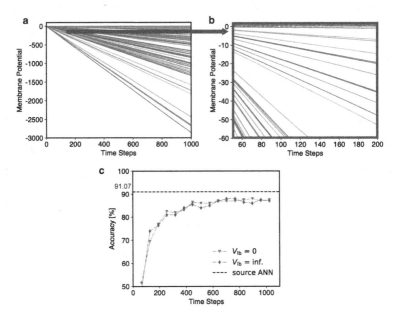

Fig. 5. Results of the demonstration experiment. **a,b.** Negative membrane potentials with no constraint are perfectly linear during the inference. **c.** No change in the inference accuracy beyond the error level, even when negative membrane potential is entirely disabled.

of neurons receive an input spike equally at each time step, thereby eliminating instability. To achieve this, we add buffers to all synapses, count the incoming spikes during inference and then pass the average spike counts to the neuron, as described in the following equation:

$$\delta_i^l(t) = r_i^l(T) = \frac{1}{T} \sum_{t=1}^{T} \Theta_i^l(t) \ , \tag{5}$$

where $\delta_i^l \in [0,1]$ represents a fractional spike whose value equals the average input spike count. It replaces the original binary spike and is sent to the neuron at each time step. Thereby, the total input potential remains the same as the original. The network needs to be computed layer by layer to accommodate this change, while the rest of the network configurations are kept the same as before.

In this case, as illustrated in Fig. 5a,b, even the slightest fluctuations in the negative membrane potentials are eliminated in the absence of a lower bound. On this basis, we set $V_{\text{lb}} = 0$ and find that even under this extreme condition, the performance is fully maintained at every time step (Fig. 5c), demonstrating that the negative membrane potentials can indeed be constrained in a lossless manner, as per our guideline. While we have only tested the case of ResNet-20 architecture, we anticipate that it will also be applicable to even deeper networks.

4   Hardware-Friendly Method

The above demo proves the effectiveness of the proposed guideline. However, it requires Multiply-and-Accumulate (MAC) operations to support fractional spikes, which can significantly compromise hardware efficiency. In this section, we present an alternative practical method that employs the least possible amount of additional hardware with the same effectiveness.

4.1   Packed Spike Format

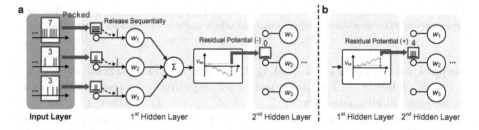

Fig. 6. Schematic diagram illustrating the proposed hardware-friendly method.

The proposed method is based on a novel packed spike format. As Fig. 6 illustrates, the process starts at the input layer, where input spike trains are accumulated over a period and then packed. The spike packets (blue boxes in Fig. 6) replace the spike trains that propagate backward. Synapses of the neuron in the next layer receive the spike packets and process them by extracting one spike per time step in the following period. Meanwhile, the membrane potential updater, which functions as the neuron's axon, accumulates the input potential. Only at the end of the period, depending on whether the residual membrane potential is positive (Fig. 6b) or negative (Fig. 6a), the neuron releases a spike packet of the corresponding value, or zero spike packet, to the next layer. This process is repeated for each subsequent layer.

This method is expected to be similarly effective to the demo, as it also conveys the statistics of spikes rather than discrete and unstable spike trains; thus, transient outliers in membrane potential will not affect results. The effectiveness of the proposed method is anticipated to be affected by the depth of spike packets. Meanwhile, while this method requires additional memory for spike packets, it is unnecessary to make significant modifications to the core of neurons since they still receive binary spike inputs and therefore require no multiplier.

4.2   Results

This section evaluates the effectiveness and efficiency of the proposed method. We use the same network configuration as before, except that additional input and inter-layer buffers are added to handle the spike packets.

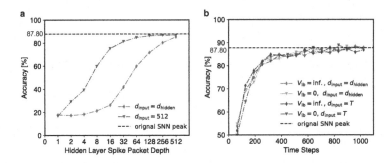

Fig. 7. **a.** Influence of the spike packet depth on inference accuracy when negative membrane potential is disabled. **b.** Effect of the proposed practical method. For both schemes the accuracies are well maintained when negative potential is disabled.

Impact on Accuracy. Regarding the depth of spike packets, we test two schemes: **Scheme 1.** The input layer uses the same spike packet depth as all subsequent hidden layers, with $d_{\text{input}} = d_{\text{hidden}} = T/k$, where T is the total inference duration. **Scheme 2.** Hidden layers use the same spike packet depth $d_{\text{hidden}} = T/k$ as in scheme 1, while the input layer uses deeper spike packets with $d_{\text{input}} = T$ in order to reinforce the effect of smoothing. To accommodate this change, neurons in the first hidden layer extract only $1/k$ of the spikes from the input spike packets each time during inference.

Figure 7a presents the impact of packet depth on accuracy for both schemes. We set the total inference duration $T = 512$, at which the original SNN is near saturation in terms of accuracy. We also set the $V_{\text{lb}} = 0$. In both schemes, the accuracies are fully maintained at $d_{\text{hidden}} = 512$ and experience degradation as d_{hidden} decreases. However, the degradation is slower in scheme 2, where the accuracy is well maintained even at $d_{\text{hidden}} = 128 = T/4$, showing that the enhancement on the input layer benefits all subsequent layers. In contrast, scheme 1 only achieves lossless performance when d_{hidden} equals the full duration.

Figure 7b further demonstrates the effectiveness of the proposed method at various inference durations. We employ $d_{\text{hidden}} = T$ and $d_{\text{hidden}} = T/4$ for schemes 1 and 2, respectively, to maximize performance. With these settings, both schemes achieve optimal performance across all inference durations, even at $V_{\text{lb}} = 0$, which allows the complete disabling of negative membrane potential in deep SNN hardware.

Impact on Storage Overhead. In this work, we assume an 8-bit quantization for the weights. At the same time, with the proposed method, we are able to substantially constrain the membrane potential to a range of $[0, 1]$. Consequently, we can perform a 7-bit quantization for the membrane potential, even lower than that of the weights.

We demonstrate a substantial reduction in the required memory for membrane potential by 41.67% for both schemes (Table 1). We anticipate that the

Table 1. Impact of the proposed practical method on the storage overhead for spiking ResNet-20 on the CIFAR-10 dataset.

Method	MP Range	Memory Usage [kB]		
		MP Memory	Spike Buffer	Total
Directly constraining	[−16, 1]	430.19	3.82	434.01
Scheme 1 (512/512)*	[0, 1]	250.95 (−179.24[†])	34.42 (+30.60[†])	285.37 (−148.64[†])
Scheme 2 (512/128)*	[0, 1]	250.95 (−179.24[†])	30.05 (+26.23[†])	281.00 (−153.01[†])

MP: membrane potential.
*: spike packet depths in the input layer and hidden layers ($d_{\text{input}}/d_{\text{hidden}}$).
[†]: difference compared to the baseline method with directly constraining.

proposed method will yield even more significant storage overhead reduction for deeper SNNs in the future as the safe V_{lb} further decreases.

Buffers for spike packets require additional memory, while, unlike membrane potential, by leveraging the convolutional topology, only a few rows of spike packets need to be retained for each channel and layer simultaneously [11] (except for the input layer in scheme 2, where all spikes within the packets cannot be extracted at once). As a result, only a small amount of additional memory for spike packets is needed, especially in scheme 2, making it the more efficient option. Furthermore, in hardware implementations, smaller spike packets can be allocated to higher-level memory with lower access power, while extensive membrane potential requires lower-level memory. Therefore, the proposed method may have a more far-reaching impact on energy efficiency.

5 Conclusion

We propose a guideline for constraining negative membrane potential in deep SNNs without sacrificing accuracy. The key insight is that the instability of spike trains, which is eliminable, mainly contributes to the accuracy degradation. On top of that, we develop a practical method for implementing this guideline which uses a novel packed spike format and requires minimal modifications to existing SNN hardware. We demonstrate the effectiveness of our method on the ResNet-20, achieving significant memory usage reduction through reduced-precision quantization of the membrane potential. Overall, our work lays the ground for future efficient hardware implementation of even deeper SNNs, which can facilitate high-performance outcomes across a wider range of applications.

References

1. Javanshir, A., Nguyen, T.T., Mahmud, M.A.P., Kouzani, A.Z.: Advancements in algorithms and neuromorphic hardware for spiking neural networks. Neural Comput. **34**, 1289–1328 (2022). https://doi.org/10.1162/neco_a_01499
2. Cao, Y., Chen, Y., Khosla, D.: Spiking deep convolutional neural networks for energy-efficient object recognition. Int. J. Comput. Vision **113**(1), 54–66 (2014). https://doi.org/10.1007/s11263-014-0788-3

3. Rueckauer, B., Lungu, I.-A., Hu, Y., Pfeiffer, M., Liu, S.-C.: Conversion of Continuous-Valued Deep Networks to Efficient Event-Driven Networks for Image Classification. Front. Neurosci. **11**, (2017). https://doi.org/10.3389/fnins.2017.00682

4. Hu, Y., Tang, H., Pan, G.: Spiking Deep Residual Networks. IEEE Trans. Neural Netw. Learn. Syst. 1–6, Early Access (2021). https://doi.org/10.1109/TNNLS.2021.3119238

5. Hwang, S., et al.: Low-Latency spiking neural networks using pre-charged membrane potential and delayed evaluation. Front. Neurosci. **15** (2021). https://doi.org/10.3389/fnins.2021.629000

6. Wang, Z., Lian, S., Zhang, Y., Cui, X., Yan, R., Tang, H.: Towards lossless ANNSNN conversion under ultra-low latency with dual-phase optimization, arXiv preprint arXiv:2205.07473 (2022)

7. Kang, Z., Wang, L., Guo, S., Gong, R., Deng, Y., Dou, Q.: ASIE: an asynchronous SNN inference engine for AER events processing. In: 2019 25th IEEE International Symposium on Asynchronous Circuits and Systems (ASYNC), pp. 48–57 (2019). https://doi.org/10.1109/ASYNC.2019.00015

8. Zhang, J., Wu, H., Wei, J., Wei, S., Chen, H.: An asynchronous reconfigurable SNN accelerator with event-driven time step update. In: 2019 IEEE Asian Solid-State Circuits Conference (A-SSCC), pp. 213–216 (2019). https://doi.org/10.1109/A-SSCC47793.2019.9056903

9. Ju, X., Fang, B., Yan, R., Xu, X., Tang, H.: An FPGA implementation of deep spiking neural networks for low-power and fast classification. Neural Comput. **32**, 182–204 (2020). https://doi.org/10.1162/neco_a_01245

10. Wang, S.-Q., Wang, L., Deng, Yu., Yang, Z.-J., Guo, S.-S., Kang, Z.-Y., Guo, Y.-F., Xu, W.-X.: SIES: a novel implementation of spiking convolutional neural network inference engine on field-programmable Gate Array. J. Comput. Sci. Technol. **35**(2), 475–489 (2020). https://doi.org/10.1007/s11390-020-9686-z

11. Zhang, L., et al.: A cost-efficient high-speed VLSI architecture for spiking convolutional neural network inference using time-step binary spike maps. Sensors (Basel). **21**, 6006 (2021). https://doi.org/10.3390/s21186006

12. Aung, M.T.L., Qu, C., Yang, L., Luo, T., Goh, R.S.M., Wong, W.-F.: DeepFire: acceleration of convolutional spiking neural network on modern field programmable gate arrays. In: 2021 31st International Conference on Field-Programmable Logic and Applications (FPL), pp. 28–32. IEEE, Dresden, Germany (2021). https://doi.org/10.1109/FPL53798.2021.00013

13. Nallathambi, A., Chandrachoodan, N.: Probabilistic spike propagation for FPGA implementation of spiking neural networks, arXiv preprint arXiv:2001.09725 (2020)

14. Hwang, S., Chang, J., Oh, M.-H., Lee, J.-H., Park, B.-G.: Impact of the sub-resting membrane potential on accurate inference in spiking neural networks. Sci. Rep. **10**, 3515 (2020). https://doi.org/10.1038/s41598-020-60572-8

15. He, K., Zhang, X., Ren, S., Sun, J.: Deep residual learning for image recognition. In: 2016 IEEE Conference on Computer Vision and Pattern Recognition (CVPR), pp. 770–778. IEEE, Las Vegas, NV, USA (2016). https://doi.org/10.1109/CVPR.2016.90

Matching Patterns of Temporal Neural Activity Using the Victor-Purpura Distance in Real-Time

Alberto Ayala$^{(\boxtimes)}$, Angel Lareo⬡, Pablo Varona⬡,
and Francisco B. Rodriguez⬡

Grupo de Neurocomputación Biológica, Departamento de Ingeniería Informática,
Escuela Politécnica Superior, Universidad Autónoma de Madrid, Madrid, Spain
`alberto.ayala@estudiante.uam.es`, {`pablo.varona,f.rodriguez`}`@uam.es`

Abstract. Many neural systems encode information by generating specific sequences of action potentials forming temporal activity patterns (codes). These systems emit functionally equivalent activity patterns with a certain variability in their temporal structure. In this work, we have implemented in real-time a closed-loop stimulation protocol for the study of temporal coding in neural systems. The stimulation was triggered by matching a target code and a code obtained from the system's activity using the Victor-Purpura distance. This protocol has been developed for the Real-Time eXperiment Interface tool. Latencies during closed-loop experiments were within strict real-time temporal constraints, thus validating the use of the protocol to study information processing in activity-dependent stimulation experiments. In addition, its functionality has been validated through a proof of concept in which we have conditioned the activity of the Hindmarsh-Rose neural model to evoke a different dynamic activity state. With this protocol, equivalence between different matching patterns can be inferred when closed-loop stimulation driven by them leads to equivalent responses. Results show that the dynamic state evoked by closed-loop stimulation is difficult to generate under open-loop stimulation (i.e, without precise activity-dependent stimulation of the system).

Keywords: Closed-loop stimulation · temporal coding · clustering · pattern matching · Hindmarsh-Rose neural model · temporal patterns of neural activity (codes)

1 Introduction

How neural systems use action potentials (or spikes) to process and transfer information is one of the main questions in neuroscience. There are several coding schemes that attempt to understand how neural systems process information. Temporal coding, the scheme this work is focused in, asserts that the precise time in the generation of spikes or inter-spike times contains relevant information in the coding process of neural systems [12].

© IFIP International Federation for Information Processing 2023
Published by Springer Nature Switzerland AG 2023
I. Maglogiannis et al. (Eds.): AIAI 2023, IFIP AICT 676, pp. 541–553, 2023.
https://doi.org/10.1007/978-3-031-34107-6_43

In neural systems, sensory-motor feedback loops are widespread. In this regard, closed-loop experimental designs are particularly suitable for studying temporal coding information processing [5]. In addition, these systems generate specific time sequences of spikes directly related with a particular function, i.e., they produce functionally equivalent neural patterns. These sequences are generated with a certain variability in their temporal structure, that is, inter-spike intervals can vary up to a certain level and still preserve its functional meaning [4,11]. This paper presents a closed-loop stimulation protocol that enables the study of temporal coding in neuronal systems considering the variability with which they encode information. It detects a possible state of the dynamical system (given by a determinate neural code), and stimulates it, allowing to analyze whether the system responses are similar, i.e. it is able to establish whether the detected neural codes are likely equivalent due to the similar responses of the dynamical system. The implemented protocol is based on the Temporal Code-Driven Stimulation (TCDS) algorithm, which acquires a neural signal, binarizes it, and stimulates the system when a specific neural code is detected [2,9,10]. To consider the intrinsic variability of information coding in neural systems a flexible code detection metric, based on the Victor-Purpura distance [16] has been implemented in real-time to expand and complement the functionality of the TCDS protocol. Neural systems usually produce spikes within or below the millisecond scale and the precise time at which they are stimulated can vary their dynamic state. Therefore, closed-loop tasks must be performed within the required precision constraints. To comply with these temporal constraints the protocol was implemented using the Real-Time eXperiment Interface (RTXI) framework [13], a software application specifically designed for real-time software development in biology and neuroscience research. The protocol performance has been analyzed by measuring latencies in real-time closed-loop experiments. Latency results in Sect. 3.1 show that this protocol complies with the strict temporal constraints for the study of temporal coding in neural systems.

In addition, a proof of concept has been designed. The implemented protocol is used to condition the activity of the Hindmarsh-Rose (HR) neuronal model [7], which is frequently used in theoretical neuroscience as well as in the implementation between hybrid circuits of living and model neurons [1,14,15]. When the protocol detects a certain dynamic state in the HR activity, it stimulates the system to generate a specific response (as described in Sect. 2.4). This proof of concept revealed that it is only possible to robustly condition the activity of the model using closed-loop stimulation. This is due to the fact that the protocol considers the variability of the temporal structure of equivalent patterns, and accurately stimulates the system producing responses with equivalent temporal characteristics and variability (as characterized by the Victor-Purpura distance) to identify them.

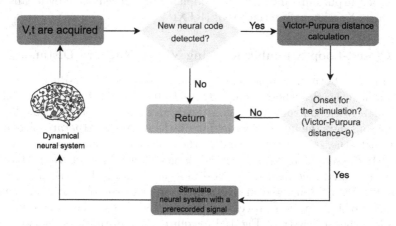

Fig. 1. Flowchart representing the real-time tasks of the implemented protocol. The protocol acquires the signal emitted by the neural system and digitizes it in binary manner forming neural codes. For each detected code, it calculates the Victor-Purpura distance to the target code. If the distance value is below a threshold the protocol matches the pattern and stimulates the system. All these tasks are executed each nominal period established by the real-time system.

2   Methods

2.1   Temporal Code-Driven Stimulation Protocol

As mentioned in the Introduction (Sect. 1) Temporal Code-Driven Stimulation (TCDS) is the base of the new implemented protocol [2,9,10]. In TCDS the neural signal is acquired in real-time and is divided into time windows whose value depends on whether or not an action potential above a certain threshold is detected, the value of the window is 1 if a spike is detected, otherwise 0. The time duration of these windows is called bin time and the values attributed to these time windows are called bits. As we mentioned above, a specific temporal sequence of these binary events is what we call code. When a code identical to the target code is identified, stimulation is delivered to the system. Bin time selection in the original work defining TCDS is guided by a maximum entropy criterion [9]. However, the bin time selected by this criterion may be excessively large, resulting in a possible loss of information (for example two spikes that occur in the same time window). As discussed in [8], to deal with this problem it is possible to decrease the bin time and increase the code size. However, a new problem arises: as the number of bits increases, the probability of exactly finding the target code decreases exponentially. To overcome this problem, we present a solution based on spike train distance metrics. More precisely, the Victor-Purpura distance, which is implemented in real-time by means of the Real-Time eXperiment Interface tool (RTXI[1]).

2.2 Closed-Loop Stimulation Using Victor-Purpura Distance

As mentioned above, the implemented protocol uses the Victor-Purpura distance to detect neural codes whose temporal structure is similar to the target code and to stimulate with controlled precision the dynamic system in real-time [3]. This protocol considers the intrinsic variability in the temporal structure of sequential activity patterns. It does not depend on the bin time that maximizes the entropy like TCDS does, and effectively matches larger sequences of neural activity that can be functionally equivalent. In addition, as mentioned in the introduction, this protocol is implemented in real-time in order to comply with the temporal constraints of information processing in neural systems. The functionality can be seen in the flowchart of Fig. 1. It acquires in real-time the signal emitted by the analyzed system, binarizes it and calculates the Victor-Purpura distance between the detected codes and the target code. The Victor-Purpura distance [16] compares the temporal synchronization between trains of action potentials. Thus, it is useful to compare the similarity between the temporal structure of neural codes. As a definition, the Victor-Purpura distance is the minimum cost of transforming one train of action potentials into another (see Eq. 1) by the following elementary steps: i) adding a single spike (cost 1), ii) deleting a single spike (cost 1), and iii) shift a single spike in the time of occurrence (cost $q * |\Delta t|$ where q is the relative sensitivity of the metric to precise timing of spikes):

$$D\left(C_a, C_b\right) = \min\left[K\left(C_a, C_1\right) + K\left(C_1, C_2\right) \ldots + K\left(C_{n-1}, C_b\right)\right]. \tag{1}$$

$D\left(C_a, C_b\right)$ is the Victor-Purpura distance between two neural codes, C_a is a detected code, C_b is the target code, and C_i are the intermediate codes generated by the elementary steps to turn C_a into C_b whose cost is $K\left(C_{i-1}, C_i\right)$. If the Victor-Purpura distance calculated by the implemented protocol is below the *limit*, it stimulates the system, closing the loop.

An example of use of the implemented protocol is shown in Fig. 2. First, the values of the parameters were selected offline: the bin time is set as the maximum value for which there is no missing information (it is not possible that two spikes occur in the same time window). Also, the metric parameters (q and *limit*) are selected based on the flexibility with which equivalent patterns are matched: the stricter the metric the more similar the temporal structure of the patterns (target code versus found code). The "Online" box shows the execution of real-time tasks that are performed in real-time. The example shows the calculation of the Victor-Purpura distance between a detected code ('11101010001') and the searched one ('11010100001'), the minimum cost of transforming the detected one into the target code consists of performing two bit shifts in time and removing a spike from the train, if the value of the distance is below the *limit* then the protocol will stimulate the system.

---

[1] Real-Time eXperiment Interface tool, RTXI, (http://rtxi.org/).

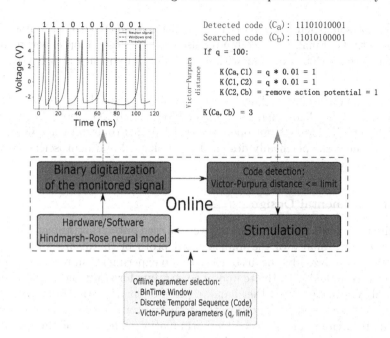

Fig. 2. Schematic of the implemented protocol. Starting from below, the parameters are selected offline. The "Online" box at the center shows the execution sequence of each real-time task. Finally, the top side of the figure shows an example of Victor-Purpura distance calculation. To calculate the distance between the detected code (C_a) '11101010001' and the target code (C_b) '11010100001' the protocol transform one into the other by two 1 bit shifts ($K(C_a, C_1)$ and $K(C_1, C_2)$) and removing 1 bit from the detected code ($K(C_2, C_b)$), as the shifts are of one bin time size (10 ms) the distance between the codes is 3 (with q = 100), if this value is below the *limit* stimulation is delivered in real-time.

2.3 Hardware-Software Architecture

Hardware Architecture. This section describes the hardware architecture of the implemented protocol that is involved in the acquisition and transmission of data in real-time. For this reason, it has been tested that, in conjunction with the software architecture, it complies with the temporal constraints explained in the Introduction (Sect. 1) through the measurement of latencies in closed-loop stimulation experiments (Sect. 2.4 and Sect. 3.1). The neural system signal is acquired in real-time through a data acquisition card (DAQ), which digitizes the signal and sends it to the software architecture using an input channel. The signal is processed and when the protocol decides, it sends a stimulus to the neural system through an output channel of the DAQ, establishing a bidirectional communication with the system (see the flowchart in Fig. 2).

In the real-time performance analysis the activity of an electronic neuron was processed. This hardware device is an electronic neuron that implements the Hindmarsh-Rose neural model [2,3,7] which is capable of reproducing the behavior of some neural systems in a realistic manner, such as bursting and spiking activity. Finally, the computer used in the closed-loop experiments has an Intel Core i7-6700 processor with 4 cores and a frequency of 3.46 GHz.

Software Architecture. The software development of the protocol[2] has been carried out in the Real-Time eXperiment Interface (RTXI) tool [13] (developed in the RTOS Xenomai[3]), an open-source hard real-time data acquisition and control framework specifically designed for biological and neuroscience research widely used by many laboratories.

2.4   Experimental Design

Two different closed-loop experiments were carried out in this project. On the one hand, the performance of the implemented protocol (hardware-software architecture) was analyzed by means of closed-loop experiments in real-time to verify whether it complied with the temporal constraints for studying temporal coding in neural systems. On the other hand, a proof of concept was designed in which the protocol was used to condition the activity of a neuronal model to evoke a different behaviour under closed-loop stimulation. The aim of this proof is to validate its use to study equivalence of variable patterns of temporal activity.

Real-Time Performance Analysis. As mentioned, neural systems encode information on the millisecond time scale, in addition the timing of stimulation must be precise. To verify that the hardware-software architecture complies with these temporal constraints several closed-loop experiments have been performed in which the latency values of the real-time tasks have been measured.

Latency is the difference between the time when a real-time task should start and the time when the real-time task actually starts. The left side of Fig. 3 shows an example of the latency calculation performed in this experiment. The instantaneous latency (L_{ins}) is calculated as the absolute value of the subtraction between the time at which the current task starts (t_i), the time at which the previous task started (t_{i-1}) and the nominal period of the system (T_{nom}). In this figure the red arrows indicate an example of the actual time of execution of two successive real-time tasks while the black arrows represent the ideal time at which they should have started. The latency values were calculated as the absolute value of the subtraction because real-time tasks can run before a nominal period after the start of the previous task execution (configured by Xenomai to reduce latency jitter), resulting in negative instantaneous latencies. An example of a negative instantaneous latency is shown on the left side of Fig. 3.

---

[2] The implementation is available in the following repository https://github.com/AlbertoAyalaV/Temporal-Code-Driven-Stimulation-and-Vcitor-Purpura-distance-protocol.

[3] Real-Time Development Software Framework Xenomai (www.xenomai.org).

In this closed-loop experiment the activity of the Hindmarsh-Rose [2,7] electronic neuron was processed in real-time. When the implemented protocol detects a burst activity it stimulates the neuron with a sine signal. The detected code was '00111101', the bin time was 10 ms, the Victor-Pupura parameters were establish to robustly detect the bursting activity (limit = 1, q = 50), the sine signal was 120 ms with 2 V of amplitude and the duration of closed-loop experiments were 120 s. For this configuration, two closed-loop experiments were carried for nominal frequencies (rate of real-time task executions per second) of 10 kHz and 20 kHz that are enough to precisely detect the events in which the information is encoded in neural systems (spikes are generated below milliseconds). Finally, the electronic neuron was configured to produce a regular bursting activity, that is, the distribution of inter-spike intervals (ISIs) and inter-burst intervals (IBIs) was regular.

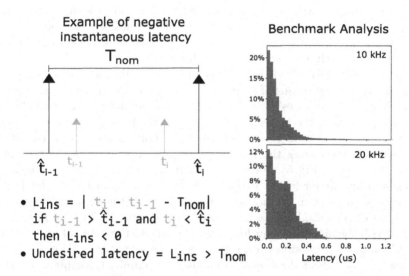

Fig. 3. Results obtained in the performance analysis. Left side shows a scheme of the instantaneous latency calculation. Right side shows the distribution of latency values obtained for a nominal frequency of 10 kHz and 20 kHz. In both cases, the average latency is under the millisecond scale, and no undesired latencies are obtained.

Conditioning Hindmarsh-Rose Neural Model Activity to Evoke Brief Bursts of Spikes. In closed-loop experiments the Hindmarsh-Rose neural model was stimulated by the implemented protocol to generate a new dynamic state in its activity. The aim of these experiments was to test the implemented protocol to detect likely functional equivalent patterns in the activity of a neural system, obtain information about the system's internal state, and evoke a different kind of behavior (a short burst of spikes) not originally showed. The parameters of the model were establish to produce a regular bursting state $(r = 0.0021, a = 1, b = 3, c = 1, d = 5, s = 4, x_1 = -8/5$, as in [7] and external

Intensity $= 1.9$) as well as in the real-time performance analysis (regular distribution of ISIs and IBIs). To simulate the intrinsic variability of temporal activity in neural systems information processing (as mentioned in Sect. 1), Gaussian noise was provided to the model input to reproduce this behaviour. In this way the system generates equivalent neural codes (bursting state) with different temporal structures (variability in the structure of ISIs). Closed-loop stimulation was triggered by robustly detecting the bursting activity of the HR model (considering its variability, as is shown in Fig. 4) and conditioning its activity to a brief bursts of spikes between bursting states. The selected stimulus was a ramp signal. A previous analysis to select the optimal stimulus parameters was performed, that is, those parameters for which the stimulus can produce brief bursts of spikes without synchronizing the activity of the neuronal model.

In addition, the stimulus signal of the closed-loop experiments was recorded, and open-loop experiments were performed by stimulating with the same signal, that is, the system was stimulated without considering the previous activity to the stimulus. The neural activity response between both methodologies was compared. It was hypothesized that it was only possible to generate brief bursts of spikes consistently in closed-loop experiments.

The state of neural activity of the dynamic system during stimulation process was characterized by means of recurrence plots [6] in closed-loop and open-loop methodologies. 18 features[4], like recurrence rate, laminarity, determinism, etc., were extracted from the activity recurrences. With these features we can automatically evaluate the differences between the original state and the conditioned state, without visualizing the HR activities generated in both dynamic states (as can be seen in Fig. 5). Please note that this quantification of recurrence plots is appropriate for future analysis with biological signals when the dynamic equations of the system are not available. Following, the Principal Component Analysis (PCA) methodology was applied to these features. The 3 principal components with the highest eigenvalue were selected and the data obtained from the closed-loop and open-loop experiments were represented in a 3D chart forming two clusters. The selected principal components maximize the explained variance of the original data (Fig. 6). Lastly, the silhouette coefficient was calculated to represent the distance between these clusters.

Finally, the hardware-software architecture was implemented in a non-real-time software system to facilitate the automation of these experiments. This implementation was used for the results in Sect. 3.2.

3   Results

3.1   Real-Time Performance Analysis

The results of the performance analysis of the implemented protocol shows that the average latency for both nominal frequencies was below milliseconds, which is necessary to accurately detect the occurrence of spikes in neural systems activity.

---

[4] Recurrence plot at a glance: http://www.recurrence-plot.tk/rqa.php.

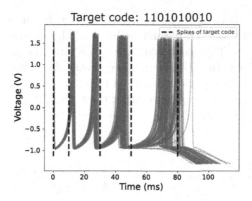

Fig. 4. Patterns matched as temporally equivalent by the protocol previous to the system stimulation in the closed-loop experiment of the proof of concept. The dashed lines show the time occurrence of the spikes in the target code. As in neural systems, there is variability in the temporal structure of the neural codes that represent the bursting state in the activity of the Hindmarsh-Rose model.

Figure 3 shows the instantaneous latency value distribution for nominal frequencies of 10 kHz and 20 kHz.

In order to establish the nominal frequency above which the use of the protocol was not feasible the term undesired latency was defined. An undesired latency is an instantaneous latency value that exceeds the nominal period of the system. When an undesired latency is obtained it is considered a critical system failure and the implemented protocol would not comply with the temporal constraints. No undesired latencies have been obtained for the two nominal frequencies, that is the protocol can be used in closed-loop studies with a nominal frequency up to 20 kHz which is enough to enable the study of information processing in neural systems. Based on the latency results, we conclude that the real-time closed-loop stimulation protocol complies with the strict temporal constraints. However, an analysis of latencies as a function of the neural code size is needed to study in more detail the performance of it in real-time closed-loop stimulation.

3.2   Analyzing Brief Bursts of Spikes Evoked by the Close-Loop Stimulation Protocol

Figure 5 shows an example of the performed closed-loop and open-loop experiments. Under closed-loop stimulation, the brief bursts of spikes are consistently generated in the Hindmarsh-Rose model activity. However, in open-loop this rarely happens. As shown in Fig. 5, in open-loop there is no control of the previous activity to the stimulation (the stimulation timing is not precise resulting in extending the bursting state in most of the stimulations). This result shows that it is essential to control the previous activity to the stimulation process as well as to consider the temporal variability of the bursting state in the neuronal model activity. This is shown in Fig. 4 where the patterns matched as functionally equivalent by the implemented protocol in closed-loop experiments have been plotted. These patterns represent the bursting state of the HR neural model activity, and it can be observed that the temporal structure of ISIs varies.

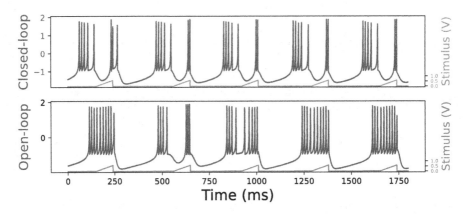

Fig. 5. Example of the Hindmarsh-Rose model activity in the performed proof of concept. The top side shows its activity in the closed-loop experiments and the stimulus signal sent to the model. The bottom side shows its activity in the open-loop experiments and the stimulus signal delivered. It is possible to consistently generate brief bursts of spikes only in the closed-loop experiment.

Finally, Fig. 6 shows the selected principal components of the open-loop and closed-loop experiments. These components represent the original data with an explained variance of 93%. Data from closed-loop experiments (blue dots in Fig. 6) are clustered in the chart while data from open-loop experiments (yellow dots in Fig. 6) are scattered. This indicates that in closed-loop sessions the brief bursts of spikes are consistently evoked in the neural model activity while in open-loop it rarely occurs. This figure shows in a global manner the results represented in the Fig. 5. In addition, the value of the silhouette coefficient is 0.31 which indicates that the two methodologies generate different neural activities under stimulation.

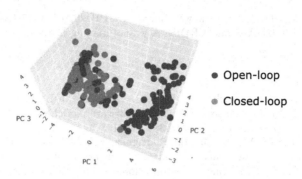

Fig. 6. Plot of the first 3 components after PCA application to the extracted features of the Hindmarsh-Rose model signal when it is stimulated in closed-loop and open-loop experiments. Figure shows that the closed-loop data are clustered while the open-loop data are spread out. Closed-loop conditions the activity of the model by consistently generating the brief busrts of spikes, however, this kind of activity is rarely generated in open-loop.

4   Conclusions

The real-time performance analysis showed that the average of latency values did not exceed milliseconds and no undesired latencies were obtained. Thus, the use of the implemented protocol is viable for frequencies up to 20kHz in closed-loop experiments. Therefore, it complies with the strict temporal constraints to study temporal coding in neural systems. In addition, we consider that it is also needed to analyze the real-time performance of the protocol as a function of the code size. As the neural patterns size increase (the number of spikes contained in each pattern could increase), the computational complexity of Victor-Purpura calculation increases, so the protocol carries out more comparisons, thus affecting to the real-time performance. The clustering analysis of the Hindmarsh-Rose model activity comparing results under open-loop and closed-loop stimulation showed that it was only possible to robustly evoke brief bursts of spikes between standard bursting states in closed-loop experiments compared to open-loop. This result showed that the dynamic activity state conditioned by closed-loop stimulation was difficult to generate if the protocol did not consider to apply pattern matching and precise stimulation to the dynamic system. Based on overall results we conclude that the implemented protocol is able to study temporal coding in neural systems by means of likely functionally equivalent pattern matching and closed-loop stimulation. The protocol enables the detection of possible dynamic states of neural systems whether closed-loop stimulation leads its activity to similar responses.

Acknowledgements. This work was funded by PID2020-114867RB-I00, PID2021-122347NB-I00 (MCIN/AEI and ERDF- "A way of making Europe").

References

1. Amaducci, R., Reyes-Sanchez, M., Elices, I., Rodriguez, F.B., Varona, P.: Rthybrid: a standardized and open-source real-time software model library for experimental neuroscience. Front. Neuroinform. **13**, 11 (2019)
2. Ayala, A., Lareo, A., Varona, P., Rodriguez, F.B.: Closed-loop temporal code-driven stimulation implemented and tested using real-time experimental interface (RTXI). In: 30th Annual Computational Neuroscience Meeting: CNS*2021-Meeting Abstracts. P153. J. Comput. Neurosci. **49**, 3–208 (2021). https://doi.org/10.1007/s10827-021-00801-9
3. Ayala, A., Lareo, A., Varona, P., Rodriguez, F.B.: Closed-loop stimulation protocol driven by flexible neural codes based on victor-purpura distance. In: 31th Annual Computational Neuroscience Meeting: CNS*2022-Meeting Abstracts. (P92). J. Comput. Neurosci. **51**, 3–101 (2022). https://doi.org/10.1007/s10827-022-00841-9
4. Carlson, B.A., Hopkins, C.D.: Stereotyped temporal patterns in electrical communication. Animal Behav. **68** (2004). https://doi.org/10.1016/j.anbehav.2003.10.031
5. Chamorro, P., Muñiz, C., Levi, R., Arroyo, D., Rodríguez, F.B., Varona, P.: Generalization of the dynamic clamp concept in neurophysiology and behavior. PLoS ONE **7** (2012). https://doi.org/10.1371/journal.pone.0040887
6. Eckmann, J.P., Kamphorst, O.O., Ruelle, D.: Recurrence plots of dynamical systems. Europhys. Lett. **4** (1987). https://doi.org/10.1209/0295-5075/4/9/004
7. Hindmarsh, J.L., Rose, R.M.: A model of neuronal bursting using three coupled first order differential equations. In: Proceedings of the Royal Society of London. Series B, Containing papers of a Biological character. Royal Society (Great Britain) , vol. 221 (1984). https://doi.org/10.1098/rspb.1984.0024
8. Lareo, A.: Study of sequential information processing in electroreception through modelling and closed-loop stimulation techniques. Ph.D. thesis, Universidad Autónoma de Madrid (2023)
9. Lareo, A., Forlim, C.G., Pinto, R.D., Varona, P., Rodriguez, F.B.: Temporal code-driven stimulation: definition and application to electric fish signaling. Front. Neuroinform. **10** (2016). https://doi.org/10.3389/fninf.2016.00041
10. Lareo, Á., Forlim, C.G., Pinto, R.D., Varona, P., Rodríguez, F.B.: Analysis of electroreception with temporal code-driven stimulation. In: Rojas, I., Joya, G., Catala, A. (eds.) IWANN 2017. LNCS, vol. 10305, pp. 101–111. Springer, Cham (2017). https://doi.org/10.1007/978-3-319-59153-7_9
11. Lareo, A., Varona, P., Rodriguez, F.B.: Modeling the sequential pattern variability of the electromotor command system of pulse electric fish. Front. Neuroinform. **16**, 64 (2022)
12. Nádasdy, Z.: Spike sequences and their consequences. J. Physiol. Paris **94** (2000). https://doi.org/10.1016/S0928-4257(00)01103-7
13. Patel, Y.A., George, A., Dorval, A.D., White, J.A., Christini, D.J., Butera, R.J.: Hard real-time closed-loop electrophysiology with the real-time experiment interface (rtxi). PLoS Comput. Biol. **13** (2017). https://doi.org/10.1371/journal.pcbi.1005430
14. Reyes-Sanchez, M., Amaducci, R., Elices, I., Rodriguez, F.B., Varona, P.: Automatic adaptation of model neurons and connections to build hybrid circuits with living networks. Neuroinformatics **18**(3), 377–393 (2020)

15. Szücs, A., Varona, P., Volkovskii, A.R., Abarbanel, H.D., Rabinovich, M.I., Selverston, A.I.: Interacting biological and electronic neurons generate realistic oscillatory rhythms. NeuroReport **11**(3), 563–569 (2000)
16. Victor, J.D., Purpura, K.P.: Nature and precision of temporal coding in visual cortex: A metric- space analysis. J. Neurophysiol. **76** (1996). https://doi.org/10.1152/jn.1996.76.2.1310

Text Mining/Transfer Learning

Thematic Modeling of UN Sustainable Development Goals: A Comparative Meta-based Approach

Harris Partaourides[✉][iD], Emily Kouzaridi[iD], Nicolas Tsapatsoulis[iD], and Constantinos Djouvas[iD]

Cyprus University of Technology, Limassol, Cyprus
c.partaourides@cut.ac.cy

Abstract. To effectively monitor academic progress towards United Nations Sustainable Development Goals (SDGs), accurate and up-to-date information is crucial. Thematic modeling with keyword-based queries have emerged as a promising tool for clustering the large amounts of publications available in academic research databases. However, the effectiveness of these bibliometric queries depends on the choice of keywords used, and there is no standardized set of keywords for tracking academic progress towards the SDGs. In this study, we performed a comparative analysis of the most used keyword-based queries, assessing their advantages and disadvantages, and identifying gaps and redundancies. Based on our findings, we performed a meta-based approach to develop a new set of keywords that is both concise and thematically representative.

Keywords: Sustainable development goals · Keyword-based queries · Meta Approach · Semantic-based Matching

1 Introduction

The United Nations Sustainable Development Goals (SDGs) were adopted in 2015 as a universal call to action to end poverty, protect the planet, and ensure that all people enjoy peace and prosperity. The 17 goals and their associated 169 targets aim to address global challenges and are intended to be achieved by 2030. The list of United Nations (UN) SDGs is presented in Table 1. Most of the SDGs have a specific goal, except SDG 17 which is a cross-cutting SDG that aims to promote collaboration and cooperation among stakeholders at all levels to achieve the other 16 SDGs.

To effectively monitor progress towards the SDGs, accurate and up-to-date information is crucial. Thematic modeling with keyword-based queries has emerged as a promising tool for tracking academic progress towards the SDGs as a set of goals [3,7] or individually [11]. These bibliometric queries enable the clustering of large amounts of publications that are publicly available in academic research databases, such as Scopus, Web of Science, and OpenAIRE. However,

© IFIP International Federation for Information Processing 2023
Published by Springer Nature Switzerland AG 2023
I. Maglogiannis et al. (Eds.): AIAI 2023, IFIP AICT 676, pp. 557–568, 2023.
https://doi.org/10.1007/978-3-031-34107-6_44

Table 1. United Nations Sustainable Development Goals

SDG	Name
1	No Poverty
2	Zero Hunger
3	Good Health and Well-being
4	Quality Education
5	Gender Equality
6	Clean Water and Sanitation
7	Affordable and Clean Energy
8	Decent Work and Economic Growth
9	Industry, Innovation, and Infrastructure
10	Reduced Inequalities
11	Sustainable Cities and Communities
12	Responsible Consumption and Production
13	Climate Action
14	Life Below Water
15	Life On Land
16	Peace, Justice, and Strong Institutions
17	Partnerships for the Goals

the effectiveness of keyword-based queries highly depends on the selection of appropriate keywords [15].

At present, there is no standardized set of keywords for tracking progress towards the SDGs. In this context, several universities and organizations have constructed their own keyword sets such as Aurora's search queries for "Mapping Research Output to the SDGs" (AUR) [12], Auckland University SDG Keyword Mapping (AUC) [14], Elsevier's 2020 (ELS20) [4], 2021 (ELS21) [9], and 2022 (ELS22) [10].

In this study, we perform a comparative analysis between the most used keyword-based queries, present their advantages and disadvantages and through a meta-based approach create a new set of keywords that is concise, semantically relevant, and easily maintainable. The refined set of keywords related to sustainable development can greatly facilitate the evaluation and monitoring of academic progress towards specific targets and goals. Moreover, by using the derived set of keywords, researchers, policymakers, and practitioners can unlock new insights into the progress being made towards a more sustainable future. This can save time and effort while helping them make more informed decisions and take more effective action towards steering research [8].

2   Background and Literature Review

Keyword-based queries involve logically combining words and phrases that are representative of the goals (and targets) defined and associated with the United

Table 2. Text size and query execution tme

SDG	AUR		AUC		ELS20		ELS21/22	
	Size(KB)	Time(s)	Size(KB)	Time(s)	Size(KB)	Time(s)	Size(KB)	Time(s)
1	2	<5	3	<5	<1	<5	409	10
2	2	<5	5	<5	1	<5	195	25
3	5	<5	8	<5	3	<5	224/226	20
4	2	<5	6	<5	2	<5	1676	-
5	3	<5	5	<5	2	<5	1030	25
6	1	<5	7	<5	2	<5	216	11
7	1	<5	6	<5	2	<5	378	35
8	3	<5	6	<5	2	<5	86	21
9	3	<5	5	<5	1	<5	341	25
10	2	<5	4	<5	1	<5	250	30
11	2	<5	7	<5	1	<5	135	22
12	2	<5	6	<5	2	<5	95	22
13	2	<5	6	<5	2	<5	148	22
14	3	<5	5	<5	1	<5	1016	50
15	3	<5	7	<5	2	<5	172	23
16	3	<5	5	<5	2	<5	85	22

Nations' SDGs policy. Aurora's, Auckland's and Elsevier's are three of the most used query sets to track academic progress towards the SDGs. All of the query sets are publicly available and can be directly executed on the Scopus Advanced Search Tool to retrieve relevant publications. Table 2 provides an overview of the query text size in Kilobytes(KB) and the estimated time required to perform each query in seconds(s).

2.1   Aurora's Search Queries

To map research output to the SDGs, AUR [12] search queries were developed using a combination of sources: the official UN definition of the goals (targets and indicators), the Sustainable Development Solutions Network compiled list of keywords [1], and keyword-combination searches utilizing Boolean and proximity operators. The AUR set is carefully crafted a) to take full advantage of Scopus Advanced Search tool's functionalities, b) use combinations of keywords to minimize false positives and c) actively avoid the use of excluding keywords ("NOT" operator) to prevent the removal of true positives.

The set's performance was evaluated through a survey of 244 researchers conducted between October 2019 and January 2020 [13]. Newer versions of the set have been released over the years, incorporating additional keywords such as synonyms, antonyms, and academic terminology. The latest version, version 5, was released in July 2021.

2.2   Auckland's Search Queries

The University of Auckland SDG Keyword Mapping set was developed using text-mining techniques that involved multiple stages of data collection and analysis [14]. Firstly, an initial list of SDG-related keywords was generated using a similar approach to the AUR's search query methodology. Next, the abstracts of relevant publications available in the Scopus academic research database were collected using these keywords.

To identify relevant sequences of words, an n-gram model was applied to mine the abstracts of academic publications. The n-gram tokens were then scored based on their frequency and counts and ranked accordingly. High-ranking keywords were examined and manually reviewed to confirm their relevance to the corresponding SDG. Additionally, both author-provided and publication index keywords were evaluated based on their counts and frequencies.

It's worth noting that the AUC set does not include a specific query for SDG 17. The methodology used to create the set aimed to identify keywords related to specific SDGs and their targets, rather than focusing on the overarching theme of partnership and collaboration present in SDG 17.

2.3   Elsevier's 2020, 2021 and 2022 Search Queries

Elsevier has been actively supporting researchers and institutions in monitoring and demonstrating progress towards the SDGs. To achieve this, the company has been generating SDG search queries since 2018. In 2020, inspired by the earlier queries, Elsevier used a new approach to map publications to the SDGs. This new approach incorporated crowd-sourced responses (customer feedback) and has significantly increased the number of search terms used to define each SDG [4]. Moreover, they used a machine learning model to improve the recall by approximately 10%.

Specifically, an n-gram model was applied to mine the title, abstract, author's keywords, and journal subject areas and define the 50K most frequent features. This is followed by a logistic regression to predict the scores for each of the SDGs. In this context, the most confident model predictions ($>.95$) are retained as SDG-related publications.

Building on this success, Elsevier further improved the search query set in 2021, resulting in the capture of twice as many articles on average compared to the 2020 version while maintaining a precision rate of over 80% [9]. The mapping also had better overlap with SDG queries from other independent projects. The latest release in 2022, entails the same search queries and ML algorithm as the 2021 version, with an exception for SDG 3 (good health and well-being). This is because, in collaboration with university partners, Elsevier agreed to add COVID-related search terms to SDG 3 [10]. To simplify the comparative analysis we omitted ELS21 in favor of the updated ELS22. Similar to AUC, all Elsevier's sets do not include SDG 17.

It's important to note that Elsevier's search queries are also being used by the Times Higher Education as part of their Impact Rankings.

3   Methodology

As in the majority of empirical studies, the methodology we follow consists of four main steps: problem formulation, data collection, data analysis, and conclusion drawing based on the collected data. We begin this section by providing a mathematical formulation of the problem we are trying to solve, while each one of the remaining steps is analysed in a different subsection.

3.1   Problem Formulation

Let $\mathcal{D}$ be a dataset of scientific publications, e,g, Scopus, OpenAire, etc. Let also $\mathcal{Q}$ a terms set used to query the dataset $\mathcal{D}$, and $\mathcal{R}^{\mathcal{Q}}$ the set of retrieved results. Assuming that $\mathcal{T}_i$ a scientific topic for which relevant publications do exist in $\mathcal{D}$ the problem of finding those publications is highly relevant to the query we execute.

Finding the publications that are relevant to each one of the SDGs in the $\mathcal{D}$ dataset is the key problem of the current study. For this purpose, we define each SDG as a different topic, i.e., $\mathcal{T}_1$ refers to SDG 1, $\mathcal{T}_2$ refers to SDG 2, etc. We also define $\mathcal{Q}_i^j$ as the j-th term set used to query $\mathcal{D}$ aiming at topic $\mathcal{T}_i$. In this context, we denote as $\mathcal{R}_i^{\mathcal{Q}^j}$ the results retrieved form the j-th query regarding the i-th topic.

Given a set of queries $\mathcal{S}_i = \{\mathcal{Q}_i^1, \mathcal{Q}_i^2, ...\}$ targeting the i-th topic we aim to develop a meta query $\mathcal{Q}_i^M$ which is based on the existing ones and provides more relevant results, being also easily interpretable by humans.

3.2   CUT's SDG Keyword Mapping

In Table 2 we observe that the extensive and detailed ELS22 entails computationally expensive queries; large file sizes and long server response times. In this context, a concise and thematically representative query set will not only benefit in terms of readability but also interpretability of the publications retrieved. Towards this end, we developed a new keyword set using ELS20 query set as a starting point, performed corrections and light improvements, and added keywords from AUC, and ELS22 [2]. Specifically, a small subset of the highest ranking keywords returned by the machine learning models of AUC and ELS22 was selected. Then the selected terms where evaluated under a semantic-based matching with the SDGs and excluding generic terms that produce false positives. This meta-based approach resulted in the Cyprus University of Technology: SDG Keyword Mapping (CUT). In Table 3 we present a subset of five keywords per SDG. The subset contains the keywords with the highest volume of publications returned. A full list of keywords and the associated queries of CUT set are publicly released[1].

A qualitative evaluation based on interpretation was carried out to verify that the new keywords match the original SDG to which they belong. Since we

---

[1] https://github.com/Partaourides/CUT_SDGs_Keyword-Mapping.

Table 3. Subset of added keywords

SDG1	SDG2	SDG3	SDG4
Child welfare	Agroforestry	Air pollution	Academic achievement
Low socioeconomic	Biocontrol	Covid-19	Academic performance
Social exclusion	Biological control	Healthcare	Scholarships
Social policy	Domestication	Pandemic	Trainees
Social security	Sustainable agriculture	Stroke	Vocational education
SDG5	SDG6	SDG7	SDG8
Feminist	Drinking water	Biodiesel	Economic activities
Lgbt	Irrigation	Fuel cells	Human capital
Marginalized	Water pollution	Power consumption	Job satisfaction
Sexism	Water resources	Wind power	Labor market
Std	Water supply	Wind turbines	Regional development
SDG9	SDG10	SDG11	SDG12
Infrastructure	Financial crisis	Building*	Energy saving
Manufacturing process	Health care access	Infrastructure	Energy use
Nanofabrication	Medicaid	Urban development	Landfill
Prototyping	Racism	Urban environment	Natural resource
Research and development	Social justice	Urban planning	Recycle
SDG13	SDG14	SDG15	SDG16
Co2	Aquaculture	Bioremediation	Community engagement
Global climate	Aquatic	Conservation	Community participation
Global temperature	Bloom	Environmental change	Human rights
Natural disasters	Conservation	Indigenous	National security
	Hydrocarbons	Restoration	Participatory approach

had a small amount of data and a predefined list of keywords, a basic approach of qualitative analysis was selected to identify the broad topics or themes represented by the keywords. This involved manually reviewing the keywords and determining the common subject or subjects they represented. We looked for similarities or connections between the keywords and considered the context or domain to which they belonged.

The primary goal of the process was not to determine whether the additional keywords comprehensively covered all aspects of every SDG. Instead, the objective was to confirm whether the topics represented by the additional keywords were included in the original sub-targets listed on the website. This required a focused analysis of the additional keywords in relation to the relevant sub-targets. By comparing the topics covered by the keywords with the content of the sub-targets, we were able to assess whether the keywords provided meaningful additional insights into the relevant SDGs. While the process did not aim to provide comprehensive coverage of every aspect of every SDG, it was still an important step in ensuring that the additional keywords were aligned with the original sub-targets and contributed to a more complete understanding of the SDGs.

It is worth mentioning that this approach, while useful for gaining insights into a small set of data, can be subject to biases and limitations. A basic approach to qualitative analysis can be a valuable tool for gaining an initial understanding of the content and themes of a small set of data. The methodology utilized to evaluate the appropriation of keywords is akin to the coding process in qualitative analysis. The coding process is a crucial step in qualitative analysis: The data are categorized and organized into meaningful themes. In a similar vein, the evaluation of keyword appropriation involves identifying and categorizing keywords into higher categories. The subjects covered by each SDG are then contrasted with these higher categories. In this particular case, the coding approach is deductive since the list of keywords is predefined and the framework for each SDG is already established. The use of a relatively limited number of keywords further reinforces the deductive approach [6]. Overall, the deductive coding process allows for a more structured analysis of the data, based on the established framework and keywords. This approach can provide insights into how the SDGs are perceived and addressed. Kovacs et al. [5] used also a simple manual form of content analysis on collected words for ordering them into higher categories according to their scientific field within psychology. One of the focuses of their study on mapping qualitative research in psychology was to explore the topics of the examined articles.

After conducting a thorough review of the lists, the results have indicated that the keywords associated with each of the SDGs are in alignment with the overall objective of their corresponding targets. This highlights the consistency and coherence in the language used to define and articulate the SDGs.

3.3 Operationalization

In the context of this study, the $\mathcal{D}$ dataset is the Scopus dataset, the topics searched $\mathcal{T}_i, i = 1, .., 16$ are the SDG topics, while $\mathcal{S}_i, i = 1, ..., 16$ are the query term sets reviewed in Sect. 2, i.e., $\mathcal{S}_1 = \{\mathcal{Q}_1^{AUC}, \mathcal{Q}_1^{AUR}, \mathcal{Q}_1^{ELS20}, \mathcal{Q}_1^{ELS22}, \mathcal{Q}_1^{CUT}\}$ are the query term sets developed by AUC, AUR, Elsevier (2020, 2022) and CUT targeting the SDG 1. For easy reference, by dropping the subscript index we mean the whole set of SDG query sets developed by each one of the compared approaches, i.e., $\mathcal{Q}^{AUR}$ is the set of queries developed by AUR for all SDGs.

By $\mathcal{R}_i^{\mathcal{Q}^j}$ we denoted the number of per year publications retrieved when executing the $\mathcal{Q}_i^j$ query. Each row in Tables 4–8 is an instance of $\mathcal{R}_i^{\mathcal{Q}^j}$ while by $\mathcal{R}^{\mathcal{Q}^j}$ we denote the number of per year and per SDG publications. Thus, each one of the Tables 4-8 is an instance of $\mathcal{R}^{\mathcal{Q}^j}$.

4   Data Collection and Comparative Analysis

Scopus Advanced Search tool was used to execute the queries and collect data for the years 2015–2022. The data collection was conducted in January 2023. The query results per year are presented in Tables 4, 5, 6, 7, and 8 for AUR, AUC, ELS20, ELS22[2], and CUT, respectively. The query file sizes and server execution time of CUT are similar to AUR, AUC and ELS20.

---

[2] We couldn't retrieve the information for SDG4 on the ELS22 set. To avoid missing values we added the average of SDG4 between AUC and ELS20.

Table 4. $\mathcal{R}^{\mathrm{AUR}}$ from 2015 to 2022 (in thousands)

SDG	2022	2021	2020	2019	2018	2017	2016	2015
1	12.6	12.1	10.5	9.7	8.9	8.1	7.4	3.9
2	9.4	8.3	6.8	5.4	4.5	4.0	3.5	3.2
3	102.1	98.8	45.1	16.9	15.5	14.5	13.4	12.0
4	17.6	16.0	13.9	12.1	10.7	9.7	8.9	8.1
5	7.4	6.7	5.8	5.0	4.7	4.2	3.8	3.4
6	30.1	27.9	24.8	21.6	19.0	17.1	15.5	13.7
7	14.6	13.2	11.8	11.5	10.1	9.1	8.1	7.3
8	9.6	9.0	9.2	7.7	6.6	6.2	5.4	5.0
9	9.5	8.1	7.0	6.2	5.4	4.8	4.2	3.8
10	5.3	5.0	4.5	4.2	3.8	3.5	3.3	2.9
11	28.5	27.5	25.0	23.9	20.4	18.0	15.6	13.4
12	29.8	27.2	22.2	19.0	16.4	14.5	12.9	11.9
13	94.7	88.4	75.8	67.5	61.4	56.1	52.0	48.3
14	31.5	32.4	29.6	26.9	25.0	22.0	21.1	20.0
15	28.6	26.1	22.1	19.3	16.6	14.9	13.3	12.2
16	14.2	13.9	12.4	12.0	10.9	10.4	9.4	8.4
17	11.8	11.4	10.6	9.7	8.5	7.9	7.0	6.8

Table 5. $\mathcal{R}^{\mathrm{AUC}}$ from 2015 to 2022 (in thousands)

SDG	2022	2021	2020	2019	2018	2017	2016	2015
1	24.8	24.3	22.2	21.1	19.7	18.4	16.5	15.9
2	126.3	125.9	109.7	96.9	88.4	81.0	77.9	74.8
3	1214.5	1221.1	1065.9	912.0	862.4	825.1	813.3	797.4
4	144.8	139.3	119.5	107.3	93.1	82.5	76.5	71.6
5	35.7	33.6	29.8	27.3	25.7	23.4	22.1	20.8
6	105.0	101.0	93.2	84.4	76.1	69.1	65.7	61.1
7	180.6	168.7	156.9	155.3	137.4	124.8	114.5	105.5
8	60.9	58.4	52.0	47.1	41.2	38.6	34.5	31.8
9	99.4	97.2	89.8	81.6	69.1	61.2	54.8	49.0
10	125.3	1232.0	109.2	95.9	88.4	82.8	77.2	72.3
11	205.8	197.3	180.2	166.2	146.5	131.6	121.2	109.1
12	145.6	137.9	124.8	116.8	101.9	92.4	82.5	74.9
13	99.5	89.2	76.1	67.0	60.7	55.9	51.3	47.5
14	71.4	71.5	65.5	59.6	55.0	49.2	47.9	45.2
15	156.3	155.1	137.3	125.3	113.2	102.5	97.4	91.5
16	70.1	70.1	65.5	62.6	59.4	57.3	51.9	46.9

This was followed by a correlation analysis to measure the degree of association between any two query sets. In our analysis, we consider the 16 SDGs as independent sample pairs and the years 2015–2022 as dependent values. Our findings are presented in Table 9, with statistical significance levels denoted by

Table 6. $\mathcal{R}^{ELS20}$ from 2015 to 2022 (in thousands)

SDG	2022	2021	2020	2019	2018	2017	2016	2015
1	3.6	3.6	3.2	2.9	2.6	2.5	2.3	2.2
2	35.3	33.7	28.5	24.8	22.0	19.3	17.6	16.3
3	939.9	964.3	861.3	744.2	701.4	672.2	662.1	645.5
4	8.9	8.5	7.5	6.6	6.1	5.2	5.0	4.5
5	13.7	12.6	10.6	6.5	8.7	7.8	7.0	6.3
6	14.7	14.3	13.1	11.7	10.6	9.3	8.8	7.9
7	122.0	112.7	102.2	100.4	87.1	78.5	69.7	62.5
8	35.0	32.4	27.9	25.5	21.6	19.8	17.3	15.7
9	13.7	12.4	11.7	10.6	9.1	8.1	7.3	6.7
10	14.9	14.1	12.5	12.1	11.1	10.6	9.6	9.0
11	46.1	46.3	42.3	39.6	34.6	29.7	25.0	21.6
12	36.2	32.0	26.6	23.4	20.1	17.9	15.5	14.0
13	65.7	60.7	51.8	45.4	4.1	37.1	35.0	32.9
14	30.6	30.6	27.4	24.9	22.6	20.4	19.6	18.5
15	34.3	34.1	30.2	27.6	25.5	22.6	21.4	19.8
16	46.4	46.3	41.8	42.7	41.1	39.8	35.8	31.9

Table 7. $\mathcal{R}^{ELS22}$ from 2015 to 2022 (in thousands)

SDG	2022	2021	2020	2019	2018	2017	2016	2015
1	19.2	17.8	15.8	15.0	13.7	13.1	11.8	10.8
2	53.3	49.9	42.4	36.6	32.5	29.1	26.6	25.0
3	613.3	606.1	521.1	416.4	392.4	374.0	365.6	350.8
4*	76.8	73.9	63.5	56.9	49.6	43.9	40.7	38.0
5	34.7	31.4	27.4	25.1	24.0	21.7	20.3	18.5
6	71.2	66.8	59.7	53.1	47.8	48.7	40.0	36.4
7	162.2	149.9	138.2	134.4	121.5	110.7	101.2	93.8
8	67.7	61.9	53.7	48.2	41.5	37.6	33.0	30.1
9	111.6	101.5	90.2	81.3	68.4	60.2	52.2	45.6
10	58.8	53.2	45.8	41.9	39.1	36.3	33.0	29.9
11	88.3	85.4	77.7	71.6	63.1	53.9	48.5	42.7
12	59.5	54.4	46.5	41.1	35.3	32.3	27.7	25.2
13	73.5	63.0	52.7	45.7	40.9	37.7	33.6	30.4
14	30.8	30.8	27.1	24.1	22.1	19.8	18.3	16.8
15	46.6	45.5	40.4	36.3	33.8	30.9	28.7	27.2
16	49.9	48.5	43.2	41.5	39.7	37.7	34.0	31.4

* for 0.05 and ** for 0.01. It's worth noting that a significance level of 0.01 indicates stronger evidence is needed to reject the null hypothesis. In this context, the analysis shows a high correlation between AUC, ELS20, ELS22, and CUT, suggesting that they can serve interchangeably as indicators for measuring SDG-related academic progress. However, there are substantial differences in the quantity and logical combinations of keywords used in each set, which hinders the explainability of the results and insights to make informed decisions. Among the three sets, ELS22 has the most extensive and extremely finetuned keyword combination for each SDG, while ELS20 is the most concise and readable. This can also be observed from the size and execution time of the queries presented in Table 2.

Table 8. $\mathcal{R}^{\mathrm{CUT}}$ from 2015 to 2022 (in thousands)

SDG	2022	2021	2020	2019	2018	2017	2016	2015
1	19.4	19.2	17.5	16.0	14.7	14.3	13.3	13.3
2	42.0	40.2	34.5	29.9	26.5	23.5	21.7	19.9
3	1071.3	1072.2	930.1	783.0	736.6	704.6	692.7	675.2
4	28.1	27.3	23.7	20.7	19.1	17.4	16.4	15.5
5	28.5	25.6	22.0	20.4	19.1	17.0	16.0	14.1
6	65.4	63.5	58.4	52.3	46.9	42.7	40.0	37.1
7	160.1	147.6	135.4	133.6	117.9	107.2	98.2	89.7
8	48.5	45.2	39.6	36.6	31.3	28.8	25.9	23.6
9	80.2	76.2	70.4	67.4	59.3	53.7	49.7	45.8
10	55.3	52.5	46.0	40.7	38.0	36.4	33.7	31.2
11	64.2	63.6	58.6	55.8	48.1	41.9	36.2	31.2
12	57.9	52.7	45.8	41.6	36.6	33.2	29.7	26.7
13	66.7	61.2	52.1	45.7	41.4	37.3	35.2	33.1
14	35.8	35.6	32.1	29.1	26.5	23.8	22.9	21.5
15	38.3	37.9	33.5	30.7	28.4	25.2	23.9	22.0
16	60.7	59.8	54.7	55.4	53.0	51.5	46.8	41.3

Table 9. Correlation Query Results (N=16 independent pairs)

	AUC	AUR	ELS20	ELS22	CUT
AUR	1.000	0.339	0.393	0.390	0.392
AUC	0.339	1.000	0.893*/**	0.891*/**	0.898*/**
ELS20	0.393	0.893*/**	1.000	0.977*/**	0.997*/**
ELS22	0.390	0.891*/**	0.977*/**	1.000	0.986*/**
CUT	0.392	0.898*/**	0.997*/**	0.986*/**	1.000

Table 10. AUR correlations per year

	2022	2021	2020	2019	2018	2017	2016	2015
AUC	0.686	0.362	0.361	0.011	0.014	0.022	0.024	0.023
ELS20	0.704	0.715	0.386	0.035	−0.008	0.048	0.052	0.051
ELS22	0.665	0.673	0.338	−0.013	−0.007	0.005	0.007	0.008
CUT	0.683	0.695	0.359	0.004	0.011	0.019	0.024	0.024

AUR query formulation being the most stringent with the definition of the SDGs has the least correlation with the others. However, a closer examination of the yearly correlation data (presented in Table 10) reveals a recent substantial increase in correlation values. This may be attributed to growing SDG awareness among academia, as well as a trend of authors incorporating SDG-related keywords in their work.

5   Conclusion and Future Work

In conclusion, we conducted a comparative analysis of various keyword-based approaches used to quantify academic progress towards achieving the SDGs. Our study revealed that existing keyword sets, such as ELS22, can be extensive and elaborate, which may pose challenges in terms of readability and interpretability of results. To address this issue, we created a new keyword set that is concise and readable while being comparable to the extensive and elaborate ELS22 set. By using a simplified list of keywords, our approach offers better explainability of results, which can assist policymakers and stakeholders in making informed decisions. Moreover, our approach is straightforward to apply to any academic research databases and SDG-oriented applications, making it a valuable tool for researchers and practitioners alike.

In addition to the current findings, there are a few areas for future work that could further improve our approach. Firstly, we aim to further simplify the keywords list to make it even more concise while remaining representative towards the SDGs. This could involve exploring the relationships between the existing keywords and identifying redundant or overlapping terms. Secondly, it would be valuable to apply our approach to different academic research databases to evaluate its generalizability and potential limitations. Thus, conducting a comparative analysis of different databases using our approach could help identify any potential issues and refine the keywords further. Finally, we aim to implement the queries on a specialized dashboard for academic policymakers and assess their impact on strategic decision-making.

Overall, the applicability and readability of the derived keyword-based set can assist the ongoing efforts to achieve the United Nations SDGs by 2030.

Acknowledgements. The work presented in the current study was undertaken in the framework of the IBA-SwafS-Support-2-2020 project "EUt- EXTRAS: European University of Technology - Experimentation to Transform Research Activities and Steering" under the contract H2020-IBA-SwafS-Support-2-2020/101035812.

References

1. Compiled list of SDG keywords by Monash university and SDSN Australia/Pacific. https://ap-unsdsn.org/wp-content/uploads/2017/04/Compiled-Keywords-for-SDG-Mapping Final 17-05-10.xlsx (2017)
2. Azad, H.K., Deepak, A.: Query expansion techniques for information retrieval: a survey. In. Process. Manag. **56**(5), 1698–1735 (2019)
3. Hassan, S.U., Haddawy, P., Zhu, J.: A bibliometric study of the world's research activity in sustainable development and its sub-areas using scientific literature. Scientometrics **99**, 549–579 (2014)
4. Jayabalasingham, B., Boverhof, R., Agnew, K., Klein, L.: Identifying research supporting the united nations sustainable development goals. Mendeley Data **1**, 1 (2019)
5. Kovács, A., Kiss, D., Kassai, S., Pados, E., Kaló, Z., Rácz, J.: Mapping qualitative research in psychology across five central-eastern european countries: Contemporary trends: A paradigm analysis. Qualitative Research in Psychology (2019)
6. Linneberg, M.S., Korsgaard, S.: Coding qualitative data: a synthesis guiding the novice. Qual. Res. J. **19**(3), 259–270 (2019)
7. Meschede, C.: The sustainable development goals in scientific literature: A bibliometric overview at the meta-level. Sustainability **12**(11), 4461 (2020)
8. Olawumi, T.O., Chan, D.W.: A scientometric review of global research on sustainability and sustainable development. J. clean. Prod. **183**, 231–250 (2018)
9. Rivest, M., Kashnitsky, Y., Bédard-Vallée, A., Campbell, D., Khayat, P., Labrosse, I., Pinheiro, H., Provençal, S., Roberge, G., James, C.: Improving the scopus and aurora queries to identify research that supports the united nations sustainable development goals (sdgs) 2021. Mendeley Data 2 (2021)
10. Roberge, G., Kashnitsky, Y., James, C.: Elsevier 2022 sustainable development goals (sdg) mapping (2022)
11. Sweileh, W.M.: Bibliometric analysis of scientific publications on "sustainable development goals" with emphasis on "good health and well-being" goal (2015–2019). Globalization and health **16**, 1–13 (2020)
12. Vanderfeesten, M., Otten, R., Spielberg, E., Kullman, L.: Search queries for "mapping research output to the sustainable development goals (sdgs)" v4.0 (2020). https://doi.org/10.5281/zenodo.3817443
13. Vanderfeesten, M., Spielberg, E., Gunes, Y.: Survey data of "mapping research output to the sustainable development goals (sdgs)" (2020). https://doi.org/10.5281/zenodo.3813230
14. Wang, W., Kang, W., Mu, J.: Mapping research to the sustainable development goals (sdgs) (2023)
15. Webber, W.: Evaluating the effectiveness of keyword search. IEEE Data Eng. Bull. **33**(1), 54–59 (2010)

Transfer Learning Through Knowledge-Infused Representations with Contextual Experts

Daniel Biermann[✉], Morten Goodwin, and Ole-Christoffer Granmo

Centre for Artificial Intelligence Research (CAIR), Department of ICT,
University of Agder, Grimstad, Norway
{daniel.biermann,morten.goodwin,ole.granmo}@uia.no

Abstract. In recent years, transfer learning in natural language processing has been dominated by incredibly large models following a pretraining-finetuning approach. A problem with these models is that the increasing model size goes hand in hand with increasing training costs. In this work, we instead evaluate the transfer learning capabilities of the recently introduced knowledge-infused representations. Previously, these infused representations have been shown to infuse experts' knowledge into a downstream model when the expert and downstream model operates on the same task domain. We extend this by investigating the effects of different expert task configurations on the performance of the downstream model. Our results show that differing expert and downstream tasks do not affect the downstream model. This indicates a desired robustness of the model towards adding irrelevant information. Simultaneously, the ability to transport important information is retained as we continue to see a significant performance improvement when adding two experts of differing tasks. Overall, this solidifies the potential knowledge-infused representations have regarding the ability to generalize across different tasks and their ability to recycle old computations for smaller new downstream models.

Keywords: Machine Learning · Text classification · Transfer learning

1 Introduction

Data-driven machine learning suffers from an inherent problem: Data-driven algorithms perform best when trained for narrowly defined tasks on a task-specific dataset, and the disadvantage is that a trained algorithm will fail if the task is changed. Moreover, the information contained in the trained algorithm for one task is, in general, of no use for another task. The trend of increasing performance by increasing the scale of the models makes training the current state-of-the-art increasingly time-consuming and expensive. The ability to effectively use previously trained models could help reduce the temporal, financial, and environmental impact of computations training models for new tasks. This

© IFIP International Federation for Information Processing 2023
Published by Springer Nature Switzerland AG 2023
I. Maglogiannis et al. (Eds.): AIAI 2023, IFIP AICT 676, pp. 569–578, 2023.
https://doi.org/10.1007/978-3-031-34107-6_45

problem lies at the heart of transfer learning, a field that investigates the transfer of knowledge between models across tasks, datasets, and architectures.

Machine learning algorithms have made incredible improvements in performance over the last decade, and transfer learning has been a significant contributor. Many state-of-the-art models use a pretraining-finetuning approach in their methodology. This pretraining-finetuning approach is rooted in transfer learning as the model is first trained on a large general dataset and subsequently finetuned on a smaller task-specific dataset. The general idea is to learn general structures in the data and finetune the learned structure for a downstream task. Examples of this approach find application in all fields of machine learning. Natural language processing has been particularly impacted through the Transformer models pretrained on vast unlabelled datasets [2,4,18].

Transfer learning methods are not limited to pretraining-finetuning methods. For example, the text-to-text transformer (T5) architecture [12] performs transfer learning on a model-based level. The idea is to train a single model to solve multiple tasks. Thus, the knowledge gained by training in one task affects all other tasks as the model parameters are shared.

A problem that can arise in both approaches is catastrophic forgetting (or catastrophic inference) [6]. While especially relevant in continual learning, it can occur in all fields of machine learning. This phenomenon occurs when adjusting the weights in a network for a new example can lead to overwriting/forgetting the knowledge that was attained in previous training. In transfer learning, this can be problematic when we forget instead of using the knowledge contained in previously trained models.

In this contribution, we investigate the transfer learning capabilities of a model that combines the output of a task-specific expert with the original input given to the expert. The model thus creates a new representation that is infused with the experts' knowledge and then given to a downstream model. This work expands on Biermann et al. [1], which have shown that knowledge infused representations benefit downstream model performance if expert and downstream models operate in the same task domain. In our investigation, we test the influence of different task domains on the downstream model performance when using knowledge-infused representations. We examine whether the information encoded in the infused representations has any positive or negative effects when considering experts and downstream models of different task domains. We further expand the model by combining the information of two experts and investigating the influence of a task-foreign expert on the performance of downstream models.

2   Related Work

This work is based on and a continuation of previous work by the authors [1]. Previously, we established that infusing the information contained in the output of an expert can be transported down to a simple downstream model if the expert and downstream model share the same task domain. Missing from this work is the important and relevant case where expert task domain and downstream task domain differ. In this work, we investigate the influence of differing expert and downstream task domains. Additionally, the previous work considered only cases with one expert, whereas in this study, we explicitly investigate the influence of multiple experts on the downstream performance in the context of transfer learning.

Transfer learning is an important field in machine learning, and with the increase in model size and computation cost over the last decade, its relevance will continue to rise. As discussed in 1, within the NLP field, transfer learning is mainly achieved through pretraining on enormous unlabelled datasets as the various GPT models show [2,8–11]. Another approach is the above-mentioned T5 transformer [12] that trains the same model parameters on subsequent tasks. Overall, the computational cost is again heavy as you have to train transformer models. In our approach, instead of finetuning and retraining transformer models, we aim to recycle and benefit from already existing and finished models. As far as we are aware, there is no other work investigating transfer learning in this direction.

This approach has the added benefit that the models that are actually trained can be made smaller. This allows for more competition across the machine learning field as smaller institutions can symbiotically benefit from the enormous models that can only be trained by a handful of large institutions. Smaller models might emphasize the problem of catastrophic forgetting again as increasing model size and dataset size have been shown to reduce the impact of catastrophic forgetting [13]. With regards to this, the here proposed model remains an elegant candidate as the nature of the finished and fixed experts prevents any form of overwriting or forgetting previously trained parameters.

3 Methods

3.1 General Architecture

The model follows the general architecture of previous work used in Biermann et al. [1] and extends it by an additional expert. Adding an additional expert allows us to test the models' response to the presence of additional experts that do not offer direct beneficial information regarding the downstream task. In contrast to the previous work, we also test the model for cases in which the expert's task domain and downstream task domain differ. The general architecture is depicted in Fig. 1. An input sequence is separately given to up to two experts and an embedding layer. The contextual experts are pretrained models that solve a specific task. The experts are contextual in the sense that they can be specifically chosen for a downstream task. The outputs of the experts are then scaled up to the embedding dimension via single linear layers and appended to the sequence itself. This corresponds to the sequential combination paradigm in our previous work. We opted to concentrate on the sequential paradigm in this work as it is suspected that the model scales better with the sequential paradigm when increasing the number of experts. Additionally, and more importantly, the sequential paradigm combined with an attention-based combination offers a natural interpretability lost in the other combination paradigm. The extended sequence is then given to an attention-based combination mechanism that reduces the sequence length back to the original input sequence length and infuses the sequence tokens with the expert's output information, yielding an information-infused new sequence representation. This infused representation is then given to a downstream model that is trained to perform a downstream task. The error is backpropagated from the downstream model to the combination mechanism when training the model. The experts are seen as finished products and are not trained or finetuned in any way.

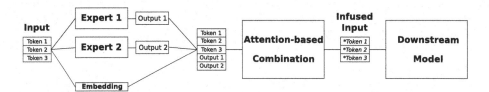

Fig. 1. Model architecture. The original input is given to contextual experts and to an embedding layer. The experts are pre-trained task-specific models. The outputs of the experts are linearly scaled, via a feed forward layer, to the embedding dimension of the sequence tokens and appended to the sequence. The combination mechanism combines the expert output and original input into a new information-infused representation. Downstream models are arbitrary, to-be-trained models.

3.2   Combination Mechanism

The goal of the combination mechanism is to take in the original input sequence appended by the expert output tokens and reduce it back to the original sequence length. Ideally, this happens in a way that the information contained in the original input tokens and the expert output tokens are fused in the new infused sequence.

We employ the same mechanism used in [1] which is based on Vaswani et al.'s scaled dot-product and multi-head attention introduced with the Transformer [16]. To reiterate, the scaled dot-product

$$\mathcal{A}(Q, K, V) = \text{softmax}(\frac{QK^T}{\sqrt{d_k}})V \qquad (1)$$

calculates an attention weight map from each word to each word in the sequence via the query Q and key K matrices and creates a new representation by multiplying and summing with the value matrix V. Q, K, and V are created from the original input, and their respective vectors show dimensionalities of $d_q = d_k, d_v$. The new representation then has the dimensionality d_v

In multi-head attention, multiple heads H_i calculate the scaled dot-product in parallel and are concatenated back into a single new representation and scaled to a final new representation via weight matrix W^O.

$$\mathcal{M}(Q, K, V) = \text{Concat}(H_1, \ldots, H_h)W^O \tag{2}$$

$$H_i = \mathcal{A}(Q_i, K_i, V_i) \tag{3}$$

This work follows the general practice and chooses $d_k = d_q = d_v = d_{emb}$, where d_{emb} is the dimension of the word embedding. To reduce the sequence length of expert output infused new representation, the sequence is cut off after reaching its original length.

For example, if we set the original sequence length as N and the number of expert outputs to e, the attention mechanism calculates $N + e$ new representation tokens. The original sequence length N is subsequently enforced by cutting off the last e tokens in the infused sequence.

3.3   Contextual Experts

The general idea is that any arbitrary model or architecture can be used as an expert as long as it is trained to perform a single task. In the sequential combination paradigm we employ in this work, it is also possible for the experts to return a single output token or a sequence of output tokens. This allows us to give the experts a certain contextual component. With contextual experts, we mean that the experts can be handpicked in the context of a downstream task. The idea is to choose experts that might offer beneficial information with regard to the downstream task. For example, in this work, we chose our experts to be a dialogue act classifier and a sentiment classifier. While not directly related to their task, one could reasonably assume that certain dialogue act correlate more with certain sentiments than others. Thus, having the information of the sentiment expert might hold benefit for a downstream model trying to solve dialogue act classification.

For the sake of simplicity, both experts chosen in this work are based on the DistilBERT model [14] implemented via the Huggingface Transformer library [17]. The experts are then fine-tuned in their respective tasks on their respective datasets.

Dialogue Act classifier (DA): The dialogue act classifier is fine-tuned on the SwitchBoard Dialogue Act corpus (SwDA) [5,15][1]. The SwDA corpus consists of transcribed phone conversations and the cleaned version contains 41 different classes. To counteract the strong class imbalance present in the dataset, the expert fine-tuned with class weights. The expert was finetuned for 5 epochs and reached a test accuracy of 0.781

Sentiment Analysis classifier (SA): The sentiment classifier is finetuned on the well-established IMDB movie reviews dataset [7]. The dataset consists of movie

---

[1] This work uses the cleaned and curated train, validation, and test splits given by https://github.com/NathanDuran/Switchboard-Corpus.

reviews and categorizes the reviews in 2 possible sentiment classes. The expert was finetuned for 2 epochs following an 80–20 training and validation split and reached a test accuracy of 0.932

3.4   Downstream Model

This architecture aims to use the information that is contained and generated by already trained experts. Thus, keeping the downstream model deliberately simple shows that simple models can benefit from this approach. A simple model further emphasizes the idea of combining computationally heavy experts with lightweight downstream models to maximize the amount of computation saved when compared to training or finetuning large models.

To this extent, the downstream model consists of a single GRU [3] layer leading into a softmax classifier consisting of 64 hidden units.

4   Experiments

To investigate the transfer learning capabilities of the proposed architecture, we perform several simulations with different expert and downstream task settings. The 'Expert Task/Downstream Task' column in Table 1 lists the different expert and downstream task combinations considered.

As a baseline, we train the downstream model in dialogue act classification (DA) or sentiment classification (SA) without adding expert output. This way, we can provide a baseline that includes any benefits that the attention mechanism may provide to the performance. This ensures that any comparisons in performance with the baseline can be more directly attributed to the addition of the expert output.

Subsequently, we first add one expert and run simulations for all possible expert- and downstream task combinations. Adding only one expert allows us to directly investigate the impact that a differing expert and downstream task have on performance. In our previous work, we only considered cases in which the expert and downstream task solve the same task.

Finally, we combine both experts and train the downstream model in each task. Adding both experts allows us to probe the effects that combining multiple expert outputs may have on each other. Mainly, we test whether adding two experts elevates the performance beyond what one expert shows or if the presence of another task-unrelated expert hinders the performance of the downstream model.

The model is trained for the same amount of epochs in all simulations using a learning rate of 2×10^{-4}. For the input sequence, we train an embedding layer to use 300-dimensional embedding vectors. The experts use their own respective tokenizers and embeddings.

Table 1. Baseline and downstream task test accuracies for different expert- and downstream task configurations. DA stands for the dialogue act classification task, and SA stands for the sentiment classification task.

Model	Accuracy
	Baseline
Dialogue Act expert	0.781
Sentiment expert	0.932
Downstream Model (DA)	0.748
Downstream Model (SA)	0.835
Expert Task/Downstream Task	Downstream
DA/DA	0.776
SA/SA	0.928
SA/DA	0.751
DA/SA	0.820
DA + SA/DA	0.776
DA + SA/SA	0.929

4.1   Results

Table 1 summarises the baseline and test accuracies for the downstream model for all performed simulations.

Comparing the expert and baseline performances for the different tasks, we see that the expert slightly outperforms the baseline by 3.3% for the DA task and more significantly by 9.4% for the SA task, respectively. Though the difference between baseline and expert performance is small, it is significant enough to see whether information has been transported from the expert to the downstream model.

As expected, in the cases where the expert and downstream model share the same task ('DA/DA' and 'SA/SA'), with 0.776 and 0.928 we see an improvement in the downstream performance close to the performance of the respective expert. This aligns with the results achieved in our previous work and the information of the expert has been transported to the downstream model. This performance improvement can not be observed when the expert and downstream task domains differ from each other. In these cases ('SA/DA' and 'DA/SA'), the downstream performance stays close to their respective baseline performances. While the DA performance of 0.751 lies slightly above the baseline, the SA performance falls slightly below the baseline with 0.820. This shows that the model does not benefit from adding the knowledge of a task-foreign expert but roughly remains around its baseline performance.

When adding task-foreign experts, one could imagine scenarios in which the expert might still hold some information. For example, in dialogue act classification and sentiment classification, it might be reasonable to assume that certain dialogue act classes correlate with certain sentiments, and thus, knowing the sentiment of a sentence might hold useful information. The simulations show that our model, with the chosen experts, tasks and datasets, could not learn and use this type of cross-benefit. While it would have been nice to observe this type of cross-benefit in our simulations, their absence does not mean that this model cannot achieve them. These cross-benefits are highly dependant on the chosen experts, the form of their output, and the chosen expert and downstream task. Some tasks are natively more beneficial to each other than more independent tasks.

What is more beneficial is that the performance does not worsen significantly when including an expert in a different task, indicating the model's ability to ignore unhelpful information that might be introduced through the expert output. Notably, this implicates a certain robustness of the model toward adding multiple experts. If the model can ignore irrelevant information, the negative effects of adding irrelevant experts becomes less problematic.

In fact, we can see this in the simulations in which both experts are added to the model (DA+SA). When both experts are added, the downstream model reaches performances of 0.776 for the DA task and 0.929 for the SA task. Both performances approach the respective expert task performance again. This solidifies the previous observations that the model can pay attention to beneficial information and can, at the same time, ignore seemingly irrelevant information.

5   Conclusion

We tested the transfer learning capabilities of the proposed model by testing different expert- and downstream task configurations. When expert and downstream tasks align, we see a clear and significant improvement in downstream model performance. When the expert and downstream tasks differ, we could see no positive effect on the downstream model performance. This behavior is expected as a task-foreign expert does not carry immediate relevant information for the downstream task. Nevertheless, as both chosen tasks are within the NLP domain one could imagine possible indirect cross-benefits the model might gain. The results indicate a limited ability of the model to benefit from possible cross-benefits between tasks. As these cross-benefits are highly dependent on the chosen tasks, it is virtually impossible to make a definite statement on the ability of this model to achieve these types of benefits. Though further investigation is warranted as examples of intuitive possible cross-benefits easily come to mind and cross-benefits may be more apparent for more nuanced tasks.

Additionally, we observe that there are no negative effects when the expert task and downstream task differ. This is a promising result as it indicates robustness regarding irrelevant experts. This is further emphasized by simulations that add two experts of different tasks simultaneously. Here, the model can again reach a downstream performance close to that of its respective expert itself. This shows that the model can pay attention to the beneficial expert information while at the same time ignoring the irrelevant expert information. It also shows that the inclusion of task-foreign experts does not hinder the models' ability to benefit from the task-relevant expert.

Overall, we have shown that this model is able to combine multiple experts without losing its ability to transport relevant and beneficial information to the downstream model. At the same time, we have shown that the model is able to ignore task-foreign information which indicates the models' robustness regarding the negative influences of irrelevant information.

This has nice implications for future applications of this approach. Our results show that adding more experts to the model shows no immediate negative impact on the performance of the model itself. Thus, possible next steps include adding more experts to the model. Adding more experts could lead to a higher probability of encountering positive cross-benefits that we could not observe with only two different tasks. Furthermore, a natural next step is to test the multi-task capabilities of this model and whether we are able better train a downstream model on multiple tasks when infusing it with expert knowledge.

Finally, this approach shows promise in making simpler models competitive again and gives an alternative to the ever-growing, large models as we effectively can 'recycle' old computations.

References

1. Biermann, D., Goodwin, M., Granmo, O.C.: Knowledge infused representations through combination of expert knowledge and original input. In: Zouganeli, E., Yazidi, A., Mello, G., Lind, P. (eds.) Nordic Artificial Intelligence Research and Development: 4th Symposium of the Norwegian AI Society, NAIS 2022, Oslo, Norway, May 31-June 1, 2022, Revised Selected Papers, vol. 1650, pp. 3–15. Springer, Cham (2023). https://doi.org/10.1007/978-3-031-17030-0_1

2. Brown, T., et al.: Language models are few-shot learners. In: Larochelle, H., Ranzato, M., Hadsell, R., Balcan, M., Lin, H. (eds.) Advances in Neural Information Processing Systems, vol. 33, pp. 1877–1901. Curran Associates, Inc. (2020). https://proceedings.neurips.cc/paper/2020/file/1457c0d6bfcb4967418bfb8ac142f6 4a-Paper.pdf

3. Cho, K., et al.: Learning phrase representations using RNN encoder-decoder for statistical machine translation. arXiv preprint: arXiv:1406.1078 (2014)

4. Devlin, J., Chang, M.W., Lee, K., Toutanova, K.: BERT: pre-training of deep bidirectional transformers for language understanding. arXiv preprint: arXiv:1810.04805 (2018)

5. Godfrey, J., Holliman, E., McDaniel, J.: Switchboard: telephone speech corpus for research and development. In: [Proceedings] ICASSP-92: 1992 IEEE International Conference on Acoustics, Speech, and Signal Processing, vol. 1, pp. 517–520 (1992). https://doi.org/10.1109/ICASSP.1992.225858

6. Kirkpatrick, J., et al.: Overcoming catastrophic forgetting in neural networks. Proc. Natl. Acad. Sci. **114**(13), 3521–3526 (2017)

7. Maas, A.L., Daly, R.E., Pham, P.T., Huang, D., Ng, A.Y., Potts, C.: Learning word vectors for sentiment analysis. In: Proceedings of the 49th Annual Meeting of the Association for Computational Linguistics: Human Language Technologies, pp. 142–150. Association for Computational Linguistics, Portland, Oregon, USA, June 2011. http://www.aclweb.org/anthology/P11-1015

8. OpenAI: Gpt-4 technical report (2023)

9. Ouyang, L., et al.: Training language models to follow instructions with human feedback. In: Advances in Neural Information Processing Systems, vol. 35, pp. 27730–27744 (2022)
10. Radford, A., Narasimhan, K., Salimans, T., Sutskever, I., et al.: Improving language understanding by generative pre-training (2018)
11. Radford, A., Wu, J., Child, R., Luan, D., Amodei, D., Sutskever, I., et al.: Language models are unsupervised multitask learners. OpenAI blog **1**(8), 9 (2019)
12. Raffel, C., et al.: Exploring the limits of transfer learning with a unified text-to-text transformer. J. Mach. Learn. Res. **21**(1), 5485–5551 (2020)
13. Ramasesh, V.V., Lewkowycz, A., Dyer, E.: Effect of scale on catastrophic forgetting in neural networks. In: International Conference on Learning Representations (2022)
14. Sanh, V., Debut, L., Chaumond, J., Wolf, T.: DistilBERT, a distilled version of BERT: smaller, faster, cheaper and lighter. arXiv preprint: arXiv:1910.01108 (2019)
15. Stolcke, A., et al.: Dialogue act modeling for automatic tagging and recognition of conversational speech. Comput. Linguist. **26**(3), 339–373 (2000)
16. Vaswani, A., et al.: Attention is all you need. In: Advances in Neural Information Processing Systems, vol. 30 (2017)
17. Wolf, T., et al.: Transformers: State-of-the-art natural language processing. In: Proceedings of the 2020 Conference on Empirical Methods in Natural Language Processing: System Demonstrations, pp. 38–45 (2020)
18. Yang, Z., Dai, Z., Yang, Y., Carbonell, J., Salakhutdinov, R.R., Le, Q.V.: XLNet: generalized autoregressive pretraining for language understanding. In: Wallach, H., Larochelle, H., Beygelzimer, A., d'Alché-Buc, F., Fox, E., Garnett, R. (eds.) Advances in Neural Information Processing Systems. vol. 32. Curran Associates, Inc. (2019). https://proceedings.neurips.cc/paper/2019/file/dc6a7e655 d7e5840e66733e9ee67cc69-Paper.pdf

Author Index

© IFIP International Federation for Information Processing 2023
Published by Springer Nature Switzerland AG 2023
I. Maglogiannis et al. (Eds.): AIAI 2023, IFIP AICT 676, pp. 579–582, 2023.
https://doi.org/10.1007/978-3-031-34107-6

Printed in the United States
by Baker & Taylor Publisher Services

Printed in the United States
by Baker & Taylor Publisher Services